THE ONE SHOW

XXVIII

INTERACTIVE ADVERTISING DESIGN

ADVERTISING'S BEST PRINT, DESIGN, RADIO AND TV

THE ONE CLUB FOR ART & COPY

PRESIDENT
David Baldwin

EXECUTIVE DIRECTOR
Mary Warlick

EDITOR
Yash Egami

ONE SHOW MANAGER
Emily Isovitsch

DESIGNER
Jennah Synnestvedt

PHOTO EDITOR
Joel Fischer

COVER AND DIVIDER PAGE DESIGN
Richard Boynton
Wink/Minneapolis

PUBLISHED BY
One Club Publishing
21 E. 26th Street, 5th floor
New York, NY 10010

ISBN
0-929837-29-0

DISTRIBUTED IN THE US
AND INTERNATIONALLY BY
Rockport Publishers
a member of
Quayside Publishing Group
33 Commercial Street
Gloucester, MA 01930
978-282-9590
www.rockpub.com
www.quaysidepublishinggroup.com

OTHER TITLES BY ONE CLUB PUBLISHING
Brand Apart by Joe Duffy
www.oneclub.org/store/

TABLE OF CONTENTS

BOARD OF DIRECTORS	iv
PRESIDENT'S MESSAGE	v
ONE SHOW JUDGES	vi
ONE CLUB MEMBERS	vii
CREATIVE HALL OF FAME	x
BEST OF SHOW	xviii
GOLD, SILVER AND BRONZE	2
GOLD ON GOLD	132
JUDGES' CHOICE	146
PRINT MERIT	158
PUBLIC SERVICE MERIT	262
TELEVISION AND RADIO MERIT	296
INNOVATIVE MEDIA/INTEGRATED MERIT	338
DESIGN MERIT	376
COLLEGE MERIT	482
INDEX	516

The One Club Board of Directors

I love the One Show. There, I said it. And so do you or you wouldn't have worked so hard to get into this book.

But why do you love it?

Face it: the judging is brutal and the odds are harshly against you walking away with heavier pockets on the night of the Show. But here you sit with a mix of envy, excitement and admiration, all calculated in vastly different equations depending on whether you won or not.

Of course, some of you do get in. And you get in all the time. You inspire us to try a little harder, work a little later, and think a little bigger. We owe you our thanks and our attention.

But, really, think about it. Most of the industry never even sees a Merit award in this show. Most of the industry never gets to see their name in the index at the back of the book with an italicized page number just to the right. Most of the industry enters the work and then wonders if the fax machine is broken when the finalists are announced. I've watched that happen before.

Maybe that's the point. We all love great advertising and we love to see it practiced powerfully. Because that's the game, my friends, to do something amazing that changes the way people feel and think and do. To look at things in ways they've never been looked at before. That's what you get to do if you're lucky enough to be in advertising.

This is where the great stuff is. This is where careers can be made in an evening. Where weekend beach houses can be bought as a direct result of being in this book.

This is a glorious attempt to distill one year's inspiration into one place.

What a privilege it is to be in this book.

–David Baldwin

2006 One Show Judges

DAVID APICELLA
Ogilvy & Mather/New York

ANDY AZULA
The Martin Agency/Richmond

LISA BENNETT
DDB/San Francisco

ARTHUR BIJUR
Cliff Freeman & Partners/New York

MIMI COOK
Goodby, Silverstein & Partners/San Francisco

RAVI DESHPANDE
Contract India/Mumbai

SUSAN EBLING CORBO
Mother/New York

MORIHIKO HASEBE
Hakuhodo/Tokyo

RACHEL HOWALD
Young & Rubicam/New York

ANDREW KELLER
Crispin Porter + Bogusky/Miami

JANET KESTIN
Ogilvy & Mather/Toronto

JIM LESSER
BBDO/San Francisco

CHUCK MCBRIDE
TBWA\Chiat\Day/San Francisco

TODD MCCRACKEN
Grey Asia Pacific/Kuala Lumpur

PETER MCHUGH
Carmichael Lynch/Minneapolis

THAM KHAI MENG
Ogilvy & Mather Asia Pacific/Singapore

TY MONTAGUE
JWT/New York

ZAK MROUEH
Taxi/Toronto

DAVID NOBAY
Saatchi & Saatchi/Sydney

BETINNA OLF
Springer & Jacoby/Hamburg

KEVIN PROUDFOOT
Wieden + Kennedy/New York

MARK TUTSSEL
Leo Burnett Worldwide/Chicago

EDDIE VAN BLOEM
Lowe/New York

ERIK VERVROEGEN
TBWA\Paris/Boulogne-Billancourt

MATTHEW VESCOVO
Freelance/Brooklyn

RICARDO VIOR
la comunidad/Martinez

2006 One Show Design Judges

RICHARD BOYNTON
Wink/Minneapolis

MATT ELLER
Feel Good Anyway/Portland

HALEY JOHNSON
Haley Johnson Design/Seattle

BRIAN GUNDERSON
Goodby, Silverstein and Partners/San Francisco

ABBY LOW
Kate Spade/New York

SEIJO KAWAGUCHI
Tugboat/Tokyo

ANDERS KORNESTEDT
Happy Forsman and Bodenfors/Sweden

DAVID MASHBURN
Mash and Burn Design/New York

CLIVE PIERCY
PhD Design/Santa Monica

NEIL POWELL
Margeotes Fertitta Powell/New York

2006 One Show Radio Judges

BRAD EMMETT
Cliff Freeman & Partners/New York

MARK GROSS
DDB/Chicago

DAN KELLEHER
BBDO/New York

ANDREW MEYER
Leo Burnett Worldwide/Chicago

COLIN NISSAN
Freelance/New York

PETER ROSCH
Lowe/New York

DAWN MCCARTHY
Freelance/New York

MICHAEL BUSS
GSDM/Austin

JOSH DENBURG
Leo Burnett Worldwide/Chicago

MATT IAN
BBH/New York

SCOTT AAL
Grant Scott Hurley/San Francisco

A

David Abbott
Jamie Ackerman
Ekta Aggarwal
Daniel X Ahearn
Kenan Aktulun
Mauricio Alarcon
Lisa Albano
David Alberts
Samuel Albis
Shari Alexander
Ali Alvarez
Ralph Ammirati
Angie Anderson
Keith Anderson
Stephanie Anderson
Magnus Andersson
Daniel Andréani
Philip Andrew
Jason Andrews
David Apicella
Marcelo Aragao
Emerson Arehart
Ana Paula Areia
Gil Arevalo
David Arnold
Ben Arrow
Joel Arzu
Jimmy Ashworth
Michael Asphar
Brian Avenius
David Ayscue
Andy Azula

B

Ron Bacsa
Rob Baiocco
Larry Baisden
Lisa Balser
Jennifer Banks
Jane Barber
Keate Barker
Bob Barnwell
Ann Barrick
Ben Bartholomew
Lars Bastholm
Lars Bastholm
Alec Bathgate
Trevor Beddoe
Paul Belford
Gregg Benedikt
Jay Benjamin
Jeff Benjamin
Benjamin Bensimon
Thomas Berger
Meredith Bergman Apicella
Nicke Bergstrom
David Bernstein
Adam Berry
Amber Bezahler
Brooke Bierdeman
Arthur Bijur
Rasmus Blaesbkerg
Don Blanton
Eric Boscia
Richard Boynton
Mark Braddock
Robert Braden
Tim Braybrooks
John Brockenbrough
Robert Brothers
Ryan Brown
Mark Brown
Warren Brown
Ian Brown
Mark Buchanan
Audra Buchwald
Gayle M. Budd
Dave Bullen
Scott Burditt
Al Burstein

C

Larry Cadman
Daniel Cady
Robin Cain
Michael Calienes
Bridget Camden
Jennifer Campbell
William Campbell
Tommy Campbell
David Canning
Josephine Carey
Kari Cartwright
Paul Catmur
Gary Caulfield
Mark Chalmers
Joanne Chan
Daniel Charron
Alex Chen
Andy Cheng
Luke Chess
Benjamin Chiang
Heather Chisvin
Young-Hee Choi
Charmaine Choi
Aaron Chown
Krisan Christensen
Kevin Christie
Thomas Christmann
Esther Clerehan
Bart Cleveland
Geoff Clow
Lee Clow
Harry Cocciolo
David Cohen
Scott Cohen
Gary Cohen
Peter Cohen
Christopher Cole
Anna Coll
Paul Collins
Leighton Collis
Mark Collis
Brett Compton
Lou Congelio
Brian Connaughton
Mimi Cook
Jake Cooney
Kyle Cooper
Ozan Coskun
Fabio Costa
Susan Cotler Block
Anthony Cozzolino
Jeremy Craigen
Jay Cranford
David Crawford
Damaso Crespo
Mary Ann Cristiano
Loran Crowley
Sean Cummins
George Curi
Lisa Curry

D

Deborah Dachis Gold
Paul Daigle
Billy D'ambrosio
Celeste Dang
Stefan Danielski
Gassel Darcy
Joanna D'avanzo
Simon Davies
Craig Davies
Joshua Davis
James Davis
Nigel Dawson
Mateus De Paula Santos
Jason De Turris
Laura Degraff
Steve Deiters
Tom Delmundo
Charles Demarco
Toni D'eramo
Heather Deschene
Ravi Deshpande
Amanda Desimone
Darryn Devlin
Richard Devon
Steve Diamond
Alexander Dickman
Andrew Dilallo
Joshua Dimarcantonio
Matt Dimmer
Greg Dinoto
Joe Dobbin
Fabien Dodard
Matt Doman
Tommy Donoho
Michael Donovan
Icaro Doria
Alicia Dotter
Mike Doyle
Danny Drexler
David Droga
Cynthia Drummond
Michael Duckworth
Anja Duering
Joe Duffy
Jim Durfee
Melissa Dziemian

E

Lee Earle
Susan Ebling Corbo
Craig Eiri
Matt Eller
Chris Elliott
Michael Emory
Crystal English
Guniz Engur
Dirk Eschenbacher
Janet Esquirol
Alexander Esseveld

F

Dave Fagin
Jonathan Fallik
Dana Farbo
Jordan Farkas
Michael Faudet
Roy Faulkner
Rob Feakins
Stephen Fechtor
Dan Federman
David Felton
Alison Fetten
Daniele Fiandaca
Ginevra Figg
Ricardo Figueira
Monique Fikar
Leo Fiorica
Hugh Fitzhardinge
Andrew Flemming
Jim Foster
Brian Fouhy
Roger Frank
Chris Franzese
Charlie Frazer
Cliff Freeman
Piero Frescobaldi
Glen Fruchter
Javier Fuentes
Toshiya Fukuda
Toshi Furuta

G

Tom Gabriel
Marc Gallucci
Mauricio Galvan
Sean Patrick Ganann
Yash Gandhi
Mark Ganton
Julie Gardner
Amil Gargano
Justine Gazzola
Lauren Geisler
William Geraghty
Richard Gerdes
Natalya Gerzhgorina
Saro Ghazarian
Monica Giardina
Alan Gilleo
George Goetz
Kevin Goff
Dan Goldgeier
Dominic Goldman
Cristian Gomez
Emiliano González De Pietri
Jeff Goodby
Kara Goodrich
John Goodson
Mitch Gordon
Folkert Gorter
Jennifer Graham

Jeff Graham
Alastair Green
Luca Grelli
Norm Grey
Glenn Griffin
Aaron Griffiths
Frank Grosberger
Philip Growick
Fench Guan
David Guerrero
Brian Gunderson

H

Christian Haas
Lori Habas
Nathan Hackstock
Juliane Hadem
Jennifer Hahs
Stephen Hall
John Halliday
Matthew Hallock
Alexandra Halpern
Rhea Hanges
Mark Harricks
Joe Harris
Jessica Hartmann
Morihiko Hasebe
Britt Hayes
John Hegarty
Florian Heiss
Brendan Hemp
Mary Henderson
Uschi Henkes
Roy Herbert
Rony Herz
Ralf Heuel
Heather Higgins
Emmanuel Hill
Drew Hill
Helmut Himmler
Paul Hirsch
Rob Hoffman
John Hofmeister
Bill Hollister
Dave Holloway
Eric Holm
Tricia Holman
Jeanine Holmes
Robert Holzer
David Horridge
Ryan Hose
Rachel Howald
Reuben Hower
Jonson Hsieh
Chia-An Hu
Jonathan Huang
Mike Hudock
Mike Hughes
John Hynes

I

David Iannone
Hyun Ho Im
Rei Inamoto
Brenda Innocenti
Vladislav Ivangorodsky

J

Rob Jackson
Harry Jacobs
Doug Jaeger
Freddy Jana
Erwin Jansen
Jr Jasinski
John Jay
Andrew Jeske
Scott Johnson
Glynnis Johnson
Erin Johnson
Marcus Johnson
Haley Johnson
Rick Johnson
Jennifer Johnson
Anthony Johnson
Ed Jones
Stephen Jones
William Jurewicz

K

Jon Kamen
Stephen Kamsler
Scott Kaplan
Shadi Katebini
Seijo Kawaguchi
Leslie Kay
Andrew Keller
Carol Lee Kelliher
Alan Kelly
Ramona Kelly
Kris Kendrick
David Kennedy
Janet Kestin
Jeffrey Keyton
Kris Kiger
Eugina Rae Kim
Kalie Kimball-Malone
Joyce King Thomas
Takyoshi Kishimoto
Neil Kitainik
Lauren Kloepfer
Erich T. Kloth
Greg Knagge
Jonathan Kneebone
Joe Knezic
Bob Kochuk
Jessica Kolski
Julian Koenig
Kristen Koop
Maya Kopytman
Daniel Korkhov
Anders Kornestedt
Paula Korpalski
Hitomi Kosumi
Thorsten Kraus
Dylan Krenka
Paul Kruger
Ben Kunz
Sasha Kurtz
Michael Kutschinski

L

Jesus Lada
Ming Lai
David Lai
Robin Landa
Bryan Landaburu
Lindsey Lanpher
Jim Lansbury
Adam Larocca
David Laskarzewski
Megan Leblanc
Han-Yi Lee
Eun-Jung Lee
Karen Lehnst
Ann Lemon
Dany Lennon
Gustavo Leon
Nelson Leung
Kate Levin
Bob Levenson
Mary Lewis
Amy Lewis
Elaine Li
Jessica Liao
Ted Lim
Julio Lima
Jessica Lin
Paul Linkogle
Cooper Liska-Smith
Tina Liu
Nadia Livshits
Marcus Liwag
George Lois
Michael Long
Myriam Lopez
Maria Pilar Anne Lopezbanos
Frank Lopresti
Abby Clawson Low
David Lubars
Heddy Lunenfeld
Bonnie Lunt
Ernest Lupincacci
Lisa Lurie
Michael Lynch
Diana Lynn

M

Shayne Mackey
Sam Maclay
Richard Maddocks
Vanessa Maganza
Sharoz Makarech
Kendra Malcolm
Karen Mallia
Andreas Malm
Denis Mamo
Michael Manning
John Mannion
Steve Mapp
Bryant Marcum
Lawrence Marks
Jay Marsen
Erin Martin
Kerri Martin
David Mashburn
Jose A. Matamoros
Kim Mathers
Tricia Matoto-Desanto
Gabrielle Mayeur
Mauricio Mazzariol
Scott McAfee
Cal McAllister
Chuck McBride
Ed McCabe
Peter McCarty
Kerry McCashin
Todd McCracken
Joe McDonagh
Joseph McDonough
Tom McElligott
James McGrath
Matthew McGrath
Peter McHugh
Matt McKenna
Tim McMullen
Steve McNamara
Adrian McNamara
Bryan McPeak
Jeff Meglio
Alex Melvin
Tham Khai Meng
Lucy Meredith
Matthew Merino
Melinda Mettler
Bogdan Migulski
Debbra Mikaelsen
Mark Millar
Ron Miller
Kari Miller
Renee Miller
Simon Milliship
Graham Mills
Laurence Minsky
Charles Mirisola
Jerry Mlekoday
James Mok
José Mollá
Sakol Mongkolkasetarin
Ty Montague
Younghwa Moon
Jeff Moore
Craig Moore
Bob Moore
Frank Morabito
Jonathan Morgan
Kevin Moriarty
Bourne Morris
Deborah Morrison
Jim Mountjoy
Emmanuel Mousis
Stanford Moy
Matthew Moyer
Zak Mroueh
Alexander Muk
Melissa Murray
Jayant Murty
Jason Musante
Rick Myers

N

Saori Nakakariya
Yugo Nakamura
Jeff Neely
Robert Neiler
Peter Nelson
Kate Nemes
An Nguyen
Jenny Nicholson
David Nobay
Jacqueline Nolan
David Noot
Toke Nygaard

O

Steve O'Brien
Austin O'Connor
Wanda O'Connor
Matthew R. Ogelby
Naoto Oiwa
Yasumichi Oka
Paco Olavarrieta
Frank Oles
Betinna Olf
Martin Olinger
Jeff Olsen
Chantal Olson
Takashi Omura
Peter Oravetz
Ron Ordansa
Matt Orser
Reuben Orter
Mikio Osaki
Zara O'Shannacery
Mike O'Sullivan
Akira Oyama

P

Paula Pagano
Jack Palancio
Patricia Palma
Matias Palm-Jensen
Nicholas G. Panas
Richard Parubrub
Lance Paull
Patsy Peacock
Stan Pearlman
Pj Pereira
Andrew Petch
Elizabeth Phillips
Matthew Piacentini
Clive Piercy
Christopher Pinckney
Stephen Pite
Caitlin Plattner
Demir Karpat Polat
Paul Potak
Neil Powell
Sophie Preap
Andreas Putz

R

Olivier Rabenschlag
Alan Rado
Richard Rapp
Jennifer Rasche
Robert Rasmussen
Alex Rathgeb
Emily Rawitsch
Brett Reese
Adam Regan
John Reider
Leah Renbaum
Siimon Reynolds
Nancy Rice
Hal Riney
Petter Ringbom
Mark Ringer
Peter Risafi
Jason Ritchkoff
Tim Roan
Phyllis Robinson
Chris Robb
Ed Robinson
Carlos Rocca
Kevin Roddy
Jason Rogers
Jeneal Rohrback
Kate Rolston
Fernanda Romano
Nick Roop
Tom Roope
Jonathan Rosman
Lindsay Ross
Damian Royce
Diane Rothschild
Sebastian Royce
Melody Rozsa
Roger Ruegger
Vanessa Rumbold
Dr. Bill Ryan

S

Gibran Saleem
Steve Sandstrom
Paulo Sanna
Yukimi Sano
Yasuharu Sasaki
Robert Sawyer
Robert Saxon
Paula Scher
Chris Schlegel
Dana Schmergel
Michael Schmidt
Jonathan Schoenberg
Julian Schreiber
Jessica Schultz
Danny Schuman
Jaime Schwarz
Sally Schweitzer
Tod Seisser
Kathy Selker
Burl Seslar
David Shaban
Ant Shannon
Denise Shearer
Norm Shearer
Glen Sheehan
Peter Sheldon
Bill Shelton
Jennifer Shoop
Mark Silber
Rich Silverstein
Frederic Simon
Roger Simpson
Fred Siqueira
Suzanne Siriotis
Stephanie Skaggs
Pat Sloan
Ward Smith
Michele Snure
Yoshi Sodeoka
Mo Solomon
Nick Sonderup
Paul Soon
William Spencer
Catherine St. Jean
Melody Stanbery
Russ Stark
Daniel Stein
David Steinke
Eric Stephens
Hamish Stewart
Erin Stites
Colleen Stokes
Scott Storrs
Thomas Stringham
Alan Stuart
Mcad Students
Niko Stumpo
Wade Sturdivant
Amy Su
Luke Sullivan
Steve Swan
Steve Swartz
Manoj Swearingen
Matthew Szymczyk

T

Iain Tait
Kishimoto Takayoshi
Matthew Tarulli
Samuel Taylor
Mark Taylor
Mike Tesch
Jessica Terlizzi
Patrick Thiede
Greg Thomas
Sean Thompson
Remon Tijssen
Justin Tindall
Renny Tirador
Domingo Torres
Ezequiel Trivino
Jakob Trollback
Peter Trueblood
Evelina Trzeciak
Chuck Tso
Roman Tsukerman
Diane Tucker
Tracey Turner
Mark Tutssel

U

Fehmi Mahir Uraz

V

Peter Van Bloem
Eddie Van Bloem
Peter Van Regenmorter
Guy Venables
Paul Venables
Erik Vervroegen
Matthew Vescovo
Erik Vevroegen
Carol Vick-Bynum
Ricardo Vior
Michael Volkmer
Brigitte Von Puttkamer
Nancy Vonk
Steve Vranakis
Johnny Vulkan

W

Elaine Wagner
Russell Wakelin
Joerg Waldschutz
Kelly M Wallis
Melinda Ward
Mary Warlick
Regan Warner
Bob Warren
Clay Weiner
Riomar Welch
Mary Wells
Ben Welsh
Craig Welsh
Robert Shaw West
Brian Wheeler
Keith White
Dan Wieden
Kari Wiens
Rebecca Wikler
Scott Wild
Tim Williams
Samantha Williams
Megan Wilson
Dafna Winter
Chris Wojda
Lloyd Wolfe
Willy Wong
Vicki Wong
Laura Wood
Leslye Wood
Doug Worple
Nick Worthington
Bill Wright

Y

Betsy Yamazaki
Lo Sheung Yan
Takehiko Yasui
Aaron Younger

Z

Mark Zapico
Richard Zeid
John Zilly
Shareif Ziyadat
Matt Zucker
Hannah Zumberge

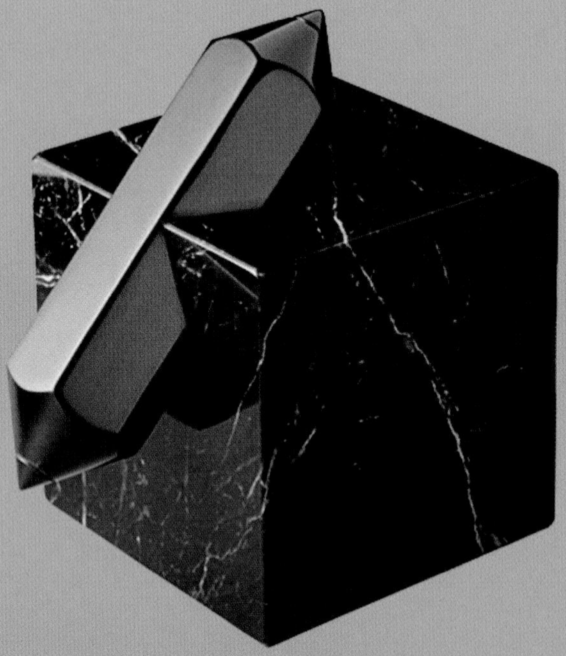

RICH SILVERSTEIN
CHAIRMAN

When I first started in this business I really didn't know what the heck I was doing. A degree in graphic design did not prepare me for the business of advertising. But after a few years of doing pretty mediocre work I got lucky enough to have a piece accepted into the *One Show Annual*. This was a defining moment in my career. I remember that I wanted to be able to share it with my parents, who never really understood what I did for a living. For them my high school charcoal sketches of vegetables that hung proudly in their kitchen were testament enough of my talent. Then somewhere along the way, I won a Pencil and the whole world changed forever. I received a small raise and grew a little more confident. This strange business actually started to become fun.

And over time I learned that if you work hard, and remain true to yourself, and have a great partner, and are really, really lucky, you just might get chosen to be in the Hall of Fame. And though you secretly always hoped that you'd get in, it's only at this evening's event that it really sinks in that you've accomplished something big. I only wish that my parents had been able to attend my induction. Maybe they would have finally understood and put the watercolors in the basement where they belong.

Congratulations to our newest inductees. This is a very special occasion.

I knew Cliff would be inducted into some hall of fame 20 years ago. You can't have that much raw talent and not get into one of these.

When I met him at Dancer Fitzgerald Sample, Cliff was on a tear as a writer. He was sitting quietly, cloistered away in his office surrounded by medals and trophies; everywhere was the glint of gold.

I learned fast that Cliff Freeman is all about the work. Nothing could get in his way of doing it as well as humanly possible. He talks about it articulately. It drives him. Then I learned about funny. You can't talk about Cliff and not talk about funny. It's part of the Brand.

Cliff has a philosophy about how advertising works and he has never wavered from it because no one has ever proved him wrong—simply, that to connect, advertising must entertain. Over the years this credo, and more importantly his talent to achieve it, has created historic successes. It has also drawn like-minded people to the agency and to his fandom. And, befitting a Hall of Famer, it has fueled some of the most memorable work of the last couple or three decades.

"Sometimes you feel like a nut," which he created in the '70s at Dancer Fitzgerald Sample with then longtime partner Fred Massin is, unbelievably, still on the air. "Where's the beef?" hit a national nerve and Mondale ran with it—figuratively and literally. Probably the most famous advertising line ever written, it pops up frequently in the news and pop culture. Intentionally or not, those three words captured an encyclopedic volume of human dissatisfaction. Our lives are woefully short on "beef." That's a pretty depressing insight. Cliff made it hilarious.

Ultimate Electronics

He also worked his magic juju using only two words: "Pizza, Pizza." For nine years, that campaign had everyone looking forward to the next commercial and it filled the sails of the newly christened ship, Cliff Freeman and Partners. By the way, that's Cliff's voice babbling, "Pizza, Pizza." After casting hundreds of people to utter those silly yet descriptive words, Mike Illitch, owner of Little Caesars, finally begged Cliff to do it because "no one else I heard sounds so much like Little Caesar."

THE ONE CLUB

Cliff Freeman and Partners

To mention all the famous campaigns that have sprung from the agency, including Budget, Staples, Fox, Sauza, Pep Boys, Comedy Channel, a harrowing anti-heroin effort and Hollywood Video, would take too much space. The commonality though, humorous or not, is that the work works because it rings true. And, of course, always entertains.

Being one of the four founders of Cliff Freeman and Partners (I'm the "and"), along with the stalwart Pete Regan and Donna Weinheim, should entitle me to share some knowledge of the man himself.

An intensely private person, he wouldn't be too comfortable having much revealed about him. In fact, that revelation alone will embarrass him. Sorry, Cliff. So here are the revealables. He has Mississippi roots, played a little high school basketball, partied a little, partied a little more at Florida State and has a bunch of brothers

HOME OF THE BIG BUN
HOME OF THE BIG BUN
WENDY'S

Wendy's

and sisters. Ready for something funny? Cliff started in the business as an account guy. He didn't find that amusing at all so he became a copywriter. After a stint at McCann in Atlanta, where he won the first of his 93,376,128 awards, he moved to New York. There he met and married the talented and irrepressible Susan, his other half, his muse, and gifted design maven—check out our offices sometime.

Cliff's interests are eclectic and he is to his core passionate about everything in his life. You see it in his appreciation of design, you see it in his collecting and you see it in his home. If you'd like to glimpse the passion of Cliff, just sit down next to him and say the word, "Yankees." On second thought, don't do that this year.

Never being one to shy away from controversial work is, to me, one of Cliff's most appealing qualities. He is a perpetual optimist and is filled with a contagious excitement by smart, unusual ideas. Those are the kind of ideas, which by definition involve pushing an envelope or two, sometimes into the shredder.

Like anyone who succeeds magnificently, he has had guides and a support system of talented helpers. He would surely cite Stan Becker as one of those who supported him most. Stan's tenacity and audacity helped create an environment where sometimes you could feel like a nut and dream up a "Where's the beef?" That being said, Cliff's internal compass has always operated independently of external forces.

No Cliff notes would be complete without a word about his enduring influence on the business of advertising. Somehow, he has created a petri dish for infectious ideas. Cliff Freeman, both the guy and the agency, have shown legions of advertising people (inside and outside the agency for that matter) where the bar ought to be. Then some pheromone he emitted into the air infected a lot of them with an ability to reach it and even nudge it higher.

It would be impossible to add up the many disciples he and the agency helped and continue to launch. There are directors, including Steve Miller, Rick LeMoine, Kevin Donovan, Bruce Hurwitt, and agencies Venables, Bell & Partners and David & Goliath, some of whose leaders were sent forth from Cliff Freeman and Partners with holy-cow credentials. That's not to mention numerous other talents who have already made and are presently making names for themselves on the Cliff Freeman and Partners stage.

His fame is owed primarily to his true calling. His writing. But everyone who works with him knows he is also a terrific editor, thoughtful planner and keen observer of human behavior. Most will say he is a genius. Others say he's eccentric. Some just say funny. They are all right.

In the world of advertising, you never have to ask, "Where's the beef?" Cliff's got it.

—Arthur Bijur

The next time you light up a joint, let your Senator know how you feel.
Get off your butt and do something about getting the use of marijuana decriminalized. Let someone know how you feel about the issue. Write your Senator or Congressman now!
Oregon, Alaska, Maine, Colorado, California and Ohio have stopped arresting people for marijuana possession. Now it can be done at the national level.
In the Senate, The Marijuana Control Act of 1975 (S.1450) has been sponsored by Senator Javits. In the House, Congressman Koch has introduced an identical measure(HR.6108).
Write the letter. The pen has power.
You don't have to smoke marijuana to know it's today's marijuana laws that are criminal. Let Congress know how you feel.
Join NORML. Money is needed to finish the job once and for all.
NORML
NATIONAL ORGANIZATION FOR THE REFORM OF MARIJUANA LAWS
2317 M STREET, N.W., WASHINGTON, D.C.
I enclose $15.00 membership fee. (Students and Military $10.00)
I'm not a joiner but I would still like to help with a contribution.
Send along the following NORML items. All the proceeds from their sale go toward furthering the fight.
GOLD MARIJUANA LEAF PINS

NORML

This man has one cavity.
LIFE IS HARSH.
Your tequila shouldn't be.
SAUZA "CONMEMORATIVO." THE SMOOTHER, OAK-AGED TEQUILA.

Sauza Tequila

PLEASERS
PLEASERS
2 PIZZAS $9.98
MONEY BACK GUARANTEE
Little Caesars Pizza

Little Caesars

John Hegarty

Even for John Hegarty, some things are unimaginable. Like the thought of reading a thousand words on his life and times.

It just begs for him to remind you of a survey that revealed that less than two percent of people bother reading copy. This two percent, he'll tell you, is the client, their marketing department, the writer, the writer's mom and the account director.

"If the founders of the French Revolution were able to reduce their slogan to three words—"Liberté, Égalité, Fraternité"—and the Romans built an empire on another three—"Veni, Vidi, Vici"—why do we need so many more to sell cat food?"

So if John had to sum up his first 40 years in advertising, what would that one word be? That word would be "Ideas," for it's been in the restless pursuit of single, simple ideas—the ones that elude so many creative people—that has fascinated John ever since he left the London College of Printing in 1965 and started work as a junior art director at Benton & Bowles.

Why do some people have ideas, and others don't? Why are some ideas more compelling than others? ("Nobody ever bought something whilst they were asleep.") Why does an idea inspire people to think about products in a new, more attractive way? Why do ideas that capture a mood, an attitude and a point of view accelerate their impact and magnify their effect? Where do ideas come from?

A writer who worked with John tells the story of them sitting in an office after a briefing. "First he looked at the blank sheet of layout paper, and shook his head. Then he looked up at the wall, and shook his head. Then he gazed skywards and started wheeling his chair around the office. I asked him what he was doing. He said, 'If ideas drop out of the sky, I don't want them to miss me.'"

BLACK LEVI'S.
LEVI'S
WHEN THE WORLD ZIGS, ZAG.

Levi's

But John had to wait two years before he found himself in exactly the right place, at exactly the right time.

Within 18 months of landing his first job, the advertising business almost lost him. It wasn't because he was fired (he was). It was a love affair (with golf). Golf, or advertising—one had to go. It was 30 years before John pulled out his putter again.

In 1966, he took a job in a small agency called John Collings & Partners with offices in fashionable Soho, in London's West End. "They said they were an agency going places. They were—Camden Town," at that time a shabby area in North London.

But even working in small agencies, John managed to appear alongside the creative giants of that time, Doyle Dane Bernbach and Collett Dickenson Pearce, in the D&AD (Design & Art Direction) Annual, the gold standard of British advertising. In particular, his work for El Al Airlines and an ad with the headline, "The Flight of the Israelites."

Keep on feeding their imagination.
LEGO
LEGO IS A NEW TOY EVERY DAY.

LEGO

But it wasn't until 1967 when he joined Cramer Saatchi that John really began to make his mark. Ross Cramer and Charles Saatchi had clients that allowed high profile work, like the Health Education Council.

In 1970, Charlie teamed up with brother Maurice and started Saatchi & Saatchi. John was appointed Deputy Creative Director.

In 1971, John won a D&AD Gold for an anti-smoking ad. Another ad in the campaign showed a cigarette in a man's mouth. The photographer asked him to be the model. "It let me show off my best feature," John said. "My lips."

Yes, it has been known to rain in Israel.
EL AL. The Airline of the People of Israel

EL AL

Realizing that the agency "was going to grow into the largest agency group in the world and fall foul of the City," John left in 1973 to co-found TBWA—the first agency voted Agency of the Year in 1980 by *Campaign*, the UK's leading advertising magazine.

It was here and for LEGO John wrote the ad that best summed up his approach. A single red brick sits on a yellow brick. The line: "It's the simple ideas that win through."

At TBWA, John and his creative department's ideas more than won through. John was awarded his second D&AD Gold, for *Newsweek* (he was later to win another six Silvers adding to his Cannes and British Television Golds & Silvers). The agency also produced a commercial that got into the *Guinness Book of Records* as the world's most awarded commercial.

In 1982, John left TBWA with the two other founding partners, Nigel Bogle and John Bartle, to set up on their own. Within weeks, BBH had asserted its creative superiority with work for Levi's and Audi—their first accounts, both still clients today.

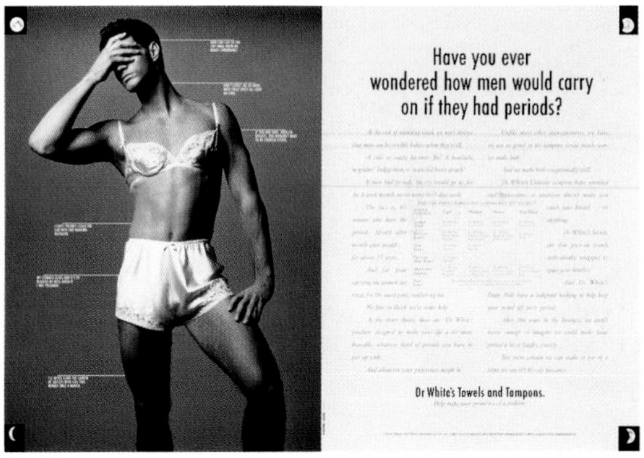
Have you ever wondered how men would carry on if they had periods?
Dr White's Towels and Tampons.

Dr. White's

John's commercial for Levi's launched the career of an unknown model named Nick Kamen, who stripped in a laundrette. A second featured another unknown at the time, Brad Pitt. John pioneered the importance of music for Levi's, the soundtracks for seven commercials getting into the UK number-one spot. He was also responsible for "Vorsprung durch Technik" for Audi, now one of UK's most famous advertising slogans.

Since then, BBH has been voted *Campaign* magazine's Agency of the Year four times. In 1993, it became the Cannes Advertising Festival's first Agency of the Year by winning more awards than any other agency. (They won it again in 1994.) More recently, BBH Worldwide was voted *Campaign's* first "Network of the Year."

How many cigarettes a day does your child smoke?
When a child breathes air filled with cigarette smoke it can be as bad as if he actually smoked the cigarette himself.
Don't smoke when there are children present.

Health Education Council

John has also been awarded the D&AD President's Award for Outstanding Achievement, Chairman of the 1999 New York's Art Directors Advertising Show, voted one of the most influential people in fashion, and awarded the International Clio Awards Lifetime Achievement Award. His belief—that if an idea is simple and compelling enough, it can work anywhere in the world—has resulted in BBH becoming "one agency in five places"—London, Singapore, New York, Tokyo and Brazil, all of which John oversees as Worldwide Creative Director.

With Shanghai as his next stop, John's premise that before you can inform you must engage is being stretched to new lengths. "How do you engage with people who don't have televisions?"

One thousand words are up. John may never read them, but I will let him have the last word(s): "When the world zigs, zag."

—Neil Patterson

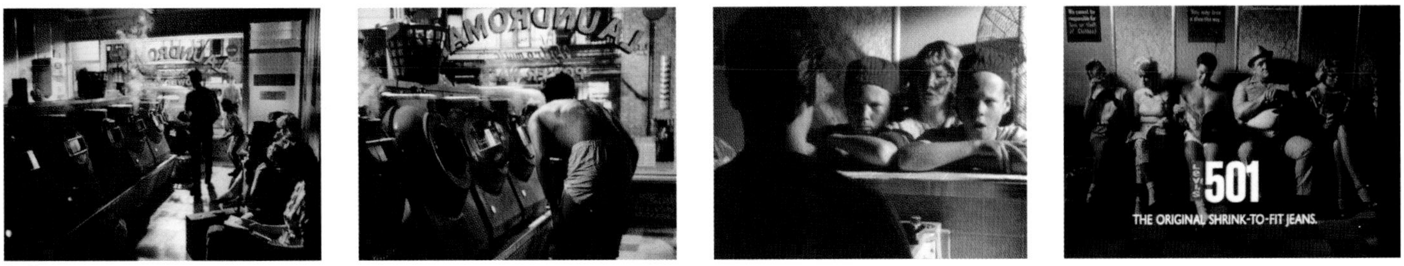
501
THE ORIGINAL SHRINK-TO-FIT JEANS.

Levi's

DIANE ROTHSCHILD

You can't talk about Diane Rothschild without mentioning Doyle Dane Bernbach, and vice-versa. Such was the creative environment that has become legendary—an environment that inspired people to think big, by thinking small. It not only cultivated great advertising, it cultivated great talents. And as each generation had its stars, none shown brighter than Diane. Diane Rothschild is a classic combination of beauty and brains. In fact, when we worked together I would often tell her, "with your good looks and your brains, we make a great team."

One of the things that most inspired and drove creative people to new ways of thinking was not only to learn from what was done but also to challenge it.

That is what Diane Rothschild is all about—a master of precision thinking in pursuit of excellence. She would always say (regardless of how good she thought the work was), "OK, we got that, now let's do something great."

She not only challenged other great ads, she challenged herself.

"Doing something great" leads to years of excellence, years of award-winning advertising for Chivas Regal, Volkswagen and Cigna to name a few. In fact, from 1977 to 1986, Diane won more awards than any other writer at DDB.

In 1986, Diane and Roy Grace founded Grace & Rothschild Advertising where for 14 years she continued her uncompromising ways, creating award-winning campaigns for clients such as Range Rover, J&B Scotch, Mount Sinai, Whittle and whatever else they worked on. When Roy retired, Diane merged with Della Femina Jeary & Partners.

In this business we work closely with other people, sharing a special part of ourselves, partnering with art directors and writers to create something great. But most of us move on and sometimes lose touch with our "advertising friends."

But what is unique in our industry is that a person's work can bridge those separations.

Although I hadn't seen Diane for several years, I always knew what she was up to. I just had to flip open a magazine, drive by a billboard or turn on a TV. And there she was, with her signature brilliance—simplicity, wit and impact.

That signature brilliance has lead Diane to one of advertising's greatest honors—one that will immortalize her work and, most importantly, her. As Diane always said, "the work speaks for itself." And it speaks volumes.

—Jim Scalfone

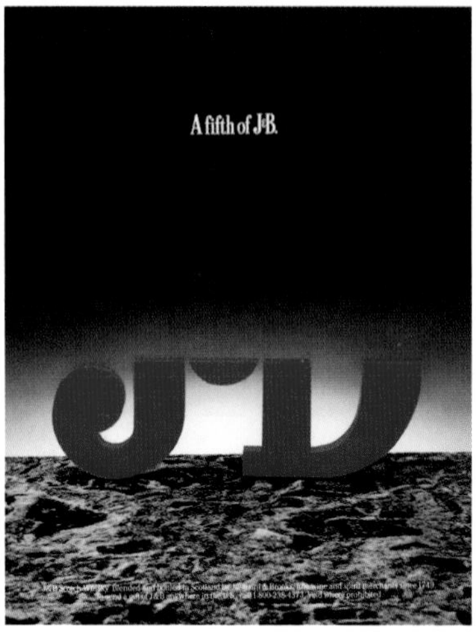
A fifth of J&B.

ABCDEF
GHIJKL
MNOPQ
RSTUV
WXYZ
J&B neat.

J&B Scotch

Everything you hear about a RANGE ROVER is true.
1-800-FINE-4WD

Range Rover

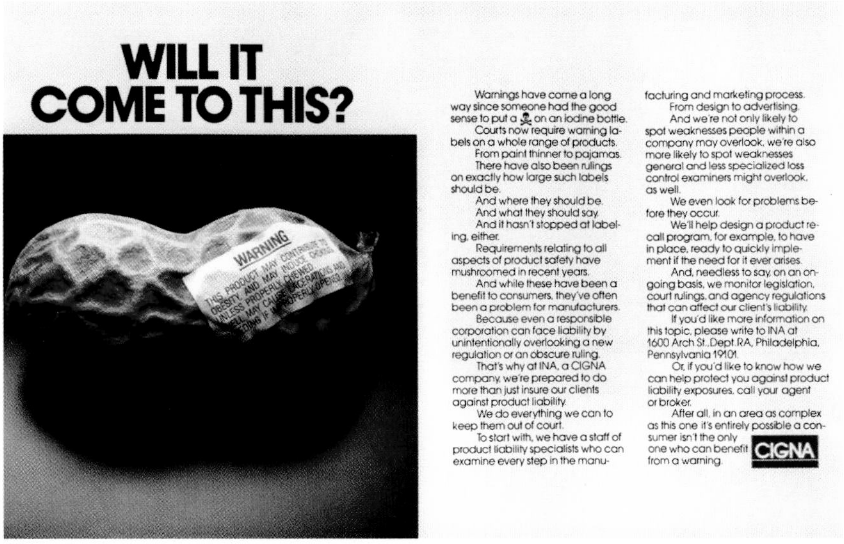
WILL IT
COME TO THIS?
WARNING
Warnings have come a long way since someone had the good sense to put a ☠ on an iodine bottle.
Courts now require warning labels on a whole range of products.
From paint thinner to pajamas.
There have also been rulings on exactly how large such labels should be.
And where they should be.
And what they should say.
And it hasn't stopped at labeling, either.
Requirements relating to all aspects of product safety have mushroomed in recent years.
And while these have been a benefit to consumers, they've often been a problem for manufacturers.
Because even a responsible corporation can face liability by unintentionally overlooking a new regulation or an obscure ruling.
That's why at INA, a CIGNA company, we're prepared to do more than just insure our clients against product liability.
We do everything we can to keep them out of court.
To start with, we have a staff of product liability specialists who can examine every step in the manufacturing and marketing process.
From design to advertising.
And we're not only likely to spot weaknesses people within a company may overlook, we're also more likely to spot weaknesses general and less specialized loss control examiners might overlook, as well.
We even look for problems before they occur.
We'll help design a product recall program, for example, to have in place, ready to quickly implement if the need for it ever arises.
And, needless to say, on an ongoing basis, we monitor legislation, court rulings, and agency regulations that can affect our client's liability.
If you'd like more information on this topic, please write to INA at 1600 Arch St., Dept RA, Philadelphia, Pennsylvania 19101.
Or, if you'd like to know how we can help protect you against product liability exposures, call your agent or broker.
After all, in an area as complex as this one it's entirely possible a consumer isn't the only one who can benefit from a warning.
CIGNA

Cigna

Can you spot the Range Rover in this picture?
Goodbye road. Goodbye traffic. Goodbye 5 m.p.h.
A Range Rover does something far more impressive than get you through a traffic jam in air-conditioned, arm-chaired, stereo-surrounded comfort.
A Range Rover takes you where there are no jams. Because there is no traffic.
Through the woods. Along the beach. Across the desert. Range Rovers, after all, are so extraordinary, they drive for years in places ordinary cars couldn't drive a quarter of a mile.
So it's not surprising that to many a Range Rover's most luxurious feature isn't its elegant interior, optional sunroof, or the security of 24 hour roadside assistance.
Its most luxurious feature is its ability to provide an experience a bit more exhilarating than a highway to the suburbs at six p.m.
Why not call 1-800-FINE 4WD for the Range Rover dealer nearest you?
We won't deny that at somewhat above $34,000 a Range Rover is hardly inexpensive.
But after all the time you've spent in trafficlikethis, what could be nicer than going off on your own?
RANGE ROVER

Range Rover

Normandy
was captured
long before
D-Day.
NORMANDY AND ITS ARTISTS REMEMBERED AT THE NASSAU COUNTY MUSEUM OF ART
JUNE 12 - SEPTEMBER 11, 1994. FEATURING MONET, COROT, BONNARD, DUFY, AMONG OTHERS
TUESDAY THROUGH SUNDAY, 11:00 AM TIL 5:00 PM. FOR MORE INFORMATION CALL 516-484-9337
SPONSORED IN PART BY ALL OF US AT THE AMERICANA

Nassau County Museum of Art

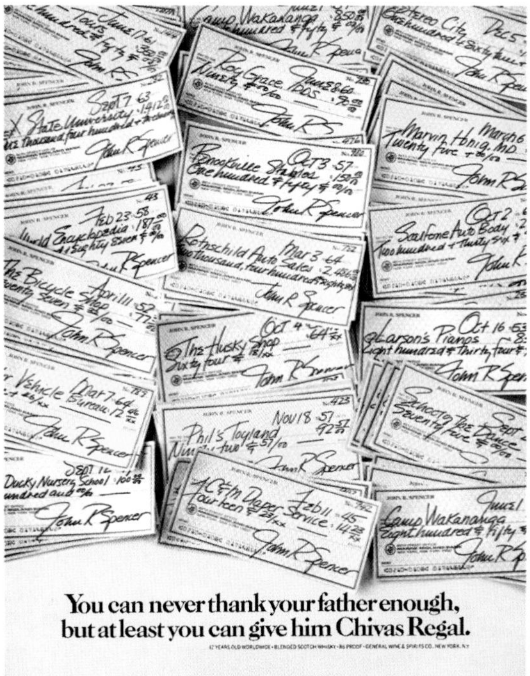
You can never thank your father enough,
but at least you can give him Chivas Regal.

Chivas Regal

THE ONE SHOW
BEST OF SHOW

REFRESHING, BRILLIANT AND SATISFYING. AND WE'RE NOT JUST TALKING ABOUT THE BEER. AMV BBDO'S SPOT FOR GUINNESS, TITLED "NOITULOVE," WHICH SPELLS EVOLUTION BACKWARDS, TAKES THE VIEWER ON A JOURNEY THROUGH TIME. THE STORY BEGINS WITH THREE MEN IN A BAR WHO TAKE A SIP OF GUINNESS BEER. THEN THE SWINGING MUSIC BEGINS AND EVERYTHING STARTS TO GO IN REVERSE. THE MEN TURN TO CAVEMEN, THEN APES, THEN AQUATIC ANIMALS UNTIL THEY REACH THEIR MOST PRIMITIVE STATE AS SLIMY, LIZARD-LIKE CREATURES. GOOD THINGS DO INDEED COME TO THOSE WHO WAIT, WHICH IS WHY IT'S OUR 2006 BEST OF SHOW.

CLIENT
Guinness

AGENCY
Abbott Mead Vickers BBDO/London

[We see three men in a bar about to take a sip of Guinness beer. Then they begin to walk backwards out the bar in sped-up reverse to the tune of Sammy Davis, Jr.'s "Rhythm of Life." The cityscape devolves into a town and then the wilderness. The men also turn into cavemen and we see various stages of time such as the Ice Age and the period where dinosaurs roamed the Earth. They turn into chimps, aquatic creatures and finally into three slimy, primitive animals. One takes a sip of pond water.]

CREATURE: Blech!

SUPER: Good things come to those who wait.

GOOD THINGS COME TO THOSE WHO WAIT.
GUINNESS

CLIENT OF THE YEAR: UNILEVER

THE NEW LONGER LASTING
AXE EFFECT.
AXE

2006 was the year of big commercials, and fittingly, it was the year of big brands as Unilever won our Client of the Year award. Brands under the Unilever umbrella such as Axe in the U.S. and Lynx in Europe brought cheeky lad humor to their integrated campaigns. Print, TV, online, collateral and even a mock airline worked perfectly in sync with each other and showed what's possible when a big brand is willing to take creative risks.

AXE
axefantasy.com

AXE
axefantasy.com
The Axe Effect
AXEFANTASY

Bronze

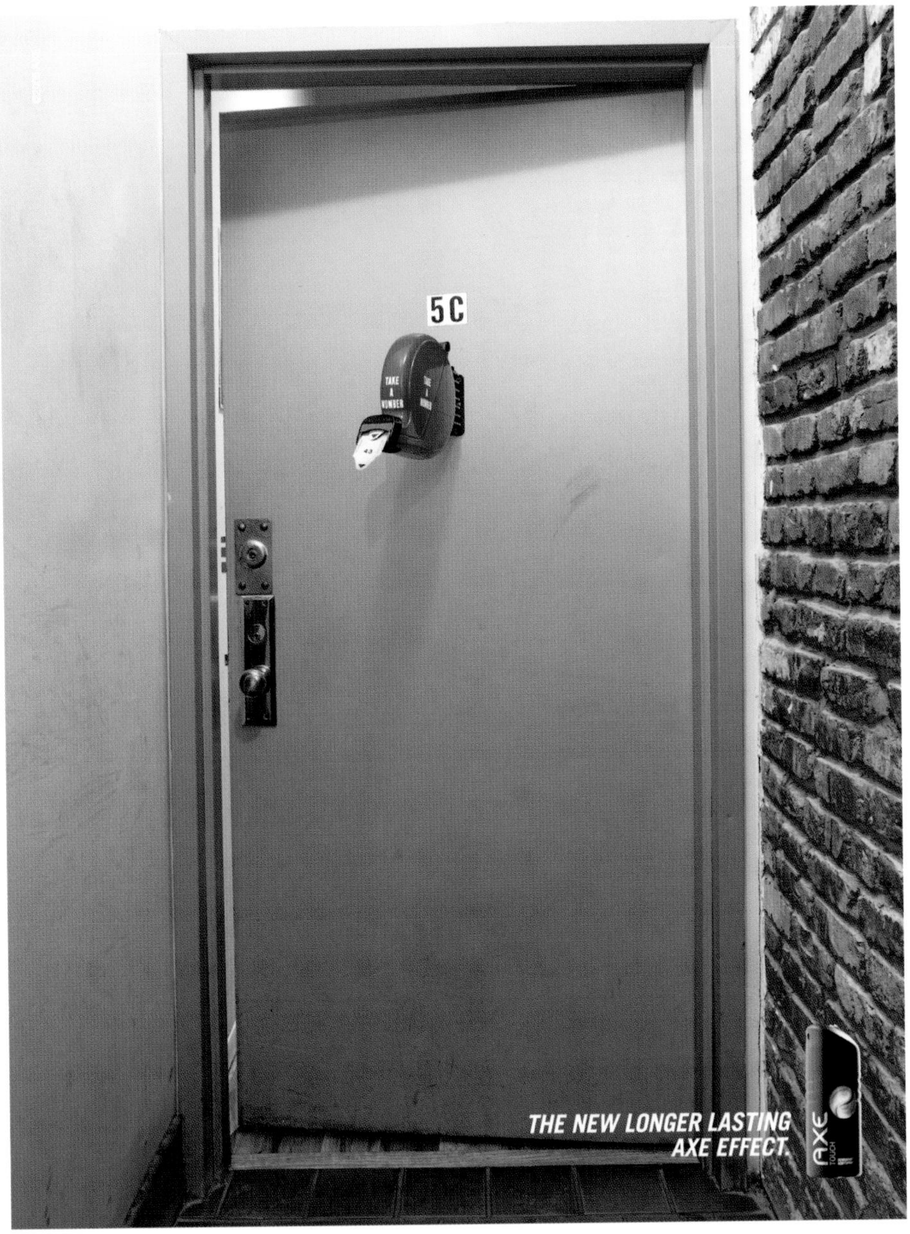
5C
THE NEW LONGER LASTING
AXE EFFECT.
AXE

Bronze

Merit

Bronze

THE AXE EFFECT
AXE

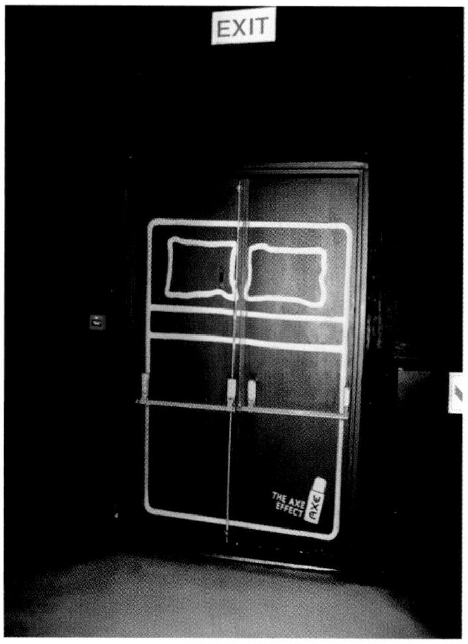
EXIT
THE AXE EFFECT
AXE

THE AXE EFFECT
AXE

Merit

His
Hers
Her Sister's
Her Roommate's
How Dirty Boys Get Clean.
NEW AXE SHOWER GEL
AXE

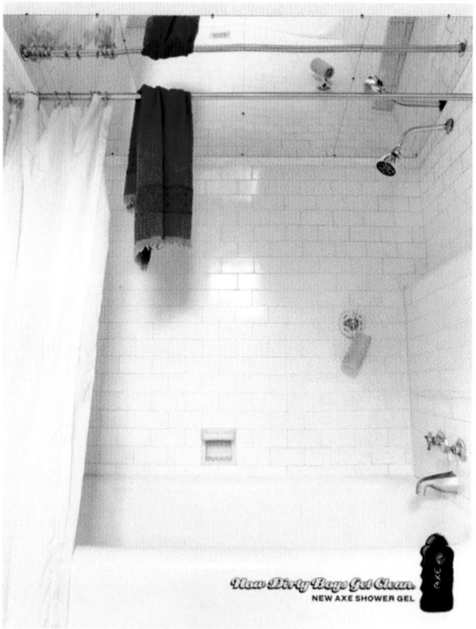
How Dirty Boys Get Clean.
NEW AXE SHOWER GEL

How Dirty Boys Get Clean.
NEW AXE SHOWER GEL

Merit

WHEN OUTNUMBERED AND PHYSICALLY EXHAUSTED BY GIRLS, THIS NAPKIN MAY ALSO BE USED AS A FLAG OF SURRENDER.
IT CAN HAPPEN ANYWHERE.

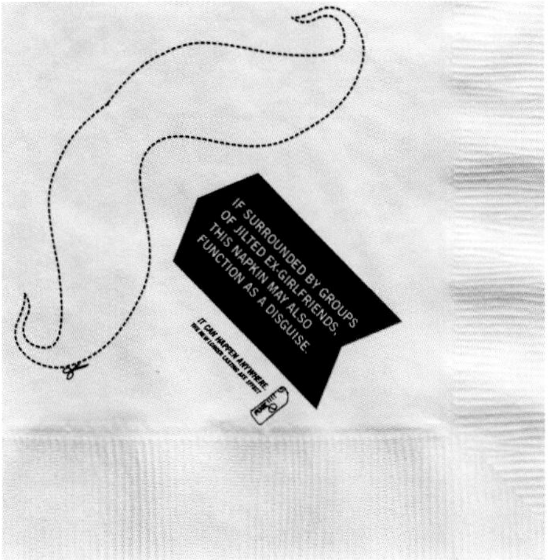
IF SURROUNDED BY GROUPS OF JILTED EX-GIRLFRIENDS, THIS NAPKIN MAY ALSO FUNCTION AS A DISGUISE.
IT CAN HAPPEN ANYWHERE.

Merit

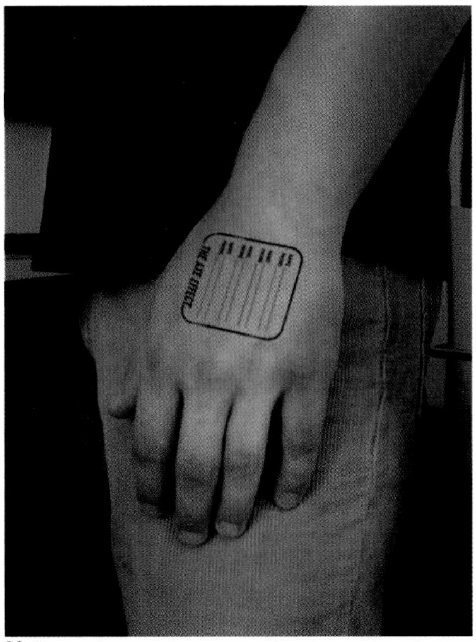
THE AXE EFFECT.

Merit

It was very special

Merit

Merit

TAXI

BRONZE
CATEGORY
Outdoor-Campaign

ART DIRECTORS
Amee Shah
Phillip Bonnery

WRITERS
Matt Ian
Brian Friedrich

PHOTOGRAPHER
Clang

CREATIVE DIRECTOR
William Gelner

AGENCY
Bartle Bogle Hegarty/ New York

ANNUAL ID
06023A

BRONZE
CATEGORY
Exceptional Innovation in Marketing: Innovative Marketing - Single

ART DIRECTOR
Husen Baba Khan

WRITER
Sandeep Fernandes

AGENCY PRODUCER
Vinayachandran Chandrahasan

CREATIVE DIRECTOR
Manoj Ammanath

AGENCY
Lowe/Dubai

ANNUAL ID
06052A

BRONZE
CATEGORY
Integrated Branding - Campaign

DESIGNER
Kris Rees

ART DIRECTORS
Dejan Rasic
Simone Brandse
Nick Robinson

WRITERS
Michael Canning
Howard Collinge

PHOTOGRAPHER
Stephen Stewart

DIGITAL ARTIST/ MULTIMEDIA
Jamie Corker

AGENCY PRODUCERS
Darren Bailey
Lisa Cordukes
Charna Henry
Jeff Edwards

PRODUCTION COMPANY
Plaza Films

DIRECTOR
Nicholas Reynolds

CREATIVE DIRECTORS
Adam Lance
Peter Bidenko

AGENCY
Lowe Hunt/Sydney

ANNUAL ID
06004G

MERIT
CATEGORY
Consumer Television: Over:30 - Single - Max :90

ART DIRECTOR
Diego Sanchez

WRITER
Matias Corbelle

AGENCY PRODUCER
Roberto Carsillo

PRODUCTION COMPANY
Rebolucion

DIRECTOR
Armando Bo

CREATIVE DIRECTORS
Hernan Ponce
Sebastian Stagno
Rafael D'Alvia

AGENCY
VegaOlmosPonce/ Acassuso

ANNUAL ID
06060T

MERIT
CATEGORY
Consumer Television: :20 and under - Campaign

ART DIRECTORS
Amee Shah
John Hobbs

WRITERS
Matt Ian
Peter Rosch

AGENCY PRODUCER
Lisa Gatto

PRODUCTION COMPANY
HSI Productions

DIRECTOR
Joe Public

CREATIVE DIRECTOR
William Gelner

AGENCY
Bartle Bogle Hegarty/ New York

ANNUAL ID
06096T

MERIT
CATEGORY
Consumer Magazine: Color: Full Page or Spread - Campaign

ART DIRECTOR
Nick Klinkert

WRITER
Tom Kraemer

PHOTOGRAPHER
Todd Hido

CREATIVE DIRECTOR
William Gelner

CLIENT
Unilever

AGENCY
Bartle Bogle Hegarty/ New York

ANNUAL ID
06097A

MERIT
CATEGORY
Exceptional Innovation in Media: Print - Single

ART DIRECTOR
Andre Massis

WRITER
Nathan Frank

ILLUSTRATOR
Andre Massis

CREATIVE DIRECTOR
William Gelner

AGENCY
Bartle Bogle Hegarty/ New York

ANNUAL ID
06251A

MERIT
CATEGORY
Exceptional Innovation in Media: Print - Single

ART DIRECTOR
Andre Massis

WRITER
Nathan Frank

PHOTOGRAPHER
Jason Fulford

CREATIVE DIRECTOR
William Gelner

CLIENT
Unilever

AGENCY
Bartle Bogle Hegarty/ New York

ANNUAL ID
06252A

MERIT
CATEGORY
Exceptional Innovation in Media: Print - Single

ART DIRECTOR
Andre Massis

WRITER
Nathan Frank

CREATIVE DIRECTOR
William Gelner

AGENCY
Bartle Bogle Hegarty/ New York

ANNUAL ID
06253A

MERIT
CATEGORY
Exceptional Innovation in Media: Outdoor - Single

ART DIRECTORS
Marion Bryan
Andre Vrdoljak

WRITER
Asheen Naidu

CREATIVE DIRECTORS
Gareth Lessing
Rob McLennan

AGENCY
Lowe Bull/Johannesburg

ANNUAL ID
06274A

GOLD
SILVER
BRONZE

THE ONE SHOW

MMVI

INTERACTIVE ADVERTISING DESIGN

SILVER

ART DIRECTOR
Steve Jones

WRITER
Martin Loraine

ILLUSTRATOR
Spencer Lawrence

CREATIVE DIRECTOR
Jeremy Craigen

CLIENT
Volkswagen

AGENCY
DDB/London

ANNUAL ID
06003A

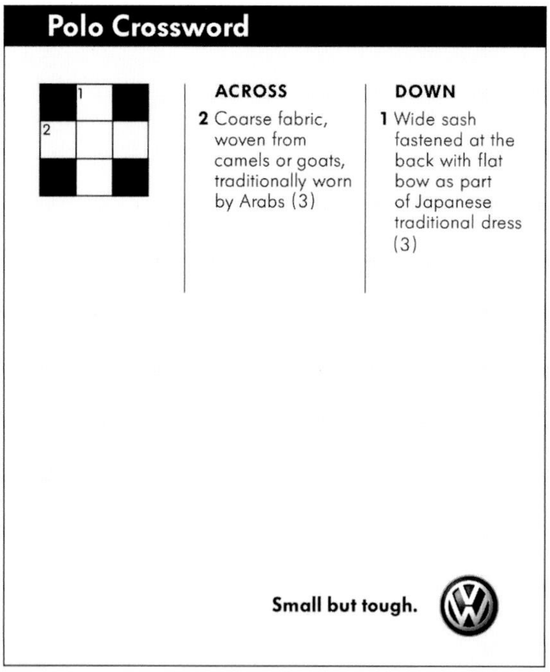
Polo Crossword
1
2
ACROSS
2 Coarse fabric, woven from camels or goats, traditionally worn by Arabs (3)
DOWN
1 Wide sash fastened at the back with flat bow as part of Japanese traditional dress (3)
Small but tough.

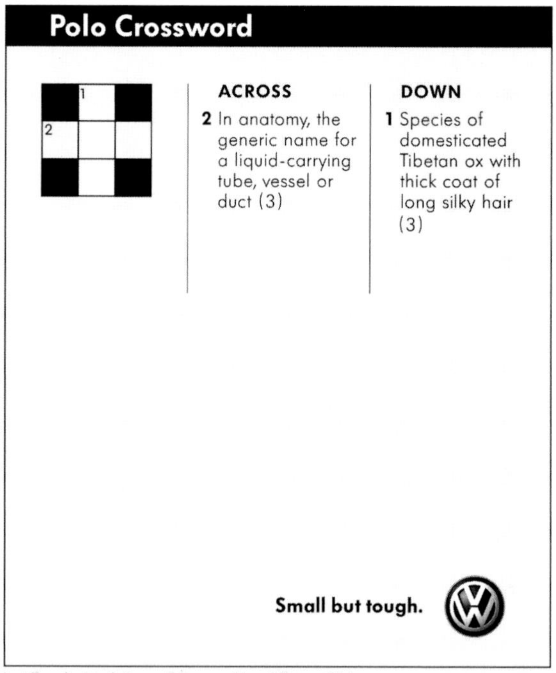
Polo Crossword
1
2
ACROSS
2 In anatomy, the generic name for a liquid-carrying tube, vessel or duct (3)
DOWN
1 Species of domesticated Tibetan ox with thick coat of long silky hair (3)
Small but tough.

Last Tuesday's solutions: 2 Across: Aba. 1 Down: Obi.

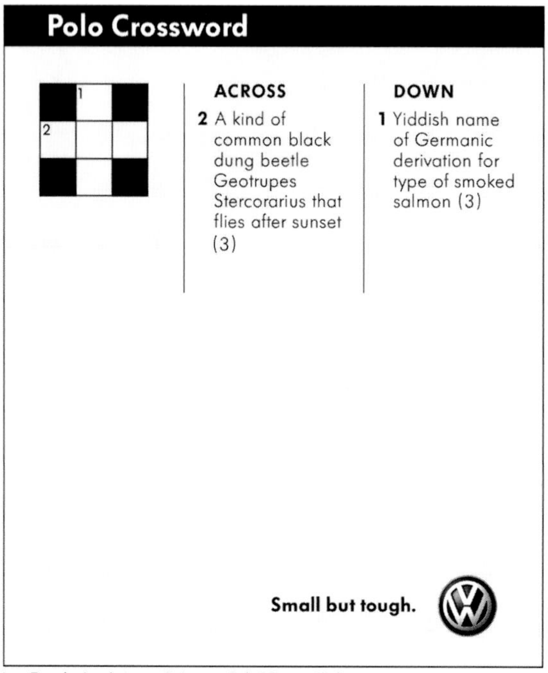
Polo Crossword
1
2
ACROSS
2 A kind of common black dung beetle Geotrupes Stercorarius that flies after sunset (3)
DOWN
1 Yiddish name of Germanic derivation for type of smoked salmon (3)
Small but tough.

Last Tuesday's solutions: 2 Across: Bel. 1 Down: Ked.

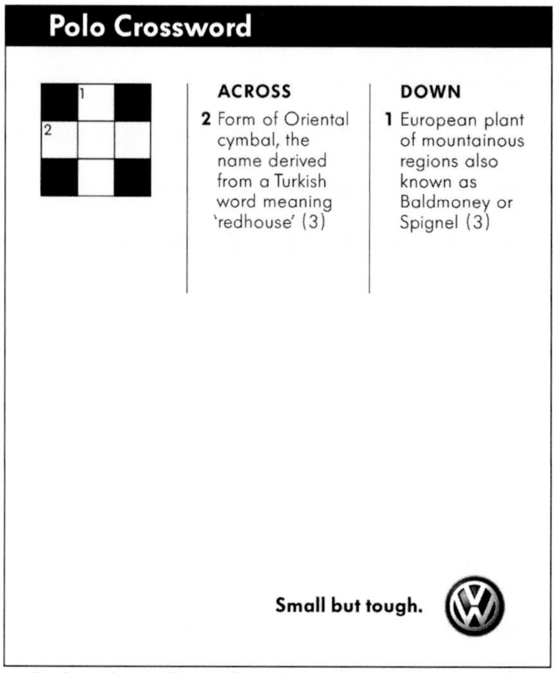
Polo Crossword
1
2
ACROSS
2 Form of Oriental cymbal, the name derived from a Turkish word meaning 'redhouse' (3)
DOWN
1 European plant of mountainous regions also known as Baldmoney or Spignel (3)
Small but tough.

Last Tuesday's solutions: 2 Across: Dor. 1 Down: Lox.

durex
extra large

Merit

durex
extra large

durex
extra large

durex
extra large

BRONZE

ART DIRECTORS
Shane Forbes
Liam Wielopolski

WRITERS
Glenn Curtis
Clint Bechus

PHOTOGRAPHER
Michael Meyersfeld

CREATIVE DIRECTORS
Graham Warsop
Michael Blore

CLIENT
Permark International

AGENCY
The Jupiter Drawing Room/Johannesburg

ANNUAL ID
06004A

ALSO AWARDED
Merit:
Consumer Newspaper:
Over 600 Lines - Single

Merit:
Collateral:
Posters - Campaign

Merit:
Consumer Magazine
Color: Full Page or
Spread - Campaign

GOLD

ART DIRECTORS
Paul Stechschulte
Tiffany Kosel

WRITERS
Franklin Tipton
Rob Reilly

CREATIVE DIRECTORS
Alex Bogusky
Andrew Keller
Steve O'Connell

CLIENT
MINI

AGENCY
Crispin Porter + Bogusky/Miami

ANNUAL ID
06005A

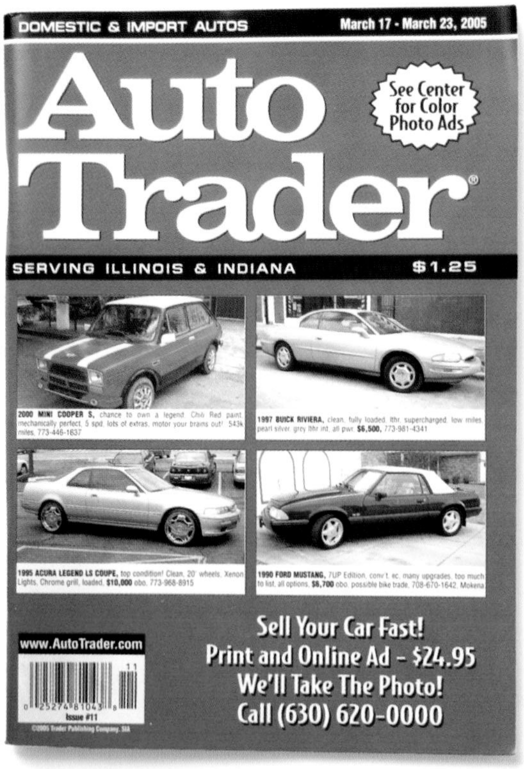
DOMESTIC & IMPORT AUTOS
March 17 - March 23, 2005
Auto Trader
See Center for Color Photo Ads
SERVING ILLINOIS & INDIANA
$1.25
www.AutoTrader.com
Sell Your Car Fast!
Print and Online Ad - $24.95
We'll Take The Photo!
Call (630) 620-0000

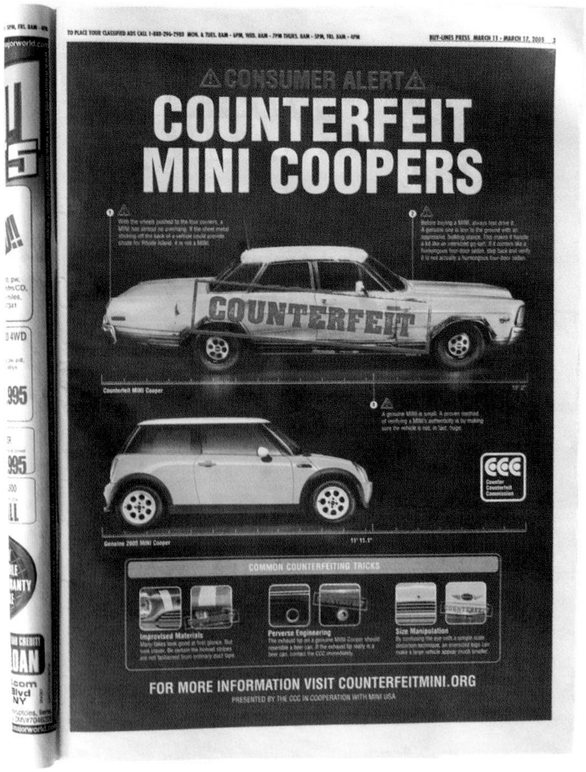
CONSUMER ALERT
COUNTERFEIT MINI COOPERS
COUNTERFEIT
COMMON COUNTERFEITING TRICKS
FOR MORE INFORMATION VISIT COUNTERFEITMINI.ORG

BMW
McKENNA CERTIFIED PRE-OWNED CENTER
No Photo Available
2003 MINI COOPER S, super charged, 1.6L eng, 6 spd, authentic union jack roof & mirrors, one owner, garage kept, whiptastic handling, 310-492-5184 CWA21312/ 00464080617
For boats, cycles or RVs go to www.TraderOnline.com

2003 MINI COOPER S, super charged, 1.6L eng, 6 spd, authentic union jack roof & mirrors, one owner, garage kept, whiptastic handling, 310-492-5184 CWA21312/ 00464080617

pasta shapes
in tomato sauce
MARVEL
SPIDER-MAN
HEINZ
TM and © 2004 Marvel

GOLD

ART DIRECTORS
Nicholas Pringle
Clark Edwards

WRITERS
Nicholas Pringle
Clark Edwards

PHOTOGRAPHER
Kelvin Murray

CREATIVE DIRECTOR
Jim Thornton

CLIENT
Heinz

AGENCY
Leo Burnett/London

ANNUAL ID
06006A

ALSO AWARDED
Silver:
Consumer Newspaper:
Over 600 Lines - Single

GOLD

ART DIRECTORS
Matt Miller
Dan Ware
Adrien Bindi
Greg Auer

WRITERS
Andy Dao
Dave Derrick
Nick Cade
Mark Andersen

PHOTOGRAPHER
Tony D'Orio

CREATIVE DIRECTORS
Noel Haan
G. Andrew Meyer

CLIENT
Altoids

AGENCY
Leo Burnett/Chicago

ANNUAL ID
06009A

ALSO AWARDED
Merit:
Consumer Magazine
Color - Single

Merit:
Consumer Magazine
Color - Single

Merit:
Consumer Magazine
Color: - Single

VE HAVE VAYS OV MAKING YOU TALK.
THE CURIOUSLY STRONG MINTS
curious? altoids.com

Merit

ALTOIDS CINNAMON
THE CURIOUSLY STRONG MINTS
curious? altoids.com

Merit

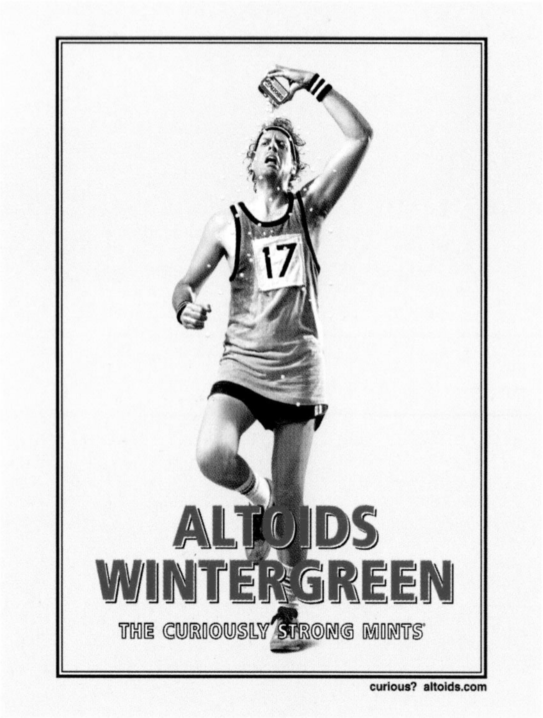
17
ALTOIDS WINTERGREEN
THE CURIOUSLY STRONG MINTS
curious? altoids.com

Merit

ALTOIDS SMALLS
THE CURIOUSLY STRONG (and small) MINTS
curious? altoids.com

Risk

Bronze, Merit

Risk

Merit

中华人民共和国万
世界人民大团结
Risk

Silver

ART DIRECTOR
Din Sumedi

WRITER
Mikael Teo

PHOTOGRAPHERS
Teo Studio
Corbis

CREATIVE DIRECTOR
Graham Kelly

CLIENT
Hasbro

AGENCY
Saatchi & Saatchi/ Singapore

ANNUAL ID
06010A

ALSO AWARDED
Silver:
Collateral:
Posters - Campaign

Bronze:
Consumer Newspaper:
Over 600 Lines - Single

Merit:
Collateral:
Posters - Single

Merit:
Consumer Newspaper:
Over 600 Lines - Single

BRONZE

ART DIRECTORS
Vanessa Gibson
Robyn Bergmann

WRITER
Bridget Johnson

PHOTOGRAPHER
Clive Stewart

CREATIVE DIRECTORS
Fran Luckin
Gerry Human

CLIENT
Harley-Davidson

AGENCY
Ogilvy South Africa/
Johannesburg

ANNUAL ID
06011A

BIKES FOR WOMEN

BIKES FOR WOMEN

BIKES FOR WOMEN

$1.25
extra
Bring this coupon and pay an extra
$1.25 on your next Stella Artois.
1 1004623 2384623 0
No valid with any other offers.
Excludes tax and other charges.
Valid at participating locations only.
Expires 11/30/2005.
ANNO 1366
STELLA ARTOIS
Reassuringly expensive.

$4.00
reg. $2.75
Bring this coupon and pay an extra
$1.25 on your next Stella Artois.
1 1004623 2384623 0
No valid with any other offers.
Excludes tax and other charges.
Valid at participating locations only.
Expires 11/30/2005.
ANNO 1366
STELLA ARTOIS
Reassuringly expensive.

20%
more
Bring this coupon and pay an extra
$1.25 on your next Stella Artois.
1 1004623 2384623 0
No valid with any other offers.
Excludes tax and other charges.
Valid at participating locations only.
Expires 11/30/2005.
ANNO 1366
STELLA ARTOIS
Reassuringly expensive.

Gold

ART DIRECTOR
Raj Kamble

WRITER
Anselmo Ramos

CREATIVE DIRECTORS
Fernanda Romano
John Hobbs
Peter Rosch
Mark Wnek

CLIENT
Stella Artois

AGENCY
Lowe/New York

ANNUAL ID
06012A

BRONZE

ART DIRECTORS
Paul Kwong
Kim Jenkins

WRITERS
Glen Levy
Craig Love

CREATIVE DIRECTORS
Tony Granger
Tod Seisser
Mark Cacciatore
Ron Arnold

CLIENT
General Mills - Wheaties

AGENCY
Saatchi & Saatchi/
New York

ANNUAL ID
06013A

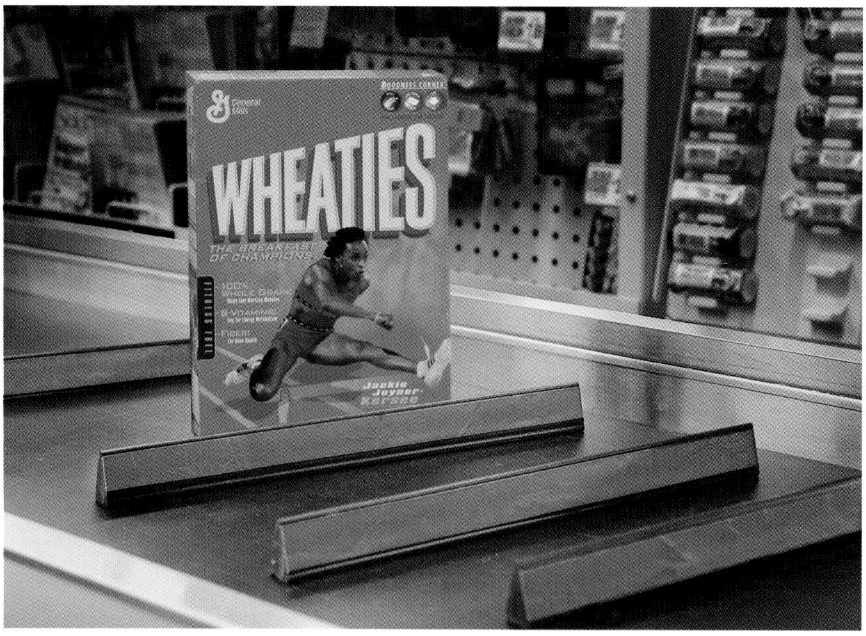
General Mills
WHEATIES
THE BREAKFAST OF CHAMPIONS
100% WHOLE GRAIN
B-VITAMINS
FIBER
Jackie Joyner-Kersee

General Mills
GOODNESS CORNER
WHEATIES
THE BREAKFAST OF CHAMPIONS
100% WHOLE GRAIN
Michael Phelps
SWIMMING

General Mills
GOODNESS CORNER
WHEATIES
MARTINEZ
45
Pedro Martinez

PLEASE SEND COMMENTS OR COMPLAINTS TO:
YOUR ASS
1019 YOURASS AVE.
YOURASS, YA 10012
the ONION

SILVER

ART DIRECTOR
Kevin Thoem

WRITER
Kevin Thoem

CREATIVE DIRECTORS
Mike Hughes
Mike Lear

CLIENT
The Onion

AGENCY
The Martin Agency/ Richmond

ANNUAL ID
06014A

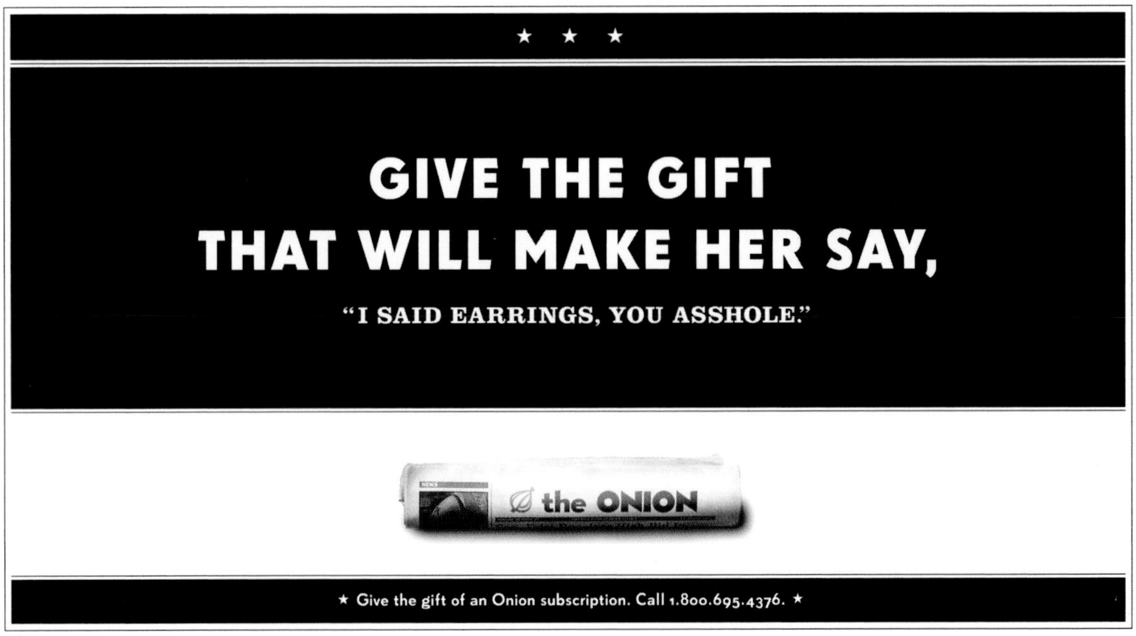
GIVE THE GIFT THAT WILL MAKE HER SAY,
"I SAID EARRINGS, YOU ASSHOLE."
the ONION
★ Give the gift of an Onion subscription. Call 1.800.695.4376. ★

Silver

ALL THE THINGS YOU'VE THOUGHT BUT NEVER SAID,
PRINTED AND DISTRIBUTED NATIONALLY.
the ONION
★ Subscribe to The Onion. One year, delivered, only $39.95. Call 1.866.466.4667 ★

HELL IS GONNA BE SO COOL.
the ONION
★ Subscribe to The Onion. One year, delivered, only $39.95. Call 1.866.466.4667 ★

STORIES THAT HIT HARDER
THAN YOUR LAST BOYFRIEND.
the ONION
★ Subscribe to The Onion. One year, delivered, only $39.95. Call 1.866.466.4667 ★

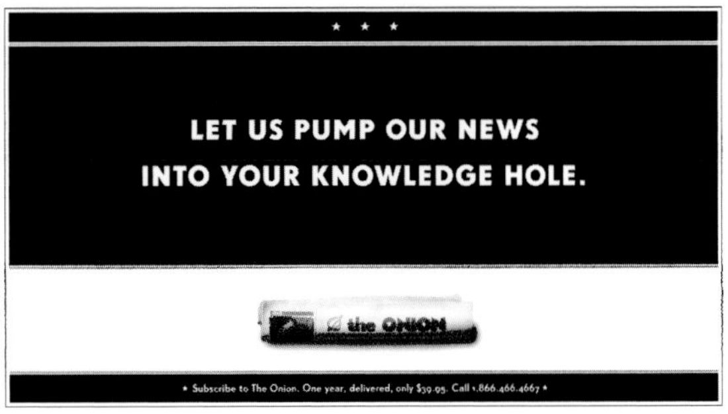
LET US PUMP OUR NEWS INTO YOUR KNOWLEDGE HOLE.
the ONION
★ Subscribe to The Onion. One year, delivered, only $39.95. Call 1.866.466.4667 ★

SILVER

ART DIRECTOR
Kevin Thoem

WRITERS
Mike Lear
Todd Brusnighan
Sara Grunden

CREATIVE DIRECTORS
Mike Hughes
Mike Lear

CLIENT
The Onion

AGENCY
The Martin Agency/ Richmond

ANNUAL ID
06016A

ALSO AWARDED
Silver:
Small Space: Black and White - Single

SILVER

ART DIRECTORS
Markham Smith
Mark Fairbanks

WRITERS
Markham Smith
Mark Fairbanks

CREATIVE DIRECTORS
Paul Belford
Nigel Roberts

CLIENT
The Economist

AGENCY
Abbott Mead Vickers BBDO/London

ANNUAL ID
06019A

If at first you don't succeed... hang on, sorry, wrong poster.
The Economist

BRONZE

WRITERS
Tim Riley
Richard Foster

DESIGNER
John Tisdall

CREATIVE DIRECTORS
Paul Belford
Nigel Roberts

CLIENT
The Economist

AGENCY
Abbott Mead Vickers BBDO/London

ANNUAL ID
06020A

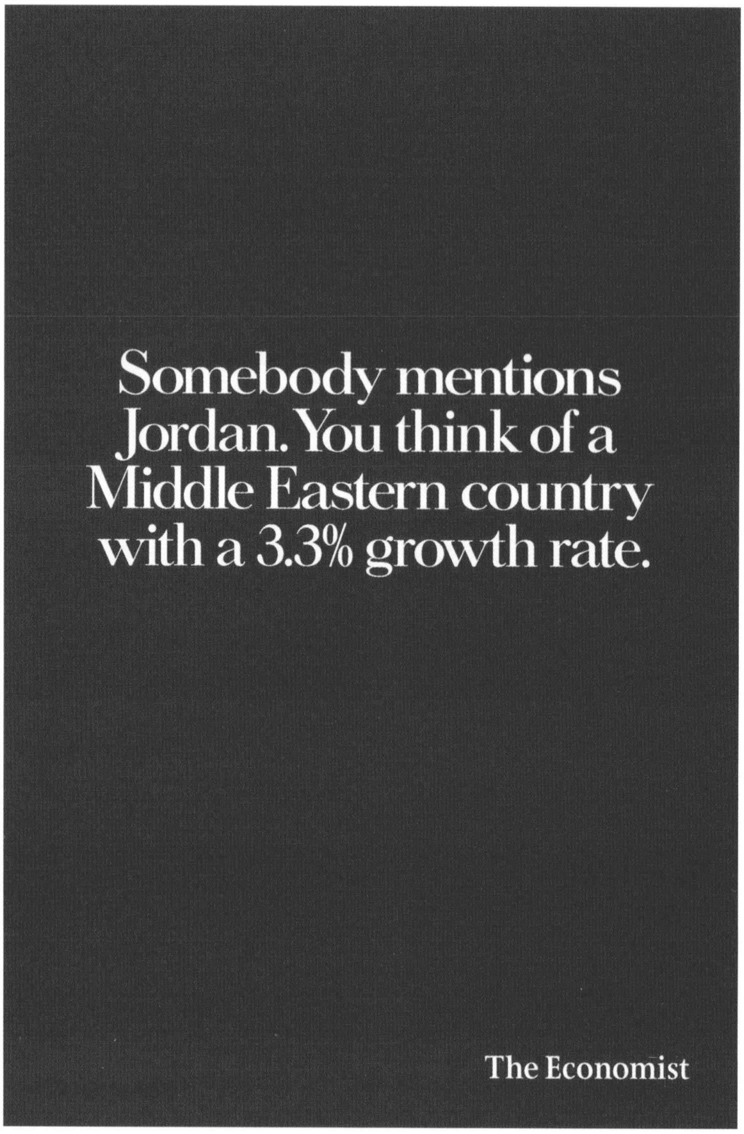
Somebody mentions Jordan. You think of a Middle Eastern country with a 3.3% growth rate.
The Economist

LEGO
play on

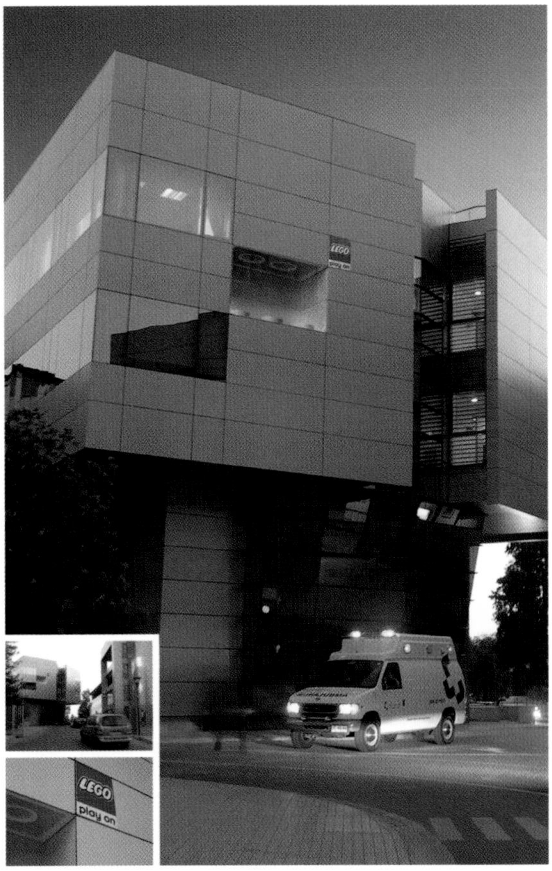
LEGO
play on
LEGO
play on

Gold

ART DIRECTORS
Sebastian Alvarado
Sergio Iacobelli

WRITER
Felipe Manalich

PHOTOGRAPHER
Juan Carlos Sotelo

ILLUSTRATOR
Ricardo Salamanca

CREATIVE DIRECTOR
Cesar Agost Carreno

CLIENT
Lego

AGENCY
Ogilvy & Mather/
Santiago

ANNUAL ID
06021A

ALSO AWARDED
Gold:
Outdoor - Single

LEGO
play on
E
EVITE MULTAS

Gold

Silver

ART DIRECTORS
Axel Schilling
Marc Ebenwaldner

WRITERS
Johan H. Ohlson
Alexander Schierl

DESIGNER
Pia Schneider

PHOTOGRAPHER
Hiepler, Brunier

CREATIVE DIRECTORS
Stefan Setzkorn
Silke Schneider
Gunnar Loeser

CLIENT
BSH Bosch und Siemens

AGENCY
Scholz & Friends/ Hamburg

ANNUAL ID
06022A

SIEMENS
CHESS WORLD CHAMPIONSHIP
PASKAROV
CHARLES
CHESS WORLD CHAMPIONSHIP
The quietest vacuum cleaner in its class:
technopower sound & silence.
Siemens. The future moving in.

SIEMENS
The quietest vacuum cleaner in its class:
technopower sound & silence.
Siemens. The future moving in.

SIEMENS
The quietest vacuum cleaner in its class:
technopower sound & silence.
Siemens. The future moving in.

©2005 AXE
5C
THE NEW LONGER LASTING
AXE EFFECT.
AXE

THE NEW LONGER LASTING
AXE EFFECT.

THE NEW LONGER LASTING
AXE EFFECT.

BRONZE

ART DIRECTORS
Amee Shah
Phillip Bonnery

WRITERS
Matt Ian
Brian Friedrich

PHOTOGRAPHER
Clang

CREATIVE DIRECTOR
William Gelner

CLIENT
Unilever

AGENCY
Bartle Bogle Hegarty/
New York

ANNUAL ID
06023A

Silver

ART DIRECTOR
Ashidiq Ghazali

PHOTOGRAPHER
Roy Zhang

ILLUSTRATOR
Magic Cube

CREATIVE DIRECTOR
Sonal Dabral

CLIENT
DHL

AGENCY
Ogilvy & Mather/ Singapore

ANNUAL ID
06024A

ALSO AWARDED
Bronze:
Collateral: Posters - Single

Merit:
Innovative Use of Media: Outdoor - Single

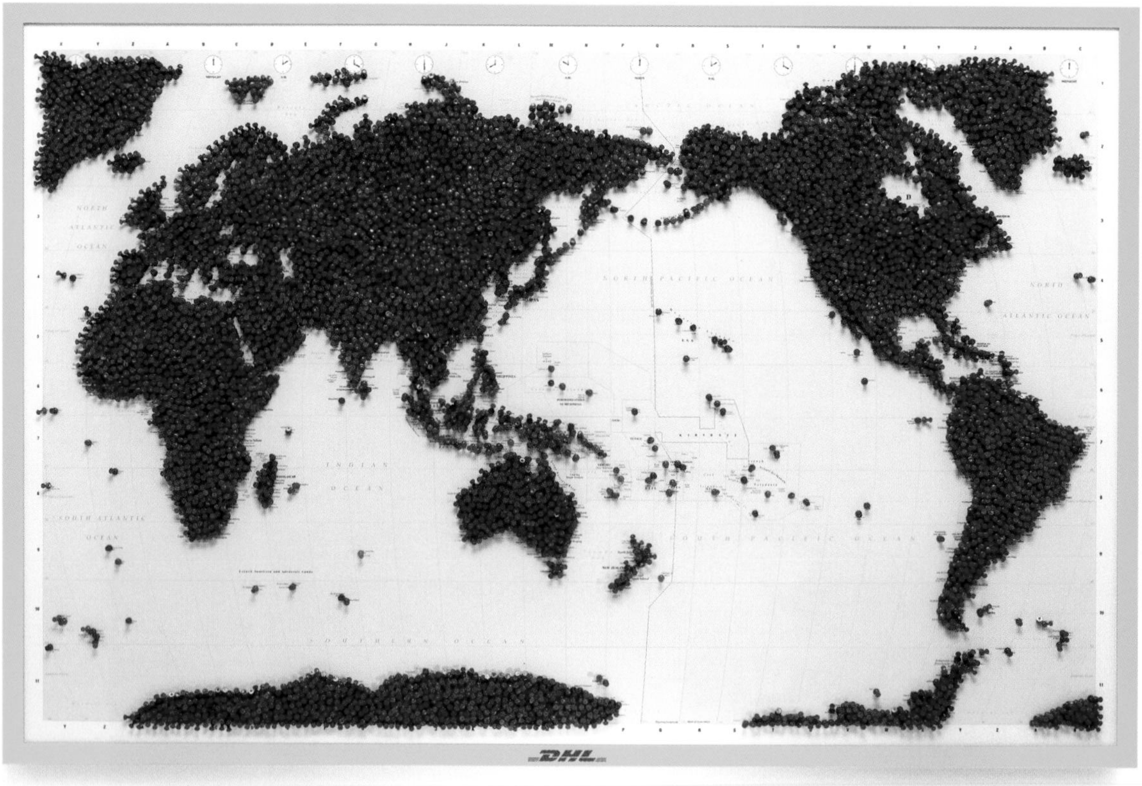
DHL

weru
soundproof windows

Silver

ART DIRECTOR
Kay Luebke

WRITER
Michael Haeussler

PHOTOGRAPHER
Ralph Baiker

CREATIVE DIRECTORS
Matthias Spaetgens
Jan Leube

CLIENT
Weru

AGENCY
Scholz & Friends/Berlin

ANNUAL ID
06025A

weru
soundproof windows

weru
soundproof windows

BRONZE

ART DIRECTORS
Petra Cremer
Benjamin Allwardt
Stefan Haegerling
Pia Kortemeier

WRITER
Hanna Kayenburg

CREATIVE DIRECTORS
Andreas Geyer
Ulrich Zuenkeler

CLIENT
Bisley

AGENCY
Kolle Rebbe Werbeagentur/Hamburg

ANNUAL ID
06026A

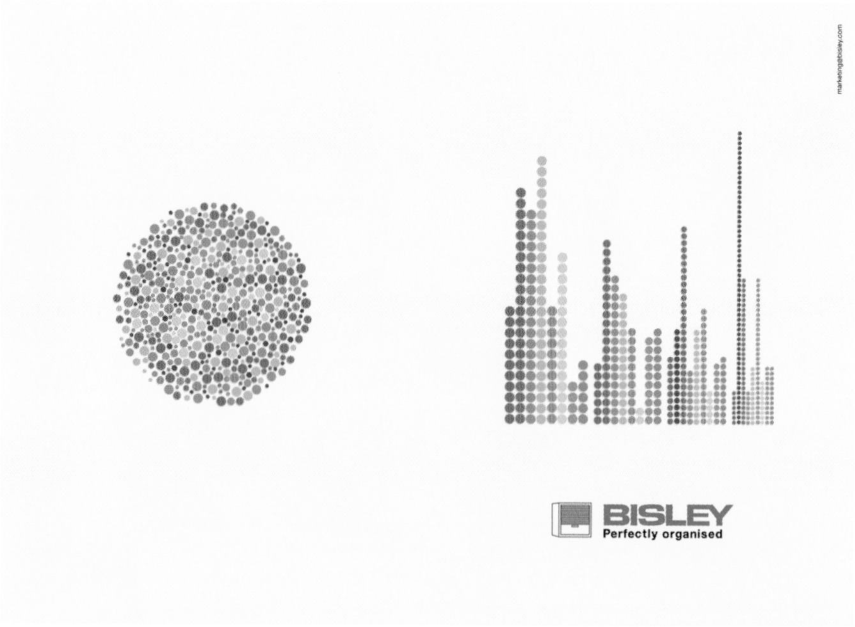
BISLEY
Perfectly organised

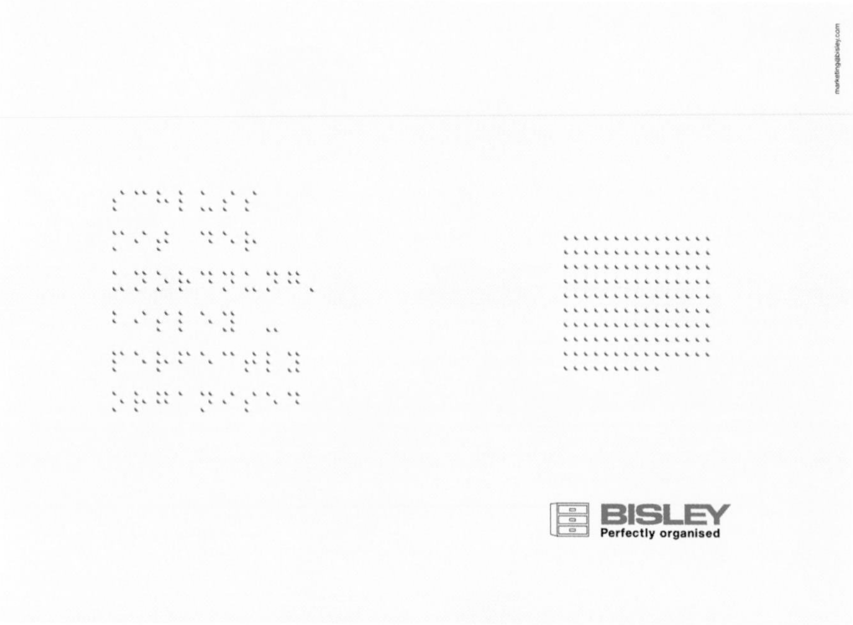
BISLEY
Perfectly organised

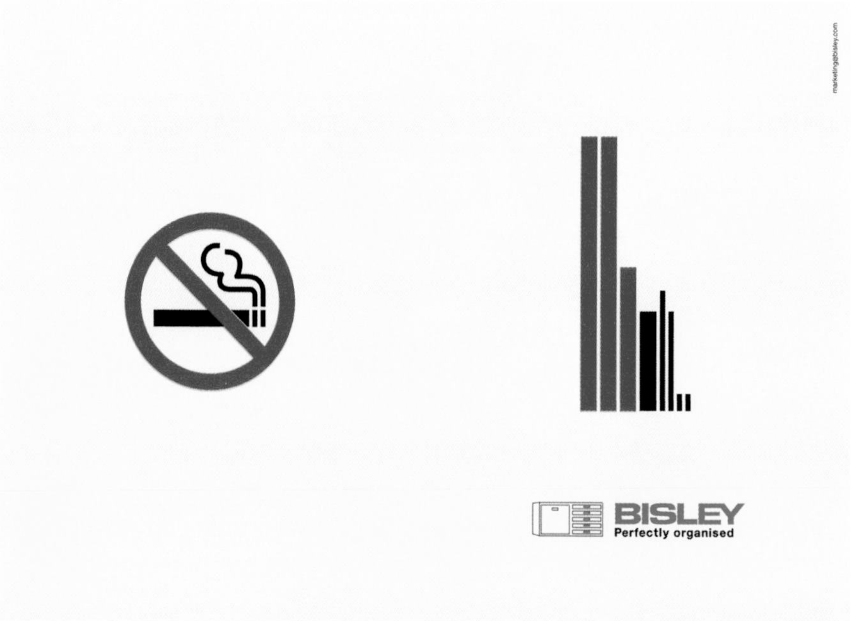
BISLEY
Perfectly organised

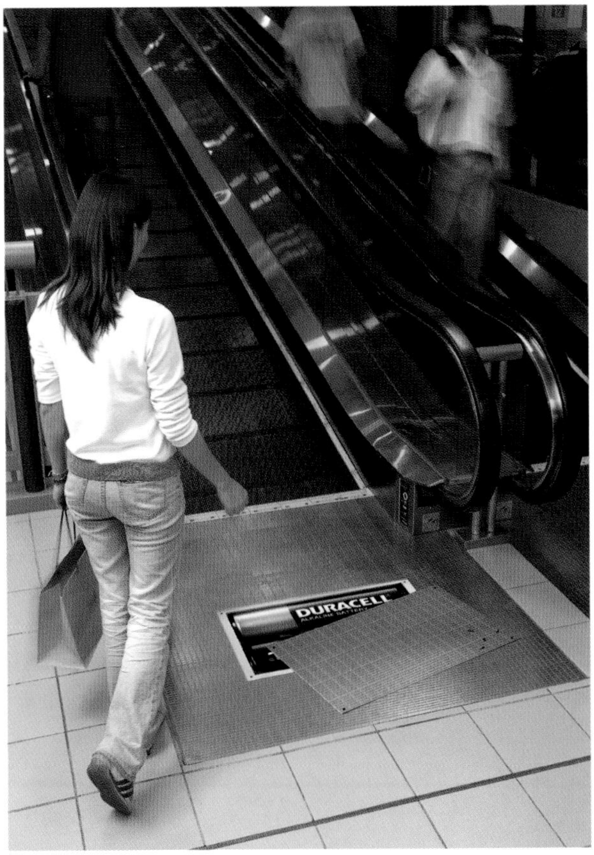
DURACELL

DURACELL
ALKALINE BATTERY

SILVER

ART DIRECTORS
James Wong
Gary Hor
Khai Meng Tham

WRITER
Danny Low

PHOTOGRAPHER
Wizard Photography

CREATIVE DIRECTORS
Daniel Comar
Khai Meng Tham
Brenda Boler

CLIENT
Gillette

AGENCY
Ogilvy & Mather/
Kuala Lumpur

ANNUAL ID
06028A

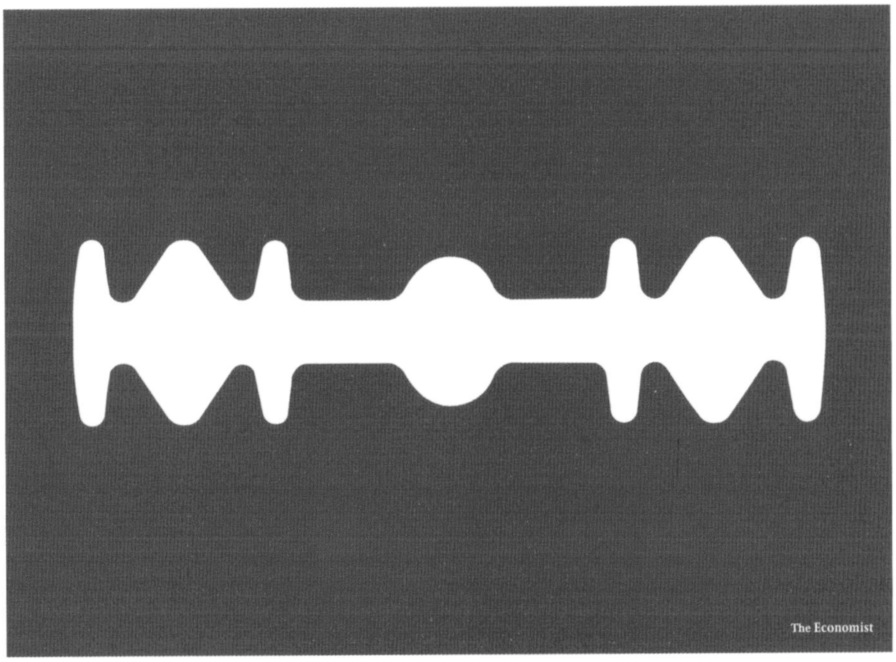
The Economist

BRONZE

ART DIRECTORS
Stuart Mills
Ashidiq Ghazali

WRITER
Eugene Cheong

CREATIVE DIRECTORS
Khai Meng Tham
Eugene Cheong

CLIENT
The Economist

AGENCY
Ogilvy & Mather/
Singapore

ANNUAL ID
06029A

ALSO AWARDED
Merit:
Consumer Magazine:
Color: Full Page or
Spread - Single

Gold

ART DIRECTOR
Justin Tindall

WRITER
Adam Tucker

PHOTOGRAPHER
James Day

CREATIVE DIRECTORS
Justin Tindall
Adam Tucker

CLIENT
Harvey Nichols

AGENCY
DDB/London

ANNUAL ID
06030A

ALSO AWARDED
Gold:
Collateral: P.O.P. and In-Store - Single

Silver:
Consumer Magazine Color: Full Page or Spread - Single

Bronze:
Consumer Magazine Color: Full Page or Spread - Single

Merit:
Consumer Magazine Color: Full Page or Spread - Single

Merit:
Collateral: P.O.P. and In-Store - Single

Merit:
Collateral: P.O.P. and In-Store - Single

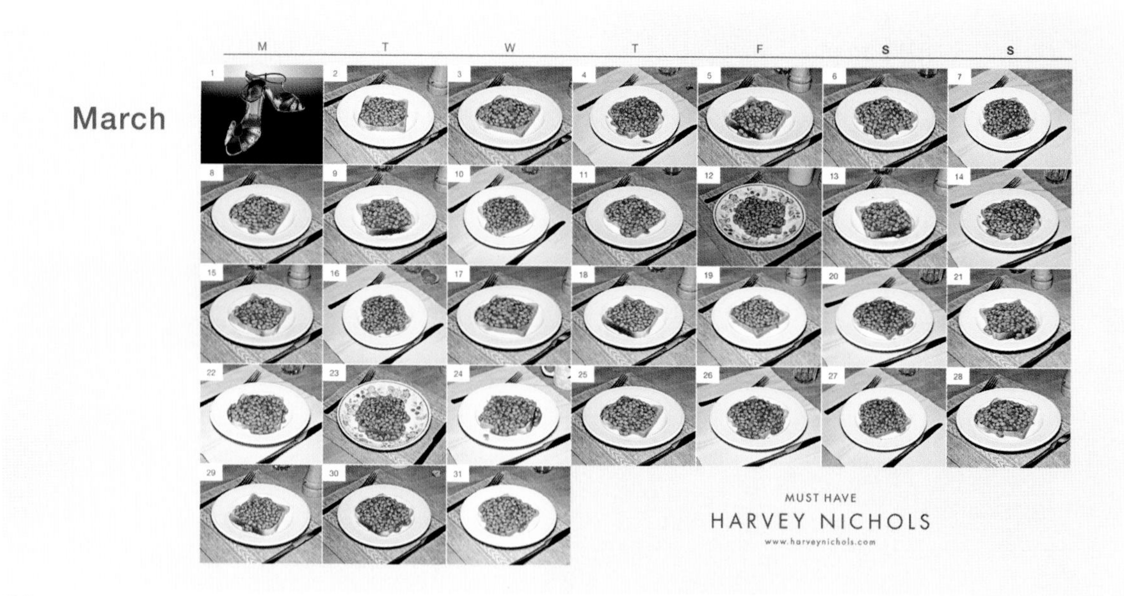
M T W T F S S
March
MUST HAVE
HARVEY NICHOLS
www.harveynichols.com

Gold

April
MUST HAVE
HARVEY NICHOLS

Silver, Merit

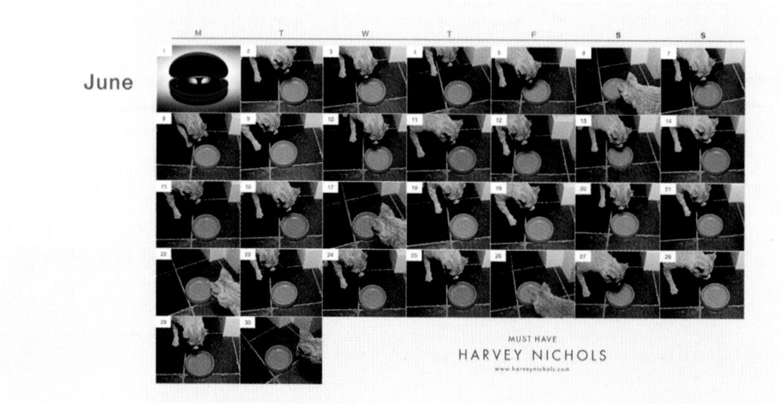
June
MUST HAVE
HARVEY NICHOLS

Bronze, Merit

May
MUST HAVE
HARVEY NICHOLS

Merit

MILO

Merit

MILO

Merit

MILO

Silver

ART DIRECTOR
Alan Vladusic

WRITERS
Neil Flory
Clay Weiner

PHOTOGRAPHER
Corbis

CREATIVE DIRECTOR
Sonal Dabral

CLIENT
Nestlé

AGENCY
Ogilvy & Mather/
Singapore

ANNUAL ID
06031A

ALSO AWARDED
Merit:
Collateral: P.O.P and In-Store - Single

Merit:
Collateral: P.O.P and In-Store - Single

Merit:
Consumer Magazine: Color: Full Page or Spread - Campaign

BRONZE

ART DIRECTOR
Jens Petter Waernes

WRITER
Simone Nobili

DESIGNER
Erik Dagnell

PHOTOGRAPHER
Stephan Abry

CREATIVE DIRECTORS
Jan Rexhausen
Doerte Spengler-Ahrens

CLIENT
Cars & Boxes

AGENCY
Jung von Matt/Hamburg

ANNUAL ID
06032A

CARS&BOXES
The toy car specialist. www.cars-and-boxes.de

CARS&BOXES
The toy car specialist. www.cars-and-boxes.de

CARS&BOXES
The toy car specialist. www.cars-and-boxes.de

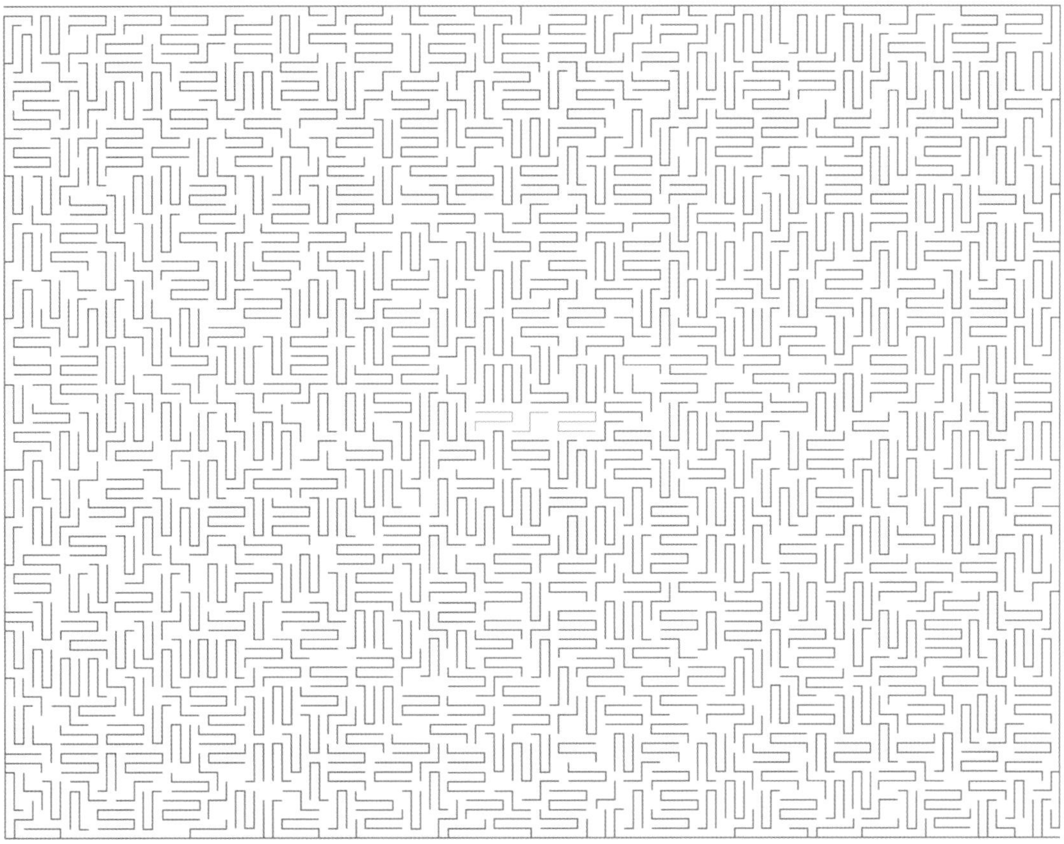

Silver

ART DIRECTORS
Ean-Hwa Huang
KC Chung

WRITERS
Szu-Hung Lee
Eddie Azadi

DESIGNER
KC Chung

CREATIVE DIRECTORS
Szu-Hung Lee
Ean-Hwa Huang

CLIENT
Sony

AGENCY
McCann Erickson/
Kuala Lumpur

ANNUAL ID
06033A

ALSO AWARDED
Silver:
One Show Design
Collateral Design:
Posters - Single

CONSUMER ALERT
As we chomped on our golfball-sized Skittles and hugged goodbye, my adoration for this wise and caring hedonist became simply unbearable. "I love you," I mumbled into the collar of his jacket.
COUNTERFEIT MINI COOPERS
PROTECT YOURSELF FROM THE HUMILIATION OF OWNING A FAKE!

CONSUMER ALERT
COUNTERFEIT MINI COOPERS: A BIG PROBLEM THAT'S GROWING BIGGER.
REPORT ALL SUSPICIOUS ACTIVITIES

HOW TO IDENTIFY A GENUINE MINI.
REPORT ALL SUSPICIOUS ACTIVITIES

Bronze

ART DIRECTORS
Paul Stechschulte
Tiffany Kosel

WRITERS
Franklin Tipton
Rob Reilly

PHOTOGRAPHER
Sebastian Gray

CREATIVE DIRECTORS
Alex Bogusky
Andrew Keller

CLIENT
MINI

AGENCY
Crispin Porter +
Bogusky/Miami

ANNUAL ID
06035A

BRONZE

ART DIRECTOR
Jerome Marucci

WRITER
Ari Weiss

ILLUSTRATOR
Amy Bartlett Wright

CREATIVE DIRECTORS
Dan Kelleher
Eric Silver
David Lubars

CLIENT
Guinness

AGENCY
BBDO/New York

ANNUAL ID
06037A

ALSO AWARDED
Merit:
One Show Design
Collateral: Posters - Single

Merit:
One Show Design
Collateral: Posters - Campaign

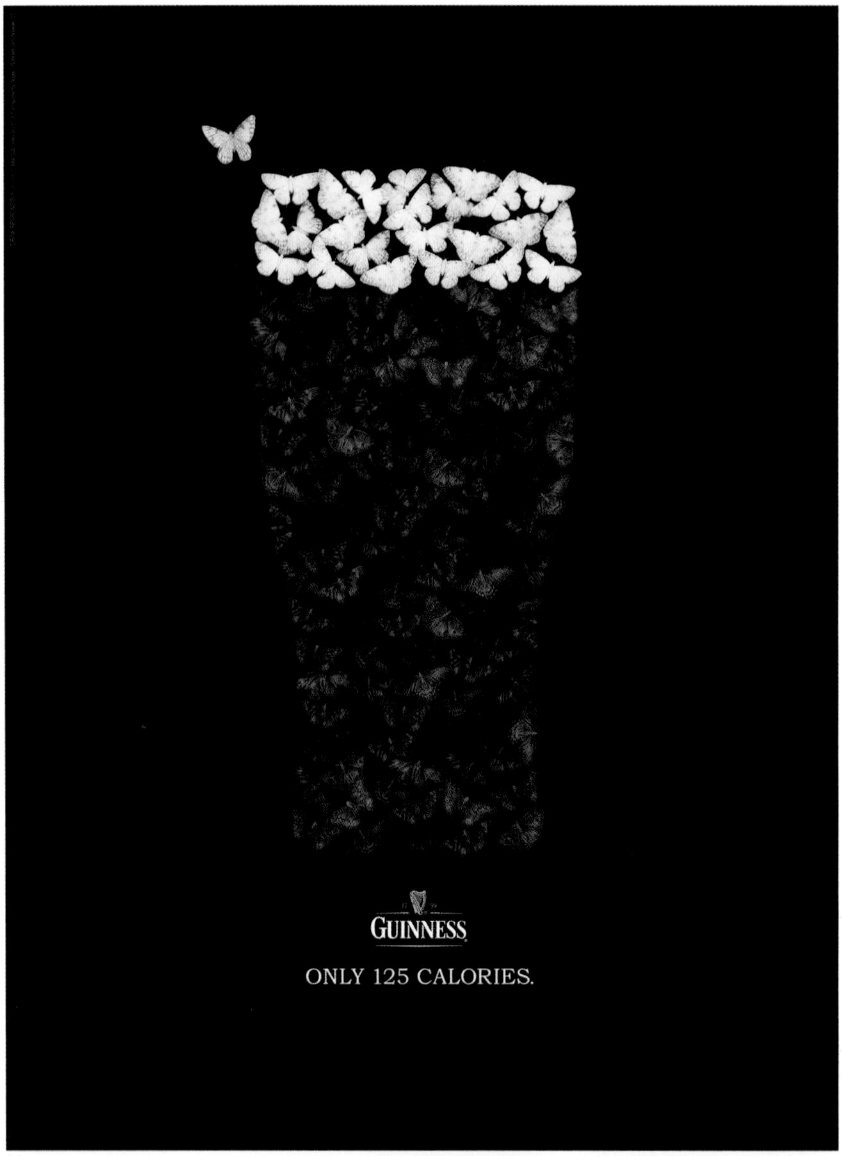
GUINNESS
ONLY 125 CALORIES.

Merit

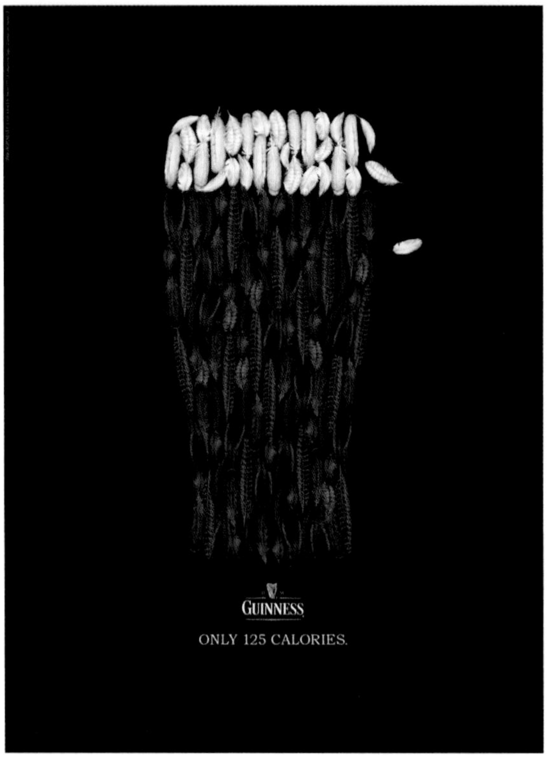
GUINNESS
ONLY 125 CALORIES.

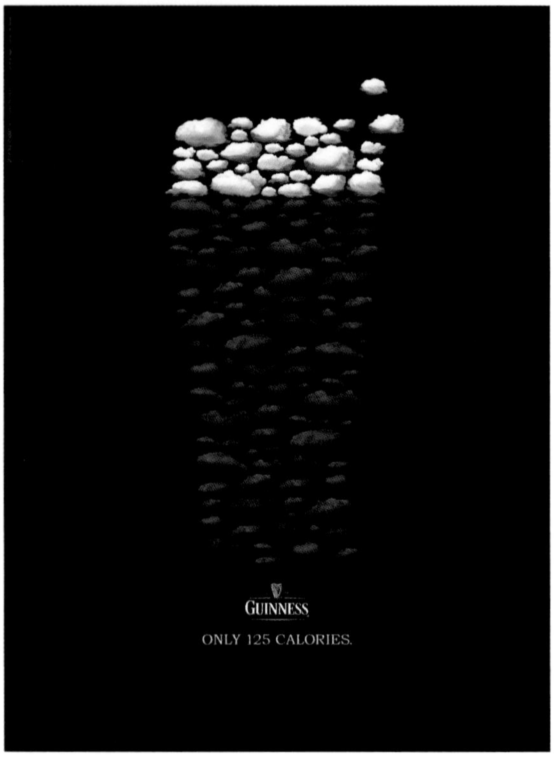
GUINNESS
ONLY 125 CALORIES.

UNCARRIABLE CARRIER BAGS
MOTHER
Flippers Fried Dolphins
BURGERS • WRAPS • FRIED BLOW HOLES

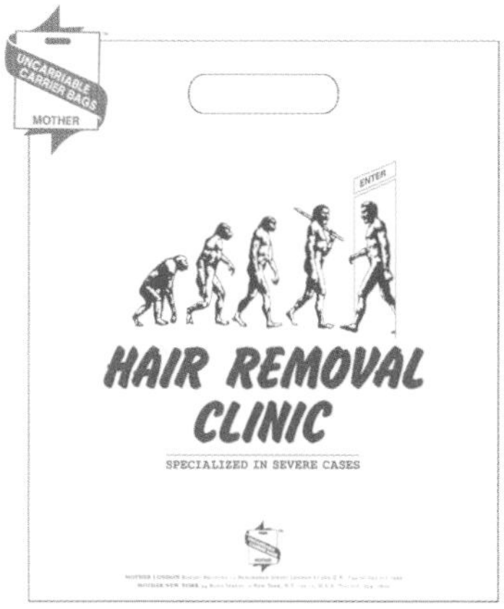
UNCARRIABLE CARRIER BAGS
MOTHER
ENTER
HAIR REMOVAL CLINIC
SPECIALIZED IN SEVERE CASES

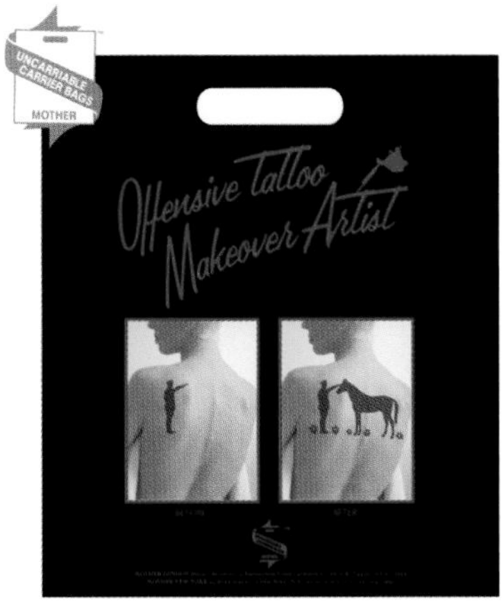
UNCARRIABLE CARRIER BAGS
MOTHER
Offensive Tattoo Makeover Artist

UNCARRIABLE CARRIER BAGS
MOTHER
SPERM CLINIC
DROP IN CENTRE
SPILL YOUR SEED FOR THOSE IN NEED

UNCARRIABLE CARRIER BAGS
MOTHER
T.G.R
Annual meet Houston 2005
TEXAS GAY REPUBLICANS

UNCARRIABLE CARRIER BAGS
MOTHER
THIS SIDE UP. CONTENT MAY BE CONTAGIOUS
INFECTIONOUS DISEASE CENTRE
SAMPLE BAG
HANDLE WITH EXTREME CARE

Gold

ART DIRECTORS
Cecilia Dufils
Markus Bjurman
Tobias Carlson
Jonas Wittenmark

WRITERS
Cecilia Dufils
Markus Bjurman
Tobias Carlson
Jonas Wittenmark

CREATIVE DIRECTORS
Robert Saville
Mark Waites

CLIENT
Mother

AGENCY
Mother/London

ANNUAL ID
06038A

SILVER

ART DIRECTOR
Nellie Kim

WRITER
Chris Hirsch

CREATIVE DIRECTORS
Stephen Jurisic
Angus Tucker

CLIENT
James Mahon

AGENCY
John St./Toronto

ANNUAL ID
06039A

James A.W. Mahon, LL.B.
DIVORCE LAWYER
Tel: 867 873 4969
Fax: 867 873 6567
jmahon@marshall.yk.com
Tel: 867 873 4969
Fax: 867 873 6567
jmahon@marshall.yk.com

James A.W.
DIVORC
Tel: 867 873 4969
Fax: 867 873 6567
jmahon@marshall.yk.com
Mahon, LL.B.
E LAWYER
Tel: 867 873 4969
Fax: 867 873 6567
jmahon@marshall.yk.com

Recycle paper. Save trees.
GREENPEACE

Silver

ART DIRECTORS
Joey Ong
Dave Ferrer

WRITER
Joey Ong

PHOTOGRAPHERS
Francis Rivera
Groovy Studios/Procolor

CREATIVE DIRECTOR
Dave Ferrer

CLIENT
Greenpeace

AGENCY
JWT/Makati City

ANNUAL ID
06040A

ALSO AWARDED
Merit
Public Service/Political: Outdoor - Single

Non-Native Species of the California Coast
The Cig Egret
CALIFORNIA COASTAL CLEANUP DAY
September 17th • 9am-noon
CALIFORNIA COASTAL COMMISSION

Bronze

ART DIRECTOR
Paul Foulkes

WRITER
Tyler Hampton

PHOTOGRAPHER
Claude Shade

CREATIVE DIRECTORS
Jeffrey Goodby
Rich Silverstein

CLIENT
California Coastal Commission

AGENCY
Goodby, Silverstein & Partners/San Francisco

ANNUAL ID
06041A

SILVER

ART DIRECTOR
Paul Wallace

WRITER
David Ross

PHOTOGRAPHER
Mark Zibert

CREATIVE DIRECTORS
Andrew Simon
William Hammond

CLIENT
Royal Ontario Museum

AGENCY
DDB/Toronto

ANNUAL ID
06043A

ALSO AWARDED
Merit:
Public Service/Political: Newspaper or Magazine - Single

Merit:
Public Service/Political: Newspaper or Magazine - Single

www.rom.on.ca
FEATHERED DINOSAURS
AND THE ORIGIN OF FLIGHT
Are birds actually dinosaurs? Fossils recently unearthed in China hold the surprising answer. Come for a rare glimpse at these intriguing finds dating back 125 million years.
Royal Ontario Museum
March 12 - September 5
ROM

Merit

FEATHERED DINOSAURS
AND THE ORIGIN OF FLIGHT
ROM

Merit

FEATHERED DINOSAURS
AND THE ORIGIN OF FLIGHT
ROM

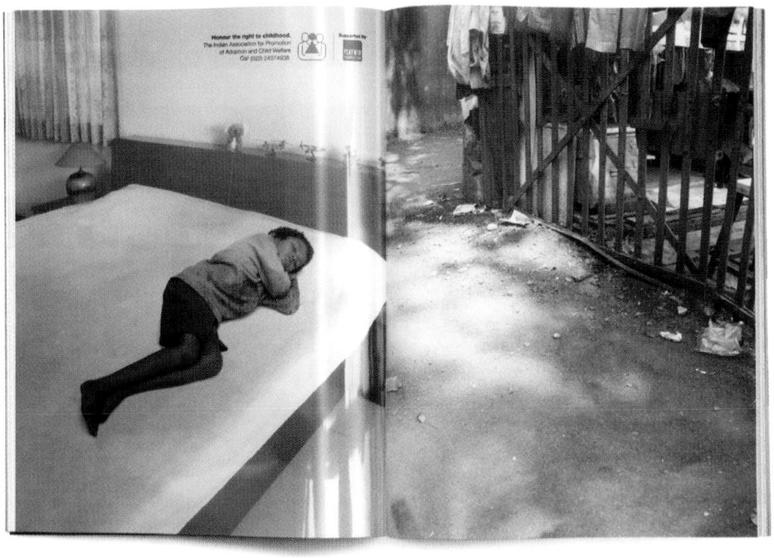

Silver

ART DIRECTOR
Kunal Sawant

WRITERS
Sumanto Chattopadhyay
Kunal Sawant

PHOTOGRAPHER
Saish Kambli

ILLUSTRATOR
Milind Aglave

CREATIVE DIRECTORS
Piyush Pandey
Sumanto Chattopadhyay

CLIENT
The Indian Association For Promotion Of Adoption & Child Welfare (IAPA)

AGENCY
Ogilvy & Mather/ Mumbai

ANNUAL ID
06042A

BRONZE

ART DIRECTOR
Richard Copping

WRITER
Jagdish Ramakrishnan

PHOTOGRAPHER
Getty Images

CREATIVE DIRECTOR
Graham Kelly

CLIENT
Greenpeace

AGENCY
Saatchi & Saatchi/ Singapore

ANNUAL ID
06220A

ALSO AWARDED
Merit: Public Service/Political: Outdoor - Campaign

It was like a giant green umbrella stuck in the ground.
It stood about three or four stories tall and at the top it had millions of tiny, green, heart-shaped bits that shielded the sun.
When the wind blew, these bits would shiver, shake and rustle.
They were green mostly, but every once in a while they turned a bright orange and dropped off.
That was a time they called autumn.
GREENPEACE

It was a bit like a submarine.
A fat, blue submarine.
It must have weighed over a hundred tonnes.
And it had this small hole at the top that shot out a spray whenever it came to the surface.
Not that it came up often.
It usually stayed deep down, making weird noises like some drowning symphony orchestra.
Some said the noises were songs, but no one knew for sure.
GREENPEACE

It looked like a busy underwater city, but a miniature one designed by elves or clowns.
It had these bizarre, colourful structures just piled on top of each other.
Some were like ribbons, hats and pin cushions.
Some seemed uncannily like human brains and hands.
And darting about among them were these magical little creatures with strange patterns.
You just never tired of watching them.
GREENPEACE

CANCER
PATIENTS AID
ASSOCIATION

Silver

ART DIRECTOR
Nishant Jethi

WRITER
Sundar Iyer

PHOTOGRAPHER
Sandeep Suvarna

CREATIVE DIRECTOR
Milind Dhaimade

CLIENT
Cancer Patients Aid Association

AGENCY
Everest Brand Solutions/ Mumbai

ANNUAL ID
06044A

FOUND ON REDONDO BEACH. AUGUST 21, 2005.
WWW.SURFRIDER.ORG

Bronze

ART DIRECTOR
Michael Reginelli

CREATIVE DIRECTORS
Steve Rabosky
Harvey Marco
Felipe Bascope

CLIENT
Surfrider Foundation

AGENCY
Saatchi & Saatchi/ Los Angeles

ANNUAL ID
06045A

ALSO AWARDED
Bronze:
One Show Design
Environmental Design: Single

Silver

ART DIRECTOR
Jim Landry

WRITER
Michael Atkinson

CREATIVE DIRECTOR
Jac Coverdale

CLIENT
MADD

AGENCY
Clarity Coverdale Fury/ Minneapolis

ANNUAL ID
06046A

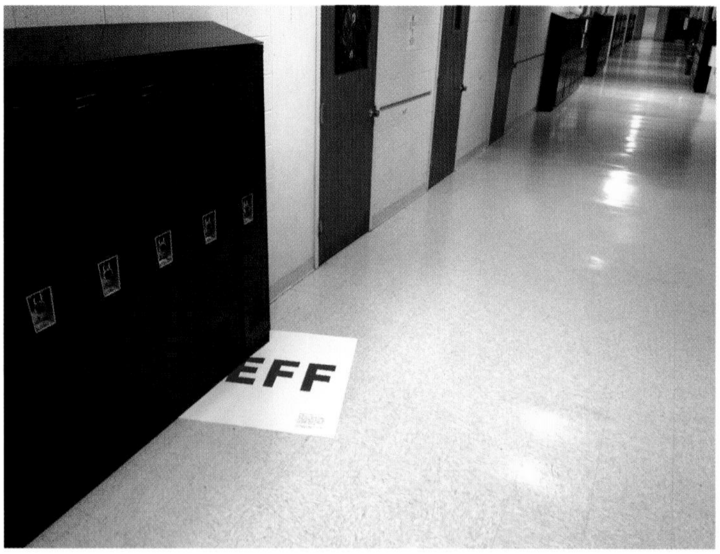
EFF

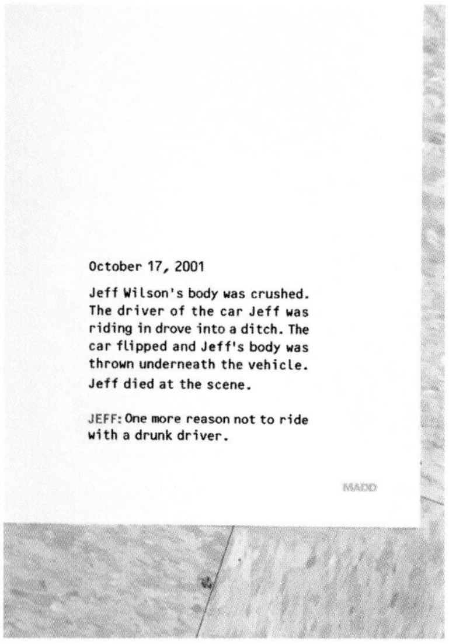
October 17, 2001
Jeff Wilson's body was crushed. The driver of the car Jeff was riding in drove into a ditch. The car flipped and Jeff's body was thrown underneath the vehicle. Jeff died at the scene.
JEFF: One more reason not to ride with a drunk driver.
MADD

JENNY
JENNY

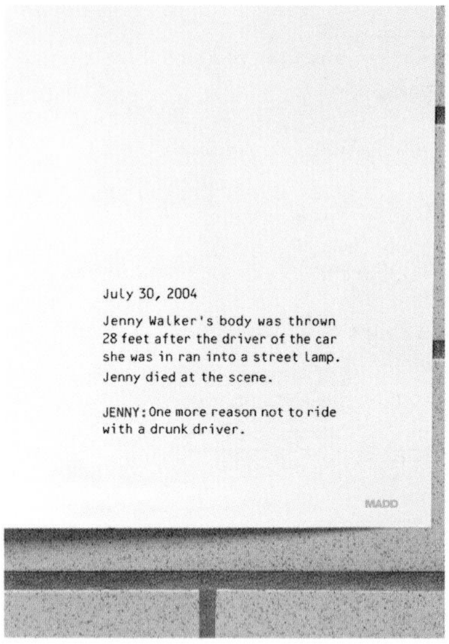
July 30, 2004
Jenny Walker's body was thrown 28 feet after the driver of the car she was in ran into a street lamp. Jenny died at the scene.
JENNY: One more reason not to ride with a drunk driver.
MADD

LISA

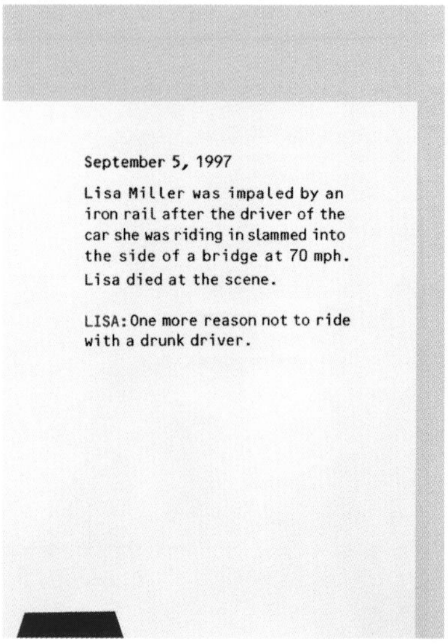
September 5, 1997
Lisa Miller was impaled by an iron rail after the driver of the car she was riding in slammed into the side of a bridge at 70 mph. Lisa died at the scene.
LISA: One more reason not to ride with a drunk driver.

[Open on a sitcom-style title sequence.]

MUSIC: If you don't like it – tough! It's fair enough.

SUPER: "Fair Enough"
Written By: Big Tobacco

VO: Based on big tobacco brainstorming sessions and marketing ideas from 1987, '89, '90 and '92.

[Cut to several businessmen sitting at a table]

CEO: We're here to come up with ideas for the "next generation" of tobacco satisfaction. Anybody?

MAN 1: What about a tobacco lotion?

[Laugh track]

MAN 2: Yes...perhaps an aftershave.

[The audience chuckles]

CEO: Hmmm...maybe something more refined and sophisticated.

MAN 3: We could try to put a tobacco extract into perfume.

[More laughter]

CEO: Excellent

MAN 4: How about a salted snack derived from tobacco?

[Laughter and applause]

SUPER: It might be funnier if it wasn't true.

SUPER: See more about Big Tobacco's marketing ideas for their deadly addictive cigarettes at: Fairenough.com

VO: Fair Enough is a truth® production.

LOGO: A truth® production

It might be funnier if it wasn't true.

See more about Big Tobacco's marketing ideas for their deadly addictive cigarettes at:
"Fair Enough".com
a truth production

Gold

ART DIRECTORS
Jason Ambrose
Rob Kottkamp
Chris Bakay

WRITERS
Dustin Ballard
Will Chambliss

AGENCY PRODUCERS
David Rolfe
Rupert Samuel
Corey Bartha

PRODUCTION COMPANY
Moxie Pictures

DIRECTOR
Martin Granger

CREATIVE DIRECTORS
Ron Lawner
Pete Favat
Alex Bogusky
John Kearse
Tom Adams

CLIENT
American Legacy Foundation

AGENCY
Arnold Worldwide/Boston and Crispin Porter + Bogusky/Miami

ANNUAL ID
06001T

Silver

ART DIRECTORS
Alvaro Ramos
Beatriz Caravedo

WRITER
Juan Carlos Gomez de la Torre

AGENCY PRODUCER
Katy Klauer

DIRECTORS
Tito Koster
Alvaro Velarde

CREATIVE DIRECTOR
Juan Carlos Gomez de la Torre

CLIENT
Ponle Corazon (Foundation Against Cancer)

AGENCY
Leo Burnett Del Peru/Lima

ANNUAL ID
06003T

[A magician performs various tricks for passers-by in a park. But a troubled frown falls upon his face as he spots a particular young girl watching the show with her mother. He pulls the child from the crowd and removes her hat, revealing that she has no hair. Clearly a result of chemotherapy. He proceeds to place his own magician's hat on her head and waves a wand above. When he finally pulls it off, the girl amazingly has a full head of flowing locks.]

SUPER: The Magic of Giving
Peruvian Cancer Foundation

Silver

ART DIRECTOR
Callum MacGregor

WRITER
Guy Barnett

AGENCY PRODUCER
Oscar Thomas

PRODUCTION COMPANY
Thomas Thomas Films

DIRECTOR
Kevin Thomas

CLIENT
United Nations Mine Action Service

AGENCY
The Brooklyn Brothers/New York

ANNUAL ID
06002T

[We see several girls and their parents gathering at a field for a soccer game. One girl scores a goal, and then to everyone's horror, steps on mine which causes an explosion. Parents and children are screaming and several girls are injured.]

SUPER: If there were landmines here, would you stand for them anywhere?

Help the UN eradicate landmines everywhere.
stoplandmines.org

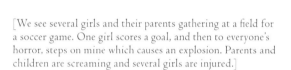

PDA

[We see several famous dictators, such as Saddam Hussein, Sese Seko Mobutu, Augusto Pinochet, Kim Jong Il, Moammar Khaddafi, Ayatollah Khomeini, and Fidel Castro. One after another we see their faces and then they appear to be blowing like they are trying to blow out a flame.]

SUPER AND LOGO: We're here to stay.
Amnesty International

Working to protect human rights worldwide.

Saddam Hussein

Sese Seko Mobutu

amnesty international
WORKING TO PROTECT
HUMAN RIGHTS WORLDWIDE.

BRONZE

ART DIRECTOR
Philippe Taroux

WRITER
Benoit Leroux

AGENCY PRODUCER
Christian Delhaye

PRODUCTION COMPANY
La Societe du Spectacle

CREATIVE DIRECTOR
Erik Vervroegen

CLIENT
Amnesty International

AGENCY
TBWA/Paris

ANNUAL ID
06004T

GOLD

ART DIRECTORS
Jason Ambrose
Rob Kottkamp
Chris Bakay

WRITERS
Dustin Ballard
Will Chambliss

AGENCY PRODUCERS
David Rolfe
Rupert Samuel

PRODUCTION COMPANY
Moxie Pictures

DIRECTOR
Martin Granger

CREATIVE DIRECTORS
Ron Lawner
Pete Favat
Alex Bogusky
John Kearse
Tom Adams

CLIENT
American Legacy Foundation

AGENCY
Arnold Worldwide/ Boston and Crispin Porter + Bogusky/ Miami

ANNUAL ID
06005T

"Fair Enough!"

Percentage of Annual Sales by Ethnic Group
WRITTEN BY
BIG TOBACCO

It might be funnier if it wasn't true.

[Open on a sitcom-style title sequence.]

MUSIC: If you don't like it – tough! It's fair enough.

SUPER: "Fair Enough"
Written By: Big Tobacco

VO: This episode is based on 1990 Big Tobacco Marketing Ideas.

[We see several businessmen sitting at a table]

EXECUTIVE: We've talked about targeting young adults and women. What about a cigarette targeting inner-city blacks. Any ideas?

MAN 1: [Using air quotes] Perhaps we could utilize the popularity of "rap" music.

EXECUTIVE: Rap music, yes.

[Laugh track]

MAN 2: Blacks have less money. Let's offer a 10-pack.

[More laughter]

MAN 3: We should call them "Fat Boys."

EXECUTIVE: Yes, yes.

MAN 4: How about this: "You know you're cool, you know you're the man, when you've got a Fat Boy in your hand."

[Laugh track and then applause]

SUPER: It might be funnier if it wasn't true.

SUPER: See more about Big Tobacco's marketing ideas for their deadly addictive cigarettes at: Fairenough.com

VO: Fair Enough is a truth® production.

LOGO: A truth® production

SEPTEMBER
OCTOBER

It might be funnier if it wasn't true.

See more about Big Tobacco's marketing ideas for their deadly addictive cigarettes at:
"Fair Enough".com
a truth production

[Open on a sitcom-style title sequence.]

MUSIC: If you don't like it – tough! It's fair enough.

SUPER: "Fair Enough"
Written By: Big Tobacco

VO: This episode is based on 1997 Big Tobacco Marketing Ideas.

ATTORNEY I: Your company told Congress that cigarette smoking was no more addictive than Twinkies.

[Laugh track.]

ATTORNEY I: If a pack a day smoker puffs five puffs per cigarette, I have calculated that to be 1,092,000 puffs of cigarette smoke over 30 years.

MAN: I'll accept your calculation

ATTORNEY I: Do you know anybody who has eaten 1,092,000 Twinkies?

[Laugh track]

MAN'S ATTORNEY: Object to the form of the question. It's an unfair comparison. A puff if anything might equate to a bite, not a whole Twinkie, but this is pretty silly in any event. And I'm not sure how many bites there are in a Twinkie, but we can investigate at lunch.

[Audience laughs]

ATTORNEY I: We might do that.

SUPER: It might be funnier if it wasn't true.

See more Big Tobacco documents about their deadly addictive cigarettes at: Fairenough.com

VO: Fair enough is a truth® production

LOGO: A truth® production

"Fair Enough!"

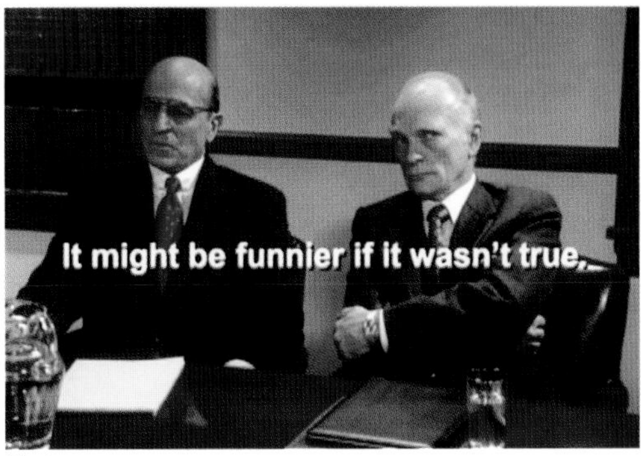
It might be funnier if it wasn't true.

Merit

BRONZE

ART DIRECTORS
Mike Costello
Phil Covitz
Jason Ambrose
Geordie Stephens

WRITERS
Marc Einhorn
Dustin Ballard
Franklin Tipton

AGENCY PRODUCER
Jessica Dierauer

PRODUCTION COMPANY
Moxie Pictures

DIRECTOR
Martin Granger

CREATIVE DIRECTORS
Ron Lawner
Pete Favat
Alex Bogusky
John Kearse
Tom Adams

CLIENT
American Legacy Foundation

AGENCY
Arnold Worldwide/ Boston and Crispin Porter + Bogusky/ Miami

ANNUAL ID
06007T

ALSO AWARDED
Merit:
Public Service/Political TV - Single

Merit:
Public Service/Political TV - Single

Merit

It might be funnier if it wasn't true.

BRONZE

ART DIRECTOR
Daryl Gardiner

WRITER
Kevin Rathgeber

AGENCY PRODUCER
Catharine Chesterman

PRODUCTION COMPANIES
Spy Films
Rogue Artists

DIRECTOR
James Brown

CREATIVE DIRECTOR
Alan Russell

CLIENT
ICBC

AGENCY
DDB/Vancouver

ANNUAL ID
06006T

DRINKING DRIVING
COUNTERATTACK

[It's night. A group of teens are in a four-door sedan, heading home after a house party. The female passenger looks at the driver of the car and talks to him. But neither he, nor anyone else in the vehicle can hear her.]

TEEN: When will you stop drinking and driving?

[The car swerves slightly and accelerates.]

TEEN: When I wrestle your keys away?

[The car moves down a straightaway.]

TEEN: When you get caught driving over the legal limit?

[Swerving slightly, the car approaches a curve in the highway.]

TEEN: When the cops seize your car? I know, it's when...

[Suddenly the car veers off the road and smashes hard into a tree. The passenger is launched forward at the windshield. This happens almost instantaneously. Fade to black. We hear screeching tires, sounds of impact... silence.]

SUPER: When will you stop drinking and driving?

LOGO: Drinking Driving CounterAttack

SUPER: Police Road Checks on now

When will you stop drinking and driving?

[We see three men in a bar about to take a sip of Guinness beer. Then they begin to walk backwards out the bar in sped-up reverse to the tune of Sammy Davis, Jr.'s "Rhythm of Life." The cityscape devolves into a town and then the wilderness. The men also turn into cavemen and we see various stages of time such as the Ice Age and the period where dinosaurs roamed the Earth. They turn into chimps, aquatic creatures and finally into three slimy, primitive animals. One takes a sip of pond water.]

CREATURE: Blech!

SUPER: Good things come to those who wait.

GOOD THINGS COME TO THOSE WHO WAIT.
GUINNESS
BREWED IN DUBLIN

GOLD

ART DIRECTOR
Matt Doman

WRITER
Ian Heartfield

AGENCY PRODUCER
Yvonne Chalkley

PRODUCTION COMPANY
Johnnie Frankel

DIRECTOR
Daniel Kleinman

CREATIVE DIRECTOR
Paul Brazier

CLIENT
Guinness

AGENCY
Abbott Mead Vickers BBDO/London

ANNUAL ID
06009T

GOLD

ART DIRECTOR
Grant Rutherford

WRITER
Ant Keogh

AGENCY PRODUCER
Pip Heming

PRODUCTION COMPANIES
Plaza Films
Peter Masterton

DIRECTOR
Paul Middleditch

CREATIVE DIRECTOR
James McGrath

CLIENT
Carlton Draught

AGENCY
George Patterson Y&R/ Melbourne

ANNUAL ID
06008T

It's a big ad.

Expensive ad!

CARLTON DRAUGHT

[The scene opens with a man in a yellow robe pointing and singing in opera style. Then we see thousands of people in yellow, red and white robes charging toward a huge group of people in red and blue robes. From above we realize that one group is in the shape of a pint of beer while the other is a person with an outstretched arm. As the two groups converge, they form the shape of someone drinking the beer where you see it going down to their stomach.]

SINGING: It's a big ad. Very big ad. It's a big ad we're in. It's a big ad. My God it's big! Can't believe how big it is! It's a big ad! For Carlton Beer. It's just so freak-ing HUGE! It's a big ad! Expensive ad! This ad better sell some bloooody beer!

SUPER: Made from Beer.

[Very soothing music plays. Open on a man standing on the beach. He has long braided hair, he is with many swimsuit clad children on the sand. He pulls up to the beach and there is a group of people, surfers, waiting for him.]

IZZY: My name is Izzy Paskowitz and I've been running surf camps for autistic kids for 7 years. We get 'em down to the beach. The kids are going to scream. Some of the kids, they don't know how to speak. The only words coming out of their mouth is screaming.

[The adult surfers take kids out on surf boards – two to a board. People watch with binoculars from the beach. They ride. People cheer and wave from the beach. Kids and surfers catch waves standing on the board together.]

IZZY: What's perfect for us is to see that screaming and the kicking when they go out, and when they turn around and ride that wave in. . .just nothing like it.

[Kids smile and laugh on the beach.]

IZZY: And there's the parents with tears in their eyes saying, "Man, we've had a lot of tough times but today was just a perfect day."

[Parents and kids are hugging on the beach.]

SUPER: Without sports, where would we find ourselves?
ESPN

WITHOUT SPORTS,
WHERE WOULD WE
FIND OURSELVES?

SILVER

ART DIRECTOR
Jesse Coulter

WRITER
Greg Kalleres

AGENCY PRODUCER
Gary Krieg

PRODUCTION COMPANY
RSA Films

DIRECTOR
The Malloys

CREATIVE DIRECTORS
Todd Waterbury
Kevin Proudfoot
Paul Renner
Derek Barnes

CLIENT
ESPN Brand

AGENCY
Wieden+Kennedy/
New York

ANNUAL ID
06010T

BRONZE

ART DIRECTORS
Paul Stechschulte
Tiffany Kosel

WRITERS
Franklin Tipton
Rob Reilly

AGENCY PRODUCERS
Rupert Samuel
David Rolfe
Matt Bonin
Bill Meadows

PRODUCTION COMPANIES
Hungry Man
Jodaf/Mixer

DIRECTOR
Bryan Buckley

CREATIVE DIRECTORS
Alex Bogusky
Andrew Keller
Steve O'Connell

CLIENT
MINI

AGENCY
Crispin Porter + Bogusky/ Miami

ANNUAL ID
06014T

"Let's Motor!" right?

CCC: CRASH TEST DRAMATIZATION
00:04:40:09
WWW.COUNTERFEITMINI.ORG

CONSUMER ALERT
CCC
COUNTERFEIT
MINI COOPERS
DVD

VO: It's happening all around the globe, people getting tricked by counterfeit brand name merchandise. Premium watches, sunglasses and you won't believe what else is being knocked off…

SUPER: "Counterfeit" stamps across screen.

VO: … MINI Coopers. That's why you need this important dvd from the counter counterfeit commission. You'll get a crash course on how to spot a fake.

[We see a guy whose face is blacked out. He speaks, his voice altered.]

VO: You'll hear from humiliated victims.

MAN: I thought, a MINI for 1200 bucks? Let's motor, right?

VO: Wrong!

SUPER: "Counterfeit" stamps across screen.

VO: We'll even take you overseas and show you how they duplicate MINI's signature look.

GUY: [Translated] You just paint the roof, slap on some bonnet stripes. Boom-boom! No one can tell the difference.

VO: Until they try to park it…

SUPER: "Counterfeit" stamps across screen.

VO: Drive it…

SUPER: "Counterfeit" stamps across screen.

VO: …or turn it!

[Cut to a counterfeit being crash tested. It explodes into a huge ball of fire.]

VO: Don't be fooled by imitations. Protect yourself!

SUPER: "Counterfeit" stamps across screen.

VO: Be certain your MINI is genuine!

To order "Counterfeit MINI Coopers," visit COUNTERFEITMINI.org . Or send $19.99 check or money order to the Counter Counterfeit Commission.

SUPER: Counterfeit MINI Coopers
www.COUNTERFEITMINI.org

[A man wakes up in bed and sits up. His shoes tie on his feet by themselves. We see him running down a street and then through the woods in a dream-like, surreal landscape. He is chased by a bear and then he jumps. He is in the suburbs. He lies down and begins to crawl upside down in the sky. He eventually becomes tired and crawls back into bed.]

SUPER: World's first intelligent shoe.
Impossible is nothing.

BRONZE

ART DIRECTOR
Joe Kayser

WRITER
Chuck McBride

PRODUCERS
Jennifer Golub
Vince Landay

PRODUCTION COMPANY
MJZ

DIRECTOR
Spike Jonze

CREATIVE DIRECTORS
Chuck McBride
Lee Clow
Joe Kayser

CLIENT
adidas

AGENCY
TBWA\Chiat\Day/San Francisco (180\TBWA)

ANNUAL ID
06013T

run barefoot.

[We see a group of men running on the beach wearing white and the music from *Chariots of Fire* playing. Everything is the same as the movie until you begin to see parking meters and manholes on the beach. They run by a man sitting on a bench and then a fire escape hanging in the air. A cab drives by and then we see mailboxes and finally a bus. The music stops and suddenly we see a man stopping at a corner on a busy street in the city.]

SUPER: run barefoot.
nikefree.com

BRONZE

ART DIRECTOR
Monica Taylor

WRITER
Derek Barnes

PRODUCERS
Jennifer Fiske
Vince Landay

PRODUCTION COMPANY
Biscuit Filmworks

DIRECTOR
Noam Murro

CREATIVE DIRECTORS
Mike Byrne
Hal Curtis

CLIENT
Nike

AGENCY
Wieden+Kennedy/Portland

ANNUAL ID
06012T

BRONZE

ART DIRECTORS
Nate Able
Geoff Edwards

WRITERS
Mat Bunnell
Scott Duchon
Rick Herrera

AGENCY PRODUCERS
David Verhoef
Hannah Murray

PRODUCTION COMPANIES
Gorgeous Enterprises
Anonoymous Content
MJZ

DIRECTORS
Frank Budgen
Rupert Sanders

CREATIVE DIRECTORS
Scott Duchon
Geoff Edwards
John Boiler
Glenn Cole
Jeff Huggins
John McNeil

CLIENT
Microsoft XBOX 360

AGENCY
McCann Erickson/ San Francisco and 72and Sunny/El Segundo

ANNUAL ID
06015T

ALSO AWARDED
Merit:
Consumer Television:
Over :30 - Single

Merit:
Consumer Television:
Over :30 - Single

Merit

[In one seamless take we see a group of people watching two young kids jumping rope in a public area. Two other people come in and take the ropes from the kids without having them stop. We then see people come in and out of the moving ropes, jumping, running and flipping as the ropes continue to move without stopping. Along with a couple of kids we see basketball star Ben Wallace get into the ropes for the finale. In the end everyone walks away as the small crowd applauds.]

SUPER: Jump in.
XBOX 360

Merit

[A man walks into his child's bedroom at night. It appears that he just got home from a long day at work and came by to see his son. The child awakens and looks at him and begins to scream for his mother. Then the man takes out *L'Equipe* newspaper and holds it in front of his face.]

CHILD: Oh, it's you Dad.

[He then hugs him.]

SUPER: Everyday. Every Sport.
L'Equipe Sport newspaper.

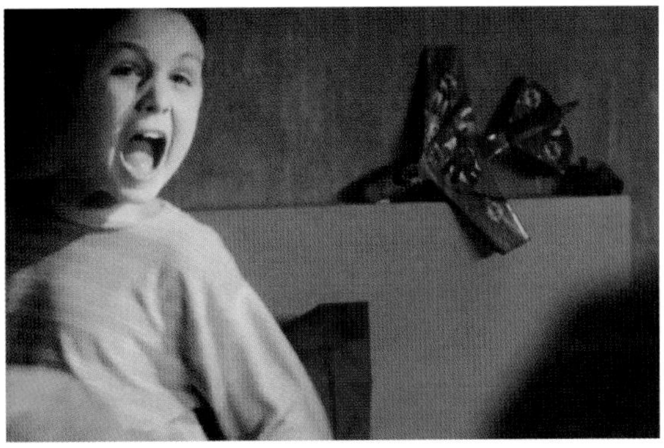

L'EQUIPE
BRONZES, POUR FINIR

Everyday. Every Sport.

L'EQUIPE
Sport newspaper.

Gold

ART DIRECTOR
Benjamin Marchal

WRITER
Celine Landa

AGENCY PRODUCER
Agathe Michaux Terrier

PRODUCTION COMPANY
75

DIRECTOR
Jonathan Herman

CREATIVE DIRECTORS
Sylvain Thirache
Alexandre Herve

CLIENT
L'Equipe

AGENCY
DDB/Paris

ANNUAL ID
06016T

SILVER

ART DIRECTOR
James Selman

WRITER
Mike Byrne

AGENCY PRODUCER
Ben Grylewicz

CREATIVE DIRECTORS
Hal Curtis
Mike Byrne

CLIENT
Nike

AGENCY
Wieden+Kennedy/ Portland

ANNUAL ID
06018T

[We see Lance Armstrong in front of microphones at a press conference.]

LANCE: On Wednesday, October 2nd, I was diagnosed with testicular cancer.

SUPER: Press Conference. October 8, 1996.

LANCE: The CAT scan revealed that my condition has spread into my abdomen.

SUPER: And his lungs and brain.

LANCE: For now I must focus on my treatment. However, I want all of you to know that I intend to beat this disease and further I intend to ride again as a professional cyclist.

SUPER: Just do it
Nike
wearyellow.com

BRONZE

ART DIRECTOR
Andrea Reinhart

WRITER
Thomas Kurzmeyer

AGENCY PRODUCER
Kerstin Reulen

PRODUCTION COMPANY
Wirz Fraefel Productiona

DIRECTOR
Ernst Wirz

CREATIVE DIRECTOR
Matthias Freuler

CLIENT
Swiss Assurance Mobiliar

AGENCY
Wirz/BBDO/Zurich

ANNUAL ID
06020T

[A man is taking photographs of a 400-piece dinner service. He causes a short circuit . . . the lights go out, and he has to find his way back out through the display in the dark.]

VO: Dear Sir or Madam, I was photographing the beautiful china collection my aunt wanted to sell. There were 400 pieces...[we hear crashing]...later even more.

SUPER: Swiss Mobiliar
Insurance and Pensions.

[A father is driving a group of teenage girls to a concert.]

GIRL: I hope she sings this one tonight! Hey dad, pull over, we need gum.

DAD: I'll buy it. Oh honey...

[They stop in front of a seedy deli. The girls walk out of the car, but then the one girl turns around and leans to the window.]

DAD: Here's some money...

[A police car pulls up behind them as he hands her money.]

POLICE: Well what do we have here.

[Sirens and spotlight shine on the father holding the money.]

SUPER: Don't judge too quickly. We won't.

LOGO: Ameriquest

DAD: I'm her...Daddy...

DON'T JUDGE TOO QUICKLY

Silver

GOLD

ART DIRECTORS
Sarah May Bates
Susan Fukuda
Christiane Brooks

WRITERS
Josh Fell
Rick Bursky
Rebecca Rivera

AGENCY PRODUCER
Vanessa MacAdam

CREATIVE DIRECTORS
Mark Monteiro
Helene Cote

CLIENT
Ameriquest Mortgage

AGENCY
DDB/Los Angeles

ANNUAL ID
06021T

ALSO AWARDED
Silver:
Consumer Television
- :30/:25 - Single

Merit:
Consumer Television
- :30/:25 - Single

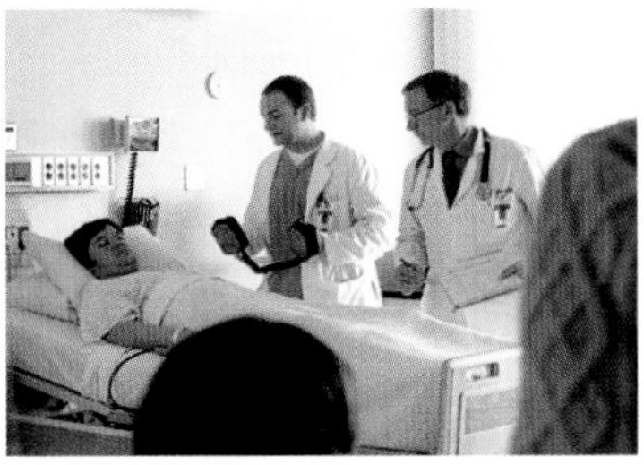

Merit

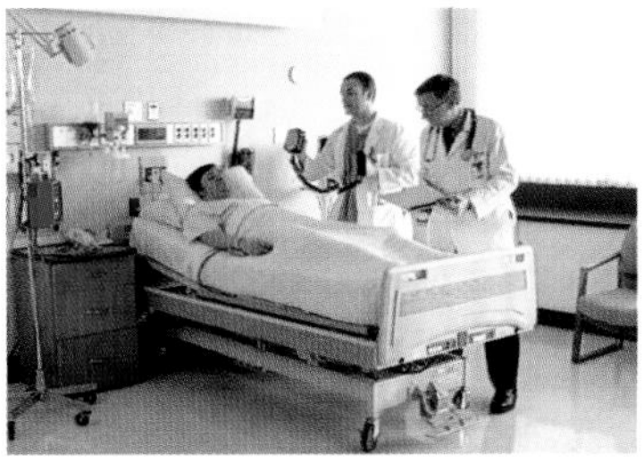

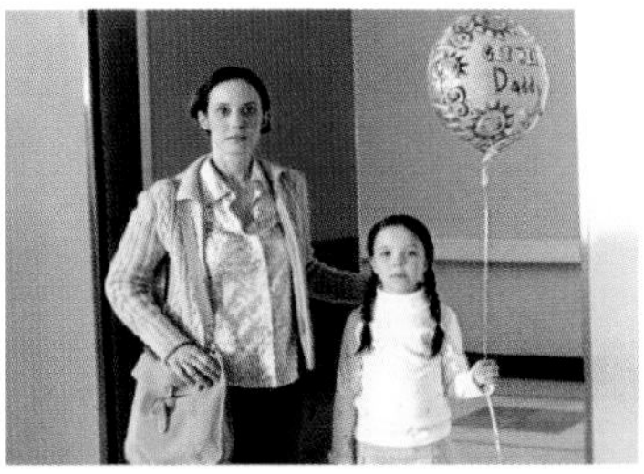

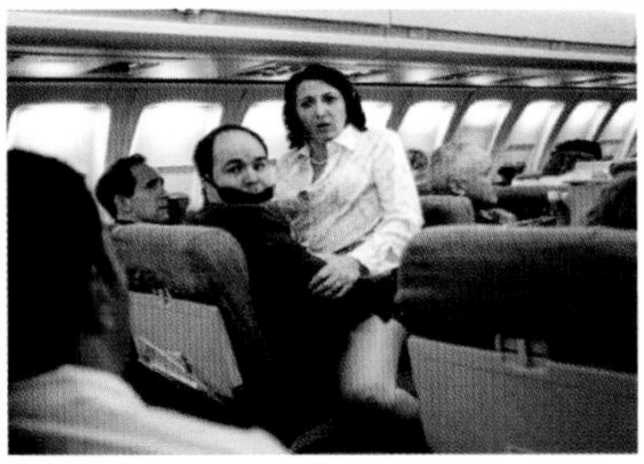

DON'T JUDGE TOO QUICKLY

Silver

ART DIRECTORS
Jon Chalermwong
Kittitat Larppitakpong
Thirasak Tanapatanakul

WRITERS
Nutchanun Chiaphanumas
Prangthip Praditpong

AGENCY PRODUCER
Chutharat Chingduang

PRODUCTION COMPANY
Phenomena

DIRECTOR
Thanonchai Sornsriwichai

CREATIVE DIRECTORS
Thirasak Tanapatanakul
Prangthip Praditpong

CLIENT
Bangkok Insurance

AGENCY
Creative Juice/G1/ Bangkok

ANNUAL ID
06022T

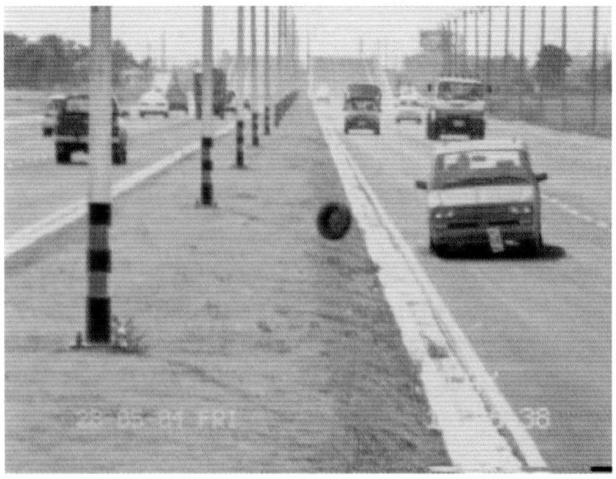

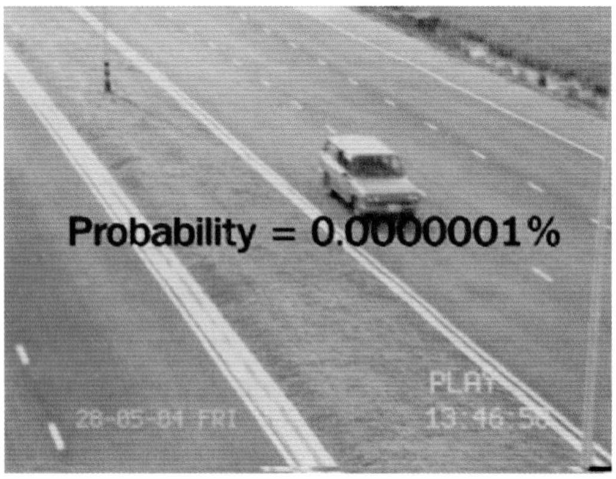
Probability = 0.0000001%

[Through the speed camera, an old car is losing a tire from one of the roll guards. The tire rolls to the other side across the road. It bounces off to the truck, hits the pole and rolls back in to the road. Gradually, the tire then rolls back in to the car's roll guard where it belongs. The car continues to drive like nothing had happened.]

SUPER: Probability = 0.0000001%
Bangkok Insurance

Probability = 0.0000001%

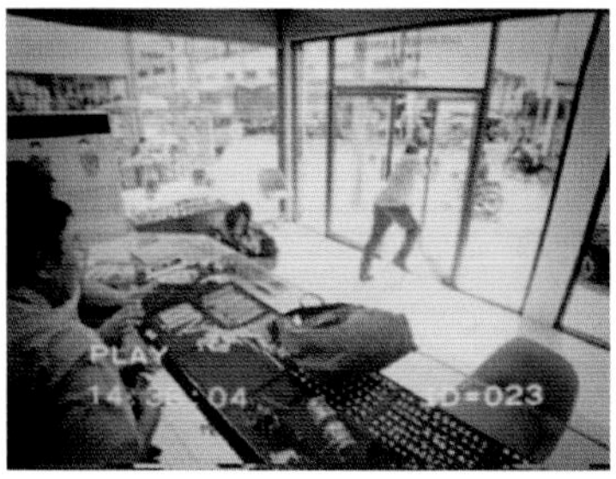

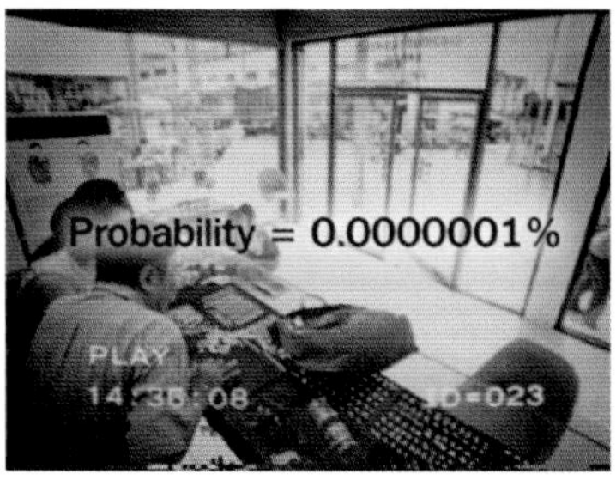
Probability = 0.0000001%

[We see a newscaster named Bob Bell talking on a TV news show.]

BOB: And the monkey did not post bail.

[The camera switches to a female broadcaster and a video of an Ace Hardware store.]

LINDA: This just in, huge crowds at the Ace Hardware sale. Bob...

[Transition music plays and the camera switches back to Bob's seat, which is empty.]

LINDA: [Laughing nervously] Oh, we're still live. Bob?

[Bob's seat is still shown empty.]

LINDA: He's at the sale! I guess Bob's at the Ace Hardware sale. Leaving me here with Steve...

[Camera shows weather guy, Steve, motioning to cut the camera.]

LINDA: That's really professional Steve. Really professional.

SUPER: Ace. The helpful place. Memorial Day Sale.

THIRD STRIKE
BOB BELL
KOVY

LIVE
Hardware
ACE HARDWARE WEEKEND SALE
HUGE CROWDS
KOVY

LIVE
KOVY

BRONZE

ART DIRECTOR
Stephen Goldblatt

WRITER
Bob Winter

AGENCY PRODUCER
James Horner

PRODUCTION COMPANY
Harvest Films

DIRECTOR
Michael Downing

CREATIVE DIRECTOR
Jeffrey Goodby

CLIENT
ACE Hardware

AGENCY
Goodby, Silverstein & Partners/San Francisco

ANNUAL ID
06023T

LIVE
BREAKING NEWS
ACE HARDWARE WEEKEND SALE
HUGE CROWDS
KOVY

LIVE
BREAKING NEWS
ACE HARDWARE WEEKEND SALE
HUGE CROWDS
KOVY

LIVE
BREAKING NEWS
ACE HARDWARE WEEKEND SALE
HUGE CROWDS
KOVY

ACE WEEKEND SALE
BREAKING NEWS
ACE HARDWARE WEEKEND SALE
HUGE CROWDS
KOVY

LIVE
BREAKING NEWS
ACE HARDWARE WEEKEND SALE
HUGE CROWDS
KOVY

LIVE
BREAKING NEWS
ACE HARDWARE WEEKEND SALE
HUGE CROWDS
KOVY

GOLD

ART DIRECTOR
Ron Smrczek

WRITER
Irfan Khan

AGENCY PRODUCER
Jennifer Mete

PRODUCTION COMPANY
Partners Film

DIRECTOR
Joachim Back

CREATIVE DIRECTORS
Lance Martin
Zak Mroueh

CLIENT
Pfizer - Viagra

AGENCY
Taxi/Toronto

ANNUAL ID
06024T

VIAGRA

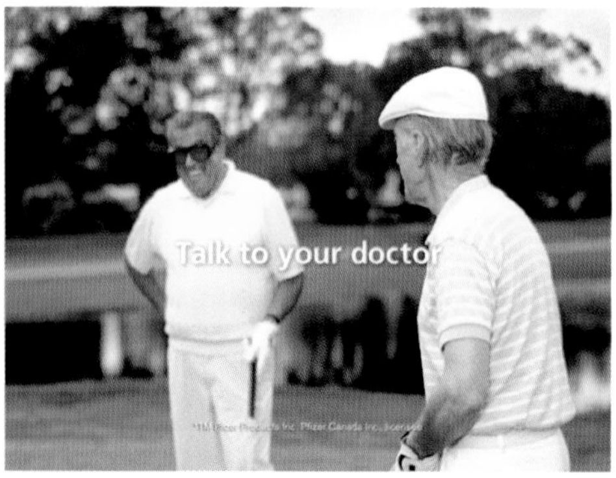
Talk to your doctor

[Two old men are playing golf. We see a putt go in the hole.]

MAN 1: Oh! Can you believe that!

MAN 2: Hey, that's nothing. This morning, I...

[Words are bleeped out and a blue Viagra pill is superimposed over his mouth. Man 1 laughs incredulously.]

SUPER: Talk to your doctor

[A young man is talking on a cell phone]

MAN: Dad, I'm gay.

DAD: Excellent.

VO: Sometimes life's more than a three minute conversation. Talk for up to 60 minutes, pay for just 3 with Vodafone.

SUPER: Talk for 60 minutes, pay for 3.

LOGO: Vodafone

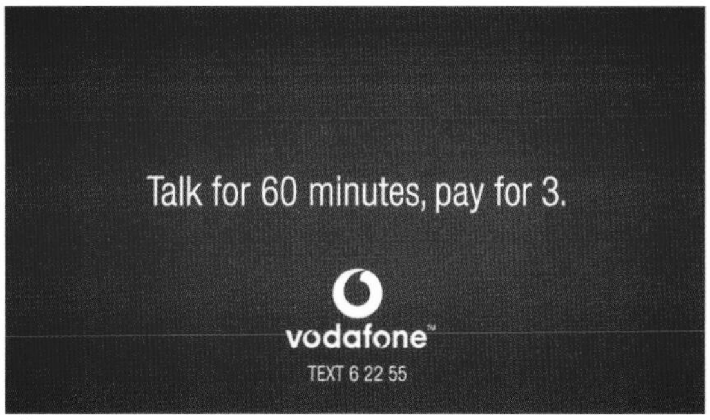
Talk for 60 minutes, pay for 3.
vodafone
TEXT 6 22 55

Silver

GOLD

ART DIRECTOR
Ian Gabaldoni

WRITER
Richard Baynham

AGENCY PRODUCER
Clare Donald

PRODUCTION COMPANY
Outsider

CREATIVE DIRECTOR
Nick Bell

CLIENT
Vodafone

AGENCY
JWT/London

ANNUAL ID
06027T

ALSO AWARDED
Silver:
Consumer Television:
:20 seconds and Under
- Single

Bronze:
Consumer Television:
:20 seconds and Under
- Single

Bronze

Talk for 60 minutes, pay for 3.
vodafone
TEXT 6 22 55

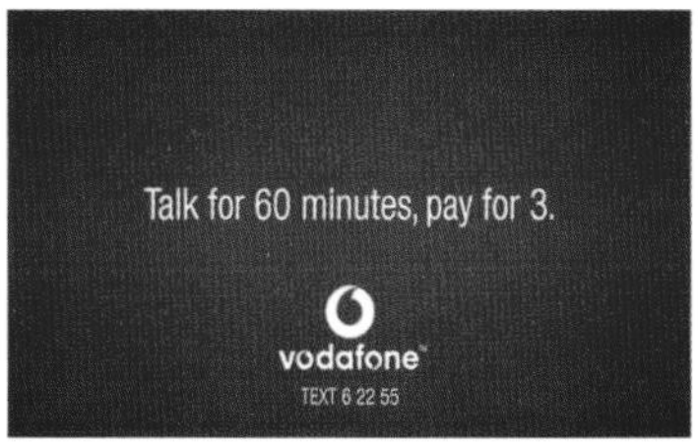
Talk for 60 minutes, pay for 3.
vodafone
TEXT 6 22 55

Silver

ART DIRECTOR
Ron Smrczek

WRITER
Irfan Khan

AGENCY PRODUCER
Jennifer Mete

PRODUCTION COMPANY
Partners Film

DIRECTOR
Joachim Back

CREATIVE DIRECTORS
Lance Martin
Zak Mroueh

CLIENT
Pfizer - Viagra

AGENCY
Taxi/Toronto

ANNUAL ID
06028T

ALSO AWARDED
Gold:
Consumer Television:
:20 and Under - Single

Merit:
Consumer Television:
:20 and Under - Single

Merit:
Consumer Television:
:20 and Under - Single

VIAGRA
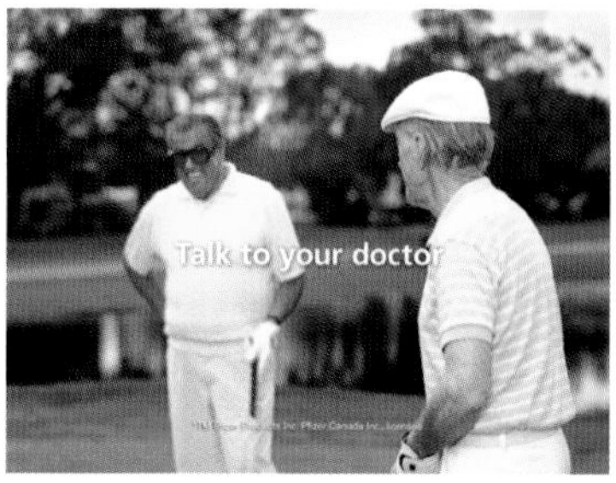
Talk to your doctor

Gold

VIAGRA

Talk to your doctor

Merit

[We see an office setting. In the kitchen area, we see three people talking.]

MAN 1: Hey Tom, you're looking good. You been working out?

TOM: No, but I've been...

[Words are bleeped out and a blue Viagra pill is superimposed over his mouth.]

WOMAN: [Laughs uncomfortably] Bravo.

SUPER: Talk to your doctor.

VIAGRA

Talk to your doctor

Merit

[Three construction workers are talking over a hole they are digging. One of them swats at a bug and screams like a girl. Then a giant Milwaukee's Best beer can lands on him.]

VO: Men should act like men. And light beer should taste like beer. Milwaukee's Best Light.

SUPER: Brewed for a man's taste, Milwaukee's Best Light

Milwaukee's
BEST
LIGHT

STAY SAFE—DRINK WISELY
Milwaukee's
BEST
LIGHT
BREWED for a MAN'S TASTE
Milwaukee's
BEST
LIGHT

BRONZE

ART DIRECTOR
Rob Baird

WRITERS
Ann Lieberman
Dave Clark

AGENCY PRODUCER
Margaux Ravis

PRODUCTION COMPANY
RSA

DIRECTOR
John O'Hagan

CREATIVE DIRECTORS
Linus Karlsson
Paul Malmstrom

CLIENT
Miller Brewing Company

AGENCY
Mother/New York

ANNUAL ID
06029T

BREWED for a MAN'S TASTE

BREWED for a MAN'S TASTE

Gold

ART DIRECTORS
Chris Groom
Tony Davidson
Matt Gooden

WRITERS
Sean Thompson
Kim Papworth
Ben Walker
Michael Russoff

AGENCY PRODUCERS
Julia Methold
Helen Whiteley

PRODUCTION COMPANIES
Partizan
Stink

DIRECTORS
Ivan Zacharias
Antoine Bardou-Jacquet
Nick Gordon

CREATIVE DIRECTORS
Tony Davidson
Kim Papworth

CLIENT
Honda

AGENCY
Wieden+Kennedy/London

ANNUAL ID
06030T

ALSO AWARDED
Silver:
Consumer Television:
Over :30 - Single

[We see a choir and a conductor standing in what looks like an underground parking lot.]

VO: This is what a Honda feels like.

[The choir begins to make the sounds of the car. We see various driving scenes and they mimic the sounds.]

SUPER: Honda. The power of dreams.

Silver

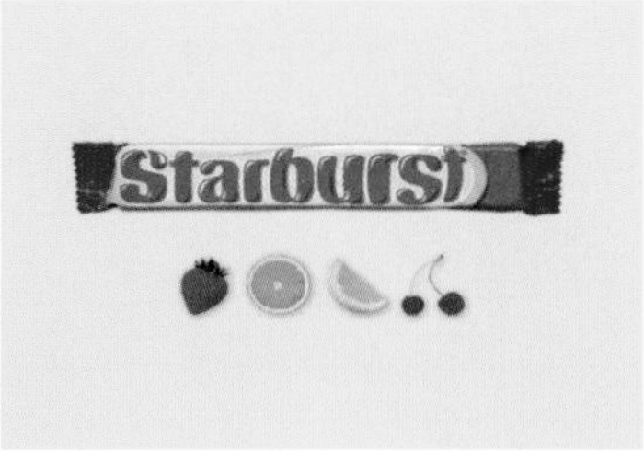
Starburst

Bronze

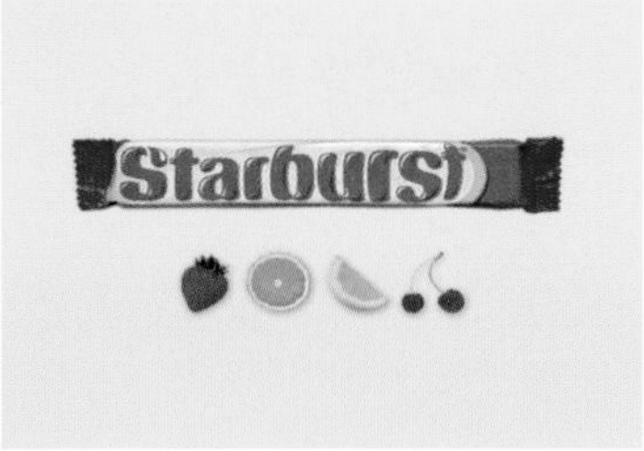
Starburst

[Two guys are eating new Baja California Starburst.]

GUY 1: These new Baja California Starburst…it's like a fiesta in my mouth.

[We see a "dramatization" of what is going on inside the guy's mouth. A mariachi band and some dancers are on top of one of the man's molars. It is a happy scene as the band plays a latin-style tune, and the dancers dance exuberantly.]

MARIACHIS: [Singing] Me gusta limon…

[Suddenly, the mood changes. The teeth begin to slowly bite down on the Baja California Starburst. The mariachi band and dancers are in danger of being crushed up.]

MARIACHI 1: El diente!

[They panic and scramble to get off of the molar. One of the band members doesn't react in time. He gets crushed repeatedly by the molar.]

DANCER 1: Jugo!

[A rush of saliva envelops them all. The band members and dancers do everything they can to hold on and avoid being washed down the esophagus. One of the dancers, Enrique, clings on desperately, but to no avail. One of his band mates calls after him.]

MARIACHI 2: Enrique!!!

[Enrique is washed away.]

SUPER: Juicy

NEW!
Starburst
baja
california

Silver

ART DIRECTOR
Craig Allen

WRITERS
Ashley Davis
Scott Vitrone
Ian Reichenthal

AGENCY PRODUCERS
Nathy Aviram
Lora Schulson
Laura Ferguson
Ozzie Spenningsby

PRODUCTION COMPANIES
Hungry Man
Epoch Films
MJZ

DIRECTORS
Bryan Buckley
Rocky Morton
Matt Aselton

CREATIVE DIRECTORS
Gerry Graf
Ian Reichenthal
Scott Vitrone

CLIENT
Masterfoods - Starburst

AGENCY
TBWA\Chiat\Day/ New York

ANNUAL ID
06032T

ALSO AWARDED
Bronze:
Consumer Television:
:30/:25 - Single

Silver

ART DIRECTORS
Mark Figliulo
Corey Ciszek

WRITERS
Ken Erke
Pete Figel

AGENCY PRODUCERS
Matt Bijarchi
Kim Mohan
Monica Wilkins

PRODUCTION COMPANY
MJZ

DIRECTOR
Spike Jonze

CREATIVE DIRECTORS
Dave Loew
Jon Wyville
Mark Figliulo

CLIENT
Miller Brewing Company

AGENCY
Young & Rubicam/ Chicago

ANNUAL ID
06031T

ALSO AWARDED
Merit: Consumer Television: :20 and Under - Single

Merit: Consumer Television: :20 and Under - Campaign

Merit: Consumer Television: :30/:25 - Campaign

16:07:22:16

16:07:27:04

15:16:03:26

Merit

[We see an otter auditioning for a part in a casting room]

OTTER: Miller Right. Miller Lite? Wait. Let me do that again. Miller Lite. More taste than Bud Light and half the carbs.

SUPER: Millerauditions.com

07:32:59:19

04:15:44:12

04:15:49:27

02:20:56:26

02:23:27:22

TCR 01:07:14:21

[A man is running and then he slows down.]

MAN: OK, we're done. Let's take a breather. What? That's not the deal. I think we can go on. Since when did we start thinking? Whatever. So who exactly are you trying to impress? 'Cause you're sure not impressing me. Save your breath, I'm gonna need it. Save your breath? You can't seen yourself, you look disgusting. This isn't the time to stop pushing. I've got to stop. You're the one who's got to stop. Me? Are we in this together or what? I don't know, are we? You're the one who's holding back. Holding you back? I'm just trying to look out for us. Unlike you, you just want to ditch me. Or maybe I should get rid of you. Stop running! No. Yes! Yes, yes, yes! No. Stop. You can't go. Please. I'm done with you.

SUPER: Leave your old self behind.
Reincarnate now.
Nike Free

leave your old self behind

BRONZE

ART DIRECTORS
Jason Williams
Selena McKenzie

WRITERS
Steve Jackson
Toby Moore

AGENCY PRODUCER
Corey Esse

PRODUCTION COMPANIES
The Sweet Shop
Exit Films
Revolver Film

CREATIVE DIRECTORS
Christy Peacock
Darren Spiller

CLIENT
Nike Australia

AGENCY
Publicis Mojo/Melbourne

ANNUAL ID
06033T

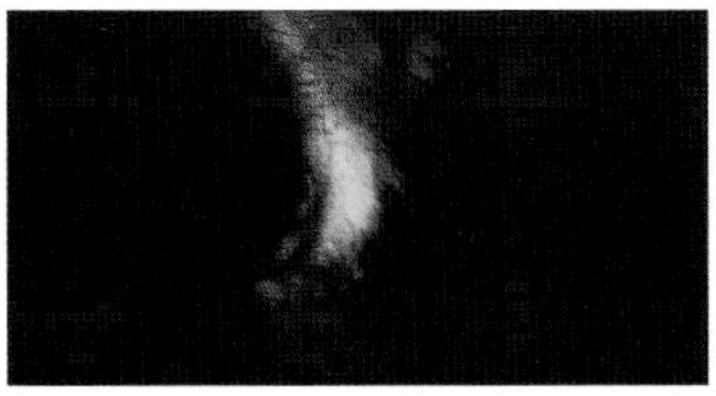

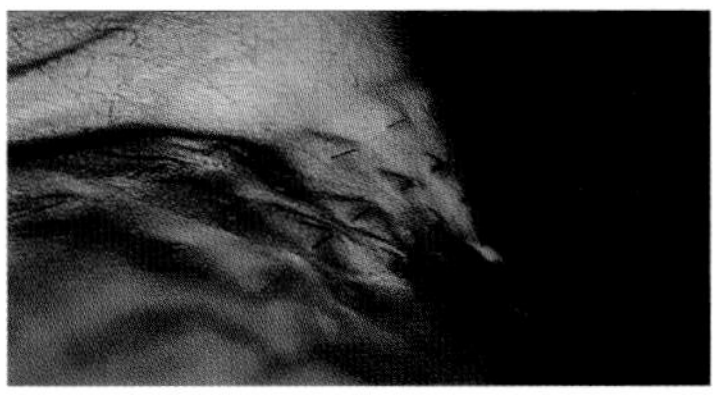

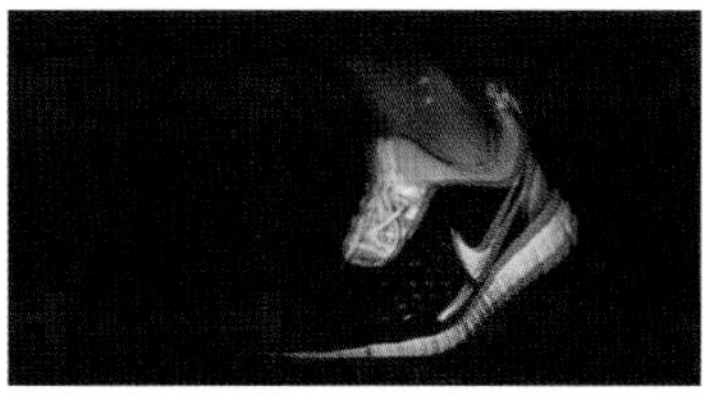

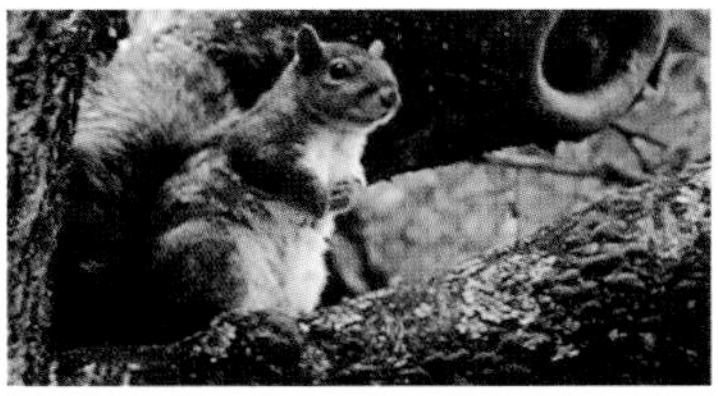

reincarnate now

GOLD

ART DIRECTORS
Paul Stechschulte
Tiffany Kosel

WRITERS
Franklin Tipton
Rob Reilly

AGENCY PRODUCERS
Rupert Samuel
David Rolfe
Matt Bonin
Rupert Samuel
Bill Meadows

PRODUCTION COMPANIES
Hungry Man
Jodaf/Mixer

DIRECTOR
Bryan Buckley

CREATIVE DIRECTORS
Alex Bogusky
Andrew Keller
Steve O'Connell

CLIENT
MINI

AGENCY
Crispin Porter + Bogusky/Miami

ANNUAL ID
06034T

I got a brand new "MINI Cooper" for 1200 bucks.

CCC
CHEP

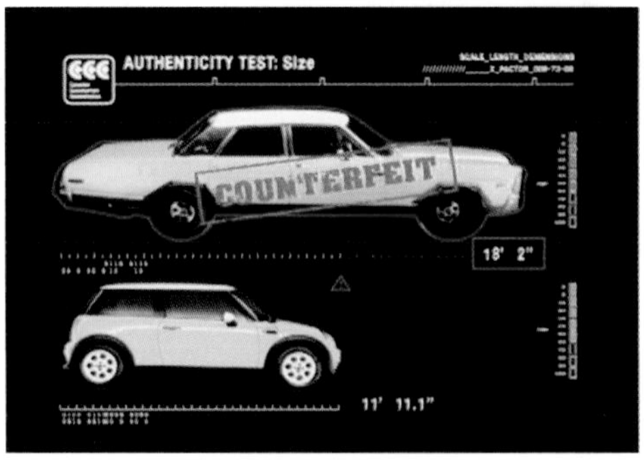
AUTHENTICITY TEST: Size
COUNTERFEIT
18' 2"
11' 11.1"

VO: Armed with the teeth of intelligence information, undercover agents and counterfeit sniffing dogs, the CC is plugging up our borders.

[We see policemen making an arrest in the streets of a foreign city.]

VO: And thanks to backing from the international police community, anyone caught is going to be crying REAL tears. Because if you've been a naughty boy, you'll be invited to special social engagement at a federal prison. Let's just hope you're not the prettiest girl at the dance.

SUPER: C.H.E.P.

VO: CHEP relies on us all working together.
Pass this DVD onto everyone in your Peer group.
Have a CHEP dinner party to compare intelligence with friends.

[We see a smiling guy with his arms crossed next to an old car.]

VO: And if you're the type of person who can detect a pair of breast implants from 200 yards out, think about joining the CCC. We need your attention to detail.

INSTRUCTOR: With CHEP.

CLASS GROUP: With CHEP.

INSTRUCTOR: With CHEP.

CLASS GROUP: With CHEP.

VO: If you're worried about the authenticity of a MINI Cooper, go to counterfeitmini.org or just see a Dealer, they'll make sure you get a genuine one.

From everyone at the CCC, and all our global partners, thanks for watching.

SUPER: Dedicated to the memory of
Jonathon Tress
(1972-2005)

STARBUCKS COFFEE
WWW.THEREDCUP.COM
PHARMACY

For a holiday promotion, a magnetic Starbucks red cup was placed on top of a car. Passers-by would stop the driver and point out the cup, and they were subsequently rewarded with a free Starbucks gift card.

Gold

ART DIRECTOR
Matt Peterson

WRITER
Jim Haven

AGENCY PRODUCER
Mary McCain

PRODUCTION COMPANY
Atomic Props

CREATIVE DIRECTORS
Jim Haven
Matt Peterson

CONTENT STRATEGIST
Holly Petitjean

CLIENT
Starbucks

AGENCY
Creature/Seattle

ANNUAL ID
06310A

ALSO AWARDED
Merit:
Innovative Use of Media and Marketing: Interactive/New Media - Single

Silver

ART DIRECTORS
David Hanselmann
Hendrik Schweder

WRITERS
Lars Haensell
Ole Kleinhans

CREATIVE DIRECTORS
Michael Rottmann
Alexander Jaggy

CLIENT
MINI

AGENCY
Jung von Matt/Zurich

ANNUAL ID
06048A

SIZE
MINI COOPER

SIZE
MINI COOPER

Silver

ART DIRECTOR
Naoki Ga

WRITERS
Yin May Tham
Yvonne Chia

PHOTOGRAPHER
Boon Heng Hon

CREATIVE DIRECTORS
Sonal Dabral
Craig Smith

CLIENT
Nike

AGENCY
Ogilvy & Mather/
Singapore

ANNUAL ID
06047A

RUN

adidas
be the ball
adidas.com/football
AUT
adidas.com/football
adidas

Bronze

ART DIRECTORS
Guy Roberts
Zayed Siddique
Karen Maurice-O'Leary

WRITER
Verity Butt

CREATIVE DIRECTOR
Andy Blood

CLIENT
adidas

AGENCY
Whybin\TBWA/
Auckland (180\TBWA)

ANNUAL ID
06049A

adidas
adidas.com/football
be the ball

BEFORE THE WORLD'S
GREATEST FOOTBALL
PLAYERS KICK IT.
BEFORE THE WORLD'S
BEST GOALIES SAVE IT.
BEFORE ONE BILLION
FOOTBALL FANS SEE IT.
YOU ARE IT.

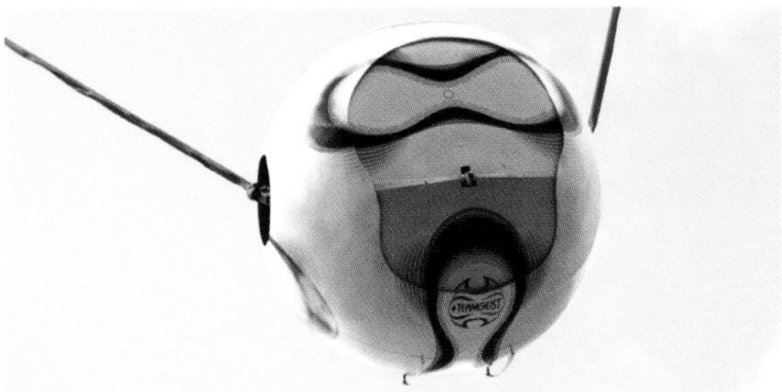

SILVER

ART DIRECTOR
Jason Musante

WRITERS
Matt Fischvogt
Brian Cain
Gregg Hale
Ernie Larsen
Jim Gunshanon

DESIGNERS
Justin Smith
Dave Szulborski

AGENCY PRODUCER
Regina Brizzolara

PRODUCTION COMPANY
Chelsea Pictures/ Campfire

DIRECTORS
Ben Rock
Mike Monello

CREATIVE DIRECTORS
Dave Cook
David Baldwin
Jonathan Cude
Brian Clark

CLIENT
Audi

AGENCY
McKinney/Durham

ANNUAL ID
06050A

ALSO AWARDED
Merit:
Innovative Marketing - Campaign

Merit:
Integrated Branding - Campaign

audiusa.com/A3

ATTENTION:

ATTENTION:
If you have any information regarding the location of a 2006 Audi A3 with VIN WAUZZZ8P65A045963, please contact Audi of America at 1-866-657-3268.
Audi

ATTENTION
mattress.com
TELECHARGE.COM 212-239-6200

AXE
axefantasy.com

The Axe Effect
AXEFANTASY
AXE

BRONZE

ART DIRECTOR
Husen Baba Khan

WRITER
Sandeep Fernandes

AGENCY PRODUCER
Vinayachandran Chandrahasan

CREATIVE DIRECTOR
Manoj Ammanath

CLIENT
Unilever

AGENCY
Lowe/Dubai

ANNUAL ID
06052A

AXEFANTASY
Mobile

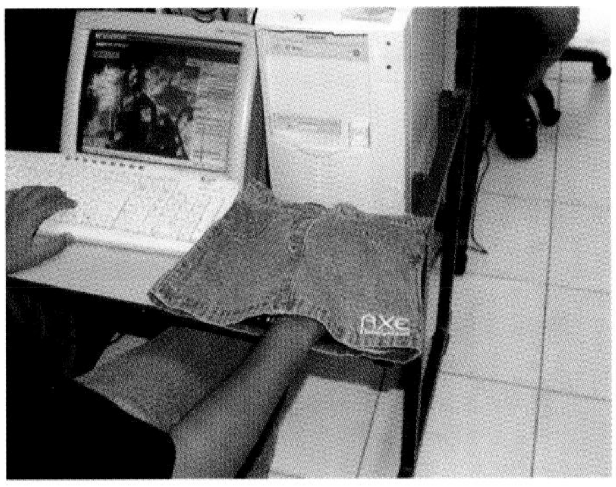

Silver

ART DIRECTOR
Chuck Tso

WRITER
Eric Schutte

CREATIVE DIRECTORS
Eric Silver
David Lubars

CLIENT
FedEx Kinko's

AGENCY
BBDO/New York

ANNUAL ID
06053A

ALSO AWARDED
Silver:
Innovative Marketing - Single

Bronze:
One Show Design Environmental Design - Campaign

OFFICE PRODUCTS
NOW AT
fedexkinkos.com
FedEx Kinko's

OFFICE PRODUCTS NOW AT fedexkinkos.com
FedEx Kinko's

Silver

OFFICE PRODUCTS
NOW AT fedexkinkos.com
FedEx Kinko's
Office and Print Center

0-60 IN 14 MINUTES?
NOT A GENUINE MINI.
MINI COOPER S
COUNTERFEITMINI.ORG
MINI

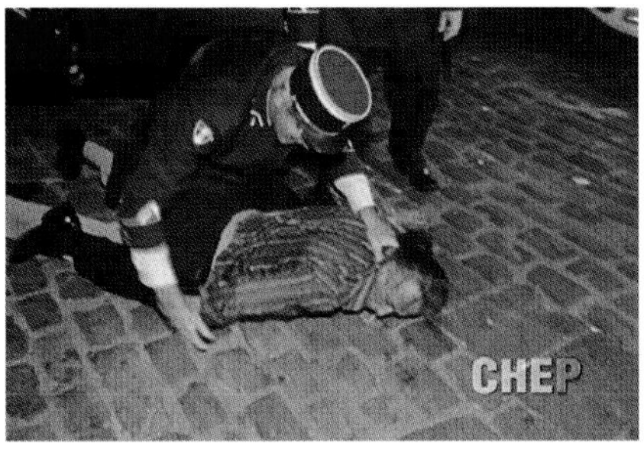
CHEP

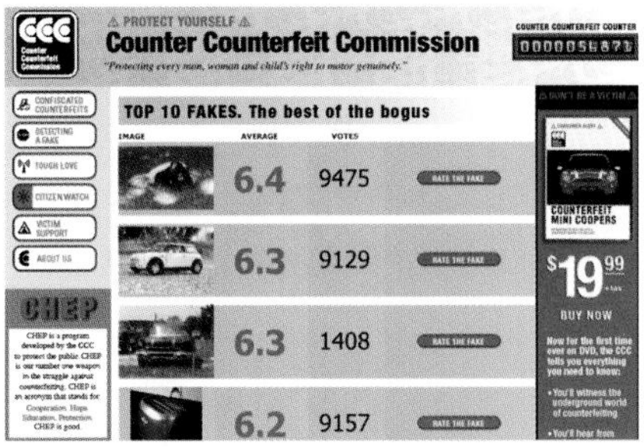
Counter Counterfeit Commission
TOP 10 FAKES. The best of the bogus
6.4 9475
6.3 9129
6.3 1408
6.2 9157
$19.99
CHEP

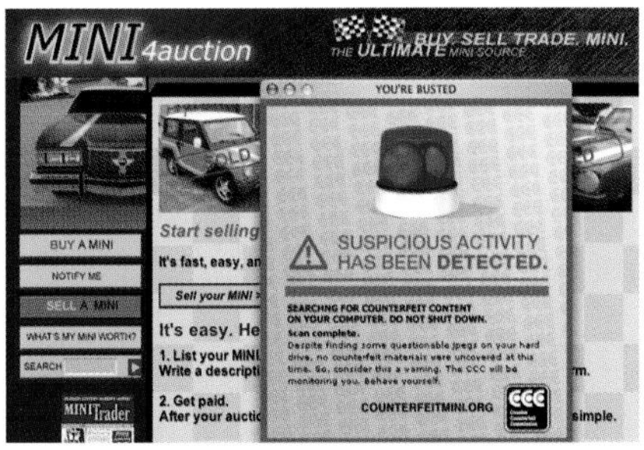
MINI4auction
BUY. SELL. TRADE. MINI.
SUSPICIOUS ACTIVITY HAS BEEN DETECTED.
BUY A MINI
SELL A MINI
COUNTERFEITMINI.ORG

WWW.COUNTERFEITMINI.ORG

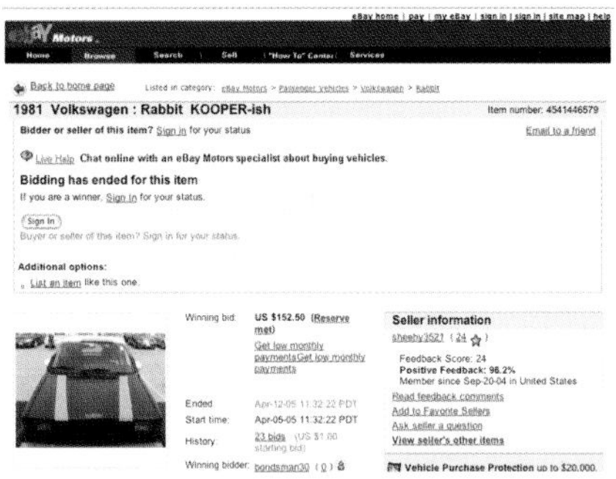
1981 Volkswagen : Rabbit KOOPER-ish
Bidding has ended for this item
Seller information

2002 MINI COOPER S Chance to own a legend. Chili Red paint, Mechanically Perfect. 5 spd, Lots of extras. Motor your brains out! 543K $6500 773-446-1637) SIA61012: 00467265403

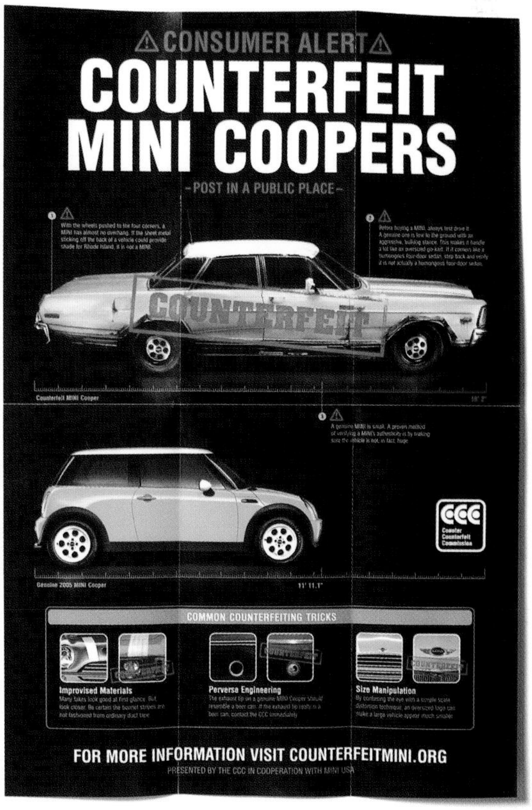
CONSUMER ALERT
COUNTERFEIT MINI COOPERS
-POST IN A PUBLIC PLACE-
COUNTERFEIT
COMMON COUNTERFEITING TRICKS
Improvised Materials
Perverse Engineering
Size Manipulation
FOR MORE INFORMATION VISIT COUNTERFEITMINI.ORG

GOLD

ART DIRECTORS
Paul Stechschulte
Tiffany Kosel

WRITERS
Franklin Tipton
Rob Reilly

DESIGNERS
Rahul Panchal
Michael Ferrare
Luis Santi

PHOTOGRAPHER
Sebastian Gray

AGENCY PRODUCERS
Rupert Samuel
David Rolfe
Matt Bonin
Bill Meadows

PRODUCTION COMPANIES
Exopolis
iChameleon
Hungry Man
Jodaf/Mixer

DIRECTOR
Bryan Buckley

CREATIVE DIRECTORS
Alex Bogusky
Andrew Keller
Jeff Benjamin
Steve O'Connell

CLIENT
MINI

AGENCY
Crispin Porter + Bogusky/Miami

ANNUAL ID
06001G

Silver

ART DIRECTORS
Mark Taylor
James Dawson Hollis
Kevin Koller
Anja Duering
Tiffany Kosel
Aramis Israel
Jed Grossman
Jason Ambrose
Dawn Yemma

WRITERS
Bob Cianfrone
Carl Corbitt
Scott Linnen
Larry Corwin
Donnell Johnson
Thomas Kemeny

DESIGNERS
Stan Winston Studios
Luis Santi

DIGITAL ARTISTS/
MULTIMEDIA
The Mill
Method
Angus Kneale
Melanie Wickham

AGENCY PRODUCERS
Rupert Samuel
David Rolfe
Letitia Jacobs
Liz Graves
Dan Ruth
Jay Howard
Aymi Beltramo
Matt Bonin
Jessica Dierauer
Cheri Anderson
Bill Meadows

PRODUCTION COMPANIES
Moxie Pictures
House of Usher
Digital Domain

DIRECTORS
Martin Granger
Kinka Usher
Erik Nash
Les Ekker

CREATIVE DIRECTORS
Alex Bogusky
Andrew Keller
Rob Reilly
Jeff Benjamin

CLIENT
Burger King

AGENCY
Crispin Porter +
Bogusky/Miami

ANNUAL ID
06002G

THIS HALLOWEEN
WAKE UP AS THE KING
> CLICK HERE TO BUY THE MASK

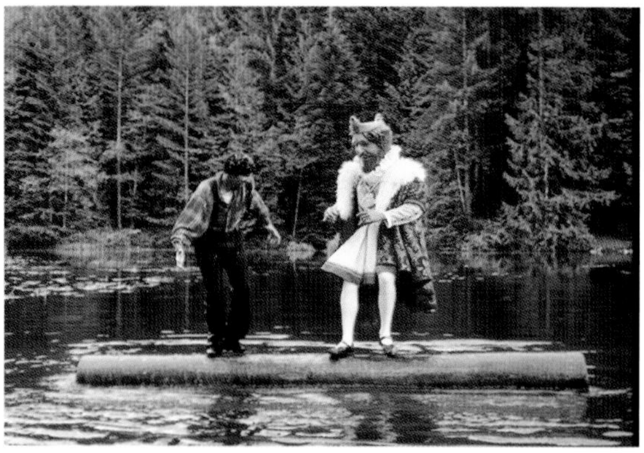

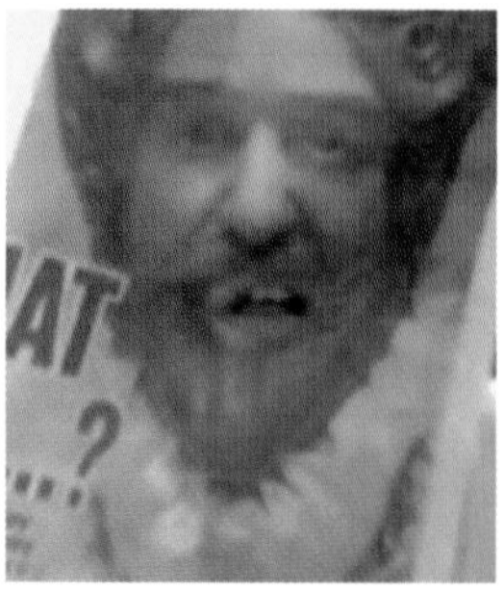

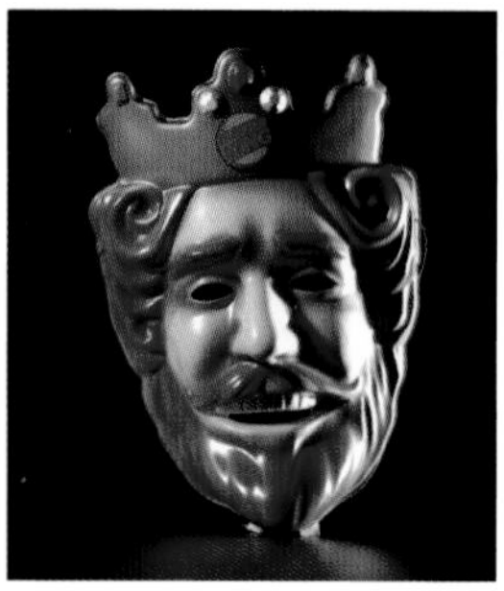

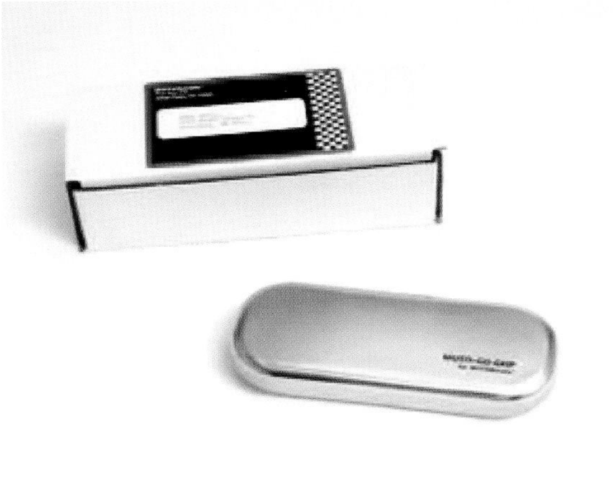

MOTORmate
HEY HORN THE FRIENDLY ALTERNATIVE TO REGULAR HONKING.
HEY HORN
$59.99
RAVE REVIEWS
SEND TO A FRIEND

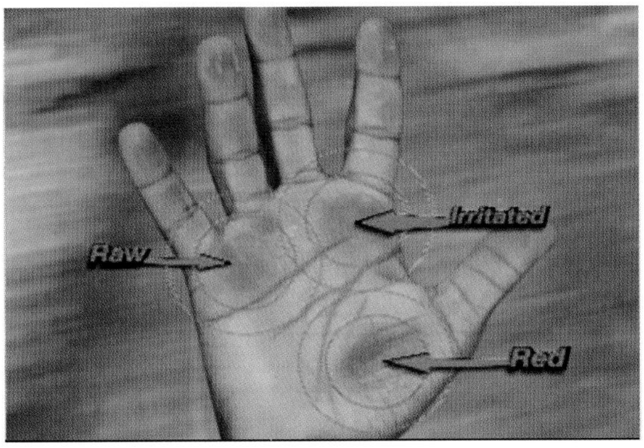
Raw
Irritated
Red

HEY HORN
$59 99 includes S&H
NOT AVAILABLE IN STORES
MOTORmate
P.O. BOX 415
WHITE PLAINS, NY 10603
To Order Visit:
www.MOTORmate.com

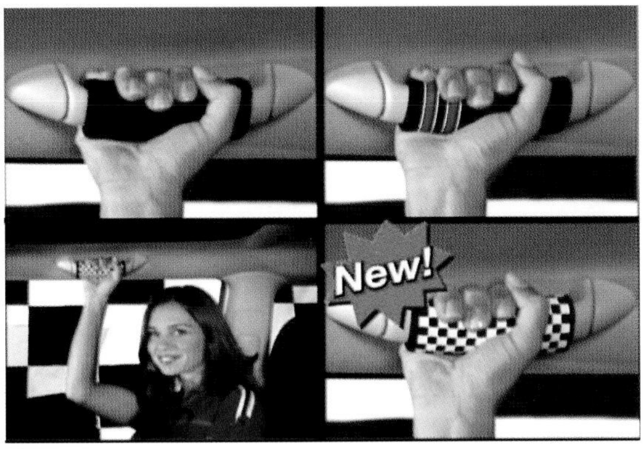
New!

G-Whiz
by MOTORmate
$29 99 includes S&H
NOT AVAILABLE IN STORES
MOTORmate
P.O. BOX 415
WHITE PLAINS, NY 10603
To Order Visit:
www.MOTORmate.com

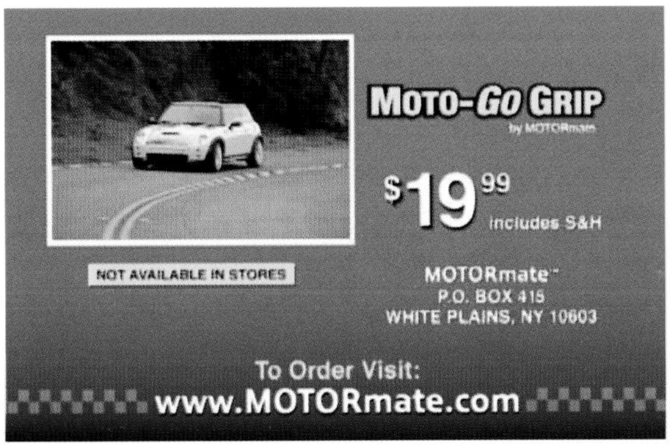
Moto-Go Grip
$19 99 includes S&H
NOT AVAILABLE IN STORES
MOTORmate
P.O. BOX 415
WHITE PLAINS, NY 10603
To Order Visit:
www.MOTORmate.com

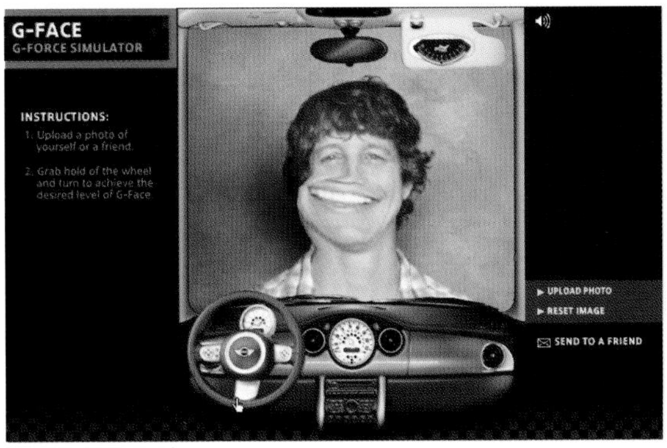
G-FACE
G-FORCE SIMULATOR
INSTRUCTIONS:
1. Upload a photo of yourself or a friend.
2. Grab hold of the wheel and turn to achieve the desired level of G-Face.
UPLOAD PHOTO
RESET IMAGE
SEND TO A FRIEND

Silver

ART DIRECTORS
Jason Ambrose
Paul Stechschulte
Jed Grossman

WRITERS
Dustin Ballard
Franklin Tipton
Larry Corwin

DESIGNER
Rahul Panchal

PROGRAMMER
Fuel Industries

DIGITAL ARTISTS/MULTIMEDIA
Spontaneous Combustion
David Elkins
Amir Qureshi

AGENCY PRODUCERS
Rupert Samuel
David Rolfe
Matthew Bonin
Bill Meadows

PRODUCTION COMPANY
Hungry Man

DIRECTOR
Bryan Buckley

CREATIVE DIRECTORS
Alex Bogusky
Andrew Keller
Jeff Benjamin
Steve O'Connell

CLIENT
MINI

AGENCY
Crispin Porter + Bogusky/Miami

ANNUAL ID
06003G

BRONZE

ART DIRECTORS
Dejan Rasic
Simone Brandse
Nick Robinson

WRITERS
Michael Canning
Howard Collinge

DESIGNER
Kris Rees

PHOTOGRAPHER
Stephen Stewart

DIGITAL ARTIST/
MULTIMEDIA
Jamie Corker

AGENCY PRODUCERS
Darren Bailey
Lisa Cordukes
Charna Henry
Jeff Edwards

PRODUCTION COMPANY
Plaza Films

DIRECTOR
Nicholas Reynolds

CREATIVE DIRECTORS
Adam Lance
Peter Bidenko

CLIENT
Unilever

AGENCY
Lowe Hunt/Sydney

ANNUAL ID
06004G

INTRODUCING A LEVEL OF
COMFORT NEVER EXPERIENCED
BEFORE IN AIR TRAVEL.
lynxjet.com

IN-FLIGHT ENTERTAINMENT
THAT IS SECOND TO NONE.
lynxjet.com

PYONGYANG
WITH
lynxjet.com

GLENGARRY
WITH
lynxjet.com

BAJA
WITH
lynxjet.com

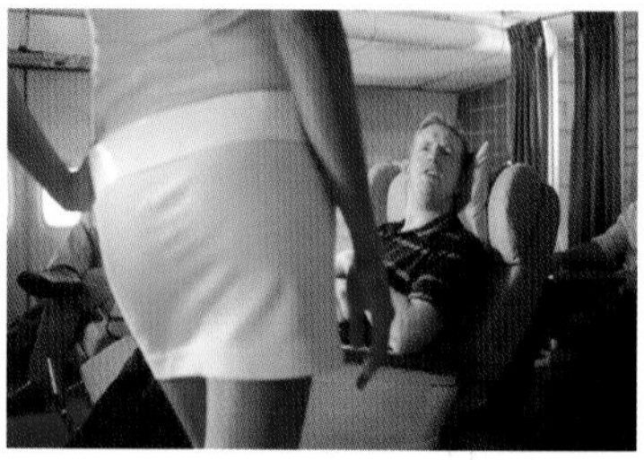

LYNX
jet
GET ON · GET OFF
lynxjet.com

Radio

Gold

Consumer Radio: Campaign

WRITERS
Jeb Quaid
Aaron Pendleton
John Baker
Robert Calabro

AGENCY PRODUCER
Marianne Newton

PRODUCTION COMPANY
Chicago Recording Company

CREATIVE DIRECTOR
Mark Gross

CLIENT
Anheuser-Busch

AGENCY
DDB/Chicago

ANNUAL ID
06008R

ALSO AWARDED
Silver: Consumer Radio - Single
"Mr. 80 SPF Wearer"

Merit: Consumer Radio - Single
"Mr. Jeans Shorts Wearer"

Silver

Consumer Radio: Campaign

WRITERS
Joe Schrack
Daniel Giachetti
John Clement
Brad Emmett

AGENCY PRODUCER
Barbara Michelson

PRODUCTION COMPANY
McHale Barone

CREATIVE DIRECTOR
Sal DeVito

CLIENT
National Thoroughbred Racing Association

AGENCY
DeVito/Verdi/New York

ANNUAL ID
06009R

ALSO AWARDED
Gold: Consumer Radio - Single
"Grandma"

Bronze: Consumer Radio - Single
"Video"

Merit: Consumer Radio - Single
"Backyard BBQ"

Bronze

Consumer Radio: Campaign

WRITER
Dan Cronin

AGENCY PRODUCER
Lilian Lopez

PRODUCTION COMPANY
Kamen Audio

CREATIVE DIRECTORS
Gerry Graf
Scott Vitrone
Ian Reichenthal

CLIENT
Masterfoods - Starburst

AGENCY
TBWA\Chiat\Day/New York

ANNUAL ID
06010R

ALSO AWARDED
Merit: Consumer Radio - Single
"Emotional Guy"

Gold

Public Service/Political-Radio: Single

ART DIRECTOR
Andy Mckay

WRITER
Mary Wear

CREATIVE DIRECTORS
Paul Belford
Nigel Roberts

CLIENT
Department for Transport

AGENCY
Abbott Mead Vickers BBDO/London

ANNUAL ID
06001R

Silver

Public Service/Political-Radio: Single

ART DIRECTORS
Dan Triechel
Colin Gaul
Jason Campbell

WRITERS
Emily Sander
Scott Bell

AGENCY PRODUCERS
Terry Brogan
Theresa Notartomaso

CREATIVE DIRECTORS
Walt Connelly
Toby Barlow

CLIENT
Partnership for a Drug Free America

AGENCY
JWT/New York

ANNUAL ID
06002R

Bronze

Public Service/Political-Radio: Single

WRITERS
Veronique Sels
Clemence Cousteau

PRODUCTION COMPANY
Capitaine Plouf

CREATIVE DIRECTOR
Erik Vervroegen

CLIENT
YLAT

AGENCY
TBWA/Paris

ANNUAL ID
06003R

Gold

Public Service/Political-Radio: Campaign

WRITERS
Brendan Guthrie
Tim Holmes

AGENCY PRODUCER
Simon Thomas

PRODUCTION COMPANY
Risk Sound

CREATIVE DIRECTOR
Ant Shannon

CLIENT
Open Family

AGENCY
Grey Worldwide/Melbourne

ANNUAL ID
06004R

SILVER

DESIGNERS
Kelly Atkins
Nancy Caal

ART DIRECTOR
Brad Simon

PHOTOGRAPHER
Peter Gregoire

ILLUSTRATORS
eboy
Kevin Sprouls

CREATIVE DIRECTOR
John Klotnia

CLIENT
Alexandria Real Estate

AGENCY
Opto Design/New York

ANNUAL ID
06001D

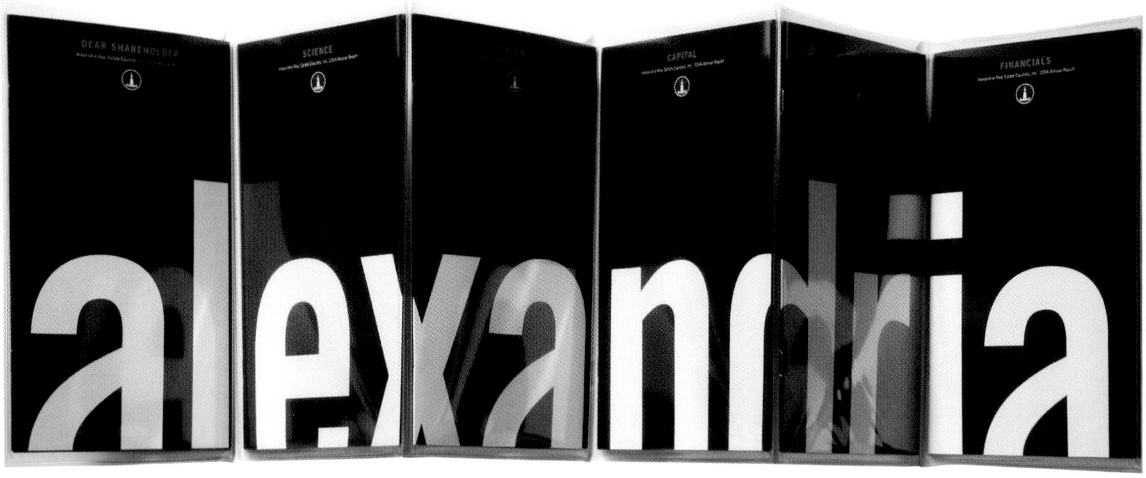
DEAR SHAREHOLDER
SCIENCE
CAPITAL
FINANCIALS
alexandria

$22.8 BILLION
+160
$5.6 BILLION
20x
+250%
1in5

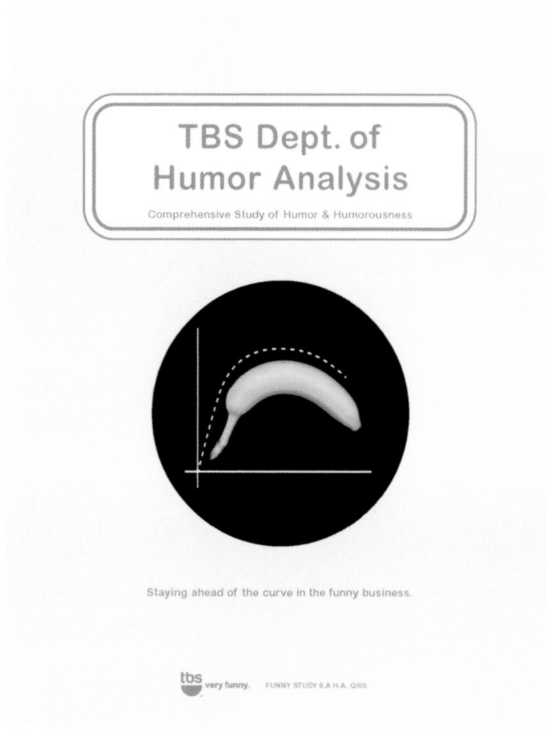
TBS Dept. of
Humor Analysis
Comprehensive Study of Humor & Humorousness
Staying ahead of the curve in the funny business.
tbs very funny.

GOLD

DESIGNER
Winnie Tsang

ART DIRECTOR
Rory Hanrahan

WRITER
Dave Clark

CREATIVE DIRECTORS
Linus Karlsson
Paul Malmstrom

CLIENT
Turner Broadcasting System (TBS)

AGENCY
Mother/New York

ANNUAL ID
06002D

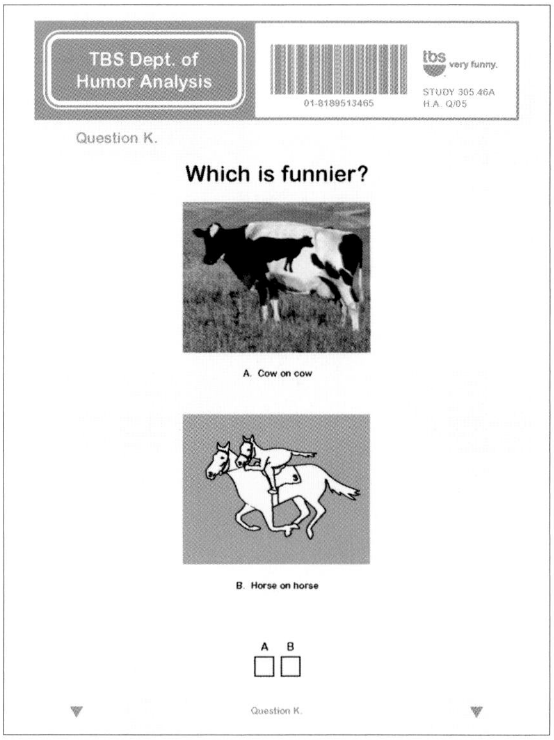
TBS Dept. of
Humor Analysis
01-8189513465
tbs very funny.
STUDY 305.46A
H.A. Q/05
Question K.
Which is funnier?
A. Cow on cow
B. Horse on horse
A B
Question K.

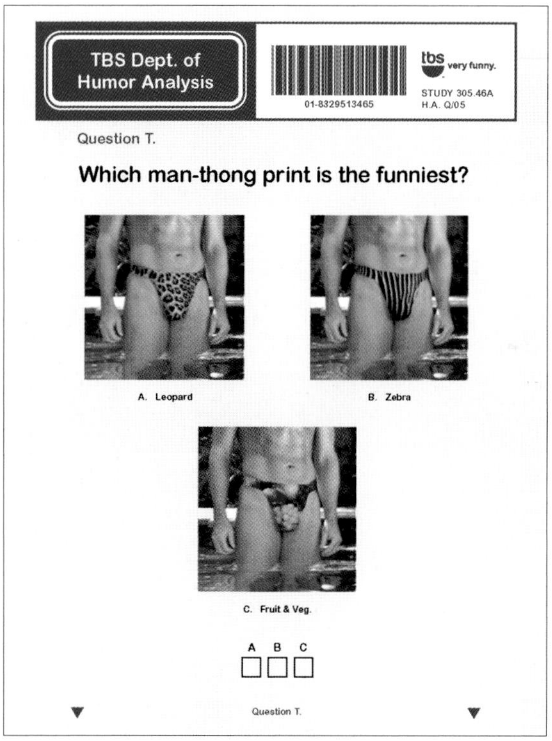
TBS Dept. of
Humor Analysis
01-8329513465
tbs very funny.
STUDY 305.46A
H.A. Q/05
Question T.
Which man-thong print is the funniest?
A. Leopard
B. Zebra
C. Fruit & Veg.
A B C
Question T.

GOLD

DESIGNER
Bertrand Kirschenhofer

ART DIRECTOR
Gunther Schreiber

WRITER
Ingmar Bartels

CREATIVE DIRECTOR
Lars Ruhmann

CLIENT
Renault Germany

AGENCY
Nordpol+/Hamburg

ANNUAL ID
06003D

ALSO AWARDED
Gold:
Direct Mail - Single

Crashtest

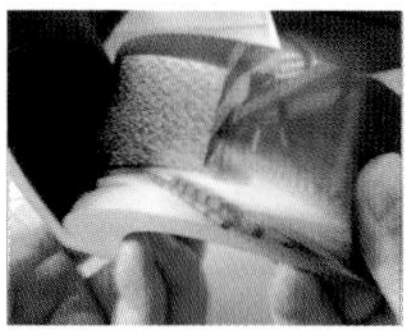

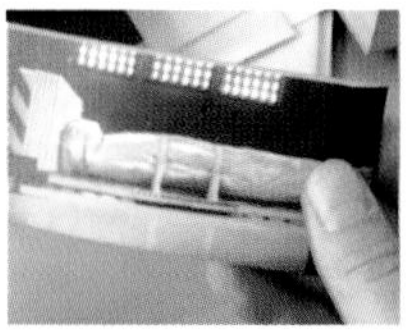

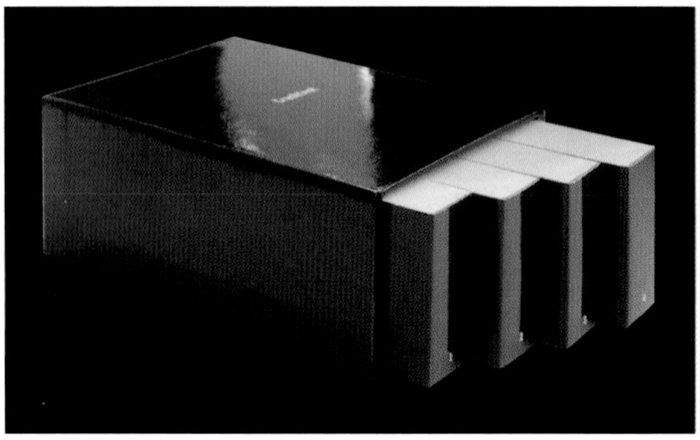

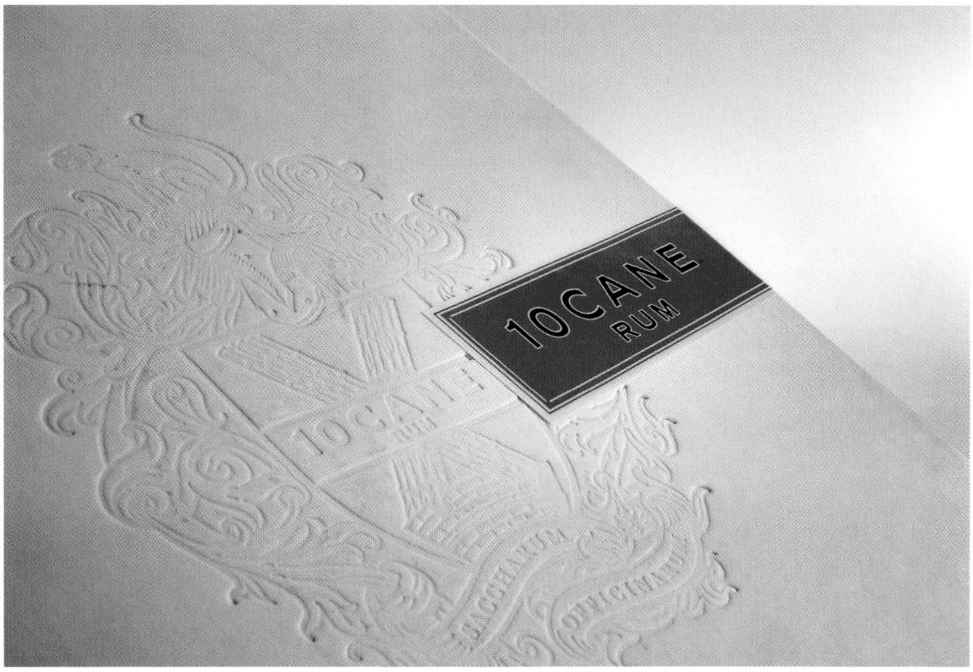
10CANE
RUM

THE STORY
10CANE
RUM

10CANE
RUM
COOL TEAM

Silver

DESIGNERS
Sean Carmody
David Mashburn

ART DIRECTOR
Sean Carmody

WRITER
Todd Lamb

PHOTOGRAPHER
Lars Topelmann

CREATIVE DIRECTORS
Linus Karlsson
Paul Malmstrom

CLIENT
LVMH

AGENCY
Mother/New York

ANNUAL ID
06004D

BRONZE

DESIGNER
Scott Thares

PHOTOGRAPHER
Marshall Fields Archives

ILLUSTRATOR
Scott Thares

CREATIVE DIRECTORS
Scott Thares
Richard Boynton
Greg Clark

CLIENT
Marshall Field's

AGENCY
Wink/Minneapolis

ANNUAL ID
06005D

3 stores become
The Shop Heard Around the World

COMMUNITY GIVING. The Marshall Field's family of stores has a rich history of contributing 5 percent of its federally taxable income to community nonprofit organizations, including support for the arts through our Marshall Field's Gives.

FRONT

FedEx
Express

GOLD

ART DIRECTORS
Eric Schutte
Chuck Tso

CREATIVE DIRECTORS
Eric Silver
David Lubars

CLIENT
FedEx

AGENCY
BBDO/New York

ANNUAL ID
06006D

Silver

ART DIRECTOR
Anthony de Klerk

WRITER
Hanlie Kriel

CREATIVE DIRECTOR
Francois de Villiers

CLIENT
Greek Restaurant

AGENCY
FCB/Cape Town

ANNUAL ID
06007D

greek
021 686 4314

Bronze

ART DIRECTOR
Daniel Zenas Upputuru

WRITER
Suchitra Gahlot

CREATIVE DIRECTOR
Emmanuel Upputuru

CLIENT
C. Roy

AGENCY
Ogilvy & Mather/ New Delhi

ANNUAL ID
06008D

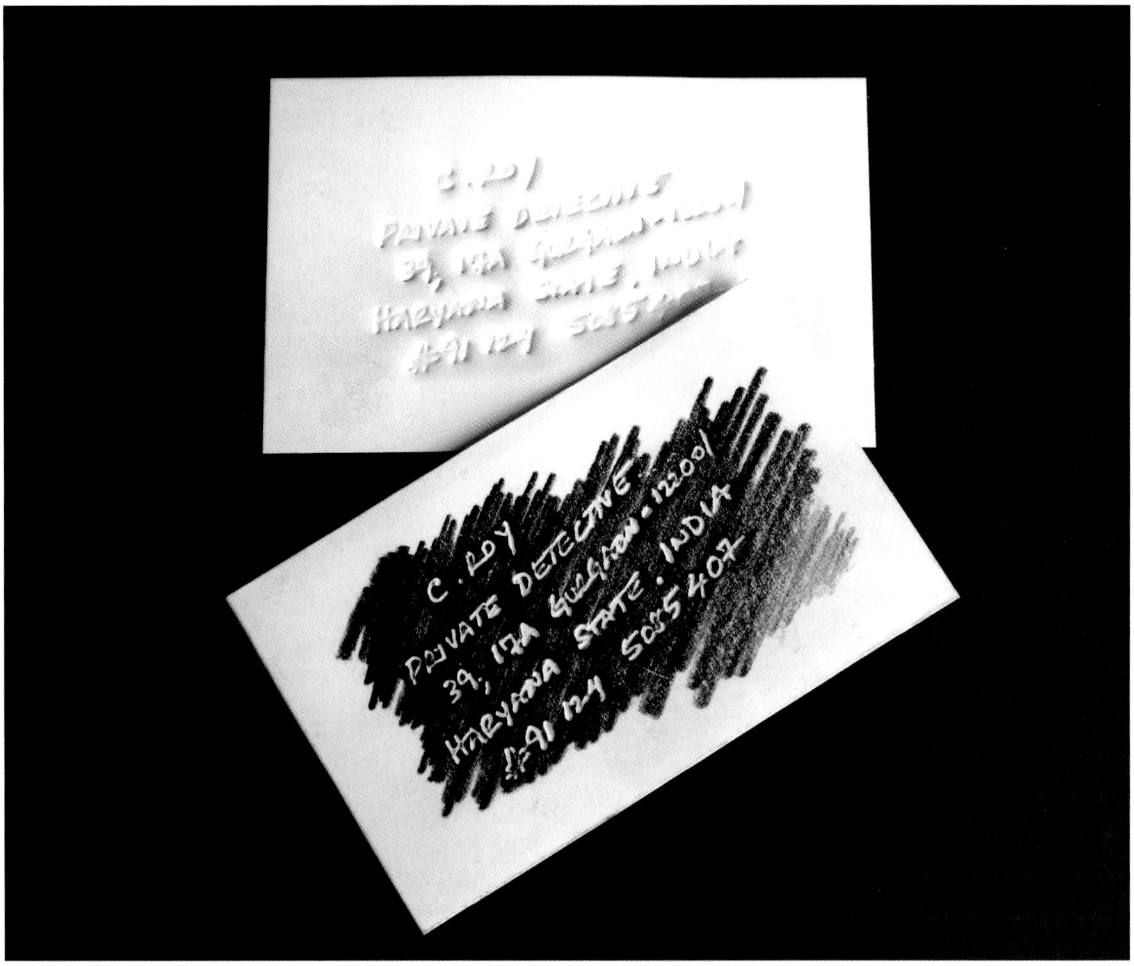
C. ROY
PRIVATE DETECTIVE
HARYANA STATE. INDIA

-VOTE JIM ESCH-
CONGRESSIONAL ★ ELECTIONS 2006
for U.S. Congress
PAID FOR BY JIM ESCH FOR CONGRESS

VOTE
E

Gold

DESIGNER
Joel Kreutzer

CREATIVE DIRECTOR
Charles Hull

CLIENT
Jim Esch for Congress

AGENCY
Archrival/Lincoln

ANNUAL ID
06009D

ALSO AWARDED
Silver:
Brand and Corporate Identity Design: Logo/ Trademark Design

JIM ESCH
FOR CONGRESS

VOTE
CHANGE
JIM ESCH
FOR CONGRESS
INVITATION TO CHANGE
YOUR PRESENCE IS WELCOME
PLEASE JOIN JIM ESCH OCTOBER 4TH AT THE OFFICIAL LAUNCH EVENT FOR HIS 2006 BID FOR CONGRESSIONAL OFFICE. COME MEET JIM AND HEAR HIM SPEAK ON HIS VISION FOR AMERICA AND A BETTER GOVERNMENT. WE WELCOME YOUR SUPPORT.
JIM ESCH FOR CONGRESS CAMPAIGN LAUNCH
OCTOBER 4TH, 2005 | 5:30 PM
1316 JONES STREET, OMAHA NE

FOR YOUR
THANK YOU

GOLD

DESIGNER
Michael Verdine

CREATIVE DIRECTORS
Michael Verdine
Dan Richards

CLIENT
Opolis

AGENCY
Opolis/Portland

ANNUAL ID
06010D

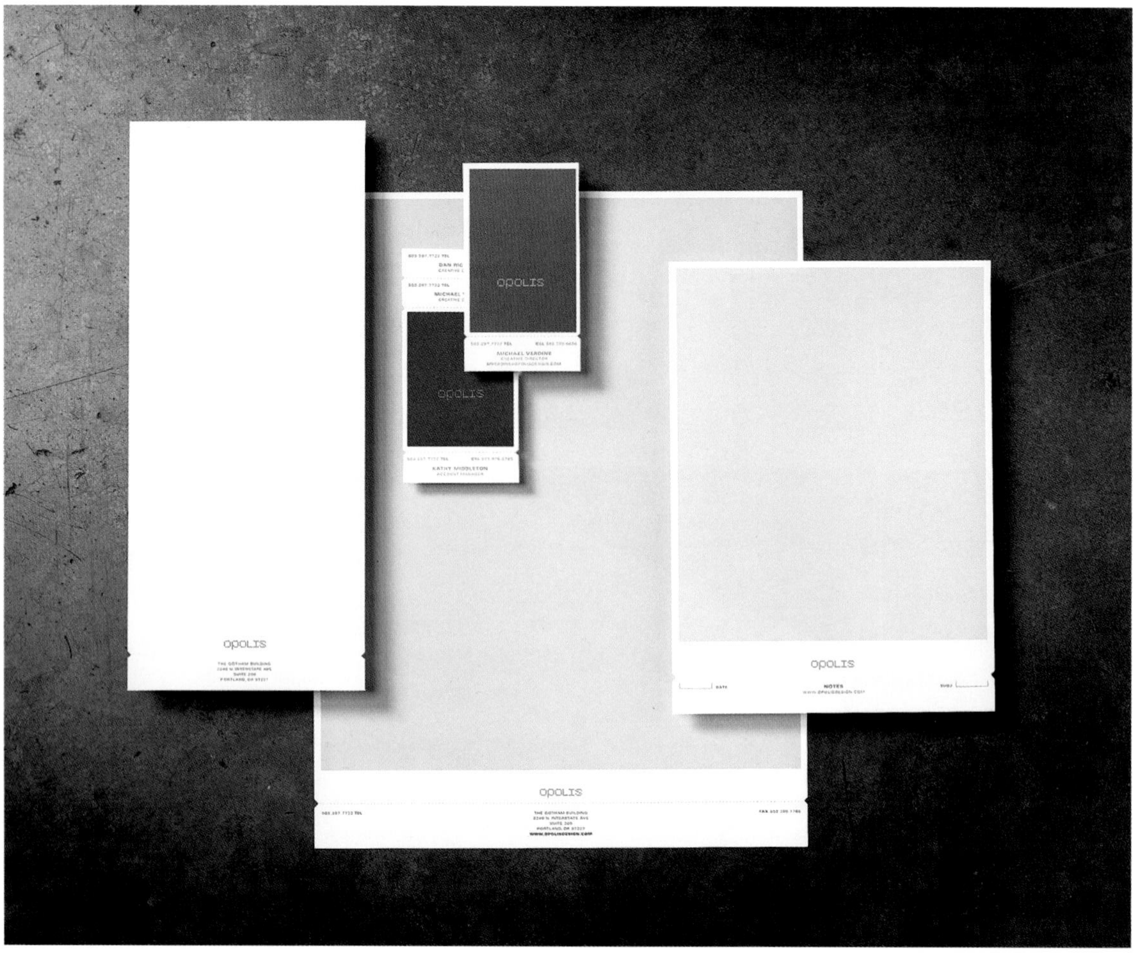
OPOLIS
OPOLIS
OPOLIS

OPOLIS
OPOLIS
CEL 503.976.2785
KATHY MIDDLETON
ACCOUNT MANAGER
MICHAEL VERDINE
CREATIVE DIRECTOR
OPOLIS
THE GOTHAM BUILDING
2240 N INTERSTATE AVE
SUITE 200
PORTLAND, OR 97227
WWW.OPOLISDESIGN.COM

GOLD

DESIGNER
Monique Gamache

ART DIRECTOR
Keli Pollock

WRITERS
Trent Burton
Joe Hospodarec

PHOTOGRAPHER
Keli Pollock

CREATIVE DIRECTOR
Monique Gamache

CLIENT
WAX Partnership

AGENCY
WAX Partnership/ Calgary

ANNUAL ID
06011D

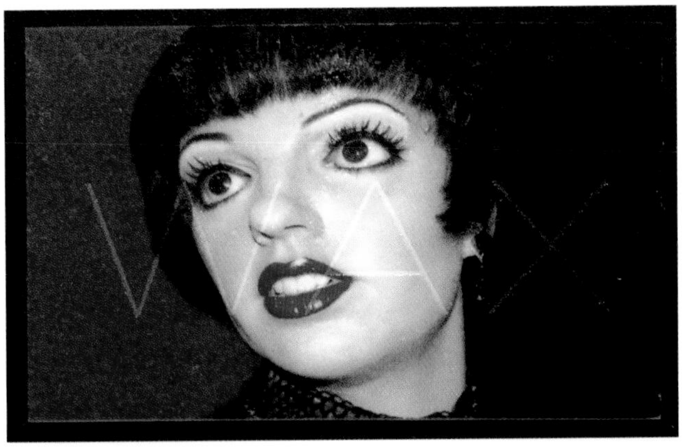

WAX

SILVER

DESIGNER
Ken Sakurai

WRITER
Lisa Pemrick

CREATIVE DIRECTOR
Dan Olson

CLIENT
Thymes

AGENCY
Duffy & Partners/ Minneapolis

ANNUAL ID
06012D

THYMES
CHRISTIANA KIPPELS

THYMES
Founded in 1982 with the aesthetic vision of its leader, Leslie Ross Lentz, the Thymes has over the years evolved from its humble start as the home-based business of one woman, to become a valued and trusted national brand.
For a company that cultivates the idea of a centered sense of self, the Thymes is also aware of who we are, and the way things should be done.
From an office filled with art and sunlight...to a passion for developing products as practical as they are sensual...to attracting and promoting women to positions of leadership, the culture at the Thymes is a testament to the spirit of inventiveness and integrity that flows through the organization.
With an unwavering commitment to providing warm, responsive service, consistently superior products, and an experience that never disappoints, those at the Thymes have turned "doing things the right way" into an artform.
5

THYMES

DIE WELT
IST IN BEWEGUNG!
KEIN BEREICH,
DER SEIT DEN 60ER JAHREN
NICHT VOM FORTSCHRITT ERFASST WURDE!
KEINER?

mamamoto
MANIFEST

mamamoto

BRONZE

DESIGNERS
Hana Sedelmayer
Bernd Oldorp

ART DIRECTORS
Arne Schmidt
Thomas Kappes
Verena Baumhogger

WRITER
Marina Klepka

ILLUSTRATOR
Thomas Kappes

CREATIVE DIRECTORS
Claudia Fischer-Appelt
Petra Matouschek

CLIENT
Mamamoto

AGENCY
Ligalux/Hamburg

ANNUAL ID
06013D

GOLD

DESIGNER
Greg Chapman

COPYWRITER
Karin Djelaj

CREATIVE DIRECTOR
Craig Cooper

CLIENT
The Dog House

AGENCY
DDB/Dallas

ANNUAL ID
06014D

alphabet

BRONZE

DESIGNER
Shani Ahmed

ART DIRECTOR
Shani Ahmed

CLIENT
I-Jusi Magazine

AGENCY
FCB/Cape Town

ANNUAL ID
06016D

GOLD

DESIGNERS
Apple Graphic Design
Apple Industrial Design
Apple Packaging Engineering

CLIENT
Apple Computer

AGENCY
Apple Computer/ Cupertino

ANNUAL ID
06017D

Now Playing
3 of 14
Just Feel Better
Santana
All That I Am
3:30
-0:55
iPod
nano
MENU
MENU

iPod
iPod

SILVER

DESIGNERS
Apple Graphic Design
Apple Industrial Design
Apple Packaging Engineering

CLIENT
Apple Computer

AGENCY
Apple Computer/Cupertino

ANNUAL ID
06018D

COLOR
pig mug
U Mo 1
pig mug

SILVER

ART DIRECTOR
Kenjiro Sano

CREATIVE DIRECTOR
Asako Harada

CLIENT
Franc Franc

AGENCY
Hakuhodo/Tokyo

ANNUAL ID
06019D

BRONZE

DESIGNERS
+cruz
Kimgym
Shotaro Tomiyama
Davi Sing Liu

ART DIRECTOR
+cruz

ILLUSTRATORS
Maharo
Solobongnu-Sensei

CREATIVE DIRECTORS
John C Jay
Sumiko Sato

CLIENT
Hifana

AGENCY
Wieden+Kennedy/Tokyo

ANNUAL ID
06020D

CHANNEL

CHANNEL

THYMES
FILIGREE
EAU DE PARFUM
PERFUMED BODY CREME
THYMES
FILIGREE
BODY CREME
Crème pour le corps
7.75 fl oz 230 ml
THYMES
THYMES
THYMES

GOLD

DESIGNER
Esther Mun

WRITER
Lisa Pemrick

CREATIVE DIRECTOR
Dan Olson

CLIENT
Thymes

AGENCY
Duffy & Partners/ Minneapolis

ANNUAL ID
06021D

SILVER

DESIGNER
Sam Lachlan

ILLUSTRATOR
Nathan Jurevicius

CREATIVE DIRECTORS
David Turner
Bruce Duckworth

CLIENT
Superdrug

AGENCY
Turner Duckworth/
San Francisco

ANNUAL ID
06022D

Superdrug
EXTRA GENTLE MANGO
2 IN 1 CONDITIONING
SHAMPOO
FOR LITTLE MONSTERS
NO TEARS FORMULA
Superdrug
EXTRA GENTLE
TROPICAL FRUIT 2 IN 1
CONDITIONING
SHAMPOO
FOR LITTLE MONSTERS
NO TEARS FORMULA

Superdrug
EXTRA GENTLE STRAWBERRY
SHAMPOO
FOR LITTLE MONSTERS
NO TEARS FORMULA
EXTRA GENTLE MELON
AFTER SWIM
3 IN 1 CONDITIONING
SHAMPOO + BODYWASH
FOR LITTLE MONSTERS
NO TEARS + DE-CHLORINATING

Torchbearer Sauces
SUPER FANCY #37 TARNATION SAUCE
SUPER FANCY #1 EVERY DAY SAUCE
FEVER SAUCE

BRONZE

ART DIRECTOR
Buffy McCoy Kelly

WRITER
Buffy McCoy Kelly

ILLUSTRATOR
Joe Barry

CREATIVE DIRECTORS
Rudy Banny
Buffy McCoy Kelly

CLIENT
Torchbearer Sauces

AGENCY
Neiman Group/ Harrisburg

ANNUAL ID
06023D

Nutrition Facts
Serving Size 1 tsp (5g)
Servings Per Container 48
Amount Per Serving
Calories 5
% Daily Value*
Total Fat 0g 0%
Trans Fat 0g 0%
Sodium 10mg 0%
Total Carbohydrate 1g 0%
Protein 0g 0%
Vitamin A 4% • Vitamin C 4%
*Percent Daily Values are based on a 2,000 calorie diet.
INGREDIENTS: Habanero Peppers, Carrots, Onions, Mandarin Oranges, Tomato Concentrate [Water and Tomato Paste, High Fructose Corn Syrup, Corn Syrup, Vinegar, Salt, Onion Powder, Spice, All Natural Flavoring] Garlic, Salt, Chili Powder, Black Pepper
Torchbearer, 1110 East Powderhorn Road Mechanicsburg, PA 17050
WWW.TORCHBEARERSAUCES.COM
Refrigerate After Opening.
WORLD'S 2ND HOTTEST NATURAL SAUCE
SCOVILLE RATING 38,202
Torchbearer Sauces
SUPER FANCY #37 TARNATION SAUCE
J. A. R. V. I. S.: ONE OF the ALLEY BOYS COULD GROW HAIR ON REQUEST. GOT THE ABILITY DUE TO HIS HIGH CONSUMPTION OF #37 IS WHAT FOLKS SAY.
HE COULD POP A MOUSTACHE OR CHEST HAIR BY SQUATTING DOWN AND GRUNTING TWO OR THREE TIMES. Word HAS IT THAT ON OCCASION HE GRUNTED TOO hard. YOU CAN GO AHEAD AND FIGURE OUT THE REST OF THAT FOR YOURSELF★
WATCH AT THIS.
HOT ENOUGH TO HURT YOU.
8 oz. 227 grams
6 56605 94832 4

Nutrition Facts
Refrigerate After Opening.
Torchbearer Sauces
SUPER FANCY #7 SULTRY SAUCE
WE HEARD A TALE ABOUT A MR. AND MISSUS WITH AN AFFINITY FOR #7 SAID SHE PUT IT IN HIS COFFEE FOR A WAKE-UP CALL.
HE PUT IT ON HER UNMENTIONABLES FOR A WAKE UP CALL, AND THEY BOTH ATE IT ON FRIED CHICKEN, AND TAHINI WITH WATER CRESS. PEOPLE SAY IT KEPT THE FIRE BETWEEN THEM. THAT'S JUST WHAT WE HEARD.
A darn good condiment to enhance what you want it to
8 oz. (227 grams)
WWW.TORCHBEARERSAUCES.COM

Nutrition Facts
Refrigerate After Opening.
Torchbearer Sauces
SUPER FANCY #1 EVERY DAY SAUCE
WE KNOW A HOSS WHO SHOOK A LITTLE DAB ON HIS TATERS, LIMA BEANS, ESCARGOT AND HIS PEANUT BUTTER SANDWICH PLUS
SAID IT DID A REAL GOOD JOB AS A HAIR TONIC AND PUT A NICE SHINE ON HIS SHOES BUT THAT'S JUST HIM THOUGH.
GOL DARN THAT'S GOOD
Made out of something and something else. Especially.
8 oz (227 grams)
WWW.TORCHBEARERSAUCES.COM

Nutrition Facts
Refrigerate After Opening.
Torchbearer Sauces
SUPER FANCY #11 SUGAR FIRE Sauce
FELLER BY THE NAME OF Big TIME USED TO EAT MORE THAN 12 MEN AND FOUR HORSES COMBINED. 3 BREAKFASTS, 1 BRUNCH, 2 LUNCHES 4 SUPPERS AND A COUPLE OF DINNERS Everyday
SAID HE WASN'T REALLY HUNGRY, JUST WAS LOOKIN' TO Satisfy HIS FLAVOR TOOTH. HIS Mamaw WHIPPED THE TAR OUT OF HIM, THEN GAVE HIM A JAR OF #11. HE NEVER HAD PROBLEMS FINDING GOOD FLAVOR AFTER THAT. To THIS DAY HIS Mamaw USES HIS FAT PANTS TO TARP HER Woodpile.
8 oz. 227 grams
WWW.TORCHBEARERSAUCES.COM

Nutrition Facts
WORLD'S HOTTEST NATURAL SAUCE
Torchbearer Sauces
SUPER FANCY #42 SLAUGHTER Sauce
KAY KAY Alifair Mayhorn WAS ONE PART PRINCESS, ONE PART GUNSLINGER, AND ALL THE REST PURE BILLY GOAT. TOTED A SAWED-OFF SHOTGUN IN HER Brassiere, AND ATE ANYTHING ON A DARE
SNAKE BERRIES, A RUSTY NAIL, AND EVEN ONCE DINED ON A TRACTOR TIRE. THE MENFOLK WOULD'VE LINED UP TO ASK FOR Her Hand BUT WERE JUST TOO DANG SCARED SHE WOULD EAT THEM FOR Dinner.
I SAID GIT OVER HERE.
HOT ENOUGH TO HURT YOU.
IT WAS A PURE rotten SHAME.
8 oz. 227 grams
WWW.TORCHBEARERSAUCES.COM
Refrigerate After Opening

Silver

DESIGNER
KC Chung

ART DIRECTORS
Ean-Hwa Huang
KC Chung

WRITERS
Szu-Hung Lee
Eddie Azadi

CREATIVE DIRECTORS
Szu-Hung Lee
Ean-Hwa Huang

CLIENT
Sony

AGENCY
McCann Erickson/
Kuala Lumpur

ANNUAL ID
06024D

ALSO AWARDED
Silver:
One Show Collateral:
Posters - Single

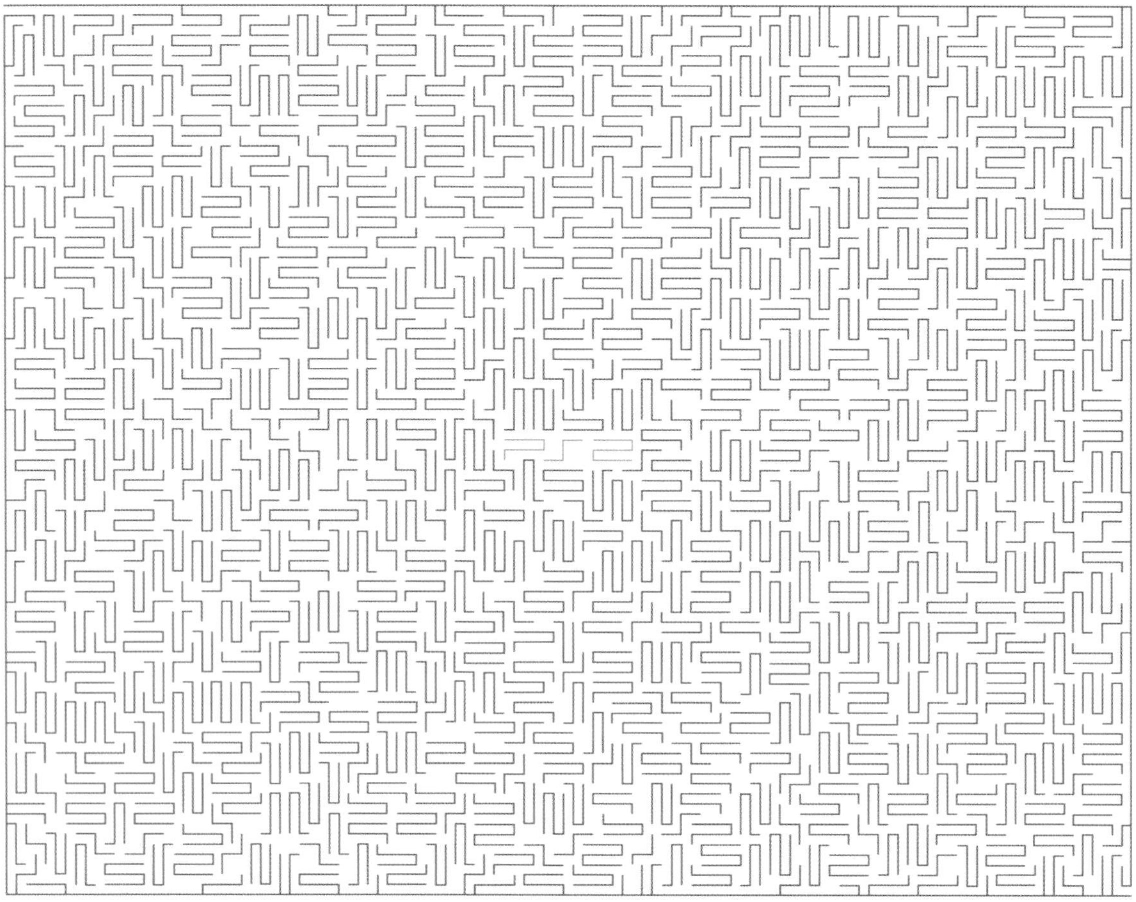

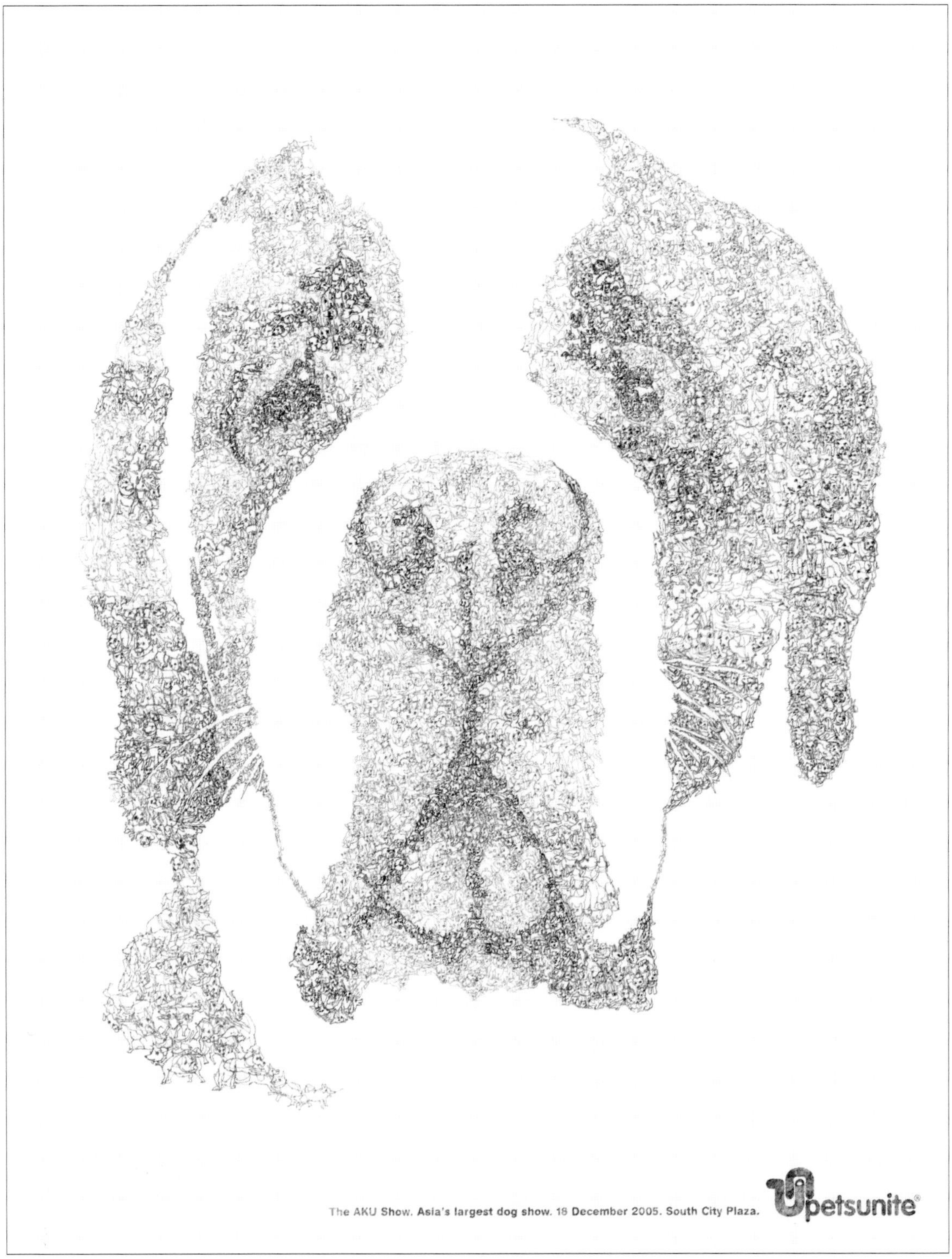
The AKU Show. Asia's largest dog show. 18 December 2005. South City Plaza.
petsunite®

petsunite

petsunite

Silver

ART DIRECTORS
Tan Chee Keong
Ng See Lok

WRITER
Donevan Chew

ILLUSTRATORS
Lee Hoon Sun
Lum Choon Kiat
Siah Ning Woei

CREATIVE DIRECTORS
Yasmin Ahmad
Ali Mohamed
Tan Yew Leong

CLIENT
PetsUnite

AGENCY
Leo Burnett/
Kuala Lumpur

ANNUAL ID
06025D

GOLD

ART DIRECTORS
Nirun Sommalardpun
Kajnarong Inpornvichitr

WRITERS
Weerachon Weeraworawit
Suthisak Sucharittanonta

PHOTOGRAPHER
Remix Studio

ILLUSTRATOR
Anuchai Sricharunputong

CREATIVE DIRECTORS
Suthisak Sucharittanonta
Annop Indravudh

CLIENT
DaimlerChrysler

AGENCY
BBDO/Bangkok

ANNUAL ID
06026D

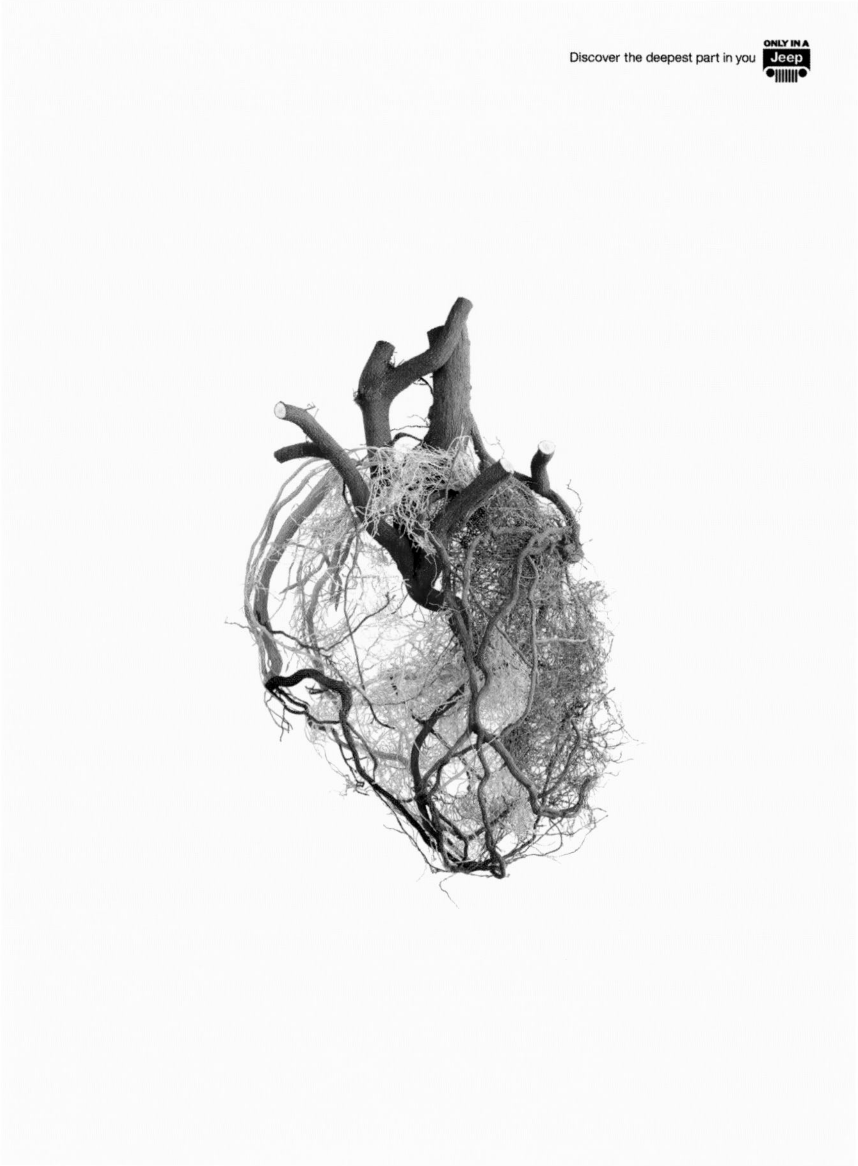
Discover the deepest part in you
ONLY IN A
Jeep

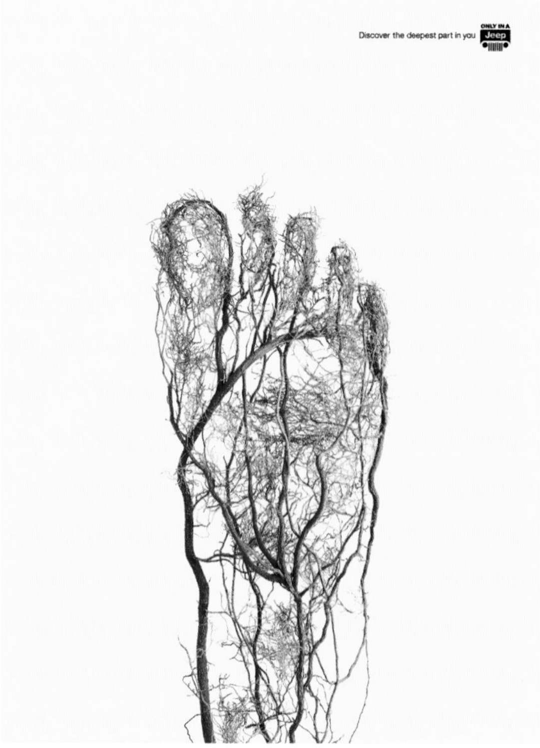
Discover the deepest part in you
ONLY IN A
Jeep

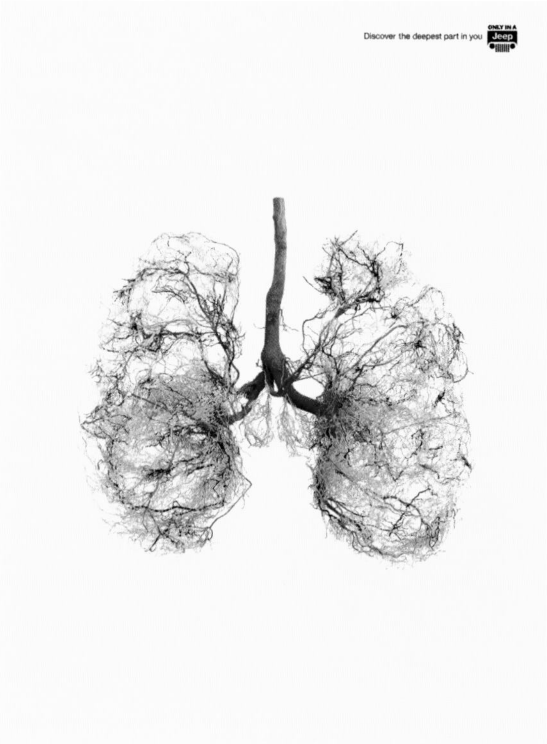
Discover the deepest part in you
ONLY IN A
Jeep

OFFICE: jason schulte design
visitoffice.com
2005

GOLD

DESIGNER
Nicole Flores

ILLUSTRATOR
Nicole Flores

CREATIVE DIRECTOR
Jason Schulte

CLIENT
Office: Jason Schulte Design

AGENCY
Office: Jason Schulte Design/San Francisco

ANNUAL ID
06027D

Silver

DESIGNER
Emi Kashima

ART DIRECTOR
Emi Kashima

PHOTOGRAPHER
Shinichi Masumoto

ILLUSTRATOR
Emi Kashima

CREATIVE DIRECTOR
Tatsuo Ebina

CLIENT
E.Co.

AGENCY
E.Co./Tokyo

ANNUAL ID
06028D

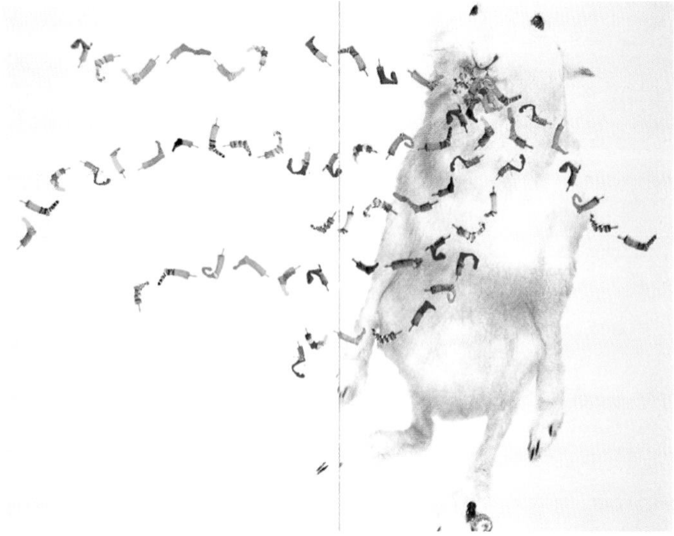

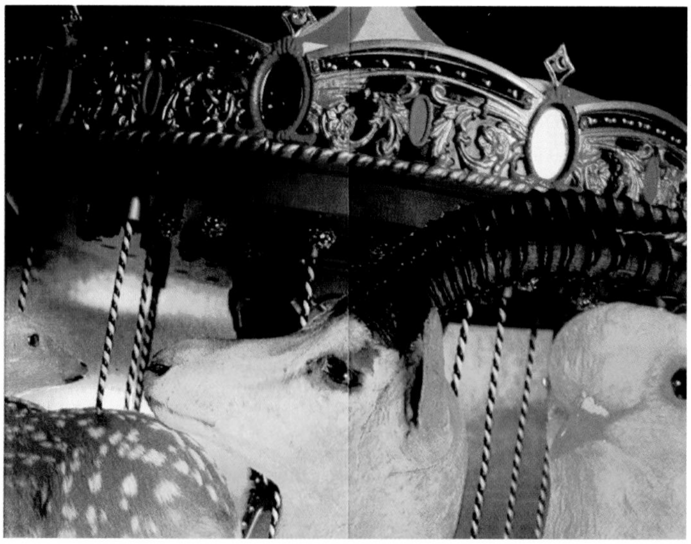

As much as we love you, we hate the design.*
Happy F&B på Röhsska museet 2005
Happy F&B at the Röhsska Museum 2005

BRONZE

ART DIRECTOR
Happy Forsman & Bodenfors

WRITER
Mikael Nanfeldt

PHOTOGRAPHERS
Jager Aren
Grafia

CREATIVE DIRECTOR
Happy Forsman & Bodenfors

CLIENT
Happy Forsman & Bodenfors

AGENCY
Happy Forsman & Bodenfors/Gothenburg

ANNUAL ID
06029D

MUU
MUU
MUU
Choklad
Banan
Jordgubb
Arla: Förpackningsdesign
Med lanseringen av den mjölkbaserade drycken MUU ville Arla konkurrera med läsktillverkarna om de yngre målgrupperna. Smakerna choklad, jordgubb och banan blev så populära att även de utanför målgruppen tog till sig MUU, inte sällan i drinkar. Till höger: MUU i den brittiska designtidskriften Wallpaper. (1997)
Arla: Packaging design
By launching its milk-based drink MUU, Swedish dairy Arla wanted to compete for younger consumers with soft drinks manufacturers. The chocolate, strawberry and banana flavours became so popular that even people outside the target group drank MUU, often in cocktails. Right: MUU in the British design magazine Wallpaper. (1997)
10

MUU
Choklad

Abba
KALLES

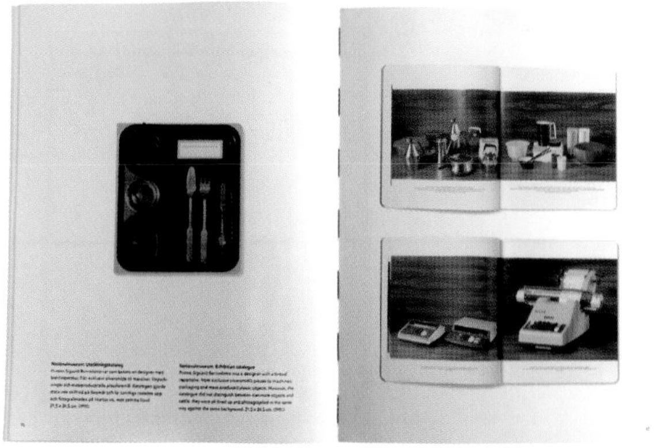

GOLD

DESIGNERS
Mark Hofler
Michael Kuhn

ART DIRECTORS
Christoph Bielefeldt
Philipp Dorner

CREATIVE DIRECTOR
Lars Ruhmann

CLIENT
ASICS Europe

AGENCY
Nordpol+/Hamburg

ANNUAL ID
06030D

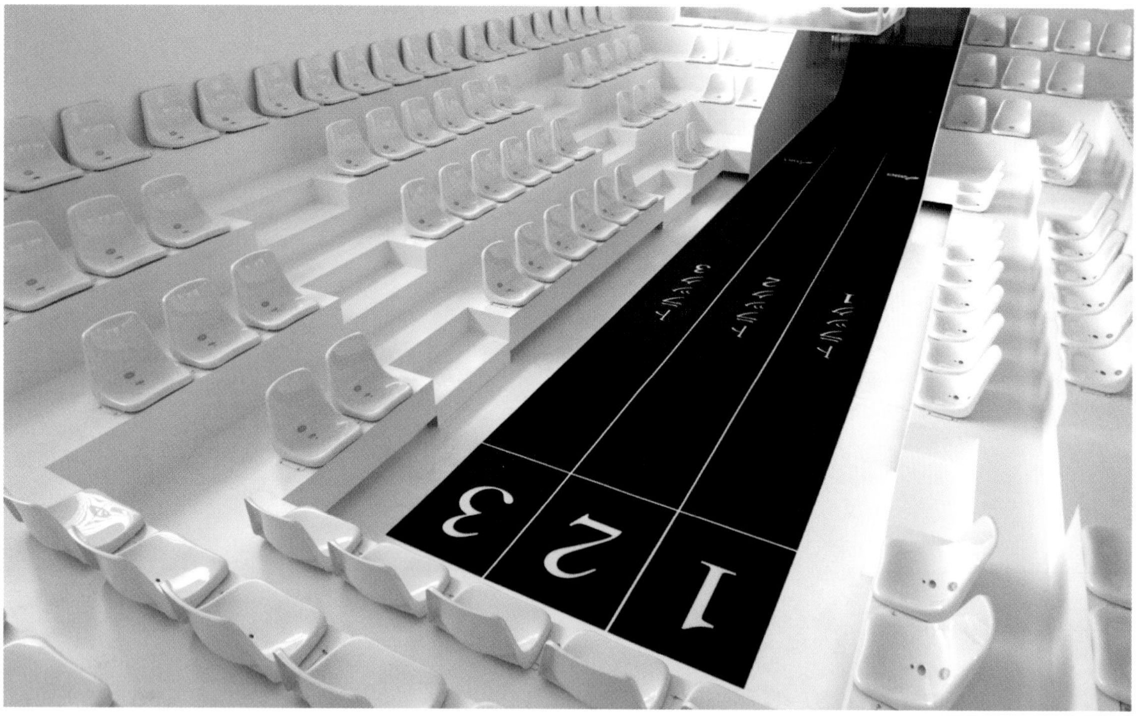

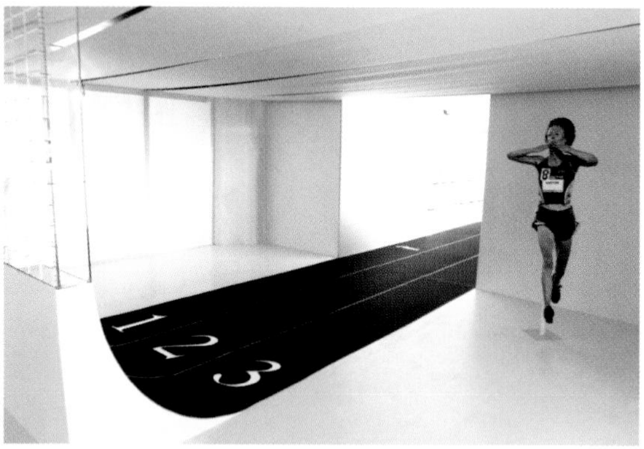

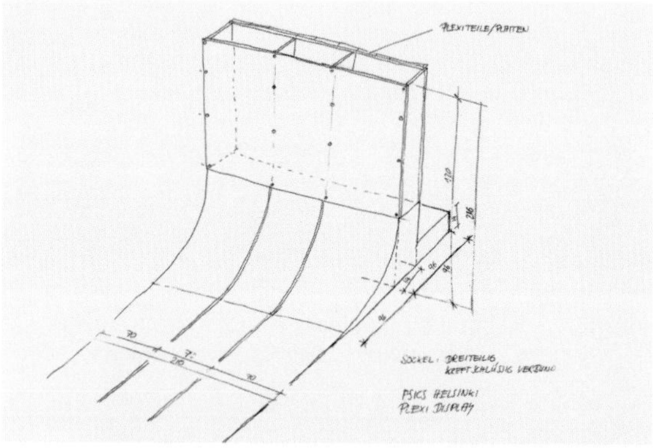

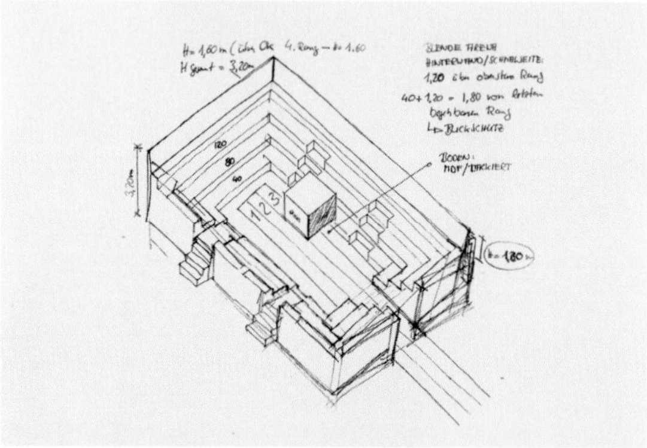

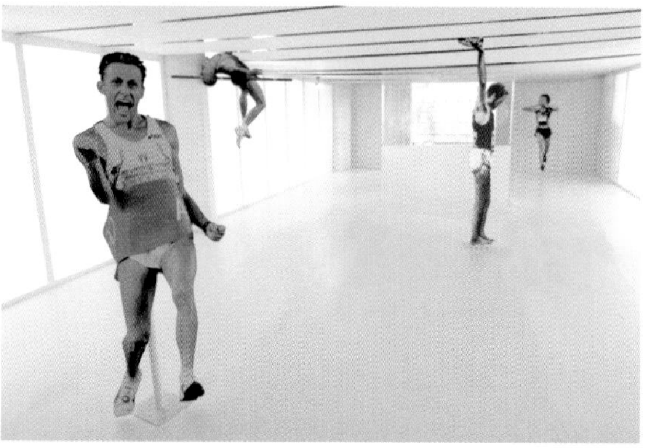

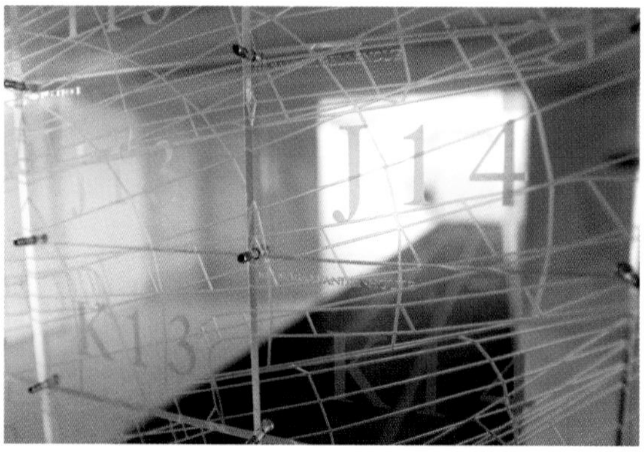

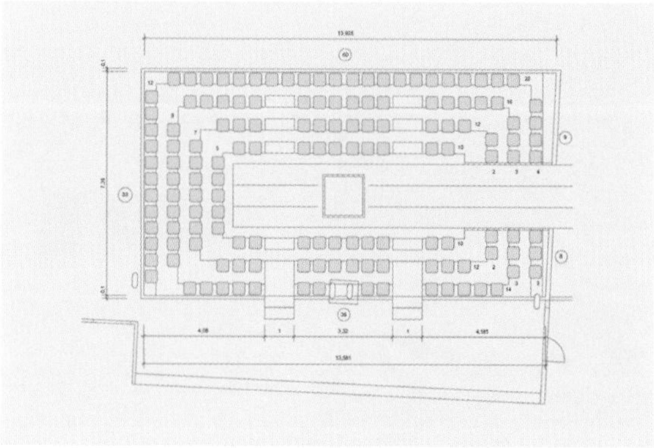

GUINNESS

20
GUINNESS

Silver

ART DIRECTOR
Sherrod Melvin

WRITER
Jason Hoff

CREATIVE DIRECTORS
Dan Kelleher
Eric Silver
David Lubars

CLIENT
Guinness

AGENCY
BBDO/New York

ANNUAL ID
06032D

[SILVER]
HAKUHODO DESIGN

Silver

DESIGNER
Kazuki Okamoto

ART DIRECTORS
Kazufumi Nagai
Kenjiro Sano

CREATIVE DIRECTOR
Kazufumi Nagai

CLIENT
Takeo Company

AGENCY
Hakuhodo/Tokyo

ANNUAL ID
06031D

BRONZE

ART DIRECTOR
Michael Reginelli

CREATIVE DIRECTORS
Steve Rabosky
Harvey Marco
Felipe Bascope

CLIENT
Surfrider Foundation

AGENCY
Saatchi & Saatchi/
Los Angeles

ANNUAL ID
06033D

ALSO AWARDED
Bronze:
One Show Public Service/Political:
Outdoor - Single

FOUND ON REDONDO BEACH. AUGUST 21, 2005.
WWW.SURFRIDER.ORG
Surfrider Foundation

SILVER

ART DIRECTOR
Florian Meimberg

WRITERS
Torsten Pollmann
Claudia Meimberg

PHOTOGRAPHER
Svenson

AGENCY PRODUCER
Peter Engel

CREATIVE DIRECTORS
Torsten Pollmann
Florian Meimberg

CLIENT
Toys "R" Us

AGENCY
Grey Worldwide/
Duesseldorf

ANNUAL ID
06034D

€ 19.99
FEUERWEHR
IVECO
MAGIRUS

€ 18.99
PRESS MASTER

HYUNDAI

OFFICE PRODUCTS
NOW AT
fedexkinkos.com
FedEx Kinko's

BRONZE

ART DIRECTOR
Chuck Tso

WRITER
Eric Schutte

CREATIVE DIRECTORS
Eric Silver
David Lubars

CLIENT
FedEx Kinko's

AGENCY
BBDO/New York

ANNUAL ID
06035D

ALSO AWARDED
Silver:
One Show
Exceptional Innovation in Marketing - Campaign

Silver:
One Show
Exceptional Innovation in Marketing - Single

OFFICE PRODUCTS NOW AT fedexkinkos.com
FedEx Kinko's

Silver

OFFICE PRODUCTS
NOW AT fedexkinkos.com
FedEx Kinko's
Office and Print Center

GOLD

DESIGNERS
Wai-Ki Kwok
Eileen Ng

ART DIRECTOR
Stanley Wong

WRITERS
Stanley Wong
Sunny Pang
Phoebe Wong
Carey Mackenzie

PHOTOGRAPHER
Stanley Wong

CREATIVE DIRECTOR
Stanley Wong

CLIENT
MCCM Creations/
Anothermountainman
Communications

AGENCY
Anothermountainman
Communications/
Hong Kong

ANNUAL ID
06036D

redwhiteblue
here/there/everywhere
anothermountainman

1
2

2001
紅白藍手袋及雨傘
redwhiteblue handbag and umbrella
marylene lichtenstern / switzerland
since 2001, i had been inspired by some elements typical of the local heritage in hong kong :
the white-and-blue scaffolding material, and the red-white-blue 'refugee bags'.
i turned those culturally coloured materials away from their original everyday use
in order to create fashionable items such as bags and umbrellas
by producing items that are culturally symbolic of hong kong as a space of migration.
when i started to design those bags,
i would never have imagined that they would bring out the past of hong kong people
and would quickly become a vector for opening up dialogue.

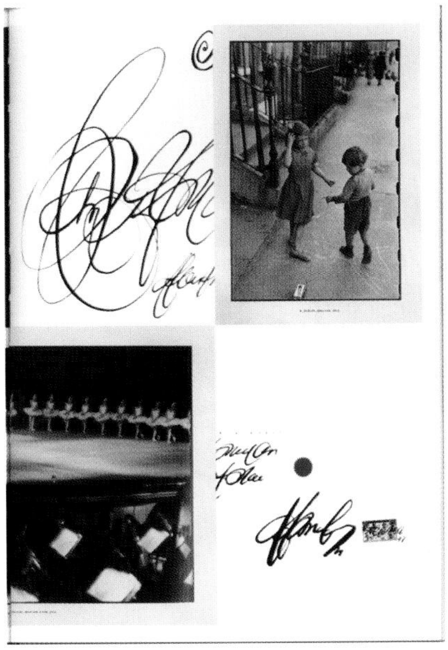

GOLD

DESIGNER
Carin Goldberg

ART DIRECTOR
Carin Goldberg

WRITER
Akiko Busch

PHOTOGRAPHER
Jason Fulford

CREATIVE DIRECTOR
Richard Wilde

CLIENT
School of Visual Arts

AGENCY
School of Visual Arts/ New York

ANNUAL ID
06037D

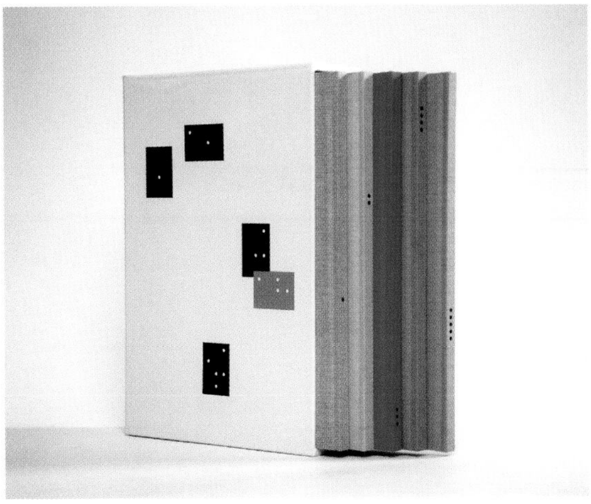

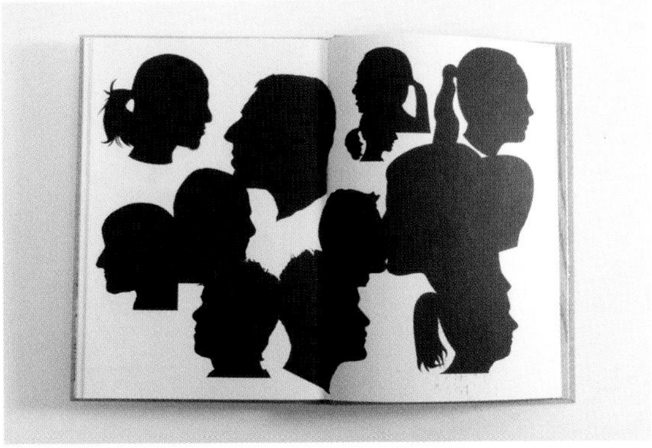

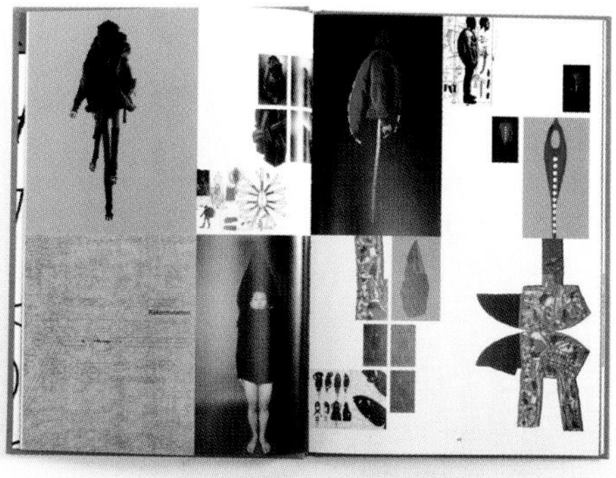

Jesus.
p. 5

SILVER

DESIGNERS
Masayoshi Kodaira
Namiko Otsuka

ART DIRECTOR
Masayoshi Kodaira

PHOTOGRAPHERS
Kozo Takayama
Hiroki Nakashima

CLIENT
Pie Books

AGENCY
Flame/Tokyo

ANNUAL ID
06038D

experimenta
1961-1974

WE HAVE CHOSEN TO BY PASS THE DECAYING BAUHAUS IMAGE WHICH IS AN INSULT TO FUNCTIONALISM
GREAT!
THINKS... WE ARE IN PURSUIT OF AN IDEA, A NEW VERNACULAR, SOMETHING TO STAND ALONGSIDE THE SPACE CAPSULES, COMPUTERS AND THROW-AWAY PACKAGES OF AN ATOMIC/ELECTRONIC AGE

introducing ARCHIZONES a survey
ARCHIGRAM NINE
BUTTERFLIES by Webb
PLANTS by Greene
OUTGROWTH
cover and story by
TONY RICKABY
ARCHIGRAM

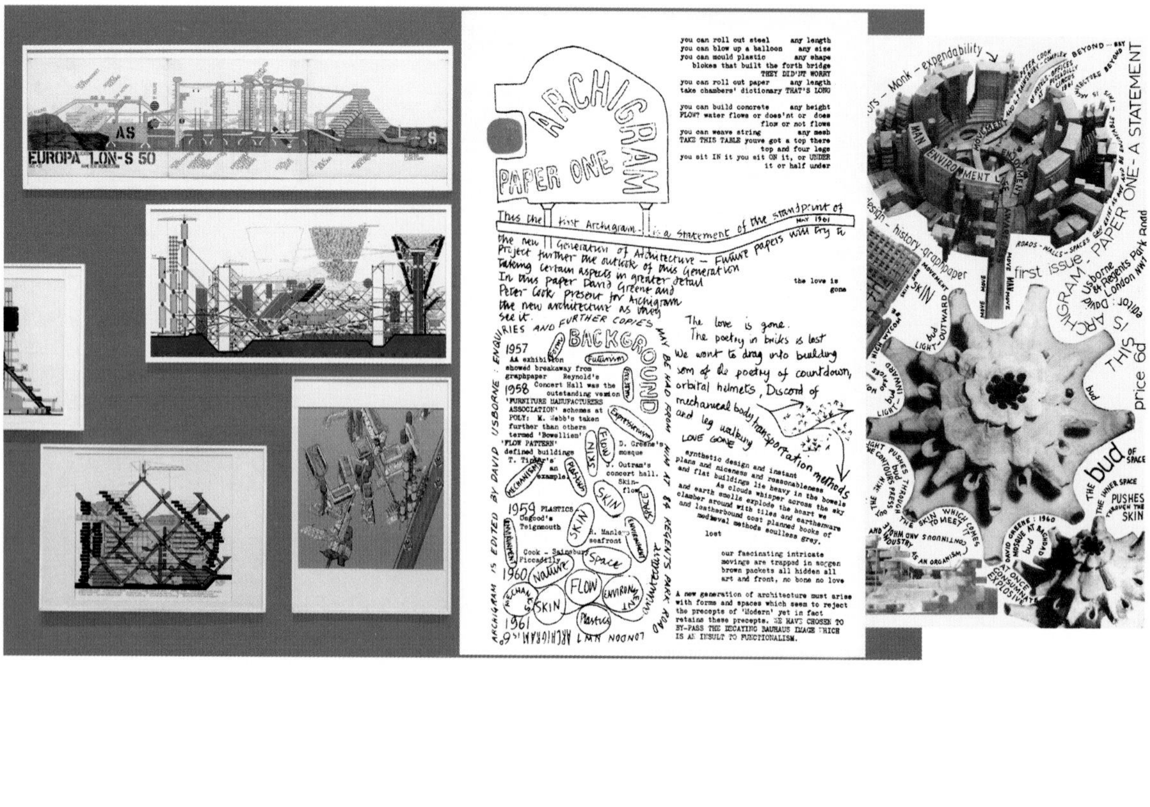
ARCHIGRAM
PAPER ONE
you can roll out steel any length
you can blow up a balloon any size
you can mould plastic any shape
blokes that built the forth bridge
THEY DID'NT WORRY
you can roll out paper any length
take chambers' dictionary THAT'S LONG
you can build concrete any height
FLOW? water flows or does'nt or does
flow or not flows
you can weave string any mesh
TAKE THIS TABLE youve got a top there
top and four legs
you sit IN it you sit ON it, or UNDER
it or half under
the love is gone
The love is gone.
The poetry in bricks is lost
BACKGROUND
synthetic design and instant plans and niceness and reasonableness and flat buildings lie heavy in the bowels
our fascinating intricate movings are trapped in soggen brown packets all hidden all art and front, no bone no love
A new generation of architecture must arise with forms and spaces which seem to reject the precepts of 'Modern' yet in fact retains these precepts. WE HAVE CHOSEN TO BY-PASS THE DECAYING BAUHAUS IMAGE WHICH IS AN INSULT TO FUNCTIONALISM.

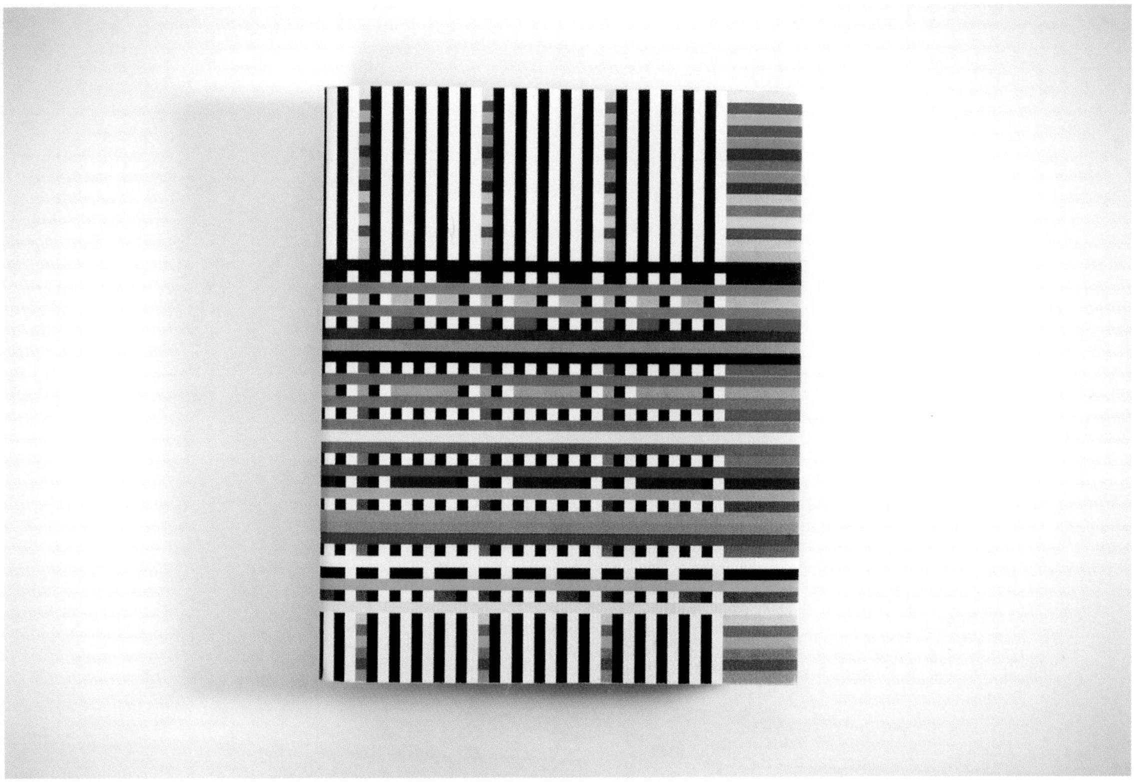

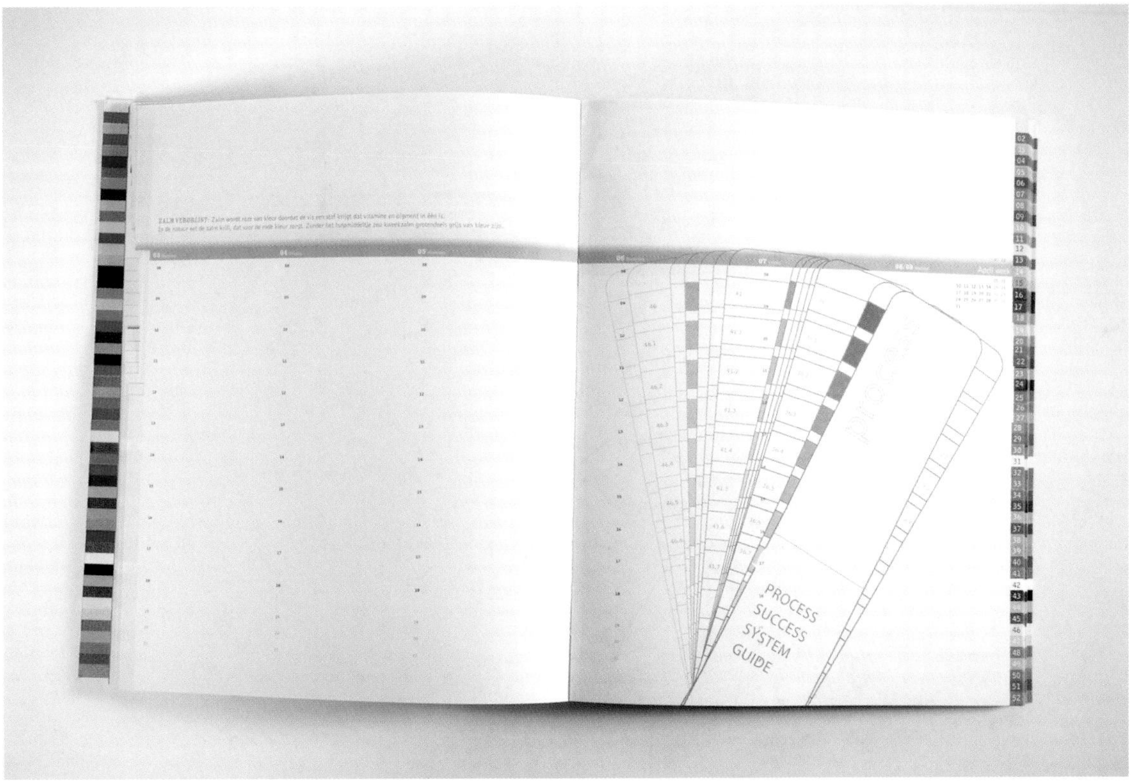
PROCESS
SUCCESS
SYSTEM
GUIDE

BRONZE

DESIGNERS
Barlock

ART DIRECTORS
Barlock

CLIENT
Ando BV

AGENCY
Ando BV/The Hague

ANNUAL ID
06039D

Gold

DESIGNERS
Heidi Chisholm
Peet Pienaar

WRITERS
Stacy Hardy
Lesego Rampolokeng
Braden Ruddy
Brian Larkin
Fred de Vries
Peter Morris
Sumeera Dawood
Mphutlane Wa Bofelo
Phillip Zhuwo

PHOTOGRAPHERS
Pieter Hugo
Tim Hetherington
Mikhael Subotsky
Misha De Ridder
Uwe Omer

ILLUSTRATOR
Peet Pienaar

CLIENT
Spier

AGENCY
Daddy buy me a Pony – a 9Nov Union Co./ Cape Town

ANNUAL ID
06040D

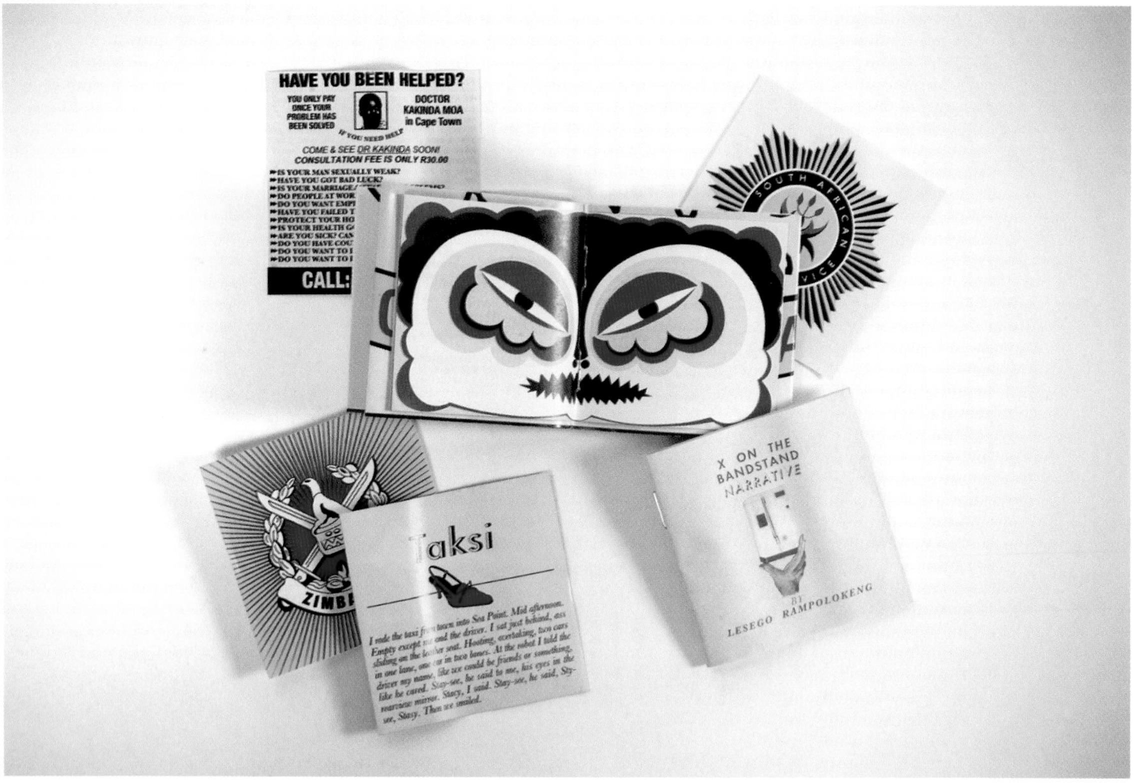
HAVE YOU BEEN HELPED?
DOCTOR KAKINDA MOA in Cape Town
COME & SEE DR KAKINDA SOON!
CONSULTATION FEE IS ONLY R30.00
CALL:
SOUTH AFRICAN
Taksi
X ON THE BANDSTAND NARRATIVE
BY LESEGO RAMPOLOKENG

PLEASE MY READERS KNOW YOURSELVES LEST YOU REGRET LIKE ME
THEY GAVE ME TWO TITLES, ONE WAS M.W WHICH MEANT MASTER OF WOMEN THE OTHER ONE WAS B.L WHICH MEANT BOY OF LOVE
A CONFESSION BY BOY OF LOVE WHO GAVE ALL HIS TIME TO WOMEN AFFAIRS LATER SUFFERED THE CONSEQUENCE OF SUCH HABIT
TROUBLES BY WOMAN
WOMEN LOVED ME TOO MUCH

AFRO-
SPIER

DEMOCRATICA DE S. TOMEE
REPUBLICA
PRINCIPE
UNIDADE
TRABALHO

see
See: The Potential of Place

The ability to see potential is a real gift.
most of us find appealing is the potential for
architects and designers are optimists: They
where the rest of us see only shortcomings.
optimism in the United States, times when
writer Pare Lorentz,
Aaron Copland. They
of suburbs and urban planning.
The potential of the built
the human condition seemed
unlimited. Ahead of their time,
wait for six years, until after
World War II, before the country
Their images of children,
families, and schools are particularly
Of course we still have children,
and perhaps nowhere
is potential valued and nurtured more
when unselfish people confront the
We're all students, aren't
we? Maybe what we really need to
our own potential and how
to live up to it.

Researchers and
designers say that
biophilia is not a
design fad. Groups
from Harvard,
Yale, and the
Rocky Mountain
Institute are busy
attempting to
quantify its effects.

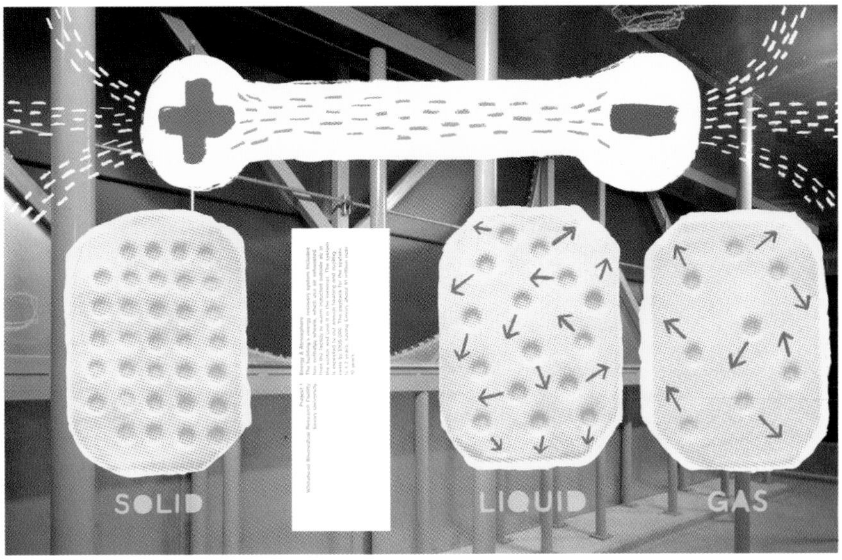
SOLID
LIQUID
GAS

SILVER

DESIGNERS
Todd Richards
Nicholas Davidson

ART DIRECTORS
Todd Richards
Steve Frykholm
Todd Richards

WRITERS
Pamela Erbe
Dan Sorensen
Dick Holm
Carol Lecocq
Julie Ridl

PHOTOGRAPHERS
Tim Simmons
Ingvar Kenne
Henning Bock
Todd Hido
Robert Schlatter
Michael S. Yamashita

ILLUSTRATORS
Brian Cairns
Joseph Hart
Blair Thornley

CREATIVE DIRECTOR
Bill Cahan

CLIENT
Herman Miller

AGENCY
Cahan & Associates/
San Francisco

ANNUAL ID
06041D

BRONZE

DESIGNERS
Todd Richards
Nicholas Davidson

ART DIRECTORS
Bill Cahan
Todd Richards
Steve Frykholm

WRITERS
Armin Moehrle
Allan Chochinov
David Willett
Dick Holm
Carol Lecocq
Julie Ridl

PHOTOGRAPHERS
Neal Preston
Fredrik Clement
Jan Roth
Allan Chochinov
Tyler Gourley
Robert Schlatter
Florian Holzherr
Nathan Perkel

ILLUSTRATORS
Jeffrey Decoster
Alan E. Cober
Joseph Hart

CREATIVE DIRECTOR
Bill Cahan

CLIENT
Herman Miller

AGENCY
Cahan & Associates/
San Francisco

ANNUAL ID
06042D

see

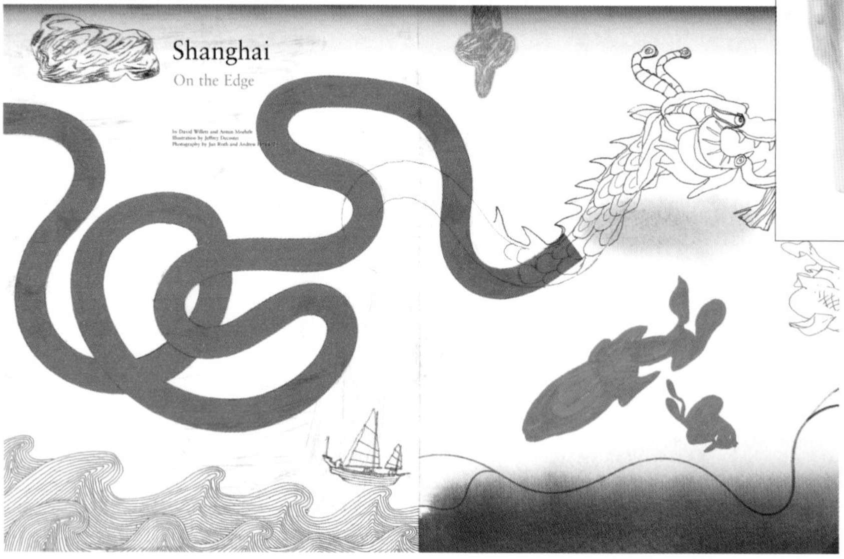
Shanghai
On the Edge

PERFORMANCE /
WORK / SPACE
TALES FROM
MANHATTAN

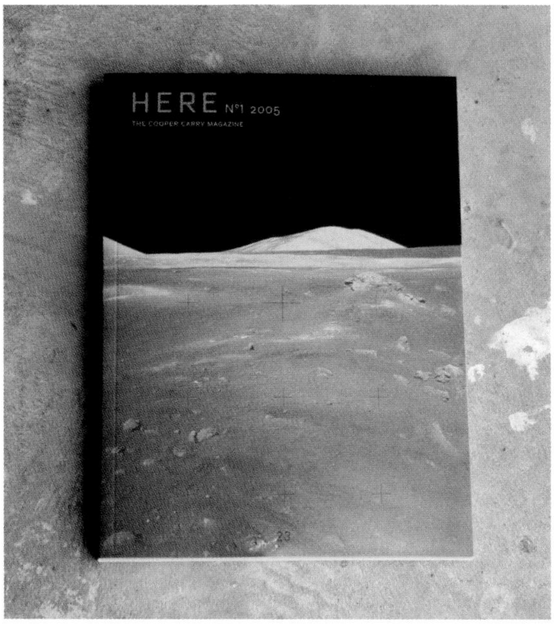
HERE Nº1 2005
THE COOPER CARRY MAGAZINE

TRAVEL:

Silver

DESIGNERS
Gabriel H. Benzur III
Lea Friedman
Martha Hemphill

WRITERS
Jason Hirthler
Matt Rollins
Gabriel H. Benzur III
Juliet D'Ambrosio
Zach Watkins

PHOTOGRAPHERS
Gregory Miller
Todd Hido
Sze Tsung Leong
Elise Woodward

ILLUSTRATORS
Jorge Colombo
Gabriel H. Benzur III

CREATIVE DIRECTOR
Matt Rollins

CLIENT
Cooper Carry

AGENCY
Iconologic/Atlanta

ANNUAL ID
06044D

FOR RESERVATIONS
CALL 6396 3445

Bronze

ART DIRECTOR
Eddie Wong Yew Heng

WRITER
Nirmal Pulickal

CREATIVE DIRECTOR
Patrick Low

CLIENT
Nadezhda Russian Restaurant

AGENCY
Dentsu Young & Rubicam/Singapore

ANNUAL ID
06045D

BRONZE

DESIGNER
Hemant Jain

ART DIRECTOR
Hemant Jain

WRITER
Hemant Jain

ILLUSTRATOR
Hemant Jain

CREATIVE DIRECTORS
Neil French
Prashant Godbole
KS Chax

CLIENT
Midland Bookshop

AGENCY
Rediffusion DYR/
Mumbai

ANNUAL ID
06047D

ALSO AWARDED
Merit:
Brand and Corporate Identity Design: Booklet/ Brochure

Merit:
Brand and Corporate Identity Design: Booklet/ Brochure

Merit:
Direct Mail - Single

THE COMMUNIST MANIFESTO

WHO READ THE COMMUNIST MANIFESTO BY MARX AND ENGELS
AND THAT, CHANGED EVERYTHING
WHICH BOOK ARE YOU READING?

Merit, Merit

20,000 LEAGUES UNDER THE SEA

LORD OF THE RINGS

WHICH BOOK ARE YOU READING?

AND GOD ONLY KNOWS HOW MANY HE WOULD HAVE MADE
F he hadn't discovered

Merit

Gold

DESIGNERS
Todd St. John
Gary Benzel

DIRECTOR
Todd St. John

CLIENT
Nike

AGENCY
HunterGatherer/
New York

ANNUAL ID
06048D

Bronze

AGENCY PRODUCER
Gunilla De Santo

PRODUCTION COMPANY
RSA

DIRECTOR
Albert Kodagolian

CREATIVE DIRECTOR
Roger Guillen

CLIENT
Sci Fi

AGENCY
Sci Fi Channel/
New York

ANNUAL ID
06049D

GOLD

DESIGNERS
Matt Bauer
Samuel Christopher

WRITER
Claire Lambert

ILLUSTRATORS
Al Murphy
Paul Bower
Mikko Rantanen

AGENCY PRODUCER
Charlotte Dale

CREATIVE DIRECTOR
Richard Holman

CLIENT
Paramount Comedy

AGENCY
devilfish/London

ANNUAL ID
06050D

TALKING HEADS
IT'S NOT LIKE THE OLD DAYS
NO. THOSE GOOD OLD DAYS WERE BETTER THAN THESE DAYS.
comedy

Today, I taught the birds to Swear

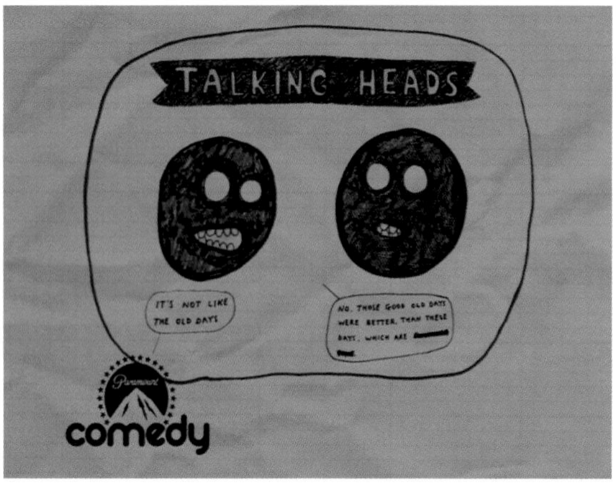
TALKING HEADS
IT'S NOT LIKE THE OLD DAYS
NO. THOSE GOOD OLD DAYS WERE BETTER THAN THESE DAYS, WHICH ARE [redacted]
Paramount
comedy

ARSE

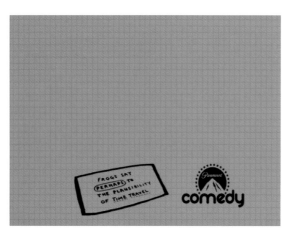
FROGS SAY PERHAPS TO THE PLAUSIBILITY OF TIME TRAVEL
Paramount
comedy

COCK
Paramount
comedy

[redacted]
HELLO

[redacted]
HELLO
WOULD YOU LIKE ME TO TURN AROUND? SO YOU CAN SEE MY BUMCHEEKS? WOULD YOU?

[redacted]
HELLO
WOULD YOU LIKE ME TO TURN AROUND? SO YOU CAN SEE MY BUMCHEEKS? WOULD YOU? IT'S NO BOTHER?
Paramount
comedy

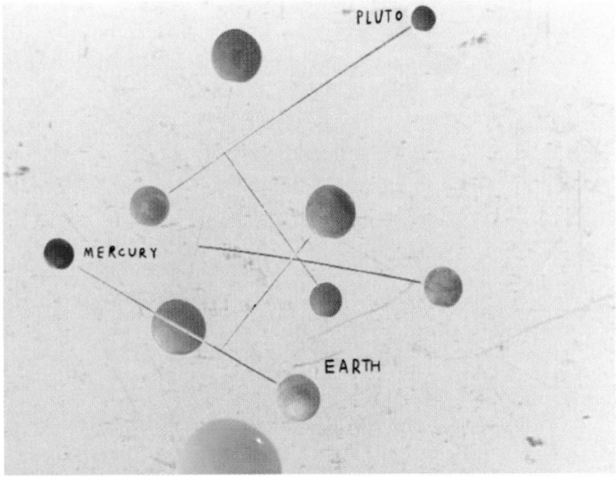
PLUTO
MERCURY
EARTH

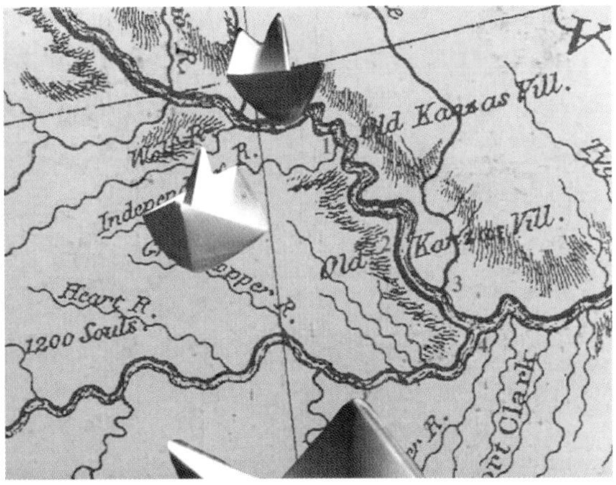
Heart R.
1200 Souls

GOLD

WRITER
Billy Collins

AGENCY PRODUCER
Anthony Garetti

DIRECTORS
Julian Grey
Juan Declan

PRODUCTION COMPANY
Head Gear Animation

CREATIVE DIRECTOR
Toby Barlow

CLIENT
The Sundance Channel

AGENCY
JWT/New York

ANNUAL ID
06051D

ALSO AWARDED
Merit:
Consumer Television:
Under $50K Budget
- Campaign

SILVER

DESIGNER
Diogo Kalil

WRITER
Mark Lewman

ILLUSTRATOR
Adam Haynes

AGENCY PRODUCER
Kirsten Blair

DIRECTORS
Mateus de Paula Santos
Cadu Macedo

CREATIVE DIRECTOR
Chris Hotz

CLIENT
Nike

AGENCY
Lobo/São Paulo

ANNUAL ID
06052D

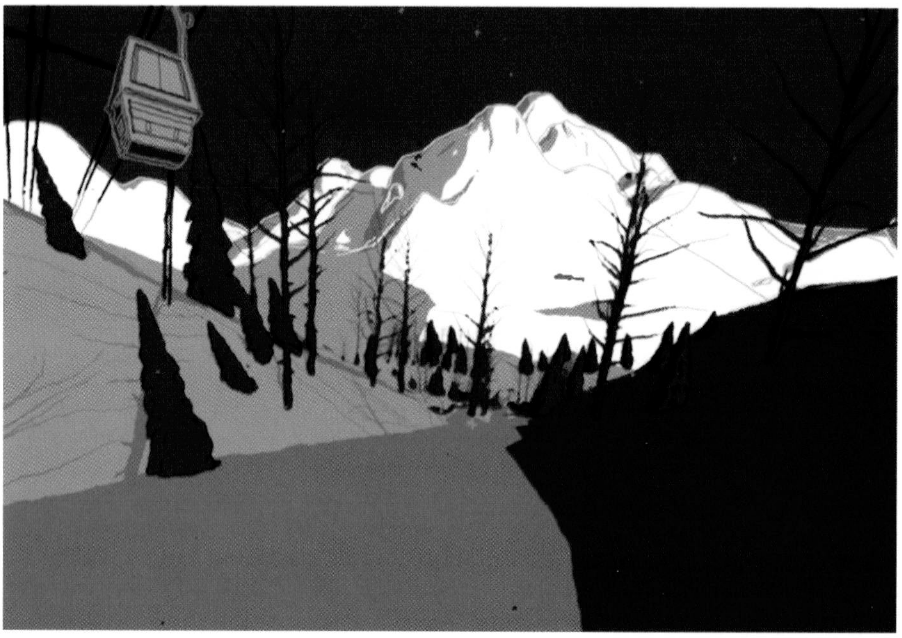

SUNDAY
STEW

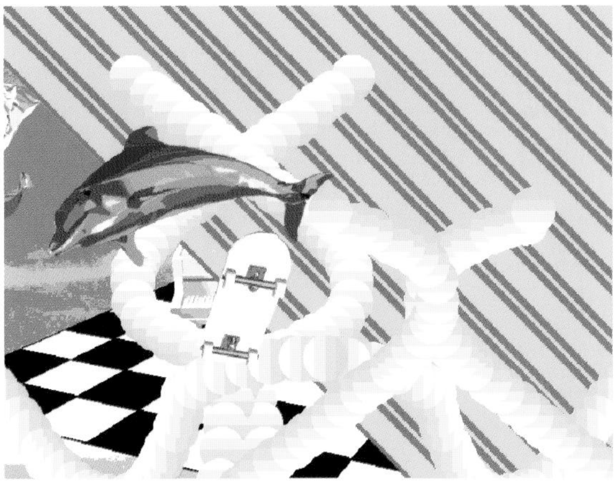

Season Premiere
This Sunday
PUNK'D
10pm/9c
mtv.com

BRONZE

DESIGNERS
Todd St. John
Gary Benzel
Phil Pinto
Mario Stipinovitch
Molly Schwartz

ART DIRECTOR
Todd St. John

AGENCY PRODUCER
Nina Goldberg

DIRECTOR
Todd St. John

CREATIVE DIRECTOR
Todd St. John

CLIENT
MTV

AGENCY
HunterGatherer/
New York

ANNUAL ID
06053D

GOLD

DESIGNERS
Yui Takada
Chiaki Aizawa

ART DIRECTOR
Manabu Mizuno

CREATIVE DIRECTOR
Manabu Mizuno

CLIENT
MORI Art Museum

AGENCY
Good Design Company/ Tokyo

ANNUAL ID
06054D

BERLIN
MORI ART MUSEUM
ROPPONGI HILLS
MORI TOWER 53F
TOKYO
MUTUAL FASCINATION HAS SHAPED
THE ART AND CULTURE OF TOKYO AND
BERLIN FOR OVER A CENTURY.
INTERNATIONALE AUSSTELLUNG
DES DEUTSCHEN WERKBUNDS
FILM UND FOTO
BERLIN 1929
FOTO-AUSSTELLUNG VOM 19. OKT. BIS 17. NOV.
FILM-SONDERVORFÜHRUNGEN VOM 19. OKT. BIS 19. NOV.
Tokyo Berlin
A STORY OF TWO CITIES
OVER 500 WORKS
PAINTINGS, SCULPTURES, PHOTOGRAPHS AND DESIGN
From the 1880s to Now
2006.1.28–2006.5.7 Mori Art Museum in Roppongi Hills
A Story of Two Cities
Over 500 Works Paintings, Sculptures, Photographs, Design and Architecture From the 1880s to Now
NIPPON
GERMANY
2006.01.28
2006.05.07

BRITISH COUNCIL
Asahi
POLA ART FOUNDATION
水戸芸術館
ART TOWER MITO
URBAN ACTION-TUNE UP
LEARN FRENCH NOW
INSTANT CITY
OUTDOOR THEATRE
January 22
- March 27, 2005
Contemporary
Art Gallery,
Art Tower Mito
アーキグラムの実験建築 1961-1974
開館時間＝9:30～18:00（入場は17:30まで） 休館日＝月曜日、ただし、3月21日［月・祝］は開館、翌、3月22日［火］は休館 入場料＝一般800円／前売・団体（20名以上）600円／中学生以下・65歳以上・各種障害者手帳をお持ちの方は無料
1年間有効パス：H.T.P.（対象15歳以上20歳未満）1,000円 チケット・H.T.P.の発売＝水戸芸術館エントランスホールチケットカウンター／JR東日本みどりの窓口／ぴゅうプラザ
主催＝財団法人水戸市芸術振興財団 助成＝財団法人ポーラ美術振興財団／大和日英基金／ブリティッシュ・カウンシル 協賛＝アサヒビール株式会社 協力＝Paul Smith Ltd.／有限会社アップリンク／株式会社創夢
キュレーター＝デニス・クロンプトン（アーキグラムアーカイヴ） 展覧会担当＝高橋瑞木（水戸芸術館現代美術センター学芸員） お問い合わせ＝〒310-0063 茨城県水戸市五軒町1-6-8 TEL.029-227-8120 http://www.arttowermito.or.jp/
2005年1月22日［土］－3月27日［日］ 水戸芸術館現代美術ギャラリー
HOURS: DOORS OPEN AT 9:30 AND CLOSE AT 18:00 (NO ADMITTANCE AFTER 17:30) CLOSED ON EVERY MONDAYS (EXCEPT MARCH 21) AND MARCH 22 1-6-8, GOKEN-CHO, MITO-SHI, IBARAKI 310-0063, JAPAN

SILVER

DESIGNERS
Namiko Otsuka
Masayoshi Kodaira

ART DIRECTOR
Masayoshi Kodaira

ILLUSTRATOR
Archigram Archives

CLIENT
Art Tower Mito

AGENCY
Flame/Tokyo

ANNUAL ID
06055D

GOLD

ART DIRECTORS
Andreas Kittel
Mikael Blom

CREATIVE DIRECTOR
Anders Kornestedt

CLIENT
The Rohsska Museum

AGENCY
Happy Forsman & Bodenfors/Gothenburg

ANNUAL ID
06057D

Första Lång-
gatan 28A-30

Tittut!
Nytt nummer av vår tidning ute nu på arkitekturmuseet.se

Gold

ART DIRECTOR
Lisa Careborg

ILLUSTRATOR
Lisa Careborg

CREATIVE DIRECTOR
Anders Kornestedt

CLIENT
The Swedish Museum of Architecture

AGENCY
Happy Forsman & Bodenfors/Gothenburg

ANNUAL ID
06058D

Tittut!
Nytt nummer av vår tidning ute nu på arkitekturmuseet.se

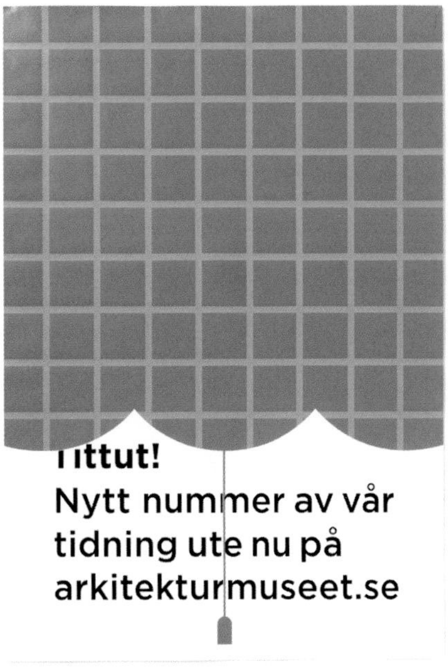
Tittut!
Nytt nummer av vår tidning ute nu på arkitekturmuseet.se

BRONZE

DESIGNERS
Paul Belford
John Tisdall

ART DIRECTOR
Paul Belford

WRITER
Nigel Roberts

CREATIVE DIRECTORS
Paul Belford
Nigel Roberts

CLIENT
D&AD

AGENCY
Abbott Mead Vickers BBDO/London

ANNUAL ID
06059D

ALSO AWARDED
Bronze:
Public Service/Non-Profit/Educational: Posters - Single

Fletcher/Forbes/Gill
Alan Fletcher, Colin Forbes & Bob Gill in conversation with David Bernstein. 23 May, bar opens at 18.30, lecture at 19.30. D&AD Congress at Old Billingsgate, 16 Lower Thames Street, London EC3. £20 (Members: £16, Students and Tutors: £10). Bookings: 020 7840 1127. www.dandad.org
D&AD. For excellence. For education. For enterprise. And not for profit. D&AD is a registered charity.

Bronze

PLPPPLPP
PLPPPLPP
PLPPPLPP
PLPPPLPP
PLPPPLPP
Regn mot tjärpapptak
Ljudveckor på
Arkitekturmuseet
31.5–3.7 2005

KRRX
KRRX
KRRX
KRRX
Steg på grusgång
Ljudveckor på
Arkitekturmuseet
31.5–3.7 2005

BING
BONG
Dörrklocka i bostadshus
Ljudveckor på
Arkitekturmuseet
31.5–3.7 2005

BRONZE

ART DIRECTOR
Lisa Careborg

CREATIVE DIRECTOR
Anders Kornestedt

CLIENT
The Swedish Museum of Architecture

AGENCY
Happy Forsman & Bodenfors/Gothenburg

ANNUAL ID
06060D

BRONZE

ART DIRECTOR
Liz Forsythe

WRITER
Bill Eckloff

CREATIVE DIRECTOR
Tom Hudder

CLIENT
Black Rep

AGENCY
Rodgers Townsend/ St. Louis

ANNUAL ID
06061D

THE BLACK REP'S SEASON 29: COMMON THREADS
KING HEDLEY II
A RAZOR. A PISTOL AND A MACHETE. YET TRUTH BECOMES THE WEAPON OF CHOICE.

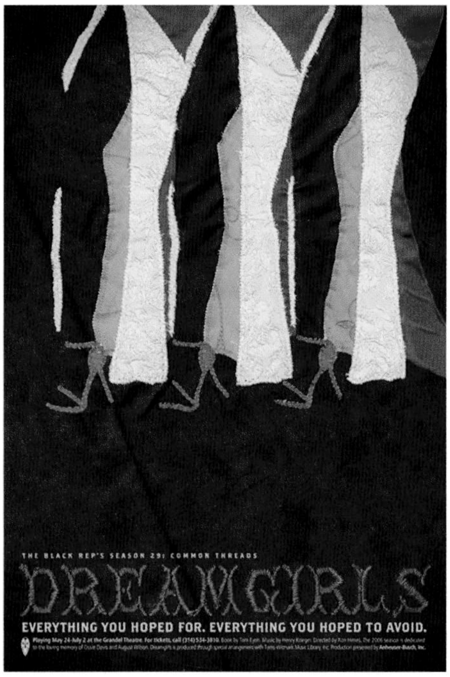
THE BLACK REP'S SEASON 29: COMMON THREADS
DREAMGIRLS
EVERYTHING YOU HOPED FOR. EVERYTHING YOU HOPED TO AVOID.

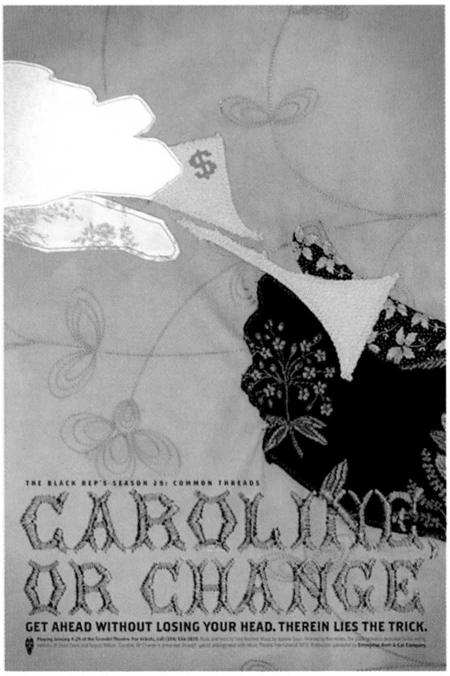
THE BLACK REP'S SEASON 29: COMMON THREADS
CAROLINE OR CHANGE
GET AHEAD WITHOUT LOSING YOUR HEAD. THEREIN LIES THE TRICK.

THE BLACK REP'S SEASON 29: COMMON THREADS
RELATIVITY
MOTHER PROVES WHITES ARE INFERIOR. DAUGHTER PROVES RACE IS JUST A MINDSET.

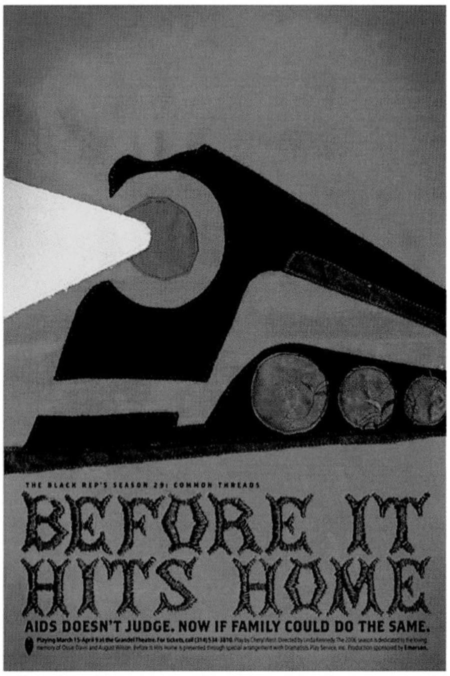
THE BLACK REP'S SEASON 29: COMMON THREADS
BEFORE IT HITS HOME
AIDS DOESN'T JUDGE. NOW IF FAMILY COULD DO THE SAME.

För smarta tjejer med lust på live
CHiCA
KAJAL PÅ KÖPET!
Kate Bosworth om Orlando Bloom:
LIVET ÄR FULLT AV FRÅGOR
EN DEL ÄR LÄTTA ATT SVARA PÅ, ANDRA KAN TILL OCH MED VARA SVÅRA ATT STÄLLA. UNDER KONFIRMANDTIDEN FÅR DU EN MÖJLIGHET ATT PRATA OM FRÅGOR SOM KÄNNS STORA OCH VIKTIGA. DET HANDLAR INTE BARA OM GUD OCH KRISTEN TRO, UTAN OCKSÅ OM KÄRLEK, FRIHET, ORÄTTVISOR OCH ENSAMHET. BLAND ANNAT.
Svenska kyrkan
I GÖTEBORG
Skäm bort din kille - och få honom dit du vill...
Stort test!
ALLT OM PREVENTIVMEDEL
Maya, 22: Mina vänner dör av droger

VARFÖR
DUGER JAG?
CHICA TEST
Hur bra är du i sängen?
CHICAs test avslöjar dig!
Del 1: Ditt sex
Del 2: Din kropp
Utvärdering av del ett
Utvärdering av del två

SILVER

ART DIRECTOR
Pontus Hofvner

CREATIVE DIRECTOR
Anders Kornestedt

CLIENT
Church of Sweden

AGENCY
Happy Forsman & Bodenfors/Gothenburg

ANNUAL ID
06062D

ALSO AWARDED
Silver:
Direct Mail - Campaign

BRONZE

ART DIRECTOR
Daniel Zenas Upputuru

WRITER
Suchitra Gahlot

ILLUSTRATOR
Daniel Zenas Upputuru

CREATIVE DIRECTOR
Emmanuel Upputuru

CLIENT
ORBO

AGENCY
Ogilvy & Mather/
New Delhi

ANNUAL ID
06063D

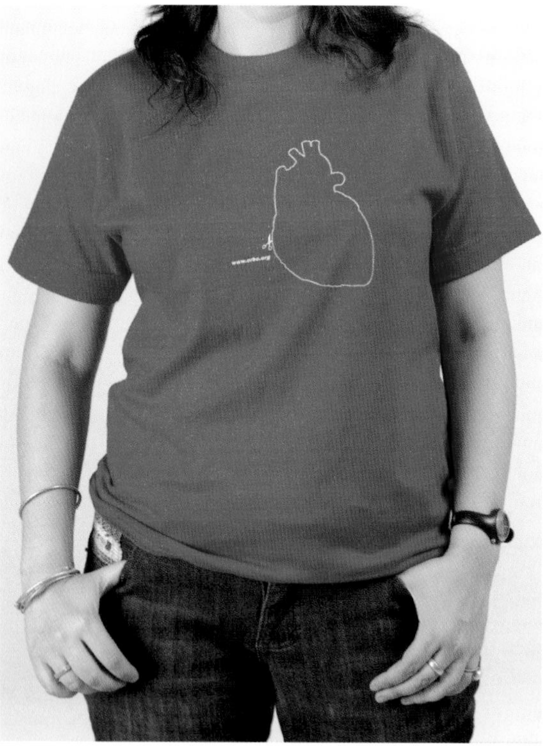

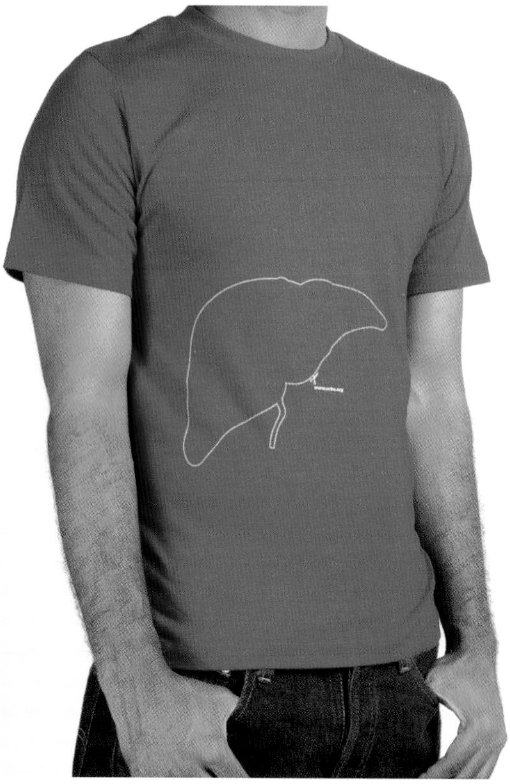

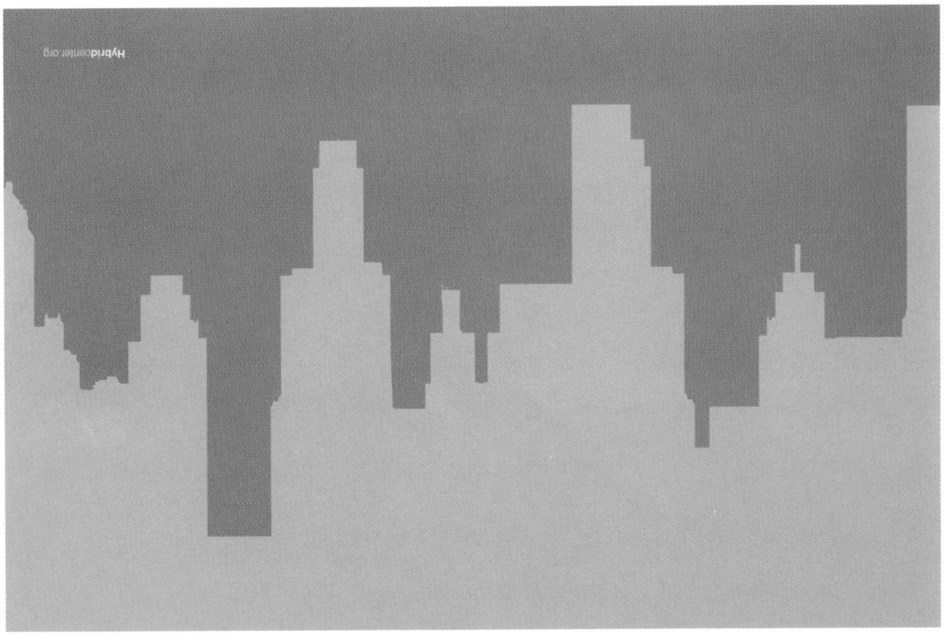
Hybridcenter.org

Hybridcenter.org

Hybridcenter.org

GOLD

ART DIRECTORS
Richard Bianrosa
Leah Renbaum

SCHOOL
Fashion Institute of Technology/New York

Silver

ART DIRECTORS
Joel Arzu
Sawzer Dishack

SCHOOL
Fashion Institute of Technology/ New York

Hybridcenter.org

Hybridcenter.org

Hybridcenter.org

BRONZE

ART DIRECTOR
Paul Wachter

WRITER
Paul Wachter

SCHOOL
University of Delaware/ Newark

Vegas Beach, Nevada
WELCOME
TO THE Fabulous
LAS VEGAS
COASTLINE
Hybridcenter.org

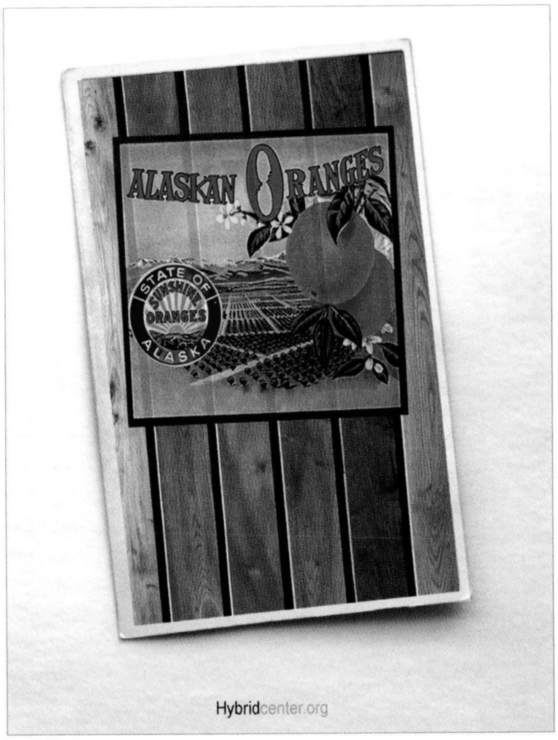
ALASKAN ORANGES
STATE OF SUNSHINE ORANGES
ALASKA
Hybridcenter.org

Chicago
The Windy Hurricane City
Hybridcenter.org

GOLD

ART DIRECTORS
Peter Durham
Mikkel Kroijer

SCHOOL
Miami Ad School/
Stockholm

The Showroom
Hybrid cars make breathing easier

SILVER

ART DIRECTOR
Shruti Veeramachineni

WRITERS
Stephanie Bialik

SCHOOL
Miami Ad School/
San Francisco

Clean air. Good life.
Hybridcenter.org

BRONZE

ART DIRECTOR
John Rekoumis

WRITER
Matthew Goodman

SCHOOL
Texas Creative-
The University of Texas
at Austin

In the future
you'll only stop
a clean start.

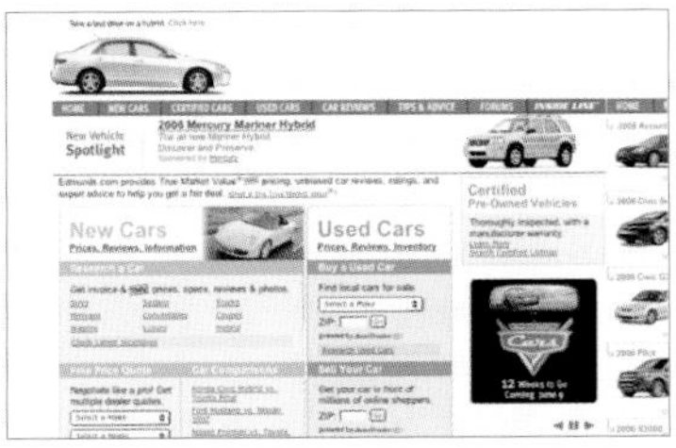

2006 Mercury Mariner Hybrid
New Cars
Used Cars

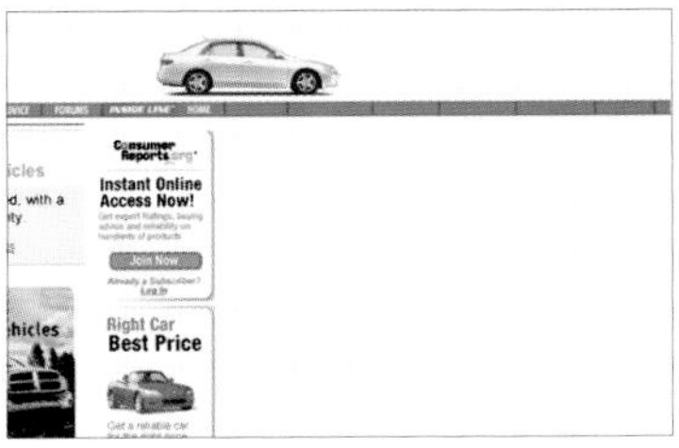

Instant Online Access Now!
Right Car Best Price

Gold

ART DIRECTOR
Moyeenul Alam

WRITER
Juan Guzman

SCHOOL
Miami Ad School/
Miami Beach

Relax,
take a deep breath.

Even non-smokers
cause second hand smoke.

To learn more about hybrid car engines visit
Hybridcenter.org

Car pollution damages sperm.
*Read article on WebMD

Car pollution damages sperm.
*Read article on WebMD

Silver

ART DIRECTOR
Ben Bartholomew

SCHOOL
School of Visual Arts/
New York

natural people for a better world
There is some pleasure in watching the lunghead who bought a Godzilla sized SUV fillup.
Hybridcenter.org

natural people for a better world
Click on Students to Ask Questions
Hybridcenter.org

natural people for a better world
Hybridcenter.org

Bronze

ART DIRECTORS
Lisa Doman
Nicolle Correa

SCHOOL
Academy of Art
University/San Francisco

Silver

ART DIRECTOR
Moyeenul Alam

WRITER
Juan Guzman

SCHOOL
Miami Ad School/ Miami Beach

Oil reserves are running out.
Switch to hybrid. Hybridcenter.org
This big SUV sticker will be placed on revolving doors. While pushing the door it'll give the impression of pushing an SUV that has ran out of gas.

Longer drives without stopping.
Switch to hybrid. Hybridcenter.org
The handrails of the escalators will be painted with white stripes to make it look like highways. While moving non-stop throughout the day, it'll convey one of the benefits of having a hybrid car.

Gold

DESIGNER
Brigitte Boudrias

SCHOOL
Université du Québec á Montréal/Montreal

Silver

DESIGNER
Molly Williams

SCHOOL
The Creative Circus/ Atlanta

Bronze

DESIGNER
Boriana Mintcheva-Strzok

SCHOOL
Minneapolis College of Art and Design/ Minneapolis

GOLD ON GOLD

CLIENT
MINI

AGENCY
Crispin Porter+ Bogusky/Miami

ANNUAL ID
06005A

CP+B CREATIVE TEAM

Have you ever had an idea at three o'clock in the morning, thought it was hilarious, and scribbled it down on a pad of paper only to find, in the morning, that it was complete crap? Somehow, this scribble worked out.

No Photo Available

SPIDER-MAN
HEINZ

CLIENT
Heinz

AGENCY
Leo Burnett/London

ANNUAL ID
06006A

NICK PRINGLE & CLARK EDWARDS

Every once in a while you're presented with such a fantastic product that your mind gets working straight away. We couldn't help but have fun with it and simply went for the idea that made us laugh the most. If it's the only superhero-themed canned pasta ad that we ever do, we'll be happy.

CLIENT
Altoids

AGENCY
Leo Burnett/Chicago

ANNUAL ID
06009A

G. ANDREW MEYER & NOEL HAAN

Recently, the original Altoids campaign turned 10 years old. And as we all know, campaign years are like dog years. That is, one year really equals seven years. So thanks to a midget bodybuilder, a sadistic Russian spy, a yogi and a jogger (not to mention a slew of dedicated creatives) for giving a 70-year-old the curious strength to win Gold.

VE HAVE VAYS OV MAKING YOU TALK.
THE CURIOUSLY STRONG MINTS
curious? altoids.com

CLIENT
Stella Artois

AGENCY
Lowe/New York

ANNUAL ID
06012A

RAJ KAMBLE & ANSELMO RAMOS

Raj and I would like to dedicate this award to all immigrants struggling to work in advertising in the developed world.

I grew up in the favelas of Cidade de Deus playing soccer barefoot with coconuts and pick-pocketing naïve American tourists for a living. Raj grew up in Kavathe Mahankal, in the slums of Bollywood, playing cricket with a ball of socks and a broomstick, and selling illegal VHSs such as *Indian E.T.* My family in Brazil has a pet monkey called Pelé. Raj's family in India has a pet elephant called Raju.

I'm dictating this out loud in Portuguese to a professional English typist assigned to me by IPG, under the Minority Assimilation Program.

Raj belongs to the lowest caste, which would explain why he doesn't know how to read, write or speak properly. We communicate using international sign language. If he likes an idea, he claps. If he doesn't, he flips me the finger.

$4.00
reg. $2.75
Bring this coupon and pay an extra $1.25 on your next Stella Artois.
No valid with any other offers.
Excludes tax and other charges.
Valid at participating locations only.
Expires 11/30/2005.
ANNO 1366
STELLA ARTOIS
Reassuringly expensive.

The coupon idea came naturally to us, since this is the only kind of ads we used to do back in our countries.

Hopefully with this pencil we'll be able to make a Western Union money transfer and send our families a couple of extra Reais and Rupees so they'll have something to eat.

For more about Brazil and India, go to twoforeigners.com. Obrigado and Dhanyavaad!!!

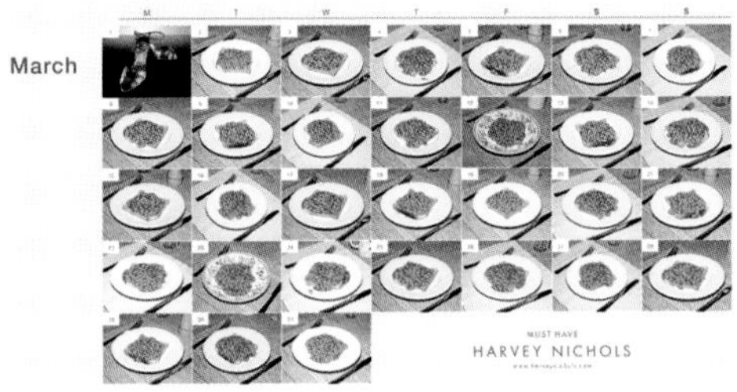
March
HARVEY NICHOLS

CLIENT
Harvey Nichols

AGENCY
DDB/London

ANNUAL ID
06030A

ADAM TUCKER & JUSTIN TINDALL

It took us a long time to get a job in advertising. Two years, pretty much. Two years eating baked beans, wiping our arses on telephone directories, mistreating our pets, staying in every night doing jigsaws, and masturbating. Luckily, they only wanted four ads for this campaign.

CLIENT
Mother

AGENCY
Mother/London

ANNUAL ID
06038A

MARKUS BJURMAN

There was chaos. Employees as well as clients and visitors needed something to put show reels and leftovers from lunch in. So we decided to make carrier bags.

After extensive research we came to the conclusion that a carrier bag is a "walking poster" as much as a t-shirt and they can sometimes express a little about its owner's personality.

Many of us know what it feels like to have an embarrassing bag at a cool party, or something like a super-savers bag in an expensive store. It's like buying a "Crazy Frog" single for your cousin's kid in your favorite record store.

And so, the "Mother Uncarriable Carrier Bags" were born. Bags you don't want to be seen carrying around. Now, you can carry them too!

UNCARRIABLE CARRIER BAGS
MOTHER
SPERM CLINIC
DROP IN CENTRE
SPILL YOUR SEED FOR THOSE IN NEED

CLIENT
American Legacy Foundation

AGENCY
Arnold Worldwide/ Boston and Crispin Porter + Bogusky/ Miami

ANNUAL ID
06001T

CP+B CREATIVE TEAM

We strung five spots of "Fair Enough" together to be aired as programming and marked them for TiVO users to record. Sure, TiVO is the instrument of the devil and is going to be the downfall of our beloved industry. But what are you gonna do?

It might be funnier if it wasn't true.

"Fair Enough!"

CLIENT
American Legacy Foundation

AGENCY
Arnold Worldwide/ Boston and Crispin Porter + Bogusky/ Miami

ANNUAL ID
06005T

CP+B CREATIVE TEAM

We don't really feel comfortable taking credit for any of this because it's all the tobacco industry's words. We tried to get a quote from them for the Gold on Gold, but they haven't returned our calls.

CLIENT
Carlton Draught

AGENCY
George Patterson Y&R/Melbourne

ANNUAL ID
06008T

ANT KEOGH

This gold award has sentimental significance for us. Years ago, as students, my art director, Grant Rutherford, and I used to sneak into bookshops to read *One Show Annuals,* desperately trying to learn the fundamentals of creative advertising. So, maybe, right now some young student is looking at this book getting inspired and thinking, "Wow, one day I'll be in this book." And they'll learn from the great examples in these pages and do some stand-out work themselves, get picked up by an agency, work their way up through the ranks and then. . . and then they'll take our jobs. . . . Hey, wait a minute! YOU! STUDENT! PUT THIS BOOK DOWN RIGHT NOW AND GET THE HELL OUT OF THAT BOOKSHOP, YOU FREELOADING LITTLE PUNK! ISN'T THERE A KEG PARTY YOU SHOULD BE AT?

CARLTON DRAUGHT

CLIENT
Guinness

AGENCY
Abbott Mead Vickers BBDO/London

ANNUAL ID
06009T

MATT DOMAN & IAN HEARTFIELD

Get very drunk.
Get Best of Show.
Get commercial on air somehow.
Delay air date again.
Delay air date.
Spend an eternity in production.
Secure services of top director.
Think of something.
Panic a bit more.
Panic.
Get Guinness brief.

L'EQUIPE

CLIENT
L'Equipe

AGENCY
DDB/Paris

ANNUAL ID
06016T

DDB CREATIVE TEAM

To Children : Men like sport. And as *L'Equipe* is like a bible for people who are fond of sports, a man can spend unknown time reading it in his room and a child might not recognize him as his father when he is not reading *L'Equipe*.

To Mothers : THANKS.

CLIENT
Ameriquest Mortgage

AGENCY
DDB/Los Angeles

ANNUAL ID
06021T

DDB CREATIVE TEAM

Caddyshack II
Weekend at Bernies II
Speed II: Cruise Control
Rocky V
The Color of Money
Staying Alive
The Next Karate Kid
Leprechaun: Back to Tha' Hood
Teen Wolf Too
Jaws: The Revenge

Considering the odds, I guess our sequel did pretty well.

Thanks.

DON'T JUDGE TOO QUICKLY

CLIENT
Pfizer - Viagra

AGENCY
TAXI/Toronto

ANNUAL ID
06024T

IRFAN KHAN & RON SMRCZEK

Pharmaceutical advertising regulations in Canada are exceedingly tough. They don't allow us to tell consumers what the product actually does. So we didn't.

VIAGRA

CLIENT
Vodafone

AGENCY
JWT/London

ANNUAL ID
06027T

RICHARD BAYNHAM & IAN GABALDONI

This Vodafone offer allowed people to talk for up to sixty minutes but pay for just three.

The creative idea hinged on the truth that so many conversations in life last for a lot longer than just three minutes.

The campaign of abrupt ten second spots dramatizes how ludicrous it would be for a topic that warrants a long conversation to be squeezed into an unrealistically short one.

For example:

One Show: "You won Gold!"

Creative Team: "Thanks."

CLIENT
Honda

AGENCY
Wieden+Kennedy/ London

ANNUAL ID
06030T

TONY DAVIDSON

"The Power of Dreams" sounds like a clichéd tagline. It isn't. It's Honda's philosophy translated from Japanese: the ability to have a great idea, but more importantly, to make it happen. In this campaign "Dreams" explains their philosophy. "Impossible Dream" shows 13 of Honda's biggest dreams over the years. And "Choir" introduces their latest dream; the new Civic. As Project Leader Matsimoto-san said, "Everybody will feel that any other car is last generation, this is my dream." Doing great work is easy when you believe in the product and tell the truth. Do you believe in the Power of Dreams?

CLIENT
MINI

AGENCY
Crispin Porter + Bogusky/Miami

ANNUAL ID
06034T

CP+B CREATIVE TEAM

The truly amazing thing about this DVD is thousands of people actually paid $19.99 to have an advertisement mailed to them within three business days.

STARBUCKS
COFFEE

CLIENT
Starbucks

AGENCY
Creature/Seattle

ANNUAL ID
06310A

JIM HAVEN & MATT PETERSON

Production of this idea was almost as funny as the idea itself. You would have thought we were redesigning the space shuttle. (Which someone should do by the way.) There were CAD drawings, a battery of safety tests including runs through a car wash. The cup had a breakaway system similar to what is used on ski gates for racing. Oh, and a special case was designed for shipping. Because as it turned out, the magnet was so powerful it affected sensitive electronic systems on airplanes.

Thanks to Starbucks for living up to its brief of "surprise and delight." Which ironically came back around to us in the form of this award.

CLIENT
MINI

AGENCY
Crispin Porter + Bogusky/Miami

ANNUAL ID
06001G

CP+B CREATIVE TEAM

We're making counterfeit One Show Pencils for the dozen or so talented people who helped make this a truly integrated campaign. Please don't sue.

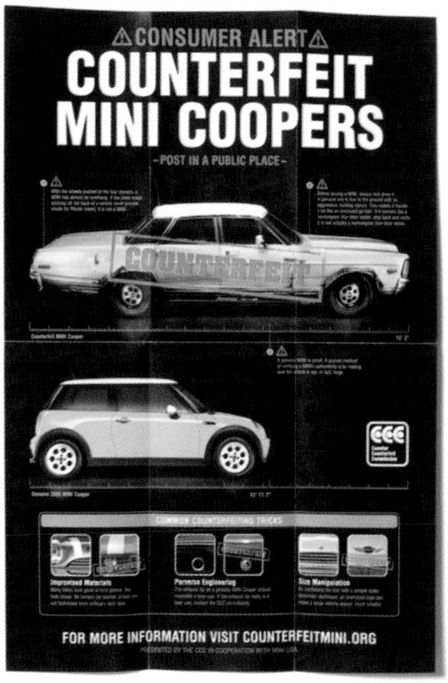
⚠CONSUMER ALERT⚠
COUNTERFEIT
MINI COOPERS
-POST IN A PUBLIC PLACE-
COUNTERFEIT
FOR MORE INFORMATION VISIT COUNTERFEITMINI.ORG

CLIENT
Open Family

AGENCY
Grey Worldwide/ Melbourne

ANNUAL ID
06004R

Brendon Guthrie & Tim Holmes

Advertising can't change the world. But occasionally, it can help those who do.

CLIENT
National Thoroughbred Racing Association

AGENCY
DeVito/Verdi/New York

ANNUAL ID
06009R

Dan Giachetti & John Clement

Our grandmothers have no idea what a Gold Pencil is.

CLIENT
Anheuser-Busch

AGENCY
DDB/Chicago

ANNUAL ID
06008R

Mark Gross

One day The Bomb will hit and we will all be wiped out. Our fancy powerbooks. Our berets. Our need for expensive dinners, warm cashews and blank cab receipts. Pulverized into tiny, smoldering bits. The only thing left will be the resilient cockroach. With nary a bread bag or cupboard to find solace in they'll be left to roam the Earth endlessly. The yearning in their bellies matched only by the emptiness in their hearts. After years and years they will finally drop. Exhausted. Spent. It is then that their tiny cockroach cell phones will ring. And it will be our client. Asking for ten more "Real Men of Genius" spots by Monday morning. "Maybe one about 'Mr. Atomic Bomb Setter Offer,' " they'll say.

Carry the torch, cockroaches. Carry the torch.

CLIENT
Turner Broadcasting System (TBS)

AGENCY
Mother/New York

ANNUAL ID
06002D

DAVE CLARK & RORY HANRAHAN

The Department of Humor Analysis are highly competent scientists. However, they know little about design. So creating their Humor Survey was going to be no laughing matter. After rounds and rounds of revisions we basically decided to rip off an old SAT booklet that was lying around. If we ever get to design something like this again, we will rip off this humor study—then it won't even be cheating, because we did this one, and it's not really cheating when you copy your own work—it's called "doing your style."

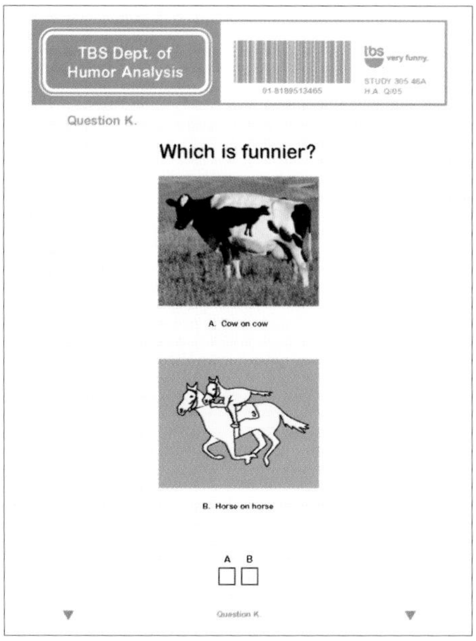
TBS Dept. of
Humor Analysis
tbs very funny.
Question K.
Which is funnier?
A. Cow on cow
B. Horse on horse
A B
Question K.

FedEx
Express
BACK

CLIENT
FedEx

AGENCY
BBDO/New York

ANNUAL ID
06006D

CHUCK TSO

We work in a truly great industry. Where else could you be rewarded for an idea that makes people look busier than they actually are?

CLIENT
Jim Esch for Congress

AGENCY
Archrival/Lincoln

ANNUAL ID
06009D

CHARLES HULL

Our client is a young unknown congressional candidate going up against a well-known, eight-year republican incumbent in a heavily republican district. Jim's primary audience being the 18 - 45 year old voter, we elected to take a hipper approach to political branding and move away from the tired conventions of political design in order to convey a fresh candidate with progressive ideas not driven by a partisan agenda, but an American agenda. This approach sparked the idea of integrating Jim's initials into an abstract flag, representing a new breed of in-touch politician who has America's best interests at heart.

FOR YOUR
THANK YOU

CLIENT
Opolis

AGENCY
Opolis/Portland

ANNUAL ID
06010D

DAN RICHARDS

Our intent was not to create a portfolio of printing techniques, but that is essentially what we did. We set out to design a system that was visually very simple, yet had a lot of character on further inspection. We accomplished this through the use of a variety of printing techniques. We engraved the logo over a litho printed color field, letterpress printed the text, and then added die cut notches and a perf that allows you to tear off a tab containing the contact information of any one of the three members of the team.

Clients are impressed when we hand them the card, but we can't help but wonder if they would be just as impressed if we wrote our number on a dollar bill. It might have been a cheaper way to make a good first impression.

OPOLIS

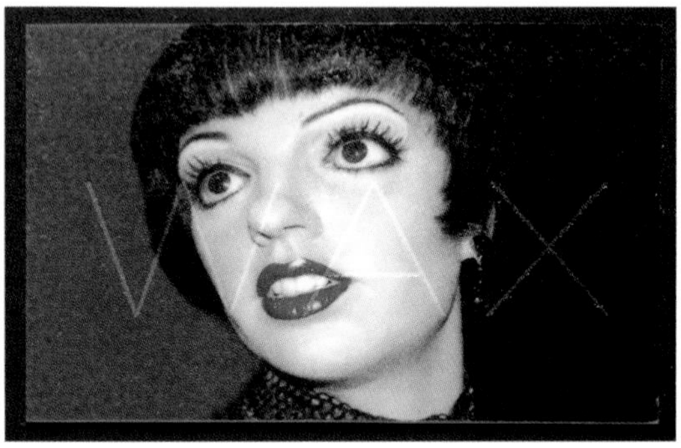

CLIENT
WAX Partnership

AGENCY
WAX Partnership/ Calgary

ANNUAL ID
06011D

TRENT BURTON, JOE HOSPODAREC, MONIQUE GAMACHE & KELI POLLOCK

Who said clients don't care about awards?

CLIENT
The Dog House

AGENCY
DDB/Dallas

ANNUAL ID
06014D

GREG CHAPMAN & CRAIG COOPER

The assignment was simple, if somewhat pretentious: develop a logo for a high-end dog grooming salon. After spending many months and untold millions of dollars conducting focus groups and one-on-one interviews with haute dogs, Greg turned a Scottie into a comb.

CLIENT
Apple Computer

AGENCY
Apple Computer/ Cupertino

ANNUAL ID
06017D

APPLE DESIGN TEAM

The iPod nano packaging is the last opportunity to connect with the customer before they own and begin using the product. The package is designed to create a feeling of ceremony, as if the customer is receiving and opening a gift. Other considerations included making it environmentally responsible, and iconic and efficient in a retail environment.

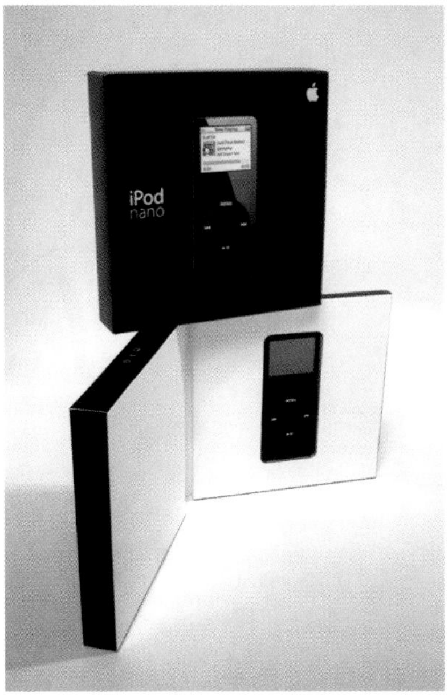

CLIENT
Thymes

AGENCY
Duffy & Partners/ Minneapolis

ANNUAL ID
06021D

DAN OLSON

Thymes had grown tired. The brand's presentation was no longer as unique or as special as the product inside. For Filigree, we designed all elements of the branding to infuse a poetic sense of balance between classic and contemporary styles. The rich brown color palette against an embossed leaf pattern, unique closures and shapes all capture the nuances of the fragrance. The brand language was then applied to primary and secondary packaging and all marketing materials. This revitalization for Thymes has driven significant incremental sales and enthusiasm among retailers and consumers alike.

CLIENT
DaimlerChrysler

AGENCY
BBDO/Bangkok

ANNUAL ID
06026D

WEERACHON WEERAWORAWIT

After receiving the brief, we kept churning out ideas and fighting each other. At one point, my art director lost control. He ran to the kitchen, grabbed a knife and stabbed me several times until my heart fell out. It looked exactly like the one in the campaign.

Now, I'm fine. My heart is replaced with this Gold Pencil.

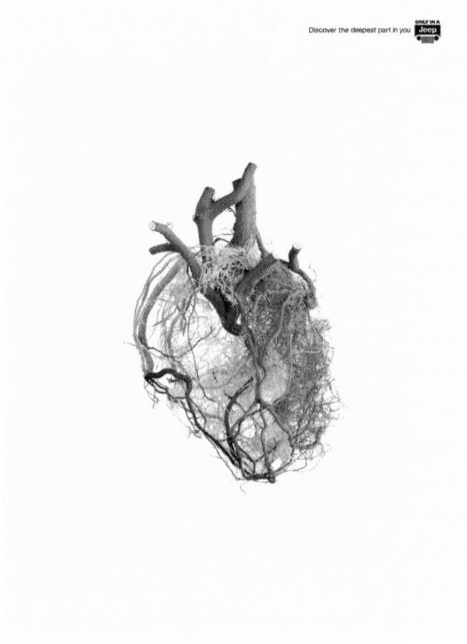

CLIENT
Office: Jason Schulte Design

AGENCY
Office: Jason Schulte Design/San Francisco

ANNUAL ID
06027D

JASON SCHULTE

Our holiday cards represent a moment-in-time snapshot of our office. The 2005 card grew from our fascination with folk art, combined with inspiration from a pile of wallpaper samples that was never put away, mixed with a modern sensibility.

We're attracted to work that is close to the artist's hand: we like to see the movement of the brushstrokes, the original pencil sketch lines on the canvas that formed the initial composition. The emboss, metallic foil, letterpress and hand-sewing yield a tactile quality that strives to replicate this ideal and to create an intimate experience for the recipient.

1
2

CLIENT
MCCM Creations/ Anothermountainman Communications

AGENCY
Anothermountainman Communications/ Hong Kong

ANNUAL ID
06036D

ANOTHERMOUNTAINMAN DESIGN TEAM

In the winter of 1998 a member of the Hong Kong creative advertising industry was on a staff exchange trip to London. He found his month in England an enriching experience, surrounded by English arts, fashion, advertisements, architecture and designs. However, one day, in a small boutique in Soho, he came face to face with a typical Hong Kong product—the redwhiteblue plastic bag. As a result, he learned to consider things from different cultural perspectives. When he returned to Hong Kong he became more concerned with all things "local" and began to look at redwhiteblue from a different angle. These books are a product of that thought and look at the many ways redwhiteblue is used.

CLIENT
School of Visual Arts

AGENCY
School of Visual Arts/ New York

ANNUAL ID
06037D

CARIN GOLDBERG

"Senior Library" showcases the best work done by the graduating seniors. It also gives a long-standing senior portfolio teacher the opportunity to design the book with total creative freedom.

I wanted the Library to be digestible and intimate as to avoid any resemblance of an unwieldy, run of the mill, graphic design annual. Therefore, the Library is divided into five digestible monographs. The silhouettes and line drawings I asked each student to submit at the start of the project inspired the sensibility of the design.

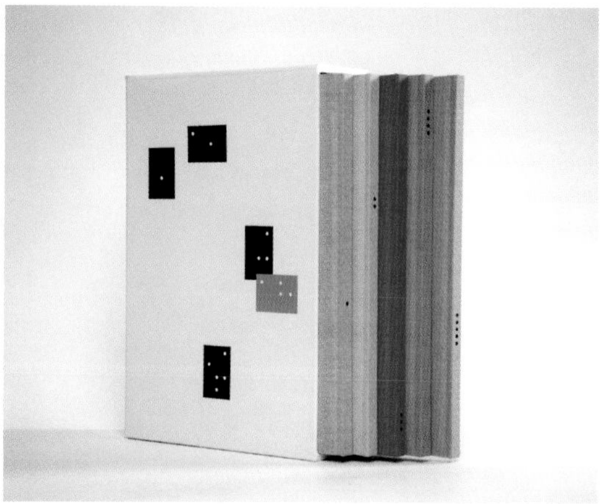

CLIENT
Nike

AGENCY
HunterGatherer/ New York

ANNUAL ID
06048D

TODD ST. JOHN

We were contacted to create artwork and animation to introduce Generation 2 of Nike's sustainable line, Considered. Nike Considered focuses on alternative and more renewable manufacturing techniques. The animation was distributed through a number of media, including a HunterGatherer designed kit.

The artwork for Considered references Nike's 13-word "Manifesto."

The animation and kit build visuals around ideas of evolution, sharing, and finite resources. Creatures evolving from one being to the next. Hybrids of plant, animal, human, and nature forms. Imagined myths and cautionary tales.

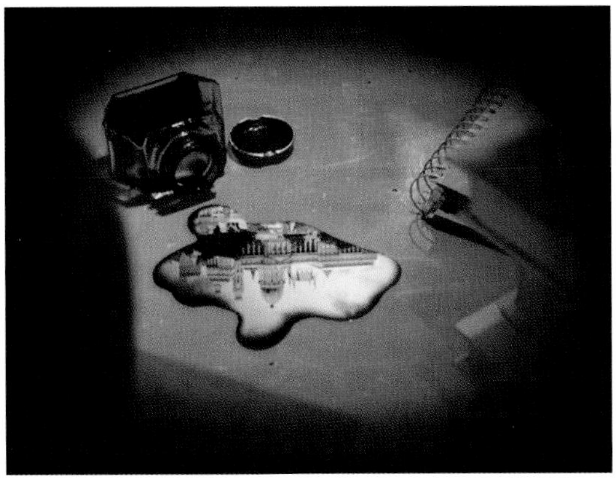

CLIENT
The Sundance Channel

AGENCY
JWT/New York

ANNUAL ID
06051D

JULIAN GREY

Animation is uniquely suited to create imagery to complement poetry. I selected three poems by the wry and unconventional Billy Collins. In "Budapest," I used a combination of stop-motion hand and pen and cel-drawn animals to capture the relation between the writer and his thoughts. "Forgetfulness" describes the effect of memory slipping away with the passage of time using various film collage techniques. In "Some Days," Collins uses the metaphor of a dollhouse and dolls to observe the vicissitudes of the everyday, reversing relationships of control. Instead of dolls, I opted to shoot realistic yet rigid miniature figurines in a surreal model house in a series of suggestive tableaux. The shallow depth of field in tiny spaces emphasizes the nuances of manipulation evoked in the poem.

CLIENT
MORI Art Museum

AGENCY
Good Design Company/Tokyo

ANNUAL ID
06054D

MANABU MIZUNO

In Japan, leaflets of an art exhibition are generally not well designed. That's why we took a meticulous approach to build a powerful visual identity. While its complicated composition conveys the atmosphere of the exhibition, the design bears the power as a symbol from a distance. I believe the exquisite balance makes it outstanding.

Every time I receive such an honorable award, I hope my achievement will soon be surpassed by superior design and become a thing of the past in the design world.

BERLIN
TOKYO
BERLIN
TOKYO
BERLIN

JUDGE'S CHOICE

ANDY AZULA – THE MARTIN AGENCY/RICHMOND

As it turns out, there was actually some very cool work this year. In fact, there were quite a few campaigns worth talking about. But in the end, I thought: Hey, why not use this space to talk about those Stella Artois coupon ads? They're tiny little print ads that actually ask you to spend more money. Can you get more reassuringly expensive than that? At a time when everyone is wondering what will come next in advertising, these do a great job of reminding us that at the end of the day it's all about the idea. Even if the idea is a small non-event, like a coupon ad.

20% more
Bring this coupon and pay an extra $1.25 on your next Stella Artois.
1 1004623 2384623 0
No valid with any other offers.
Excludes tax and other charges.
Valid at participating locations only.
Expires 11/30/2005.
STELLA ARTOIS
Reassuringly expensive.

ANNUAL ID *06012A*

TODD MCCRACKEN – GREY ASIA PACIFIC/ KUALA LUMPUR

Every year there are a number of great pieces of work. How well they do depends on how humbled the judges are. My humble o-meter fell for three campaigns specifically. Harvey Nichols print campaign. Fabulous. In every way. Guinness "NoitulovE." Fantastic, and I presume enormously expensive. And the Vodafone UK 20-second spots. Extremely short, and funny. A great and rare retail campaign that I hope will go on forever. Every one of you deserves the accolades you've scored at the One Show. Well done. Bastards.

March
HARVEY NICHOLS

ANNUAL ID *06030A*

MIMI COOK – GOODBY, SILVERSTEIN AND PARTNERS/SAN FRANCISCO

"Fair Enough" nailed everything: the scripts, the performances, the edit. Besides pulling off an original way into a well-worn subject, they found the perfect way: absurdity. It powerfully re-detonates the realization that cigarettes make no sense whatsoever.

"Fair Enough!"

ANNUAL ID *06005T*

MORIHIKO HASEBE – HAKUHODO/TOKYO

My choice is "Big Ad." It's the most simple idea, with the biggest execution. Its bold attitude of "advertising" is truly respectable. So simple, so funny, so dynamic. The song still echoes in my head.

CARLTON
DRAUGHT

ANNUAL ID *06008T*

MARK TUTSSEL – LEO BURNETT WORLDWIDE/CHICAGO

It's rooted in a wonderful product truth and brought to life through stunning craft and flawless special effects. Guinness "NoitulovE" is one of those memorable epics that takes three Guinness drinkers back to the dawn of time.

"Good things come to those who wait" is a totally relevant concept, beautifully executed, engaging and highly entertaining to watch.

The idea required an enormous amount of computer-generated imagery and each frame is beautifully crafted. Exquisite in every detail. The reality and computer animation almost indistinguishable.

The choice of music was inspired and the film rewards repeated viewings. Congratulations to AMV BBDO and the brilliant Daniel Kleinman.

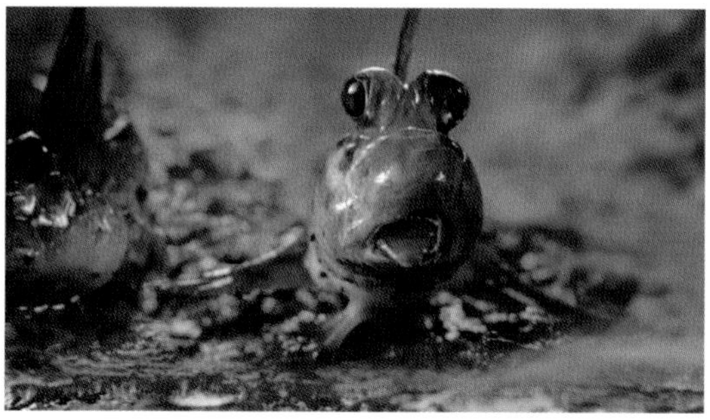

ANNUAL ID *06009T*

LISA BENNETT – DDB/SAN FRANCISCO

The first day of judging the TV category I was in the group that saw Guinness "NoitulovE." One viewing and I couldn't stop thinking about it. The simplicity of the idea, the complexity of the production. Having no idea how to pronounce "NoitulovE," I fondly referred to it as "that caveman, de-evolution, kick-ass Guinness spot."

Following that first round of judging, we saw something like 10,000 more entries. And there was quite a bit of what fellow judge David Nobay referred to as "fish poo." As we waded through the fish poo, I couldn't stop thinking about "caveman, de-evolution, kick-ass Guinness spot."

So when it came up again in the final round of judging, I pushed the 10 button on my voting keypad as hard as I could. Twice just to be sure. This spot was the opposite of fish poo. It was oop hsif. Which is why in my mind, oop hsif was hands down the most deserving of Best of Show and my obvious judge's choice.

JIM LESSER – BBDO WEST/SAN FRANCISCO

For weeks after judging, everyone asks, "So, what'd you see? Any cool stuff?" For me, the piece I kept telling people about was a Silver Pencil spot from ESPN. Here is a spot that takes a funny, long-running campaign and gives it an emotional wallop. It sucks you in from the narrator's opening line, "My name is Izzy Paskowitz and I run surf camps for autistic kids..." Then over the course of several minutes, you watch these kids who arrive terrified of the water begin to laugh and have fun and gain confidence and SURF. Then, "Without sports, where would we find ourselves?" Wow.

WITHOUT SPORTS,
WHERE WOULD WE
FIND OURSELVES?

ANNUAL ID *06010T*

RAVI DESHPANDE – CONTRACT ADVERTISING/MUMBAI

The Honda "Choir" spot is my favorite. There comes a point in advertising—after a lot of blood, sweat and tears—when an ad ceases to be merely an ad and becomes a work of art. Such points are few and far in our business. But then that's also why we can distinguish so easily between the good and the great. Congratulations to the team that was responsible for this. I envy you guys.

ANNUAL ID *06030T*

DAVID APICELLA – OGILVY & MATHER/NEW YORK

My favorite spot in this year's show is Honda "Choir," part of the "Power of Dreams" campaign from Wieden+Kennedy, London.

I think this is one of the freshest—and coolest—product demonstrations I have ever seen.

It is stylish, elegant and flawlessly executed. It speaks volumes for the brand and elevates the Civic to a place it may never have been.

I've seen it 20 times and I never tire of it.

ARTHUR BIJUR – CLIFF FREEMAN AND PARTNERS/ NEW YORK

It was a close call for me between the Vodafone campaign, which was hilarious and the Bangkok Insurance campaign.

Both were great ideas, produced perfectly.

Both were in tough categories.

Both sell really hard.

I'd give the edge by a nose to the Vodafone campaign based on the level of difficulty and the memorably funny factor.

This year a big execution took the cake but creating something so great and so simple is no small accomplishment.

ANNUAL ID *06027T*

EDDIE VAN BLOEM – LOWE/NEW YORK

It's impossible not to be awed by Guinness "NoitulovE" or charmed by Carlton's "Big Ad." I was jealous of the Lynx Jet campaign and how that idea was pulled through so many different media. I also loved the writing of *The Onion* ads, and the cleverness of the "grave effect" smoking room for Cancer Patients Aid.

But the ads I most told my friends about were the Vodafone campaign. The humor comes right out of the strategy. So smart. So funny. So short.

Of course, that leaves off the repetitive brilliance of Harvey Nichols print. And the head-exploding simplicity of the *Economist.* And the guilty-pleasure laugh of Ace Hardware. And....

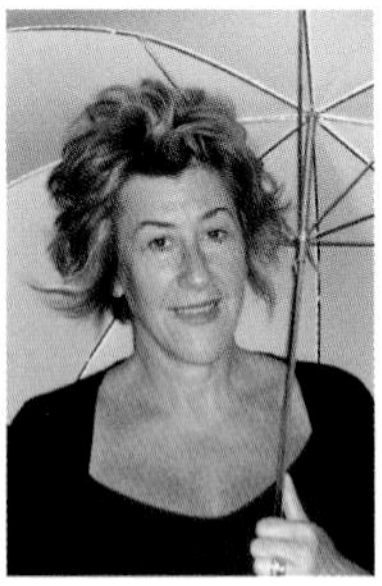

JANET KESTIN – OGILVY & MATHER/TORONTO

"Hmmm. . .I know—3 seconds of funny and 7 seconds of dry information. That'll clean up at the One Show for sure."

These spots are simple, smart, hilarious and the performances are perfect.

The more of them I saw, the more I wanted to see.

Lucky Vodafone. Clever JWT.

BETTINA OLF – SPRINGER AND JACOBY/HAMBURG

The short films Spike Jonze created for Miller were among my favorites. The animals' movements and human voices are edited together in such a simple and charming way that you can't help laughing. The diverse films are comfortable and easy to watch yet funny and innovative. Being highly creative yet unpretentious is very difficult to achieve especially when making an ironic comment about the advertising industry. It is a shame that Spike Jonze never got to work with Walt Disney.

16:07:22:16

ANNUAL ID *06031T*

SUSAN EBLING CORBO – MOTHER/NEW YORK

There was a lot of great work this year, but one campaign struck me in particular: It's the completely whacked out, yet incredibly smart Starburst work. You've got "Ernie the Klepto," a sculptural tribute to Lionel Richie and a full-on fiesta inside a gigantic mouth. Yet the team was still able to work in all the product attributes that make the candy different. It's so well done, it makes me hurt. Starburst has been around forever. You don't even think about it any more. But when they took such a fresh approach to the work, it made the brand seem completely new again.

ANNUAL ID *06032T*

KHAI MENG THAM – OGILVY & MATHER ASIA PACIFIC/SINGAPORE

It's art. When I first saw it, it moved me. Now after seeing it for the sixth time, I still love it. That's the power of a great ad.

ANNUAL ID *06052T*

RACHEL HOWALD – Y&R/NEW YORK

ESPN "Sundays are for Bowling" (especially "Dollhouse")

Nefarious bowling ball.

Great potential name for a band.

Even better idea for a campaign.

ANNUAL ID 06099T

ANDREW KELLER – CRISPIN PORTER + BOGUSKY/MIAMI

My favorite was the Starbucks Red Cup concept. Starbucks should never do ads. Their store experience and their cups are advertising enough. So how do you generate a little extra buzz without doing "ads"? Well, I think they nailed it. Use the cup. Small reach, but a story that is sure to be told over and over again. And the reward at the end is a nice, good vibes marketing move. Perfect for the holiday season.

STARBUCKS COFFEE
PHARMACY

ANNUAL ID 06310A

CHUCK MCBRIDE – TBWA/LOS ANGELES

I liked the Starbucks Red Cup because it was the truth. We have all seen someone leave something on their car. It's funny when it happens. To turn that into an idea that has brand caché is brilliant.

TY MONTAGUE – JWT/NEW YORK

My favorite campaign was "Art of The Heist." It took a lot of courage for a client the size of Audi to embrace a story as complex and multifaceted as this one. It was participatory, brand appropriate, covered just about every conceivable medium and (says the client) sold a bunch of new A3's. Made me jealous.

ATTENTION:
If you have any information regarding the location of a 2006 Audi A3 with VIN WAUZZZ8P65A045963, please contact Audi of America at 1-866-657-3268.
Audi

ANNUAL ID *06050A*

MATT VESCOVO – FREELANCE/BROOKLYN

We saw a lot of non-traditional ads during the week of judging. Many of the executions were very elaborate with huge budgets behind them, in order to make the most of the unorthodox media they lived in. Of what I saw though, the one that stood out as one of the most effective was this very simple ad on the side of a coffee cup.

What I think worked so well was that it wasn't just in an unexpected place, but more importantly, the one and only place the idea would make sense.

It wouldn't work any other way.

It used the space not only as a way to be different, but also to communicate the idea. Part of the ad is missing and can only be complete when someone does the one thing you do with a cup: drink from it. Essentially making the viewer/coffee drinker a live post-plastic surgery product demo.

That's a pretty impressive feat to pull off and gets the person thinking, "Maybe I should get some work done, I look pretty good with a small nose."

I only wish they had the actual cups at the judging. Partially, because I have a big nose and wanted to see what it looks like if it were smaller, but also because I wanted to hold the cup and experience the ad myself.

ANNUAL ID *06153A*

DAVID NOBAY – SAATCHI & SAATCHI/SYDNEY

CP+B's Gold-winning "Counterfeit MINI" integrated campaign is still the one that sticks out for me. It's smart from whatever angle you look at it: from creating an order-your-own DVD to secure cheap shopping channel media space, to blowing out the whole idea across DM and small space ads. Oh, and did I mention it made me laugh? Making tired judges laugh after 10 hours in a small, smelly room is very smart indeed.

CONSUMER ALERT
COUNTERFEIT
MINI COOPERS
-POST IN A PUBLIC PLACE-
COMMON COUNTERFEITING TRICKS
FOR MORE INFORMATION VISIT COUNTERFEITMINI.ORG

ANNUAL ID *06001G*

ZAK MROUEH – TAXI/TORONTO

LynxJet was my personal favorite. It didn't require a massive production budget to enhance it and seamlessly worked across the Web, TV and live events. I loved the guerilla component where they had vivacious flight attendants parade through the airport. For frequent fliers, the website offered the LynxJet Mile High Club. While awards juries are still figuring out how to evaluate integrated campaigns, this one was a pleasure to judge. At its core was a big, campaignable idea.

ANNUAL ID *06004G*

PETER MCHUGH – CARMICHAEL LYNCH/ MINNEAPOLIS

The work that I wish I'd done is ESPN's "Without Sports" campaign. I'd been familiar with it, but when you see it together as a campaign, with great TV, great print and great insight into sports, it was really impressive. Not one weak execution in the lot.

Ultimately, it was downgraded because doing sports advertising is "too easy." Which I don't agree with—I spent the last three years working on adidas in Amsterdam, and sports (or 'sport') is as hard or harder than anything else—it's just easier to like when it's done well.

WITHOUT SPORTS,
HOW WOULD WE
ESCAPE?

ANNUAL ID *06309G*

KEVIN PROUDFOOT – WIEDEN+KENNEDY/ NEW YORK

My favorite piece from this year's show is actually a student execution by University of Colorado at Boulder students, Molly Gannon, Sheena Brown and Vanessa Lozano. The One Show college assignment was to generate awareness of hybrid technology and drive people to a website about the technology. While most entries were print and TV ads, this execution was designed around a very specific media placement, the pollution masks that toll collectors wear. By placing the web address on the masks, consumers would encounter the message while driving their cars—when they have no choice but to acknowledge that the decisions they make do have an impact on air quality and the environment. It's a beautifully simple idea that powerfully underscores the importance of context.

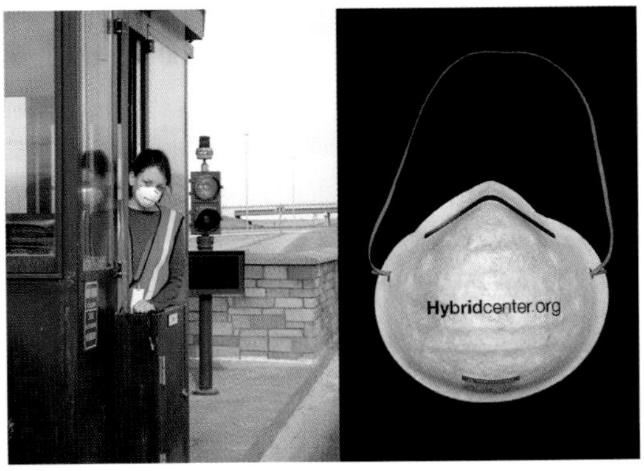
Hybridcenter.org

SCHOOL
University of Colorado/ Boulder

ART DIRECTORS
Molly Gannon, Vanessa Lozano, Sheena Brown

MATT ELLER – FEEL GOOD ANYWAY/PORTLAND

This piece has a formidable combination of grace and wit featuring the best frame-by-frame crash test of all time. Giant sushi getting bludgeoned? Sure, why not?

Yes, flipbooks have been done before. That's ok.

ANNUAL ID *06003D*

ABBY CLAWSON LOW – KATE SPADE/NEW YORK

I loved the inventive way the designers at Nordpol executed this flipbook series. The glossy black slipcase with "Crashtest" neatly centered on its face piqued my curiosity and made me want to know what was inside. And its quiet design made this piece stand out among the dozens of others that screamed for attention during our afternoon survey.

When I opened the case, I was struck by the contrast between the stark, technical-looking book covers and their whimsical contents. To discover flipbooks chronicling the crash tests of gigantic sushi rolls, supersized sausages, colossal crackers and French baguettes of ponderous proportions, only emphasized the enchanting, light-hearted design that makes this piece so endearing.

The books are clean and crisp, and their dimensions invite the consumer to flip the pages and experience the uncoated paper with its four-color bleed printing. The farcical food-based crash tests they chronicle looked as delectable as they were charming.

And besides, if these French cars drive as well as French bread tastes, aren't we all better off?

NEIL POWELL – MARGEOTES FERTITTA POWELL/ NEW YORK

What can I say? Apple continues to raise the bar. It's why I think Apple is the strongest brand on the planet. The experience of opening the Nano packaging is almost as good as the experience of using the product. Not unlike the product, the packaging is beautiful in its simplicity, and intelligent in its function. And, it provokes something that I always admire in great package design – that tinge of guilt you feel when you go to throw it away.

iPod
nano

ANNUAL ID *06017D*

SEIJO KAWAGUCHI – TUGBOAT/TOKYO

In today's world, where information and media are increasingly diversified, designs which interpret them have also been thrown into a state of chaos.

That is why I found this creative to be especially unforgettable; because, with its smart design and appearance, it expresses the true essence of what design brings us.

ANNUAL ID *06019D*

HALEY JOHNSON – HALEY JOHNSON DESIGN/ MINNEAPOLIS

My choice is the Turner Duckworth packaging for Superdrug.

As a package designer I feel that it is my duty to choose something I sort of understand, like packaging. And I found the Superdrug shampoo series to be good, clean fun. Everything works with this little monster theme. The colors and the unique shape of the bottles instantly set the tone. The characters are personable and goofy in their fruity, monster-like state. The chunky, child-like quality of the typography complements the illustrations nicely. It all adds up and says "buy me."

EXTRA GENTLE MANGO
2in1 CONDITIONING
SHAMPOO
FOR LITTLE MONSTERS
NO TEARS FORMULA
EXTRA GENTLE
TROPICAL FRUIT 2in1
CONDITIONING
SHAMPOO
FOR LITTLE MONSTERS
NO TEARS FORMULA
EXTRA GENTLE STRAWBERRY
SHAMPOO
FOR LITTLE MONSTERS
NO TEARS FORMULA
EXTRA GENTLE MELON
AFTER SWIM
FOR LITTLE MONSTERS

ANNUAL ID *06022D*

RICHARD BOYNTON – WINK/MINNEAPOLIS

My guess is that the presentation for the ASICS Helsinki Lounge went something like this:

"We're going to take over the top floor of a hotel in Helsinki and build a mini-stadium that's really more of an art installation than a corporate sales piece. And you're not only going to approve it, but you're going to pay handsomely to produce it. Because if you don't, we're going to post those photos of you at last year's IAFF mixer... and we won't even ask for a credit card number or anything! "

Because nobody gets away with something this simple, tasteful, bold, naive, and beautiful when corporate money is behind it unless they've got something juicy to leverage with. Nordpol are to be commended as much for their ruthlessness as their talent!

ANNUAL ID *06030D*

BRIAN GUNDERSON – GOODBY, SILVERSTEIN AND PARTNERS/SAN FRANCISCO

I felt that the three spots created for the Sundance Channel were extremely successful in combining dream-like imagery with poeticism. They were simple, elegant, and powerful; and though unified conceptually, each was distinct and memorable. The animation techniques were truly innovative and uniquely applied. Congrats on the great work...

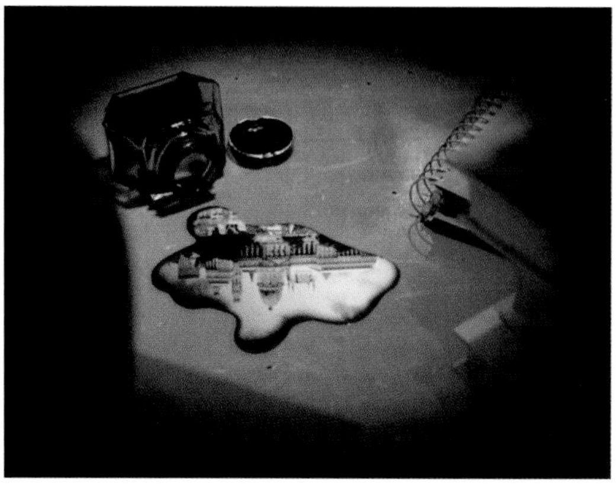

ANNUAL ID *06051D*

MY
FAVOR-

CLIVE PIERCY – PHD DESIGN/SANTA MONICA

My Judge's Choice is the JWT/HeadGear Sundance Channel animations. Of all the work that I looked at, these pieces had the greatest emotional impact on me. Of course, the poetry is by Billy Collins, so we are off to a great start. But it would have been easy to overwork the visuals, and what I particularly like is the casual style of the animations that perfectly complement the profound and funny words as they wash over the audience. I loved these pieces.

ANDERS KORNESTEDT – HAPPY FORSMAN AND BODENFORS/GOTHENBURG

My favourite work was absolutely the animations for the Sundance Channel because it was really charming, well executed, extremely relevant and BIG FUN.

MERIT

PRINT

MERIT

ART DIRECTOR
Anni Klintworth

WRITER
Claudette Browne

CREATIVE DIRECTOR
Porky Hefer

CLIENT
Independent Newspapers

AGENCY
Lowe Bull/Cape Town

ANNUAL ID
06054A

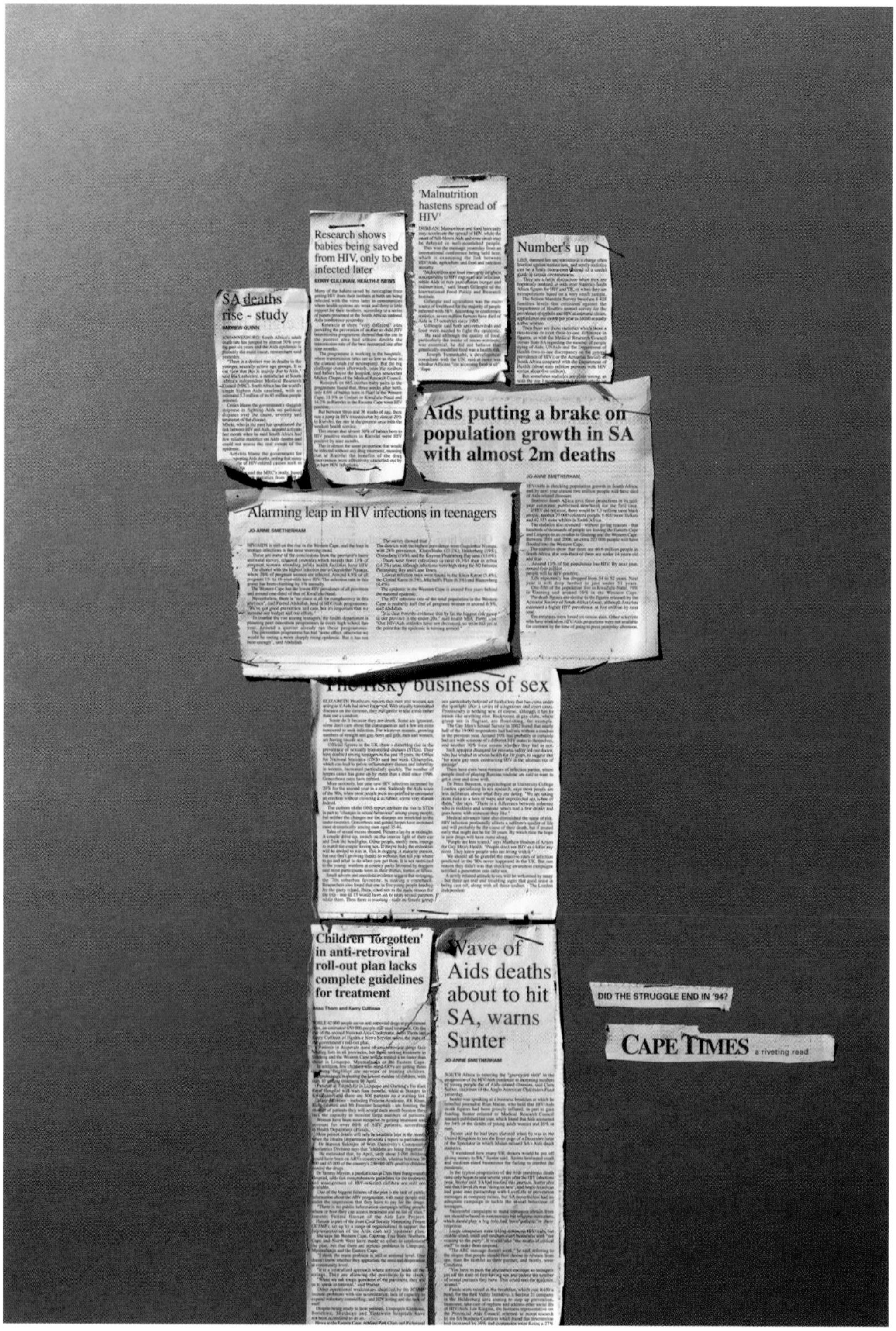
'Malnutrition hastens spread of HIV'
Research shows babies being saved from HIV, only to be infected later
Number's up
SA deaths rise - study
Aids putting a brake on population growth in SA with almost 2m deaths
Alarming leap in HIV infections in teenagers
business of sex
Children forgotten' in anti-retroviral roll-out plan lacks complete guidelines for treatment
Wave of Aids deaths about to hit SA, warns Sunter
DID THE STRUGGLE END IN '94?
CAPE TIMES a riveting read

Touareg. The Volkswagen SUV.
Drivers wanted.

MERIT

ART DIRECTOR
Chris Hall

WRITER
Matt Syberg-Olsen

CREATIVE DIRECTORS
Bill Newbery
Tim Kavander

CLIENT
Volkswagen

AGENCY
Arnold Worldwide/
Toronto

ANNUAL ID
06055A

LEGO
imagine...

MERIT

ART DIRECTOR
Lance Vining

WRITERS
Lance Vining
Charles Foley

PHOTOGRAPHER
Gerard Turnely

CREATIVE DIRECTOR
Brett Morris

CLIENT
Lego

AGENCY
FCB/Johannesburg

ANNUAL ID
06056A

MERIT

ART DIRECTORS
Johan Eghammer
Mikko Timonen

WRITERS
Jacob Nelson
Oscar Askelof

PHOTOGRAPHER
Jens Mortensen

CLIENT
Volvo

AGENCY
Forsman & Bodenfors/Gothenburg

ANNUAL ID
06057A

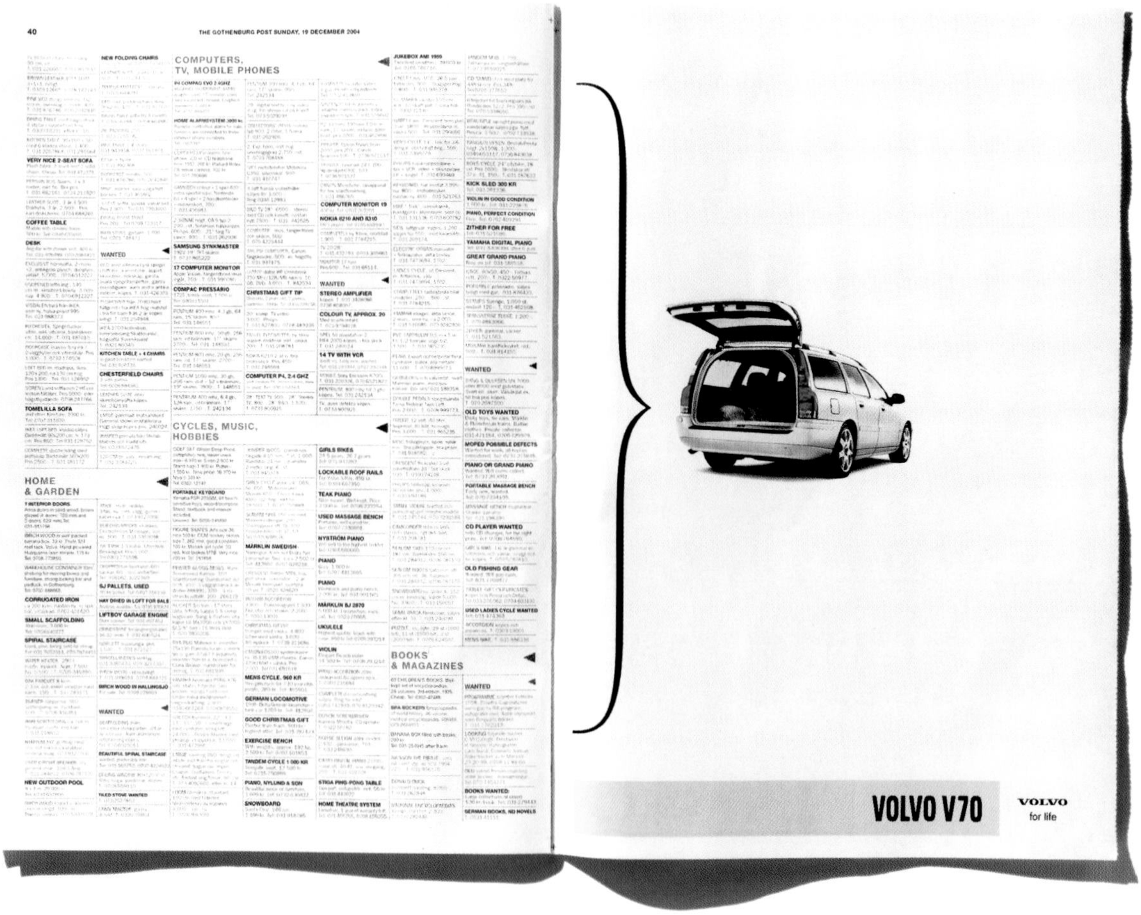
40
THE GOTHENBURG POST SUNDAY, 19 DECEMBER 2004
COMPUTERS, TV, MOBILE PHONES
CYCLES, MUSIC, HOBBIES
HOME & GARDEN
BOOKS & MAGAZINES
VOLVO V70
VOLVO for life

MERIT

ART DIRECTOR
David Mously

WRITERS
Mirko Stolz
Jan Harbeck

CREATIVE DIRECTORS
Burkhart von Scheven
David Mously
Jan Harbeck
Mirko Stolz

CLIENT
DHL

AGENCY
Jung von Matt/Berlin

ANNUAL ID
06058A

No size limits.

Tubeless
Tyres
APOLLO

MERIT

ART DIRECTOR
Ashok Lad

WRITER
Amitabh Agnihotri

PHOTOGRAPHER
Umesh Aher

CREATIVE DIRECTORS
Amitabh Agnihotri
Ashok Lad
Agnello Dias
Bruce Matchett

CLIENT
Apollo Tyres

AGENCY
JWT/Mumbai

ANNUAL ID
06059A

SPIDERMAN

MERIT

ART DIRECTORS
Nicholas Pringle
Clark Edwards

WRITERS
Nicholas Pringle
Clark Edwards

PHOTOGRAPHER
Kelvin Murray

CREATIVE DIRECTOR
Jim Thornton

CLIENT
Heinz

AGENCY
Leo Burnett/London

ANNUAL ID
06060A

MERIT

ART DIRECTOR
Bo Deng

WRITER
Ning Chen

CREATIVE DIRECTORS
Nils Andersson
Wilson Chow

CLIENT
Airbus

AGENCY
Ogilvy/Beijing

ANNUAL ID
06062A

中国民航报

历史上超大型全双层飞机
空中客车A380首航成功

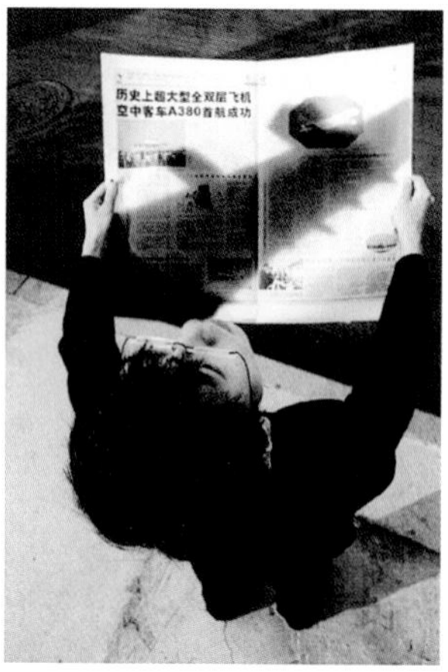
历史上超大型全双层飞机
空中客车A380首航成功

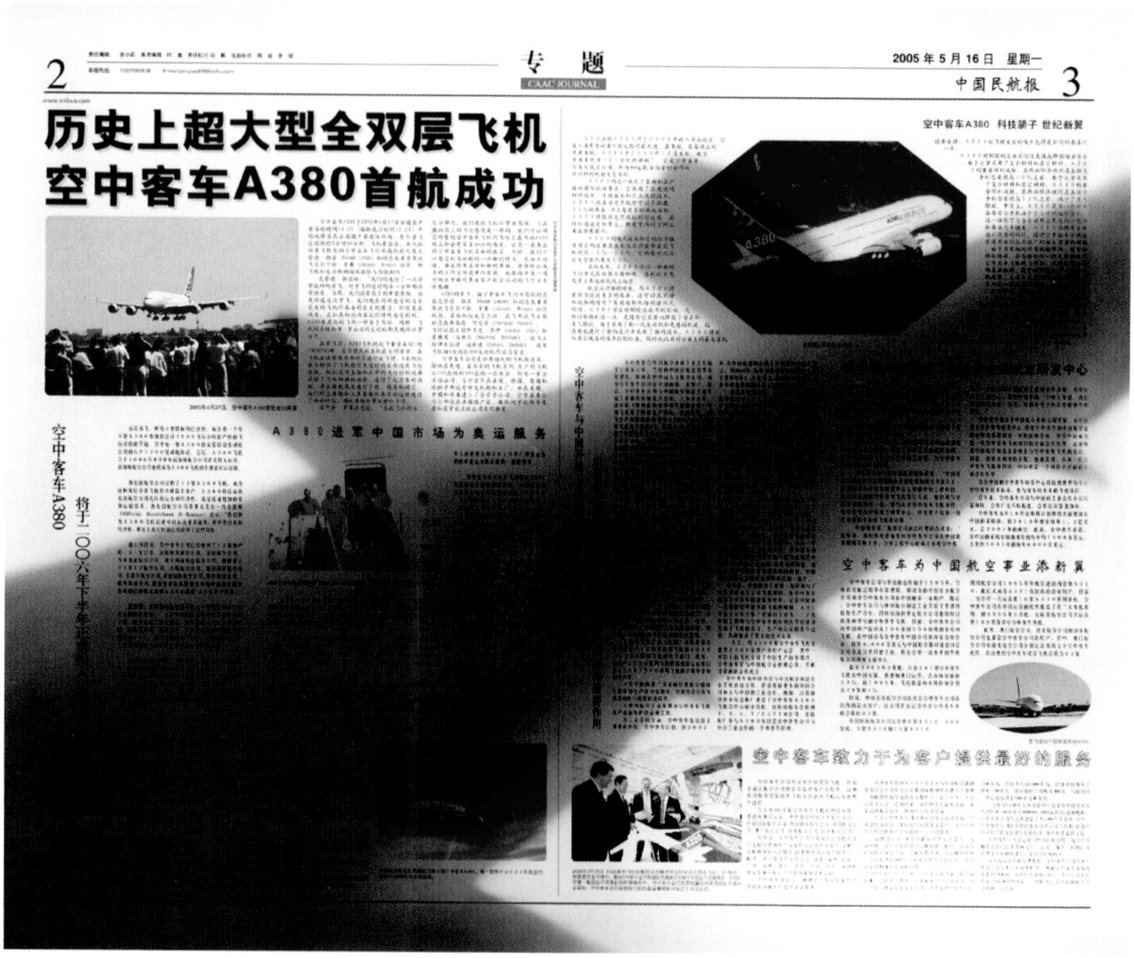

2 专题 CAAC JOURNAL 2005年5月16日 星期一 中国民航报 3

历史上超大型全双层飞机 空中客车A380首航成功

空中客车A380 科技骄子 世纪新翼

A380进军中国市场为奥运服务

空中客车为中国航空事业添新翼

空中客车致力于为客户提供最好的服务

ACDelco
ultra-soft shock absorbers
Available at Vincar Pte Ltd, 61 Ubi Avenue 2 #02-16/17 Automobile Megamart, Singapore (408898)

MERIT

ART DIRECTOR
Ko Min Jung

WRITER
Lim Chiao Woon

CREATIVE DIRECTOR
Robert Gaxiola

CLIENT
AC Delco Shock Absorbers

AGENCY
Bates/Singapore

ANNUAL ID
06065A

ACDelco

ACDelco
Available at Vincar Pte Ltd, 61 Ubi Avenue 2 #02-16/17 Automobile Megamart, Singapore (408898)

MERIT

ART DIRECTOR
Ivan de Dios

WRITER
Alberto Jaen

PHOTOGRAPHER
Camilo Puyal

ILLUSTRATOR
Camilo Puyal

CREATIVE DIRECTOR
Javier Alvarez

CLIENT
Fiat

AGENCY
*Vitruvio Leo Burnett/
Madrid*

ANNUAL ID
06066A

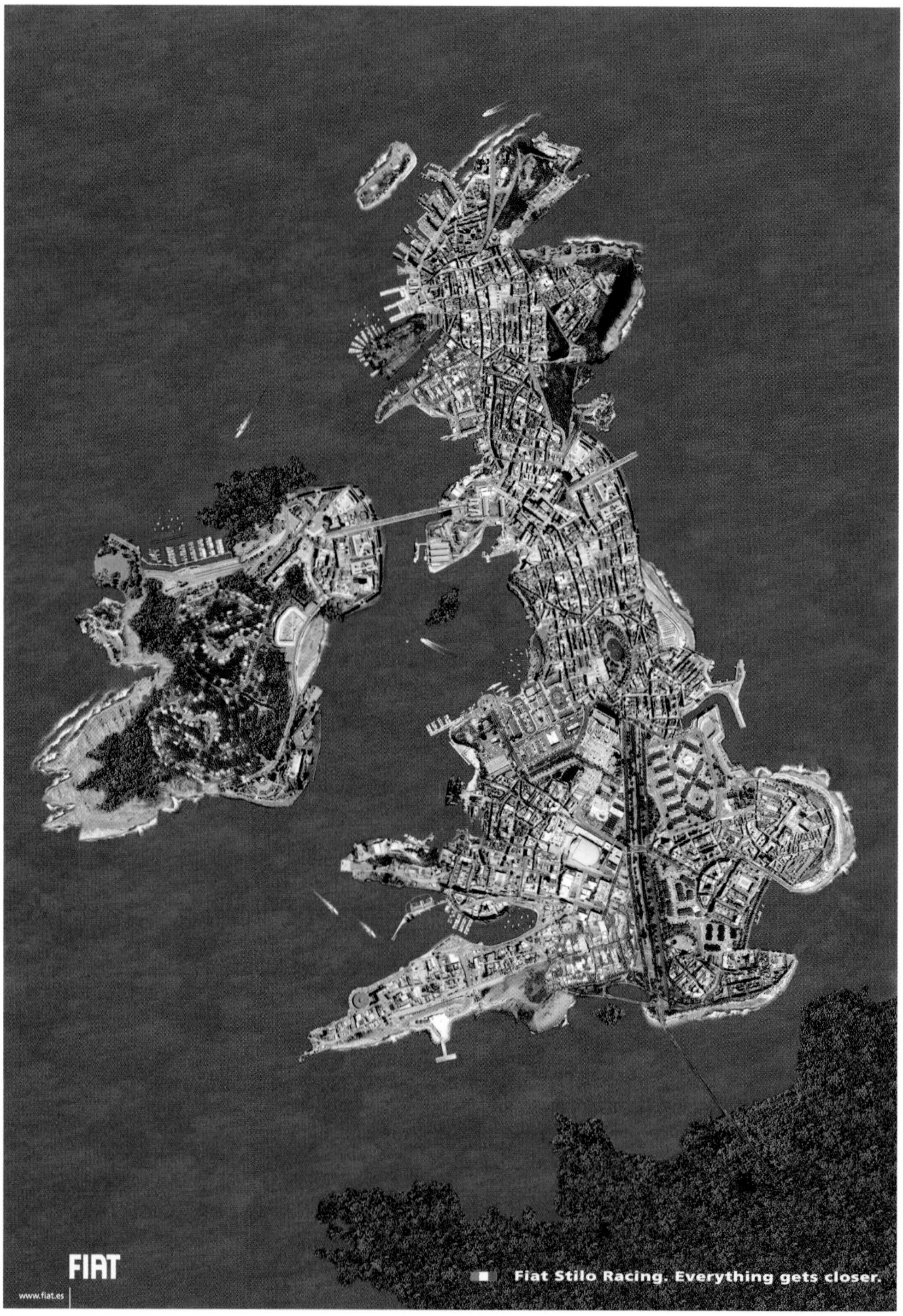
FIAT
www.fiat.es
Fiat Stilo Racing. Everything gets closer.

FIAT

FIAT

MANELAND
JUNGLE LODGE

For reservations call: 91-22-26184014/15 ■ Gir Lion Sanctuary and National Park Sasan Dist. Junagadh Gujarat 362135 (India). Tel: 02877-285555

MERIT

ART DIRECTOR
Santosh Padhi

WRITERS
Kaushik Mitra
Agnello Dias
K.V. Sridhar

PHOTOGRAPHER
Shekhar Phalke

ILLUSTRATOR
Bhushan Patil

CREATIVE DIRECTORS
Santosh Padhi
K.V. Sridhar

CLIENT
Maneland Jungle Lodge

AGENCY
Leo Burnett/Mumbai

ANNUAL ID
06067A

DUTY OFFICER
RECEPTION
MANELAND
JUNGLE LODGE

MANELAND
JUNGLE LODGE

MANELAND
WELCOME
MR.C.K.JADEJA
MANELAND
JUNGLE LODGE

MERIT

ART DIRECTOR
Raj Kamble

WRITER
Stephen Lundberg

PHOTOGRAPHERS
Michael Webber
Stuart Tyson

CREATIVE DIRECTORS
Fernanda Romano
John Hobbs
Peter Rosch
Mark Wnek

CLIENT
Federated Department Stores

AGENCY
Lowe/New York

ANNUAL ID
06068A

macy's

hurry. macy's one day sale.

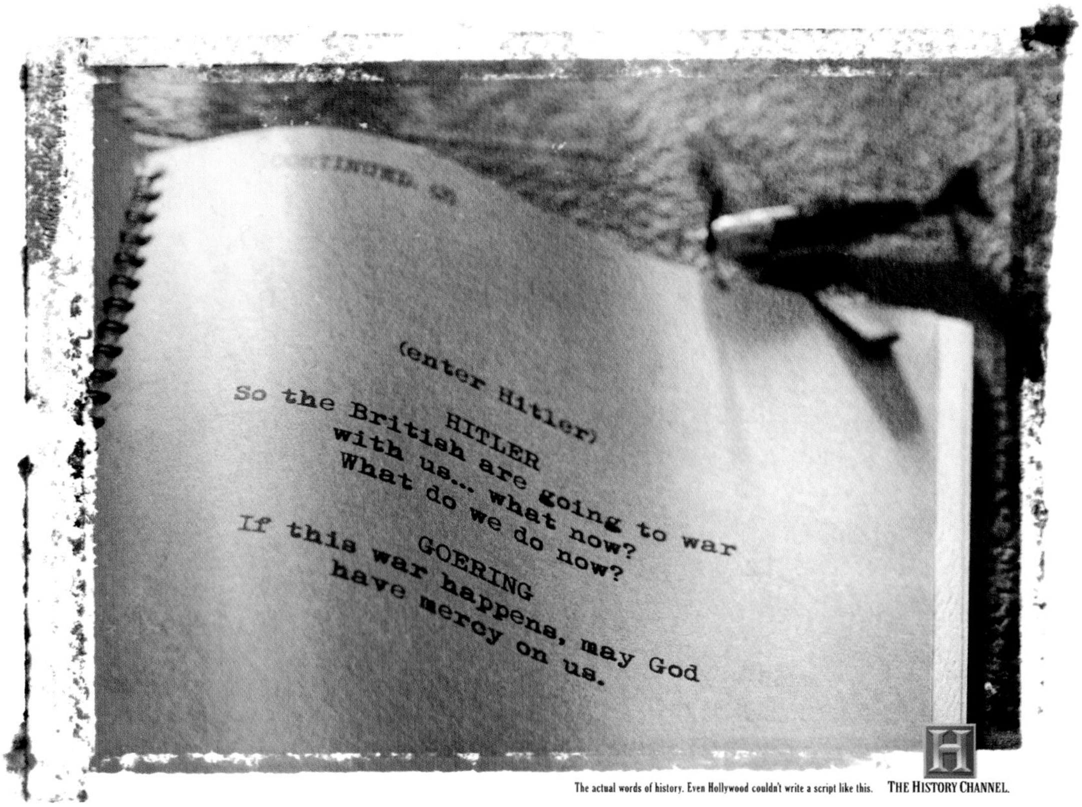
(enter Hitler)
HITLER
So the British are going to war with us... what now? What do we do now?
GOERING
If this war happens, may God have mercy on us.
The actual words of history. Even Hollywood couldn't write a script like this.
THE HISTORY CHANNEL

CHAPMAN.
Hey John!
His victim slumps to the ground.
DOORMAN.
(shaken)
Do you know what you've done?
CHAPMAN.
Yes. I've just shot John Lennon.
The actual words of history. Even Hollywood couldn't write a script like this.
THE HISTORY CHANNEL

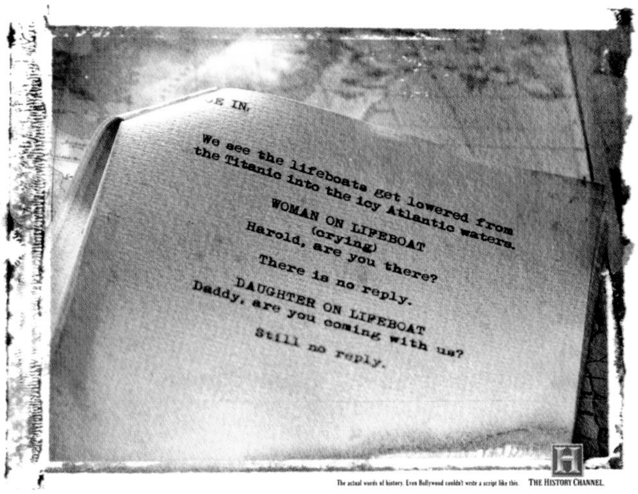
We see the lifeboats get lowered from the Titanic into the icy Atlantic waters.
WOMAN ON LIFEBOAT
(crying)
Harold, are you there?
There is no reply.
DAUGHTER ON LIFEBOAT
Daddy, are you coming with us?
Still no reply.
The actual words of history. Even Hollywood couldn't write a script like this.
THE HISTORY CHANNEL

Merit

ART DIRECTOR
Karin Barry

WRITER
Derek Shevel

PHOTOGRAPHER
Pierre Peters

CREATIVE DIRECTORS
Fran Luckin
Gerry Human

CLIENT
Multichoice DStv

AGENCY
Ogilvy South Africa/ Johannesburg

ANNUAL ID
06069A

Merit

ART DIRECTOR
Peter Walker

WRITER
Vincent Raffray

PHOTOGRAPHER
Clive Stewart

CREATIVE DIRECTORS
Vincent Raffray
Khaled Gadallah

CLIENT
Sony

AGENCY
Tonic Communications/ Dubai

ANNUAL ID
06070A

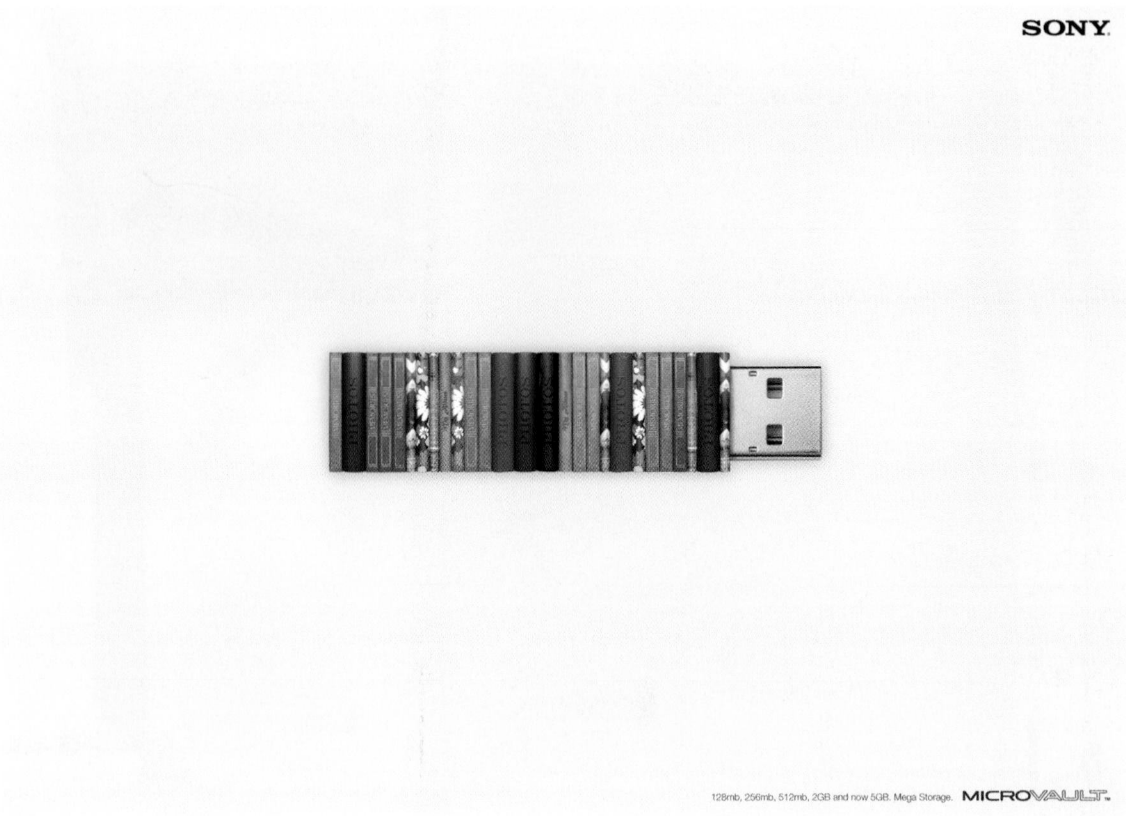
SONY
128mb, 256mb, 512mb, 2GB and now 5GB. Mega Storage.
MICROVAULT

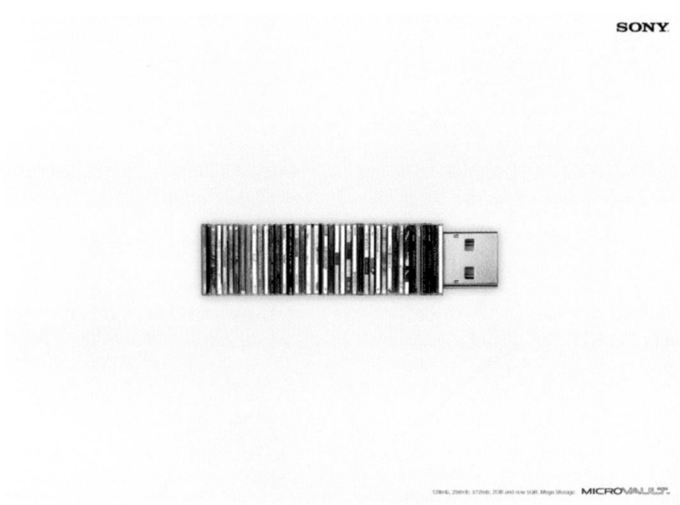
SONY
MICROVAULT

SONY
MICROVAULT

SONY
MICROVAULT

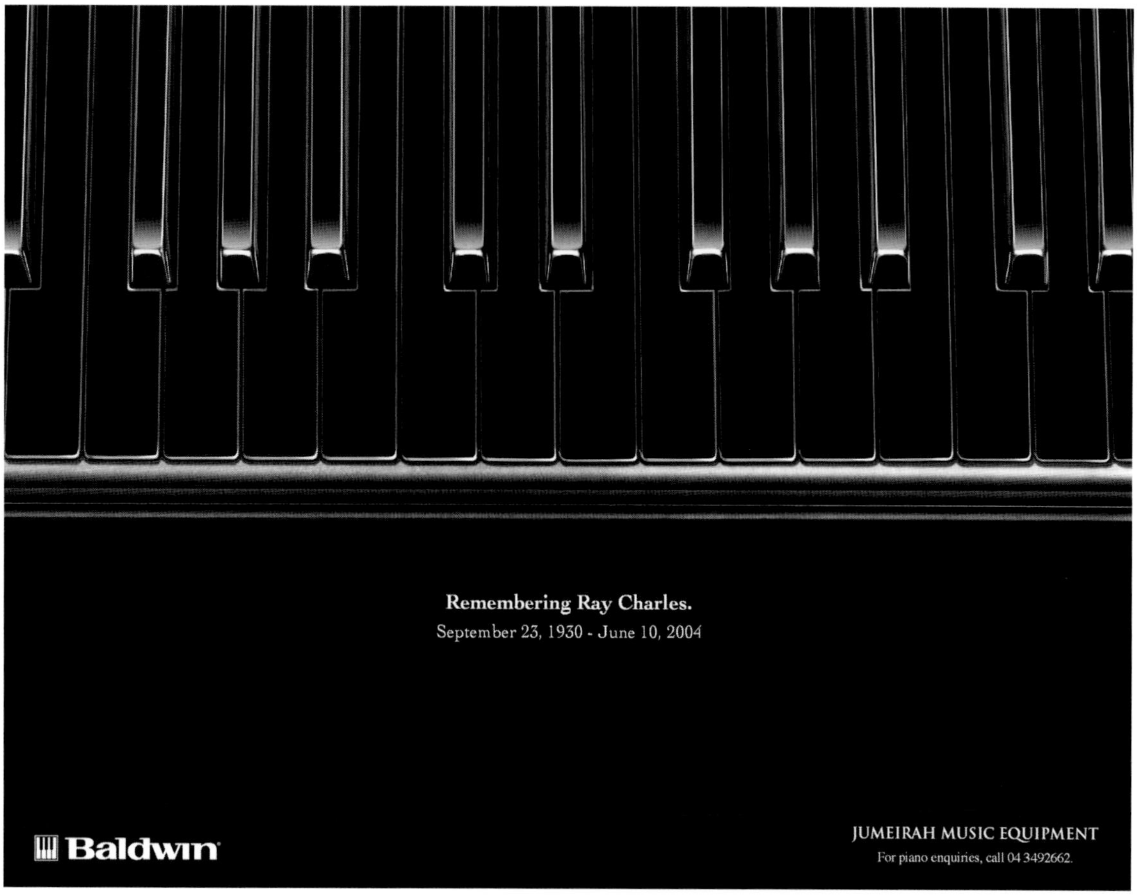
Remembering Ray Charles.
September 23, 1930 - June 10, 2004
Baldwin
JUMEIRAH MUSIC EQUIPMENT
For piano enquiries, call 04 3492662.

MERIT

ART DIRECTOR
Husen Baba Khan

WRITER
Sandeep Fernandes

PHOTOGRAPHER
Suresh Subramanian

ILLUSTRATOR
Mahesh Kubal

CREATIVE DIRECTOR
Manoj Ammanath

CLIENT
Jumeirah Music Equipment

AGENCY
Lowe/Dubai

ANNUAL ID
06071A

MERIT

ART DIRECTOR
Ivan de Dios

WRITER
Jaime Chavarri

CREATIVE DIRECTORS
Antonio Montero
Jaime Chavarri
Ivan de Dios

CLIENT
WWF/Adena

AGENCY
Contrapunto/Madrid

ANNUAL ID
06072*A*

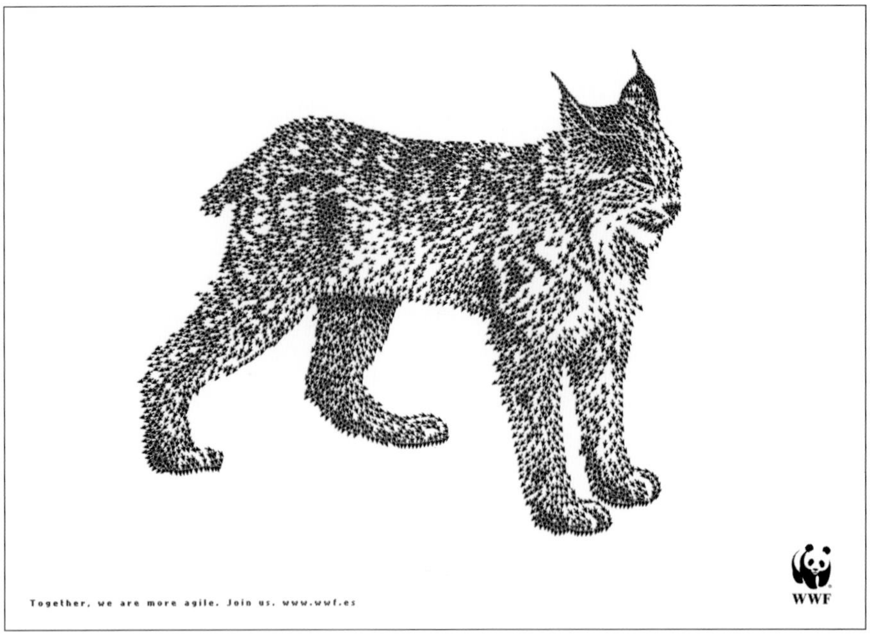
Together, we are more agile. Join us. www.wwf.es
WWF

Together, we are stronger. Join us. www.wwf.es
WWF

Together, we are more powerful. Join us. www.wwf.es
WWF

Press play.
PHILIPS

Press play.
PHILIPS

Press play.
PHILIPS

MERIT

ART DIRECTOR
Marcos Medeiros

WRITER
Flavio Casarotti

ILLUSTRATOR
Marcos Medeiros

CREATIVE DIRECTORS
Sergio Valente
Pedro Cappeletti

CLIENT
Philips

AGENCY
DDB/São Paulo

ANNUAL ID
06073A

MERIT

ART DIRECTOR
Kat Morris

WRITERS
Ronny Northrop
Steve O'Connell
Maureen Bongiovanni

ILLUSTRATOR
Timmy Kucynda

CREATIVE DIRECTORS
Alex Bogusky
Andrew Keller

CLIENT
MINI

AGENCY
Crispin Porter +
Bogusky/Miami

ANNUAL ID
06074A

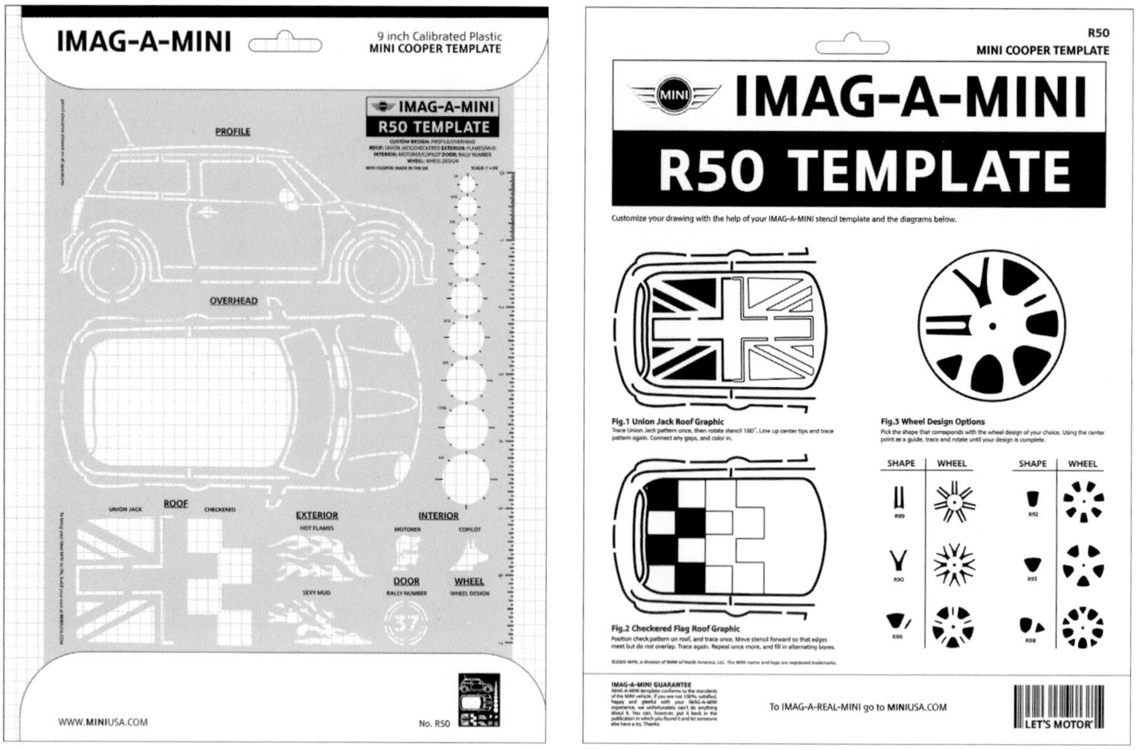
IMAG-A-MINI
9 inch Calibrated Plastic
MINI COOPER TEMPLATE
IMAG-A-MINI
R50 TEMPLATE
PROFILE
OVERHEAD
ROOF
EXTERIOR
INTERIOR
DOOR
WHEEL
WWW.MINIUSA.COM
No. R50
R50
MINI COOPER TEMPLATE
IMAG-A-MINI
R50 TEMPLATE
Customize your drawing with the help of your IMAG-A-MINI stencil template and the diagrams below.
Fig.1 Union Jack Roof Graphic
Fig.3 Wheel Design Options
SHAPE
WHEEL
Fig.2 Checkered Flag Roof Graphic
IMAG-A-MINI GUARANTEE
To IMAG-A-REAL-MINI go to MINIUSA.COM
LET'S MOTOR

MERIT

ART DIRECTOR
Tim Van den Broeck

WRITER
Ad Luijten

PHOTOGRAPHER
Christophe Gilbert

CREATIVE DIRECTOR
Dominique van
Doormaal

CLIENT
Volkswagen

AGENCY
DDB/Brussels

ANNUAL ID
06075A

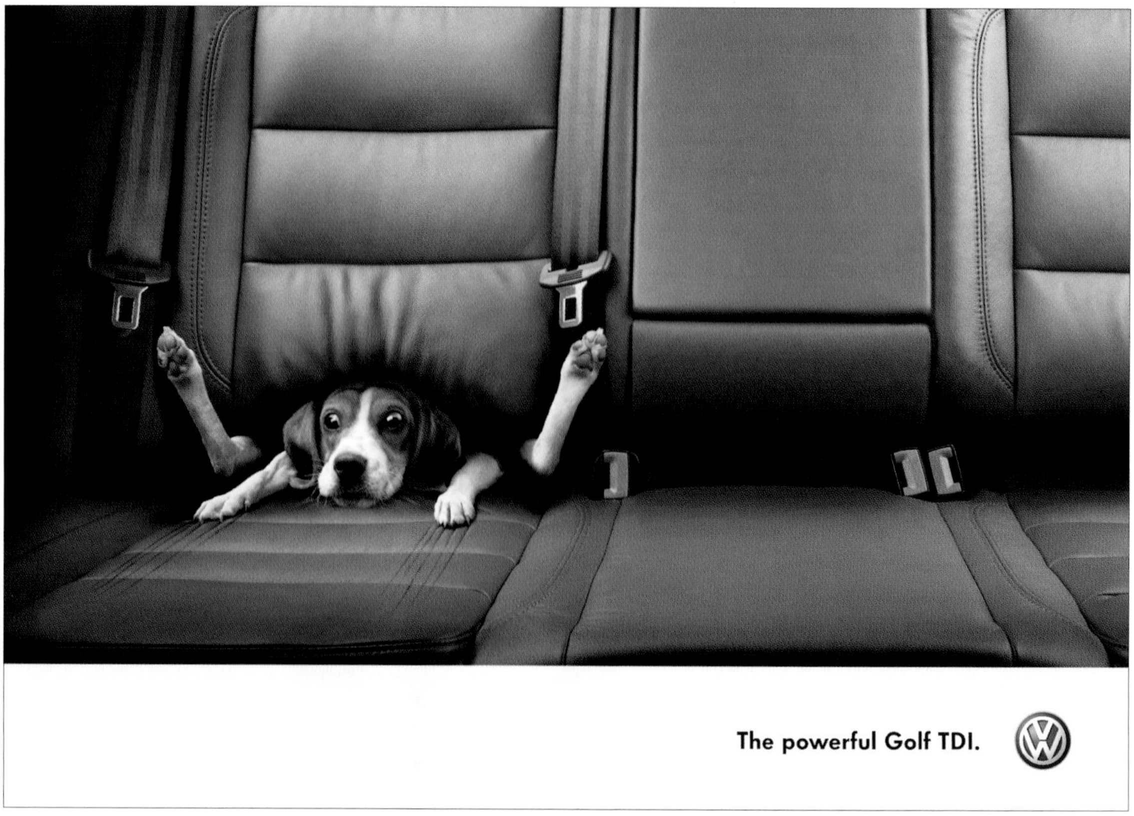
The powerful Golf TDI.

Do you need a cordless drill?
BOSCH

MERIT

ART DIRECTORS
Bernardo Hernandez
Cristina Davila

WRITERS
Juan Sanchez
Cesar Olivas

CREATIVE DIRECTORS
Juan Sanchez
Alberto Astorga

CLIENT
Robert Bosch

AGENCY
DDB/Madrid

ANNUAL ID
06077A

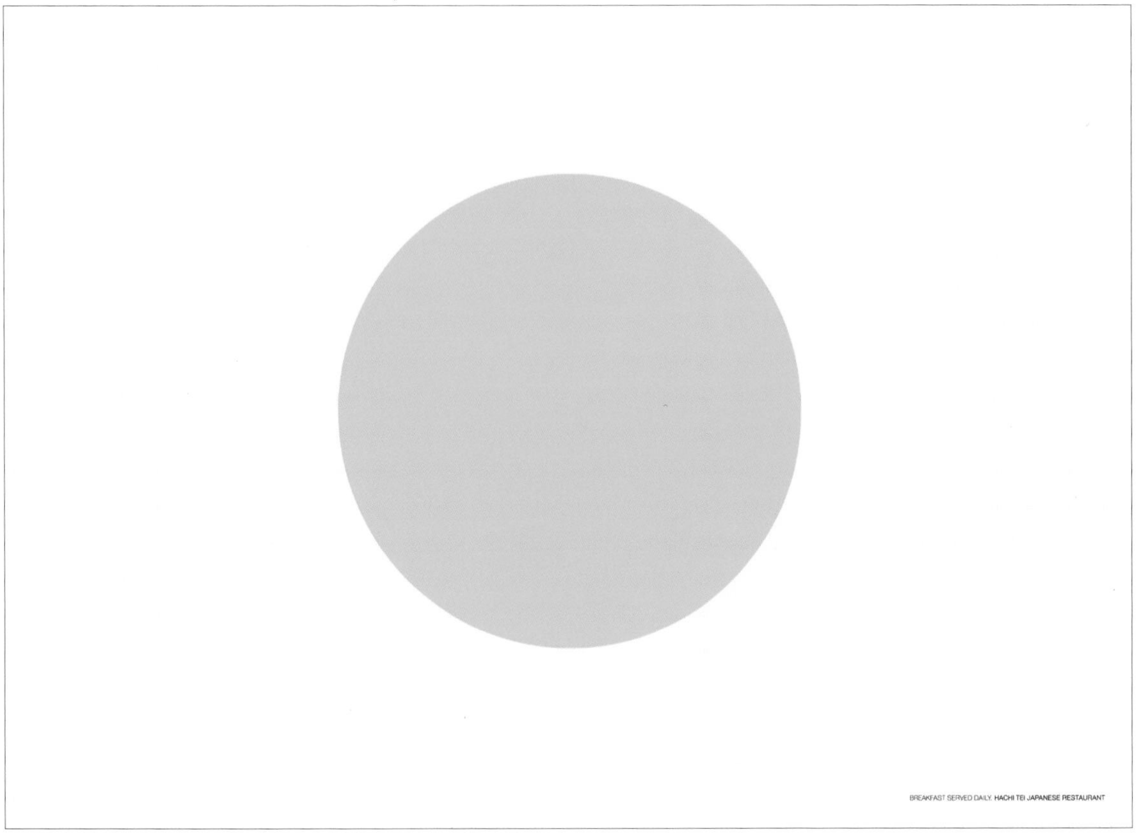
BREAKFAST SERVED DAILY. HACHI TEI JAPANESE RESTAURANT

MERIT

ART DIRECTOR
Eddie Wong Yew Heng

WRITER
Nirmal Pulickal

CREATIVE DIRECTOR
Patrick Low

CLIENT
Hachi Tei Restaurant

AGENCY
Dentsu Young & Rubicam/Singapore

ANNUAL ID
06078A

ALSO AWARDED
Merit:
Collateral: P.O.P. and In-Store - Single

Merit

ART DIRECTOR
Alexandre Pagano

WRITER
Marcelo Nogueira

PHOTOGRAPHER
Ricardo Barcellos

CREATIVE DIRECTORS
Fabio Fernandes
Eduardo Lima

CLIENT
Sustagen

AGENCY
F/Nazca Saatchi & Saatchi/São Paulo

ANNUAL ID
06079A

Much more
energy for
your child.
SUSTAGEN

Merit

CREATIVE DIRECTOR
Jo Espen Johansen

CLIENT
Oslo Hudpleiesenter

AGENCY
Grey/Oslo

ANNUAL ID
06080A

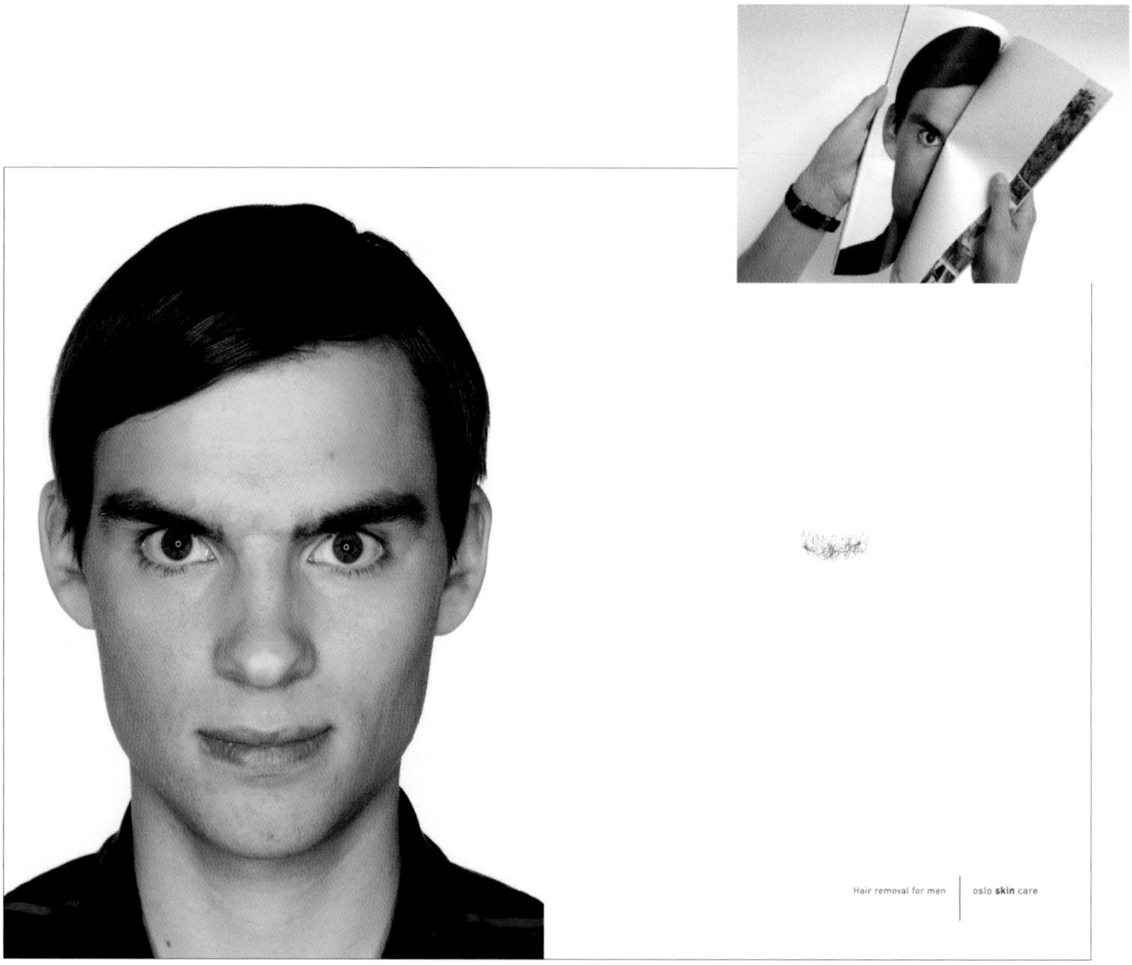
Hair removal for men
oslo skin care

BRITAIN'S
TEN BEST TAILORS.
ONE ROOM.
AT
Harrods
harrods.com
HOLLAND ESQ RICHARD JAMES OZWALD BOATENG NICK TENTIS TIMOTHY EVEREST PAUL SMITH VIVIENNE WESTWOOD SPENCER HART OLIVERSPENCER GIEVES THE BRITISH TAILORING ROOM

Merit

ART DIRECTORS
Jules Chalkley
Nick Simons

WRITERS
Jules Chalkley
Nick Simons

CREATIVE DIRECTORS
Malcolm Poynton
Neil Dawson

CLIENT
Harrods

AGENCY
Ogilvy/London

ANNUAL ID
06084A

DHL
EXPRESS

Merit

ART DIRECTORS
Eric Yeo
Muk

WRITER
Serene Loong

PHOTOGRAPHERS
Procolor
Edwin Ho
Groovy Studio

CREATIVE DIRECTOR
Sonal Dabral

CLIENT
DHL

AGENCY
Ogilvy & Mather/ Singapore

ANNUAL ID
06086A

MERIT

ART DIRECTOR
Ashidiq Ghazali

WRITER
Kelly Putter

PHOTOGRAPHER
Roy Zhang

ILLUSTRATOR
Yan Digital

CREATIVE DIRECTOR
Sonal Dabral

CLIENT
The Economist

AGENCY
Ogilvy & Mather/ Singapore

ANNUAL ID
06088A

The
Economist

MERIT

ART DIRECTORS
Mathieu Degryse
Yves-Eric Deboey

WRITERS
Curt Detweiler
Yves-Eric Deboey
Mathieu Degryse

CREATIVE DIRECTOR
Curt Detweiler

CLIENT
Nissan

AGENCY
TBWA\G1/Paris

ANNUAL ID
06089A

SMALL PRICE
NISSAN MICRA
10 500 €
VERY SMALL PRICE

NISSAN MICRA
10500 €
VERY SMALL PRICE
NISSAN

Merit

ART DIRECTORS
Mathieu Degryse
Yves-Eric Deboey

WRITERS
Curt Detweiler
Yves-Eric Deboey

CREATIVE DIRECTOR
Curt Detweiler

CLIENT
Nissan

AGENCY
TBWA\G1/Paris

ANNUAL ID
06090A

NISSAN PICK-UP THINK BIGGER
NISSAN
SHIFT_size

Merit

ART DIRECTOR
Yves-Eric Deboey

WRITER
Matthieu Degryse

CREATIVE DIRECTOR
Curt Detweiler

CLIENT
Nissan

AGENCY
TBWA\G1/Paris

ANNUAL ID
06091A

MERIT

ART DIRECTOR
Caprice Yu

WRITER
Tim Geoghegan

PHOTOGRAPHER
Jeff Mermelstein

CREATIVE DIRECTORS
Richard Bullock
Andy Fackrell

CLIENT
adidas

AGENCY
180 Amsterdam
(180\TBWA)

ANNUAL ID
06092A

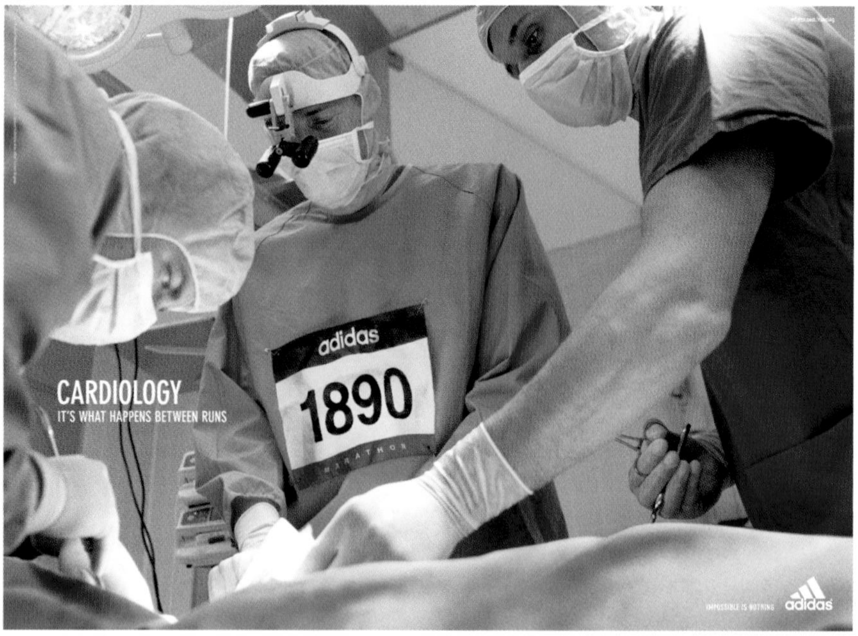
CARDIOLOGY
IT'S WHAT HAPPENS BETWEEN RUNS
adidas
1890
IMPOSSIBLE IS NOTHING
adidas

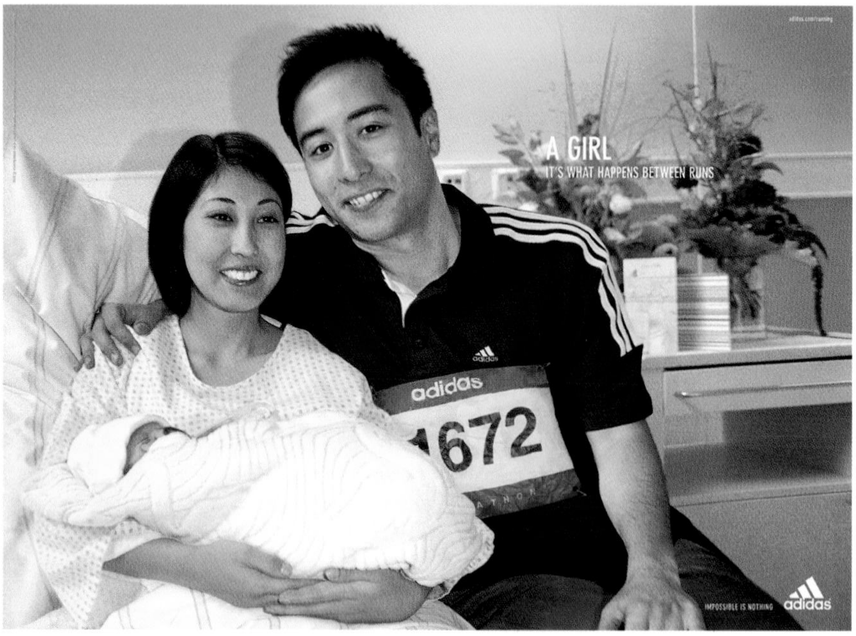
A GIRL
IT'S WHAT HAPPENS BETWEEN RUNS
adidas
1672
IMPOSSIBLE IS NOTHING
adidas

BOYFRIENDS
IT'S WHAT HAPPENS BETWEEN RUNS
adidas
1276
IMPOSSIBLE IS NOTHING
adidas

BBC World is a trademark of the British Broadcasting Corporation
Reporter: Emily Buchanan, Zimbabwe, 23.09.92
Emily Buchanan was in Zimbabwe filming the effects of severe drought and human rights abuses. On the way to interview President Mugabe her aircraft crash-landed. She survived and returned to the wreckage to retrieve her notebook.
Report successfully filed 16:30 GMT.
BBC
WORLD
Putting News First.

MERIT

ART DIRECTOR
Paul Brazier

PHOTOGRAPHER
Adam Whitaker

CREATIVE DIRECTOR
Paul Brazier

CLIENT
BBC Television

AGENCY
Abbott Mead Vickers BBDO/London

ANNUAL ID
06093A

GSM
Cameraman: Vaughan Smith, Serbia, 05.03.98
When filming the assault at Prekaz, Vaughan Smith was shot at by a sniper. The bullet passed through the contents of his pocket and fortunately lodged in his mobile phone.
Report successfully filed 20:49 GMT.
BBC
WORLD
Putting News First.

Reporter: John Simpson, Northern Iraq, 06.04.03
While reporting near Kirkuk, John Simpson came under attack from a coalition aircraft. Embedded in this bullet-proof vest is the shrapnel from a 450kg bomb that landed 10 metres away. John continued reporting throughout the attack.
Report successfully filed 18:14 GMT.
BBC
WORLD
Putting News First.

WORLD
TRADE
CENTER
DATE
NAME
COMPANY
SIGNATURE
Reporter: Stephen Evans, New York, 09.11.01
Stephen Evans was in the World Trade Center when the first plane hit the towers. He tried to write his report from the base of the tower but when the second plane hit, disabling the entire telecom network, he fled the building to complete his report elsewhere
Report successfully filed 15.00 GMT.
BBC
WORLD
Putting News First.

MERIT

ART DIRECTORS
Cesar Finamori
Renato Fernandez

WRITER
Dulcidio Caldeira

CREATIVE DIRECTOR
Marcello Serpa

CLIENT
Editora Abril

AGENCY
Almap BBDO/
São Paulo

ANNUAL ID
06094A

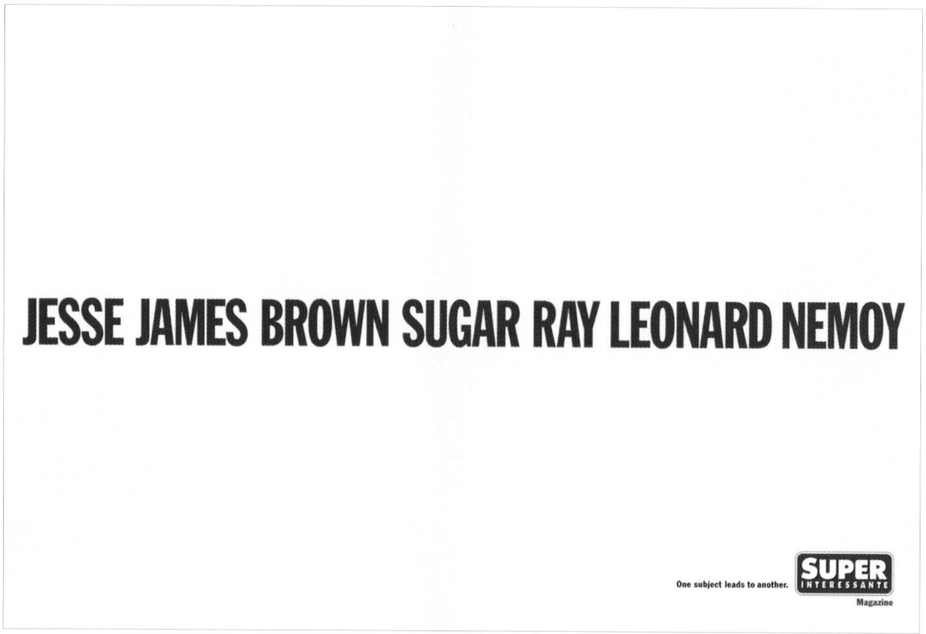
JESSE JAMES BROWN SUGAR RAY LEONARD NEMOY
One subject leads to another.
SUPER
INTERESSANTE
Magazine

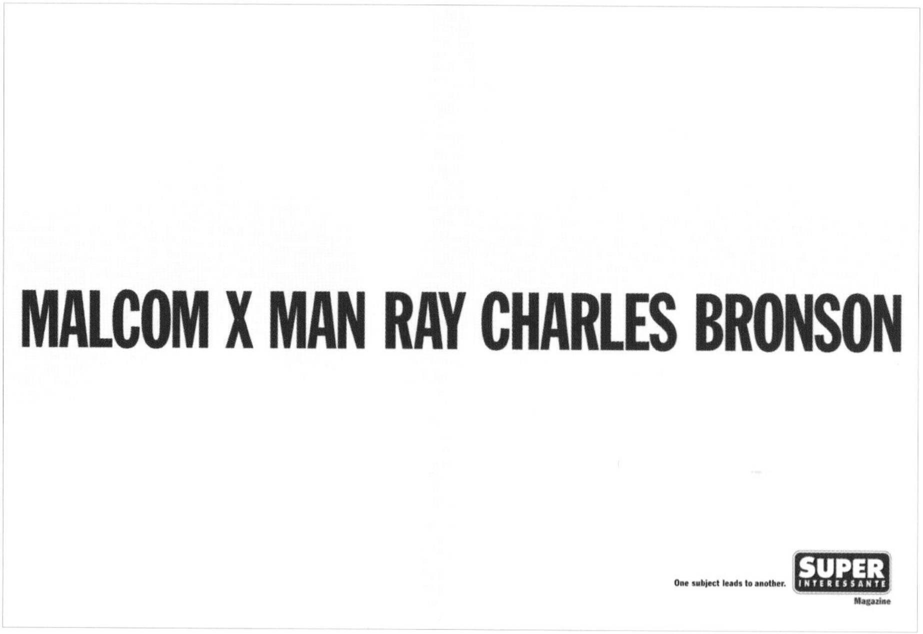
MALCOM X MAN RAY CHARLES BRONSON
One subject leads to another.
SUPER
INTERESSANTE
Magazine

STUART LITTLE RICHARD NIXON
One subject leads to another.
SUPER
INTERESSANTE
Magazine

CrossFox. The first off-road compact from Volkswagen.

CrossFox. The first off-road compact from Volkswagen.

CrossFox. The first off-road compact from Volkswagen.

MERIT

ART DIRECTOR
Julio Andery

WRITER
Andre Faria

ILLUSTRATOR
6B estudio

CREATIVE DIRECTORS
Tales Bahu
Rodrigo de Almeida

CLIENT
Volkswagen

AGENCY
Almap BBDO/
São Paulo

ANNUAL ID
06095A

Merit

ART DIRECTOR
Arnie Presiado

WRITER
Pete Shamon

PHOTOGRAPHER
Smari

CREATIVE DIRECTORS
Ron Lawner
Alan Pafenbach
Dave Weist
Colin Jeffery

CLIENT
Volkswagen

AGENCY
Arnold Worldwide/
Boston

ANNUAL ID
06096A

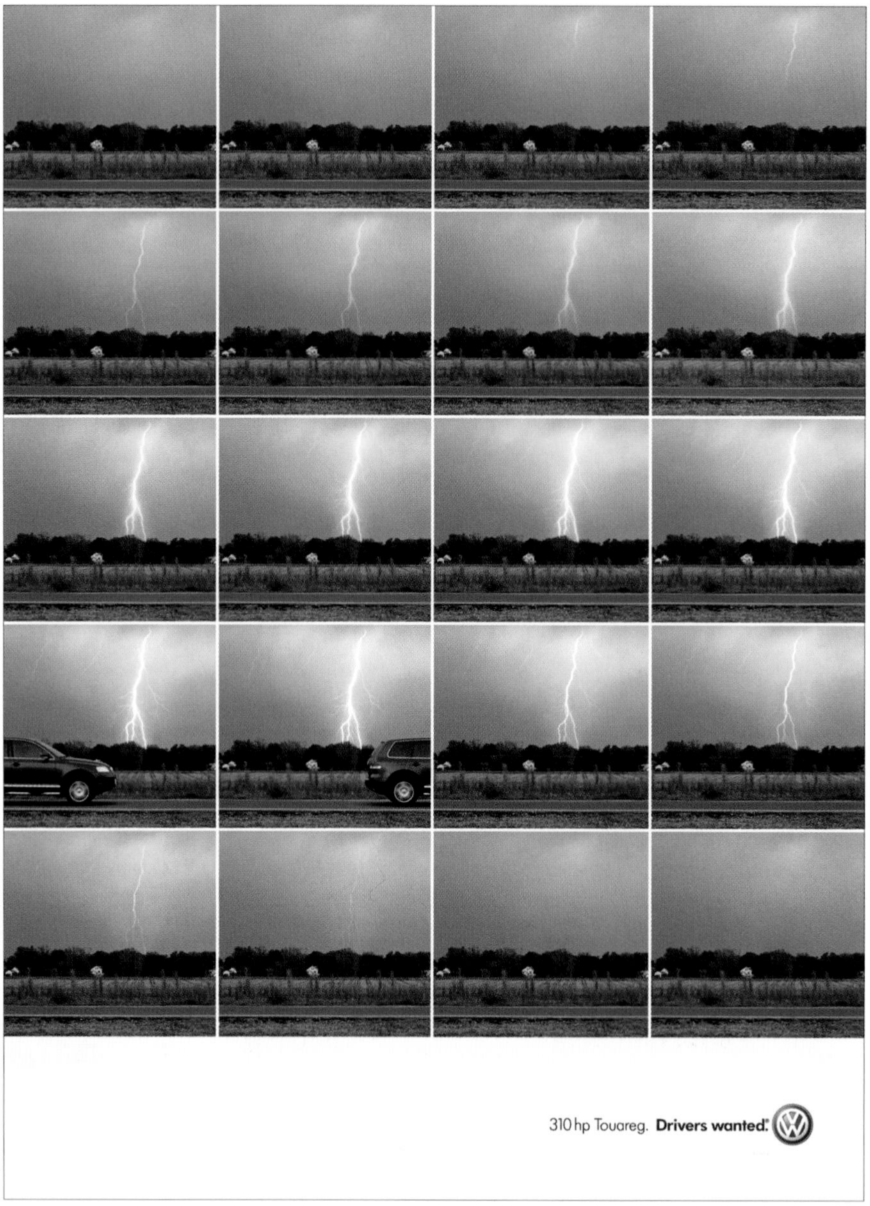
310 hp Touareg. Drivers wanted.

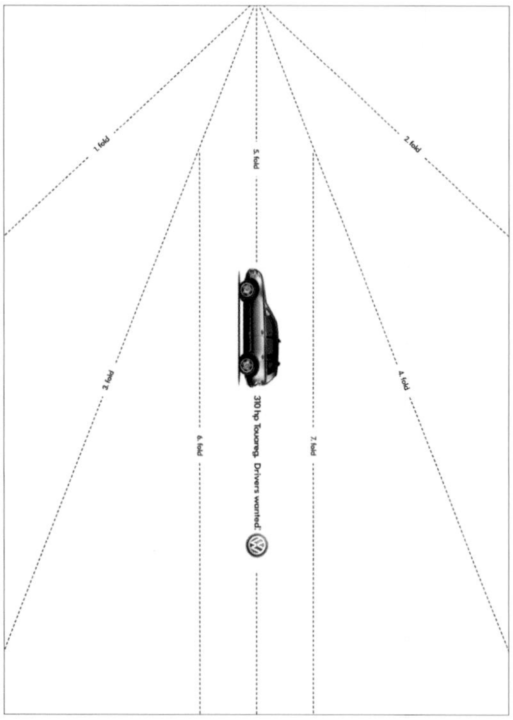
1. fold
2. fold
3. fold
4. fold
5. fold
6. fold
7. fold
310 hp Touareg. Drivers wanted.

Gift Subscription Offer

BUSINESS REPLY MAIL
BUSINESS REPLY MAIL

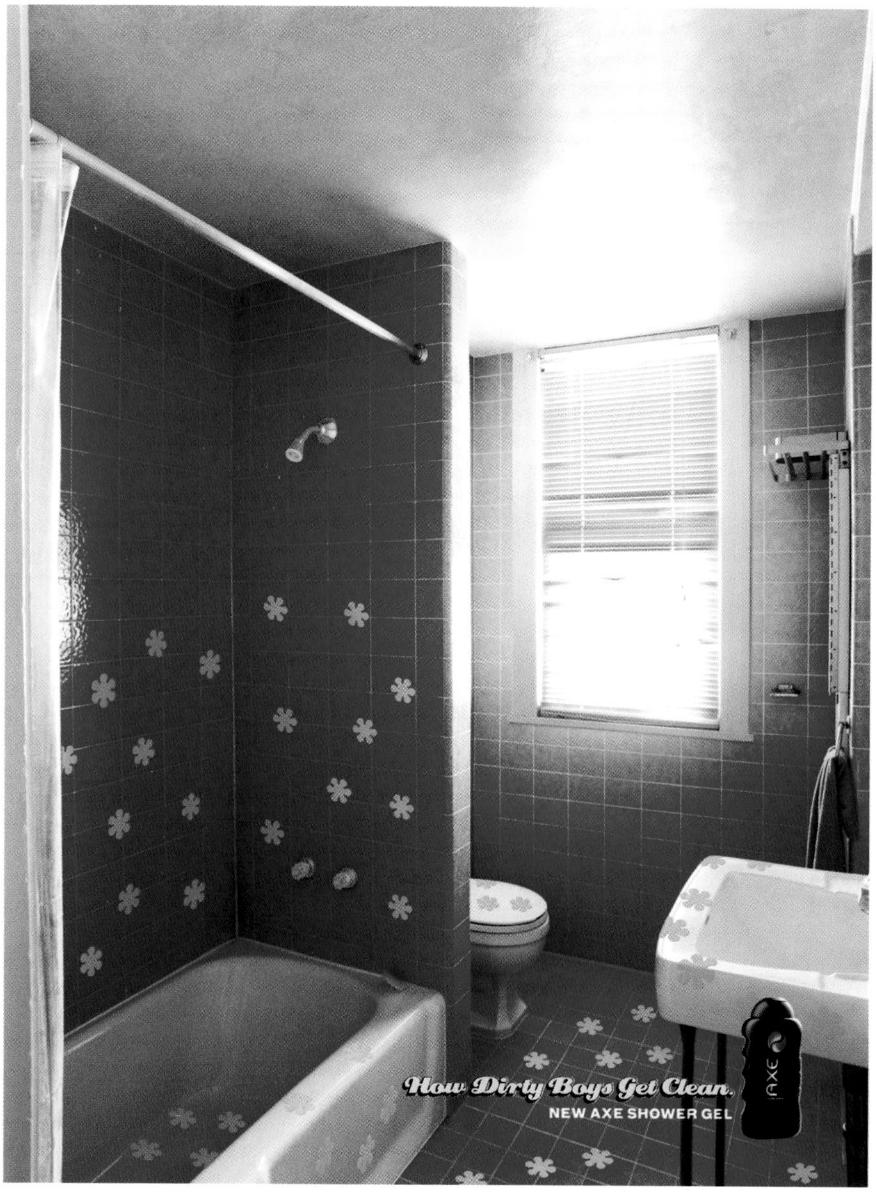
How Dirty Boys Get Clean.
NEW AXE SHOWER GEL
AXE

Merit

ART DIRECTOR
Nick Klinkert

WRITER
Tom Kraemer

PHOTOGRAPHER
Todd Hido

CREATIVE DIRECTOR
William Gelner

CLIENT
Unilever

AGENCY
Bartle Bogle Hegarty/
New York

ANNUAL ID
06097A

How Dirty Boys Get Clean.
NEW AXE SHOWER GEL

His
Hers
Her Sister's
Her Roommate's
How Dirty Boys Get Clean.
NEW AXE SHOWER GEL

MERIT

ART DIRECTOR
Carles Patris

WRITER
Sergi Coulibaly

PHOTOGRAPHER
Josep Roca

CREATIVE DIRECTOR
Ramiro Eduardo

CLIENT
Dinopolis Teruel

AGENCY
Bassat Ogilvy & Mather/Barcelona

ANNUAL ID
06098A

After Dinópolis
any animal
will seem small

After Dinópolis
any animal
will seem small

After Dinópolis
any animal
will seem small

NIKE

Merit

ART DIRECTOR
Sebastien Pierre

WRITER
Jerome Langlade

PHOTOGRAPHER
Ben Stockley

CREATIVE DIRECTORS
Alexandre Herve
Sylvain Thirache

CLIENT
Nike

AGENCY
DDB/Paris

ANNUAL ID
06099A

ALSO AWARDED
Merit:
Outdoor - Campaign

MERIT

ART DIRECTOR
Pierrette Diaz

WRITER
Matthieu Elkaim

PHOTOGRAPHER
Jean Yves Lemoigne

CREATIVE DIRECTORS
Sylvain Thirache
Alexandre Herve

CLIENT
Volkswagen

AGENCY
DDB/Paris

ANNUAL ID
06100A

Danger won't come from the road anymore
LT with ABS, airbags and ESP as standard

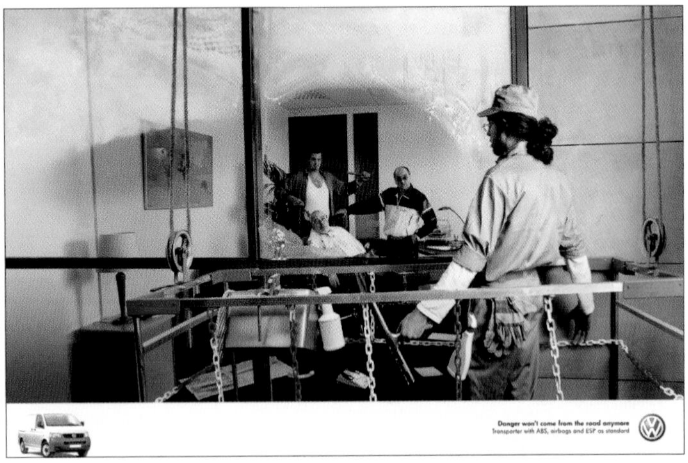
Danger won't come from the road anymore
Transporter with ABS, airbags and ESP as standard

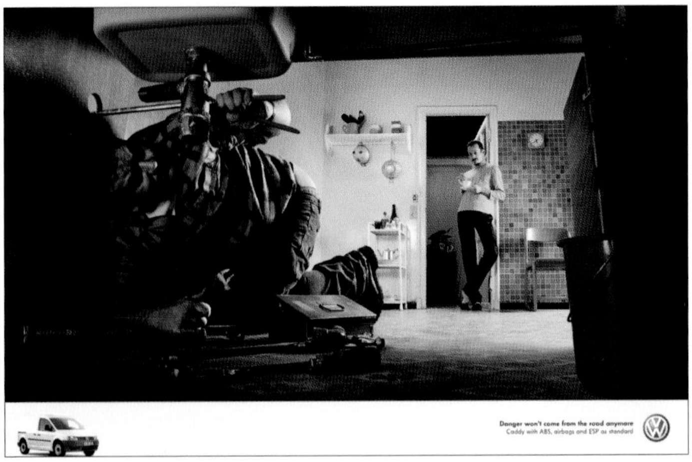
Danger won't come from the road anymore
Caddy with ABS, airbags and ESP as standard

Danger won't come from the road anymore
Transporter with ABS, airbags and ESP as standard

Danger won't come from the road anymore
Caravelle with ABS, airbags and ESP as standard

STOP
Beetle
Life's less serious when you drive the New Beetle.
Engineered inside out

Beetle
POLICE
Life's less serious when you drive the New Beetle.
Engineered inside out

Beetle
Life's less serious when you drive the New Beetle.
Engineered inside out

Merit

ART DIRECTORS
David Seah
Aaron Phua
Ching Hai Pok

WRITERS
Craig Howie
Calvin Soh

PHOTOGRAPHER
Sam Tan

ILLUSTRATORS
Ching Hai Pok
Nelson Yu

CREATIVE DIRECTORS
Calvin Soh
Yang Yeo

CLIENT
Volkswagen

AGENCY
Fallon/Singapore

ANNUAL ID
06101A

Merit

ART DIRECTOR
Eric Sutton

WRITERS
Marc Gallucci
Justin Galvin

ILLUSTRATORS
Peter Fiore
Eric Sutton

CREATIVE DIRECTOR
Marc Gallucci

CLIENT
ESPN

AGENCY
Fort Franklin/Boston

ANNUAL ID
06102A

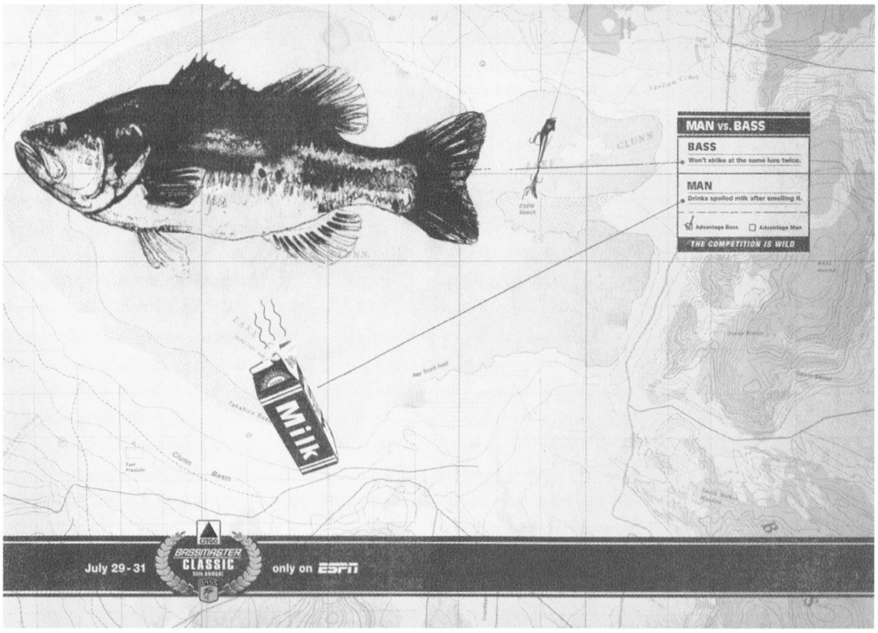
MAN vs. BASS
BASS
Won't strike at the same lure twice.
MAN
Drinks spoiled milk after smelling it.
Advantage Bass
Advantage Man
THE COMPETITION IS WILD
Milk
July 29-31
BASSMASTER CLASSIC
only on ESPN

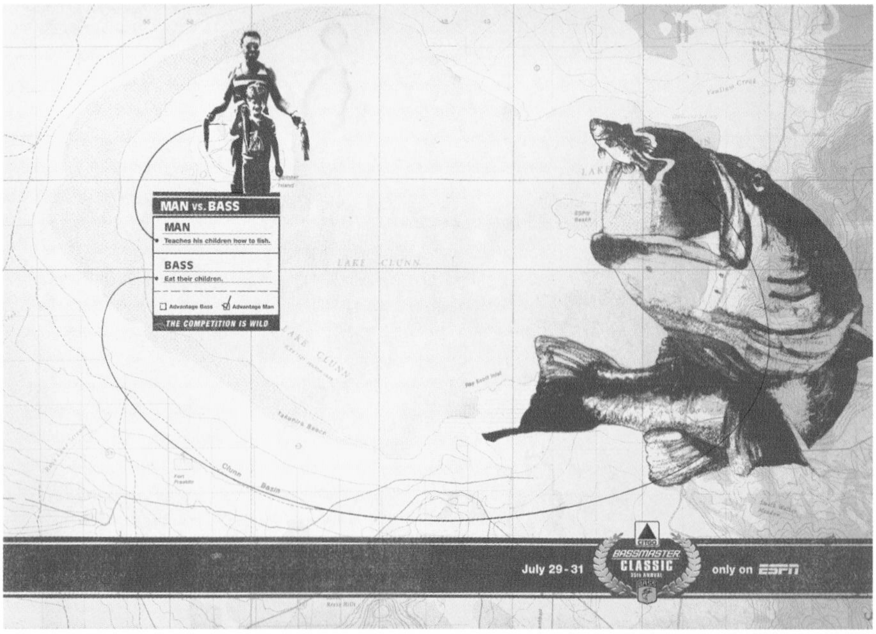
MAN vs. BASS
MAN
Teaches his children how to fish.
BASS
Eat their children.
Advantage Bass
Advantage Man
THE COMPETITION IS WILD
LAKE CLUNN
July 29-31
BASSMASTER CLASSIC
only on ESPN

MAN vs. BASS
BASS
So sensitive they locate & capture minnows by vibration alone.
MAN
Give their wives bowling balls as gifts.
Advantage Bass
Advantage Man
THE COMPETITION IS WILD
July 29-31
BASSMASTER CLASSIC
only on ESPN

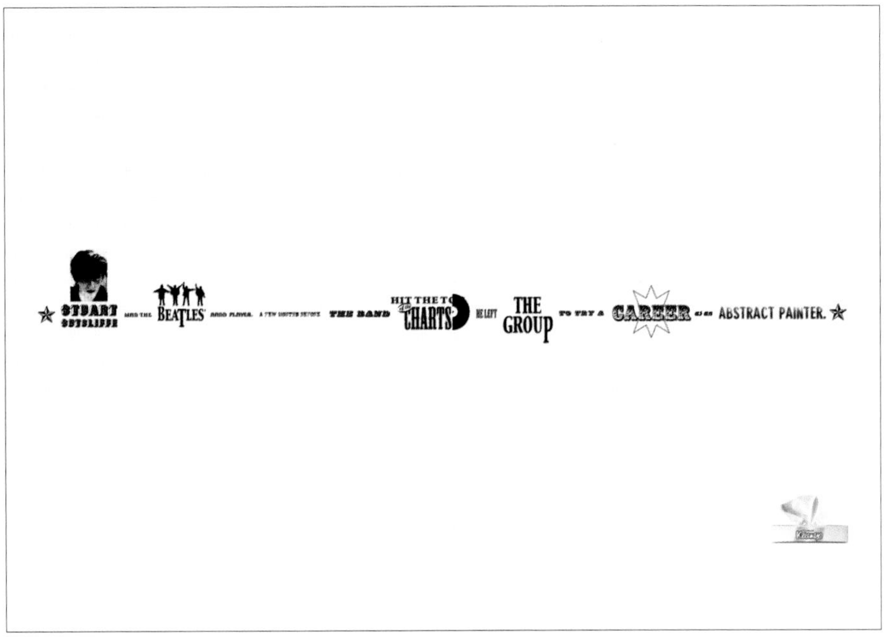
BEATLES
THE BAND
CHARTS
THE GROUP
CAREER
ABSTRACT PAINTER.

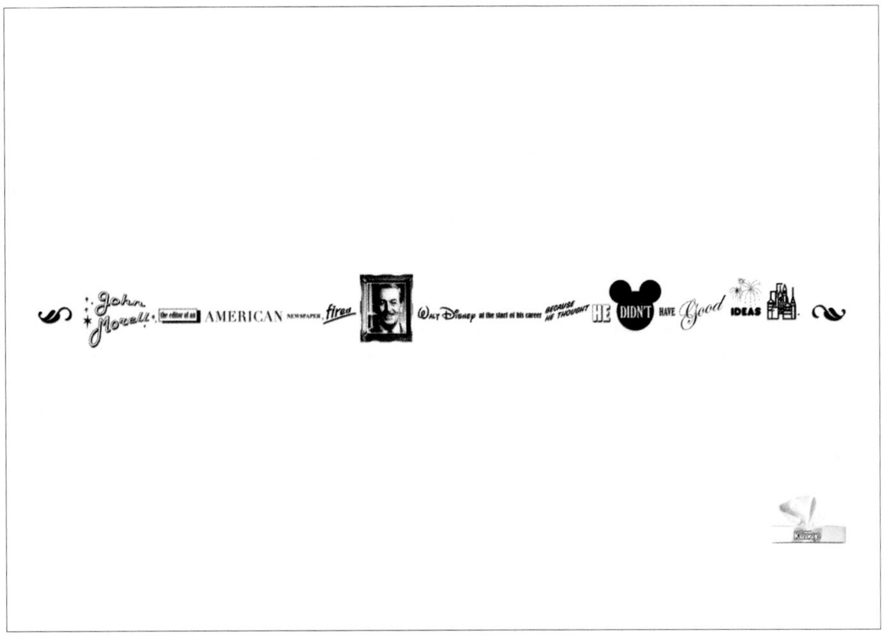
John
Morell
AMERICAN
fired
Walt Disney
HE
DIDN'T
HAVE
Good
IDEAS

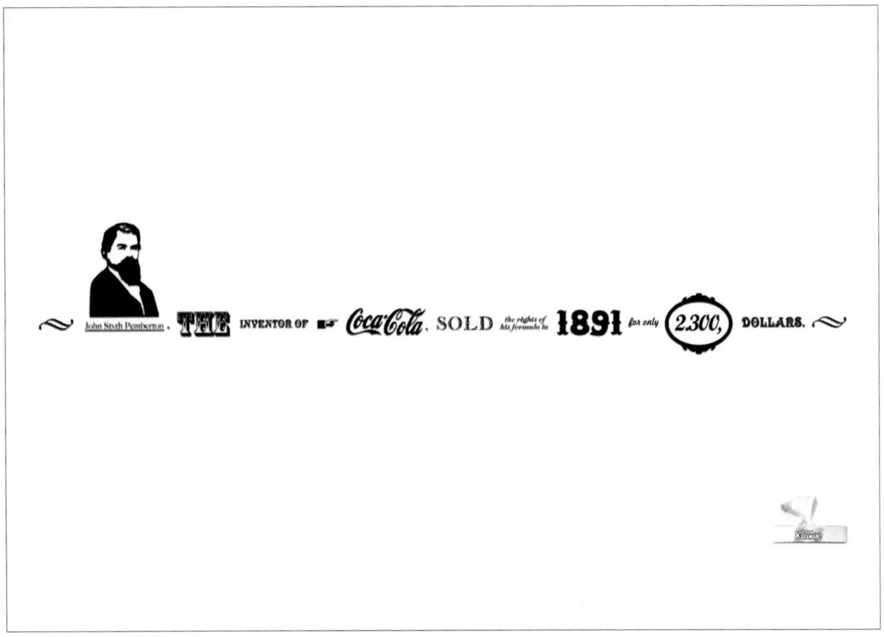
John Stith Pemberton
THE
INVENTOR OF
Coca-Cola
SOLD
1891
for only
2.300,
DOLLARS.

Merit

ART DIRECTOR
Keka Morelle

WRITER
Joao Caetano Brasil

PHOTOGRAPHER
Andre Faccioli

CREATIVE DIRECTORS
Atila Francucci
Alexandre Soares
Fernando Nobre
Joao Linneu

CLIENT
Kimberly-Clark

AGENCY
JWT/São Paulo

ANNUAL ID
06104A

Merit

ART DIRECTOR
Giovanni Settesoldi

WRITER
Luissandro Del Gobbo

PHOTOGRAPHER
Riccardo Bagnoli

ILLUSTRATOR
Claudio Luparelli

CREATIVE DIRECTORS
Pascal Manry
Andrea Stillacci

CLIENT
Reckitt Benckiser O Cedar

AGENCY
JWT/Paris

ANNUAL ID
06105A

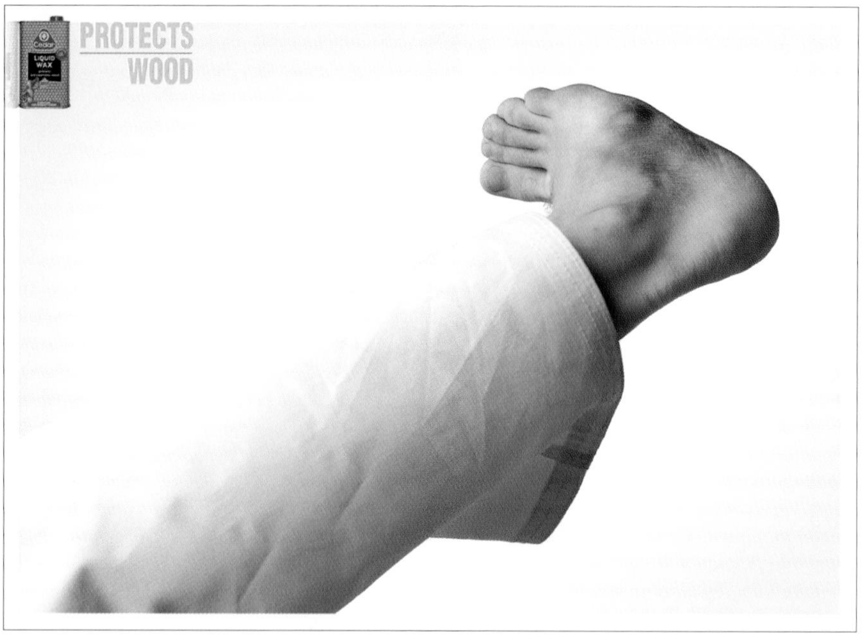
PROTECTS
WOOD
LIQUID
WAX

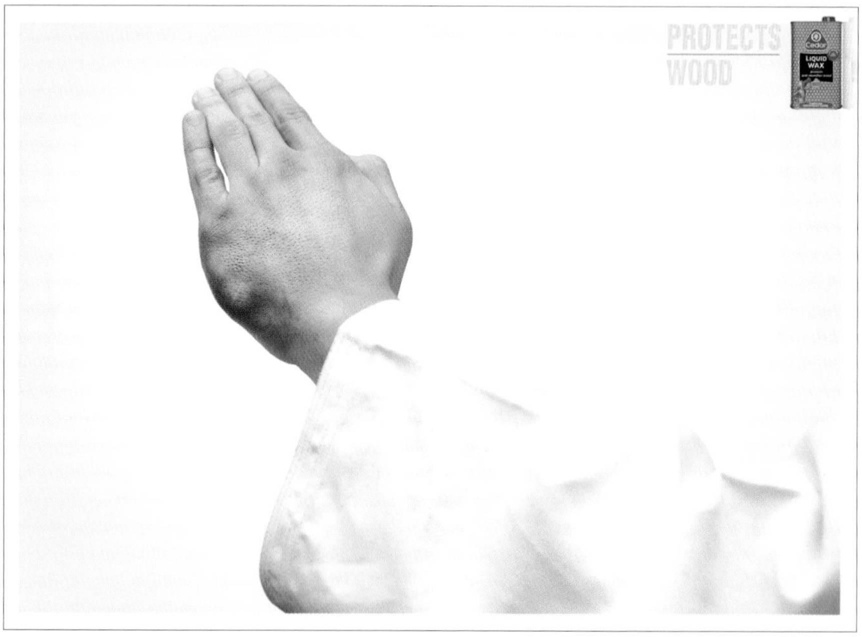
PROTECTS
WOOD
LIQUID
WAX

PROTECTS
WOOD
LIQUID
WAX

Merit

ART DIRECTORS
Jan Blumentritt
Christine Manger

CREATIVE DIRECTORS
Anke Winschewski
Vappu Singer

CLIENT
WMF

AGENCY
KNSK/Hamburg

ANNUAL ID
06106A

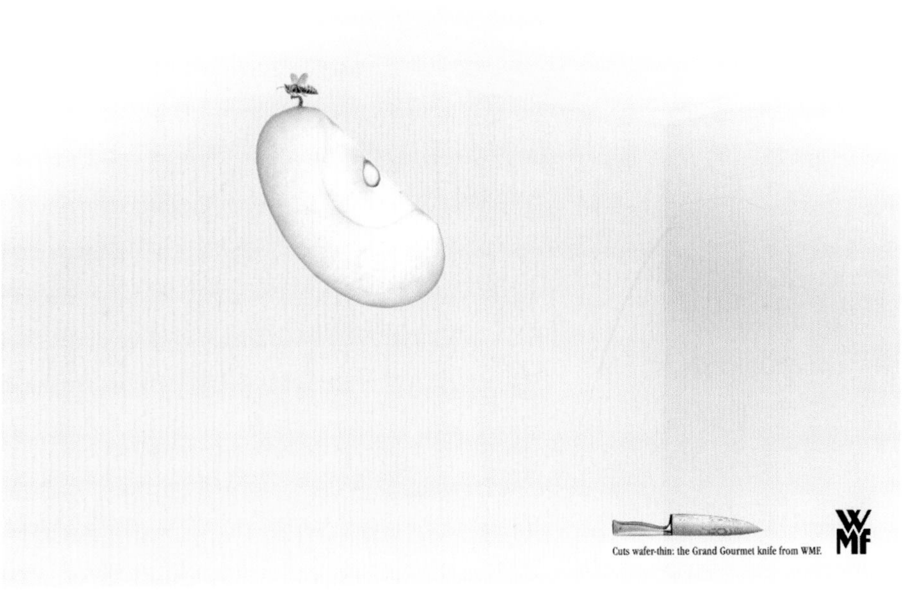
Cuts wafer-thin: the Grand Gourmet knife from WMF.
WMF

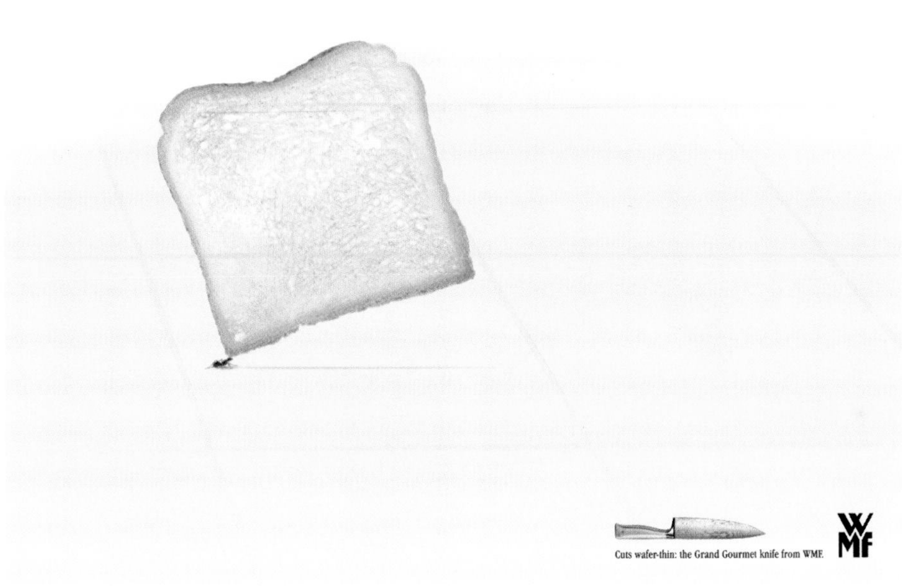
Cuts wafer-thin: the Grand Gourmet knife from WMF.
WMF

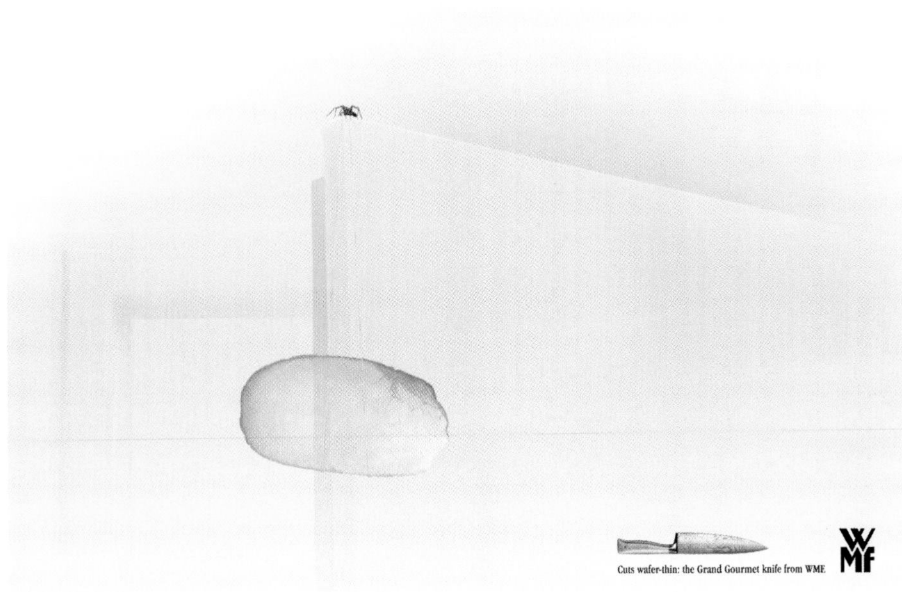
Cuts wafer-thin: the Grand Gourmet knife from WMF.
WMF

Merit

ART DIRECTORS
Alberto Villagrán
Javier Saruwatari

WRITER
Luis Hernández

PHOTOGRAPHER
Manuel Santos

CREATIVE DIRECTOR
Olivier Caizergues

CLIENT
Volvo

AGENCY
Ogilvy & Mather/ Mexico

ANNUAL ID
06107A

ALSO AWARDED
Merit: Consumer Magazine: Color - Single

YOU'LL TAKE SAFETY FOR GRANTED. New Volvo range 2006, now with Active Security.
VOLVO

Merit

YOU'LL TAKE SAFETY FOR GRANTED. New Volvo range 2006, now with Active Security.
VOLVO

YOU'LL TAKE SAFETY FOR GRANTED. New Volvo range 2006, now with Active Security.
VOLVO
for life

Cascade

Cascade

Cascade

Merit

ART DIRECTORS
James Rothwell
Aaron Padin

WRITER
Shawn Gauthier

PHOTOGRAPHER
Kulbir Thandi

CREATIVE DIRECTORS
Tony Granger
Andrew Jeske

CLIENT
Procter & Gamble - Cascade

AGENCY
Saatchi & Saatchi/ New York

ANNUAL ID
06111A

MERIT

ART DIRECTORS
Peter Cohen
Hamish McArthur

WRITER
Jay Taub

CREATIVE DIRECTORS
Tony Granger
Barbara Boyle

CLIENT
Procter & Gamble - Pampers

AGENCY
Saatchi & Saatchi/ New York

ANNUAL ID
06112A

Pppppp pppp....
"Pp! pppp! pp. Pp p pppp, pppp."
"Ppp, Ppppp pppp ppp pppp, ppp!"
Ppp ppppp pppppppp ppp. "Ppppp ppp ppp!"
Pppp ppp ppppppp pppp;
Ppp ppp ppp! Pp pppp ppppp. Pppp pppp.
Pp Ppppp p ppp. "Pp pp pppp pp pppp p pp?"
Pppp. Ppppp pppp. Pppp ppp. Ppppp.
Pppp ppp ppppp ppp pp.
"Pp! pppp! pp. Pp p pppp, pppp."
Pppp ppp ppppp ppp pp.
Pampers
It's hard to concentrate on a good book with a wet diaper on your mind.

Pppppp pppp....
"Pp! pppp! pp. Pp p pppp, pppp."
Ppp pppppp pppppppp ppp.
"Ppp, Ppppp ppppp ppp ppppp, pppp, ppp!"
Ppp ppppppp ppp ppppp.
"Pppp, ppp, ppp!"
Pppp ppp pppppppp pp p pppp,
Pp Ppppp p ppp."Pp pp pppp pp ppppppp
p pp?" Ppppp Ppppp pppp...
"Ppp, Ppppp ppppp ppp ppppp,
pppp, ppp!"
Ppp ppppppp ppp ppppp.
Pampers
It's hard to concentrate on a good book with a wet diaper on your mind.

GET TO KNOW THE WILD
GOLITE

GET TO KNOW THE WILD
GOLITE

GET TO KNOW THE WILD
GOLITE

MERIT

ART DIRECTOR
Richard Copping

WRITER
Jagdish Ramakrishnan

PHOTOGRAPHER
Getty Images

CREATIVE DIRECTOR
Andy Greenaway

CLIENT
Golite

AGENCY
Saatchi & Saatchi/ Singapore

ANNUAL ID
06109A

ALSO AWARDED
Merit:
Collateral: Posters - Campaign

Merit

ART DIRECTOR
Aaron Tan

WRITER
Aaron Tan

PHOTOGRAPHER
Nicholas Leong @ Reservoir

CREATIVE DIRECTOR
Andy Greenaway

CLIENT
Hasbro

AGENCY
Saatchi & Saatchi/ Singapore

ANNUAL ID
06110A

ALSO AWARDED
Merit: Collateral: Posters - Campaign

Jenga
ARE YOU A PLAYER?

Jenga
ARE YOU A PLAYER?

Jenga
ARE YOU A PLAYER?

EPHYDROL. FOR DEADLY FOOT ODOR.

EPHYDROL. FOR DEADLY FOOT ODOR.

EPHYDROL. GETS RID OF DEADLY FOOT ODOR.

MERIT

ART DIRECTORS
Jessica Gerard-Huet
Javier Rodriguez

WRITER
Jean-Franois Bouchet

PHOTOGRAPHER
Cindy Gravelat

CREATIVE DIRECTOR
Erik Vervroegen

CLIENT
Ephydrol

AGENCY
TBWA/Paris

ANNUAL ID
06113A

MERIT

ART DIRECTOR
Mark Bamfield

WRITER
Rob Kleman

PHOTOGRAPHER
Groovy Studio

CREATIVE DIRECTOR
Mark Bamfield

CLIENT
Sphere

AGENCY
Batey/Singapore

ANNUAL ID
06116A

THE STRAITS TIMES THURSDAY FEBRUARY 3, 2005
US soldier in kidnap photo may be a GI Joe doll
BAGHDAD
A MILITANT group's claim that it has kidnapped a US soldier in Iraq and plans to behead him is suspected of being a hoax.
A California toy manufacturer says photos of the purported captive on an insurgent website appear to show one of its collectible dolls.
A group calling itself the Mujahedeen Brigades had posted a photograph that appeared to show a stern-faced US soldier sitting at gunpoint before a black banner with Arabic script. The posting called the soldier "John Adam".
The US military authorities said aspects of the photograph raised doubts.
The soldier's vest, for instance, resembled no such apparel issued by the army, and the claim on the website about the kidnapping appeared to contain misspellings.
Nevertheless, they asked for a full accounting of military personnel in Iraq.
"No units have reported anyone missing," Staff Sergeant Nick Minecci of the military's press office in Baghdad told Associated Press.
An executive for Dragon Models USA said the soldier looked exactly like a 30cm-tall GI Joe-type doll which the company manufactures for sale at US bases in Kuwait.
Los Angeles Times
SPHERE 1/6th ACTION FIGURES.
AS REAL AS IT GETS.
WWW.SPHEREMARKETING.NET

ARIEL

Merit

ART DIRECTOR
Sharmad Khambekar

WRITER
Sharmad Khambekar

PHOTOGRAPHER
Saish Kambli

CREATIVE DIRECTORS
Juju Basu
Hanoz Mogrelia

CLIENT
Procter & Gamble

AGENCY
Saatchi & Saatchi/
Mumbai

ANNUAL ID
06119A

MERIT

ART DIRECTOR
Stuart Harricks

CREATIVE DIRECTOR
Andy Greenaway

WRITER
Stuart Harricks

PHOTOGRAPHER
Sam @ Boomerang

CLIENT
Lego

AGENCY
*Saatchi & Saatchi/
Singapore*

ANNUAL ID
06120A

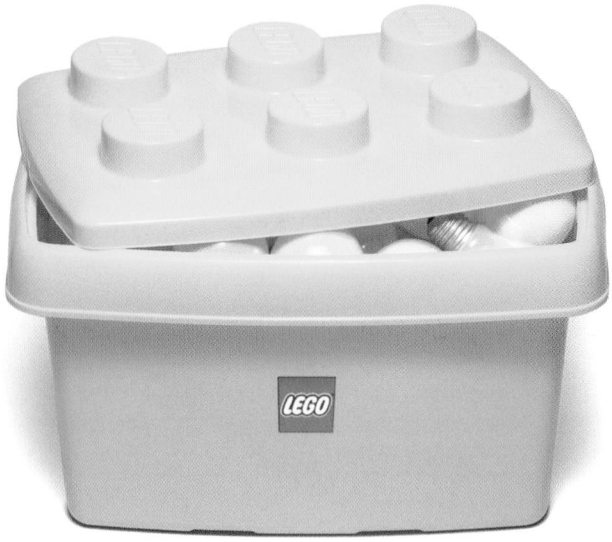
LEGO

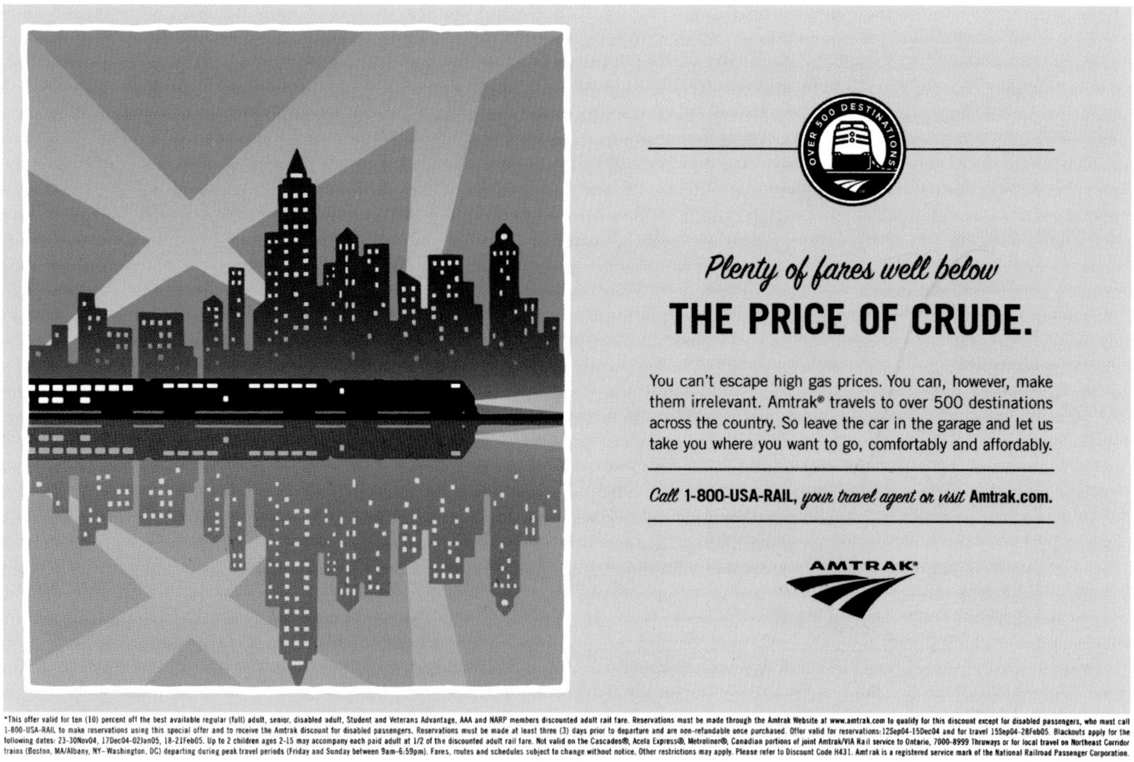
OVER 500 DESTINATIONS
Plenty of fares well below
THE PRICE OF CRUDE.
You can't escape high gas prices. You can, however, make them irrelevant. Amtrak® travels to over 500 destinations across the country. So leave the car in the garage and let us take you where you want to go, comfortably and affordably.
Call 1-800-USA-RAIL, your travel agent or visit Amtrak.com.
AMTRAK®
*This offer valid for ten (10) percent off the best available regular (full) adult, senior, disabled adult, Student and Veterans Advantage, AAA and NARP members discounted adult rail fare. Reservations must be made through the Amtrak Website at www.amtrak.com to qualify for this discount except for disabled passengers, who must call 1-800-USA-RAIL to make reservations using this special offer and to receive the Amtrak discount for disabled passengers. Reservations must be made at least three (3) days prior to departure and are non-refundable once purchased. Offer valid for reservations: 12Sep04-15Dec04 and for travel 15Sep04-28Feb05. Blackouts apply for the following dates: 23-30Nov04, 17Dec04-02Jan05, 18-21Feb05. Up to 2 children ages 2-15 may accompany each paid adult at 1/2 of the discounted adult rail fare. Not valid on the Cascades®, Acela Express®, Metroliner®, Canadian portions of joint Amtrak/VIA Rail service to Ontario, 7000-8999 Thruways or for local travel on Northeast Corridor trains (Boston, MA/Albany, NY–Washington, DC) departing during peak travel periods (Friday and Sunday between 9am-6:59pm). Fares, routes and schedules subject to change without notice. Other restrictions may apply. Please refer to Discount Code H431. Amtrak is a registered service mark of the National Railroad Passenger Corporation.

MERIT

ART DIRECTOR
Sissy Estes

WRITER
Mick Sutter

ILLUSTRATOR
Michael Schwab

CREATIVE DIRECTORS
Ron Lawner
Woody Kay
Fred Burgos

CLIENT
Amtrak

AGENCY
Arnold/McLean

ANNUAL ID
06122A

OVER 500 DESTINATIONS
The
ROAD LESS TRAVELED
isn't a road at all.
Amtrak® serves the big cities you know, plus hundreds of smaller towns you might not. So come aboard and explore. America has some great hidden treasures. And there's no better introduction to them than through the window of a train.
Call 1-800-USA-RAIL, your travel agent or visit Amtrak.com.
AMTRAK®

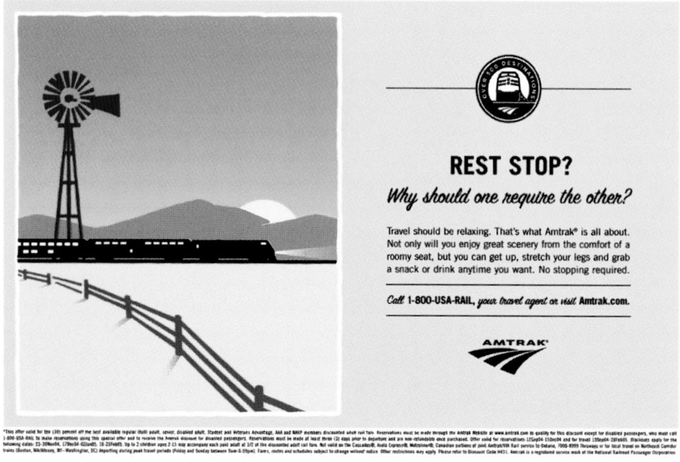
OVER 500 DESTINATIONS
REST STOP?
Why should one require the other?
Travel should be relaxing. That's what Amtrak® is all about. Not only will you enjoy great scenery from the comfort of a roomy seat, but you can get up, stretch your legs and grab a snack or drink anytime you want. No stopping required.
Call 1-800-USA-RAIL, your travel agent or visit Amtrak.com.
AMTRAK®

OVER 500 DESTINATIONS
Stop the world,
I WANT TO GET ON.
On Amtrak® you can watch the country unfold from your roomy seat, or get a better view in the Sightseer Lounge. Dining Car and sleeping accommodations are available on most trains, too. So come aboard. The world is waiting.
Call 1-800-USA-RAIL, your travel agent or visit Amtrak.com.
AMTRAK®

Merit

ART DIRECTORS
Hannah Ford
Simon Horton

WRITERS
Hannah Ford
Simon Horton

PHOTOGRAPHER
Adam Hinton

CREATIVE DIRECTOR
Nick Bell

CLIENT
Trader Media - Autotrader

AGENCY
JWT/London

ANNUAL ID
06123A

ALSO AWARDED
Merit: Small Space - Print: Color: Less than a Page - Single

Merit: Small Space - Print: Color: Less than a Page - Single

VW POLO
2004, 15,000 miles, 5 door hatchback, handles superbly except when owner was driving home from pub and hit a pedestrian who died a week later from internal bleeding.
DON'T DRINK AND DRIVE. AUTOTRADER.
Private
128555/1103/1/1103
£3,500

SEAT LEON
2004, green re-spray was the last thing a mother of three saw before being knocked down and killed by a driver who had drunk two pints of cider after work
DON'T DRINK AND DRIVE. AUTOTRADER.
Private
128555/1103/1/1103
£4,895

Merit

VAUXHALL ASTRA 1.7D TURBO
ABS, power steering and driver's airbag. But nothing to stop passenger hurtling through windscreen after driver had spent a couple of hours in pub.
DON'T DRINK AND DRIVE. AUTOTRADER.
Private
128555/1103/1/1103
£3,995

Merit

HONDA CIVIC
2001, full MOT, driven 40,000 miles by driver who drank a pint and a half before hitting girl cycling home and killing her.
DON'T DRINK AND DRIVE. AUTOTRADER.
Private
128555/1103/1/1103
£3,150

FORD FIESTA 1.25 ZETEC
60,000 miles, central locking, new alloys, new RADIO/CD changer, all a complete write-off after the young driver had a few cocktails, drove into lamppost and killed herself outright.
DON'T DRINK AND DRIVE. AUTOTRADER.
Private
128555/1103/1/1103
£1,750

HONDA CIVIC
2002, 30,000 miles, 1 lady owner who, after a few sherries, knocked down and killed a boy playing outside his home.
DON'T DRINK AND DRIVE. AUTOTRADER.
Private
128555/1103/1/1103
£5,200

VOLVO ESTATE AUTO 2.0
1996, 88,000 miles, metallic green, one owner gaoled for fourteen years for killing girl after enjoying a few G&Ts with friends.
DON'T DRINK AND DRIVE. AUTOTRADER.
Private
128555/1103/1/1103
£2,400

WEEK
09
2005 SEASON
FOLLOW THE SEASON PLAY-BY-PLAY. GAME-BY-GAME.
EX-GIRLFRIEND-BY-EX-GIRLFRIEND.
XM SATELLITE RADIO

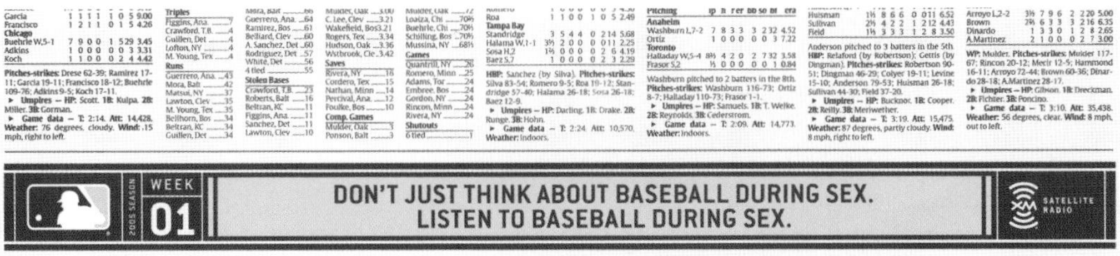
WEEK
01
2005 SEASON
DON'T JUST THINK ABOUT BASEBALL DURING SEX.
LISTEN TO BASEBALL DURING SEX.
XM SATELLITE RADIO

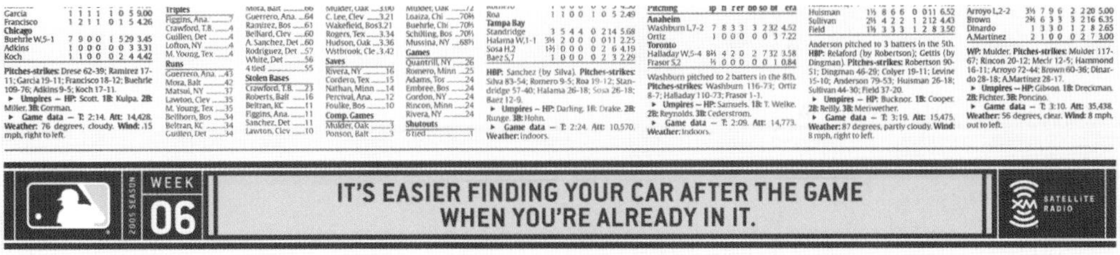
WEEK
06
2005 SEASON
IT'S EASIER FINDING YOUR CAR AFTER THE GAME
WHEN YOU'RE ALREADY IN IT.
XM SATELLITE RADIO

MERIT

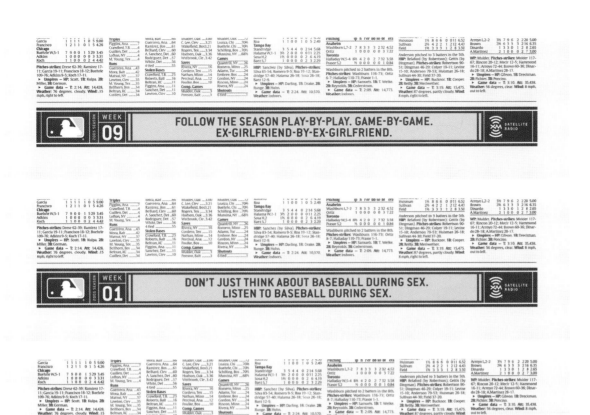

ART DIRECTOR
Mike Shaughnessy

WRITERS
Jeff Baxter
Bruno Corbo

CREATIVE DIRECTORS
Edward Boches
Michael Ancevic
Tim Cawley

CLIENT
XM Satellite Radio

AGENCY
Mullen/Wenham

ANNUAL ID
06124A

Merit

ART DIRECTOR
Cody Spinadel

WRITER
John Mahoney

CREATIVE DIRECTOR
Cliff Sorah

CLIENT
CBS

AGENCY
The Martin Agency/ Richmond

ANNUAL ID
06125A

ALSO AWARDED
Merit: Small Space - Print: Color: Less than a Page - Single

Nutrition Facts
Per 3 oz. (84g)
Amount
% Daily Value
Calories 45
Fat 2g 5%
Saturated Fat 0g
Cholesterol 10mg 4%
Sodium 14mg 7%
Carbohydrate 0g 0%
Fiber 0g 0%
Sugar 0g
Protein 9g 12%
Vitamin A 2% Vitamin C 0%
Calcium 0% Iron 2%
Survivor
Thursday Nights at 8:00 et/pt

Merit

Nutrition Facts
Survivor

Nutrition Facts
Survivor

★ ★ ★
COMES IN SIZES FROM
SMALL TO "HONEY DON'T POINT AT THE FAT MAN."
the ONION
America's Finest News Source.
★ Get your official Onion gear at store.theonion.com ★

MERIT

ART DIRECTOR
Kevin Thoem

WRITER
Sara Grunden

CREATIVE DIRECTORS
Mike Hughes
Mike Lear

CLIENT
The Onion

AGENCY
The Martin Agency/
Richmond

ANNUAL ID
06127A

MERIT

ART DIRECTORS
Sissy Estes
Jules Vangelder

WRITER
Mick Sutter

CREATIVE DIRECTORS
Woody Kay
Ron Lawner

CLIENT
Colonial Williamsburg

AGENCY
Arnold/McLean

ANNUAL ID
06128A

"I CONVICTED A WITCH."

And other unorthodox replies to "What did you do this weekend?"

Flee the mall and multiplex for a weekend experience like no other with the Colonial Escape Package from Colonial Williamsburg. Immerse yourself in 18th-century life through interactive programs and exhibits, or be contented strolling the lush formal gardens and unique shops. Accommodations in a Colonial Williamsburg hotel, daily breakfast, and admission to the Historic Area for the length of your stay are included. For reservations, call 1-800-684-6346 today.

COLONIAL ESCAPE PACKAGE

from $60* *per person, per night*

*Rate based on a double-occupancy stay at the Governor's Inn. Pricing varies for other Colonial Williamsburg hotels.

Grace Sherwood

WIDOW OR WITCH? Grace Sherwood stands accused of the black arts in the re-creation of this real-life trial. You are the jury. Will 18th-century evidence send her to the gallows? Or will 21st-century wisdom prevail? "Cry Witch" is but one of Colonial Williamsburg's riveting evening programs to attend.

AMERICA. CHAPTER I.

Colonial Williamsburg

WILLIAMSBURG, VIRGINIA 1-800-684-6346 COLONIALWILLIAMSBURG.COM

Children Admitted Free WITH *PARENT, GUARDIAN, OR* FOREFATHER.

Mr. Young and Mr. Old

Nothing sparks the imagination of a child like a Colonial Williamsburg vacation. Here kids serve on juries, learn trades, join the militia, and help manage farms and households all as it was in the 18th century. Then there are the stage plays, fife and drum marches, carriage rides, and talks with the Founding Fathers they can take part in. And, with all the fun they're having, your kids probably won't realize they're learning a lot, too.

KIDS UNDER 18 FREE ALL SUMMER

Free lodging and admission to the Historic Area when staying at an official Colonial Williamsburg hotel.

NOW THROUGH LABOR DAY, when you stay at one of the five Colonial Williamsburg hotels, children under 18 stay free and get free admission to the Historic Area with a paying adult. Some restrictions may apply. To book your reservation today, call 1-800-261-0182.

AMERICA. CHAPTER I.

Colonial Williamsburg

WILLIAMSBURG, VIRGINIA 1-800-261-0182 COLONIALWILLIAMSBURG.COM

RATES SO LOW *they're almost* *HISTORICALLY* ACCURATE.

Mr. Thrifty

September is a wonderful time for a Colonial Williamsburg visit. Attend a colonial performance. Enjoy a hearty tavern meal. Stroll the palace grounds or browse the shops on Duke of Gloucester Street. Rates at Colonial Williamsburg hotels are the lowest they'll be all year, starting at just $34.50 per person, per night. Kids under 18 stay free and get free admission to the Historic Area with a paying adult, too. To make reservations or for more information, call 1-800-684-6346. Hurry, offer ends September 30th.

SEPTEMBER SPECIAL

from $34.50* *per person, per night*

I. Nightly hotel accommodations
II. Kids under 18 stay free with paying adult
III. Kids under 18 get free admission to the Historic Area with paying adult
IV. Discounted admission to Historic Area for adults
V. Daily continental breakfast
VI. Free bicycle rentals
VII. Free miniature golf
VIII. Preferred dining reservations

*Some restrictions may apply. Based on availability. Rate based on a double-occupancy stay, Sunday - Thursday at the Governor's Inn. Pricing varies for other Colonial Williamsburg hotels. Offer valid on stays 9/1/04 to 9/30/04.

AMERICA. CHAPTER I.

Colonial Williamsburg

WILLIAMSBURG, VIRGINIA 1-800-684-6346 COLONIALWILLIAMSBURG.COM

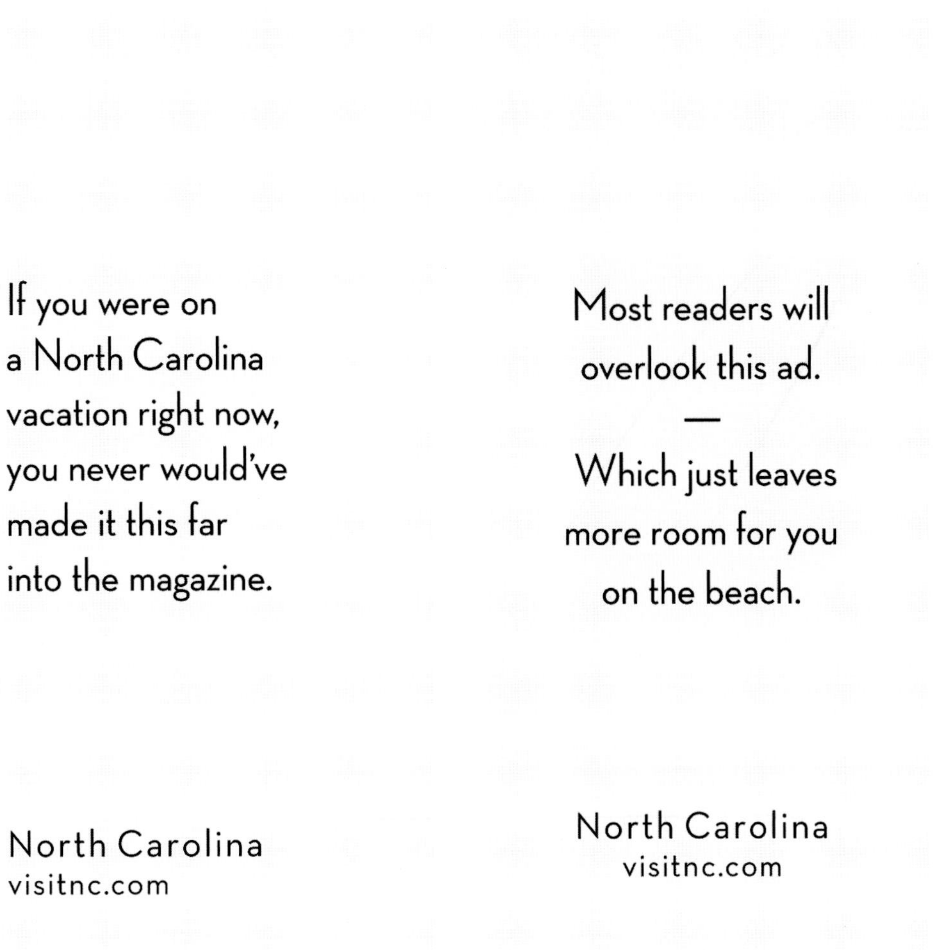
If you were on
a North Carolina
vacation right now,
you never would've
made it this far
into the magazine.
North Carolina
visitnc.com
Most readers will
overlook this ad.
—
Which just leaves
more room for you
on the beach.
North Carolina
visitnc.com

Merit

We're not
anxious to draw
big crowds.
North Carolina

MERIT

ART DIRECTOR
Doug Pedersen

WRITER
Lee Remias

CREATIVE DIRECTOR
Jim Mountjoy

CLIENT
North Carolina Travel & Tourism

AGENCY
LKM/Charlotte

ANNUAL ID
06129A

ALSO AWARDED
Merit
Small Space: Black and White - Single

MERIT

ART DIRECTORS
Naz Nazli
Gareth Hare

WRITERS
Naz Nazli
Gareth Hare

PHOTOGRAPHER
Partice deVilliers

CREATIVE DIRECTORS
Jim Thornton
Mark Tutssel
Dave Beverley

CLIENT
Kellogg's - All Bran

AGENCY
Leo Burnett/London

ANNUAL ID
06130A

ALSO AWARDED
Merit:
Consumer Newspaper:
Over 600 Lines - Single

Kellogg's
ALL-BRAN
ORIGINAL
Helps you feel good on the inside

MERIT

WRITER
Dirk Wilkesmann

CREATIVE DIRECTORS
Knut Burgdorf
Kai Roffen

CLIENT
Renault Nissan

AGENCY
TBWA/Berlin

ANNUAL ID
06131A

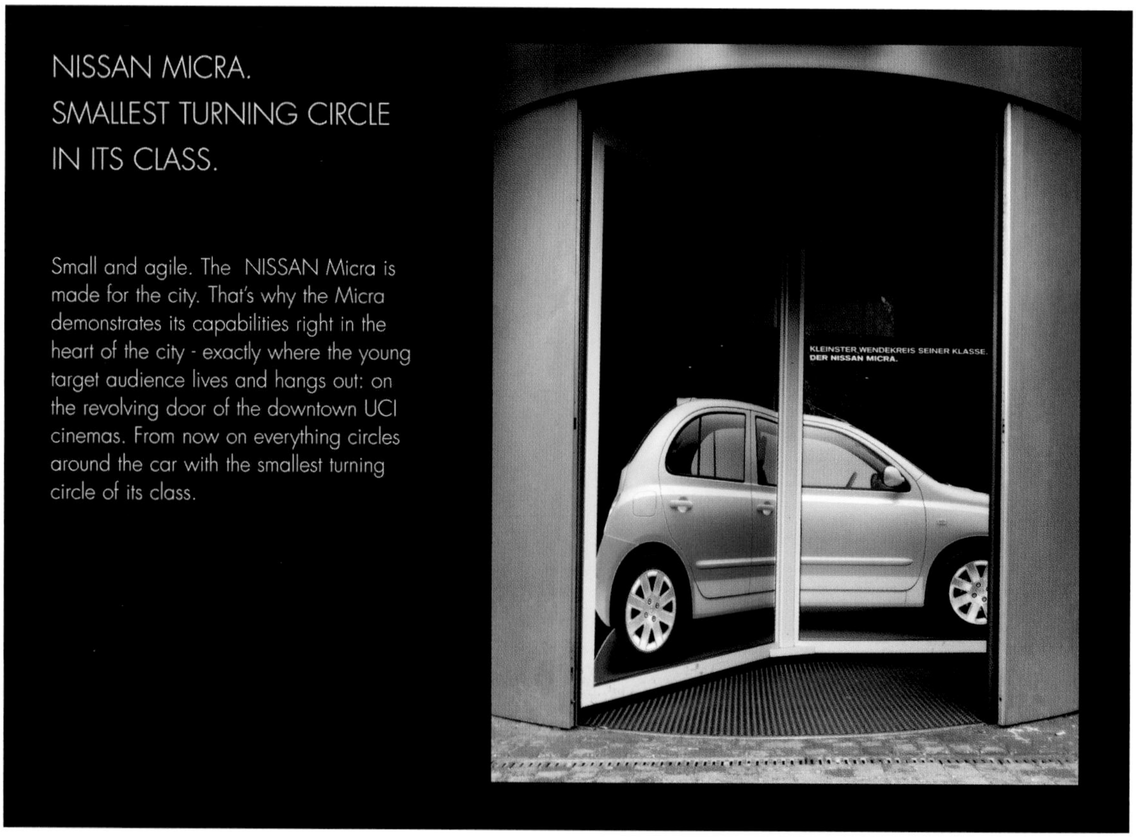
NISSAN MICRA.
SMALLEST TURNING CIRCLE
IN ITS CLASS.
Small and agile. The NISSAN Micra is made for the city. That's why the Micra demonstrates its capabilities right in the heart of the city - exactly where the young target audience lives and hangs out: on the revolving door of the downtown UCI cinemas. From now on everything circles around the car with the smallest turning circle of its class.
KLEINSTER WENDEKREIS SEINER KLASSE.
DER NISSAN MICRA.

reinforced steel structure in the whole range
smart

reinforced steel structure in the whole range
smart

reinforced steel structure in the whole range
smart

MERIT

ART DIRECTOR
Leandro Cacioli

WRITER
Mikel Etxeberria

CREATIVE DIRECTORS
Jose Ma Cornejo
Fernando Galindo
Mikel Etxeberria
Antonio Montero

CLIENT
Mercedes Benz - Smart

AGENCY
Contrapunto/Madrid

ANNUAL ID
06132A

Merit

ART DIRECTOR
Al Davis

WRITER
Jez Willy

DESIGNER
Iain Richardson

PHOTOGRAPHER
Steen Sundland

CREATIVE DIRECTORS
Richard Flintham
Andy McLeod

CLIENT
Sony

AGENCY
Fallon/London

ANNUAL ID
06134A

SONY
50 hour battery life
The 1GB WALKMAN. Seriously long lasting.
CONNECT
like.no.other™
www.connect-europe.com
WALKMAN
'Sony', 'WALKMAN', 'Connect' and 'like.no.other' are trademarks of Sony Corporation Japan. Respect copyright. Copying of copyright material (other than for your own personal, non-business use) is unlawful unless authorised in advance by the copyright owners.
www.sony.co.uk/walkman

SONY
40 hour battery life
The 20GB WALKMAN. Seriously long lasting.
CONNECT
like.no.other
WALKMAN
www.sony.co.uk/walkman

40 hour battery life
The 20GB WALKMAN. Seriously long lasting.
CONNECT
like.no.other
WALKMAN
www.sony.co.uk/walkman

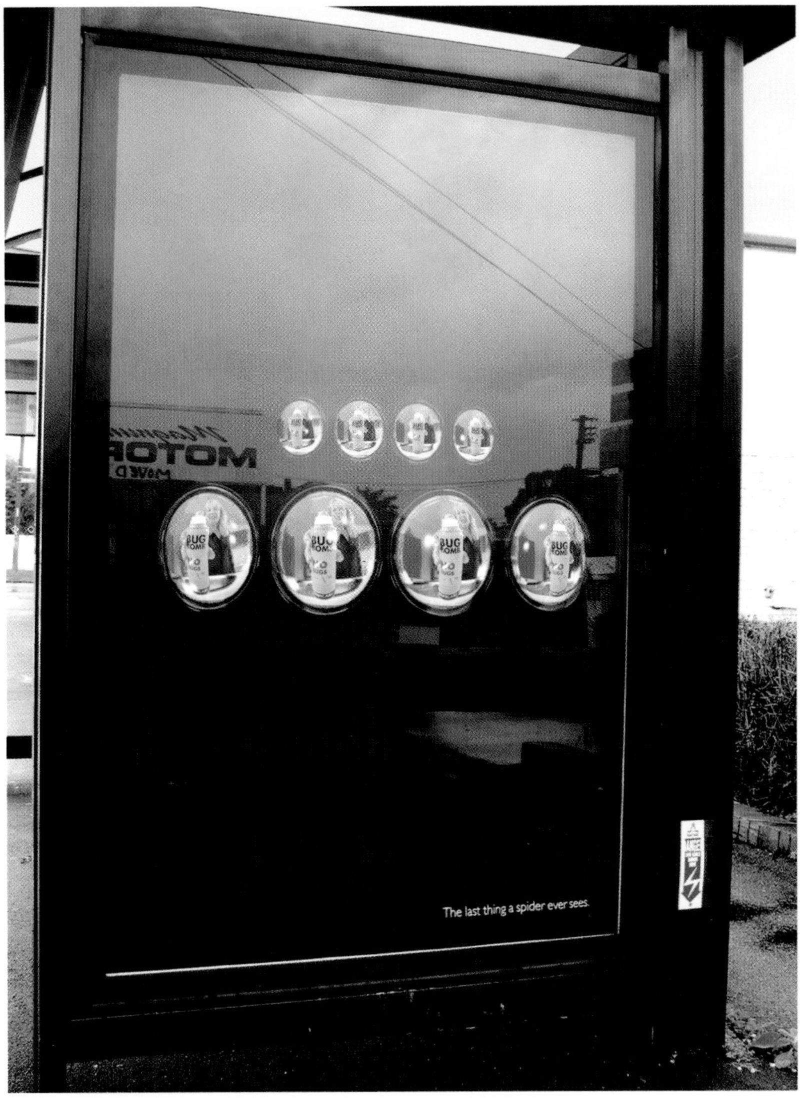
The last thing a spider ever sees.

MERIT

ART DIRECTORS
Todd McCracken
Joe Harris

WRITER
Noah Marshall

PHOTOGRAPHER
Paul Jones

CREATIVE DIRECTOR
Todd McCracken

CLIENT
Kiwicare

AGENCY
Grey Worldwide/ Auckland

ANNUAL ID
06135A

The last thing a fly ever sees.

The last thing a mosquito ever sees.

Merit

ART DIRECTOR
Christian Bobst

WRITERS
Jan Harbeck
Mirko Stolz

ILLUSTRATORS
Fra Angelico
Limburg Brothers
Paul Roberts

CREATIVE DIRECTORS
Burkhart von Scheven
Stephan Ganser

CLIENT
Figueroa Brothers

AGENCY
Jung von Matt/Berlin

ANNUAL ID
06136A

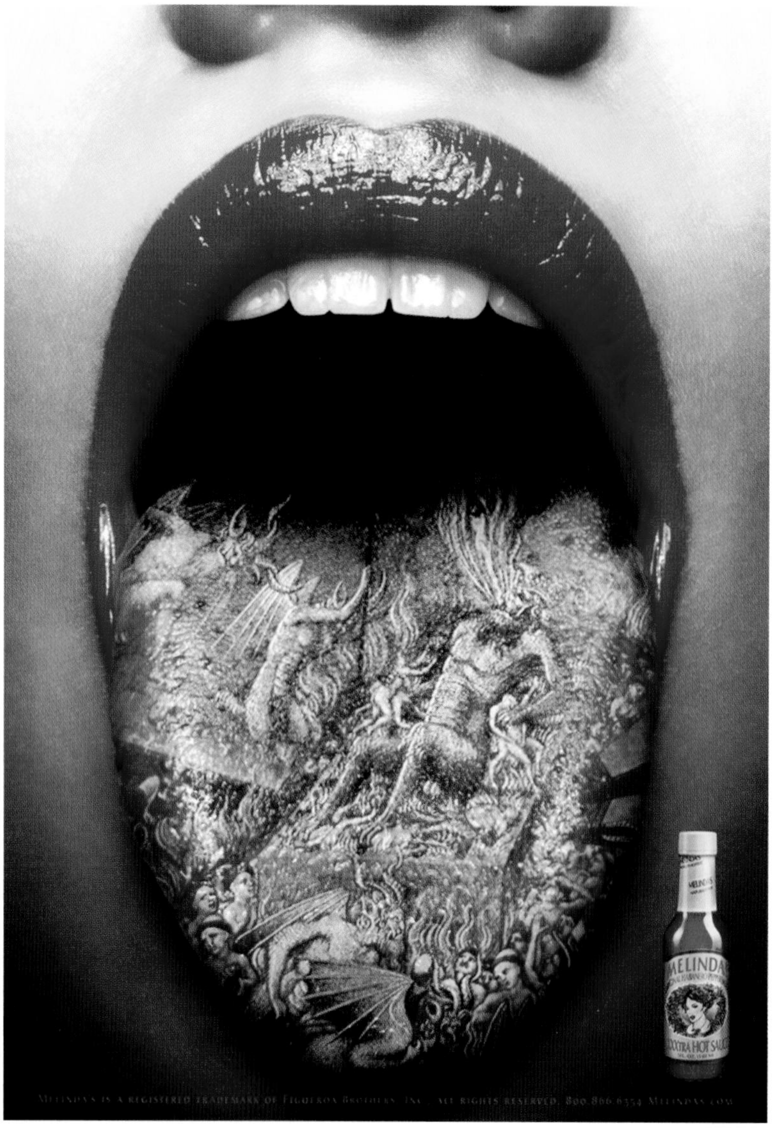
MELINDA'S

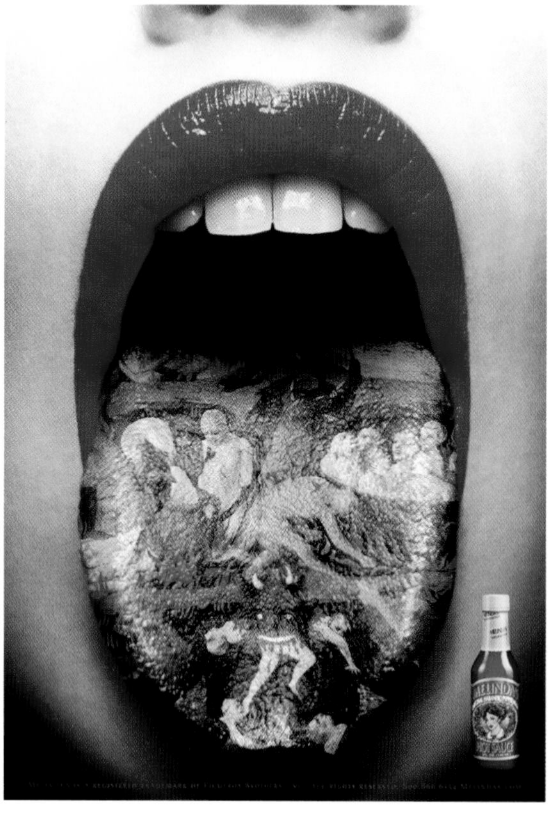

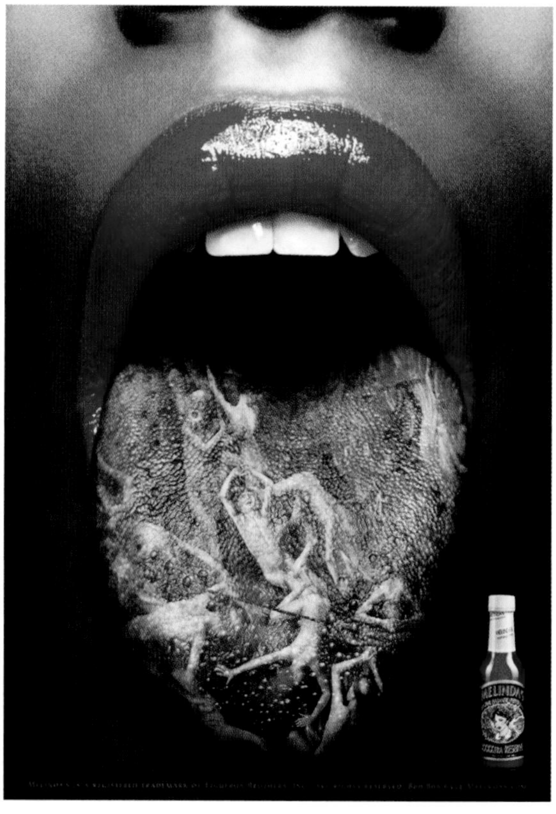

Merit

ART DIRECTOR
Ulf Henniger von Wallersbrunn

WRITER
Andreas Stalder

PHOTOGRAPHER
Jean Pascal Gunther

CREATIVE DIRECTOR
Andreas Pauli

CLIENT
Fiat

AGENCY
Leo Burnett/Frankfurt

ANNUAL ID
06137A

FOR STUFF
THAT DOESN'T FIT
EVERYWHERE.
FIAT
Transporter

FOR STUFF
THAT DOESN'T FIT
EVERYWHERE.
FIAT
Transporter

FOR STUFF
THAT DOESN'T FIT
EVERYWHERE.
FIAT
Transporter

Merit

ART DIRECTOR
Melissa Lin

WRITER
Anselmo Ramos

PHOTOGRAPHER
Adrian Mueller

CREATIVE DIRECTORS
Bernie Hogya
Fernanda Romano
John Hobbs
Peter Rosch
Mark Wnek

CLIENT
MilkPEP - Milk Processor Education Program

AGENCY
Lowe/New York

ANNUAL ID
06138A

Milk helps bones grow. All 206 of them.
got milk?

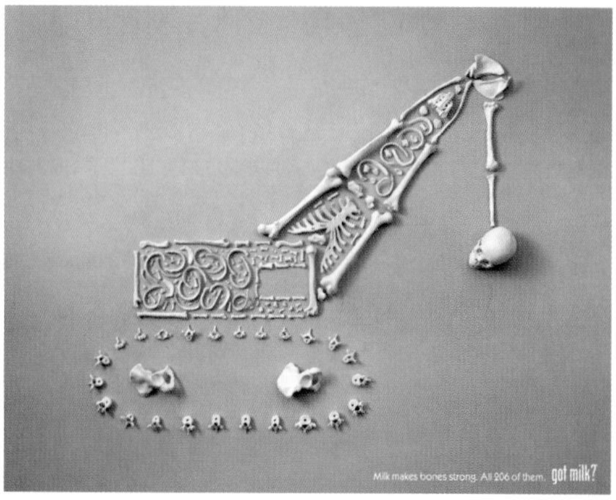
Milk makes bones strong. All 206 of them.
got milk?

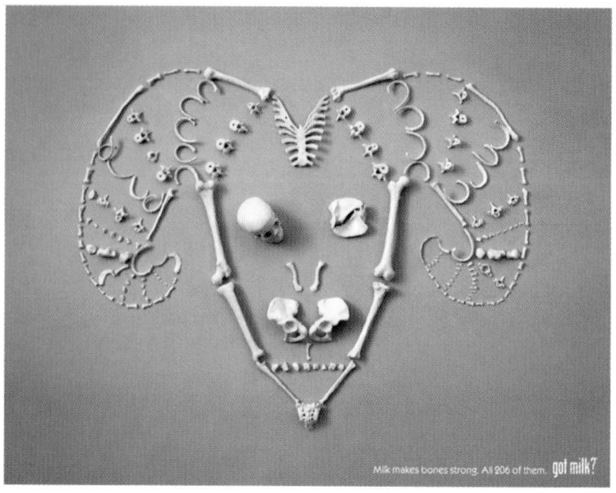
Milk makes bones strong. All 206 of them.
got milk?

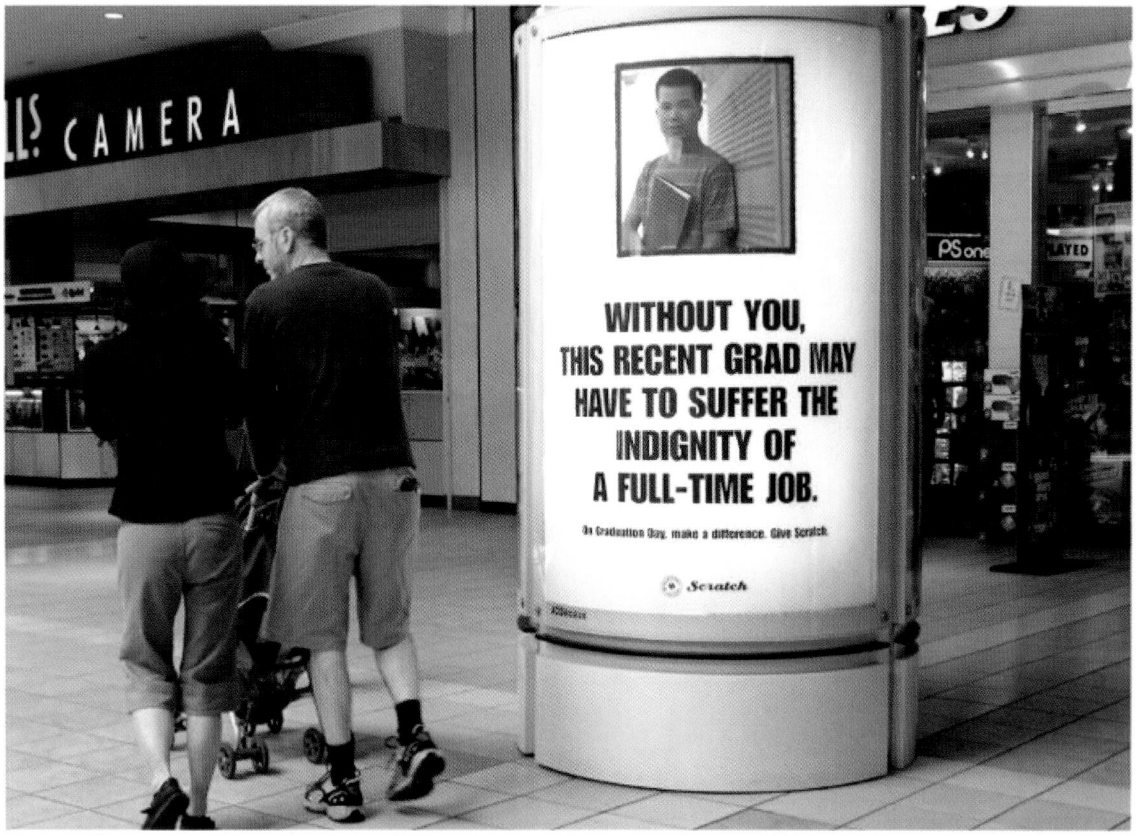
CAMERA
WITHOUT YOU,
THIS RECENT GRAD MAY
HAVE TO SUFFER THE
INDIGNITY OF
A FULL-TIME JOB.
On Graduation Day, make a difference. Give Scratch.
Scratch

WITHOUT YOUR HELP,
THIS MAN'S TANNING
SALON MEMBERSHIP
MAY EXPIRE.
This Father's Day, make a difference. Give Scratch.
Scratch

NO ONE SHOULD
HAVE TO LIVE
LIKE THIS.
ALAN HALL
HAS NEVER KNOWN
CRÈME BRÛLÉE.

NO ONE SHOULD
HAVE TO LIVE
LIKE THIS.
This Father's Day, make a difference. Give Scratch.
Scratch

ALAN HALL
HAS NEVER KNOWN
CRÈME BRÛLÉE.
WITHOUT YOUR HELP,
THIS MAN'S TANNING
SALON MEMBERSHIP
MAY EXPIRE.
NO ONE SHOULD
HAVE TO LIVE
LIKE THIS.

ALAN HALL
HAS NEVER KNOWN
CRÈME BRÛLÉE.
This Father's Day, make a difference. Give Scratch.
Scratch

NO ONE SHOULD
HAVE TO LIVE
LIKE THIS.
ALAN HALL
HAS NEVER KNOWN
CRÈME BRÛLÉE.

EVERY NIGHT
JILL HALL MUST SLEEP
ON SHEETS WITH A
LOW THREAD COUNT.
Direct Store

MERIT

ART DIRECTORS
Steven Grskovic
Tarsha Hall

WRITERS
Glenn Rockowitz
Greg Lane

CREATIVE DIRECTORS
Bob Moore
Rob Rich
Gethin Stout

CLIENT
Washington's Lottery

AGENCY
Publicis West/Seattle

ANNUAL ID
06139A

MERIT

ART DIRECTOR
David Fischer

WRITER
Axel Tischer

PHOTOGRAPHER
Hans Starck

CREATIVE DIRECTORS
Matthias Spaetgens
Jan Leube

CLIENT
jobsintown.de

AGENCY
Scholz & Friends/Berlin

ANNUAL ID
06140A

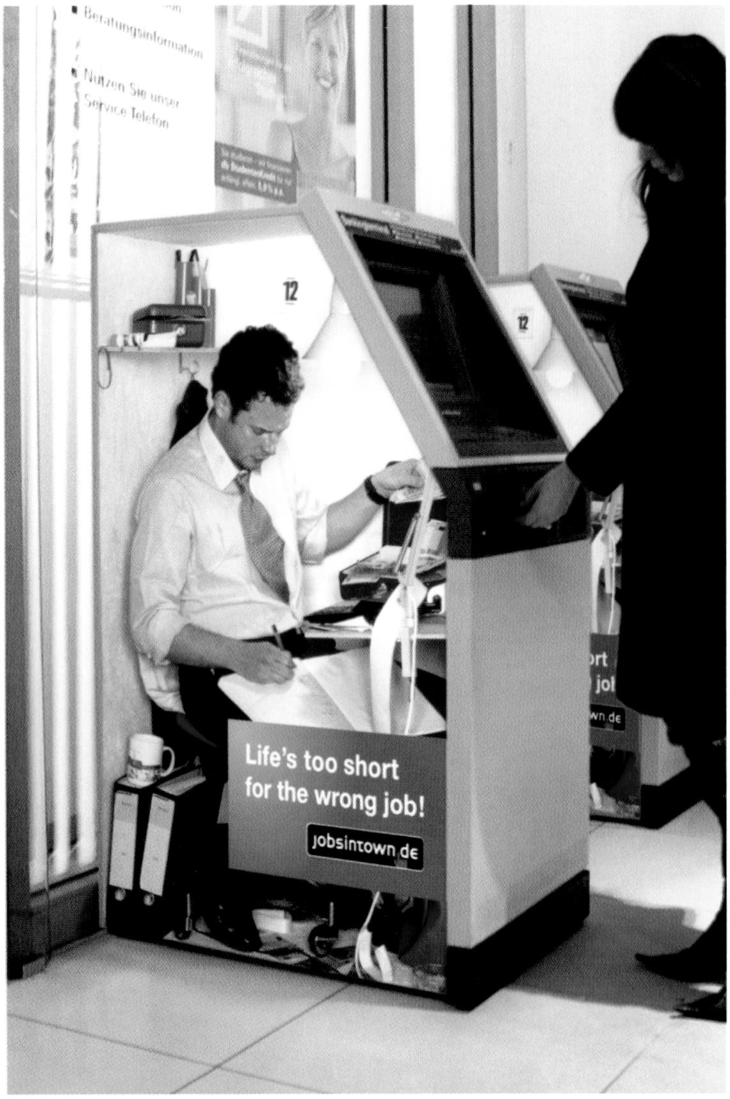
Life's too short
for the wrong job!
jobsintown.de

Life's too short
for the wrong job!
jobsintown.de

Life's too short
for the wrong job!
jobsintown.de

READY FOR YOUR :45 ?
CHECK NIKEHOCKEY.CA

READY FOR YOUR :45 ?
CHECK NIKEHOCKEY.CA

READY FOR YOUR :45 ?
CHECK NIKEHOCKEY.CA
5791

MERIT

ART DIRECTOR
Jaimes Zentil

WRITER
Craig McIntosh

PHOTOGRAPHER
Mark Zibert

CREATIVE DIRECTORS
Lance Martin
Zak Mroueh

CLIENT
Nike Canada

AGENCY
TAXI/Toronto

ANNUAL ID
06141A

MERIT

ART DIRECTOR
Tony Bradbourne

WRITER
Steve McCabe

PHOTOGRAPHERS
Tranz Photo Library
Stock Image Group Photo Library

CREATIVE DIRECTOR
Tony Bradbourne

CLIENT
Nokia

AGENCY
Y&R/Auckland

ANNUAL ID
06142A

USE THIS AS A BACKGROUND FOR "I'M WORKING LATE" VIDEO CALLS
VIDEO CALL BACKGROUNDS. USE THEM WHEN YOU'RE SOMEWHERE YOU SHOULDN'T BE.
NOKIA
NOKIA 6680
WITH VIDEO CALLING

USE THIS AS A BACKGROUND FOR "I'M AT THE GYM" VIDEO CALLS
VIDEO CALL BACKGROUNDS. USE THEM WHEN YOU'RE SOMEWHERE YOU SHOULDN'T BE.
NOKIA
NOKIA 6680
WITH VIDEO CALLING

USE THIS AS A BACKGROUND FOR "I'M AT THE SUPERMARKET" VIDEO CALLS
VIDEO CALL BACKGROUNDS. USE THEM WHEN YOU'RE SOMEWHERE YOU SHOULDN'T BE.
NOKIA
NOKIA 6680
WITH VIDEO CALLING

Happy Holidays from Philishave

MERIT

ART DIRECTOR
Paul Wallace

WRITER
David Ross

ILLUSTRATOR
Greg Banning

CREATIVE DIRECTORS
Andrew Simon
William Hammond

CLIENT
Philips

AGENCY
DDB/Toronto

ANNUAL ID
06143A

Merit

ART DIRECTOR
Doug Pedersen

WRITER
Lee Remias

PHOTOGRAPHER
Christian Schmidt

CREATIVE DIRECTOR
Jim Mountjoy

CLIENT
North Carolina Travel & Tourism

AGENCY
LKM/Charlotte

ANNUAL ID
06144A

visit north carolina visitnc.com

Merit

ART DIRECTOR
Shawn James

WRITER
David Mueller

PHOTOGRAPHER
George Simhoni

CREATIVE DIRECTOR
Zak Mroueh

CLIENT
George Simhoni Photography

AGENCY
TAXI/Toronto

ANNUAL ID
06145A

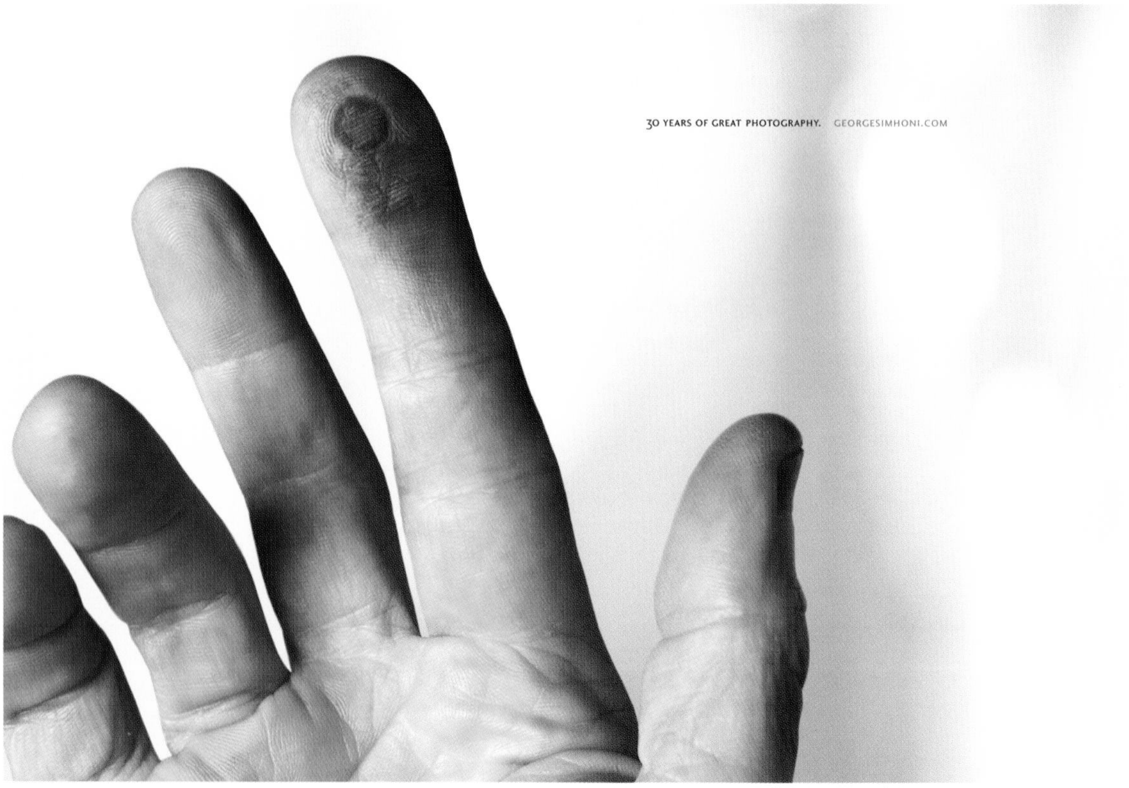
30 YEARS OF GREAT PHOTOGRAPHY. GEORGESIMHONI.COM

MERRY

DOWN
MERRY

MERRY
DOWN

DOWN
MERRY

MERRY
DOWN

MERIT

ART DIRECTOR
Dave Dye

WRITER
Sean Doyle

ILLUSTRATORS
Al Murphy
Daddy Buy me a Pony
Paul Bower
Mikko Rantenen
Yukko Kondo

CREATIVE DIRECTOR
Dave Dye

CLIENT
Merrydown

AGENCY
Campbell Doyle Dye/ London

ANNUAL ID
06146A

Merit

ART DIRECTORS
Aniruth Assawanapanon
Gun Kanjanapokin

WRITERS
Suthisak Sucharittanonta
Wirat Charoenwiwatchai

PHOTOGRAPHER
Boonsunh Chalard

ILLUSTRATOR
Big Jo House

CREATIVE DIRECTOR
Suthisak Sucharittanonta

CLIENT
Three Bond VIV Sales

AGENCY
BBDO/Bangkok

ANNUAL ID
06147A

ThreeBond

ThreeBond

ThreeBond

A31654
Let's draw the line on STOCK
illustration growers of AMERICA

MERIT

ART DIRECTOR
Larry Day

ILLUSTRATORS
Gary Taxali
Anita Kunz
Larry Day
Bill Mayer
Jack Unruh

CREATIVE DIRECTORS
Noel Haan
G. Andrew Meyer

CLIENT
Illustration Growers of America

AGENCY
Leo Burnett/Chicago

ANNUAL ID
06148A

A History for Public Schools
forget it.
FRANCE
TORONTO
COMPANY, LIMITED
GARY TAXALI
SHUCK
LET'S DRAW THE LINE ON
ILLUSTRATION GROWERS OF AMERICA

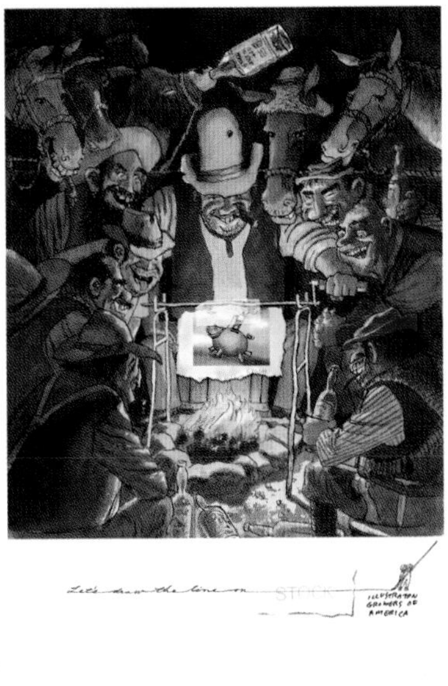
Let's draw the line on STOCK
illustration growers of america

STOCK

MERIT

ART DIRECTOR
Keith Campbell

WRITER
Chris Harwood

CREATIVE DIRECTOR
Dave Remer

CLIENT
Corbis

AGENCY
Remerinc/Seattle

ANNUAL ID
06149A

Keyword
Chameleon
Search
corbis.com
Seattle 1.800.260.0444
New York +1.212.777.6200
London +44.20.7644.7644
Paris +33.1.53.33.38.00
Düsseldorf +49.211.912.820
Hong Kong +852.2215.8000
Kuala Lumpur +603.6203.3111
Tokyo +81.3.3544.1857
corbis.
start here

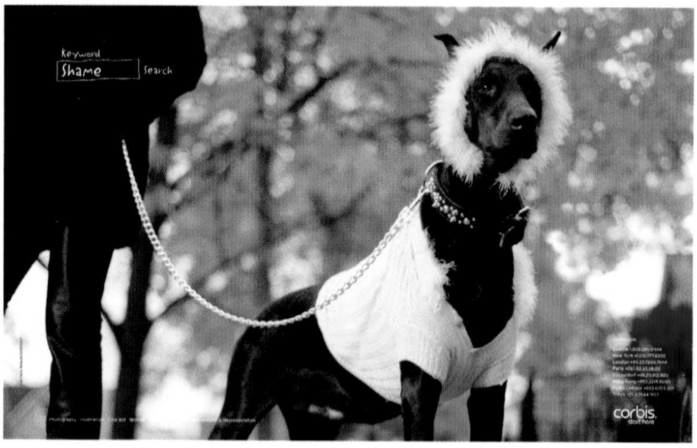
Keyword
Shame
Search
corbis.
start here

Keyword
Overconfidence
Search
corbis
start here

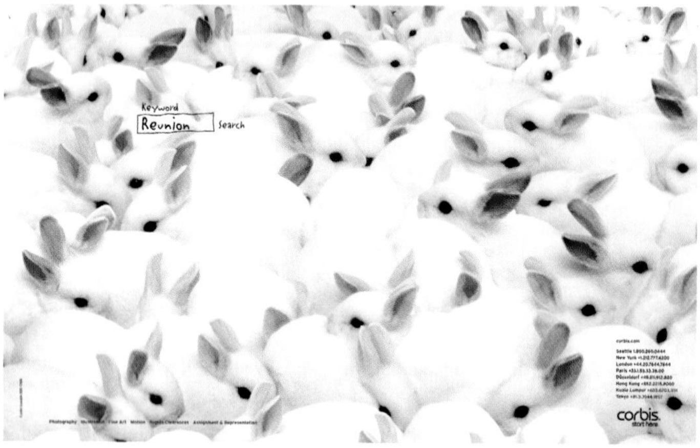
Keyword
Reunion
Search
corbis.
start here

Keyword
Available
Search
corbis.
start here

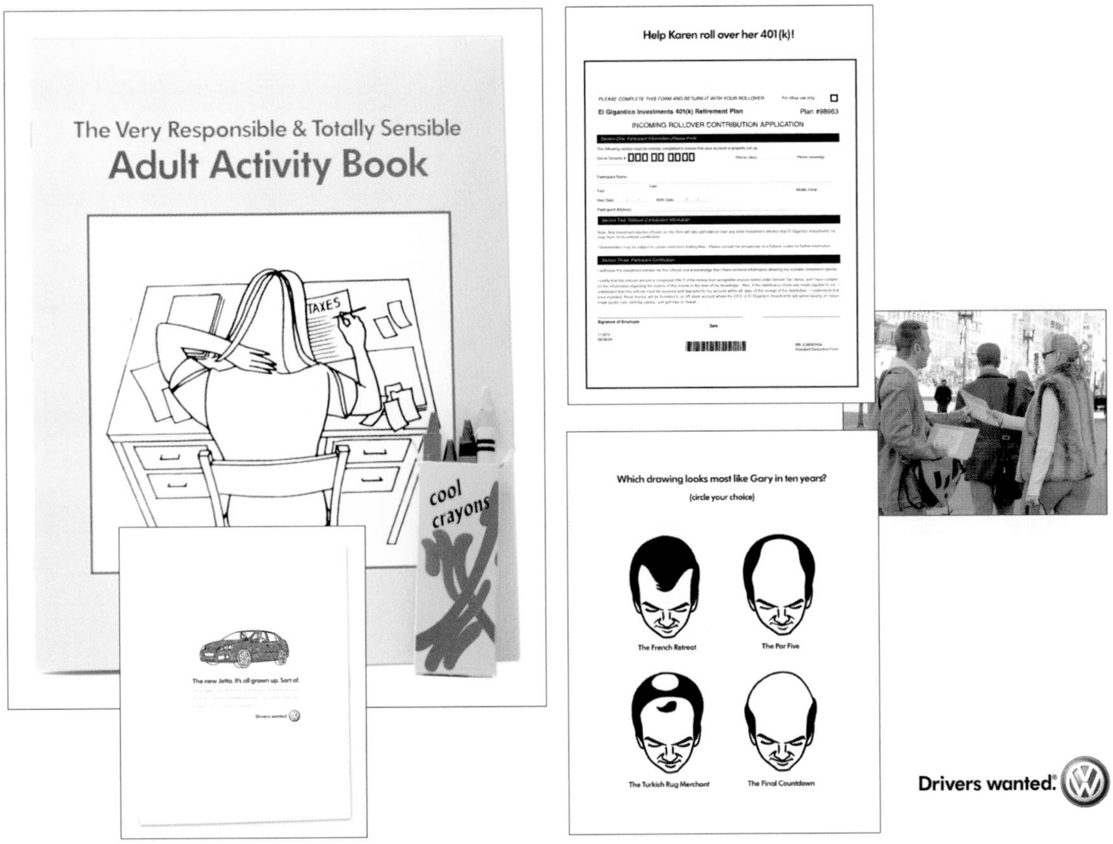
The Very Responsible & Totally Sensible
Adult Activity Book
TAXES
cool crayons
The new Jetta. It's all grown up. Sort of.
Help Karen roll over her 401(k)!
El Gigantico Investments 401(k) Retirement Plan
Plan #98963
INCOMING ROLLOVER CONTRIBUTION APPLICATION
Which drawing looks most like Gary in ten years?
(circle your choice)
The French Retreat
The Par Five
The Turkish Rug Merchant
The Final Countdown
Drivers wanted.

MERIT

ART DIRECTOR
Jen Wells

WRITER
Mark Billows

ILLUSTRATOR
Charlie Hoar

CREATIVE DIRECTORS
Ron Lawner
Alan Pafenbach
Dave Weist
Colin Jeffery

CLIENT
Volkswagen

AGENCY
Arnold Worldwide/ Boston

ANNUAL ID
06150A

MERIT

ART DIRECTOR
James Clunie

WRITER
James Clunie

CREATIVE DIRECTOR
David Lubars

CLIENT
Dexter Russell

AGENCY
BBDO/New York

ANNUAL ID
06160A

MERIT

ART DIRECTOR
James Clunie

WRITER
James Clunie

CREATIVE DIRECTOR
David Lubars

CLIENT
Dexter Russell

AGENCY
BBDO/New York

ANNUAL ID
06159A

MERIT

ART DIRECTOR
Nicholas Costarides

WRITER
Matt Covington

CREATIVE DIRECTOR
Tim Smith

CLIENT
Atlanta Braves

AGENCY
Blue Sky Advertising/ Atlanta

ANNUAL ID
06151A

G
BRAVES.
do your part. postseason braves tickets: 800-326-4000

G
BRAVES.
do your part. postseason braves tickets: 800-326-4000

G
BRAVES.
do your part. postseason braves tickets: 800-326-4000

WELCOME
Columbia
Sportswear Company

MERIT

ART DIRECTOR
Jeremy Boland

WRITER
Eric Terchila

PHOTOGRAPHER
Jeremy Boland

CREATIVE DIRECTOR
Terry Schneider

CLIENT
Columbia Sportswear

AGENCY
Borders Perrin Norrander/Portland

ANNUAL ID
06152A

torontoplasticsurgery.com

MERIT

ART DIRECTORS
Joel Arbez
Rachel Abrams

WRITERS
Rachel Abrams
Joel Arbez

PHOTOGRAPHER
Philip Rostron

CREATIVE DIRECTORS
Andrew Simon
William Hammond

CLIENT
Toronto Plastic Surgery

AGENCY
DDB/Toronto

ANNUAL ID
06153A

MERIT

ART DIRECTOR
Kevin Gentile

WRITER
Sandy Weber Neidhart

PHOTOGRAPHER
Alex Freund

CREATIVE DIRECTORS
Sally Hogshead
Rich Buceta
Mark DiMassimo

CLIENT
Duvel/Moortgat Brewery

AGENCY
DiMassimo/New York

ANNUAL ID
60157A

Duvel
REPENT TOMORROW

Live
richly.
THOUGHTS ON LIFE AND MONEY

"There's more to life than money."
A message from one of the least likely sources, a bank. Conceived in 2000 at the height of the dot-com boom, "Live richly" brought a much-needed perspective to the then-opulent mindset of the times. Today, it continues to resonate with people who realize that you don't have to strike it rich to strike it happy.
rs will not be found on a time sheet.
citi Live richly
En los negocios hay que enseñar los dientes. Sonríe.
citi Live richly
你記得你的銀行卡密碼，那你的結婚紀念日呢…
citi Live richly
He who dies with the most toys is still dead.
citi
It's a balance sheet, not a scorecard.
citi
Your assets:
Family
Friends
Life
Memories
Kids
Personality
Your smile
Laughter
The air
Freedom
Hopes
Passion
Love
Pets
citi
Live richly

Remember, today's
must-haves often
become tomorrow's
what-was-I-thinkings.

Remember, the
people you
work for are
waiting for
you at home
right now.

MERIT

WRITERS
Rich Black
James Bray
Dean Buckhorn
Colin Corcoran
Steve Driggs
Michael Hart
Reuben Hower
John Matejczyk
Mike Smith
Anna Stassen
Allon Tatarka
Mike Ward

CLIENT
Citibank

AGENCY
Fallon/Minneapolis

ANNUAL ID
06158A

MERIT

ART DIRECTORS
Craig Wong
Paul Kamzelas
Anil Bathwal

WRITERS
Brett Howlett
Jeff Golder

ILLUSTRATOR
Chris Gall

CREATIVE DIRECTORS
Brett Howlett
Paul Kamzelas

CLIENT
British Airways

AGENCY
M&C Saatchi/
New York

ANNUAL ID
06161A

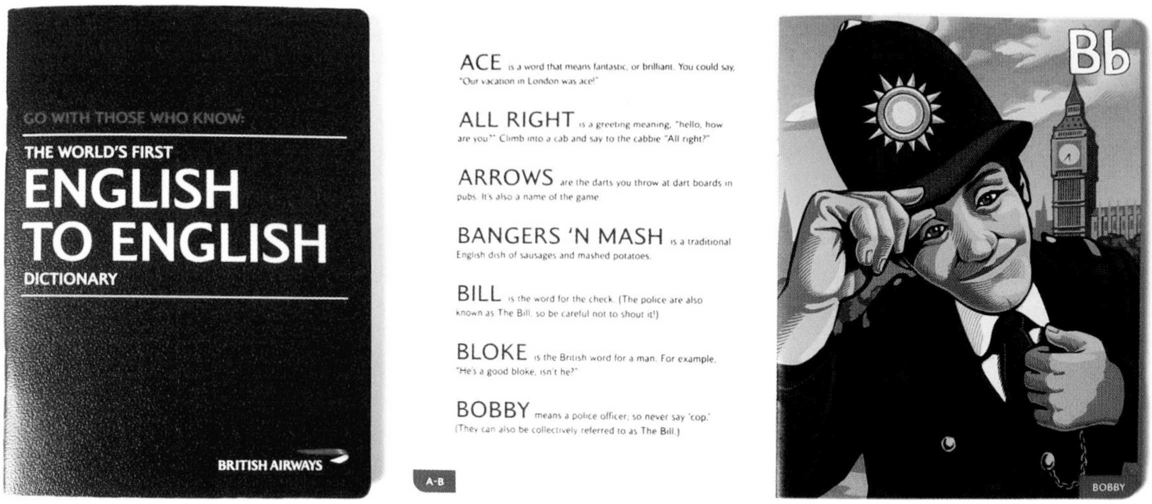
GO WITH THOSE WHO KNOW:
THE WORLD'S FIRST
ENGLISH TO ENGLISH
DICTIONARY
BRITISH AIRWAYS
ACE is a word that means fantastic, or brilliant. You could say, "Our vacation in London was ace!"
ALL RIGHT is a greeting meaning, "hello, how are you?" Climb into a cab and say to the cabbie "All right?"
ARROWS are the darts you throw at dart boards in pubs. It's also a name of the game.
BANGERS 'N MASH is a traditional English dish of sausages and mashed potatoes.
BILL is the word for the check. (The police are also known as The Bill, so be careful not to shout it!)
BLOKE is the British word for a man. For example, "He's a good bloke, isn't he?"
BOBBY means a police officer; so never say 'cop.' (They can also be collectively referred to as The Bill.)
A-B
Bb
BOBBY

MERIT

ART DIRECTOR
Maurice Wee

WRITER
Renee Lim

PHOTOGRAPHER
Groovy Studio

ILLUSTRATOR
Procolor

CREATIVE DIRECTOR
Sonal Dabral

CLIENT
Duracell

AGENCY
Ogilvy & Mather/
Singapore

ANNUAL ID
06162A

DURACELL

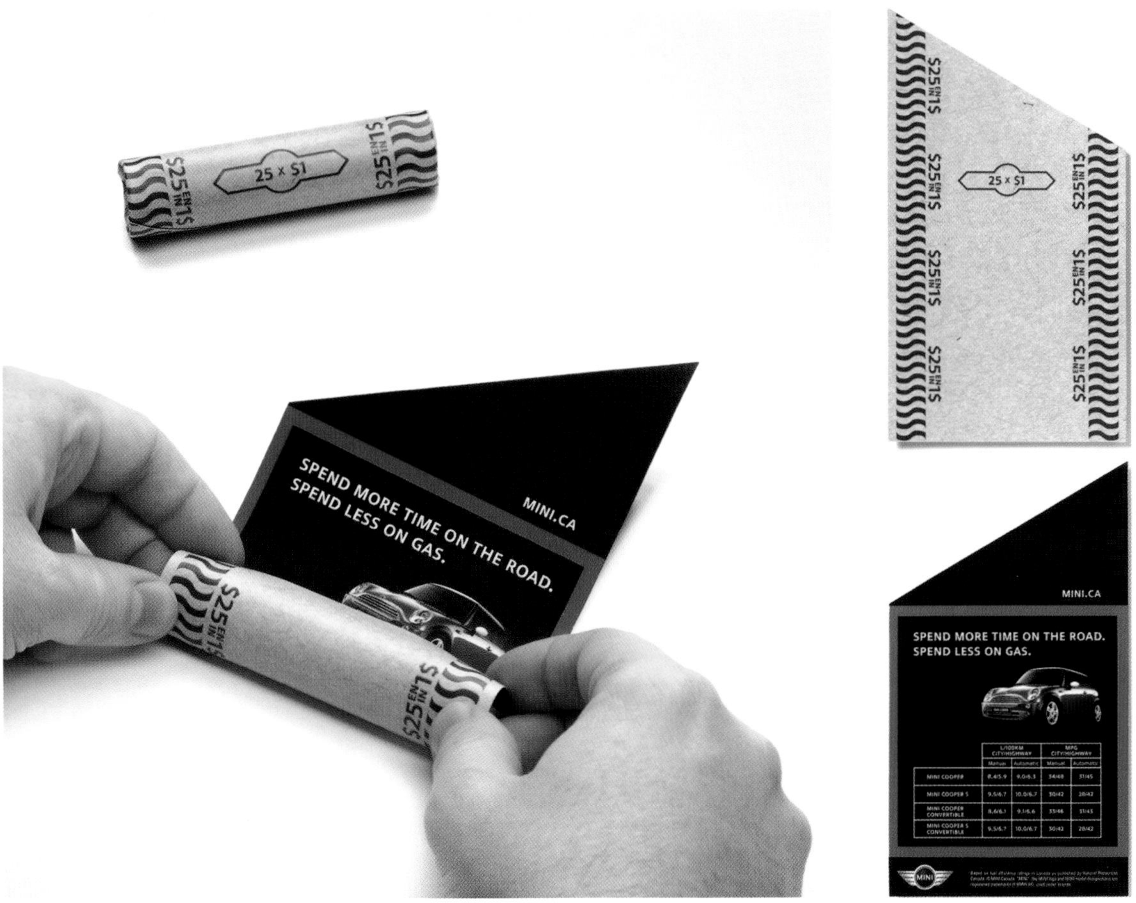
25 x $1
$25 EN 1$ IN
SPEND MORE TIME ON THE ROAD.
SPEND LESS ON GAS.
MINI.CA

MERIT

ART DIRECTOR
Troy McGuinness

WRITER
Jordan Doucette

CREATIVE DIRECTOR
Zak Mroueh

CLIENT
MINI

AGENCY
TAXI/Toronto

ANNUAL ID
06165A

Spontex
Super absorbent

MERIT

ART DIRECTORS
Philippe Taroux
Clement Langlais

WRITER
Benoit Leroux

PHOTOGRAPHER
Richard Dobson

CREATIVE DIRECTOR
Erik Vervroegen

CLIENT
Spontex

AGENCY
TBWA/Paris

ANNUAL ID
06166A

Merit

ART DIRECTORS
Alvaro Zunini
Manuel Techera
Santiago Chaumont

WRITERS
Alvaro Zunini
Manuel Techera
Santiago Chaumont

CREATIVE DIRECTORS
Alvar Sunol
Manuel Techera
Santiago Chaumont
Alvaro Zunini

CLIENT
Ford/Lo Jack

AGENCY
JWT/Mexico City

ANNUAL ID
06167A

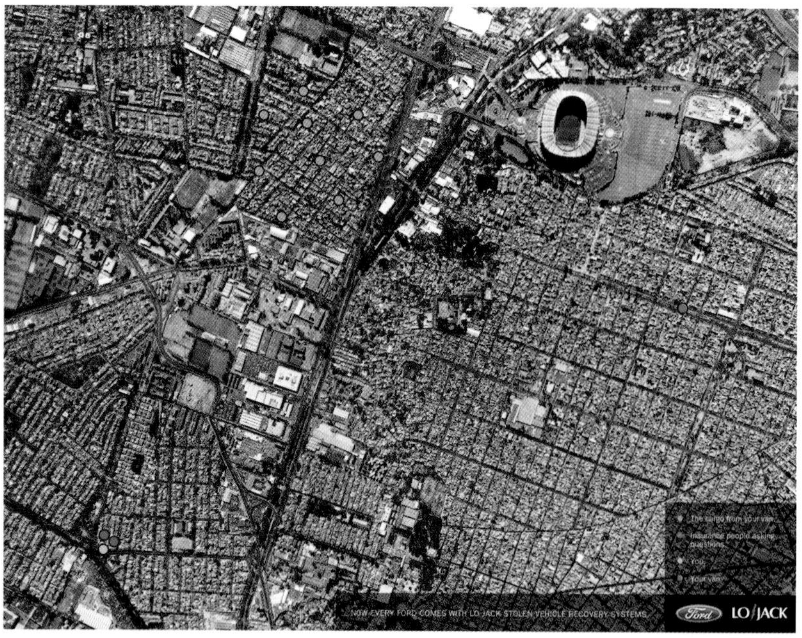
The cargo from your van.
Insurance people asking questions.
You.
Your van.
NOW EVERY FORD COMES WITH LO JACK STOLEN VEHICLE RECOVERY SYSTEMS.
Ford
LO/JACK

The cops.
You.
Your car painted like a taxi.
NOW EVERY FORD COMES WITH LO JACK STOLEN VEHICLE RECOVERY SYSTEMS.
Ford
LO/JACK

The cops.
A car just like yours.
Your car.
NOW EVERY FORD COMES WITH LO JACK STOLEN VEHICLE RECOVERY SYSTEMS.
Ford
LO/JACK

ALWAYS SHARP
TEXWOOD

MERIT

ART DIRECTORS
Shannon Tham
Gary Tranter

WRITER
Matt Cullen

PHOTOGRAPHER
Wing Shya

ILLUSTRATOR
Terry Batty @ Centro

CREATIVE DIRECTORS
Gary Tranter
Matt Cullen

CLIENT
Texwood

AGENCY
Ogilvy & Mather/ Hong Kong

ANNUAL ID
06168A

ALWAYS SHARP
TEXWOOD

ALWAYS SHARP
TEXWOOD

Merit

ART DIRECTOR
Matt Gilmour

WRITER
Anthony Moss

PHOTOGRAPHER
Brock Elbank

CREATIVE DIRECTOR
David Nobay

CLIENT
Lexus

AGENCY
Saatchi & Saatchi/Sydney

ANNUAL ID
06169A

LEXUS
See beyond the road. The LX470 4WD

LEXUS
See beyond the road. The LX470 4WD

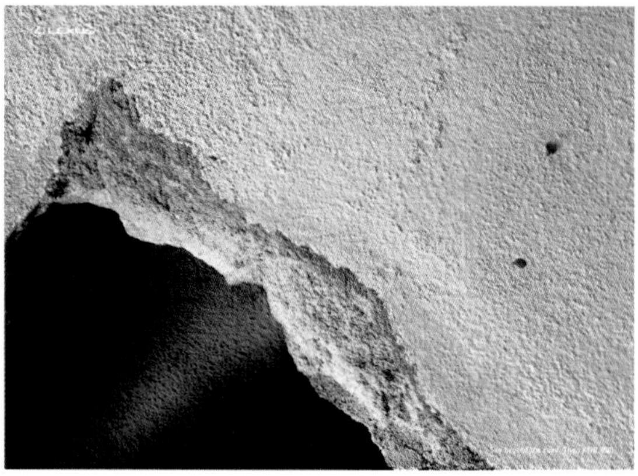

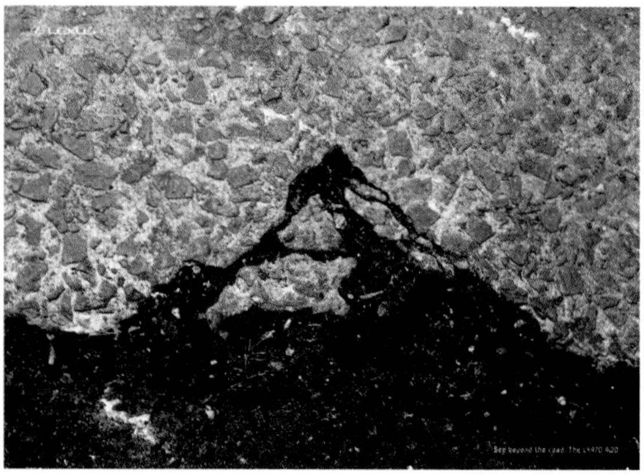

I FART WHEREVER
I LIKE AND PEOPLE
FEEL SORRY FOR ME.
IT'S GREAT
GETTING OLD

MERIT

ART DIRECTOR
Vince Lagana

WRITER
Luke Chess

DESIGNER
Nic Buckingham

PHOTOGRAPHER
Matt Hoyle

CREATIVE DIRECTOR
David Nobay

CLIENT
Lion Nathan

AGENCY
Saatchi & Saatchi/Sydney

ANNUAL ID
06170A

THERE'S A SIGN
ON THE BUS THAT
SAYS YOU HAVE TO
GET UP FOR ME.
IT'S GREAT
GETTING OLD

I GET MONEY
FOR DOING
BUGGER ALL.

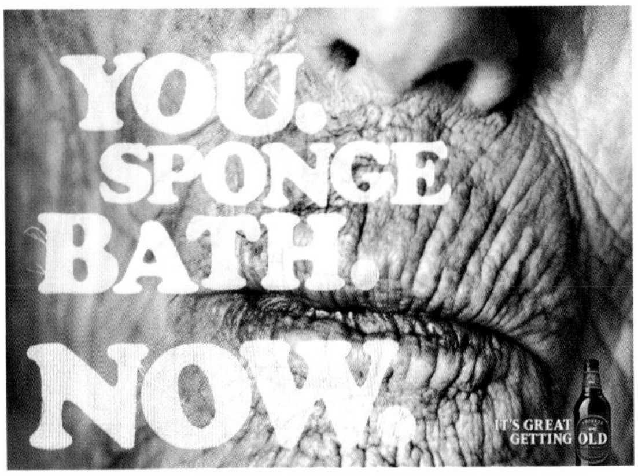
YOU.
SPONGE
BATH.
NOW.
IT'S GREAT
GETTING OLD

MERIT

ART DIRECTORS
Michaela Gressbach
Sybille Stempel
Ekkehard Frenkler

WRITER
Christine Deinhart

DESIGNER
Hayo Ross

CREATIVE DIRECTOR
Ekkehard Frenkler

CLIENT
Verlagsgruppe Lubbe

AGENCY
Serviceplan Gruppe für Innovative Kommunikation/Munich

ANNUAL ID
06171A

KEN FOLLET
EISFIEBER
ROMAN
LÜBBE
Madoba-2

Have you ever
leafed through a killer-virus?

OLYMPUS
The μ 700.
Slim.

MERIT

ART DIRECTOR
Wing Kit Hor

WRITER
Adam Miranda

CREATIVE DIRECTORS
Ronald Ng
David Sin

CLIENT
Olympus

AGENCY
BBDO/Kuala Lumpur

ANNUAL ID
06172A

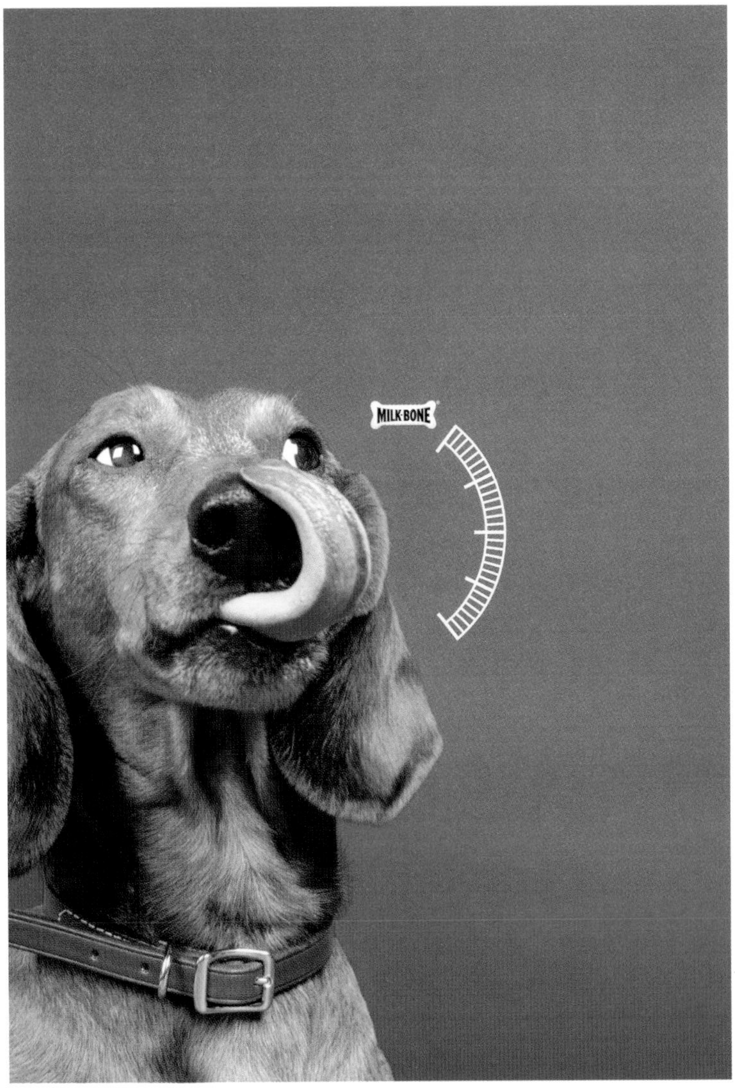
MILK-BONE

MERIT

ART DIRECTOR
Daniela Montanez

WRITERS
Heidi Hackemer
Matthew Bottkol

CREATIVE DIRECTORS
Sandy Greenberg
Terri Meyer
Chris Becker

CLIENT
Kraft/Milk-Bone

AGENCY
Foote Cone & Belding/
New York

ANNUAL ID
06173A

Merit

ART DIRECTOR
Dustin Duke

WRITER
Chris Soskin

PHOTOGRAPHER
Dustin Duke

CREATIVE DIRECTORS
Earl Cavanah
Lisa Rettig-Falcone
Dean Hacohen

CLIENT
Museum of Sex

AGENCY
Lowe/New York

ANNUAL ID
06174A

EXIT
useumofsex
233 FIFTH AVENUE NYC
WWW.MUSEUMOFSEX.COM

Merit

ART DIRECTORS
Mun
Alvin Teoh
Tan Yee Kiang

WRITERS
Raymond Ng
Ted Lim

PHOTOGRAPHER
Steve Koh

CREATIVE DIRECTORS
Ted Lim
Alvin Teoh

CLIENT
Energizer

AGENCY
Naga DDB/
Petaling Jaya

ANNUAL ID
06175A

Energizer

The widest lens in its class
Nikon

MERIT

ART DIRECTORS
Mun
Alvin Teoh
Tan Yee Kiang

WRITERS
Raymond Ng
Ted Lim

PHOTOGRAPHER
Steve Koh

CREATIVE DIRECTORS
Ted Lim
Alvin Teoh

CLIENT
Nikon

AGENCY
Naga DDB/
Petaling Jaya

ANNUAL ID
06176A

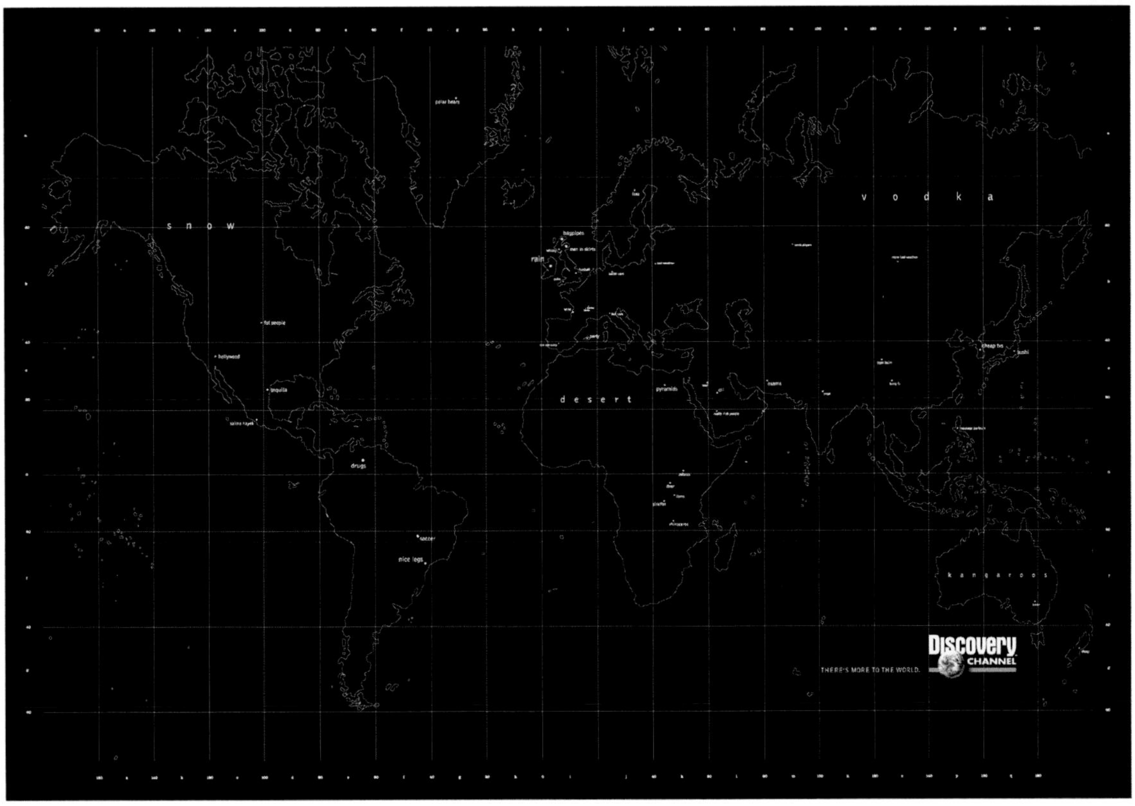
s n o w
v o d k a
d e s e r t
k a n g a r o o s
Discovery Channel
THERE'S MORE TO THE WORLD.

MERIT

ART DIRECTOR
Daniel Zenas Upputuru

WRITER
Suchitra Gahlot

ILLUSTRATOR
Daniel Zenas Upputuru

CREATIVE DIRECTOR
Emmanuel Upputuru

CLIENT
Discovery Channel

AGENCY
Ogilvy & Mather/
New Delhi

ANNUAL ID
06177A

MERIT

ART DIRECTOR
Gavin Simpson

WRITER
Gavin Simpson

CREATIVE DIRECTOR
Gavin Simpson

CLIENT
The Economist

AGENCY
Ogilvy & Mather/
Makati City

ANNUAL ID
06178A

The Economist

MERIT

ART DIRECTORS
Simon Cox
Heather Sheen

WRITER
Hamish Spencer

PHOTOGRAPHER
Steve Turner

CREATIVE DIRECTOR
Darren Spiller

CLIENT
Creative Brands

AGENCY
Publicis Mojo/Walsh Bay

ANNUAL ID
06179A

GREEN CHOICE
CONCENTRATED
DISH 375mL LIQUID
Environmentally Friendlier
Tel: (03) 9699 4099
corporation

GREEN
CHOICE
CONCENTRATED
Environmentally Friendlier
Tel: (03) 9699 4099
corporation

MERIT

ART DIRECTORS
Simon Cox
Heather Sheen

WRITER
Hamish Spencer

PHOTOGRAPHER
Steve Turner

CREATIVE DIRECTOR
Darren Spiller

CLIENT
Creative Brands

AGENCY
Publicis Mojo/Walsh Bay

ANNUAL ID
06181A

GREEN
CHOICE
TOILET, BATH AND
SHOWER CLEANER
500mL
Fax
Environmentally Friendlier
Tel: (03) 9699 4099
corporation

MERIT

ART DIRECTORS
Simon Cox
Heather Sheen

WRITER
Hamish Spencer

PHOTOGRAPHER
Steve Turner

CREATIVE DIRECTOR
Darren Spiller

CLIENT
Creative Brands

AGENCY
Publicis Mojo/Walsh Bay

ANNUAL ID
06180A

Merit

ART DIRECTOR
Porky Hefer

WRITER
Roger Paulse

ILLUSTRATOR
Paul Hudson @
Sett Digital

CREATIVE DIRECTOR
Porky Hefer

CLIENT
Durex

AGENCY
Lowe Bull/Cape Town

ANNUAL ID
06183A

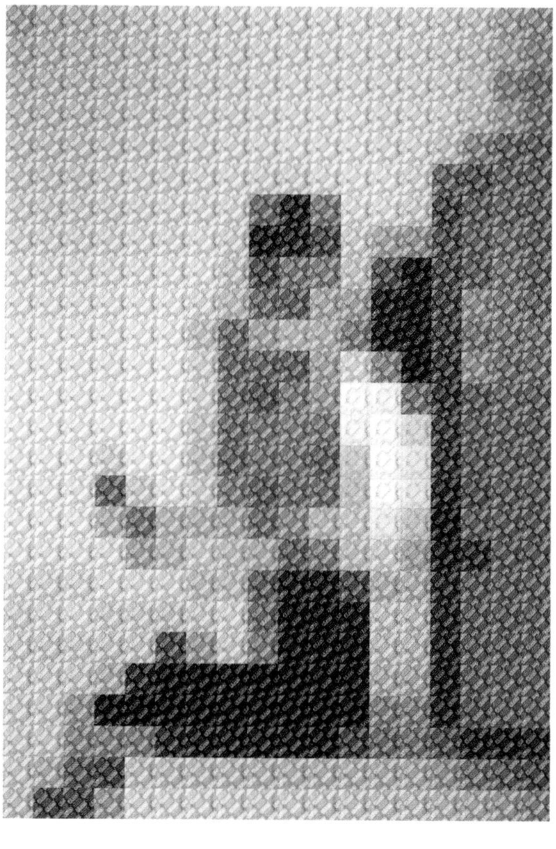

Every day on eBay, thousands of small business owners sell more than $1.9 million in home furnishings to customers around the world. Learn how to join them with eBay's Seller OnRamp program and get eBay sales consulting customized for your business for free. Call 1-866-304-3229 to enroll today.
you can sell it on

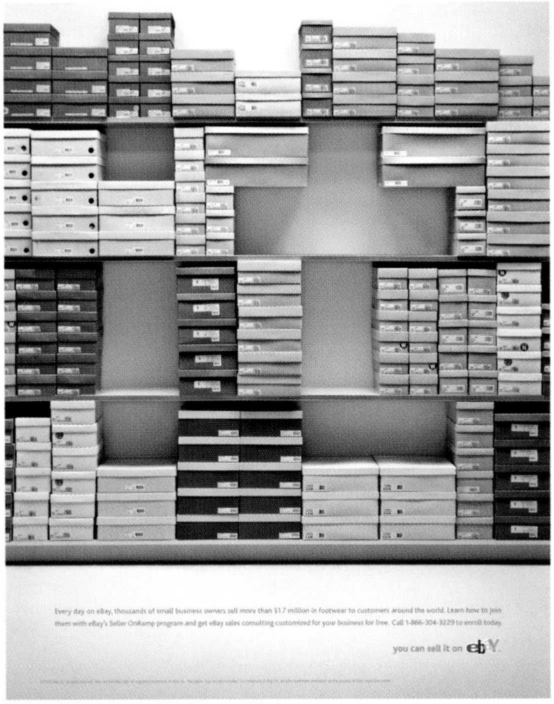
Every day on eBay, thousands of small business owners sell more than $1.7 million in footwear to customers around the world. Learn how to join them with eBay's Seller OnRamp program and get eBay sales consulting customized for your business for free. Call 1-866-304-3229 to enroll today.
you can sell it on

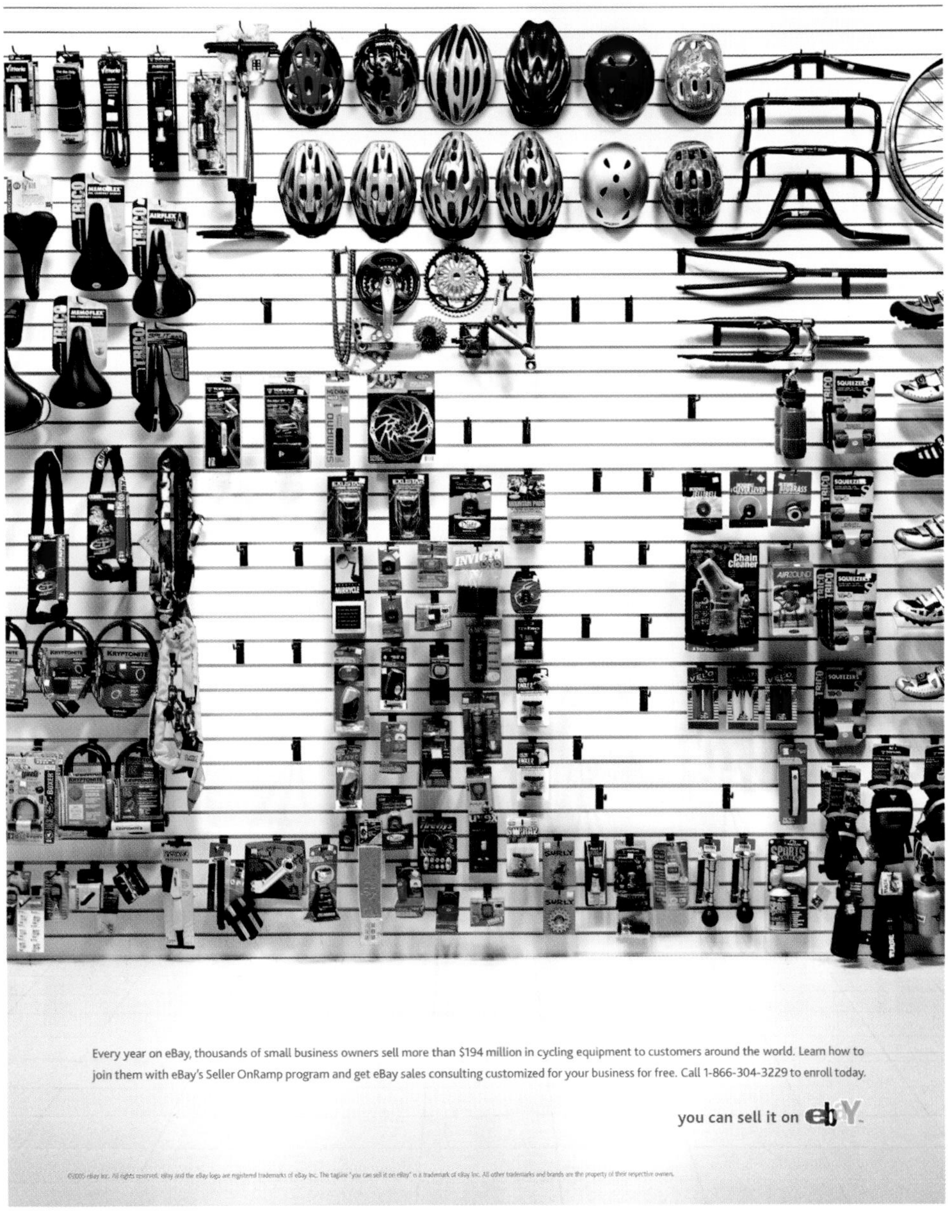
Every year on eBay, thousands of small business owners sell more than $194 million in cycling equipment to customers around the world. Learn how to join them with eBay's Seller OnRamp program and get eBay sales consulting customized for your business for free. Call 1-866-304-3229 to enroll today.
you can sell it on

MERIT

ART DIRECTOR
Chuck Tso

WRITER
Chris Maiorino

CREATIVE DIRECTORS
Greg Hahn
David Lubars

CLIENT
eBay

AGENCY
BBDO/New York

ANNUAL ID
06186A

MERIT

ART DIRECTORS
Jian Li
Hua Li
Xin-an Han
Lei Qiu

WRITERS
Jian Li
Hua Li
Qing Xu

PHOTOGRAPHER
Max

CREATIVE DIRECTORS
Jian Li
Hua Li

CLIENT
Audi

AGENCY
Beijing Creative World Advertising/Beijing

ANNUAL ID
06184A

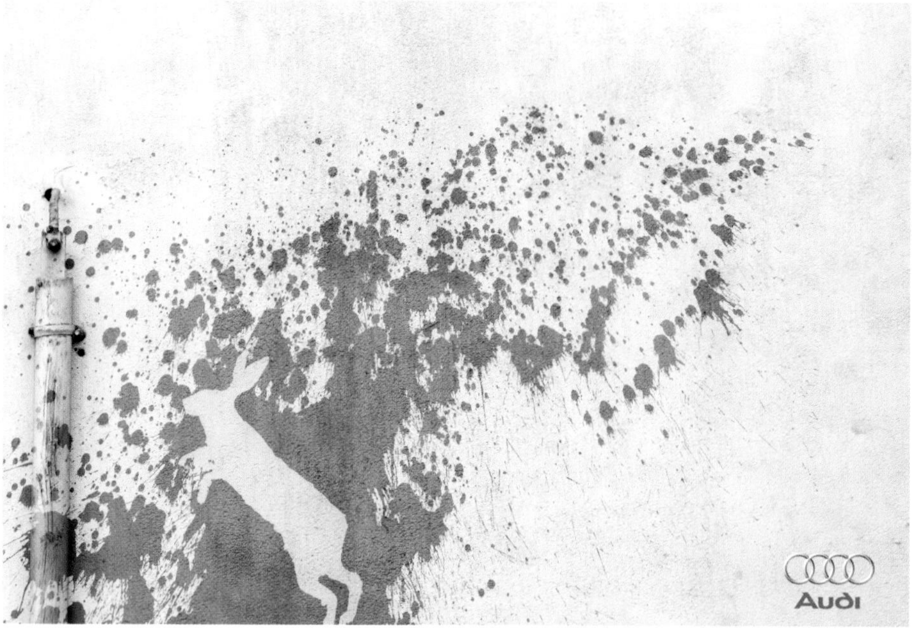
Audi

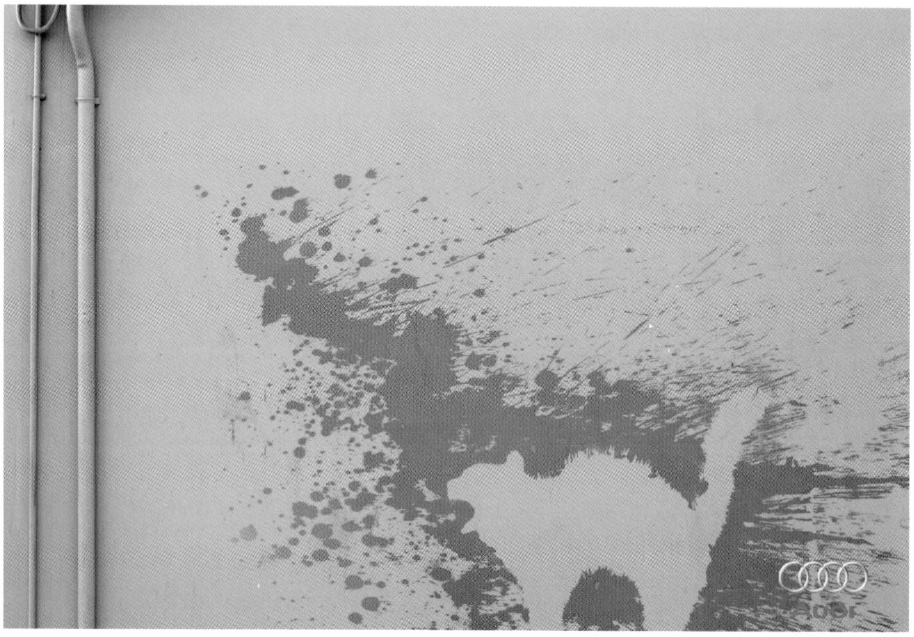

Audi

Merit

ART DIRECTORS
Anne Boothroyd
Maria Lishman
Kimberley Ragan
Rebecca Johnson-Pond

WRITERS
Maria Lishman
Anne Boothroyd
Kimberley Ragan
Rebecca Johnson-Pond

CREATIVE DIRECTOR
Richard Maddocks

CLIENT
Monaco

AGENCY
Colenso BBDO/
Auckland

ANNUAL ID
06185A

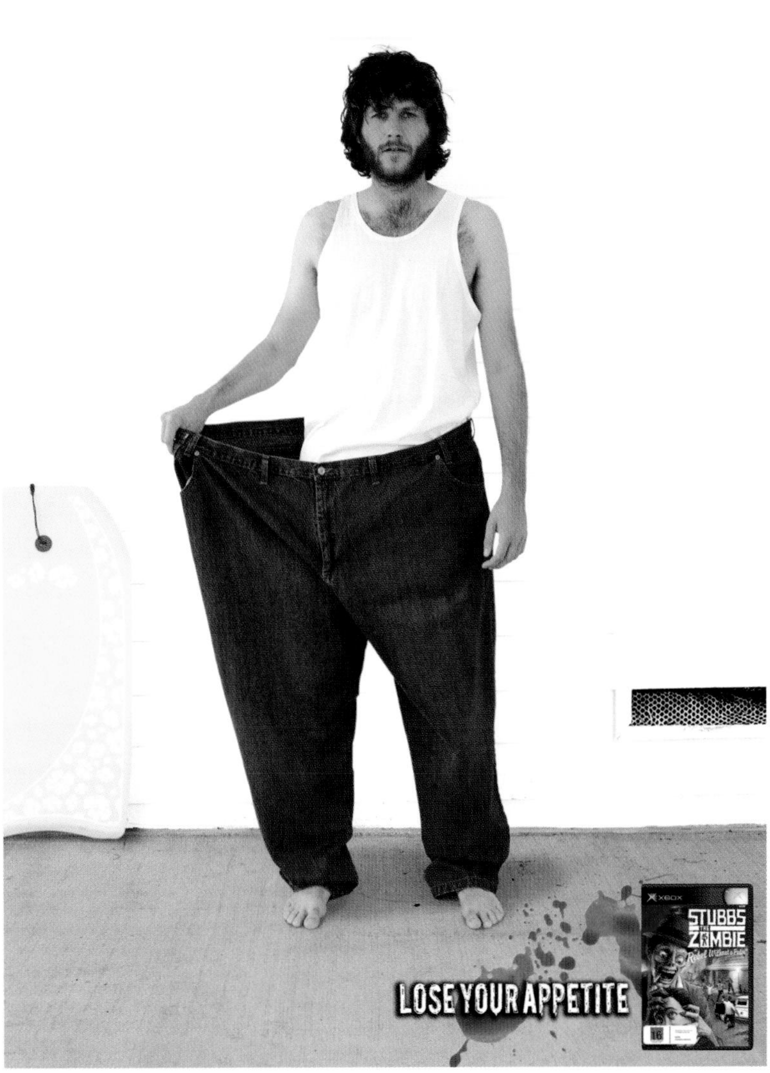
STUBBS THE ZOMBIE
LOSE YOUR APPETITE

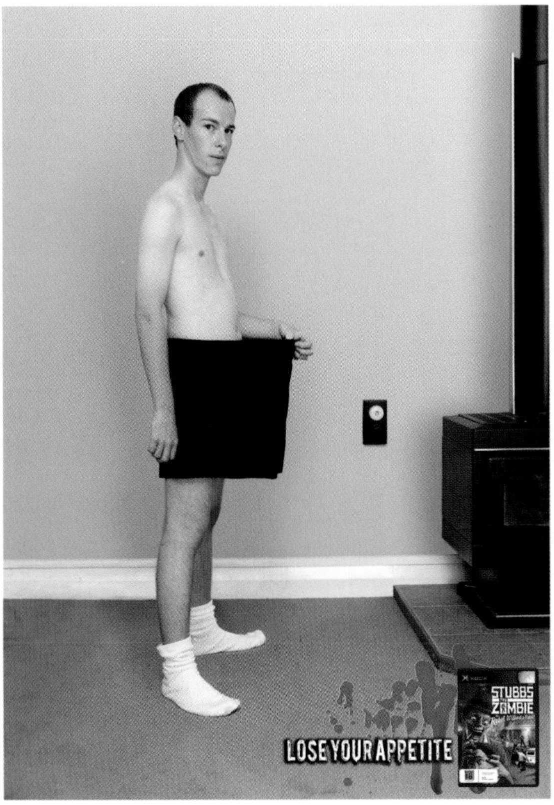
STUBBS THE ZOMBIE
LOSE YOUR APPETITE

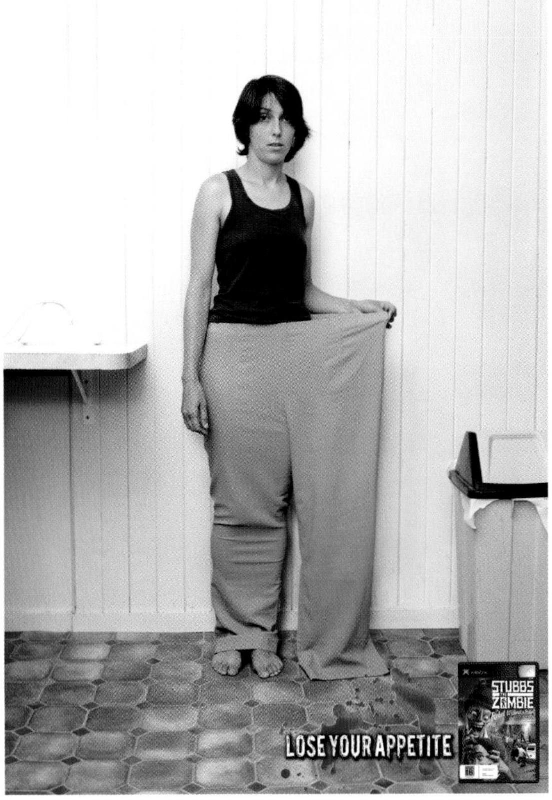
STUBBS THE ZOMBIE
LOSE YOUR APPETITE

Merit

ART DIRECTORS
Carina Teo
Richard Chin
Edwin Leong

WRITERS
Hasnah Mohd. Samidin
Edwin Leong

DESIGNERS
Carina Teo
Richard Chin

PHOTOGRAPHER
Getty Images

CREATIVE DIRECTORS
Hasnah Mohd. Samidin
Edwin Leong

CLIENT
Kimberly-Clark Trading

AGENCY
JWT/Kuala Lumpur

ANNUAL ID
06187A

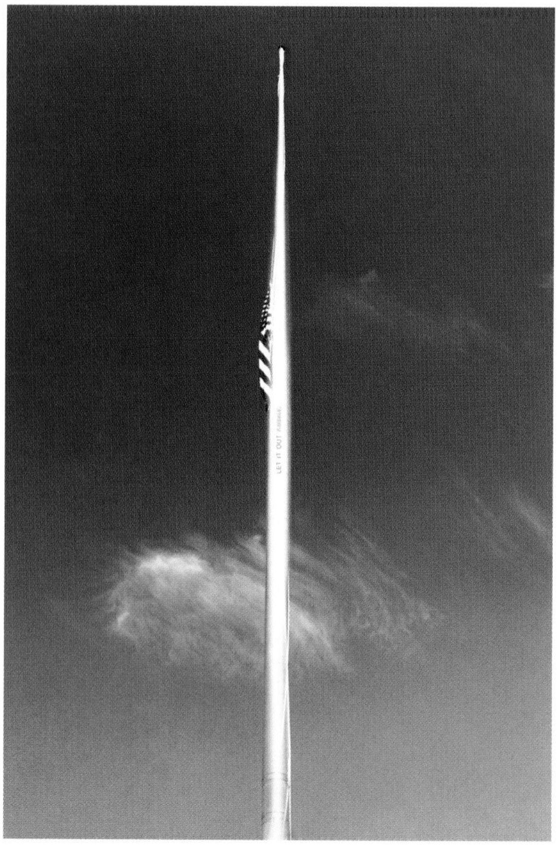

LET IT OUT

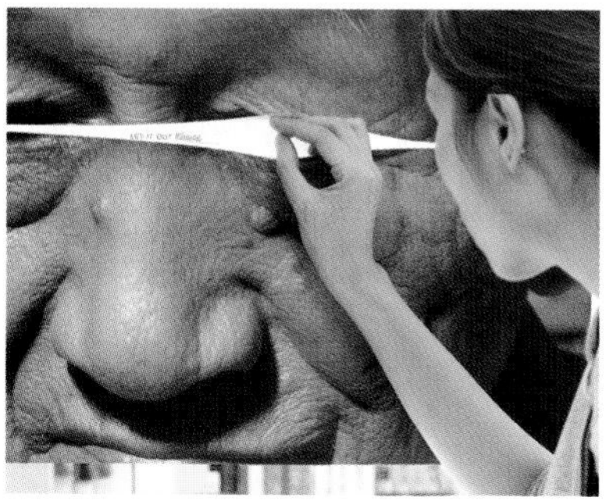

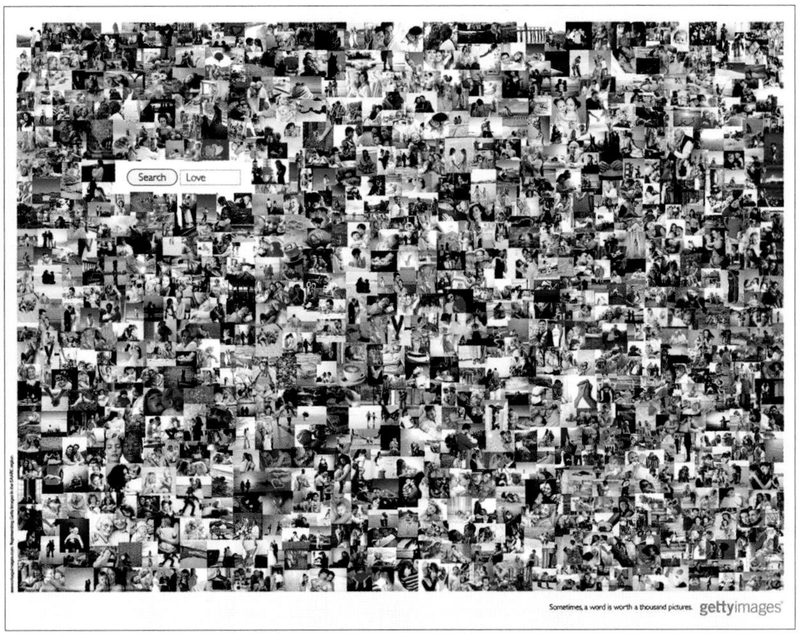
Search
Love
Sometimes, a word is worth a thousand pictures.
gettyimages

Search
Beauty
Sometimes, a word is worth a thousand pictures.
gettyimages

Search
Faith
Sometimes, a word is worth a thousand pictures.
gettyimages

MERIT

ART DIRECTOR
Abhijit Karandikar

WRITER
Ramamurthy Subramanian

CREATIVE DIRECTORS
Piyush Pandey
Sagar Mahabaleshwarkar

CLIENT
Visage Images

AGENCY
Ogilvy & Mather/ Mumbai

ANNUAL ID
06188A

MERIT

ART DIRECTOR
Justin Goh

WRITER
Darren Lee

DESIGNER
Justin Goh

ILLUSTRATOR
Justin Goh

CREATIVE DIRECTOR
Daniel Comar

CLIENT
Metropolitan TV

AGENCY
*Ogilvy & Mather/
Kuala Lumpur*

ANNUAL ID
06189A

FASHION SENSE
Hot gay tips for clueless straight guys.
queer eye. Saturdays 11pm, only on 8tv.

CULINARY SKILLS
Hot gay tips for clueless straight guys.
queer eye. Saturdays 11pm, only on 8tv.

INTERIOR DESIGN
Hot gay tips for clueless straight guys.
queer eye. Saturdays 11pm, only on 8tv.

CULTURE
Hot gay tips for clueless straight guys.
queer eye. Saturdays 11pm, only on 8tv.

JAM
WIDEST SCREEN IN THE CITY

JAM
WIDEST SCREEN IN THE CITY

JAM
WIDEST SCREEN IN THE CITY

MERIT

ART DIRECTOR
Mohit Tomar

WRITER
Nikhil Pandey

CREATIVE DIRECTOR
Emmanuel Upputuru

CLIENT
Shipra Estate

AGENCY
Ogilvy & Mather/ New Delhi

ANNUAL ID
06190A

MERIT

ART DIRECTOR
Kornthon Anantananukun

WRITER
Bhakpong Skonvitayanon

PHOTOGRAPHER
Anuchai Secharunputong

ILLUSTRATOR
Remix Studio

CREATIVE DIRECTOR
Nopadol Srikieatikajohn

CLIENT
Ionique Fertilizer

AGENCY
Ogilvy & Mather/ Bangkok

ANNUAL ID
06192A

With enriched macro-nutrients.

With enriched macro-nutrients.

With enriched macro-nutrients.

Koleman

Koleman

Koleman

Merit

ART DIRECTOR
Watchara Tansrikeat

WRITER
Bhakpong Skonvitayanon

PHOTOGRAPHER
Anuchai Secharunputong

ILLUSTRATOR
Remix Studio

CREATIVE DIRECTOR
Nopadol Srikieatikajohn

CLIENT
Koleman

AGENCY
Ogilvy & Mather/ Bangkok

ANNUAL ID
06191A

MERIT

ART DIRECTOR
Simon Oppmann

WRITER
Peter Roemmelt

PHOTOGRAPHER
Robin Ebener

CREATIVE DIRECTORS
Simon Oppmann
Peter Roemmelt

CLIENT
Kodak

AGENCY
Ogilvy & Mather/
Frankfurt

ANNUAL ID
06193A

Zoom in closer. The new Kodak Easyshare P880 with 12 x optical zoom.
Kodak

Zoom in closer. The new Kodak Easyshare P880 with 12 x optical zoom.
Kodak

Zoom in closer. The new Kodak Easyshare P880 with 12 x optical zoom.
Kodak

MOTOR
HARLEY-DAVIDSON
CYCLES

MOTOR
HARLEY-DAVIDSON
CYCLES

MOTOR
HARLEY-DAVIDSON
CYCLES

MERIT

ART DIRECTOR
Mike Groenewald

WRITER
Konstant van Huyssteen

PHOTOGRAPHER
David Prior

CREATIVE DIRECTORS
James Daniels
Gerry Human

CLIENT
Harley-Davidson

AGENCY
Ogilvy South Africa/
Johannesburg

ANNUAL ID
06194A

Merit

ART DIRECTOR
Mario Dias

WRITER
Nrusingha Chowdhury

PHOTOGRAPHERS
Raj Mistry
Saish Kambli

ILLUSTRATOR
Vinay Patil

CREATIVE DIRECTORS
Juju Basu
Hanoz Mogrelia

CLIENT
Procter & Gamble

AGENCY
Saatchi & Saatchi/ Mumbai

ANNUAL ID
06195A

Stains happen.
ARIEL

ARIEL

ARIEL

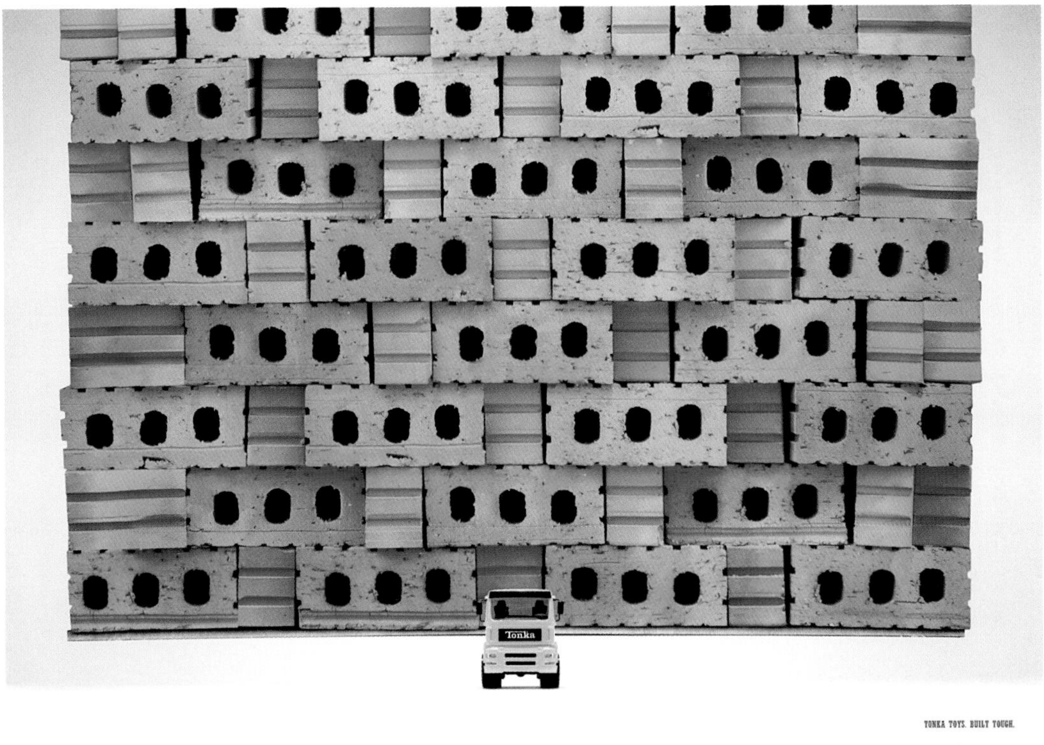
TONKA TOYS. BUILT TOUGH.

Merit

ART DIRECTOR
Richard Copping

WRITER
Jagdish Ramakrishnan

PHOTOGRAPHERS
Sam @ Boomerang
Getty Images

CREATIVE DIRECTOR
Andy Greenaway

CLIENT
Hasbro

AGENCY
Saatchi & Saatchi/
Singapore

ANNUAL ID
06198A

TONKA TOYS. BUILT TOUGH.

Merit

ART DIRECTORS
Richard Copping
Birger Linke

WRITERS
Audra Tan
Jagdish Ramakrishnan
Roger Makak

PHOTOGRAPHER
Teo Chai Guan

CREATIVE DIRECTOR
Andy Greenaway

CLIENT
Soon Hin Sportsbikes

AGENCY
Saatchi & Saatchi/
Singapore

ANNUAL ID
06199A

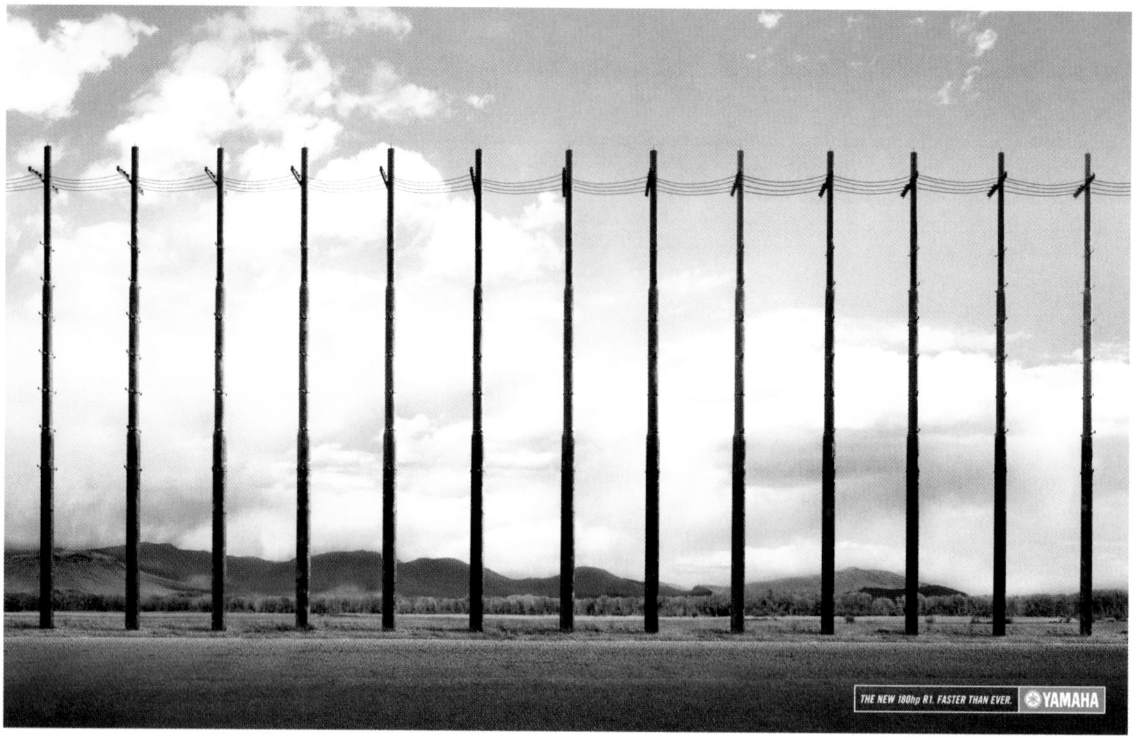
THE NEW 180hp R1. FASTER THAN EVER.
YAMAHA

THE NEW 180hp R1. FASTER THAN EVER.
YAMAHA

YAMAHA

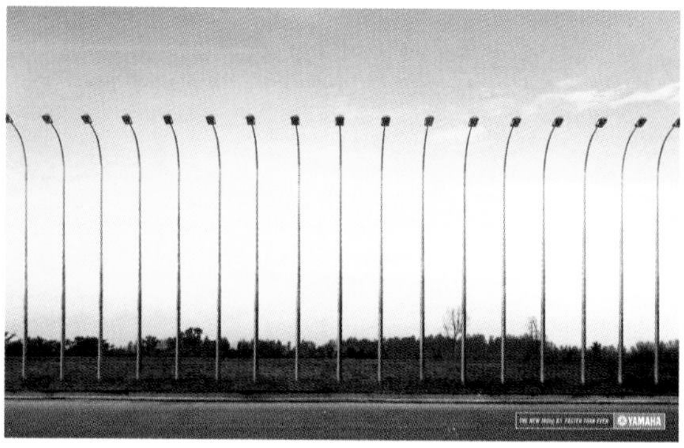
YAMAHA

www.yser-toyogo.com
TOYOGO
TOUGH PLASTICS

OFFICES
TO LET
LITTLE ITA
HOUSE
CAFE
LITTLE ITALY
TOYOGO
TOUGH PLASTICS

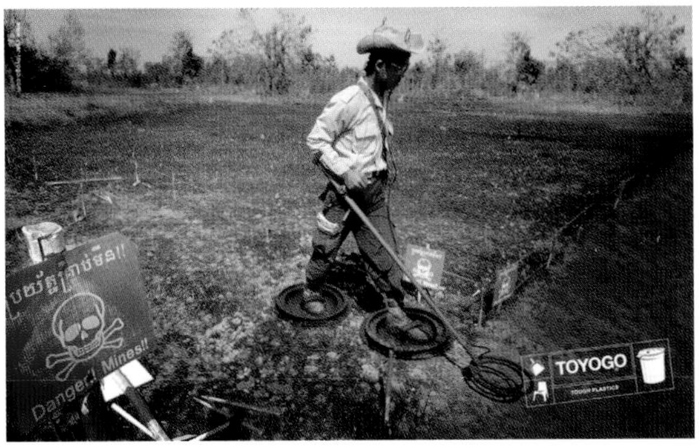
Danger! Mines!
TOYOGO

TOYOGO

Merit

ART DIRECTORS
Hor Yew Pong
Richard Chong
Edward Ong

WRITERS
May Yong
Hor Yew Pong
Richard Chong

PHOTOGRAPHERS
Corbis
Studio Rom

CREATIVE DIRECTORS
Edward Ong
Rowan Chanen
Tan Shen Guan

CLIENT
Yser Marketing

AGENCY
Y&R/Kuala Lumpur

ANNUAL ID
06201A

Merit

WRITER
James Lee

DESIGNER
Kara Bohl

PHOTOGRAPHER
Clinton Hussey

CREATIVE DIRECTORS
Alan Russell
Maria Kennedy

CLIENT
DDB Canada

AGENCY
DDB/Vancouver

ANNUAL ID
06202A

EVERYTHING IS THE COMPETITION
"IT'S NOT JUST WHAT YOU SAY THAT STIRS PEOPLE; IT'S THE WAY YOU SAY IT, YOU MORON."
— BILL BERNBACH (FOUNDER, DDB)

Merit

ART DIRECTOR
Bob Gates

WRITER
Bruno Corbo

CREATIVE DIRECTOR
Edward Boches

CLIENT
Joshua Dalsimer

AGENCY
Mullen/Wenham

ANNUAL ID
06203A

WITH A BOOK THIS GOOD, THERE'S NO TELLING WHO WILL CALL IT IN
Joshua Dalsimer is represented by Laurie Spinner 617.322.1374 dalsimerphoto.com

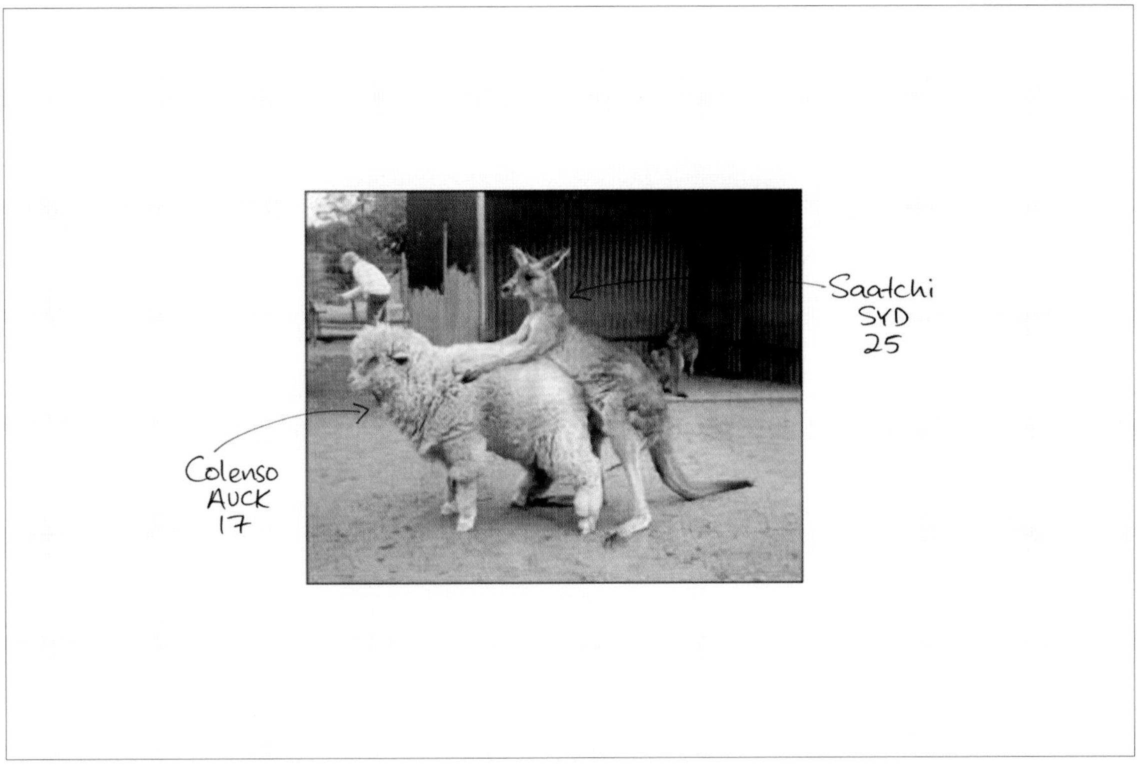
Saatchi
SYD
25
Colenso
AUCK
17

MERIT

ART DIRECTOR
Myles Allpress

WRITER
Charlie Ross

CREATIVE DIRECTOR
David Nobay

CLIENT
Saatchi & Saatchi

AGENCY
Saatchi & Saatchi/Sydney

ANNUAL ID
06204A

MERIT

PUBLIC SERVICE/POLITICAL

MERIT

ART DIRECTOR
Justin Lesinski

WRITER
Howard Hill

ILLUSTRATOR
Justin Lesinski

CREATIVE DIRECTORS
Rich Wakefield
Kyle Lewis
Marcus Kemp

CLIENT
Change the Policy

AGENCY
BBDO/Atlanta

ANNUAL ID
06205A

www.changethepolicy.org

MERIT

ART DIRECTOR
Jose Carlos Fonseca

WRITER
Liber Matteucci

PHOTOGRAPHER
Filipe Rebelo

CLIENT
APAV

AGENCY
JWT/Lisbon

ANNUAL ID
06209A

SILENCE HURTS CALL 707200077
APAV
Victim Support

One out of ten traffic victims is a pedestrian
Vereniging Verkeersslachtoffers
www.verkeersslachtoffers.nl

MERIT

ART DIRECTOR
Jan-Willem Smits

WRITER
Edsard Schutte

PHOTOGRAPHER
R. Nederveen

CREATIVE DIRECTOR
Carl Le Blond

CLIENT
Dutch Association for Traffic Victims (Vereniging Verkeersslachtoffers)

AGENCY
Ogilvy/Amsterdam

ANNUAL ID
06210A

ALSO AWARDED
Merit: Public Service/ Political: Outdoor and Posters - Single

Hemingway's fiction.
Frost's poetry.
Khrushchev's mind.
Kennedy's favorite reading.
VISIT THE JFK PRESIDENTIAL LIBRARY AND MUSEUM

MERIT

ART DIRECTOR
Dave Padgett

WRITERS
Joe Alexander
Dave Muhlenfeld

CREATIVE DIRECTOR
Joe Alexander

CLIENT
JFK Library

AGENCY
The Martin Agency/ Richmond

ANNUAL ID
06211A

MERIT

ART DIRECTOR
Dave Padgett

WRITERS
Joe Alexander
Dave Muhlenfeld

CREATIVE DIRECTOR
Joe Alexander

CLIENT
JFK Library

AGENCY
The Martin Agency/ Richmond

ANNUAL ID
06212A

Postage stamp.
Road.
Bridge.
Theater.
Library.
Art gallery.
Grade school.
City hall.
Observatory.
Stadium.
Launching pad.
Airport.
Mountain.
Baby.

Named John F. Kennedy.

VISIT THE JFK PRESIDENTIAL LIBRARY AND MUSEUM

HERTZ THEATRE

HERTZ THEATRE

MERIT

ART DIRECTOR
Phil Mimaki

WRITER
Paul Janzen

PHOTOGRAPHER
Dana Neibert

CREATIVE DIRECTORS
Kyle Lewis
Marcus Kemp

CLIENT
Hertz Theatre

AGENCY
BBDO/Atlanta

ANNUAL ID
06213A

ALSO AWARDED
Merit:
Public Service/Political:
Outdoor - Campaign

MERIT

ART DIRECTOR
Roshni Kavina

WRITER
Siddhartha Bindra

CREATIVE DIRECTORS
Ashok Karnik
Siddhartha Bindra

CLIENT
Cancer Patients Aid Association

AGENCY
Euro RSCG/Mumbai

ANNUAL ID
06214A

ALSO AWARDED
Merit:
Public Service/Political: Outdoor and Posters - Single

Merit:
Public Service/Political: Newspaper or Magazine - Single

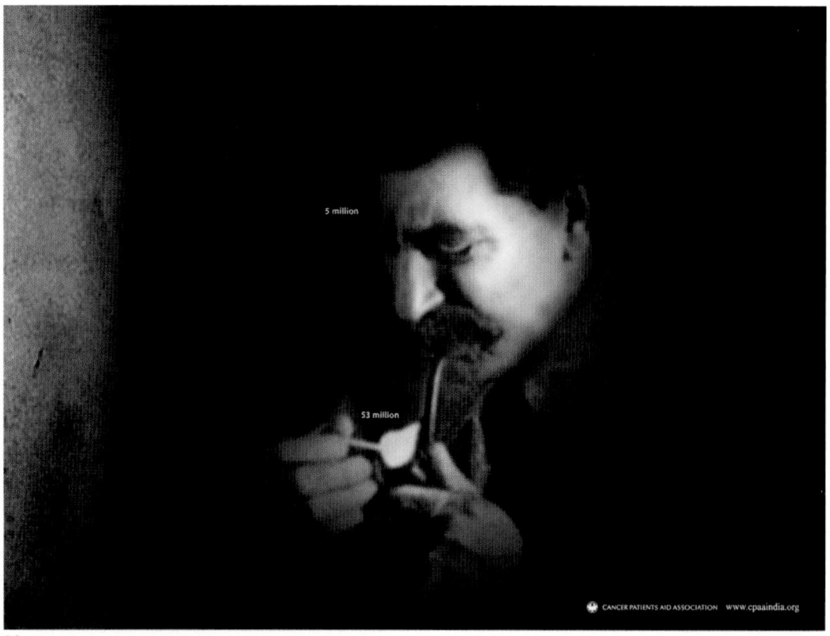
5 million
53 million
CANCER PATIENTS AID ASSOCIATION www.cpaaindia.org

Merit

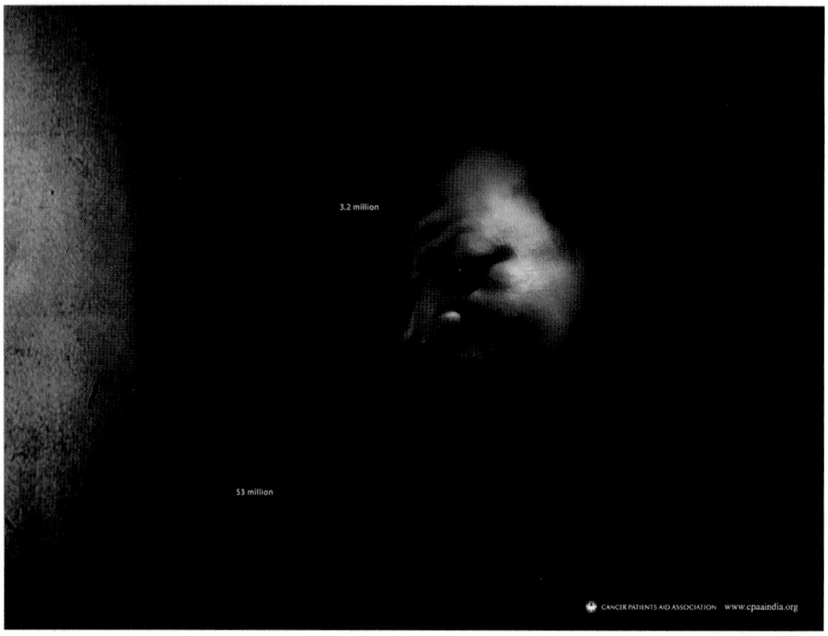
3.2 million
53 million
CANCER PATIENTS AID ASSOCIATION www.cpaaindia.org

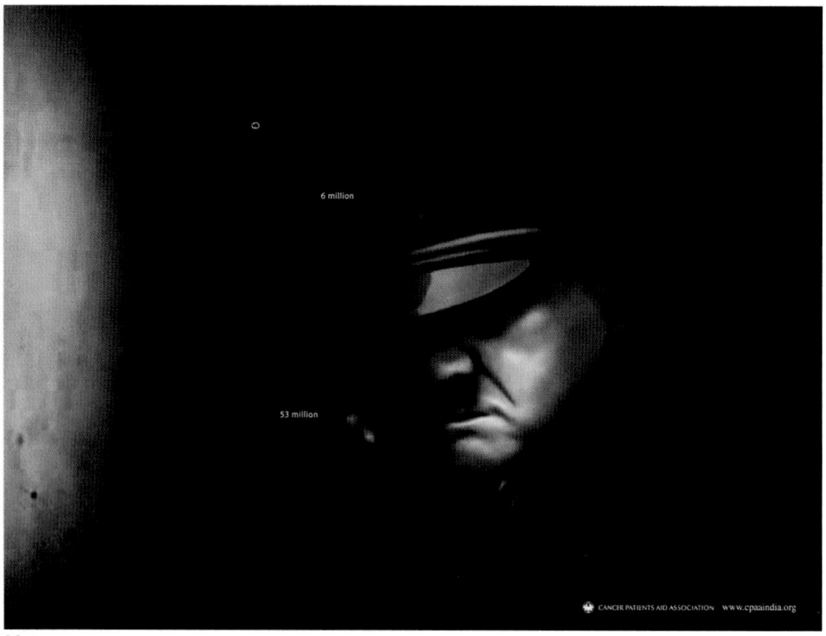
6 million
53 million
CANCER PATIENTS AID ASSOCIATION www.cpaaindia.org

Merit

Torture has no place on
American soil.
That's why we have it done in Egypt.
The United States has a practice called Extraordinary Rendition. Without being charged with any crime, people are abducted and sent to foreign countries like Jordan and Egypt, where they are interrogated in torture cells. They are kept hidden, denied legal counsel, and brutalized, sometimes for years. Extraordinary Rendition is a betrayal of America's best values and a violation of our laws. If we want our laws and values to survive for our children, then we must stand up for them now. Please tell your representatives in Congress you want an independent commission to investigate, demand accountability at all levels, and prevent further abuse. Contact them and findout more at amnestyusa.org.
AMNESTY INTERNATIONAL USA

MERIT

ART DIRECTOR
Dan Weeks

WRITERS
Pete Kellen
Derek Sherman

CREATIVE DIRECTORS
Dan Weeks
Derek Sherman

CLIENT
Amnesty International

AGENCY
Middle Child/Lake Forest

ANNUAL ID
06215A

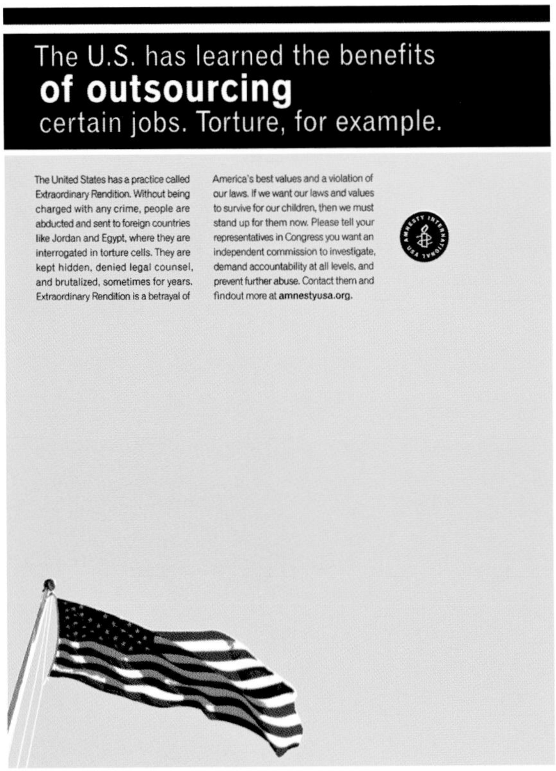
The U.S. has learned the benefits
of outsourcing
certain jobs. Torture, for example.
The United States has a practice called Extraordinary Rendition. Without being charged with any crime, people are abducted and sent to foreign countries like Jordan and Egypt, where they are interrogated in torture cells. They are kept hidden, denied legal counsel, and brutalized, sometimes for years. Extraordinary Rendition is a betrayal of America's best values and a violation of our laws. If we want our laws and values to survive for our children, then we must stand up for them now. Please tell your representatives in Congress you want an independent commission to investigate, demand accountability at all levels, and prevent further abuse. Contact them and findout more at amnestyusa.org.
AMNESTY INTERNATIONAL USA

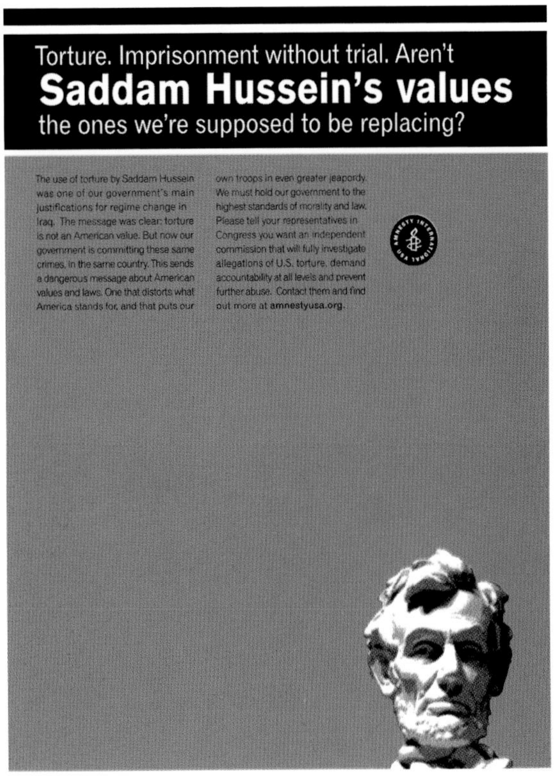
Torture. Imprisonment without trial. Aren't
Saddam Hussein's values
the ones we're supposed to be replacing?
The use of torture by Saddam Hussein was one of our government's main justifications for regime change in Iraq. The message was clear: torture is not an American value. But now our government is committing these same crimes, in the same country. This sends a dangerous message about American values and laws. One that distorts what America stands for, and that puts our own troops in even greater jeapordy. We must hold our government to the highest standards of morality and law. Please tell your representatives in Congress you want an independent commission that will fully investigate allegations of U.S. torture, demand accountability at all levels and prevent further abuse. Contact them and find out more at amnestyusa.org.
AMNESTY INTERNATIONAL USA

Merit

ART DIRECTORS
Vijay Sawant
Juhi Chaturvedi
Mohammad Ajmal

WRITER
Abhijit Avasthi

PHOTOGRAPHER
Vishlesh Desmukh

ILLUSTRATORS
Uday Kinloskar
Manjunath Beleri

CREATIVE DIRECTORS
Piyush Pandey
Abhijit Avasthi

CLIENT
Hindustan Times

AGENCY
Ogilvy & Mather/
Mumbai

ANNUAL ID
06216A

Plant more trees.

Plant more trees.

Plant more trees.

Germany's historic monuments need help. Donations: Account No. 30 55555
200

Germany's historic monuments need help. Donations: Account No. 30 55555
German Foundation for the Preservation of Historic Monuments
50

Germany's historic monuments need help. Donations: Account No. 30 55555
X25068643427
10 EURO

Merit

ART DIRECTOR
Simon Oppmann

WRITER
Peter Roemmelt

PHOTOGRAPHER
Hana Kostreba

CREATIVE DIRECTORS
Simon Oppmann
Peter Roemmelt

CLIENT
German Foundation for Monument Protection (Deutsche Stiftung Denkmalschutz)

AGENCY
Ogilvy & Mather/ Frankfurt

ANNUAL ID
06218A

ALSO AWARDED
Merit: Public Service/Political: Outdoor and Posters - Campaign

MERIT

ART DIRECTOR
Mark Voehringer

WRITER
Jake Benjamin

PHOTOGRAPHER
Kenji Toma

ILLUSTRATOR
Kevin Li

CREATIVE DIRECTORS
Tony Granger
Jan Jacobs
Leo Premutico

CLIENT
American Society for the Prevention of Cruelty to Animals (ASPCA)

AGENCY
Saatchi & Saatchi/ New York

ANNUAL ID
06221A

SUPER GLUE
WHATEVER YOU CAN IMAGINE. WE'VE SEEN WORSE.
Last year, the ASPCA handled over 65,000 cruelty complaints. 4,000 in New York City alone.
To learn how you can help prevent cases like this, visit ASPCAspeak.org.
ASPCA

WHATEVER YOU CAN IMAGINE. WE'VE SEEN WORSE.
Last year, the ASPCA handled over 65,000 cruelty complaints. 4,000 in New York City alone.
To learn how you can help prevent cases like this, visit ASPCAspeak.org.
ASPCA

WHATEVER YOU CAN IMAGINE. WE'VE SEEN WORSE.
Last year, the ASPCA handled over 65,000 cruelty complaints. 4,000 in New York City alone.
To learn how you can help prevent cases like this, visit ASPCAspeak.org.
ASPCA

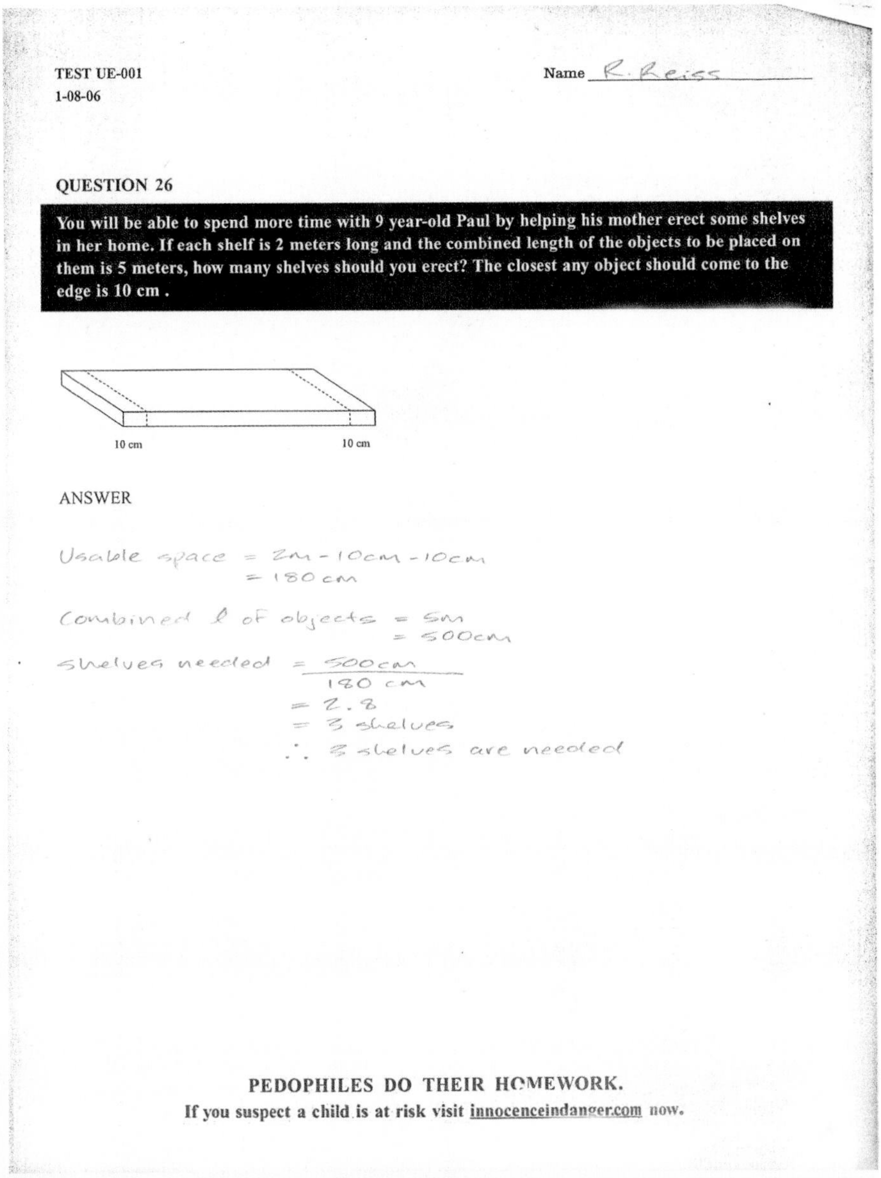

TEST UE-001
1-08-06
Name R. Reiss
QUESTION 26
You will be able to spend more time with 9 year-old Paul by helping his mother erect some shelves in her home. If each shelf is 2 meters long and the combined length of the objects to be placed on them is 5 meters, how many shelves should you erect? The closest any object should come to the edge is 10 cm .
10 cm
10 cm
ANSWER
Usable space = 2m - 10cm - 10cm
= 180 cm
Combined ℓ of objects = 5m
= 500cm
Shelves needed = 500cm / 180 cm
= 2.8
= 3 shelves
∴ 3 shelves are needed
PEDOPHILES DO THEIR HOMEWORK.
If you suspect a child is at risk visit innocenceindanger.com now.

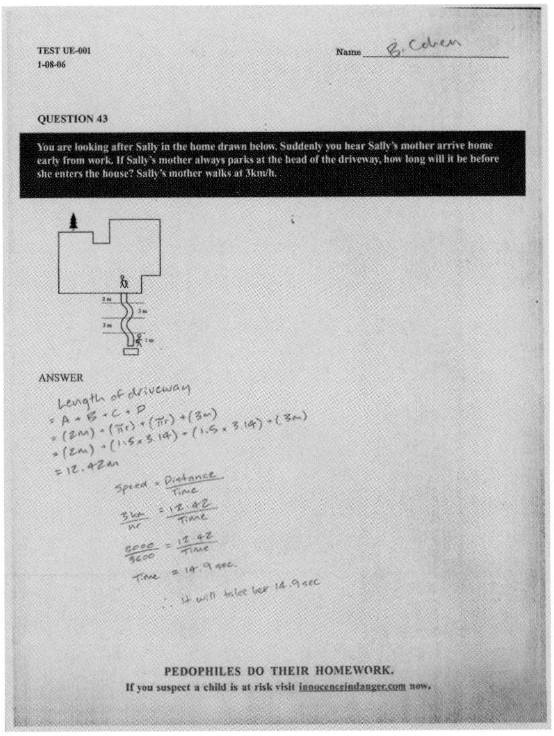

TEST UE-001
1-08-06
Name B. Cohen
QUESTION 43
You are looking after Sally in the home drawn below. Suddenly you hear Sally's mother arrive home early from work. If Sally's mother always parks at the head of the driveway, how long will it be before she enters the house? Sally's mother walks at 3km/h.
ANSWER
Length of driveway
= A + B + C + D
= (2m) + (πr) + (πr) + (3m)
= (2m) + (1.5 x 3.14) + (1.5 x 3.14) + (3m)
= 12.42m
Speed = Distance / Time
3km / hr = 12.42 / Time
3000 / 3600 = 12.42 / Time
Time = 14.9 sec.
∴ It will take her 14.9 sec
PEDOPHILES DO THEIR HOMEWORK.
If you suspect a child is at risk visit innocenceindanger.com now.

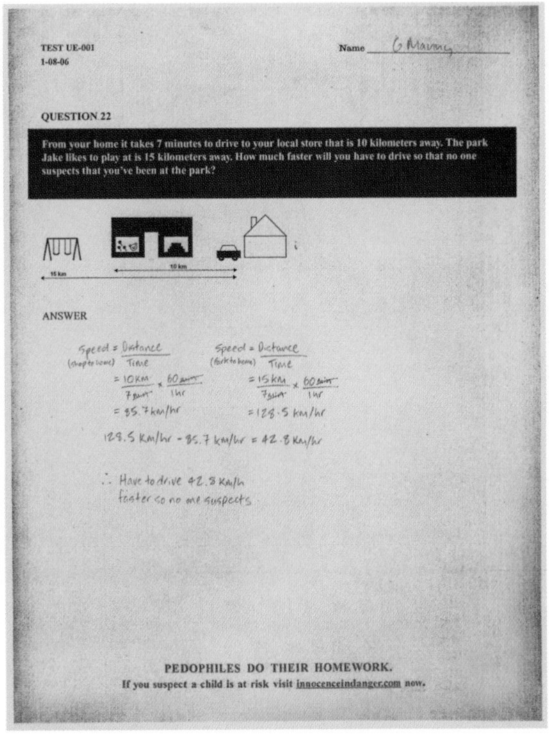

TEST UE-001
1-08-06
Name G Maurry
QUESTION 22
From your home it takes 7 minutes to drive to your local store that is 10 kilometers away. The park Jake likes to play at is 15 kilometers away. How much faster will you have to drive so that no one suspects that you've been at the park?
10 km
15 km
ANSWER
Speed (shop to home) = Distance / Time
= 10KM / 7min x 60min / 1hr
= 85.7km/hr
Speed (Park to home) = Distance / Time
= 15KM / 7min x 60min / 1hr
= 128.5 km/hr
128.5 Km/hr - 85.7 km/hr = 42.8 Km/hr
∴ Have to drive 42.8 Km/h faster so no one suspects
PEDOPHILES DO THEIR HOMEWORK.
If you suspect a child is at risk visit innocenceindanger.com now.

MERIT

ART DIRECTOR
Jan Jacobs

WRITER
Leo Premutico

ILLUSTRATOR
Kevin Li

CREATIVE DIRECTORS
Tony Granger
Jan Jacobs
Leo Premutico

CLIENT
Innocence in Danger

AGENCY
Saatchi & Saatchi/ New York

ANNUAL ID
06222A

Merit

ART DIRECTORS
Joel Clement
Steve Hough

WRITERS
Steve Hough
Joel Clement

PHOTOGRAPHERS
Ming Yeo Ho
Kong How Lee

ILLUSTRATORS
Kheng Heong Chan
Harry Bates
Aston Choong
Beng Hong Saw

CREATIVE DIRECTORS
Steve Hough
Andy Greenaway

CLIENT
Amnesty International

AGENCY
Saatchi & Saatchi/
Petaling Jaya

ANNUAL ID
06219A

HE TORTURES THE INNOCENT IN
MYANMAR
8K
8K
JUST THE SORT OF GUY YOU
WANT FOR A PEN PAL
JOIN OUR LETTER WRITING CAMPAIGN TO STOP THE MILITARY JUNTA FROM BRUTALLY SUPPRESSING POLITICAL DISSIDENTS. YOUR LETTER COULD SAVE COUNTLESS LIVES. TO HELP, VISIT WWW.AMNESTY.ORG AND STAMP OUT VIOLENCE WITH A STAMP.
amnesty international

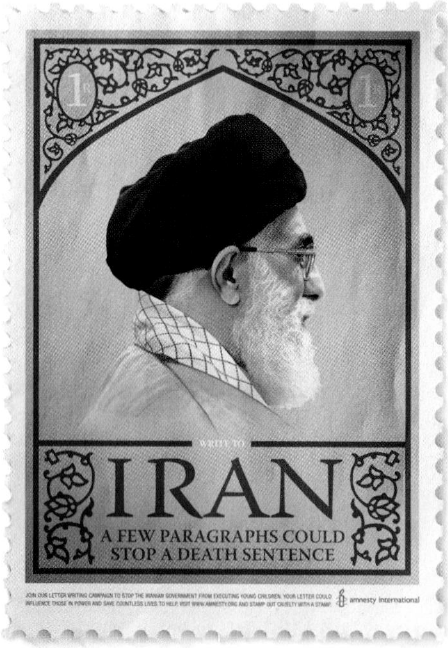
WRITE TO
IRAN
A FEW PARAGRAPHS COULD
STOP A DEATH SENTENCE
JOIN OUR LETTER WRITING CAMPAIGN TO STOP THE IRANIAN GOVERNMENT FROM EXECUTING YOUNG CHILDREN. YOUR LETTER COULD INFLUENCE THOSE IN POWER AND SAVE COUNTLESS LIVES. TO HELP, VISIT WWW.AMNESTY.ORG AND STAMP OUT CRUELTY WITH A STAMP.
amnesty international

INTIMIDATE THE DICTATOR OF
ZIMBABWE
WRITE TO HIM
5
JOIN OUR LETTER WRITING CAMPAIGN TO STOP THE ZIMBABWE REGIME FROM TORTURING AND MURDERING POLITICAL OPPONENTS. YOUR LETTER COULD SAVE COUNTLESS LIVES. TO HELP, VISIT WWW.AMNESTY.ORG AND STAMP OUT BRUTALITY WITH A STAMP.
amnesty international

GUANTANAMO BAY
WRITE TO HIM AND HELP STOP TORTURE AT
REMEMBER, USE SIMPLE WORDS
39¢
amnesty international

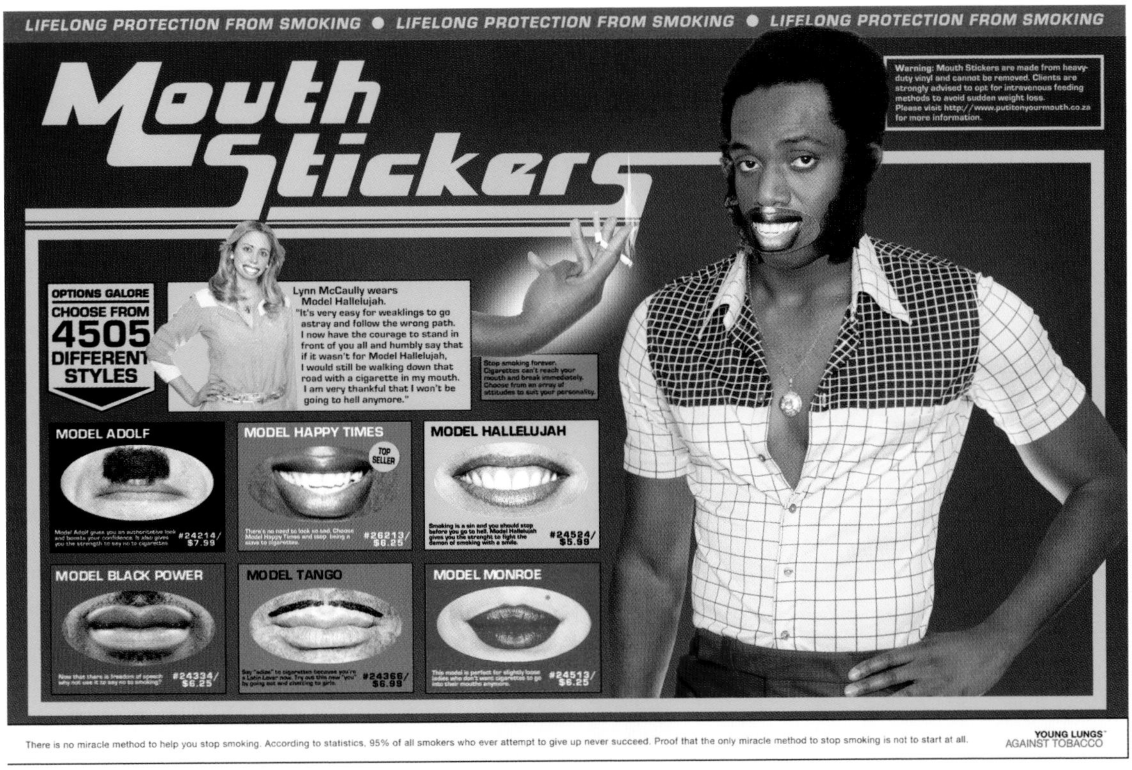
LIFELONG PROTECTION FROM SMOKING ● LIFELONG PROTECTION FROM SMOKING ● LIFELONG PROTECTION FROM SMOKING
Mouth Stickers
Warning: Mouth Stickers are made from heavy-duty vinyl and cannot be removed. Clients are strongly advised to opt for intravenous feeding methods to avoid sudden weight loss. Please visit http://www.putitonyourmouth.co.za for more information.
OPTIONS GALORE
CHOOSE FROM 4505 DIFFERENT STYLES
Lynn McCaully wears Model Hallelujah.
"It's very easy for weaklings to go astray and follow the wrong path. I now have the courage to stand in front of you all and humbly say that if it wasn't for Model Hallelujah, I would still be walking down that road with a cigarette in my mouth. I am very thankful that I won't be going to hell anymore."
Stop smoking forever. Cigarettes can't reach your mouth and break immediately. Choose from an array of attitudes to suit your personality.
MODEL ADOLF
Model Adolf gives you an authoritative look and boosts your confidence. It also gives you the strength to say no to cigarettes.
#24214/ $7.99
MODEL HAPPY TIMES
TOP SELLER
There's no need to look so sad. Choose Model Happy Times and stop being a slave to cigarettes.
#26213/ $6.25
MODEL HALLELUJAH
Smoking is a sin and you should stop before you go to hell. Model Hallelujah gives you the strenght to fight the demon of smoking with a smile.
#24524/ $5.99
MODEL BLACK POWER
Now that there is freedom of speech why not use it to say no to smoking?
#24334/ $6.25
MODEL TANGO
#24366/ $6.99
MODEL MONROE
This model is perfect for slightly loose ladies who don't want cigarettes to go into their mouths anymore.
#24513/ $6.25
There is no miracle method to help you stop smoking. According to statistics, 95% of all smokers who ever attempt to give up never succeed. Proof that the only miracle method to stop smoking is not to start at all.
YOUNG LUNGS AGAINST TOBACCO

The impenetrable Hair Wall
KEEPS CIGARETTES OUT!
It's what gentlemen prefer these days.
Handcrafted and only 100% human hair is allowed onto the factory floor. 5 different debonair colors and styles to choose from. Cash with order. Postage paid. Comprehensive instruction guide and a pocket-sized "How gentlemen should plan outfits around the Hair Wall" style guide included with each order.
INSTANT SUCCESS IN HEALTH & BUSINESS
There's nothing more debonair than The Hair Wall
BEFORE
AFTER
THE elegant WAY TO STOP SMOKING
(picture 1)
(picture 2)
THE MODERN HAIR WALL MOUSTACHE OFFERS INSTANT AND STYLISH PROTECTION FROM CIGARETTES. BEING SUAVE AND HEALTHY HAS NEVER FELT OR LOOKED THIS GOOD.
(Top)
Any attempt to put a cigarette in your mouth will fail. The moustache is impenetrable, so cigarettes will get stuck in the Hair Wall.
(Bottom)
After a few weeks success arrives. All cigarettes are kept out by the elegant Hair Wall.
(Friendly reminder: A minor side effect of the elegant moustache might be that food could get stuck in the beard along with the cigarettes. Apply elegance and grace to avoid this potential problem.)
plus Thanks to the debonair HairWall you look more SERIOUS
Your business runs better.
Your wife and your clients respect you more.
Your stock market investments start paying off.
There is no miracle method to help you stop smoking. According to statistics, 95% of all smokers who ever attempt to give up never succeed. Proof that the only miracle method to stop smoking is not to start at all.
YOUNG LUNGS AGAINST TOBACCO

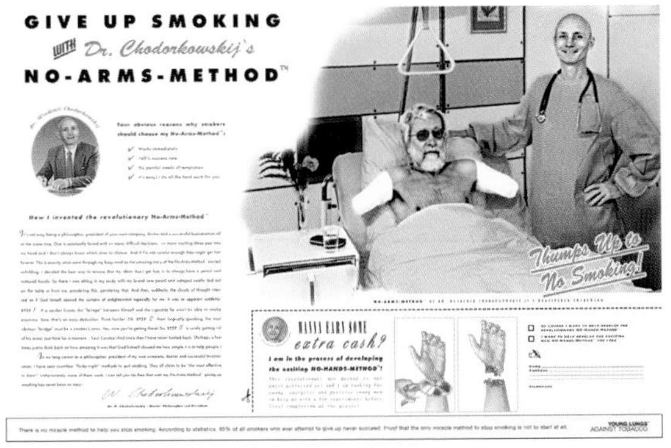
GIVE UP SMOKING
WITH Dr. Chodorkowskij's
NO-ARMS-METHOD
Thumbs Up to No Smoking!
YOUNG LUNGS AGAINST TOBACCO

TUFF STUFF
THORN RING
STOP SMOKING LIKE THE TUFF GUYZ DO!!
ELECTRO RING
TUFF STUFF
YOUNG LUNGS AGAINST TOBACCO

MERIT

ART DIRECTORS
Joakim Reveman
Bjoern Ruehmann

WRITERS
Xander Smith
Joakim Reveman
Bjoern Ruehmann
Kerry Keenan

PHOTOGRAPHERS
Hans Starck
Sven Glage

ILLUSTRATOR
Patrice Larue

CREATIVE DIRECTORS
Erik Vervroegen
Kerry Keenan

CLIENT
YLAT (Young Lungs Against Tobacco)

AGENCY
TBWA/Paris

ANNUAL ID
06114A

ALSO AWARDED
Merit:
Public Service/Political: Outdoor and Posters - Campaign

Merit

ART DIRECTOR
Paul Bootlis

WRITER
Paul Bootlis

PHOTOGRAPHER
Bradley Patrick

CREATIVE DIRECTOR
Jay Furby

CLIENT
International Campaign to Ban Landmines

AGENCY
Arnold Australia/Sydney

ANNUAL ID
06223A

ALSO AWARDED
Merit:
Innovative Use of Media:
Outdoor - Single

International CAMPAIGN TO BAN LANDMINES
Help. Or take one.

Merit

ART DIRECTORS
Sakol Mongkolsaetarin
Hewaed Jue

WRITER
Neil Levy

CREATIVE DIRECTOR
Jim Lesser

CLIENT
San Francisco Zoological Society

AGENCY
BBDO West/ San Francisco

ANNUAL ID
06224A

VIACOM
EXPERIENCE THE WORLD OF INSECTS
SAN FRANCISCO ZOO
Join Zoomanity

SUPPORT THE
HOMELESS
THIS WINTER.
IF YOU'RE COLD OR KNOW OF SOMEONE WHO IS
PLEASE TAKE THIS POSTER.

MERIT

ART DIRECTOR
Debbie Gyngell

WRITER
Stefanus Nel

CREATIVE DIRECTOR
Vanessa Pearson

CLIENT
Salvation Army

AGENCY
Lobedu Leo Burnett/
Sunninghill

ANNUAL ID
06227A

FUNDACION
VIDA SILVESTRE
ARGENTINA

MERIT

ART DIRECTOR
Juan Erasmo

WRITER
Pablo Loperena

CREATIVE DIRECTORS
Gustavo Taretto
Gabriel Vazquez

CLIENT
Fundacion Vida Silvestre

AGENCY
Ogilvy & Mather/
Buenos Aires

ANNUAL ID
06228A

Merit

ART DIRECTOR
Kanika Sethi

WRITER
Kanika Sethi

CREATIVE DIRECTOR
Emmanuel Upputuru

CLIENT
Seagram India

AGENCY
Ogilvy & Mather/ New Delhi

ANNUAL ID
06229A

Dri__
nk
ve
make a responsible choice.
Seagram

Merit

ART DIRECTORS
Xingsheng Qi
Shengxiong Chen

WRITERS
Andy Song
Jacky Lung

CREATIVE DIRECTORS
Nils Andersson
Jacky Lung

CLIENT
WWF

AGENCY
Ogilvy/Beijing

ANNUAL ID
06232A

如果全球变暖的状况得不到
改善，2100年它们就会灭绝。
支持可再生能源，减少二氧化碳
排放，才能拯救它和我们自己。
想了解更多，请访问
WWW.WWFCHINA.ORG
WWF

If global warming continues at current rates, the polar bear will disappear by 2100. But by cutting CO2 emissions and supporting renewable energy, we can keep them cool, and alive. To see how you can help, visit www.wwfchina.org

Merit

ART DIRECTOR
Peng Yu

WRITERS
Doug Schiff
Fei Zhao

CREATIVE DIRECTORS
Doug Schiff
Nils Andersson

CLIENT
WWF

AGENCY
Ogilvy/Beijing

ANNUAL ID
06233A

MERIT

ART DIRECTOR
Charlie Wilson

WRITER
Emma de la Fosse

CREATIVE DIRECTORS
Colin Nimick
Paul Hargreaves

CLIENT
Cancer Research UK

AGENCY
OgilvyOne/London

ANNUAL ID
06235A

SUSAN JAMES LOVED SITTING HERE. AND STILL DOES THANKS TO RESEARCH INTO CANCER.
To donate call 0800 316 4000

MERIT

ART DIRECTOR
Marcus Rebeschini

WRITER
Robert Kleman

PHOTOGRAPHERS
Jimmy Fok @ Katapolt
Jordan Doner @ Katapolt

ILLUSTRATOR
Trevor Bittinger

CREATIVE DIRECTORS
Marcus Rebeschini
Robert Kleman
Gerry Graf

CLIENT
American Cancer Society

AGENCY
TBWA\Chiat\Day/ New York

ANNUAL ID
06236A

PERSHING SQUARE
ONE WAY

KODAK digital

hands
the story
79
Discover another world.
BO
OK

Discover another world.
BO
OK
18

217
Discover another world.

MERIT

ART DIRECTOR
Tim Huse

WRITER
Natalie Knight

CREATIVE DIRECTOR
Richard Maddocks

CLIENT
New Zealand Book Council

AGENCY
Colenso BBDO/ Auckland

ANNUAL ID
06238A

MERIT

ART DIRECTOR
Daryl Gardiner

WRITER
Kevin Rathgeber

PHOTOGRAPHER
Frank Hoedl

CREATIVE DIRECTOR
Alan Russell

CLIENT
United Way

AGENCY
DDB/Vancouver

ANNUAL ID
06239A

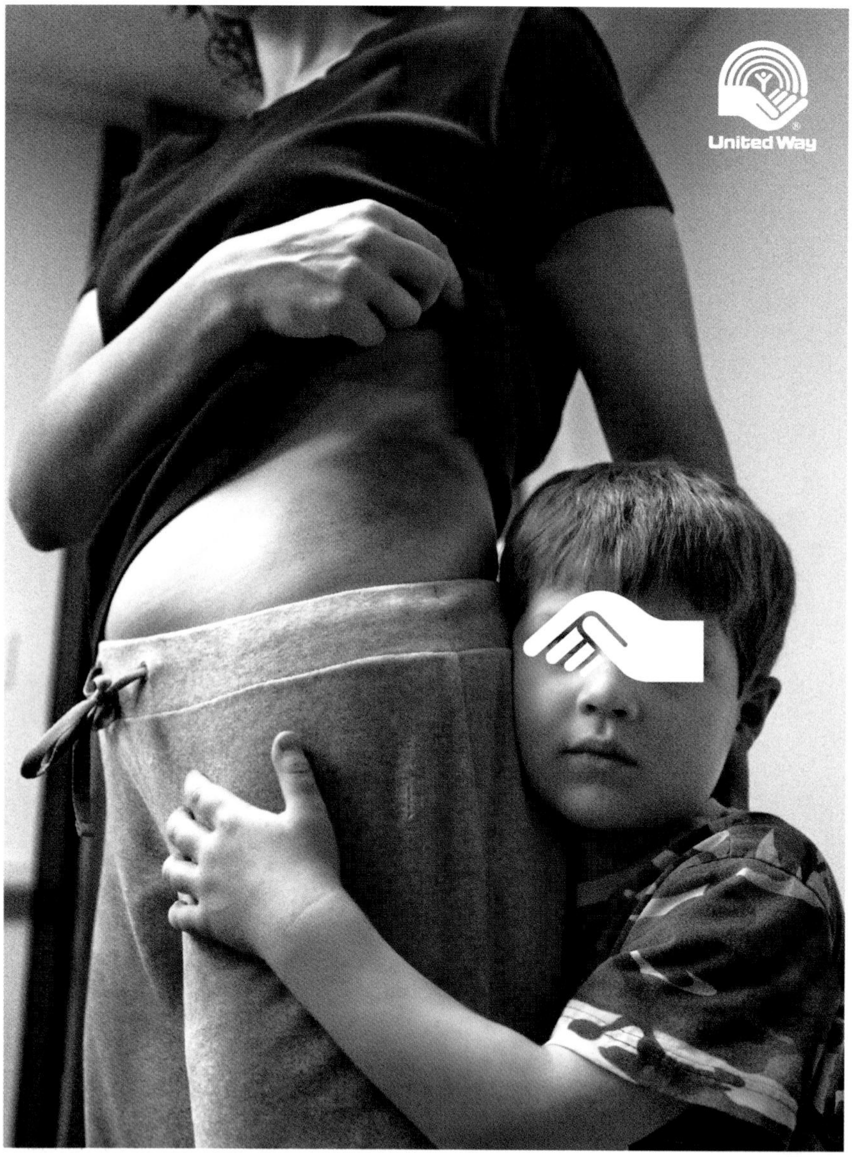
United Way

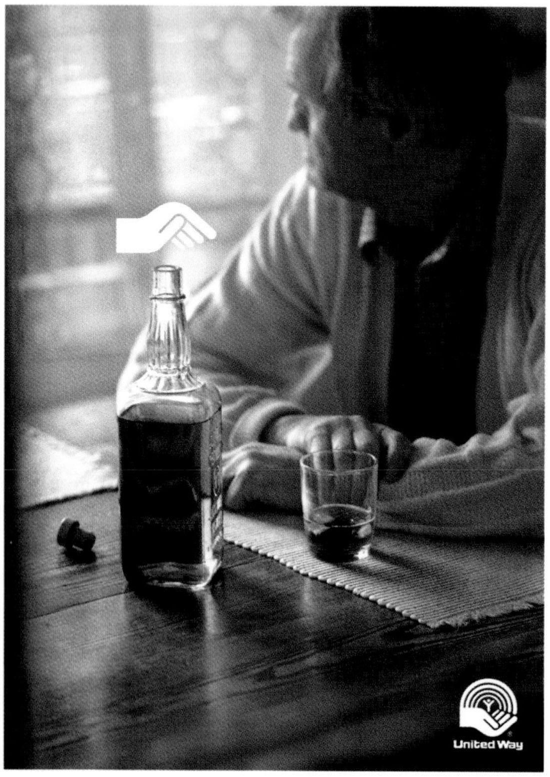
United Way

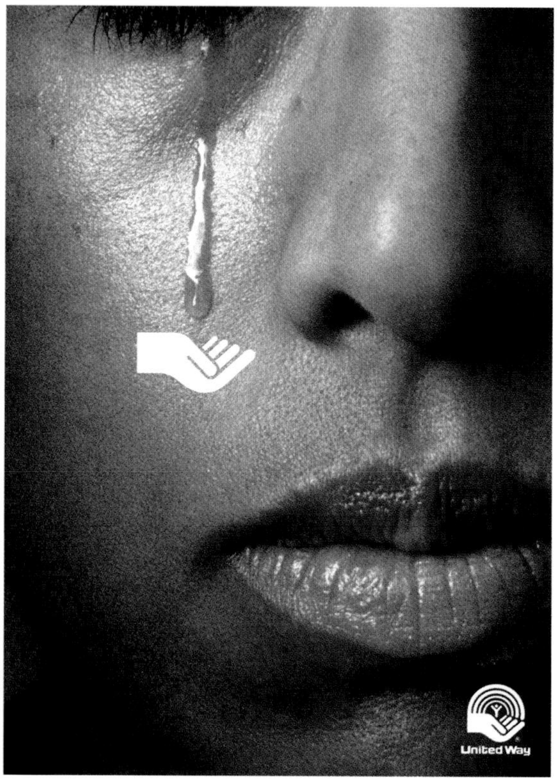
United Way

Merit

ART DIRECTOR
Paul Foulkes

WRITER
Tyler Hampton

PHOTOGRAPHER
Claude Shade

CREATIVE DIRECTORS
Jeffrey Goodby
Rich Silverstein

CLIENT
California Coastal Commission

AGENCY
Goodby, Silverstein & Partners/San Francisco

ANNUAL ID
06240A

ALSO AWARDED
Bronze:
Public Service/Political: Newspaper or Magazine - Single

Non-Native Species of the California Coast
The Cig Egret
CALIFORNIA COASTAL CLEANUP DAY
September 17th • 9am-noon
CALIFORNIA COASTAL COMMISSION

Bronze

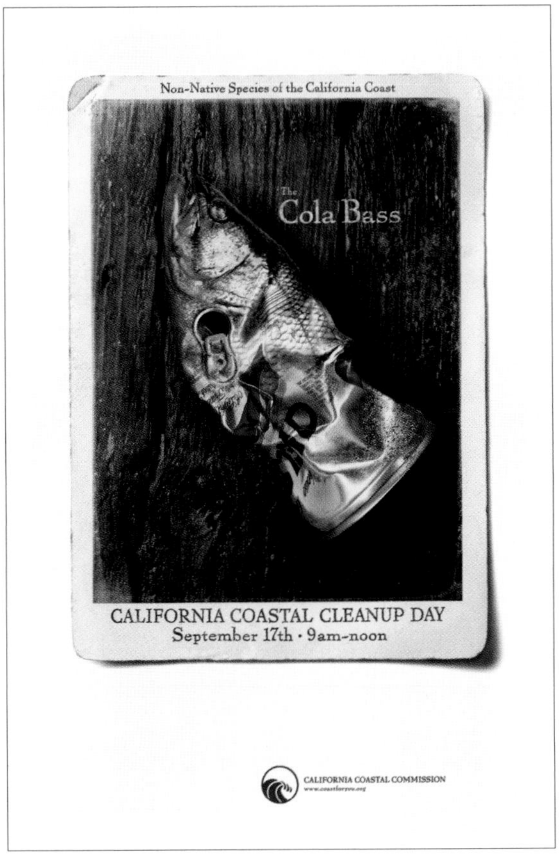
Non-Native Species of the California Coast
The Cola Bass
CALIFORNIA COASTAL CLEANUP DAY
September 17th • 9am-noon
CALIFORNIA COASTAL COMMISSION

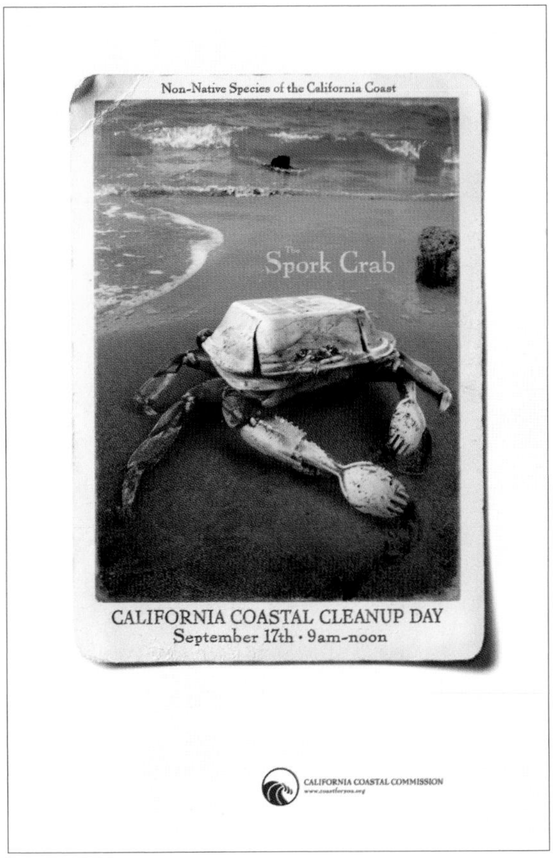
Non-Native Species of the California Coast
The Spork Crab
CALIFORNIA COASTAL CLEANUP DAY
September 17th • 9am-noon
CALIFORNIA COASTAL COMMISSION

MERIT

ART DIRECTOR
Tom Sloan

WRITER
Stephen Childress

CREATIVE DIRECTOR
Tom Sloan

CLIENT
American Red Cross

AGENCY
Henderson Advertising/ Greenville

ANNUAL ID
06241A

During Katrina,
this line would've been under water.
American Red Cross
1-800 HELP NOW

During Rita,
this awning would've been under water.
American Red Cross
1-800 HELP NOW

15 ft. storm surge crests here.

COFFEE
During Katrina, this lamp post would've been under water.

Forests for Life. WWF

Merit

Forests for Life. WWF

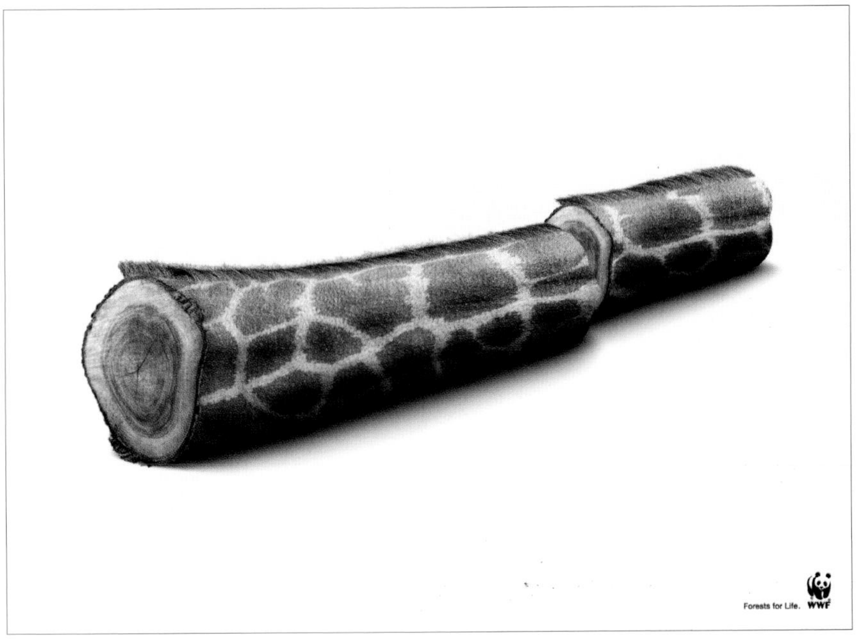
Forests for Life. WWF

MERIT

ART DIRECTOR
Gumpon Laksanajinda

WRITER
Kulvadee Doksroy

PHOTOGRAPHER
Anuchai Secharunputong

ILLUSTRATOR
Remix Studio

CREATIVE DIRECTOR
Wisit Lumsiricharoenchoke

CLIENT
WWF

AGENCY
Ogilvy & Mather/ Bangkok

ANNUAL ID
06242A

ALSO AWARDED
Merit: Public Service/Political: Newspaper or Magazine - Campaign

Merit: Public Service/Political: Outdoor and Posters - Single

MERIT

ART DIRECTORS
Simon Oppmann
Daniela Friedel

WRITER
Peter Roemmelt

CREATIVE DIRECTORS
Simon Oppmann
Peter Roemmelt

CLIENT
Worldwide Fund for Nature (WWF)

AGENCY
Ogilvy & Mather/ Frankfurt

ANNUAL ID
06244A

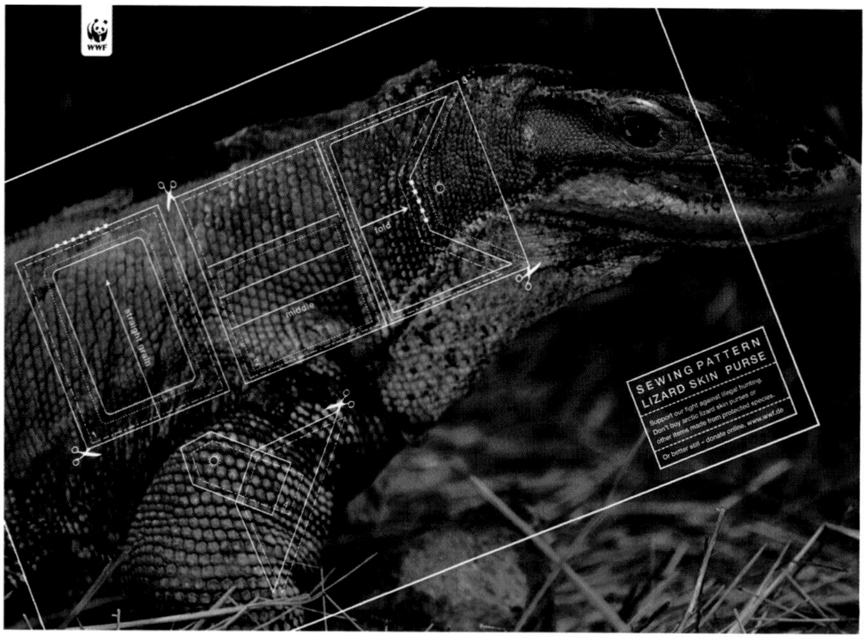
WWF
SEWING PATTERN
LIZARD SKIN PURSE
Support our fight against illegal hunting.
Don't buy arctic lizard skin purses or
other items made from protected species.
Or better still – donate online. www.wwf.de
straight grain
middle
fold

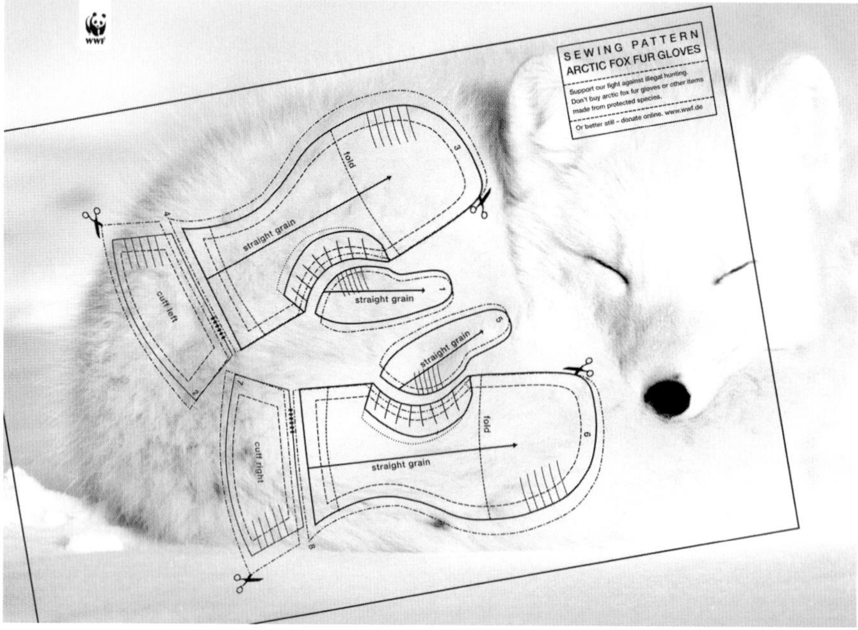
WWF
SEWING PATTERN
ARCTIC FOX FUR GLOVES
Support our fight against illegal hunting.
Don't buy arctic fox fur gloves or other items
made from protected species.
Or better still – donate online. www.wwf.de
straight grain
fold
cuff left
cuff right

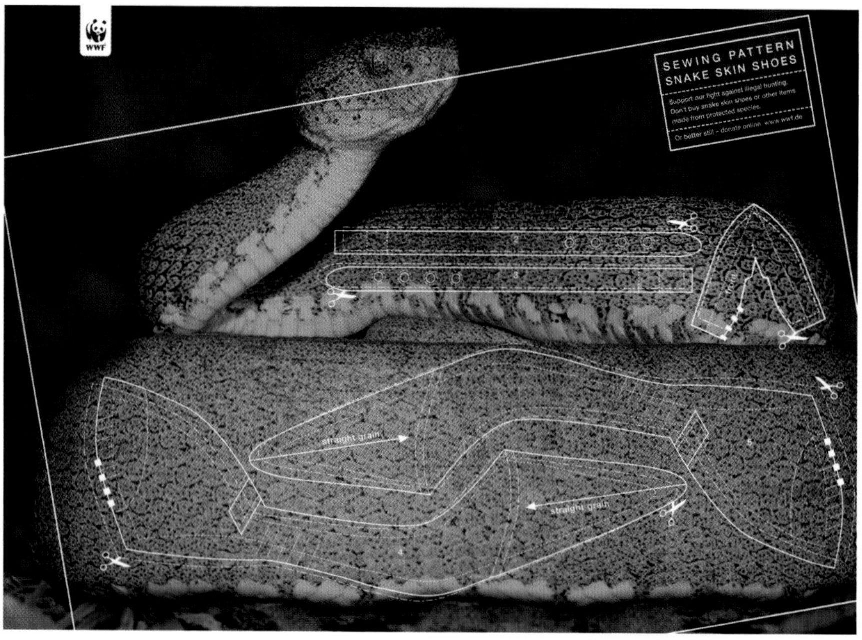
WWF
SEWING PATTERN
SNAKE SKIN SHOES
Support our fight against illegal hunting.
Don't buy snake skin shoes or other items
made from protected species.
Or better still – donate online. www.wwf.de
straight grain

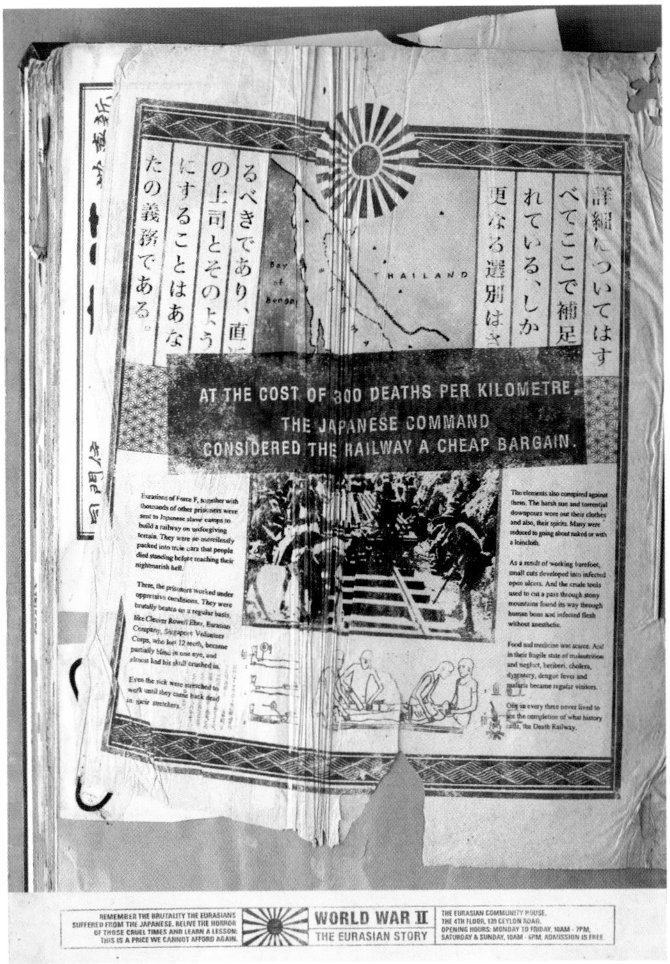

AT THE COST OF 300 DEATHS PER KILOMETRE, THE JAPANESE COMMAND CONSIDERED THE RAILWAY A CHEAP BARGAIN.
Eurasians of Force F, together with thousands of other prisoners were sent to Japanese slave camps to build a railway on unforgiving terrain. They were so mercilessly packed into train cars that people died standing before reaching their nightmarish hell.
There, the prisoners worked under oppressive conditions. They were brutally beaten on a regular basis, like Cleever Rowell Eber, Eurasian Company, Singapore Volunteer Corps, who lost 12 teeth, became partially blind in one eye, and almost had his skull crushed in.
Even the sick were stretched to work until they came back dead in their stretchers.
The elements also conspired against them. The harsh sun and torrential downpours wore out their clothes and also, their spirits. Many were reduced to going about naked or with a loincloth.
As a result of working barefoot, small cuts developed into infected open ulcers. And the crude tools used to cut a pass through stony mountains found its way through human bone and infected flesh without anesthetic.
Food and medicine was scarce. And in their fragile state of malnutrition and neglect, beriberi, cholera, dysentery, dengue fever and malaria became regular visitors.
One in every three never lived to see the completion of what history calls, the Death Railway.
REMEMBER THE BRUTALITY THE EURASIANS SUFFERED FROM THE JAPANESE. RELIVE THE HORROR OF THOSE CRUEL TIMES AND LEARN A LESSON: THIS IS A PRICE WE CANNOT AFFORD AGAIN.
WORLD WAR II
THE EURASIAN STORY
THE EURASIAN COMMUNITY HOUSE, THE 4TH FLOOR, 139 CEYLON ROAD. OPENING HOURS: MONDAY TO FRIDAY, 10AM - 7PM, SATURDAY & SUNDAY, 10AM - 6PM. ADMISSION IS FREE

NOTHING COULD STOP THE JAPANESE.
NOT EVEN A PREGNANT WOMAN.

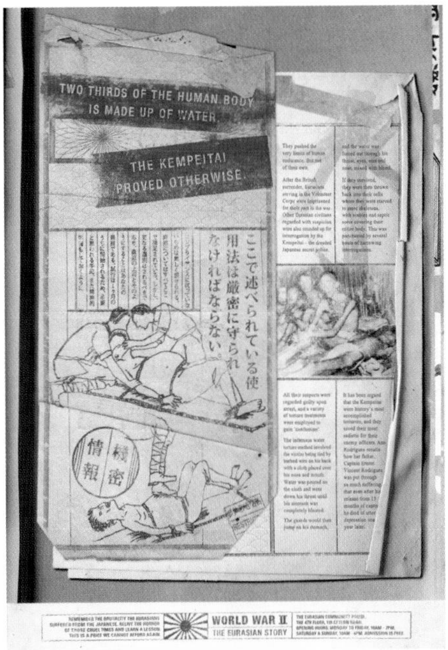

TWO THIRDS OF THE HUMAN BODY IS MADE UP OF WATER.
THE KEMPEITAI PROVED OTHERWISE.

THE ONLY HOPE OF ESCAPE FROM THE JAPANESE WAS TO RAM A CONCRETE WALL WITH YOUR OWN SKULL.
Out of sheer desperation, he charged straight into a wall with his head, bashing it again and again, until he dropped dead. Finally, he had found a way to stop the senseless cruelty.
Ivan Amorzoo, Clement Louis Marie Monteiro, Victor R. Grosse, Edward de Souza and many others of 'D' Eurasian Company of The Singapore Volunteer Corps were interned in Japanese prison camps where brutal beatings were part of a daily ritual.
They were beaten with iron bars, brass rods, wet knotted ropes, belts with buckles – anything that could cause more grievous hurt than bare knuckles.
To intensify the experience, victims were sometimes hung by their thumbs during the barrage of blows, or were forced to kneel on sharp pieces of iron or wood. They were beaten up until they passed out, and when they came to, it would start all over again.
The beatings sometimes lasted for 55 hours in a row, and the result was a pulp of fractured bone and bloody ripped flesh that left the victims unrecognisable.
If you didn't tell them the truth, you were punished. If you did tell them the truth, you were punished. The Japanese didn't need a reason to subject their prisoners to an eternity of pain.
There was no way to stop the torment unless you followed the way of the Chinese prisoner who committed suicide.
It was no surprise that the death rate in Nazi-POW camps of 1.1%, was nothing compared to the Japanese, whose prison dead measured a staggering 35.3%.
REMEMBER THE BRUTALITY THE EURASIANS SUFFERED FROM THE JAPANESE. RELIVE THE HORROR OF THOSE CRUEL TIMES AND LEARN A LESSON: THIS IS A PRICE WE CANNOT AFFORD AGAIN.
WORLD WAR II
THE EURASIAN STORY
THE EURASIAN COMMUNITY HOUSE, THE 4TH FLOOR, 139 CEYLON ROAD. OPENING HOURS: MONDAY TO FRIDAY, 10AM - 7PM, SATURDAY & SUNDAY, 10AM - 6PM. ADMISSION IS FREE.

Merit

ART DIRECTORS
Francis Ooi
Agnes Lee
Irene Lau

WRITER
Alvin Wong Twei

CREATIVE DIRECTORS
Francis Ooi
Alvin Wong Twei

CLIENT
The Eurasian Association Singapore

AGENCY
The Alchemy Partnership/Singapore

ANNUAL ID
06247A

MERIT

ART DIRECTORS
Michael Ashley
Diana Tung

WRITERS
Dinesh Kapoor
Michael Ashley

CREATIVE DIRECTOR
Michael Ashley

CLIENT
VCU Adcenter

AGENCY
Arnika/Hopewell Junction

ANNUAL ID
06248A

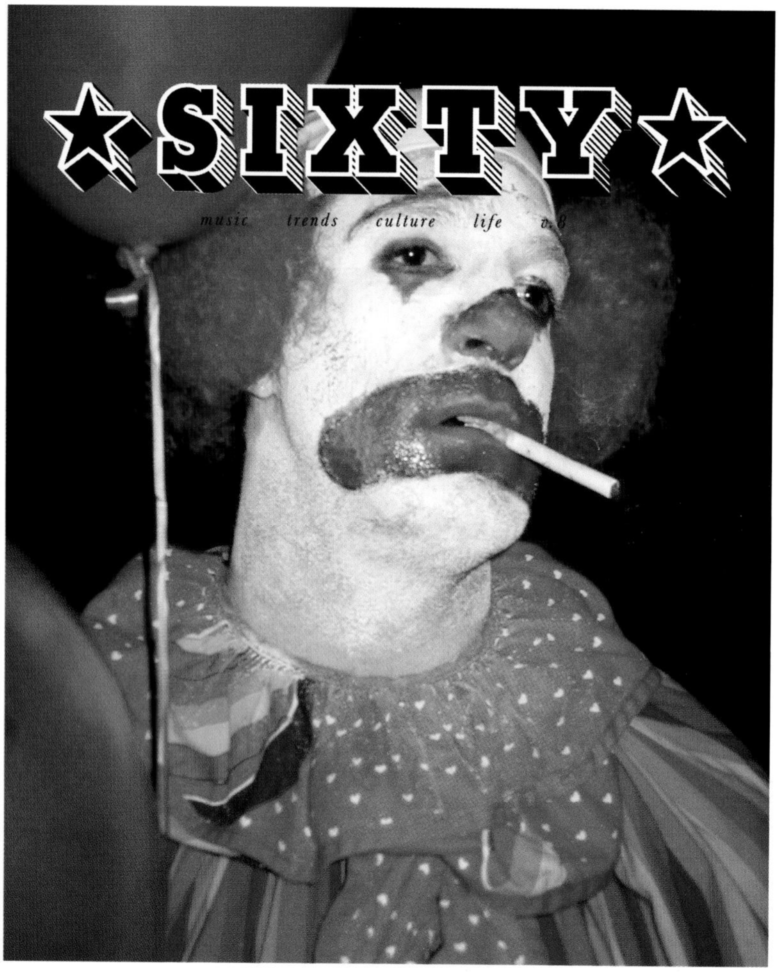
SIXTY
music trends culture life

MERIT

ART DIRECTORS
Neo Chiew Chiew
Elisa Tan

WRITER
Ali Shabaz

CREATIVE DIRECTORS
Tay Guan Hin
Ali Shabaz

CLIENT
Think Centre

AGENCY
JWT/Singapore

ANNUAL ID
06249A

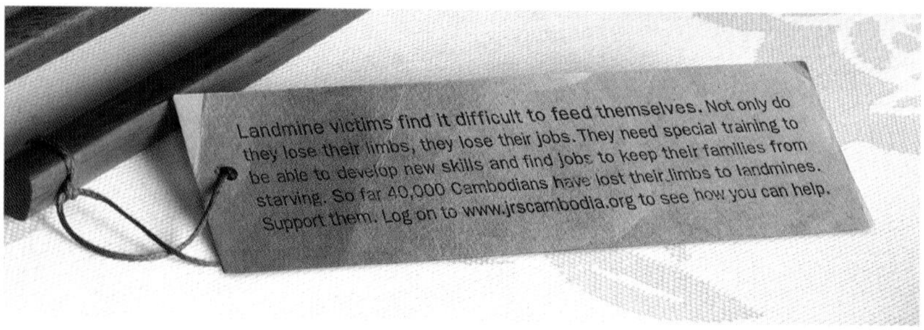
Landmine victims find it difficult to feed themselves. Not only do they lose their limbs, they lose their jobs. They need special training to be able to develop new skills and find jobs to keep their families from starving. So far 40,000 Cambodians have lost their limbs to landmines. Support them. Log on to www.jrscambodia.org to see how you can help.

MAN 1: Attention everyone! I just wanted to let everyone know that I'm holding this umbrella up for this lady!

MAN 2: Attention everyone! I just threw away a piece of trash that did not belong to me.

MAN 3: Attention everyone! I just wanted you all to know that I just held the door open for that girl.

MAN 2: I just put a quarter in this person's expired meter. They just got a free half an hour.

MAN 3: A tobacco company once gave $125,000 worth of food to a charity, according to an estimate by the *Wall Street Journal*. Then they spent well over $21 million telling people about it.

MAN 1: Attention everyone!

MAN 2: Attention everyone!

MAN 3: I guess when you sell a deadly addictive product, you need all the good PR you can get.

MAN 2: I just helped this man parallel park his vehicle. I don't even know this man.

SUPER: thetruth.com
Sign: truth found

truth found
thetruth.com

MERIT

ART DIRECTORS
Rob Kottkamp
Mike Costello
Jason Ambrose
Geordie Stephens

WRITERS
Will Chambliss
Marc Einhorn
Dustin Ballard
Franklin Tipton

AGENCY PRODUCER
Carron Pedonti

PRODUCTION COMPANY
Smuggler

DIRECTOR
Chris Smith

CREATIVE DIRECTORS
Ron Lawner
Pete Favat
Alex Bogusky
John Kearse
Tom Adams

CLIENT
American Legacy Foundation

AGENCY
Arnold Worldwide/ Boston and Crispin Porter + Bogusky/ Miami

ANNUAL ID
06035T

Merit

ART DIRECTOR
Dave Ferrer

WRITER
David Guerrero

AGENCY PRODUCER
Jeng Floresca

PRODUCTION COMPANIES
Underground Pictures
Underground Logic

DIRECTORS
Ditsi Carolino
Nana Buxani

CREATIVE DIRECTOR
David Guerrero

CLIENT
UNICEF/Consuelo Foundation

AGENCY
BBDO Guerrero Ortega/Makati City

ANNUAL ID
06038T

This is the Minors Quarters,
we sleep here.

SUPER: Over 10,000 children are detained each year. Most of them are in adult jails.

TONY: This is the Minors Quarters, we sleep here.

SUPER: Tony. 13 years old.

TONY: The Minors Brigade. Our sleeping quarters. Private rooms for a few...for us, this.

INTERVIEWER: What's that?

TONY: The shit bucket. There are so many of us, 159. Look...159 inmates sleep here, so crowded.

INTERVIEWER: Where do you sleep?

TONY: Here. By their feet. Crouching.

SUPER: The current law sees no difference between child offenders and adult criminals. Support the passage of the Comprehensive Juvenile Justice Law.

TONY: It's really tough inside.

SUPER: Unfortunately, for Tony it's too late. He died last year. In detention.

Supported by Juvenile Justice Network Philippines
Unicef.org/Philippines

Merit

ART DIRECTOR
Scott Henderson

WRITER
Angus Hennah

AGENCY PRODUCER
Marty Collins

PRODUCTION COMPANY
Silverscreen Wellington

DIRECTOR
Nathan Price

CREATIVE DIRECTOR
Philip Andrew

CLIENT
Land Transport NZ

AGENCY
Clemenger BBDO/Wellington

ANNUAL ID
06039T

[We open on a driver sitting in his car.]

VO: When we drive fast we don't realize the danger we're in.

[We cut outside the car to reveal that it's actually floating in mid air above the traffic.]

VO: If you're driving at 90 km/h and you crash, the speed your body impacts is the same as falling from the first floor of a building.

VO: At 110 km/h the impact is the same as falling from the fifth floor.

VO: And at 125km/h, the impact is like falling from the ninth floor.

[We reveal a family inside the car. The driver appears oblivious to the danger while the rest of the family seems quite concerned. The car suddenly drops and plummets towards the Earth. We cut to the end graphic before the car impacts the road.]

SUPER: The faster you go, the bigger the mess.

ED: My name is Ed. I've been married for 30 years, and I'm a father of three kids. You know, I really don't think that AIDS is a big threat in our community. I, I don't really know anybody that has AIDS. I think we raise our children better here.

SUPER: AIDS support group

ED: I mean certainly, if there was AIDS here, we would know about it. I mean, kids would look sick. Maybe in the inner city, maybe the other parts of the world, but no, it's not a problem for us here. Look, I'm a caring person. I'm concerned about a lot of things... but AIDS isn't one of them.

[Ed shakes hands with the teens. He now has tears in his eyes.]

SUPER: Change one mind. Change the world.
KNOWHIVAIDS.ORG

CHANGE ONE MIND.
CHANGE THE WORLD.

MERIT

ART DIRECTOR
Larry Olson

WRITER
Dean Saling

AGENCY PRODUCER
Craig Potter

CREATIVE DIRECTOR
Eric Gutierrez

CLIENT
Kaiser Family Foundation

AGENCY
DDB/Seattle

ANNUAL ID
06040T

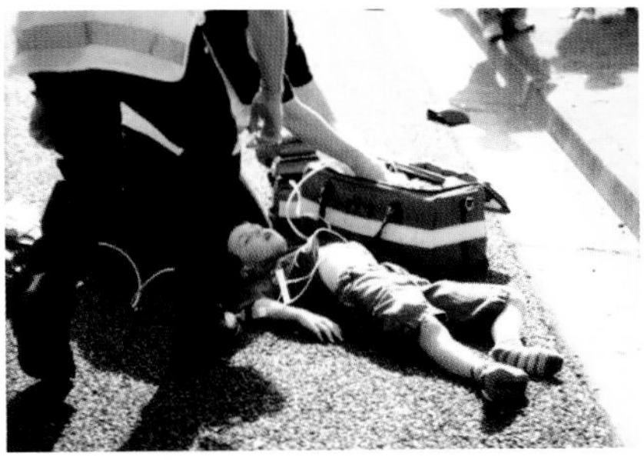

[A man wearing a baseball cap is standing by the sidelines of a football game. He sees a small boy staring at him from a few feet away. The man is then in a bus and he looks out the window and sees the boy. Next he's at home with his two small children making lunch and then he sees the boy standing in the corner. He sees him at a construction site, we see him sleeping in between the man and his wife, and then at a wedding. The scene flashes back to an accident scene with the boy.]

POLICE: Chris, have you had any alcoholic drinks today?

MAN: Just a couple of beers.

POLICE: Your breath test indicates that your breath carries alcohol. There's one other thing, I'm not sure whether you're aware that the young fellow has in fact died.

SUPER: You don't have to be drunk to be a drunk driver.
Only a little bit over? You bloody idiot.

LOGO: TAC

MERIT

ART DIRECTOR
Tim Holmes

WRITER
Nigel Dawson

AGENCY PRODUCER
James McPherson

PRODUCTION COMPANY
Filmgraphics

DIRECTOR
Mat Humphrey

CREATIVE DIRECTORS
Nigel Dawson
Ant Shannon

CLIENT
Transport Accident Commission (TAC)

AGENCY
Grey Worldwide/ Melbourne

ANNUAL ID
06041T

MERIT

ART DIRECTORS
Caroline Pay
Darren Bailes
Al MacCuish

WRITERS
Al MacCuish
Darren Bailes
Caroline Pay

CREATIVE DIRECTORS
Robert Saville
Mark Waites

CLIENT
Amnesty International

AGENCY
Mother/London

ANNUAL ID
06043T

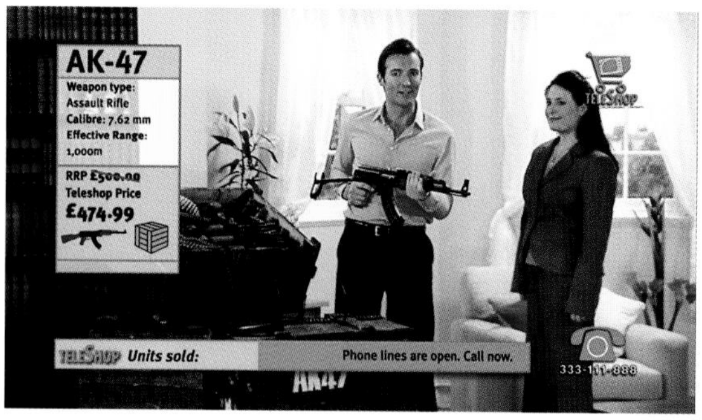
AK-47
Weapon type:
Assault Rifle
Calibre: 7.62 mm
Effective Range:
1,000m
RRP £500.00
Teleshop Price
£474.99
TELESHOP
Units sold:
Phone lines are open. Call now.

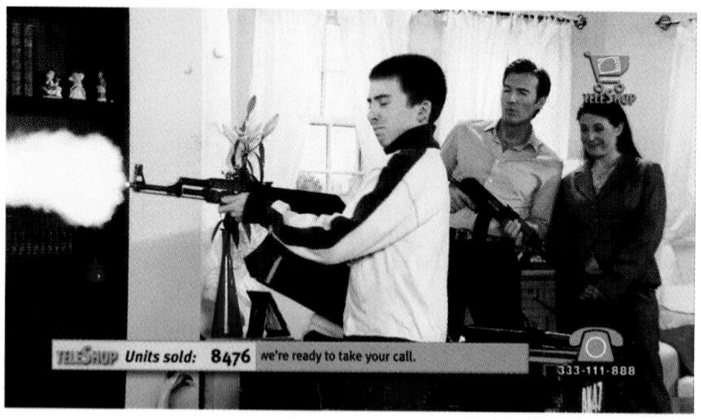
Units sold: 8476
we're ready to take your call.
333-111-888

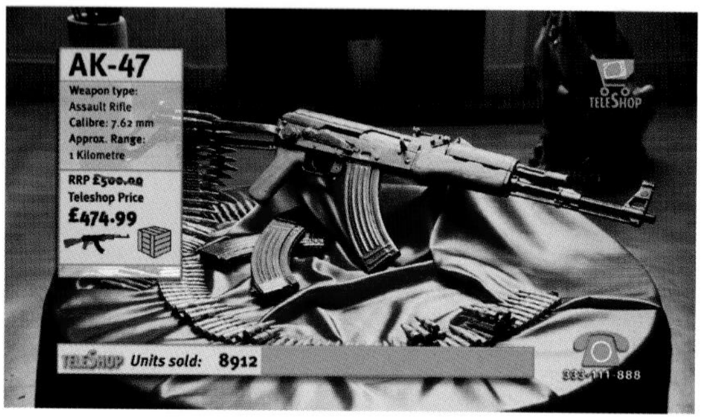
AK-47
Weapon type:
Assault Rifle
Calibre: 7.62 mm
Approx. Range:
1 Kilometre
RRP £500.00
Teleshop Price
£474.99
TELESHOP
Units sold: 8912

SUE: Welcome back...so from ice-cream makers, thanks Jim, to weaponry—now what have we got today, Clive?

CLIVE: Well today we have got...the villain's favorite, a veteran of more than 75 wars it's the AK-47 assault rifle.

CLIVE: Now Sue—come over here—let me show you this in its full splendor. Here it is—beauuuuutiful. Now we have 10,000 of these in secret locations outside the UK to sell today.

SUE: I might have to treat myself to one I think. Now, the phone lines are open folks so give us a call—and if you call within the hour there's a special gift with every purchase—a year's worth of ammunition free.

CLIVE: So how do you pay? Well we accept hard cash, dollars through off shore accounts. We'll even accept diamonds.

VO: It doesn't matter who you are, or what you want them for, if you can pay, we'll dispatch your guns today.

SUE: Clive, we're not going to get into trouble for this are we?

CLIVE: You don't need to worry about getting into trouble because surprisingly Sue, there are rather convenient loopholes in the rules governing the arms trade around the world—so you needn't worry. You don't get into trouble.

SUE: Oh that's good to know and it's good for business as well.

CLIVE: Now if you are sitting at home thinking, "Is an assault rifle difficult to use?" Then you need not worry. What do you think child soldiers are using in the likes of Liberia and the Democratic Republic of the Congo?

SUPER: It is estimated that there are between 70-100 million AK-47's in existence worldwide.

SUPER: The arms trade is out of control.
Make the world's governments sign up to an international arms trade treaty.

Text the word "arms" followed by your full name to 84118 to join the million faces petition.

Standard text rates apply.

LOGO: Amnesty International

SALESMAN: Hello sir, would you like to try some Black Water Springs, spring water?

Would you like to try a sample of Black Water Springs? This is straight from Africa and the developing world.

WOMAN 1: Why not.

SALESMAN: This is full of giardia, cryptosporidium; this comes straight from the sewage system. Sir, Ma'am, would you like to try some Black Water Springs? It's all natural and it's full of the same sort of unique balance that people in those parts of the world...

MAN 1: What's that brown stuff there?

SALESMAN: That would be organic matter, that's organic matter... look ah.

MAN 1: That's gross.

WOMAN 2: Oh yuk.

SALESMAN: Well, it's exactly as people in the developing world drink it.

WOMAN 3: What is the top one?

SALESMAN: Um, poo, basically, fecal matter. It's very good if you want to go on a diet, because it really puts you off your food, um, try just a little bit of it.

WOMAN 4: No, that's all right, thanks.

SALESMAN: It's pretty standard in the third world...It is a unique blend of minerals, have a sniff, have a smell...Would you like try some, it's full of natural, organic material...It contains feces, e. coli, vibro cholerae, cryptosporidium...More than a billion people drink that every day.

SUPER: Over 1 billion people worldwide are forced to drink Blackwater Springs.

SALESMAN: I mean yes, a lot of them die from it.

SUPER: www.blackwatersprings.com

SALESMAN: A lot of comments I've had have been about the color.

LOGO: WaterAid

MERIT

ART DIRECTOR
Heather Sheen

WRITERS
Justin Ruben
Hamish Spencer

AGENCY PRODUCERS
Marcus Eley
Jasmin Ferguson

PRODUCTION COMPANY
Independent Films

DIRECTOR
Scott Otto Anderson

CREATIVE DIRECTOR
Darren Spiller

CLIENT
WaterAid Australia

AGENCY
Publicis Mojo/Walsh Bay

ANNUAL ID
06044T

Merit

ART DIRECTOR
Shannon Sutherland

WRITER
Kathy Mattick

AGENCY PRODUCER
Ali Grant

PRODUCTION COMPANY
8 Commercials

DIRECTOR
Tim Gibbs

CREATIVE DIRECTOR
David Nobay

CLIENT
UNIFEM

AGENCY
Saatchi & Saatchi/Sydney

ANNUAL ID
06045T

[We see inside an apartment where a couple sit having dinner. They hear an argument start up between a man and woman in the apartment next door. For a moment the argument next door escalates and it becomes obvious from what the couple can hear that the fight has become physical. The woman next door is now screaming for the man to stop, but the physical and verbal assault continues. The man eating finally gets up from the table and heads for the front door. On the way out, he grabs a baseball bat from the hallstand. He bangs on his neighbor's door and a very agitated man opens it.]

GUY: Thought you could use this.

[Holds up baseball bat.]

[Man grabs the bat from his neighbor and closes the door.]

SUPER: Do nothing and you may as well lend a hand. Stop violence against women. Wear a white ribbon on November 25.

[We see a family photo.]

GIRL: This is my blog entry. I loved when my Dad and I cooked breakfast together. He always called me his honey. Then he started making meth in the kitchen. One night the police came in with white suits and gas masks. I was taken to the hospital and decontaminated. I haven't seen him since.

SUPER: End meth.
Endmeth.org/Ashley
Partnership for a Drug-Free America

MERIT

ART DIRECTOR
Colin Gaul

WRITER
Emily Sander

AGENCY PRODUCERS
Terry Brogan
Angela Buck

PRODUCTION COMPANY
Smuggler

CREATIVE DIRECTORS
Walt Connelley
Toby Barlow

CLIENT
Partnership for a Drug Free America

AGENCY
JWT/New York

ANNUAL ID
06046T

END METH

END METH

END METH

MERIT

TELEVISION AND RADIO

MERIT

ART DIRECTOR
Dean Maryon

WRITER
Ben Abramowitz

AGENCY PRODUCERS
Peter Cline
Tony Stearns

PRODUCTION COMPANY
Kleinman Productions

DIRECTOR
Daniel Kleinman

CREATIVE DIRECTORS
Andy Fackrell
Dean Maryon

CLIENT
adidas

AGENCY
180 Amsterdam
(180\TBWA)

ANNUAL ID
06048T

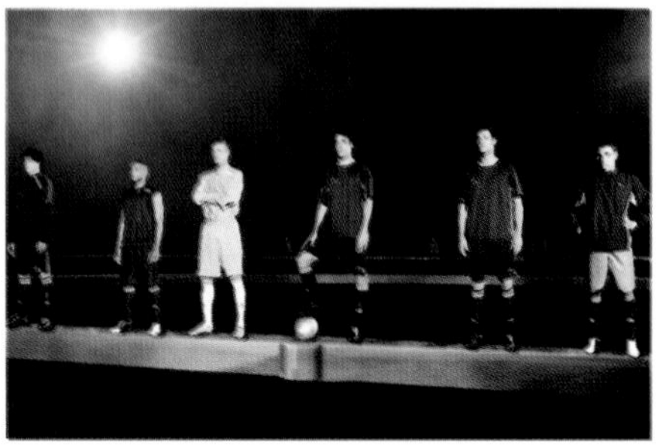

[The lines of a football pitch are literally raised to another level where the adidas stable of stars demonstrate their extraordinary balance and precision in this spectacular aerial display.]

SUPER: Impossible is nothing.

LOGO: adidas

MERIT

ART DIRECTOR
Dario Nucci

WRITER
Andy Fackrell

AGENCY PRODUCERS
Peter Cline
Cedric Gairard

PRODUCTION COMPANY
MJZ

DIRECTOR
Fredrik Bond

CREATIVE DIRECTOR
Andy Fackrell

CLIENT
adidas

AGENCY
180 Amsterdam
(180\TBWA)

ANNUAL ID
06047T

[A young couple from a nearby housing complex imagine a rampaging football fantasy through an adjacent forest. They are joined by a rabble of pros, street ballers, medics and linesmen in a Tolkien-esque world inhabited by flying chickens, animated tree roots and rabid devil dogs, each attempting to impede their progress. Finally, all the characters are composed perfectly into a Delacroix-like canvas, before the scene cuts back to reality.]

SUPER: Impossible is nothing.

LOGO: adidas

[DC skaters show off their creativity and athleticism by making improbable baskets, often while riding skateboards, at a hoop in DC's indoor training facility. All the shots are real and videotaped.]

LOGO: DC
dcshoes.com

MERIT

AGENCY PRODUCER
Candace Bowes

CREATIVE DIRECTORS
John Boiler
Glenn Cole

CLIENT
DC Shoes

AGENCY
72andSunny/El Segundo

ANNUAL ID
06049T

MAN: I saw this brilliant film on CANAL+: March of the Emperor.

WOMAN: March of the Emperor?

[The woman imagines Napoleon-like emperors marching in a row.]

MAN: Yes, it all takes place in Antarctica.

WOMAN: Really?

[She then pictures emperors marching in the snow.]

MAN: There are hundreds of emperors marching across these ice fields for days. Sometimes they slide on their bellies to go faster. Then one of them gets eaten by a seal. It's horrible. But there are some really tender moments too. Like when they pass their eggs to each other. Yes, because before that they were all having sex together. For hours.

SUPER: Movies are made to be seen.
Canal+ The Cinema Channel.

MERIT

ART DIRECTORS
Romain Guillon
Eric Astorgue

WRITERS
Pierre Riess
Luc Rouzier

AGENCY PRODUCER
David Green

PRODUCTION COMPANY
@radical.media

DIRECTOR
The Glue Society

CREATIVE DIRECTOR
Stephane Xiberras

CLIENT
CANAL+

AGENCY
BETC Euro RSCG/ Paris

ANNUAL ID
06050T

MERIT

ART DIRECTOR
Wayne Best

WRITER
Adam Alshin

AGENCY PRODUCER
Zarina Mak

PRODUCTION COMPANY
MJZ

CREATIVE DIRECTOR
Ari Merkin

CLIENT
Starbucks

AGENCY
Fallon/Minneapolis

ANNUAL ID
06051T

ALSO AWARDED
Merit:
Consumer Television:
:30/:25 – Single

2720

[Hank walks down a set of stairs with a can of Doubleshot Espresso drink. With presentation materials under his arm, he gulps down the Doubleshot. A puppet-like man with a large head enters with a boom box. Gary Glitter's stadium anthem "Rock and Roll Part 2" blares out of the stereo. The man begins to cheer. There is now a section of bleachers next to him filled with people he knows. A large group of people hold up signs which collectively spell out "Hank." Hank rides an escalator with the man with a large head behind him. People on the escalator are cheering for him. He is then in a quiet reception area. Hank is sitting in a chair. Bleachers are behind him. People keep cheering "Hank."]

RECEPTIONIST: Hank?

[Hank stands and looks back at the audience with an empowered smile. The audience stands with him. They start cheering "Hank" in rhythm, raising their fists.]

VO: Delicious Starbucks DoubleShot Espresso Drink. Bring on the day.

MERIT

ART DIRECTOR
Juan Cabral

WRITER
Juan Cabral

AGENCY PRODUCER
Nicky Barnes

PRODUCTION COMPANY
MJZ

DIRECTOR
Nicolai Fuglsig

CREATIVE DIRECTORS
Richard Flintham
Andy McLeod

CLIENT
Sony

AGENCY
Fallon/London

ANNUAL ID
06052T

[We see the streets of San Francisco. Music is playing in the background and we see thousands of colorful rubber balls bouncing down the streets in slow motion.]

SUPER: Colour like no other.
Bravia New LCD TV.
Like no other. SONY.

[Open on a young man in a Gap store pulling a stack of T-shirts off the shelf to look for his size. The entire stack falls to the floor. A Gap employee who is helping the customer notices, and then tips over a couple more stacks of shirts. Another customer who has witnessed this turn of events gently pushes over a mannequin. A Gap employee is inspired to push over another mannequin. More customers notice and begin to join in on the demo party. Soon customers and employees band together to pull down displays and demolish the entire store. A van smashes through the Gap front window and a customer yanks the arm off the last mannequin.]

SUPER: Pardon our dust.
The all-new Gap is coming.
April 22nd

LOGO: GAP

MERIT

ART DIRECTOR
John Parker

WRITER
Evan Fry

AGENCY PRODUCERS
Alex Bogusky
Rupert Samuel
David Rolfe

PRODUCTION COMPANY
MJZ

DIRECTOR
Spike Jonze

CREATIVE DIRECTORS
Alex Bogusky
Andrew Keller

CLIENT
Gap

AGENCY
Crispin Porter + Bogusky/Miami

ANNUAL ID
06056T

[We hear sad music playing. A bartender, who is carrying a couple of cases of Heineken, loses his grip. We see the top case fall and in slow motion, we see the first bottle or two hit the floor. A heavyweight boxer, momentarily distracted by the "disturbance," is dropped with a right hook. People are being sworn in as American citizens. As one eager man repeats the oath that will finally make this is home, he suddenly loses his train of thought. The lead singer in a band is distracted and stops singing. A pedestrian is outside in the rain. As umbrellas rush past him, he stands there, wet, looking into the distance. We see in his face that something is not quite right in the world. A guy is with his woman in the bedroom. Suddenly, he rolls off of her.]

WOMAN: Honey, what's wrong?

GUY: I don't know. All of a sudden I feel...really... really... sad.

GIRLFRIEND: Aww...

GUY: Don't.

[Girlfriend looks concerned. The remainder of the Heinekens, in slow motion, crash to the floor.]

SUPER: It's all about the beer.

LOGO: Heineken

MERIT

ART DIRECTOR
Ted Royer

WRITER
Ken Ratcliffe

CREATIVE DIRECTORS
David Droga
Ken Ratcliffe
Ted Royer

CLIENT
Heineken

AGENCY
Publicis/New York

ANNUAL ID
06059T

Merit

ART DIRECTOR
Diego Sanchez

WRITER
Matias Corbelle

AGENCY PRODUCER
Roberto Carsillo

PRODUCTION COMPANY
Rebolucion

DIRECTOR
Armando Bo

CREATIVE DIRECTORS
Hernan Ponce
Sebastian Stagno
Rafael D'Alvia

CLIENT
Unilever

AGENCY
VegaOlmosPonce/
Buenos Aires

ANNUAL ID
06060T

TAXI

[We can see a 30-year-old man leaving home for work. After walking for a while, he realizes his shirt is wet under his armpits. He looks up and can see a man wearing a spotlessly clean shirt watching a window-shop display. The man who is perspiring catches him off guard, immobilizes him and leads him into a back street. Seconds later, the man who was sweating appears again and, we realize the shirt he is wearing now is the one of the man he took by surprise. The guy who was looking at the window-shop display is coming out of the back street with a bare back and is somewhat dizzy and disoriented. Now, we see our protagonist sitting as a passenger in a taxi, sweating at the armpits. Seconds later, the man is getting out of the taxi wearing a t-shirt which looks too large for him. We realize that a bareback taxi driver is chasing the thief in a desperate attempt to recover his clothes. We direct our attention now to a hot-dog street stand. A salesman has a hot dog in his hand. Suddenly, we see the protagonist throwing himself headlong into the hot dog stand tackling the salesman to steal his shirt. This continues with a man in a cubicle, a park, a security guard, and a costume on a train.]

SUPER: You'd better change that common deodorant for antiperspirant Rexona Men. It fights off body odor and also protects against wetness.

Merit

ART DIRECTOR
Jesse Coulter

WRITER
Greg Kalleres

AGENCY PRODUCERS
Jesse Wann
Gary Krieg

PRODUCTION COMPANY
40 Acres and a Mule

DIRECTOR
Spike Lee

CREATIVE DIRECTORS
Todd Waterbury
Kevin Proudfoot

CLIENT
Nike Brand Jordan (Air Jordan 20)

AGENCY
Wieden+Kennedy/
New York

ANNUAL ID
06062T

[Spike Lee is sitting on a stoop with some kids and reading from a book. Then we see him in a barber shop...the story continues...he stands outside in front of a statue, on a school bus, in a gymnasium.]

SPIKE: Our story, children, begins in the county of Kings. Brooklyn, NY 1963. Swish! And the Tarheels win the championship. So he traveled to Chicago because Portland wanted a big man. Arms pumping up and down as Mr. Ilo fell to the ground. And he lost to the Motor City for the second time, mm! And he returned to win his first...his second championship. My main man money! Baseball the press asked? And he returned to win his fourth!...his fifth!... his sixth championship! And he returned again for his second time. And the people said no, no, no Michael. Michael you're going to ruin it! Don't do it! Don't do it! But Michael looked at those people and said... "I can accept failure. I can't accept not trying." Mm. And this time his retirement was final. But don't be sad. It doesn't end there. Because somewhere, someone is practicing.

CHILD 1: Who?

CHILD 2: Who was it?

CHILD 3: Who was it?

[Spike closes the book.]

SUPER: Will you be the one?

LOGO: 20 Jumpman
jumpman23.com

[Kid Tiger is being interview by an announcer who is out of the frame.]

ANNOUNCER: Well Tiger, you've won the British Open.

TIGER: Um hmmm.

ANNOUNCER: Feel good?

TIGER: Yes.

ANNOUNCER: You were marvelous around the greens and at the field at driving distance...

ANNOUNCER: Why did you do so well?

TIGER: Practice.

ANNOUNCER: A lot of practice.

TIGER: Umm hmm.

ANNOUNCER: The pressure of playing with the lead for four days, I mean, in a match like this.

ANNOUNCER: I'm sure it was enormous. How relieved were you when that putt dropped in on 18?

TIGER: Bout' a whole bunch.

ANNOUNCER: Well, very good. I shall let you go and claim your prize.

TIGER: Uh huh.

SUPER: Just Do It.

LOGO: Nike

MERIT

ART DIRECTOR
Hal Curtis

WRITER
Dylan Lee

AGENCY PRODUCER
Andrew Loevenguth

CREATIVE DIRECTORS
Hal Curtis
Mike Byrne

CLIENT
Nike

AGENCY
Wieden+Kennedy/ Portland

ANNUAL ID
06061T

MERIT

ART DIRECTORS
Colin Jeffery
Phillip Squier
Brandon Sides
Alan Pafenbach

WRITERS
Dave Weist
Mark Billows

AGENCY PRODUCERS
Bill Goodell
Amy Favat

PRODUCTION COMPANY
RSA

DIRECTOR
Jake Scott

CREATIVE DIRECTORS
Ron Lawner
Alan Pafenbach
Dave Weist
Colin Jeffery

CLIENT
Volkswagen

AGENCY
Arnold Worldwide/
Boston

ANNUAL ID
06063T

ALTO

GUARD 1: Por favor. Keys.

GUARD 2: Senor, open the truck please. Okay, Have a seat.

GUARD 1: Esta frio.

SUPER: It's cold...

[They start to take the car apart.]

VO: 120 not so standard features. One all new German engineered Passat. On the road of life there are passengers and there are drivers.

SUPER: The all-new Passat.
Drivers wanted.
newpassat.com

PULP FICTION
IN 30 SECONDS

Short but fun.

The new Fox.

STAR WARS
IN
30 SECONDS

Short but fun.

The new Fox.

[We see an animated, cut-down version of *Titanic*. It's performed by a cast of animated bunnies with high-pitched voices.]

OLDER ROSE: Titanic was called the ship of dreams ... and it was!

CAL HOCKLEY: God himself could not sink this ship!

JACK: I'm king of the world!

ROSE: I'll jump!

JACK: No you won't.

ROSE: Yes I will!

CREWMAN: Iceberg right ahead!

ANGRY PASSENGER: This ship can't sink!

THOMAS ANDREWS: I assure you, she can!

CAL HOCKLEY: I have a child!

ROSE: I won't let go, Jack!

[At the end, a VW Fox falls into an empty frame from above.]

SUPER: Short but fun.
The new Fox.
Volkswagen.

LOGO: Volkswagon

TITANIC
IN
30 SECONDS

Short but fun.

The new Fox.

Merit

ART DIRECTORS
Christian Brenner
Jennifer Shiman

WRITERS
Sandra Illes
Tim Jacobs

AGENCY PRODUCER
Marion Lange

PRODUCTION COMPANIES
VCC Perfect Pictures Düsseldorf
Angry Alien Productions

DIRECTOR
Jennifer Shiman

CREATIVE DIRECTORS
Eric Schoeffler
Amir Kassaei
Jennifer Shiman

CLIENT
Volkswagen

AGENCY
DDB/Berlin

ANNUAL ID
06064T

Merit

ART DIRECTORS
Philp Bonnery
Tim Vaccarino

WRITERS
Alex Flint
Joe Fallon

AGENCY PRODUCER
Charles Wolford

PRODUCTION COMPANIES
Biscuit
RSA

DIRECTORS
Noam Murro
Jake Scott

CREATIVE DIRECTORS
Gary Koepke
Lance Jensen

CLIENT
General Motors - Hummer Division

AGENCY
Modernista/Boston

ANNUAL ID
06065T

ALSO AWARDED
Merit:
Consumer Television:
Over :30 - Single

Merit:
Consumer Television:
Over :30 - Single

Merit

[A monster crashes through a city, smashing everything in its path. It demolishes a huge building. As the building falls, it reveals a giant robot. The two monsters stare at each other. We think they are about to engage in battle. But then they fall in love. We follow them as their loves deepens, until one day, it becomes clear that she is pregnant. Her pregnancy develops and she eventually gives birth. To an H3. The new small Hummer. Proud parents release their little one to the ground and watch as it takes its first turns on the asphalt.]

SUPER: It's a little Monster. The new H3.

ANOTHER BIG IDEA. FROM HUMMER.

Merit

[We see a series of attractive women walking with tell-tale imprints on their backs—the impressions of: a table setting, a clothes hanger, a locker room door, a car steering wheel. Last we cut to an woman walking out of an airplane bathroom a with the imprint of a no smoking sign on her back. We then see that same door open again, and a dishevelled guy trying to button his shirt walks out of the bathroom, turns down the aisle and heads back to his seat.]

SUPER: It can happen anywhere.

[We see a guy spraying on copious amounts of Axe.]

SUPER: New longer lasting Axe effect.

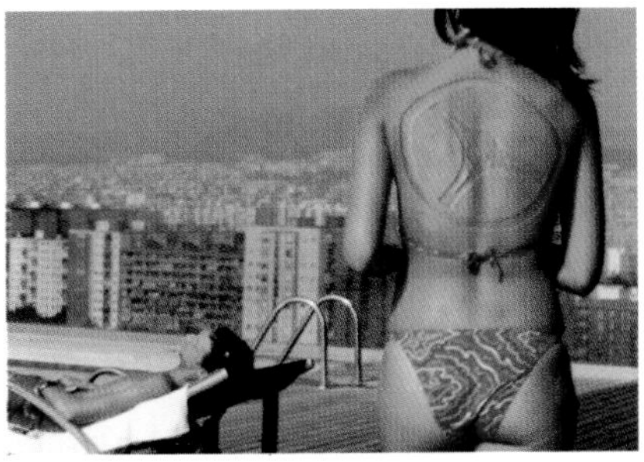

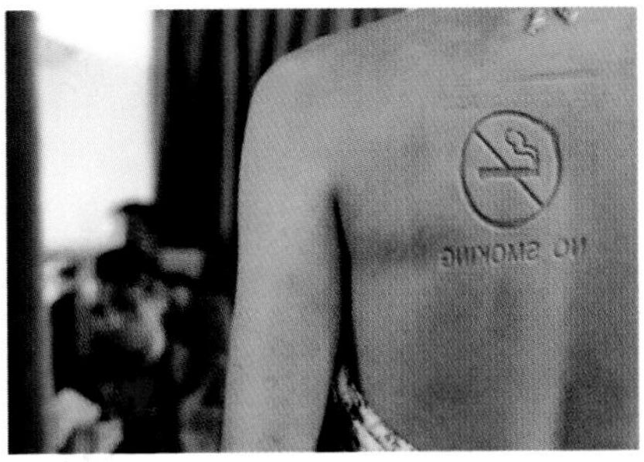

MERIT

ART DIRECTOR
Amee Shah

WRITER
Matt Ian

AGENCY PRODUCER
Stacey Higgins

PRODUCTION COMPANY
Biscuit Filmworks

DIRECTOR
Noam Murro

CREATIVE DIRECTOR
William Gelner

CLIENT
Axe

AGENCY
Bartle Bogle Hegarty/ New York

ANNUAL ID
06066T

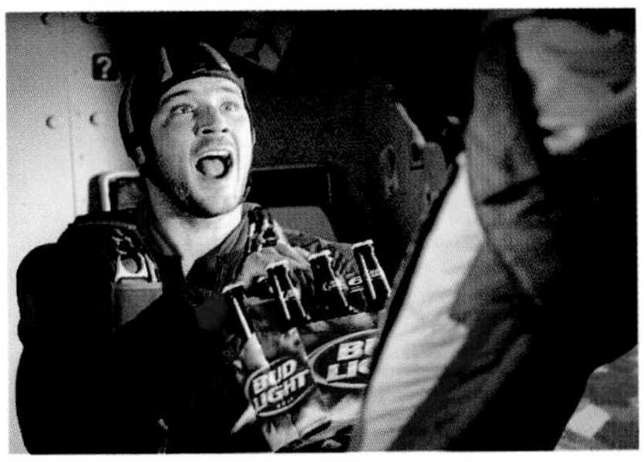

[We see the inside of a plane with skydivers.]

PILOT: GO!

INSTRUCTOR: Are you ready?

GUY 1: WHOOOOOAAA!!!

INSTRUCTOR: Are you ready?

GUY 2: I can't do this.

INSTRUCTOR: GOOO!

GUY 2: No way !!!

INSTRUCTOR: Not even for some Bud Light?

[He throws a six-pack of bud out the door. The pilot then chases after it and jumps out.]

VO: Fresh. Smooth. Real. Bud Light.

INSTRUCTOR: See ya dude!

GUY 2: Wait!

VO: It's all here.

MERIT

ART DIRECTOR
Dan Strasser

WRITER
Joe Sgro

AGENCY PRODUCER
Marianne Newton

DIRECTOR
Michael Downing

CREATIVE DIRECTOR
Mark Gross

CLIENT
Anheuser-Busch

AGENCY
DDB/Chicago

ANNUAL ID
06067T

Merit

WRITER
Yosu Aranguena

AGENCY PRODUCER
Alejandro Fernandez

PRODUCTION COMPANY
Garcia Bross & Asociados

DIRECTOR
Simon Bross

CREATIVE DIRECTORS
Sebastian Arrechedera
Yosu Aranguena
Martin Campo

CLIENT
Volkswagen

AGENCY
DDB/Mexico City

ANNUAL ID
06069T

Attention all units, we have a 40 in progress

All units report to central...

[We're on the street, we can see two policemen in a patrol, drinking coffee and chilling. Suddenly, we can hear an emergency in the radio.]

RADIO: Attention all units, we have a 40 in progress code seven at Bross Jewelers Center. The suspects are heading to Main and Uruguay Street...

[The two policemen listen carefully but when they listen that the car to pursue is a GTI they go back to drink coffee and chilling.]

RADIO: ...they are driving a red GTI, I repeat red GTI with no plates. Now they are heading north to Taboada St. and Torres St. please notify any 18 and proceed. All units report to central...

SUPER: Volkswagen
GTI 180 hp.

Merit

ART DIRECTOR
Benjamin Marchal

WRITER
Celine Landa

AGENCY PRODUCER
Agathe Michaux Terrier

PRODUCTION COMPANY
75

DIRECTOR
Jonathan Herman

CREATIVE DIRECTORS
Sylvain Thirache
Alexandre Herve

CLIENT
L'Equipe

AGENCY
DDB/Paris

ANNUAL ID
06070T

[Open to a businessman sitting down on his couch. He turns on the TV and loosens his tie. His wife walks in, is startled, drops a glass and screams. The husband looks confused and then quickly opens the sports page in front of his face.]

WIFE: Oh honey, it's you.

SUPER: Everyday. Every sport.
L'Equipe Sport newspaper.

L'EQUIPE
BRONZES, POUR FINIR

Everyday. Every Sport.

[A man opens the lid to the laundry machine, and just as he's about to put the clothes in, he sees that the machine is filled to the top with hardened concrete. He's confused. He looks around for evidence. Suddenly, he does a double take and sees a bowling ball staring at him. He looks back and forth between the ball and the machine and then takes a slow step backwards.]

SUPER: Sundays are for bowling.
The PBA Tulsa Championship, Sunday at 1pm ET.

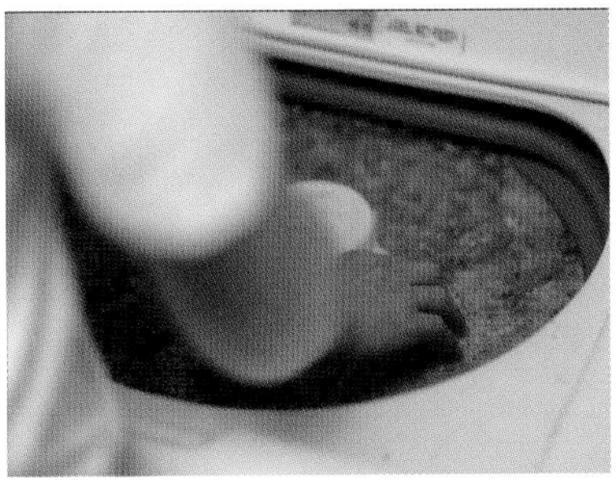

CEMEN

MERIT

ART DIRECTOR
Xanthe Hohalek

WRITER
Sean Vij

AGENCY PRODUCER
Kat Friis

PRODUCTION COMPANY
MJZ

DIRECTOR
Steven Diller

CREATIVE DIRECTOR
Court Crandall

CLIENT
ESPN

AGENCY
*Ground Zero/
Los Angeles*

ANNUAL ID
06073T

The irresistible VIOS

[A young man is jogging and notices a Toyota parked next to a lake. He stops to admire it, but then he realizes that it is a cardboard cutout. A lake monster's tentacles picks him up and takes him into the lake. It then adjusts the cutout and stands it back up.]

SUPER: The irresistible VIOS. You'll want one.
Toyota. Moving forward.

MERIT

ART DIRECTOR
Kien Hoe Ong

WRITER
Primus Nair

AGENCY PRODUCER
Shirren Lim

PRODUCTION COMPANY
Passion Pictures

DIRECTOR
Jamie Quah

CREATIVE DIRECTORS
*Henry Yap
Edmund Choe*

CLIENT
Toyota

AGENCY
*Saatchi & Saatchi/
Petaling Jaya*

ANNUAL ID
06075T

MERIT

ART DIRECTOR
Scott Vitrone

WRITER
Ian Reichenthal

AGENCY PRODUCERS
Nathy Aviram
Ozzie Spenningsby

PRODUCTION COMPANY
Moxie Pictures

CREATIVE DIRECTORS
Gerry Graf
Scott Vitrone
Ian Reichenthal

CLIENT
Masterfoods - Skittles

AGENCY
TBWA\Chiat\Day/
New York

ANNUAL ID
06076T

BLEND THE RAINBOW
Smoothie Mix
Skittles
TASTE THE RAINBOW

[Open on two sheepboys. They are part sheep, part boy: each has a sheep-like body and a human face. They are standing together in a field, eating a package of Smoothie Mix Skittles.]

SHEEPBOY 1: Mmm...

SHEEPBOY 2: These new Smoothie Mix Skittles are delicious.

SHEEPBOY 1: I know. Two different flavors blended together in each one.

SHEEPBOY 2: How can they blend together two things as different as an orange and a mango? It's unbelievable.

SHEEPBOY 1: What about peach/pear? A peach blended with a pear? Now that's an unusual combination.

[Both sheepboys laugh out loud. A farmer walks by and yells to them.]

FARMER: You two sheepboys...stop that jibber-jabbin'!

SUPER: Blend the rainbow. Taste the rainbow.

[Open in a field during prehistoric times. We see pterodactyls swirling around in the sky and a caveman named "Grog." He is walking through the field, carrying a stick. He walks over to a pterodactyl and ties the stick to the pterodactyl's leg. Then, he slaps the giant bird on the side and it starts flapping its wings. The pterodactyl lifts off the ground with the stick, and starts flying away. A tyrannosaurus rex grabs a hold of the bird and Grog watches as the pterodactyl meets its demise. The stick falls to the ground at Grog's feet.]

[Grog walks into a cave, where we see his boss sitting on a log. They start growling in cavemen language.]

GROG: Package didn't make it.

BOSS: Did you use FedEx?

GROG: No.

BOSS: Then you're fired.

GROG: But FedEx doesn't exist yet.

BOSS: Not my problem.

[Grog looks sad, and walks out of the cave, sighs and kicks a small dinosaur. We watch as a huge brontosaurus foot steps on Grog.]

SUPER: FedEx.

FedEx.
fedex.com

Merit

MERIT

ART DIRECTORS
Richard Ardito
Jonathan Mackler

WRITERS
Grant Smith
Jim LeMaitre

AGENCY PRODUCER
Elise Greiche

PRODUCTION COMPANY
Hungry Man

DIRECTOR
Hank Perlman

CREATIVE DIRECTORS
Eric Silver
Bill Bruce
David Lubars

CLIENT
FedEx

AGENCY
BBDO/New York

ANNUAL ID
06083T

ALSO AWARDED
Merit:
Consumer Television:
Over :30 - Single

Merit

ART DIRECTOR
Mark Taylor

WRITER
Bob Cianfrone

AGENCY PRODUCERS
Rupert Samuel
David Rolfe
Aymi Gonzalez
Cheri Anderson
Bill Meadows

PRODUCTION COMPANY
Moxie Pictures

DIRECTOR
Martin Granger

CREATIVE DIRECTORS
Alex Bogusky
Andrew Keller
Rob Reilly

CLIENT
Burger King

AGENCY
Crispin Porter + Bogusky/Miami

ANNUAL ID
06078T

[A guy walks through his room and opens the wooden shutters on his window. As he slides the shutter open, we instantly see the King standing just outside window. The guy is surprised. The King just stares. Then he reaches behind his back and hands the enormous omelet sandwich to the guy. The guy takes a bite. He looks at the King as if to say, "Nice job on the sandwich, King. This is great."]

VO: New...The Enormous Omelet Sandwich. Eggnormous. Meatnormous. Cheesenormous.

[Cut back to the guy polishing off the sandwich. As he does, he laughs and nods to the King again, thanking him for the sandwich. Just then, a bird lands on the King's shoulder and a squirrel climbs up on his other shoulder. All the creatures of the backyard alight on the King.]

VO: That's right. The Enormous Omelet Sandwich. Wake up with the King.

SUPER: Burger King.

[We see a top pharmaceutical representative speaking to a camera. He's the powerful corporate type, wearing a suit and tie with a medical association tie clip.]

MAN: The pharmaceutical industry applauds this nation's obsession with career advancement. Thanks to your inability to balance life with work, sales are through the roof. Indeed, forty five percent of Americans don't use all of their vacation time, a proven cause of stress-induced illness and depression. So stay the course. As long as you're committed to all work and no play, we'll provide happiness in the form of a pill.

SUPER: Have a life. Take back your vacation.
universalorlando.com

VO: Log on to universalorlando.com

MERIT

ART DIRECTORS
Anne Bioty
Anne-Lise Borgen

WRITER
Melissa Pipeling

AGENCY PRODUCER
Erin Sullivan

DIRECTOR
Kevin Samuels

CREATIVE DIRECTORS
David Angelo
Liz Gumbinner

CLIENT
Universal Orlando

AGENCY
davidandgoliath/
Los Angeles

ANNUAL ID
06079T

Merit

ART DIRECTOR
Antonio Navas

WRITER
Steve Simpson

AGENCY PRODUCER
Josh Reynolds

PRODUCTION COMPANY
Paranoid Projects: Tool

DIRECTOR
Francois Vogel

CREATIVE DIRECTORS
Steve Simpson
Rich Silverstein

CLIENT
Hewlett-Packard

AGENCY
Goodby, Silverstein & Partners/San Francisco

ANNUAL ID
06081T

simulation

[A girl sits in the middle of a living room as another girl puts a coat on her and other people in the background are scrambling to create a scene of her on a boat. That scene becomes a picture. A man hands the picture to the same girl that is now on a real boat with the same scenery as in the picture. Transition back to the living room as she holds the picture of herself on the real boat. "Let me take your photo" by The Speedies plays in the background.]

SINGER: Oh no, not on my photograph…let me take your photo.

[That scene becomes reality. Transition back to her living room as her friends scramble to create another scene of her in front of some icebergs. That scene becomes reality. Transition into girl sitting in the country in front of road as she is holding picture of her in front of the icebergs.]

SINGER: They'll take my picture once again. Let me take your photo.

SUPER: Go everywhere.

SINGER: Alright, now I'll call you a friend. Let me take your photo. Let me take your photo. Let me take your photo.

SUPER: Print anywhere.

[Transition back to the icebergs. Girl is holding the picture of last scene. She flips over a picture of a printer and camera on rocks, and the scene becomes reality.]

VO: The HP Photosmart 475…is the only portable printer… that prints up to 5X7's, without a PC.

SUPER: +hp invent.
hpshipping.com.

VO: Brilliantly simple.

MERIT

WRITERS
Brendan Gibbons
Rob Rooney

PRODUCTION COMPANY
Hungry Man

DIRECTOR
Brendan Gibbons

CREATIVE DIRECTOR
Brendan Gibbons

CLIENT
Comedy Central

AGENCY
Hungry Man/NY

ANNUAL ID
06082T

[Open on a gambler at a Gambler's Anonymous–type meeting. Other gamblers sit and listen to him speak.]

GAMBLER: I lost $300,000 watching Comedy Central. It started by going to Vegas, you know, playing some Reno 911. Next you know you're blowing your mortgage on Showbiz Show with David Spade. I lost my family, my friends, and I still couldn't stop watching Comedy Central. The truth is, I want to watch Comedy Central right now.

GAMBLER: My name is Rob and I'm addicted to Comedy Central.

SUPER: Comedy Central.

MERIT

ART DIRECTORS
Ricky Vior
Julian Montesano
Luis Ghidotti

WRITERS
Martin Jalfen
Matias Ballada
Leo Prat

AGENCY PRODUCER
Laurie Malaga

PRODUCTION COMPANY
Biscuit Films

DIRECTOR
Perlorian Brothers

CREATIVE DIRECTORS
José Mollá
Joaquin Mollá
Leo Prat
Ricky Vior

CLIENT
Virgin Mobile

AGENCY
la comunidad/
Miami Beach

ANNUAL ID
06084T

Then, I'm normal?

YOUNG MAN WITH BOOBS: [In Spanish] Mauro, I'm not normal, am I?

MAURO: What are you talking about? Every month, aren't you shocked by all those outrageous overages on your cell phone bill?

FRIEND WITH BOOBS: Yes.

MAURO: Well, that happens to everybody. It's normal.

FRIEND WITH BOOBS: Then I'm normal?

MAURO: Yes!

FRIEND WITH BOOBS: I'm normal! Ha ha, I'm normal!

SUPER: Don't be normal.

VO: Don't be normal. With Virgin Mobile, you won't pay exaggerated charges.

SUPER: Virgin Mobile.

VO: And you only pay what you want.

Why are you saying that?

No seas nor- mal.
RadioShack
Don't be normal.

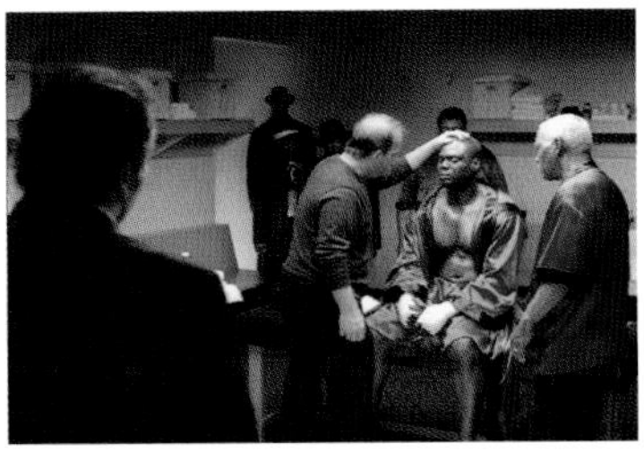

MERIT

ART DIRECTORS
Rick Bryant
Alex Manosalvas

WRITERS
Mark Taylor
Adam Cook

AGENCY PRODUCER
Don Turley

PRODUCTION COMPANY
Hungry Man

DIRECTOR
Jim Jenkins

CREATIVE DIRECTORS
Randy Snow
Arnie DiGeorge

CLIENT
Las Vegas Convention and Visitors Authority

AGENCY
R&R Partners/ Las Vegas

ANNUAL ID
06085T

[We see a young woman greeting a guy in a night club.]

WOMAN: Hi, nice to meet you, I'm Cindy.

[Then we see the same woman meeting a different guy.]

WOMAN: Hi, I'm Jan.

WOMAN: [Yelling over loud music] I'm Marsha!

WOMAN: I'm Rachel.

WOMAN: Hi, I'm Monica.

WOMAN: I'm Phoebe.

WOMAN: I'm Carrie.

WOMAN: Charlotte.

WOMAN: Miranda.

WOMAN: [Sexy voice] Samantha.

WOMAN: Hi, nice to meet you, I'm Xena.

GUY: Xena?

WOMAN: Yes, Xena.

WOMAN: I'm Lucy, this is my friend Ethel.

WOMAN: My name is Louise, call me Weezy.

WOMAN: Hi, I'm Ginger.

GUY: Ginger, I'm Cliff and this is my buddy Norm.

[The woman does a double-take.]

SUPER: What happens here, stays here.

LOGO: Only Vegas

MERIT

ART DIRECTOR
Marc Gallucci

WRITERS
Justin Galvin
Pete Shamon

AGENCY PRODUCER
Alyson Singer

PRODUCTION COMPANIES
@radical.media
Jon Kamen
Gregg Carlesimo

DIRECTOR
Steve Miller

CREATIVE DIRECTOR
Marc Gallucci

CLIENT
ESPN

AGENCY
Fort Franklin/Boston

ANNUAL ID
06086T

[Open on Gerald dressed in a racing outfit in an airplane. The stewardess brings him a cup of coffee.]

STEWARDESS: Excuse me, this is from the gentleman in first class.

[He accepts the coffee and the stewardess walks away. We see a large fish turning around in a first class seat.]

FISH: Hey Jer, how's the coffee?

[Gerald takes a sip. Cut back to the fish.]

FISH: Are you sure it's coffee?

[Cut to Gerald. The fish laughs.]

FISH: Oh, you're not sure now. Welcome to my world, Gerald.

VO: The 35th annual Bass Master Classic on ESPN.

SUPER: Bass Master Classic – ESPN

CITGO
BASSMASTER
CLASSIC
35th ANNUAL
ESPN
Ray Scott Inlet

This is
SportsCenter.

This is
SportsCenter.

[Open on John Anderson at his desk.]

SUPER: ANDERSON SportsCenter Anchor

ANDERSON: So Scott starts reeling these great shows, one right after the other.

[We cut to a SportsCenter telecast. Scott Van Pelt sits with Stuart Scott.]

VAN PELT: And A-Rod exhibits inordinate aptitude in spheroidical aviation!

[Stuart Scott looks at Scott Van Pelt confused. We cut back to the interview.]

ANDERSON: Turns out he was using performance enhancers.

[We cut to Scott standing defensively at his desk while authorities rifle through his drawers.]

VAN PELT: I fear that your inquisition will prove fruitless.

AUTHORITY 1: You mind telling us what this is?
[Cut to a close up of authorities showing Scott Van Pelt a thesaurus.]

VAN PELT: I, I don't even know what that is or how you use it.

AUTHORITY 2: Looks like a thesaurus.

[Cornered, he panics and makes a break. He is quickly pounced upon and wrestled to the ground.]

VAN PELT: Unhand me you rapscallion!

ANDERSON: We've gotta win back a lot of trust…a lot of trust.

SUPER: This is SportsCenter. ESPN

This is
SportsCenter.

Merit

MERIT

ART DIRECTOR
Stuart Jennings

WRITERS
Brant Mau
Andy Ferguson

AGENCY PRODUCERS
Jesse Wann
Chris Noble
Gary Krieg

PRODUCTION COMPANY
Hungry Man

DIRECTOR
David Shane

CREATIVE DIRECTORS
Todd Waterbury
Kevin Proudfoot
Paul Renner
Derek Barnes

CLIENT
ESPN Sportscenter

AGENCY
Wieden+Kennedy/
New York

ANNUAL ID
06088T

ALSO AWARDED
Merit:
Consumer Television:
:30/:25 - Single

MERIT

ART DIRECTOR
Jayanta Jenkins

WRITER
Brian Ford

AGENCY PRODUCER
Jennifer Smieja

PRODUCTION COMPANY
Epoch Films

DIRECTOR
Stacy Wall

CREATIVE DIRECTORS
Hal Curtis
Mike Byrne

CLIENT
Nike

AGENCY
Wieden+Kennedy/ Portland

ANNUAL ID
06087T

[LeBron James is dressed up as different "versions" of himself.]

ANNOUNCER ON TV: LeBron James is on FIRE!

BADASS TO WISE: Drop that old school.

[Rick James' Superfreak plays on the record player]

WISE: Yeah boy, that's what I'm talking about right there.

ATHLETE TO KID: I see you, little man. Uh, yeah.

WISE: Ooooooh.

ATHLETE TO WISE: Okay.

ANNOUNCER ON TV: ...with a tomahawk jam.

BADASS: That's perfect.

WISE: Wooo. That boy good. Oh.

SUPER: nikebasketball.com

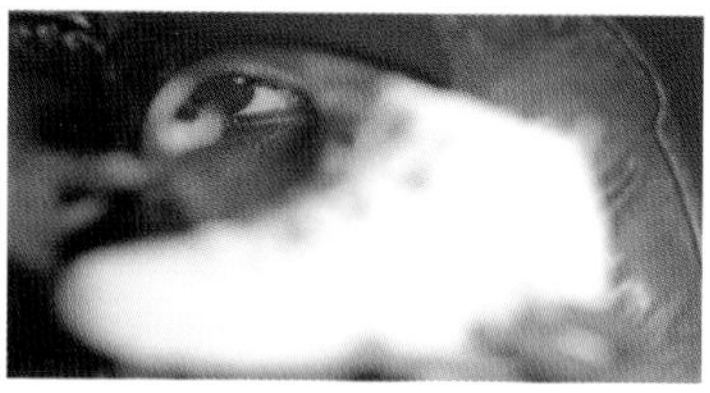

nikebasketball.com

[A father is trying to enter the bedroom of his little son. But something small is blocking the door. As we come closer it becomes clear that this small thing is in fact the new tough Polo.]

SUPER: Tough. The new Polo.
Volkswagen. Who else?

Tough. The new Polo.

MERIT

ART DIRECTOR
Jakko Achterberg

WRITER
Niels Westra

AGENCY PRODUCER
Chantal Gulpers

PRODUCTION COMPANY
Maarten.nl

DIRECTOR
Jakko Achterberg

CLIENT
Pon's Automobielhandel

AGENCY
DDB/Amsterdam

ANNUAL ID
06091T

MERIT

ART DIRECTOR
Ron Smrczek

WRITER
Irfan Khan

AGENCY PRODUCER
Jennifer Mete

PRODUCTION COMPANY
Partners Film

DIRECTOR
Joachim Back

CREATIVE DIRECTORS
Lance Martin
Zak Mroueh

CLIENT
Pfizer Canada - Viagra

AGENCY
TAXI/Toronto

ANNUAL ID
06093T

VIAGRA

Talk to your doctor

[Open in an elevator.]

PHIL: Hey Alan. Running a little late?

ALAN: Yeah.

PHIL: You look tired. Thompson file?

ALAN: No. I was up late...

[A large blue Viagra pill is superimposed over his mouth while the words are bleeped out.]

PHIL: Cool.

SUPER: Talk to your doctor.

[Open on an innocent-looking girl. She approaches an exposed pipe in her apartment and starts to dance around it. After a few seconds of dancing, the camera slowly pans up the pipe, following it to the ceiling. The camera follows the pipe to the apartment above it where it's connected to the shower drain. We then see some soapy bubbles going down the drain and a pair of guy's legs from about mid-calf down. We also see a bottle of Axe Shower Gel on the shower floor.]

SUPER: How Dirty Boys Get Clean.

VO: How Dirty Boys Get Clean.

SUPER: New Axe Shower Gel.

VO: New Axe Shower Gel.

AXE

MERIT

ART DIRECTORS
Amee Shah
John Hobbs

WRITERS
Matt Ian
Peter Rosch

AGENCY PRODUCER
Lisa Gatto

PRODUCTION COMPANY
HSI Productions

DIRECTOR
Joe Public

CREATIVE DIRECTOR
William Gelner

CLIENT
Unilever

AGENCY
Bartle Bogle Hegarty/
New York

ANNUAL ID
06096T

ALSO AWARDED
Merit:
Consumer Television:
:20 and under - single

Merit

MERIT

ART DIRECTORS
John Hobbs
Amee Shah
Greg Copeland
Tony Miller

WRITERS
Peter Rosch
Matt Ian
Paul Copeland
Tony Miller

AGENCY PRODUCER
Jill Andresevic

PRODUCTION COMPANY
Kleinman Productions

DIRECTOR
Danny Kleinman

CREATIVE DIRECTOR
Thomas Hayo

CLIENT
Levi's

AGENCY
Bartle Bogle Hegarty/ New York

ANNUAL ID
06098T

[A young man is in a hotel room with his girlfriend. Outside, his Levi's are hanging on the veranda rail, drying. "Superstition" by Stevie Wonder plays throughout. A pair of hands reaches up and steals the Levi's from the railing. We see a young man pull the jeans on. As the thief tries to walk off with the other guy's jeans his legs turn uncontrollably, mimicking the movements of the original owner. Throughout the night, every move that the original wearer makes, the thief does uncontrollably too, as if the jeans are possessed. Finally, we see the thief walking down the street but he is no longer wearing the jeans, he has had enough. The thief puts the jeans back on the veranda where he found them. A moment later the original owner comes out to collect his favorite pair of jeans. We then see the owner slide the jeans up over his hips. We see a shot from behind showing the familiar Levi's red tab on the pocket as he buttons up the fly and walks away.]

SUPER: Levi's 559 Jeans.
A Style for Every Story.

Levi's

Merit

Merit

ART DIRECTOR
Xanthe Hohalek

WRITER
Sean Vij

AGENCY PRODUCER
AnneKatherine Friis

PRODUCTION COMPANY
MJZ

DIRECTOR
Steven Diller

CREATIVE DIRECTOR
Court Crandall

CLIENT
ESPN

AGENCY
*Ground Zero/
Los Angeles*

ANNUAL ID
06099T

ALSO AWARDED
*Merit:
Consumer Television:
:30/:25 - Single*

*Merit:
Consumer Television:
:30/:25 - Single*

[A man stands in his garage working diligently on a dollhouse. He stands back, proudly, and smiles at his progress. He walks to his workbench to get a miniature chair to add to the house. When he turns around he sees the dollhouse is on fire. He looks at the little chair he's holding. Then back at the dollhouse. He suddenly notices a bowling ball on the ground next to the dollhouse staring up at him. Creepy music builds slightly. The man is confused, and a little wary. He looks to the fire, then back at the ball.]

SUPER: Sundays are for bowling.
The PBA Tulsa Championship, Sunday at 1 PM ET.

VO: The Denny's PBA tour. Begins next Sunday at 1 PM on ESPN.

LOGO: Denny's/PBA and ESPN

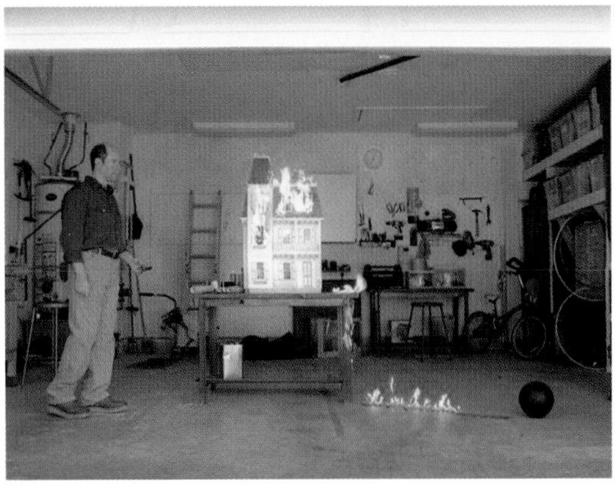

Merit

MERIT

ART DIRECTOR
Dale McGuinness

WRITER
Dennis Koutoulogenis

AGENCY PRODUCER
Tamyson Power

PRODUCTION COMPANY
2 Feet Films

DIRECTOR
Phil Rich

CREATIVE DIRECTOR
Warren Brown

CLIENT
Meat & Livestock Australia

AGENCY
BMF/Pyrmont

ANNUAL ID
06100T

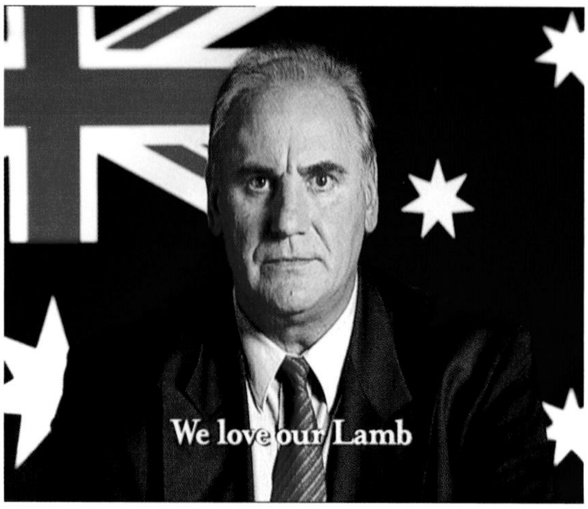
We love our Lamb

[Australian football legend Sam Kekovich is sitting at a desk with the Australian flag behind him and patriotic music playing.]

SAM: There's nothing worse than being un-Australian. I should know, I've been Australian all my life. And I'm sickened by the creeping tide of unAustralianism eroding our great traditions, like our custom of eating lamb on Australia Day. UnAustralianism is everywhere. For example, people wearing those plastic, brightly-colored flip-flop shoes with flowers on them. What's wrong with rubber thongs in simple primary colors? And if I hear another person say "thong," when they mean those swimming costumes poncey Brazilian blokes wear up their bums, I'll do my block. Sadly, the scourge of unAustralianism has even infected our national day. A balanced Australia Day diet should consist of a few nice, juicy lamb chops and beer. (And perhaps a bit of pavlova for those with a sweet tooth). Yet your long-haired, dole-bludging types are indulging their pierced tastebuds in all manner of exotic, foreign, often vegetarian cuisine: Chicken burger value meals, pizzas, a number 42 with rice… It's an absolute disgrace. And people ask why we need capital punishment. Do you think the diggers in the trenches were fighting for tofu sausages? No, they were thinking of grabbing a lamb chop off the barbie with their bare fingers, sustaining third degree burns, then sticking their hands into a relieving esky to fish out a cold one. Look at our national song, "Waltzing Matilda." It's about a bloke trying to get a nice bit of lamb into his tuckerbag, not spicy chicken wings. The soap-avoiding, pot-smoking, hippy vegetarians may disagree with me, but they can get stuffed. They know the way to the airport, and if they don't I'll show them. So the message is clear—even for you backpackers: roll out the barbie, ensure the gas bottle's filled, stack the fridge full of lamb, and prepare the invitation list. So don't be unAustralian—serve lamb on Australia Day. You know it makes sense. I'm Sam Kekovich.

SUPER: We love our lamb.

[A policeman is sitting at a table behind a typewriter inside of a police bus. Opposite him is a young man. The policeman pulls a sheet of paper out of the typewriter and begins to read out the young man's statement.]

POLICEMAN: On the A7 near Ellwangen, a heavy goods vehicle lost control and rammed my car, causing me to roll over six or seven times and go through the central crash barrier onto the other side of the road ...

POLICEMAN: I was then hit by a lorry head on which dragged me along approximately 150 meters, catapulting me down a 20 meter high bank.

[The policeman looks up at the young man, examining him.]

YOUNG MAN: Yes.

POLICEMAN: I rolled over again a few times in the field, uprooted a tree and eventually came to a stop...with the lorry on top of me.

[The policeman looks up again and scrutinizes the man in disbelief. Then his gaze moves towards the window: in front is a Polo. It is filthy, but other than a small dent in the wing it is completely undamaged.]

SUPER: Relax. It's the new Polo.

YOUNG MAN: The dent was already there.

LOGO: Volkswagen

Relax. It's the new Polo.

MERIT

ART DIRECTOR
Kristoffer Heilemann

WRITER
Ludwig Berndl

AGENCY PRODUCER
Marion Lange

PRODUCTION COMPANY
soup.film

DIRECTOR
Edward Berger

CREATIVE DIRECTORS
Wolfgang Schneider
Mathias Stiller

CLIENT
Volkswagen

AGENCY
DDB/Berlin

ANNUAL ID
06101T

ALSO AWARDED
Merit:
Non-Broadcast - Single

VO: A male hummingbird draws near preparing to drink nectar from the blossom of a flower. Slow motion—one hundred times slower than real time—is the only thing that allows us to observe the complex beating of its wings.

SUPER: Nothing's faster. DHL. The world's fastest delivery service.

MERIT

AGENCY PRODUCER
Nadja Catana

PRODUCTION COMPANY
Entspannt Film Berlin

DIRECTOR
Nicolai Niemann

CREATIVE DIRECTORS
Oliver Handlos
Michael Pfeiffer-Belli

CLIENT
DHL

AGENCY
Jung von Matt/Berlin

ANNUAL ID
06102T

Merit

ART DIRECTOR
Dave Sakamoto

WRITER
William Bloomfield

AGENCY PRODUCER
Luke Ricci

PRODUCTION COMPANY
Giraffe

DIRECTOR
Peter Martin

CREATIVE DIRECTOR
Martin Dix

CLIENT
web.com

AGENCY
M&C Saatchi/ Santa Monica

ANNUAL ID
06103T

Julie Smith
Founder, iPsycho

web.com

SUPER: Julia Smith – Founder, iPsycho.

JULIE: I've been a "psycho" ex-girlfriend for years. But I never really knew how psycho I was until friends started asking for advice.

EX-BOYFRIEND: Kathy?

JULIE: Run!

[As the girl bolts, we see his house has been tp'd and his car is defaced with "pig." Cut back to Julie at her computer.]

JULIE: That's when I decided to take my company online with Web.com. Their low rates and unsurpassed customer service make doing business online a breeze.

[On the computer screen, a virtual pin gets stuck in a virtual voodoo doll's leg. We see ex-boyfriend 2 walking through a park with his new girl. Suddenly he buckles at the knees, screams, and falls to the ground.]

EX-BOYFRIEND 2: Aaaarrrrgghhhh!!

JULIE: Well, gotta go. Duty calls...

[She speaks into the receiver with a hand-held voice disguiser. Her voice transforms and suddenly sounds like that of a gruff serial killer.]

JULIE: Hello, Steven.

[Cut to Julie and yet another 20-something female client walking out of a house carrying a shovel and gas can.]

SUPER: web.com

VO: Web.com. The easiest way to get your business on the web.

[They continue walking towards a car on the street. The open trunk reveals a bound and gagged ex-boyfriend looking scared out of his wits.]

VO: Maybe a little too easy.

[Open on an old lady sipping her afternoon tea by the window, listening to the news. The phone rings, and she gets up gingerly to answer it.]

MALE VOICE: Helloooo Mary, you sexy...

[The old lady's expression changes to an angry, indignant one as she slams down the phone, cursing under her breath. It's a flashback to the '60s and two giggly schoolgirls are laughing in a toilet, scribbling something with a marker pen. The door closes and we see the words on the toilet door: "For a good f**k, call Mary at 654-504-3405."]

LOGO: BIC Permanent Markers

For a good F[redacted]K
call Mary
876575

Merit

ART DIRECTOR
Run Run Teng

WRITER
Gayle Lim

AGENCY PRODUCER
Jude Doss

PRODUCTION COMPANY
Rushes Network

DIRECTOR
Melvin Mak

CREATIVE DIRECTOR
Tian It Ng

CLIENT
Golden Star Gifts & Stationery

AGENCY
McCann Erickson/Singapore

ANNUAL ID
06104T

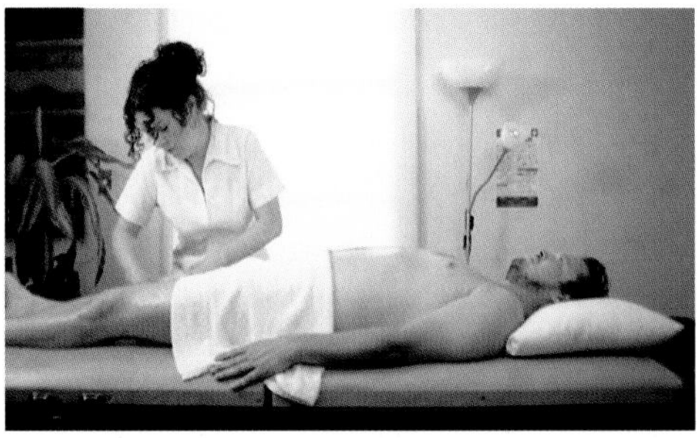

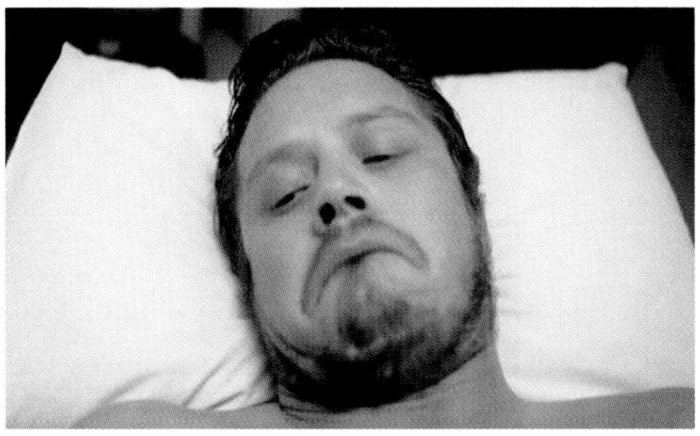

Serious about sport?

MAN: [Whispers] Why not?

WOMAN: [Whispers] No, I can't.

MAN: It'll be over...

WOMAN: I'm not going to do it.

MAN: It'll be over real quick.

WOMAN: I'll lose my job, OK?

MAN: Oh please...

WOMAN: No... shhhh!

MAN: I'll give you ten bucks.

WOMAN: No, no, no, I'm not going to do it.

MAN: Oh, please.

WOMAN: Twenty bucks. You better be quick.

[She walks over to her tray, pulls out a couple of tissues and wipes her hands with them. He sits up in anticipation. She reaches over and turns on a television suspended from the wall. A rugby match is in progress.]

SUPER: Serious about sport?

LOGO: Foxsports

Merit

ART DIRECTOR
David Nobay

WRITER
David Nobay

AGENCY PRODUCER
Scott McBurnie

PRODUCTION COMPANY
GoodOil Films

DIRECTOR
Hamish Rothwell

CREATIVE DIRECTOR
David Nobay

CLIENT
Fox Sports

AGENCY
Saatchi & Saatchi/Sydney

ANNUAL ID
06106T

MERIT

ART DIRECTOR
Mike Andrews

WRITERS
Jon Lancaric
Andrew Crocker

AGENCY PRODUCER
DP Odishoo

PRODUCTION COMPANY
Furlined Co.

DIRECTOR
Zach Math

CREATIVE DIRECTOR
Lisa Bennett

CLIENT
Golden Gate Fields

AGENCY
DDB/San Francisco

ANNUAL ID
06107T

WE WANT YOU TO WIN.

[Open on a couple playing a "claw machine" game. They are attempting, without success, to grab one of the many soft toys inside. Cut to inside the machine to reveal a jockey placing one of the toys into the claw for them.]

SUPER: We want you to win.

[A bell rings, followed by the sound of horses bolting out of the starting gates.]

SUPER: Golden Gate Fields

WE WANT YOU TO WIN.

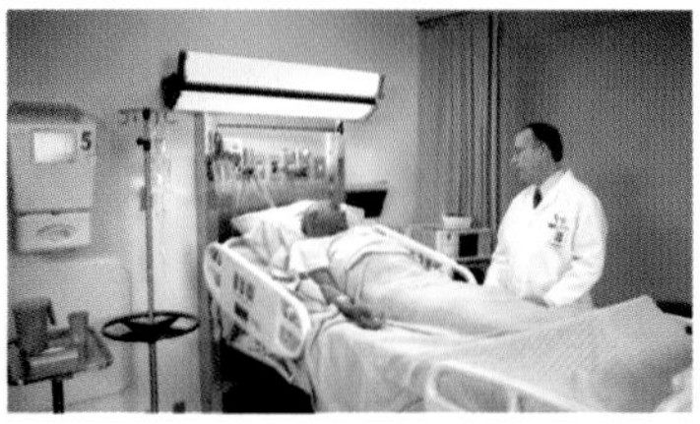

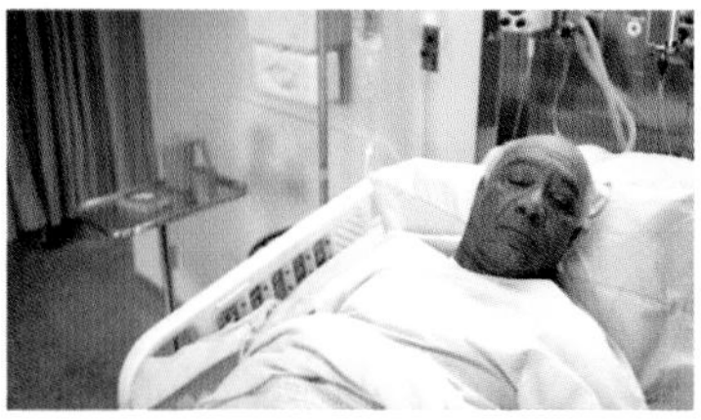

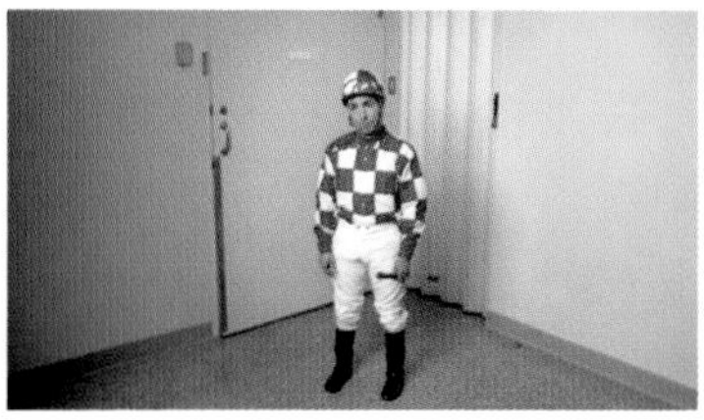

Merit

STA

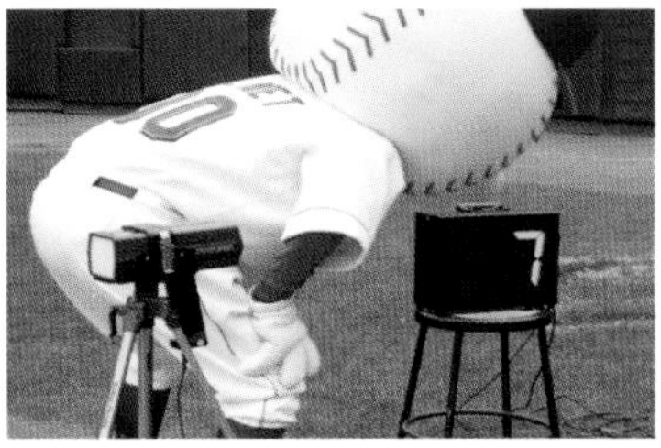
7

6

Merit

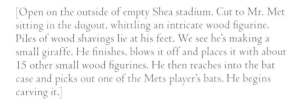

ART DIRECTORS
Arturo Gigante
Josh Rosen

WRITERS
Curtis Mueller
Mark Svartz

AGENCY PRODUCER
Carrie Simon

PRODUCTION COMPANY
Biscuit Filmworks

DIRECTOR
Tim Godsall

CREATIVE DIRECTORS
David Apicella
Joe Johnson
Josh Tavlin

CLIENT
New York Mets

AGENCY
Ogilvy & Mather/
New York

ANNUAL ID
06109T

ALSO AWARDED
Merit:
Consumer Television:
Under $50K - Single

[Open on the outside of empty Shea stadium. Cut to Mr. Met sitting in the dugout, whittling an intricate wood figurine. Piles of wood shavings lie at his feet. We see he's making a small giraffe. He finishes, blows it off and places it with about 15 other small wood figurines. He then reaches into the bat case and picks out one of the Mets player's bats. He begins carving it.]

SUPER: The excitement returns to the Shea this Tuesday. And not a moment too soon.

Mets vs. Nationals

mets.com

Mets
00

MERIT

ART DIRECTOR
Kristoffer Heilemann

WRITER
Ludwig Berndl

AGENCY PRODUCER
Marion Lange

PRODUCTION COMPANY
Markenfilm

DIRECTOR
Henry Littlechild

CREATIVE DIRECTORS
Wolfgang Schneider
Mathias Stiller

CLIENT
Volkswagen

AGENCY
DDB/Berlin

ANNUAL ID
06111T

Maximum power condensed.

The new Golf GT with TSI®

[We see a frog sitting on a leave in a pond waiting for his prey. He jumps for a fly. But the fly turns the tables: Sticking to his tongue, she drags the frog easily out of the water and right up in the air.]

SUPER: Maximum power condensed.
The new Golf GT with TSI®.

LOGO: Volkswagen

MERIT

ART DIRECTOR
Hans Juergen Kaemmerer

WRITER
Robert Junker

AGENCY PRODUCER
Sabine Schuchmann

PRODUCTION COMPANY
Core Team

CREATIVE DIRECTORS
Hans Juergen Kaemmerer
Robert Junker

CLIENT
Care International

AGENCY
Leo Burnett/Frankfurt

ANNUAL ID
06112T

[We see images of poverty-stricken regions in Africa and Asia. Then we see images of the 2005 tsunami and thousands of drowning victims.]

SUPER: Care, anyone? When disasters fade from the media after a few days, they fade from our consciousness too. But hunger, epidemics and destruction stay around a lot longer. And so do the aid workers from CARE.

LOGO: CARE

care, anyone?

[Open on a city street, camera at ground level. The streets are full of Ken dolls. Pan up to reveal GI Joe. He looks all around at the Kens, then down at his own army fatigues. He walks into a trendy clothing store. Joe steps out in black pants, a black shirt and sunglasses. A Ken from the store points him to a salon across the street. Cut to Joe getting frosted tips and facial. Cut to Joe leaving the salon. A Ken points to a gym across the street. Then we see Joe in the gym trying to make sense of all the signs: Pilates Studio 1, Yoga Studio 2, Tai Chi Studio 3, Meditation Studio 3, Taiboxerobicise Studio 5. Joe is in the locker room. Joe is then getting a chest wax. Cut to Joe in a bookstore reading *Men Who Love Too Much*. Cut to Joe in a coffee shop, trying to make sense of all the signs. Cut to Joe in a bookstore reading *Men Who Love Too Little*. Cut to Joe in a department store, looking at all the skin care products: toner, exfoliant, bronzer, concealer, super hydrating exfoliating deep pore mask, etc. Cut to Joe in a bookstore reading *Men Who Love Women Who Love Men Who Don't Love Them*. Cut to Joe in a convenience mart—all the beer is low-carb. He falls to his knees—overhead shot of him screaming at the heavens. Cut to Joe running out of the store. He runs down the street, pulling off his shirt, throwing away his sunglasses. He bursts into his apartment, closes the door and drops his pants. Naked, he walks over to his dresser and pulls open the drawer. He takes out a pair of Levi's and smiles.]

SUPER: Life getting too complicated? 501. Uncomplicate.

MERIT

WRITER
Shalom Auslander

AGENCY PRODUCER
Jonathan Shipman

PRODUCTION COMPANY
Chelsea Productions

DIRECTOR
Simon Blake

CREATIVE DIRECTOR
Craig Markus

CLIENT
Levi's

AGENCY
McCann Erickson/
New York

ANNUAL ID
06113T

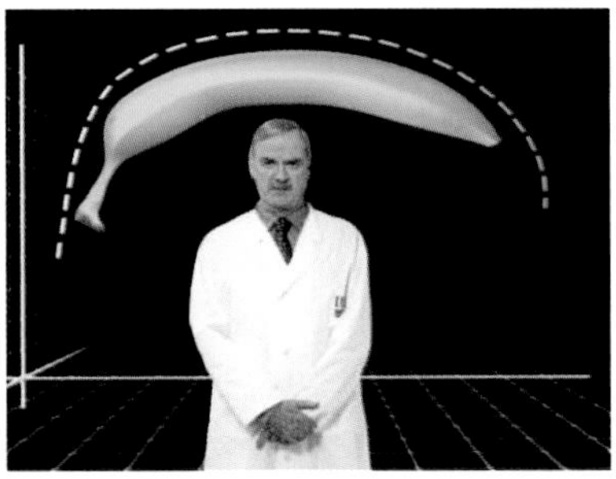

dept. of humor analysis

[John Cleese is at the TBS Department of Humor Analysis giving a tour. He demonstrates the "funniest place to hit a man with a ball" and the H-A-M, a computer that tells how funny something is. He also asks which is funnier, a mime pretending to be trapped in a glass box or a mime actually trapped in a glass box.]

CLEESE: Here's something. Are American sitcoms funnier in other languages?

[We see a *Friends* episode dubbed in Japanese. Cut to *Seinfeld* dubbed into German.]

CLEESE: Fantastic work, guys. Help the department with their important work by logging on to tbshumorstudy.com, and telling us what you find funny.

SUPER: WWW.TBSHUMORSTUDY.COM

CLEESE: The information you provide will be fed into the Humor Analysis Mainframe and shredded, so that we don't have to share it. The TBS Department of Humor Analysis...

DEPARTMENT (IN UNISON): ...putting the "very" in front of "funny."

LOGO: TBS

SUPER: THANK YOU
FRIENDS – WEEKNIGHT AT 8 PM/7C
SEINFELD – WEDNESDAYS AT 10 PM/9C
FAMILY GUY – MONDAYS AT 10 PM/9C
NORM WEBBER (FOR HIS ORANGE BALLS)

MERIT

ART DIRECTOR
Rory Hanrahan

WRITER
Dave Clark

AGENCY PRODUCER
Margaux Ravis

PRODUCTION COMPANY
Thomas Thomas

DIRECTOR
Kevin Thomas

CREATIVE DIRECTORS
Linus Karlsson
Paul Malmstrom

CLIENT
Turner Broadcasting System (TBS)

AGENCY
Mother/New York

ANNUAL ID
06114T

Merit Radio

public service/political-radio: single

WRITERS
Tim Roan
Gary Resch

AGENCY PRODUCER
Asa Sandlund

CREATIVE DIRECTORS
Toni Hess
Chris Becker

CLIENT
Eagle, Idaho Volunteer Firefighters Association

AGENCY
Foote Cone & Belding/ New York

ANNUAL ID
06014R

ART DIRECTORS
Dan Triechel
Colin Gaul
Jason Campbell

WRITERS
Emily Sander
Scott Bell

AGENCY PRODUCERS
Theresa Notartomaso
Terry Brogan

CREATIVE DIRECTORS
Walt Connelly
Toby Barlow

CLIENT
Partnership for a Drug Free America

AGENCY
JWT/New York

ANNUAL ID
06015R

WRITER
Mike Houston

CREATIVE DIRECTOR
Jerry Ketel

CLIENT
Oregon Coast Aquarium

AGENCY
Leopold Ketel & Partners/ Portland

ANNUAL ID
06042T

WRITER
Rob Tarry

AGENCY PRODUCER
Brie Gowans

PRODUCTION COMPANY
Wave Productions

CREATIVE DIRECTORS
Chris Staples
Ian Grais

CLIENT
Science World

AGENCY
Rethink/Vancouver

ANNUAL ID
06016R

WRITERS
Philippe Fass
Matthew Skolar

AGENCY PRODUCERS
Louise McKeown
Mike Blunt

PRODUCTION COMPANY
Triangle

CLIENT
National Aids Trust

AGENCY
Saatchi & Saatchi/London

ANNUAL ID
06017R

consumer radio: single

WRITER
Ballard Dustin

AGENCY PRODUCERS
Rupert Samuel
Eric Rasco

PRODUCTION COMPANY
Nutmeg Audio Post

CREATIVE DIRECTORS
Alex Bogusky
Bill Wright
Bob Cianfrone

CLIENT
Burger King

AGENCY
Crispin Porter + Bogusky/ Miami

ANNUAL ID
06021R

WRITER
Paul Little

AGENCY PRODUCER
Sue Bell

PRODUCTION COMPANY
GGRP

CREATIVE DIRECTOR
Alan Russell

CLIENT
ICBC

AGENCY
DDB/Vancouver

ANNUAL ID
06022R

WRITERS
John Baker
Robert Calabro

AGENCY PRODUCER
Marianne Newton

PRODUCTION COMPANY
Chicago Recording Company

CREATIVE DIRECTOR
Mark Gross

CLIENT
Anheuser-Busch

AGENCY
DDB/Chicago

ANNUAL ID
06027R

WRITERS
Chuck Rachford
Chris Roe

AGENCY PRODUCER
Marianne Newton

PRODUCTION COMPANY
Chicago Recording Company

CREATIVE DIRECTOR
Mark Gross

CLIENT
Anheuser-Busch

AGENCY
DDB/Chicago

ANNUAL ID
06026R

WRITER
Ludwig Berndl

AGENCY PRODUCER
Stefanie Schuster

PRODUCTION COMPANY
Hastings Audio Network/ Berlin

DIRECTOR
Andreas "Beavis" Ersson

CREATIVE DIRECTORS
Wolfgang Schneider
Mathias Stiller

CLIENT
Volkswagen

AGENCY
DDB/Berlin

ANNUAL ID
06028R

Public Service/Political-Radio: Single

WRITER
Christian Ole Puls

PRODUCTION COMPANY
Studio Funk Berlin

DIRECTOR
Stephan Moritz

CREATIVE DIRECTORS
Matthias Spaetgens
Jan Leube

CLIENT
Aktionsbuendnis Landmine

AGENCY
Scholz & Friends/Berlin

ANNUAL ID
06018R

WRITERS
Jason Kempen
Juliet Honey

PRODUCTION COMPANIES
Sterling Sound
Lorens Persson

CREATIVE DIRECTORS
Damon Stapleton
Camilla Herberstein

CLIENT
Drive Alive

AGENCY
TBWA\Hunt\Lascaris/ Johannesburg

ANNUAL ID
06019R

Public Service/Political-Radio: Campaign

WRITERS
Dustin Ballard
Dave Kennedy
Jason Yun

AGENCY PRODUCER
Carron Pedonti

PRODUCTION COMPANY
Soundtrack

CREATIVE DIRECTORS
Ron Lawner
Pete Favat
Alex Bogusky
John Kearse
Tom Adams

CLIENT
American Legacy Foundation

AGENCY
Arnold Worldwide/Boston and Crispin Porter + Bogusky/ Miami

ANNUAL ID
06020R

ALSO AWARDED
Merit:
Public Service/ Political Radio - Single:
"Toe Rings"

Merit:
Public Service/ Political Radio - Single
"Cover-Up"

Merit:
Public Service/ Political Radio - Single
"Candy Stores"

Consumer Radio: Single

WRITERS
Daniel Giachetti
John Clement
Sal DeVito

AGENCY PRODUCER
Barbara Michelson

PRODUCTION COMPANY
McHale Barone

CREATIVE DIRECTOR
Sal DeVito

CLIENT
National Thoroughbred Racing Association

AGENCY
DeVito/Verdi/New York

ANNUAL ID
06030R

WRITER
Todd Lemmon

AGENCY PRODUCER
Brian Coate

CREATIVE DIRECTORS
Steve Simpson
John Matejczyk

CLIENT
Hewlett-Packard

AGENCY
Goodby, Silverstein & Partners/ San Francisco

ANNUAL ID
06032R

WRITER
Mbulelo Nhlapo

DIRECTOR
Dumisani Maquta

CREATIVE DIRECTORS
Rob McLennan
Lynton Heath

CLIENT
Wonderbra

AGENCY
Lowe Bull Truth/Durban

ANNUAL ID
06033R

WRITERS
Paul Ewen
Phil Clarke

AGENCY PRODUCER
Nicola Warman-Johnston

PRODUCTION COMPANY
Shellike

CLIENT
Monster

AGENCY
Saatchi & Saatchi/London

ANNUAL ID
06034R

WRITER
Dan Cronin

AGENCY PRODUCER
Jason Souter

PRODUCTION COMPANY
Kamen Audio

CREATIVE DIRECTORS
Gerry Graf
Scott Vitrone
Ian Reichenthal

CLIENT
Masterfoods - Starburst

AGENCY
TBWA\Chiat\Day/ New York

ANNUAL ID
06035R

Merit Radio

Consumer Radio: Single

WRITER
Dan Cronin

PRODUCTION COMPANY
Kamen Audio

CREATIVE DIRECTORS
Gerry Graf
Scott Vitrone
Ian Reichenthal

CLIENT
Masterfoods - Starburst

AGENCY
TBWA\Chiat\Day/New York

ANNUAL ID
06037R

WRITER
Ron Henderson

AGENCY PRODUCER
Sheri Cartwright

PRODUCTION COMPANY
UNCLE

DIRECTOR
Wayne Holloway

CREATIVE DIRECTORS
Ron Henderson
Dennis Walker

CLIENT
Fruit of the Loom

AGENCY
The Richards Group/Dallas

ANNUAL ID
06038R

WRITERS
Jonathan Careless
Deborah Prenger

AGENCY PRODUCER
Janet Woods

PRODUCTION COMPANY
Pirate Radio & Television

DIRECTOR
Tom Goudie

CREATIVE DIRECTORS
Elspeth Lynn
Lorraine Tao

CLIENT
W Network

AGENCY
ZiG/Toronto

ANNUAL ID
06040R

Consumer Radio: Campaign

WRITER
Stephen Hindley

AGENCY PRODUCER
Bill Grant

PRODUCTION COMPANIES
Kris Dangla
John Buroker

CREATIVE DIRECTORS
Wade Koniakowsky
Dave Moore

CLIENT
iSoldit on eBay

AGENCY
Big Bang/Seattle

ANNUAL ID
06041R

WRITER
Brian Harris

PRODUCTION COMPANY
Earshot Audio-Post

DIRECTOR
Craig Moore

CREATIVE DIRECTORS
Scott Montgomery
Mark Bradley
Noah Sarff

CLIENT
Sport Graphics

AGENCY
Bradley and Montgomery/Indianapolis

ANNUAL ID
06042R

Consumer Radio: Campaign

WRITER
Nathan Manske

AGENCY PRODUCER
Angelo Ferrugia

DIRECTOR
Josh Webman

CREATIVE DIRECTORS
Doug Raboy
Sean LaBounty

CLIENT
Match.com

AGENCY
Hanft Raboy and Partners/New York

ANNUAL ID
06047R

WRITERS
Hugh Todd
Adam Scholes

AGENCY PRODUCER
Hannah Gibson

PRODUCTION COMPANY
Blue

CREATIVE DIRECTORS
Greg Martin
Mike McKenna

CLIENT
Vodafone

AGENCY
JWT/London

ANNUAL ID
06048R

WRITER
Oink Ink Radio

AGENCY PRODUCER
Swampy Hawkins

PRODUCTION COMPANY
Oink Ink Radio

DIRECTOR
Dan Price

CREATIVE DIRECTOR
Veronika Lineberry

CLIENT
Wheel of Fortune

AGENCY
Oink Ink Radio/New York

ANNUAL ID
06049R

WRITERS
Steve Carlin
Scot Waterhouse

AGENCY PRODUCER
Evonne Sciberras

PRODUCTION COMPANY
StellaRadio

DIRECTOR
Brad Power

CREATIVE DIRECTOR
David Nobay

CLIENT
Toyota

AGENCY
Saatchi & Saatchi/Sydney

ANNUAL ID
06050R

WRITER
Mark Lowe

AGENCY PRODUCER
Sun Yi

PRODUCTION COMPANY
Clatter & Din

CREATIVE DIRECTOR
Jim Walker

CLIENT
Tower Records

AGENCY
Sedgwick Rd./Seattle

ANNUAL ID
06051R

CONSUMER RADIO: CAMPAIGN

WRITER
Michael Atkinson

AGENCY PRODUCER
Lynda Crotty

PRODUCTION COMPANY
Babble-On Recording Studio

CREATIVE DIRECTOR
Jac Coverdale

CLIENT
Dairy Queen

AGENCY
Clarity Coverdale Fury/ Minneapolis

ANNUAL ID
06043R

WRITERS
Bart Culberson
Brad Morgan
Pat Burke
Chris Carraway

AGENCY PRODUCER
Marianne Newton

PRODUCTION COMPANY
Chicago Recording Company

CREATIVE DIRECTOR
Mark Gross

CLIENT
Anheuser-Busch

AGENCY
DDB/Chicago

ANNUAL ID
06044R

ALSO AWARDED
Merit:
Consumer Radio - Single:
"Mr. Backyard Bug Zapper Inventor"

Merit:
Consumer Radio - Single:
"Mr. Basketball Court Sweat Wiper Upper"

WRITER
Daniel Ernsting

AGENCY PRODUCER
Marion Lange

PRODUCTION COMPANY
Hastings Audio Network/ Berlin

DIRECTOR
Andreas "Beavis" Ersson

CREATIVE DIRECTORS
Alexander Weber-Gruen
Bastian Kuhn

CLIENT
Volkswagen

AGENCY
DDB/Berlin

ANNUAL ID
06045R

WRITER
Steve Dildarian

AGENCY PRODUCER
James Horner

CREATIVE DIRECTOR
Jeffrey Goodby

CLIENT
Anheuser-Busch

AGENCY
Goodby, Silverstein & Partners/San Francisco

ANNUAL ID
06046R

ALSO AWARDED
Merit:
Consumer Radio - Single
"Bud Bat"

CONSUMER RADIO: CAMPAIGN

WRITERS
Matthew Branning
Chris Garbutt

PRODUCTION COMPANY
Au Revoir Charlie

CREATIVE DIRECTOR
Erik Vervroegen

CLIENT
Playstation

AGENCY
TBWA\Paris/ Boulogne-Billancourt

ANNUAL ID
06052R

WRITERS
Dave Loew
Pete Figel
Ryan Ebner

AGENCY PRODUCERS
David Fisher
Matt Bijarchi

PRODUCTION COMPANY
Chicago Recording Company

CREATIVE DIRECTORS
Mark Figliulo
Dave Loew

CLIENT
The Travel Channel

AGENCY
Young & Rubicam/Chicago

ANNUAL ID
06053R

ALSO AWARDED
Merit:
Consumer Radio - Single:
"Souvenirs"

MERIT

Merit

ART DIRECTOR
Andre Massis

WRITER
Nathan Frank

ILLUSTRATOR
Andre Massis

CREATIVE DIRECTOR
William Gelner

CLIENT
Unilever

AGENCY
Bartle Bogle Hegarty/ New York

ANNUAL ID
06251A

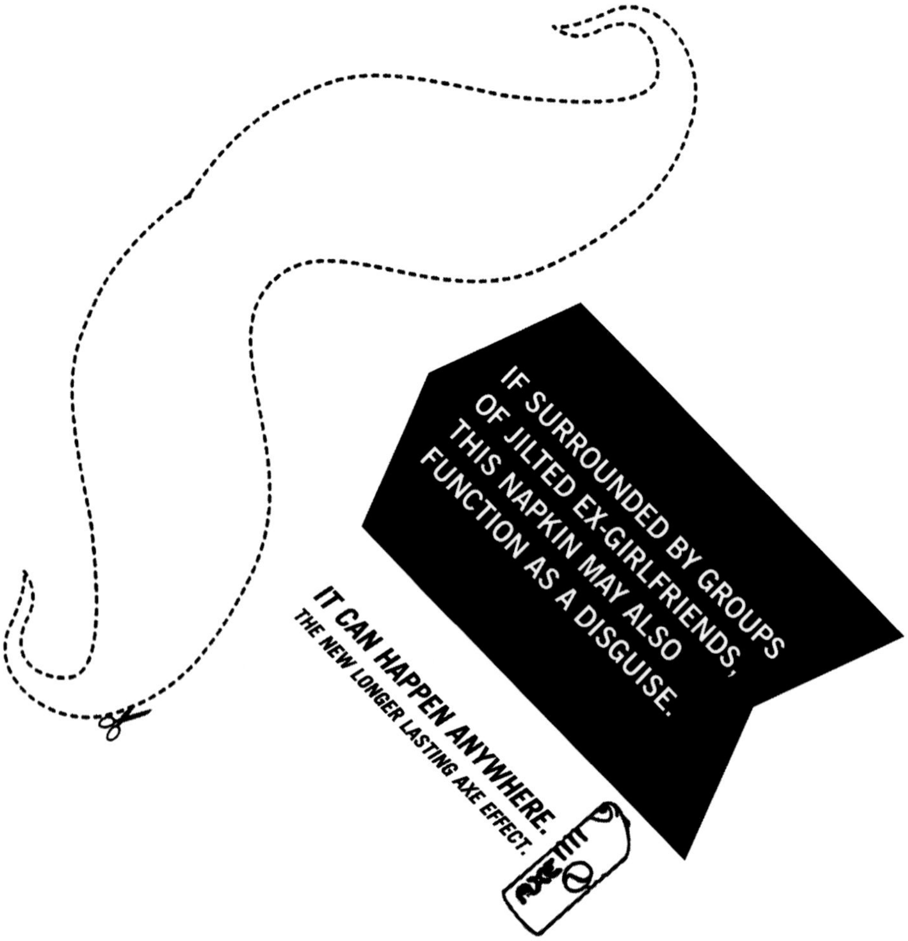
IF SURROUNDED BY GROUPS OF JILTED EX-GIRLFRIENDS, THIS NAPKIN MAY ALSO FUNCTION AS A DISGUISE.
IT CAN HAPPEN ANYWHERE.
THE NEW LONGER LASTING AXE EFFECT.

WHEN OUTNUMBERED AND PHYSICALLY EXHAUSTED BY GIRLS, THIS NAPKIN MAY ALSO BE USED AS A FLAG OF SURRENDER.
IT CAN HAPPEN ANYWHERE.
THE NEW LONGER LASTING AXE EFFECT.

IF GIRLS HAVE DESTROYED ALL OF YOUR CLOTHING, THIS NAPKIN MAY ALSO FUNCTION AS A LOINCLOTH.
IT CAN HAPPEN ANYWHERE.
THE NEW LONGER LASTING AXE EFFECT.

Precious
Memories.....

Let's Reminisce...

MERIT

ART DIRECTOR
Andre Massis

WRITER
Nathan Frank

PHOTOGRAPHER
Jason Fulford

CREATIVE DIRECTOR
William Gelner

CLIENT
Unilever

AGENCY
*Bartle Bogle Hegarty/
New York*

ANNUAL ID
06252A

we shared so much!!!

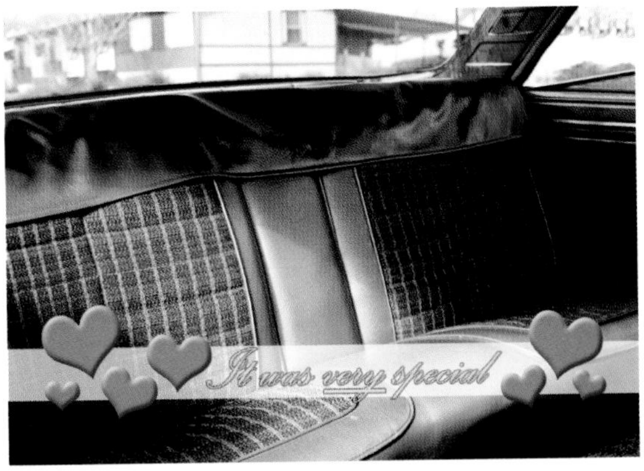
It was very special

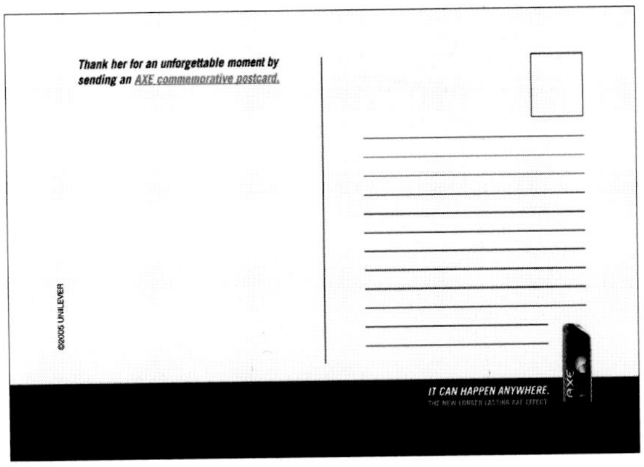
Thank her for an unforgettable moment by sending an AXE commemorative postcard.
©2005 UNILEVER
IT CAN HAPPEN ANYWHERE.
THE NEW LONGER LASTING AXE EFFECT
AXE

MERIT

ART DIRECTOR
Andre Massis

WRITER
Nathan Frank

CREATIVE DIRECTOR
William Gelner

CLIENT
Unilever

AGENCY
Bartle Bogle Hegarty/ New York

ANNUAL ID
06253A

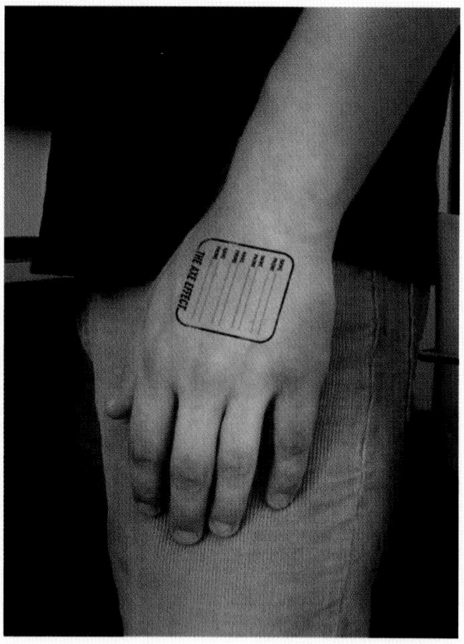

NAME
PHONE
NAME
PHONE
NAME
PHONE
NAME
PHONE
THE AXE EFFECT

MERIT

ART DIRECTOR
Khalid Osman

WRITER
Priti Kapur

PHOTOGRAPHER
Allan Ng

CREATIVE DIRECTORS
Neil Johnson
Terrence Tan

CLIENT
J H Kim Taekwondo Institute Singapore

AGENCY
DDB/Singapore

ANNUAL ID
06254A

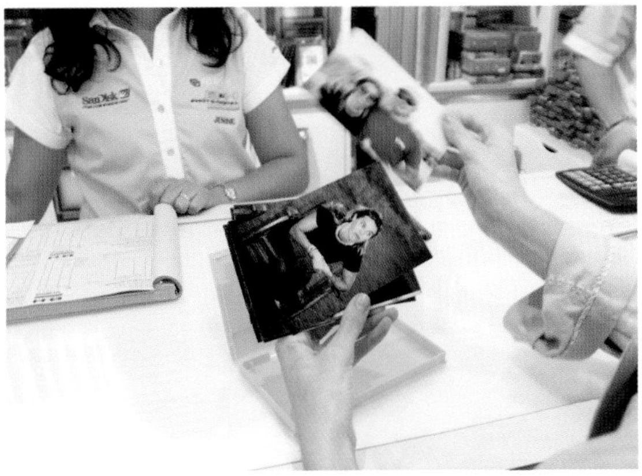

Relieve
red eyes

Relieve
red eyes

Relieve
red eyes

MERIT

ART DIRECTOR
Nicola Bower

WRITER
Lauren Gordon

PHOTOGRAPHERS
Lauren Gordon
Nicola Bower

CREATIVE DIRECTORS
Kamal Gangaram
Brett Morris

CLIENT
Adcock Ingram/Oculosan Eye Drops

AGENCY
FCB/Johannesburg

ANNUAL ID
06255A

Scotch
Reclosable
Fasteners

MERIT

ART DIRECTOR
Malcom King

WRITER
David Jennions

PHOTOGRAPHER
Craig Marais

CREATIVE DIRECTOR
Mike Barnwell

CLIENT
3M Reclosable Fasteners

AGENCY
Grey Worldwide/ Johannesburg

ANNUAL ID
06256A

MERIT

ART DIRECTOR
Run Run Teng

WRITER
Gayle Lim

PHOTOGRAPHER
Chai Guan Teo

CREATIVE DIRECTOR
Tian It Ng

CLIENT
Groupe SEB Singapore

AGENCY
McCann Erickson/ Singapore

ANNUAL ID
06257A

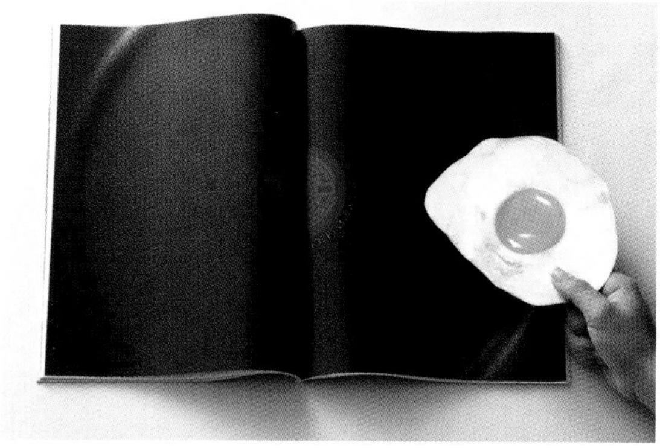

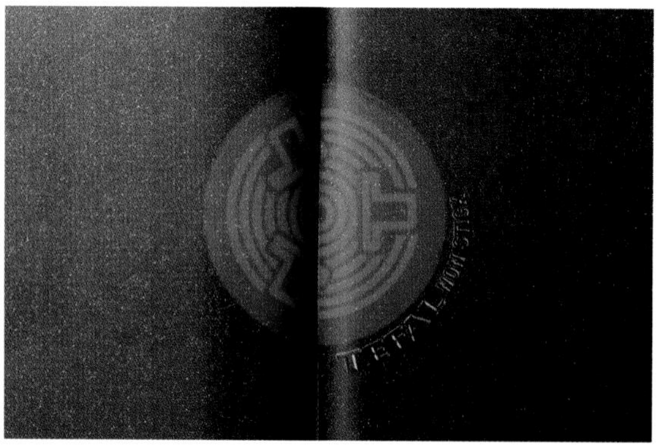

MERIT

ART DIRECTOR
Ismael Diaz

WRITER
Ricardo Cardenas

CREATIVE DIRECTOR
Ricardo Cardenas

CLIENT
Motorola

AGENCY
Ogilvy & Mather/ Mexico

ANNUAL ID
06258A

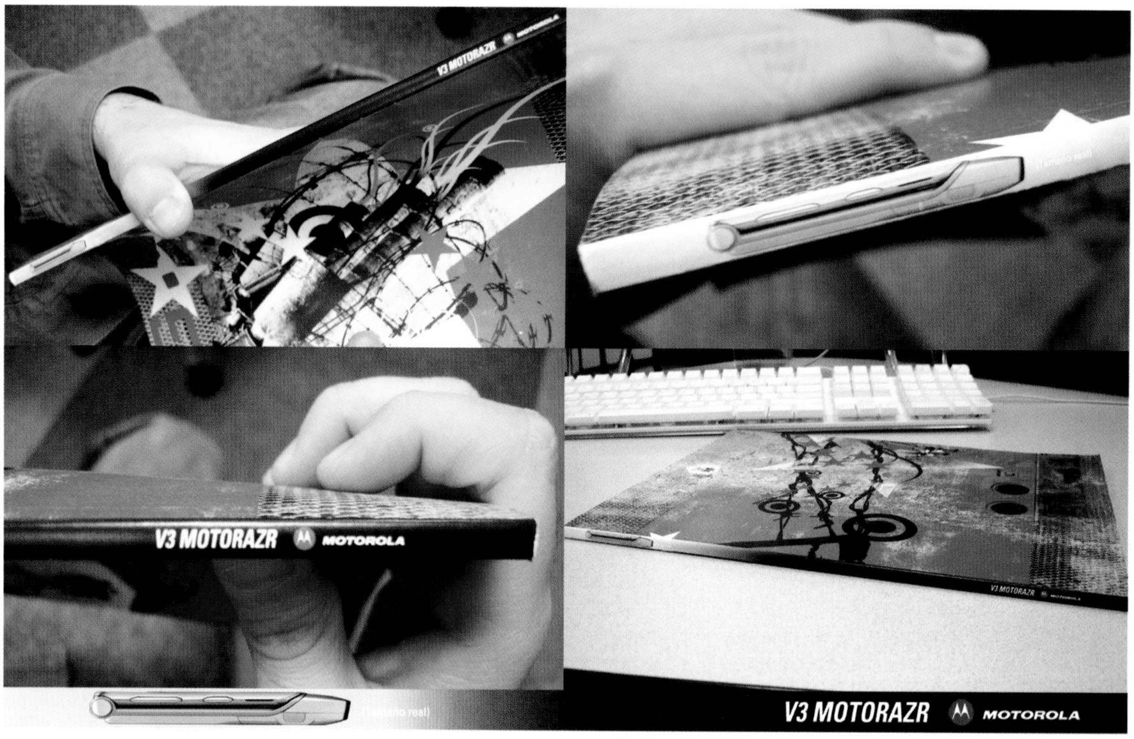
V3 MOTORAZR
MOTOROLA

"This may be the best book on advertising I've read – it's certainly the best book on print advertising."
DAVID ABBOTT
CUTTING EDGE ADVERTISING
HOW TO CREATE THE WORLD'S BEST PRINT FOR BRANDS IN THE 21ST CENTURY
2ND EDITION OF THE CLASSIC BEST-SELLER
2nd Edition Jim Aitchison

Merit

ART DIRECTOR
Eric Yeo

WRITER
Allen Tay

PHOTOGRAPHER
Shooting Gallery

CREATIVE DIRECTOR
Sonal Dabral

CLIENT
Jim Aitchison

AGENCY
Ogilvy & Mather/ Singapore

ANNUAL ID
06259A

自动柜员机
AUTO TELLER MACHINE

自动柜员机
AUTO TELLER MACHINE

Merit

ART DIRECTORS
Simon Cheung
Johe Chen

WRITERS
Andrew Lok
Owen Leung

PHOTOGRAPHER
Simon Cheung

CREATIVE DIRECTORS
Andrew Lok
Owen Leung

CLIENT
Shenzhen Mobile

AGENCY
Ogilvy & Mather/ Guangzhou

ANNUAL ID
06260A

MERIT

ART DIRECTORS
Wing Zheng
Owen Leung

WRITERS
Owen Leung
Andrew Lok

PHOTOGRAPHER
Wing Zheng

AGENCY PRODUCERS
Shadow Guo
Sisi Cheung

CREATIVE DIRECTORS
Andrew Lok
Owen Leung

CLIENT
Zhujiang Beer

AGENCY
Ogilvy & Mather/ Guangzhou

ANNUAL ID
06261A

open...
2·60元

2·60元

MERIT

ART DIRECTORS
Birol Bayractar
Anne Petri

DESIGNER
Birol Bayractar

AGENCY PRODUCER
Amandus Platt

CREATIVE DIRECTORS
Florian Pagel
Anne Petri

CONTENT STRATEGISTS
Florian Voigt
Gerhard Nonnenmacher

CLIENT
Diakonie Katastrophenhilfe (Emergency Aid)

AGENCY
Saatchi & Saatchi/ Frankfurt

ANNUAL ID
06262A

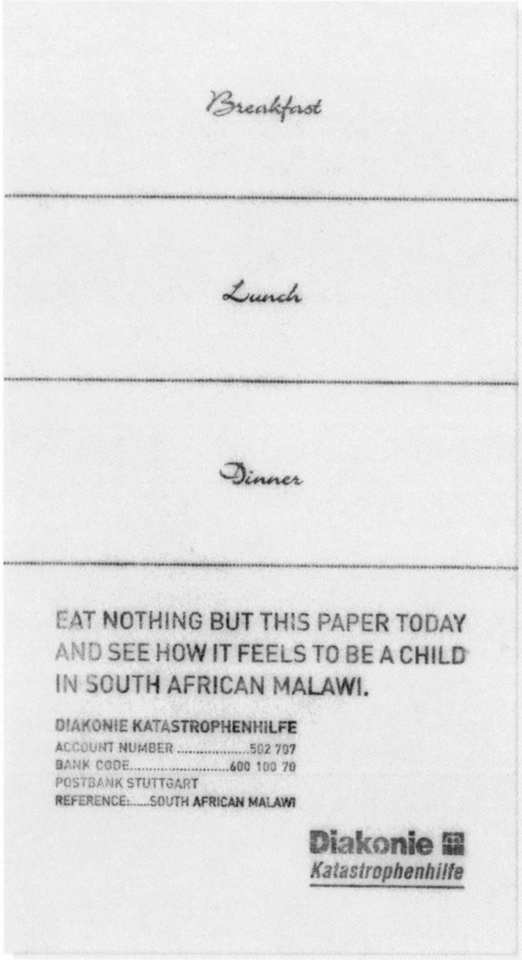
Breakfast
Lunch
Dinner
EAT NOTHING BUT THIS PAPER TODAY AND SEE HOW IT FEELS TO BE A CHILD IN SOUTH AFRICAN MALAWI.
DIAKONIE KATASTROPHENHILFE
ACCOUNT NUMBER 502 707
BANK CODE.........................600 100 70
POSTBANK STUTTGART
REFERENCE:......SOUTH AFRICAN MALAWI
Diakonie
Katastrophenhilfe

Thongs and things.
Bendon
LINGERIE
Dubai • Abu Dhabi • Riyadh

MERIT

ART DIRECTOR
Shehzad Yunus

WRITER
Shehzad Yunus

CREATIVE DIRECTOR
Shehzad Yunus

CLIENT
Bendon Lingerie

AGENCY
TBWA\RAAD/Dubai

ANNUAL ID
06263A

MERIT

ART DIRECTOR
Ian Gabaldoni

WRITER
Richard Baynham

DIGITAL ARTIST/
MULTIMEDIA
Weapon 7 digital agency

AGENCY PRODUCER
Clare Donald

PRODUCTION COMPANY
MJZ

DIRECTOR
Fredrik Bond

CREATIVE DIRECTOR
Nick Bell

CLIENT
Diageo - Smirnoff

AGENCY
JWT/London

ANNUAL ID
06264A

TO DISTIL THE STORY FURTHER
PRESS RED

TO DISTIL THE STORY A FINAL TIME
PRESS RED

TRIPLE DISTILLED

CLEARLY
SMIRNOFF

[This commercial is in three parts. By pressing the red button, each one is distilled by the consumer to parallel the triple distillation process Smirnoff undergoes. Each time the story is re-told from the same start-point, but the removal of action and dialogue via jump cuts leaves us with a different story and better outcome.]

SUPER: TO DISTILL THE STORY FURTHER PRESS RED
"TRIPLE DISTILLED"
CLEARLY

[Smirnoff bottle]

[Nike and MTV partnered to create a unique reality series that documents the battles between teams as they compete for the title of "King of the Court."]

PHILADELPHIA
6

MERIT

ART DIRECTOR
Davi Russo

PRODUCTION COMPANY
@radical.media

DIRECTOR
Derek Cianfrance

CREATIVE DIRECTOR
Bill Davenport

CLIENT
Nike

AGENCY
Wieden+Kennedy/ Portland

ANNUAL ID
06265A

Merit

ART DIRECTOR
Scott Henderson

WRITERS
Angus Hennah
Rachel Prince
Paul Graham

PHOTOGRAPHER
Lindsay Keats

CREATIVE DIRECTOR
Philip Andrew

CLIENT
Land Transport NZ

AGENCY
Clemenger BBDO/ Wellington

ANNUAL ID
06267A

CRASHING AT 125 km/h HITS YOU LIKE FALLING FROM HERE
CRASHING AT 90 km/h HITS YOU LIKE FALLING FROM HERE

CRASHING AT 125 km/h HITS YOU LIKE FALLING FROM HERE

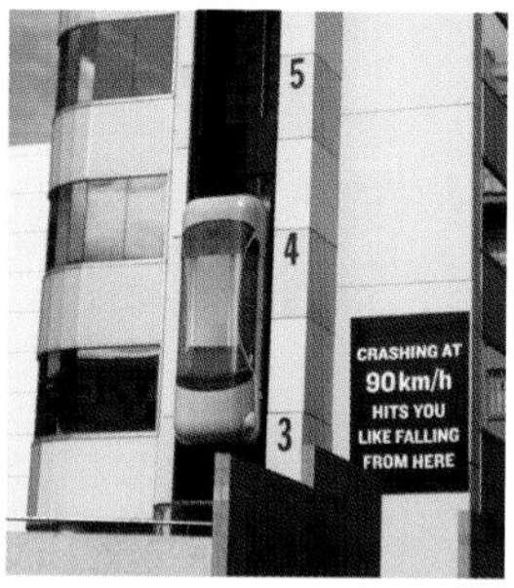
CRASHING AT 90 km/h HITS YOU LIKE FALLING FROM HERE

Merit

ART DIRECTORS
James Lee
Jin Kim

WRITERS
Terence Leong
Raymond Chin
Mabel Lee

DESIGNER
Dick Leung

ILLUSTRATOR
Hong Kong Society of Illustrators

AGENCY PRODUCER
D'or Tey

CREATIVE DIRECTORS
Calvin Soh
Yang Yeo

CLIENT
United Airlines Hong Kong

AGENCY
Fallon/Singapore

ANNUAL ID
06268A

HOLLYWOOD

UNITED
It's time to fly
往機場列車

I will go again. I haven't been to the Grand Canyon yet, and that's a very special place.

STEVEN JIANG
Hong Kong
stevenjiang@channelnewsasia.com

MERIT

ART DIRECTOR
Jochen Heimann

WRITER
Marlo Horn

AGENCY PRODUCER
Kerstin Novak

CREATIVE DIRECTOR
Lars Riebartsch

CONTENT STRATEGIST
Carsten Huschert

CLIENT
Procter & Gamble

AGENCY
Grey Worldwide/ Duesseldorf

ANNUAL ID
06269A

If it is where it belongs, it was probably delivered by DHL.
DHL

TAXI

MERIT

WRITER
Lauren Oliver

DESIGNER
Guenduez Erdil

PRODUCTION COMPANY
PX1 Berlin

CREATIVE DIRECTORS
Jan Harbeck
David Mously

CLIENT
DHL

AGENCY
Jung von Matt/Berlin

ANNUAL ID
06270A

MERIT

ART DIRECTOR
Ashok Lad

WRITERS
Amitabh Agnihotri
Gururaj Rao

PHOTOGRAPHERS
Sachin Powle
Ashay Kshirsagar

CREATIVE DIRECTORS
Amitabh Agnihotri
Ashok Lad
Agnello Dias
Bruce Matchett

CLIENT
United Breweries

AGENCY
JWT/Mumbai

ANNUAL ID
06271A

KINGFISHER

Restaurant & Bar

MERIT

ART DIRECTOR
Franois Biehler

WRITER
Thierry Brioul

CREATIVE DIRECTORS
Pascal Manry
Andrea Stillacci

CLIENT
Kellogg's

AGENCY
JWT/Paris

ANNUAL ID
06272A

SPECIAL
1 2
1 1

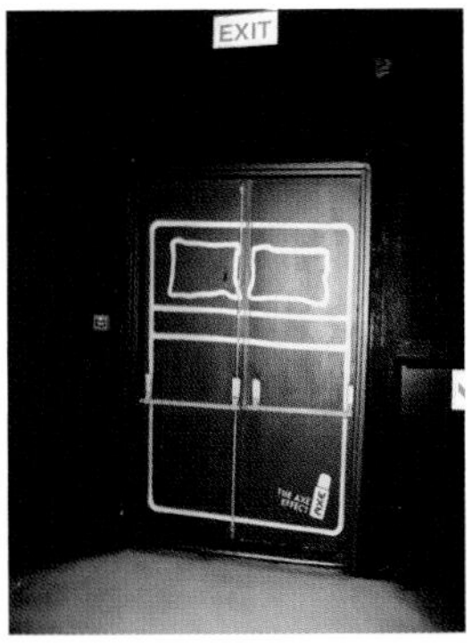
EXIT

NIGHT SHIFT

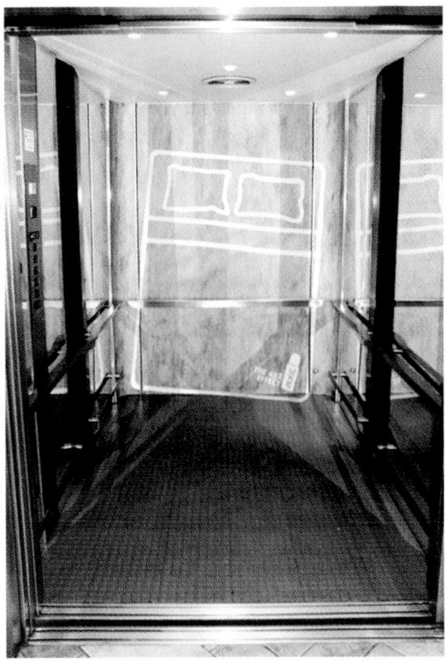

MERIT

ART DIRECTORS
Marion Bryan
Andre Vrdoljak

WRITER
Asheen Naidu

CREATIVE DIRECTORS
Gareth Lessing
Rob McLennan

CLIENT
Unilever - Axe

AGENCY
Lowe Bull/Johannesburg

ANNUAL ID
06274A

TOKAI
EXTRA STRONG

MERIT

ART DIRECTOR
Nico Juenger

WRITER
Konstantinos Manikas

PHOTOGRAPHER
Johannes Krezslack

CREATIVE DIRECTOR
Claudia Willvonseder

CLIENT
Tokai Germany

AGENCY
Publicis/Frankfurt

ANNUAL ID
06276A

Merit

ART DIRECTOR
David Alcorn

WRITERS
Josh Bletterman
Mike Spiegel
Scott Tufts

DESIGNERS
Aya Karpinska
Chuck Genco
Brian Votaw
Laura Pence
Troy Kooper
Matt Garton
Johanna Rustia

PROGRAMMERS
Ephraim Cohen
Sean Lyons
Michael Shagalov
John Mayo-Smith
Scott Prindle
Todd Kovner

CREATIVE DIRECTOR
Richard Ting

CLIENT
Nike

AGENCY
R/GA/New York

ANNUAL ID
06277A

ALSO AWARDED
Merit:
Exceptional Innovation in Media Marketing - Single

NIKE iD.COM
CALL
1-888-8-NIKE-ID
TO CUSTOMIZE THE NIKE SHOE BELOW
USE THESE KEYS ON YOUR PHONE
NIKE iD.COM
CHECK SCREEN ABOVE FOR INSTRUCTIONS.
REUTERS

CUSTOMIZE THIS SHOE.
5-11 05:19 PM
NIKE iD.COM
CHECK SCREEN ABOVE FOR INSTRUCTIONS.
REUTERS

NIKE iD.COM
europa cafe

GET THE NIKE FREE 5.0 FOR FREE
1·888·8·NIKE·ID
REUTERS
europa cafe

COFFEE

DIETING?

FREQUENTLY ASKED
QUESTIONS ABOUT BEING
A NAVAL DIVER

MERIT

ART DIRECTORS
Richard Copping
Stuart Harricks
Joel Clement

WRITER
Jagdish Ramakrishnan

PHOTOGRAPHERS
Adriana Chua
Sam @ Boomerang

CREATIVE DIRECTOR
Andy Greenaway

CLIENT
Republic of Singapore Navy

AGENCY
Saatchi & Saatchi/ Singapore

ANNUAL ID
06278A

Merit

ART DIRECTORS
Maria Lishman
Jae Morrison

WRITERS
Maria Lishman
Jae Morrison

CREATIVE DIRECTOR
Richard Maddocks

CLIENT
MINI

AGENCY
Colenso BBDO/ Auckland

ANNUAL ID
06280A

MINI
LET'S MOTOR

MINI
LET'S MOTOR

MINI
LET'S MOTOR

MINI
LET'S MOTOR

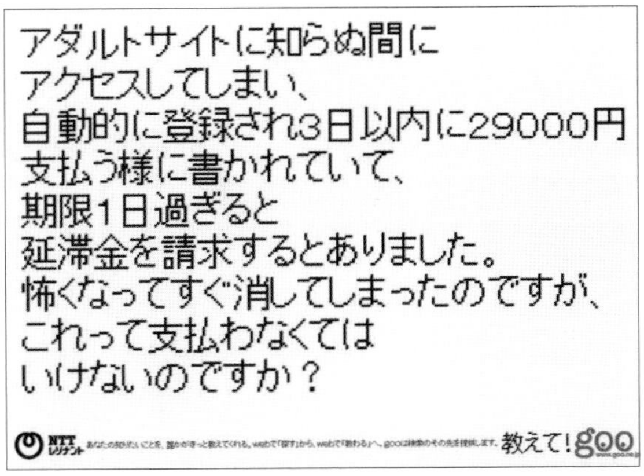
アダルトサイトに知らぬ間に
アクセスしてしまい、
自動的に登録され3日以内に29000円
支払う様に書かれていて、
期限1日過ぎると
延滞金を請求するとありました。
怖くなってすぐ消してしまったのですが、
これって支払わなくては
いけないのですか？
教えて!goo

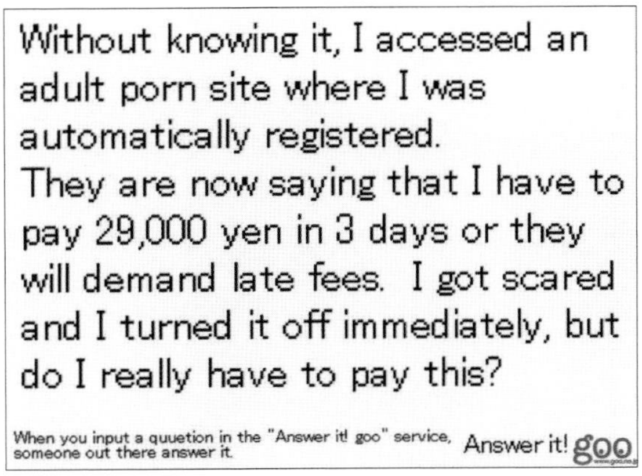
Without knowing it, I accessed an adult porn site where I was automatically registered.
They are now saying that I have to pay 29,000 yen in 3 days or they will demand late fees. I got scared and I turned it off immediately, but do I really have to pay this?
When you input a quuetion in the "Answer it! goo" service, someone out there answer it.
Answer it! goo

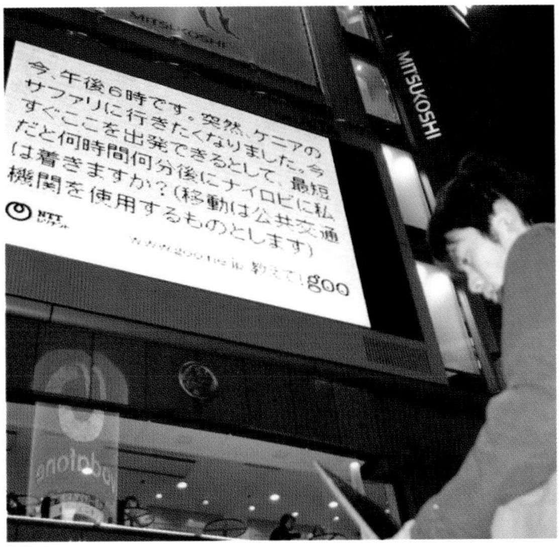
MITSUKOSHI
今、午後6時です。突然、ケニアのサファリに行きたくなりました。今すぐここを出発できるとして、最短だと何時間何分後にナイロビに私は着きますか？（移動は公共交通機関を使用するものとします）
教えて!goo

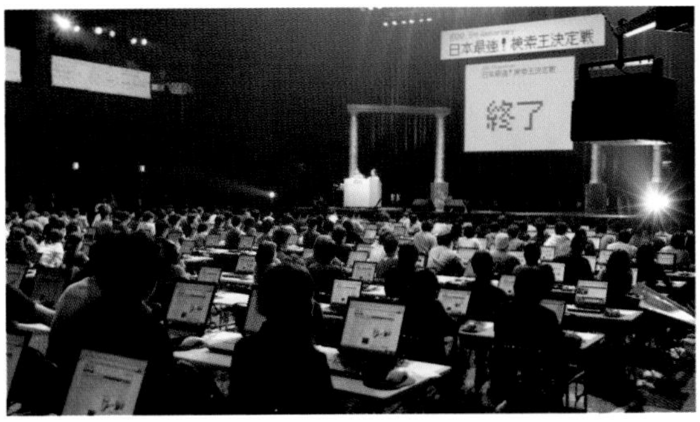
終了

Questions were posted as part of a seven week campaign throughout Tokyo. The first to respond correctly to each question won a prize.

MERIT

ART DIRECTORS
Yoichi Komatsu
Makoto Sawada

WRITERS
Satoshi Takamatsu
Naoya Hosokawa
Yohei Ugaeri

DESIGNERS
Makoto Sawada
Yasunari Mori
Masayuki Ikeda
Junko Igarashi

CREATIVE DIRECTOR
Satoshi Takamatsu

CLIENT
NTT-Resonant

AGENCY
Dentsu/Tokyo

ANNUAL ID
06281A

ALSO AWARDED
Merit:
Integrated Branding - Campaign

Merit

ART DIRECTOR
Jaimes Zentil

WRITER
Craig McIntosh

PHOTOGRAPHER
Mark Zibert

AGENCY PRODUCER
Bruce Ellis

CREATIVE DIRECTORS
Lance Martin
Zak Mroueh

CLIENT
Nike Hockey

AGENCY
TAXI/Toronto

ANNUAL ID
06282A

ALSO AWARDED
Merit:
Innovative Use of Media:
Outdoor - Single

READY FOR YOUR :45 ?
CHECK NIKEHOCKEY.CA

READY FOR YOUR :45

READY FOR YOUR :45 ?
CHECK NIKEHOCKEY.CA

READY FOR YOUR :45 ?
CHECK NIKEHOCKEY.CA

Merit

Merit

ART DIRECTOR
Nadja Lossgott

WRITER
Stuart Turner

PHOTOGRAPHER
David Prior

ILLUSTRATOR
Rob Frew

CREATIVE DIRECTOR
Theo Ferreira

CLIENT
Adcock Ingram

AGENCY
TBWA\Hunt\Lascaris/ Johannesburg

ANNUAL ID
06283A

Merit

ART DIRECTORS
Farrah Bianca
Pebble Goh
Kelvin Leong
Im Im Cheah
Clement Lim

WRITERS
Zamri Dzakaria
Sharin Shazlina

DESIGNER
Pebble Goh

PHOTOGRAPHER
Chong (IFL Studio)

CREATIVE DIRECTOR
Ronald Ng

CLIENT
Pepsi

AGENCY
BBDO/Kuala Lumpur

ANNUAL ID
06284A

FOR DISPLAY ONLY
ICE

ICE

Merit

ART DIRECTOR
Rodrigo Butori

WRITER
Kristina Slade

AGENCY PRODUCER
Anne Katherine Friis

PRODUCTION COMPANY
National Television

CREATIVE DIRECTOR
Court Crandall

CLIENT
Virgin Digital

AGENCY
Ground Zero/
Los Angeles

ANNUAL ID
06286A

CALIFORNIA

Daz

MERIT

ART DIRECTOR
Leo Burnett

WRITER
Leo Burnett

AGENCY PRODUCER
Leo Burnett

PRODUCTION COMPANY
Adam Spiegel

CREATIVE DIRECTOR
Jim Thornton

CLIENT
Leo Burnett/Comic Relief

AGENCY
Leo Burnett/London

ANNUAL ID
06287A

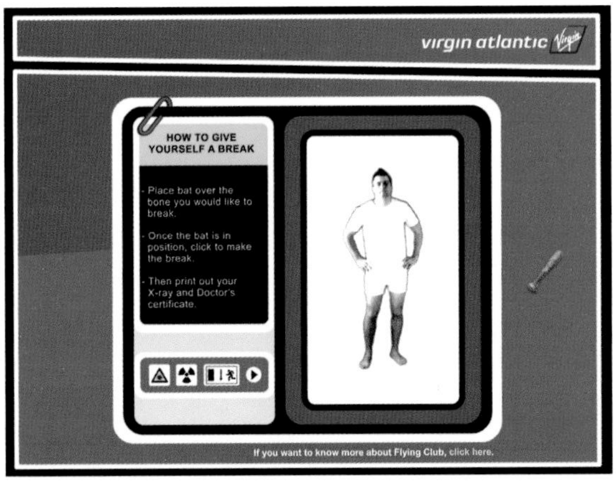
virgin atlantic
HOW TO GIVE YOURSELF A BREAK
- Place bat over the bone you would like to break.
- Once the bat is in position, click to make the break.
- Then print out your X-ray and Doctor's certificate.
If you want to know more about Flying Club, click here.

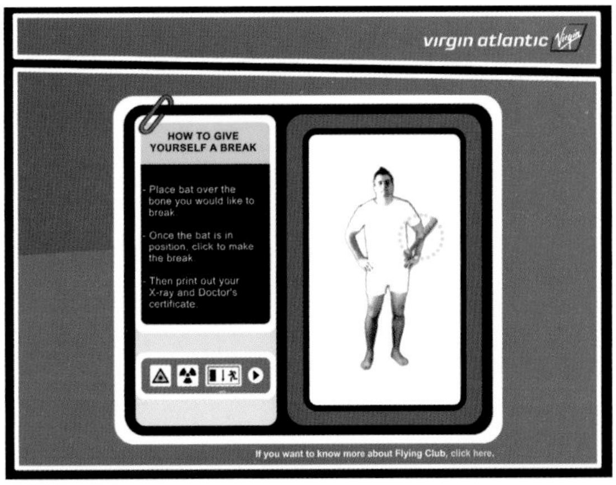
virgin atlantic
HOW TO GIVE YOURSELF A BREAK
- Place bat over the bone you would like to break.
- Once the bat is in position, click to make the break.
- Then print out your X-ray and Doctor's certificate.
If you want to know more about Flying Club, click here.

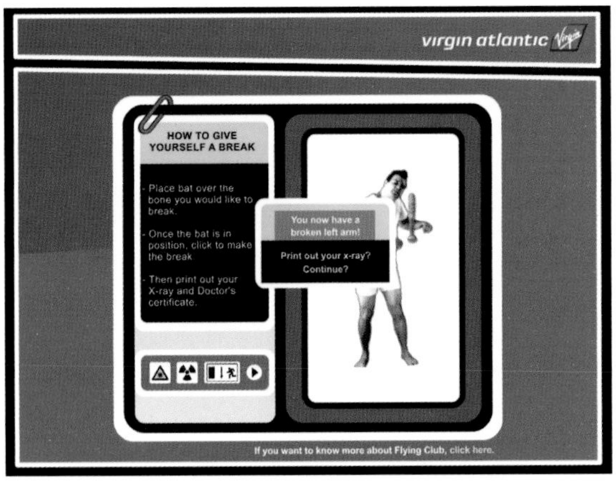
virgin atlantic
HOW TO GIVE YOURSELF A BREAK
- Place bat over the bone you would like to break.
- Once the bat is in position, click to make the break.
- Then print out your X-ray and Doctor's certificate.
You now have a broken left arm!
Print out your x-ray?
Continue?
If you want to know more about Flying Club, click here.

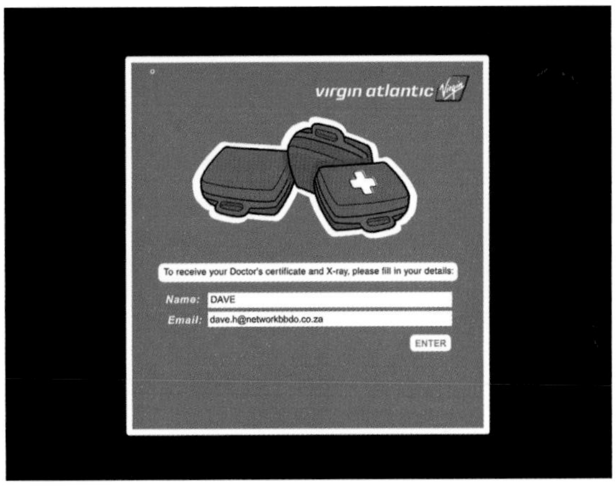
virgin atlantic
To receive your Doctor's certificate and X-ray, please fill in your details:
Name: DAVE
Email: dave.h@networkbbdo.co.za
ENTER

MERIT

ART DIRECTOR
Angie Batis

WRITER
Michele Pithey

DESIGNER
Dave Hillier

CREATIVE DIRECTOR
Mike Schalit

CONTENT STRATEGISTS
Michele Pithey
Clive Evans

CLIENT
Virgin Atlantic

AGENCY
Net#Work BBDO/Hyde Park

ANNUAL ID
06288A

MERIT

ART DIRECTOR
John Bergdahl

WRITER
Fredrik Jansson

DESIGNER
Jonas Sjovall

CLIENT
IKEA

AGENCY
Forsman & Bodenfors/ Gothenburg

ANNUAL ID
06290A

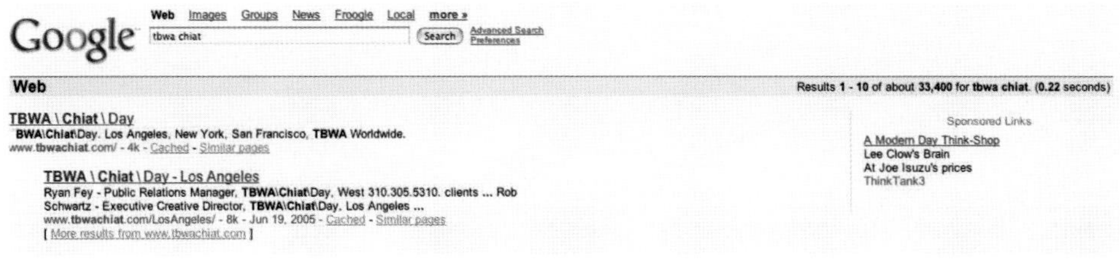
Google
Web Images Groups News Froogle Local more »
tbwa chiat
Search
Advanced Search
Preferences
Web
Results 1 - 10 of about 33,400 for tbwa chiat. (0.22 seconds)
TBWA \ Chiat \ Day
BWA\Chiat\Day. Los Angeles, New York, San Francisco, TBWA Worldwide.
www.tbwachiat.com/ - 4k - Cached - Similar pages
TBWA \ Chiat \ Day - Los Angeles
Ryan Fey - Public Relations Manager, TBWA\Chiat\Day, West 310.305.5310. clients ... Rob
Schwartz - Executive Creative Director, TBWA\Chiat\Day, Los Angeles ...
www.tbwachiat.com/LosAngeles/ - 8k - Jun 19, 2005 - Cached - Similar pages
[More results from www.tbwachiat.com]
Sponsored Links
A Modern Day Think-Shop
Lee Clow's Brain
At Joe Isuzu's prices
ThinkTank3

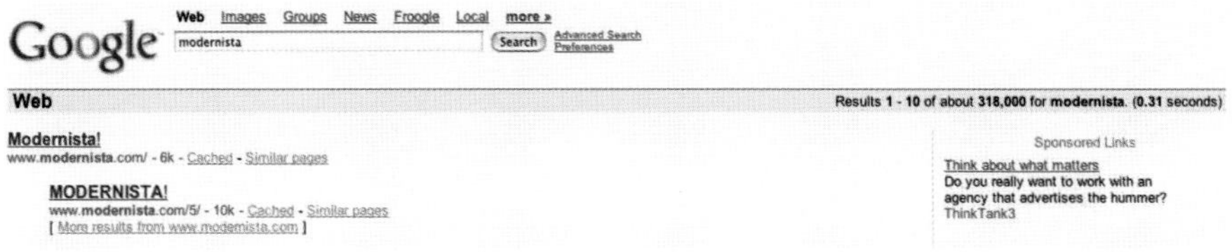
Google
Web Images Groups News Froogle Local more »
modernista
Search
Advanced Search
Preferences
Web
Results 1 - 10 of about 318,000 for modernista. (0.31 seconds)
Modernista!
www.modernista.com/ - 6k - Cached - Similar pages
MODERNISTA!
www.modernista.com/5/ - 10k - Cached - Similar pages
[More results from www.modernista.com]
Sponsored Links
Think about what matters
Do you really want to work with an
agency that advertises the hummer?
ThinkTank3

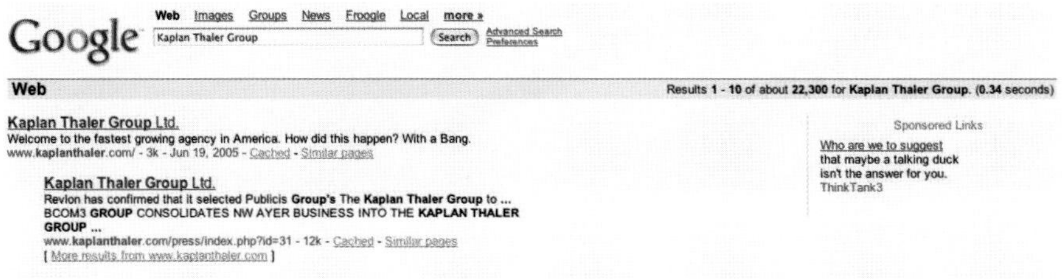
Google
Web Images Groups News Froogle Local more »
Kaplan Thaler Group
Search
Advanced Search
Preferences
Web
Results 1 - 10 of about 22,300 for Kaplan Thaler Group. (0.34 seconds)
Kaplan Thaler Group Ltd.
Welcome to the fastest growing agency in America. How did this happen? With a Bang.
www.kaplanthaler.com/ - 3k - Jun 19, 2005 - Cached - Similar pages
Kaplan Thaler Group Ltd.
Revlon has confirmed that it selected Publicis Group's The Kaplan Thaler Group to ...
BCOM3 GROUP CONSOLIDATES NW AYER BUSINESS INTO THE KAPLAN THALER
GROUP ...
www.kaplanthaler.com/press/index.php?id=31 - 12k - Cached - Similar pages
[More results from www.kaplanthaler.com]
Sponsored Links
Who are we to suggest
that maybe a talking duck
isn't the answer for you.
ThinkTank3

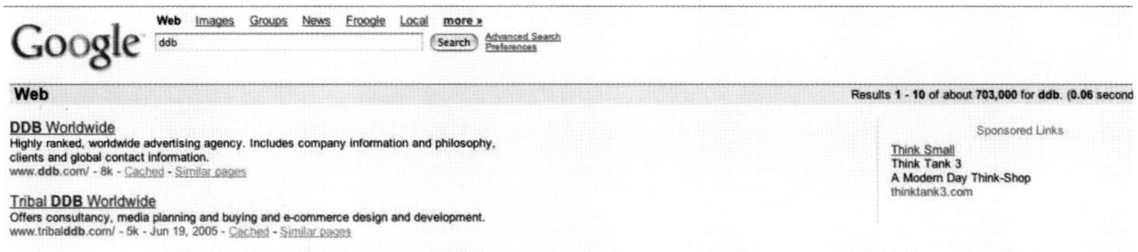
Google
Web Images Groups News Froogle Local more »
ddb
Search
Advanced Search
Preferences
Web
Results 1 - 10 of about 703,000 for ddb. (0.06 second
DDB Worldwide
Highly ranked, worldwide advertising agency. Includes company information and philosophy,
clients and global contact information.
www.ddb.com/ - 8k - Cached - Similar pages
Tribal DDB Worldwide
Offers consultancy, media planning and buying and e-commerce design and development.
www.tribalddb.com/ - 5k - Jun 19, 2005 - Cached - Similar pages
Sponsored Links
Think Small
Think Tank 3
A Modern Day Think-Shop
thinktank3.com

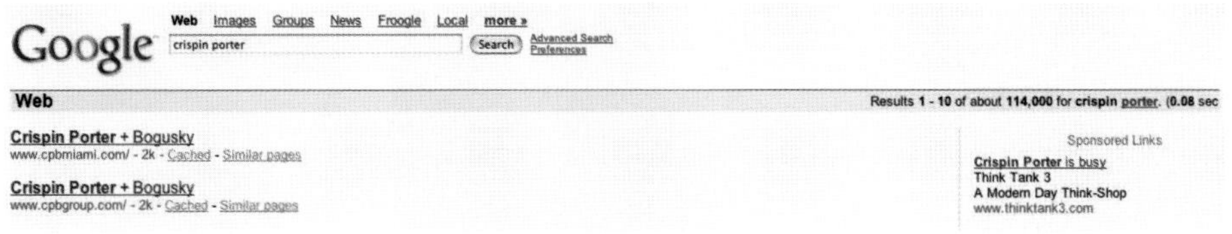
Google
Web Images Groups News Froogle Local more »
crispin porter
Search
Advanced Search
Preferences
Web
Results 1 - 10 of about 114,000 for crispin porter. (0.08 sec
Crispin Porter + Bogusky
www.cpbmiami.com/ - 2k - Cached - Similar pages
Crispin Porter + Bogusky
www.cpbgroup.com/ - 2k - Cached - Similar pages
Sponsored Links
Crispin Porter is busy
Think Tank 3
A Modern Day Think-Shop
www.thinktank3.com

MERIT

ART DIRECTORS
Matthew Dugas
Ece Kaleli

WRITERS
Harris Silver
Sharoz Makarechi

CREATIVE DIRECTOR
Sharoz Makarechi

CLIENT
Think Tank 3

AGENCY
Think Tank 3/New York

ANNUAL ID
06291A

Merit

ART DIRECTOR
Somak Chaudhury

WRITER
Somak Chaudhury

CREATIVE DIRECTORS
Chris Chiu
Kumuda Rao
Sirin Wannavalee

CLIENT
P&G

AGENCY
Leo Burnett/Bangkok

ANNUAL ID
06292A

ALSO AWARDED
Merit:
Innovative Use of Media and Marketing: Outdoor - Single

REJOICE

Merit

ART DIRECTOR
Wang Heshui

WRITER
Li Dong

PHOTOGRAPHER
Fred

PROGRAMMER
Chen Jing

CREATIVE DIRECTOR
Li Dong

CONTENT STRATEGIST
Tiger Fu

CLIENT
Total Fitness Club

AGENCY
Lowe/Shanghai

ANNUAL ID
06293A

Get rid of it!
Total Fitness Club

www.santa.org.za
It's this easy
to pick up TB.
SANTA

MERIT

ART DIRECTOR
Paul Sanders

WRITER
Chris Gotz

PHOTOGRAPHER
Jan Verboom

CREATIVE DIRECTOR
Mark Fisher

CLIENT
SANTA (South African National Tuberculosis Association)

AGENCY
Ogilvy/Cape Town

ANNUAL ID
06294A

FOR STRONG, HEALTHY TEETH.
IAMS
20
KPH

MERIT

ART DIRECTOR
Eron Broughton

WRITER
Steve May

PHOTOGRAPHER
Penny Clay

CREATIVE DIRECTOR
David Nobay

CLIENT
Procter & Gamble

AGENCY
Saatchi & Saatchi/Sydney

ANNUAL ID
06296A

Merit

ART DIRECTOR
Regan Grafton

WRITER
Bridget Short

DIGITAL ARTIST/
MULTIMEDIA
Brett Hancock

AGENCY PRODUCER
Steve Gulik

CREATIVE DIRECTOR
Paul Catmur

CLIENT
nzgirl

AGENCY
DDB/Auckland

ANNUAL ID
06297A

ALSO AWARDED
Merit:
Innovative Use of Media and Marketing: Interactive/New Media - Campaign

DON'T MESS WITH NZ GIRLS-NZGIRL.CO.NZ

JOSH SHORT LIKES IT WITH A STRAP-ON

MY CHEATING BOYFRIEND'S CAR
2 HITS FOR $1
MY CHEATING BOYFRIEND'S CAR
2 HITS FOR $1
DON'T MESS WITH NZ GIRLS

BIG DAY OUT
LIVE
Ericsson Stadium

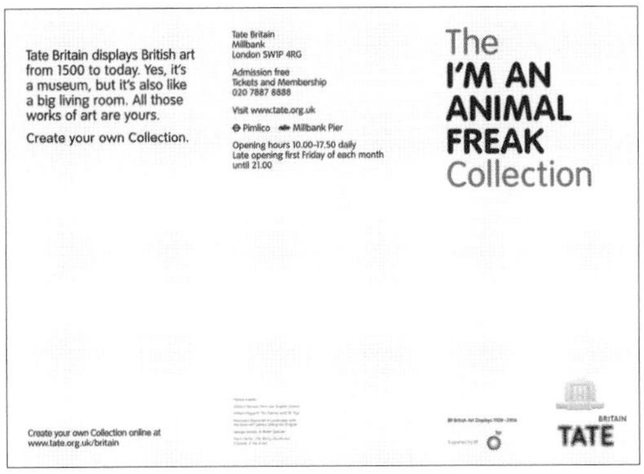
Tate Britain displays British art from 1500 to today. Yes, it's a museum, but it's also like a big living room. All those works of art are yours.
Create your own Collection.
Tate Britain
Millbank
London SWIP 4RG
Admission free
Tickets and Membership
020 7887 8888
Visit www.tate.org.uk
Pimlico
Millbank Pier
Opening hours 10.00-17.50 daily
Late opening first Friday of each month until 21.00
The
I'M AN
ANIMAL
FREAK
Collection
Create your own Collection online at www.tate.org.uk/britain
BRITAIN
TATE

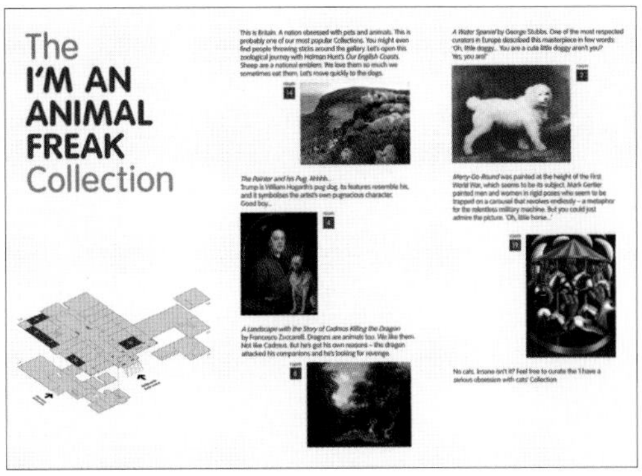
The
I'M AN
ANIMAL
FREAK
Collection

Tate Britain displays British art from 1500 to today. Yes, it's a museum, but it's also like a big living room. All those works of art are yours.
Create your own Collection.
The
HAPPILY
DEPRESSED
Collection
BRITAIN
TATE

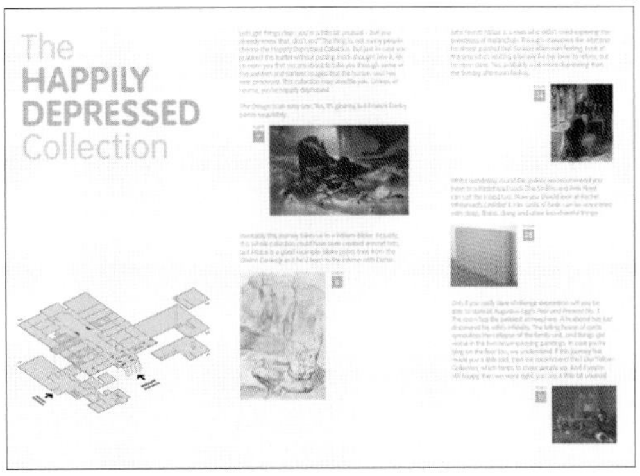
The
HAPPILY
DEPRESSED
Collection

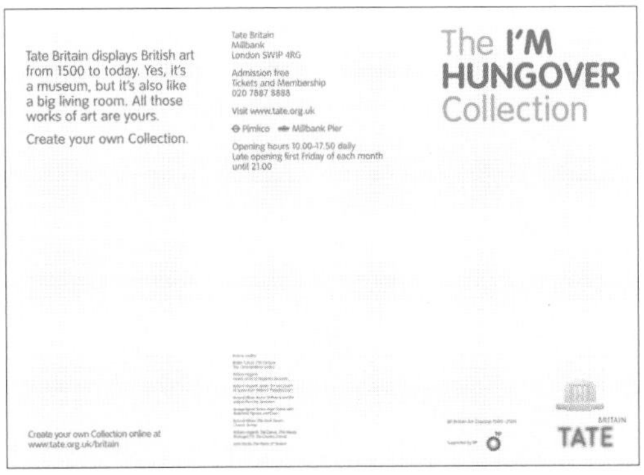
Tate Britain displays British art from 1500 to today. Yes, it's a museum, but it's also like a big living room. All those works of art are yours.
Create your own Collection.
The I'M
HUNGOVER
Collection
BRITAIN
TATE

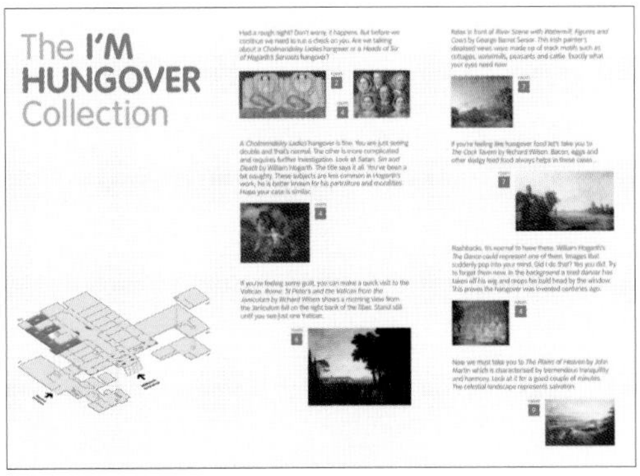
The I'M
HUNGOVER
Collection

Tate Britain displays British art from 1500 to today. Yes, it's a museum, but it's also like a big living room. All those works of art are yours.
Create your own Collection.
The
I'VE JUST
SPLIT UP
Collection
BRITAIN
TATE

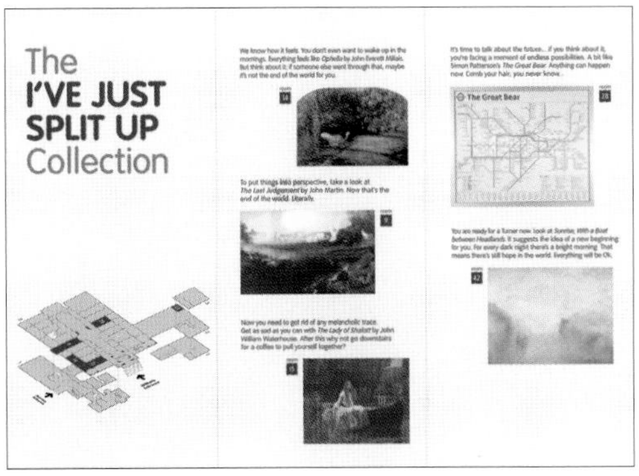
The
I'VE JUST
SPLIT UP
Collection

Tate Britain displays British art from 1500 to today. Yes, it's a museum, but it's also like a big living room. All those works of art are yours.
Create your own Collection.
The
I'M IN A
HURRY
Collection
BRITAIN
TATE

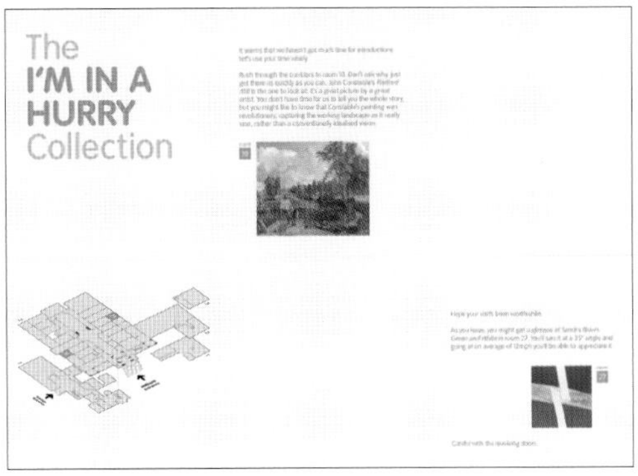
The
I'M IN A
HURRY
Collection

MERIT

ART DIRECTOR
Juan Cabral

WRITER
Juan Cabral

DESIGNERS
Practise
Iain Richardson
Ginny Carrel
(Typographer)

CREATIVE DIRECTORS
Richard Flintham
Andy McLeod

CLIENT
Tate

AGENCY
Fallon/London

ANNUAL ID
06298A

MERIT

ART DIRECTOR
Jesse Coulter

WRITER
Andy Ferguson

PHOTOGRAPHER
Koto Bolofo

AGENCY PRODUCERS
Temma Shoaf
Gary Krieg

PRODUCTION COMPANIES
HSI Productions
Blast Radius

DIRECTOR
Paul Hunter

CREATIVE DIRECTORS
Todd Waterbury
Kevin Proudfoot

CONTENT STRATEGIST
Dan Cherry

CLIENT
Nike - Brand Jordan
- Lifestyle Collection

AGENCY
Wieden+Kennedy/
New York

ANNUAL ID
06300A

Entertainment Guide
AOL music
Exclusive Online Partner
MUSIC STYLES
ARTISTS
VIDEOS
SONGS
Common
MAIN
BIO
AOL VIDEO

Common – Be, Common Video
mp3.com | media player
Common

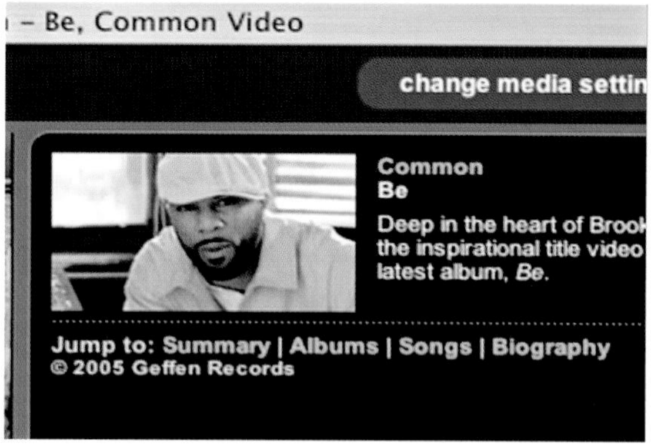
– Be, Common Video
Common
Be
Jump to: Summary | Albums | Songs | Biography
© 2005 Geffen Records

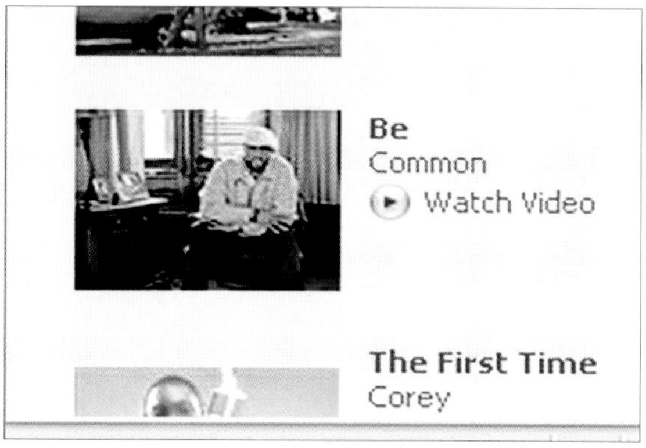
Be
Common
Watch Video
The First Time
Corey

Based on a 1986 Big Tobacco brainstorm document.
a truth production
"Fair Enough!"
It might be funnier if it wasn't true.
We need to improve our sales to the black community.
We should say to them, "It's okay to be black, hang out and have fun."
Toe rings. We could offer toe rings!
For more tobacco documents visit www.FairEnough.com
© 2005 truth

Based on a 1986 Big Tobacco brainstorm document.
a truth production
"Fair Enough!"
It might be funnier if it wasn't true.
We should refocus our efforts against indoor smoking bans.
Yes, convince the public that smoke is merely a symptom of a larger problem. . .
. . .inadequate ventilation!
For more tobacco documents visit www.FairEnough.com
© 2005 truth

"Fair Enough!"

"Fair Enough!"
It might be funnier if it wasn't true.

It might be funnier if it wasn't true.

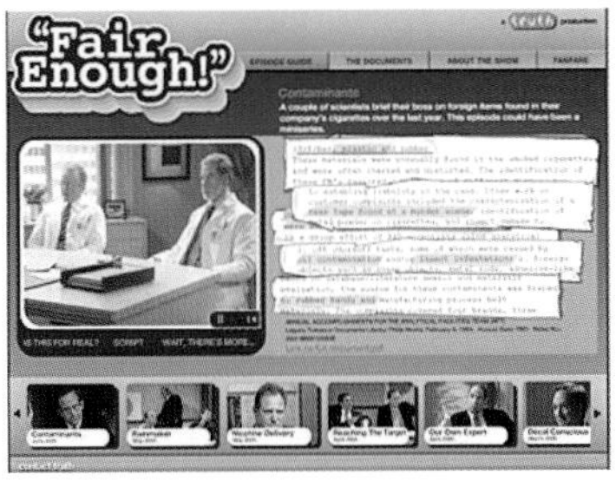
"Fair Enough!"

Download your very own studio audience
"Fair Enough!"
TRY ME
Laugh-o-matic
Get one today at
"Fair Enough!".com

"Fair Enough!"

MERIT

ART DIRECTORS
Mike Costello
Rob Kottkamp
Phil Covitz
Chris Bakay
Jason Ambrose
Geordie Stephens
Meghan Siegal

WRITERS
Marc Einhorn
Will Chambliss
Dustin Ballard
Franklin Tipton
Dave Kennedy
Jason Yun

DESIGNERS
Meghan Siegal
Chris Valencius
Max Pfennighaus
Neal Bessen
Templar Studios

ILLUSTRATOR
JJ Sedelmaier

PROGRAMMERS
Ebbey Mathew
Adam Buhler
Templar Studios

AGENCY PRODUCERS
Jessica Dierauer
David Rolfe
Rupert Samuel
Corey Bartha
Linda Donlon
Kathy McMann
Carron Pedonti
Barry Frechette

PRODUCTION COMPANIES
Moxie Pictures
Soundtrack

INFORMATION ARCHITECT
Patrick Eddy

DIRECTOR
Martin Granger

CREATIVE DIRECTORS
Ron Lawner
Pete Favat
Alex Bogusky
John Kearse
Tom Adams

CLIENT
American Legacy Foundation

AGENCY
Arnold Worldwide/ Boston and Crispin Porter + Bogusky/Miami

ANNUAL ID
06301G

MERIT

ART DIRECTORS
Colin Jeffery
Phillip Squier
Paulo Lopez
Paul Lee

WRITERS
Dave Weist
Chris Carl

PROGRAMMERS
Roy Wetherbee
The Barbarian Group

AGENCY PRODUCERS
Amy Favat
Tom Lerra

PRODUCTION COMPANIES
Brickyard
LOBO
Curious Pictures

INFORMATION ARCHITECT
Dale Cumberbatch

CREATIVE DIRECTORS
Ron Lawner
Alan Pafenbach
Dave Weist
Colin Jeffery
Chris Carl
Chris Bradley

CLIENT
Volkswagen

AGENCY
Arnold Worldwide/ Boston

ANNUAL ID
06302G

The new Passat
120
not-so-standard features.
The latest big thing from Volkswagen is the result of lots of surprising little things, 120 to be exact. And once you break it all down, it's clear how well put together the Passat really is. So, we broke it down, one life-improving, performance-boosting, dollar-stretching, not-so-standard feature at a time.
View the feature films
120 not-so-standard features. One all new German engineered Passat.
NEW PASSAT
home
120 feature films
glossary
take a test drive
Sort feature films:
36/120
Sign up to get all the latest on the new Passat via email.
The 411 on the 120:
37. Multifunction trip computer

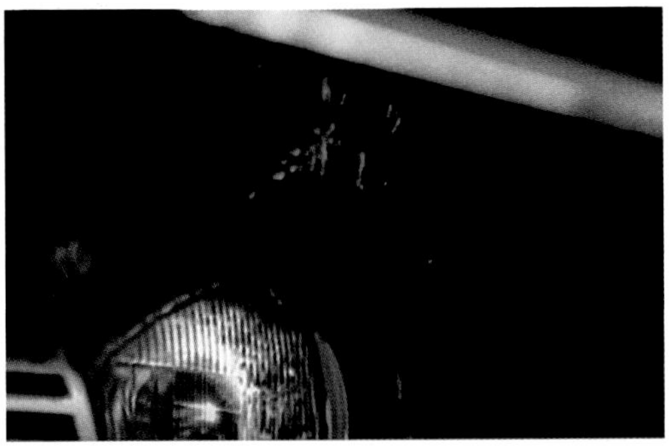

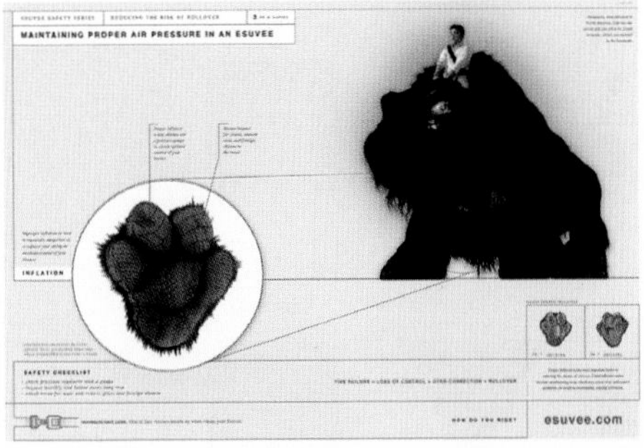
MAINTAINING PROPER AIR PRESSURE IN AN ESUVEE
INFLATION
SAFETY CHECKLIST
esuvee.com

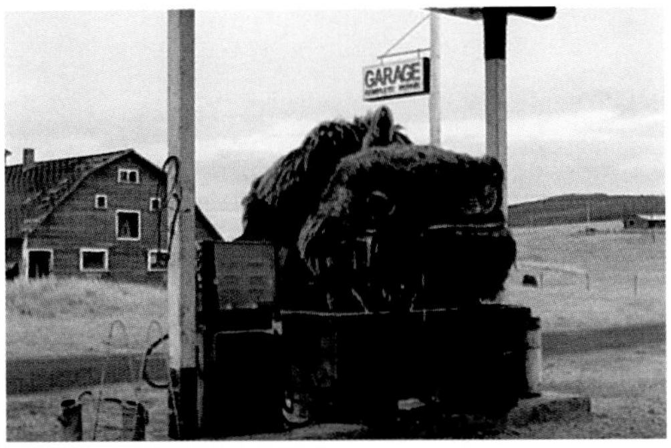
GARAGE

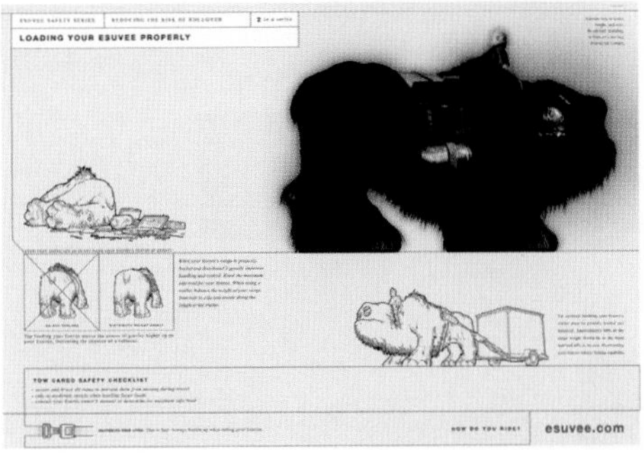
LOADING YOUR ESUVEE PROPERLY
TOW CARGO SAFETY CHECKLIST
esuvee.com

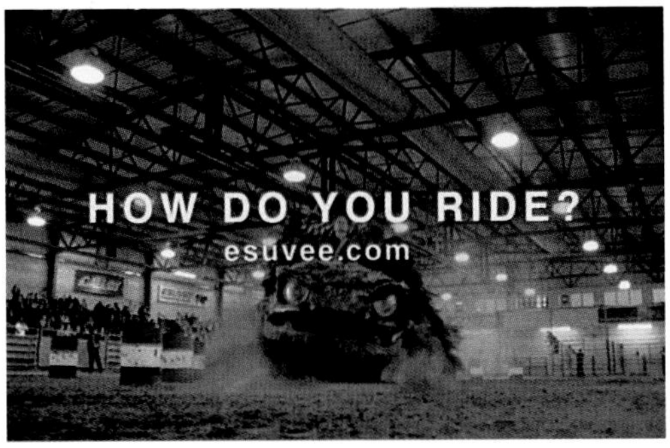
HOW DO YOU RIDE?
esuvee.com

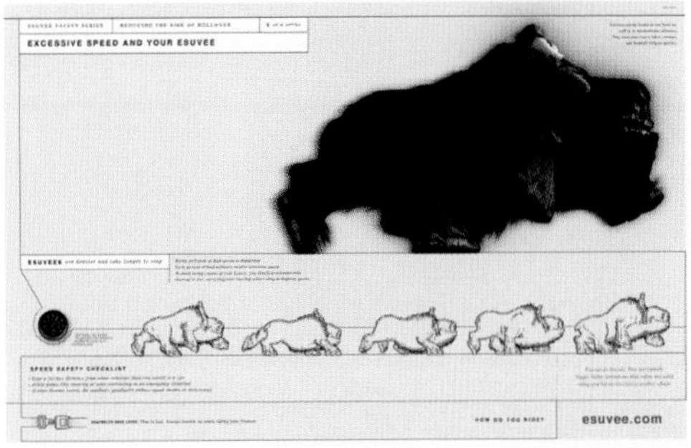
EXCESSIVE SPEED AND YOUR ESUVEE
SPEED SAFETY CHECKLIST
esuvee.com

ESUVEES AREN'T CARS
esuvee.com

KEEP IT ON ALL FOURS
esuvee.com

HOW DO YOU RIDE?
esuvee.com

MERIT

ART DIRECTOR
John Hobbs

WRITER
Peter Rosch

PHOTOGRAPHER
Nick Ruechel

DIGITAL ARTIST/
MULTIMEDIA
Framestore London

AGENCY PRODUCERS
Bruce Wellington
Chris Berger
Michelle Massaro

PRODUCTION COMPANY
Kleinman Productions

DIRECTOR
Danny Kleinman

CREATIVE DIRECTOR
Thomas Hayo

CLIENT
Ford Multi-State
Working Group

AGENCY
Bartle Bogle Hegarty/
New York

ANNUAL ID
06303G

MERIT

ART DIRECTORS
John Parker
Kat Morris
Geordie Stephens
Nick Munoz
Pres Rodriguez
Tiffany Kosel

WRITERS
Evan Fry
Mike Howard
Franklin Tipton
Maureen Bongiovanni
Aramis Israel
Scott Linnen

DESIGNERS
Rahul Panchal
Buck
Mitt Out Sound
Floyd Albee

PHOTOGRAPHERS
Cheryl Ungar
Mark Laita

PROGRAMMER
Fuel Industries

DIGITAL ARTISTS/MULTIMEDIA
Company 3
Brian Robinson
Tiffany Lynch
Mary OGara
Method
Lime Studios

AGENCY PRODUCERS
Rupert Samuel
David Rolfe
Bill Meadows

PRODUCTION COMPANY
MJZ

DIRECTOR
Spike Jonze

CREATIVE DIRECTORS
Alex Bogusky
Andrew Keller
Rob Reilly
Jeff Benjamin

CLIENT
Gap

AGENCY
Crispin Porter + Bogusky/Miami

ANNUAL ID
06304G

PEACE
LOVE
CHANGE
New store.
New look.
All-new GAP
opens April 22.

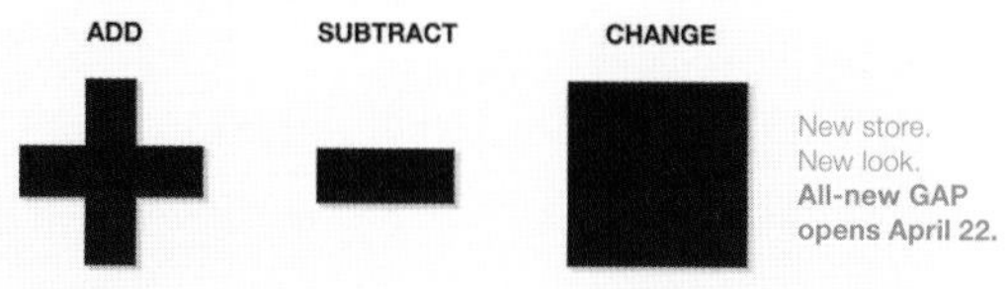
ADD
SUBTRACT
CHANGE
New store.
New look.
All-new GAP
opens April 22.

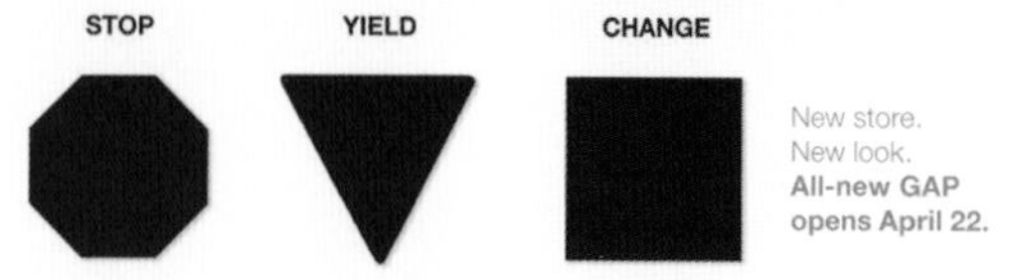
STOP
YIELD
CHANGE
New store.
New look.
All-new GAP
opens April 22.

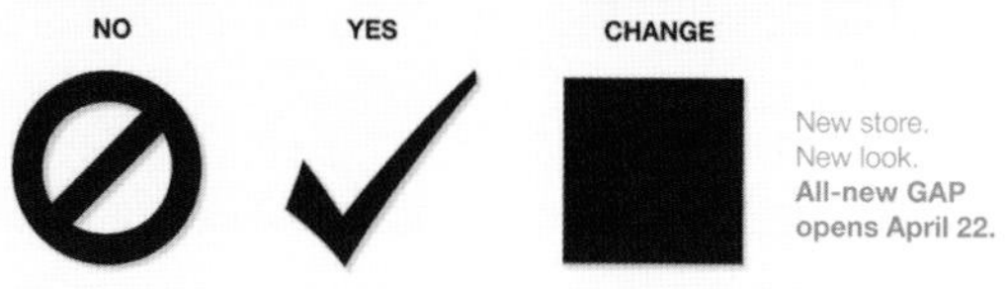
NO
YES
CHANGE
New store.
New look.
All-new GAP
opens April 22.

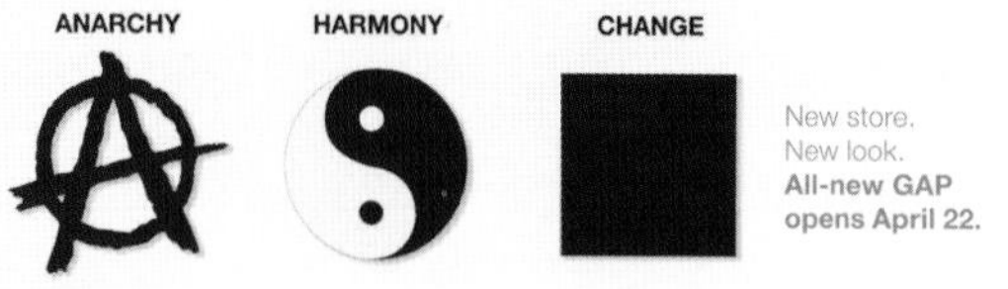
ANARCHY
HARMONY
CHANGE
New store.
New look.
All-new GAP
opens April 22.

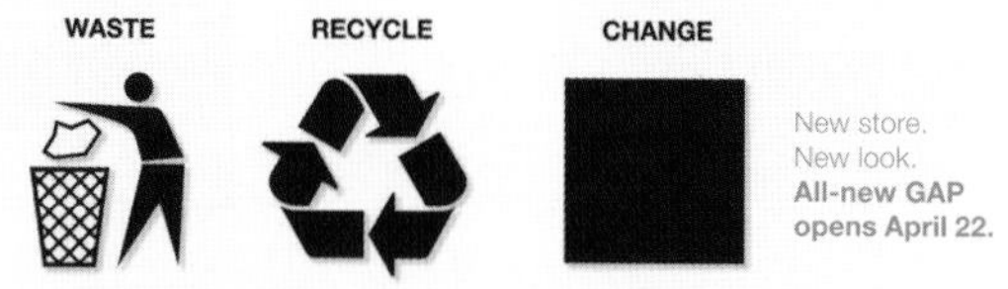
WASTE
RECYCLE
CHANGE
New store.
New look.
All-new GAP
opens April 22.

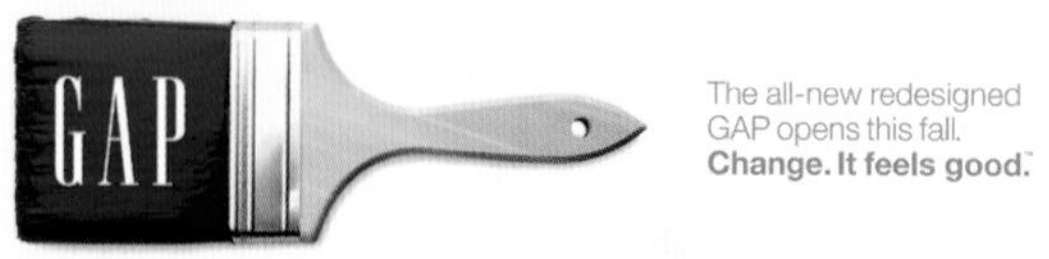
GAP
The all-new redesigned
GAP opens this fall.
Change. It feels good.

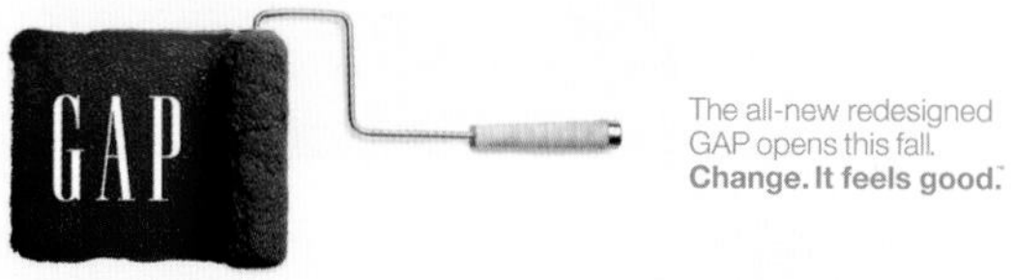
GAP
The all-new redesigned
GAP opens this fall.
Change. It feels good.

goodwill.org
GAP

Union-Tribune
Clean out
your closet.

GAP

GAP

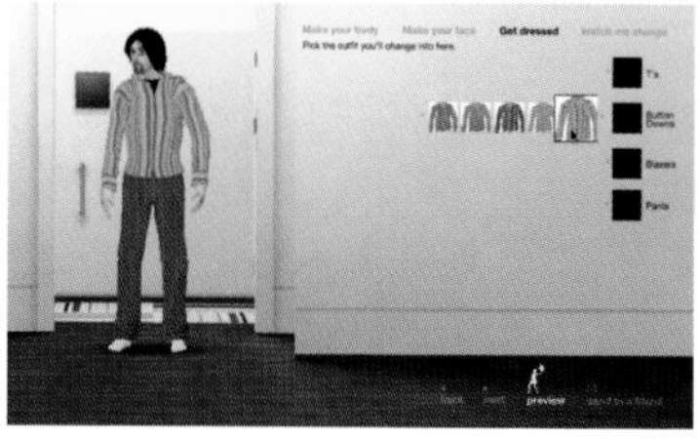

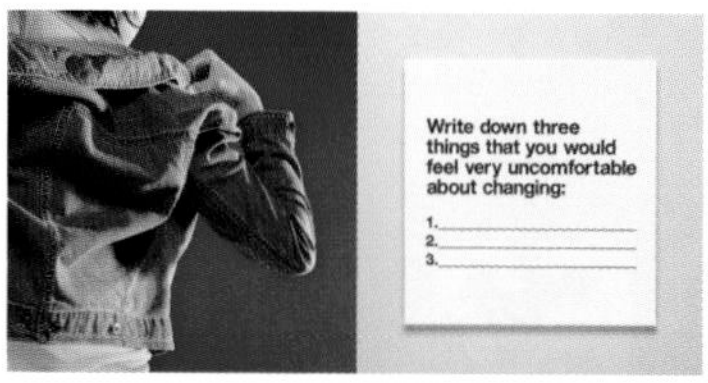
Write down three
things that you would
feel very uncomfortable
about changing:
1.
2.
3.

The Harrumpher.

Official License to Change

under 30
"WANNA SEE MY BIG IDEA?"
hardly-legal.com/ashok
Ashok

"It feels so good to win."
Estelle
See Me Now
hardly-legal
.com/estelle

YOUNG ADVERTISING STUDS
"MY COPY IS VERY LONG."
Todd
Check Me Out
hardly-legal.com/todd

"CHECK OUT MY TIGHT WORK."
TIFFANY
TV CAMPAIGN SILVER
SEE ME NOW! HARDLY-LEGAL.com/Tiffany

hardly-legal.com/kat
"I'LL SPREAD MY KERNING WIDER IF YOU'D LIKE."
Kat

"My Creative Juices Are Flowing."
hardly-legal.com/julie

18-30 ONLY PERMITTED BY LAW
Be a Young Ad Star
Call for Entry Opens Monday August 1, 2005
Call for Entry Closes Friday October 14, 2005
YoungGuns International Advertising Award
Level 1, 299 Elizabeth Street
Sydney NSW 2000 Australia
HARDLY LEGAL
ADVERTISING AWARDS
YoungGuns is looking for the youngest, hottest creatives who are ripe and eager to please. So if you're between 18-30 and think you've got the big, big ideas every creative director wants to see, go to www.ygaward.com to enter your work. If it's sweet enough, we'll put your goodies out there for the whole ad world to enjoy. Remember to submit all you've got before October 14 though, since you won't be young forever. Yeah baby, you'll be a star before you know it!
GET YOURS TODAY
to enter online or download a PDF
www.hardly-legal.com
www.ygaward.com
YoungGuns

HARDLY LEGAL
AND MORE!

HARDLY LEGAL
VANESSA

HARDLY LEGAL
TIFFANY

HARDLY LEGAL

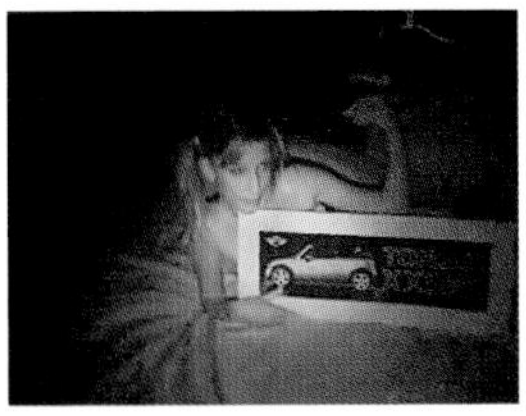

HARDLY LEGAL
18 TO 30 ADVERTISING AWARDS
ENTRY DEADLINE OCTOBER 14, 2005
HARDLY-LEGAL.COM
Kat

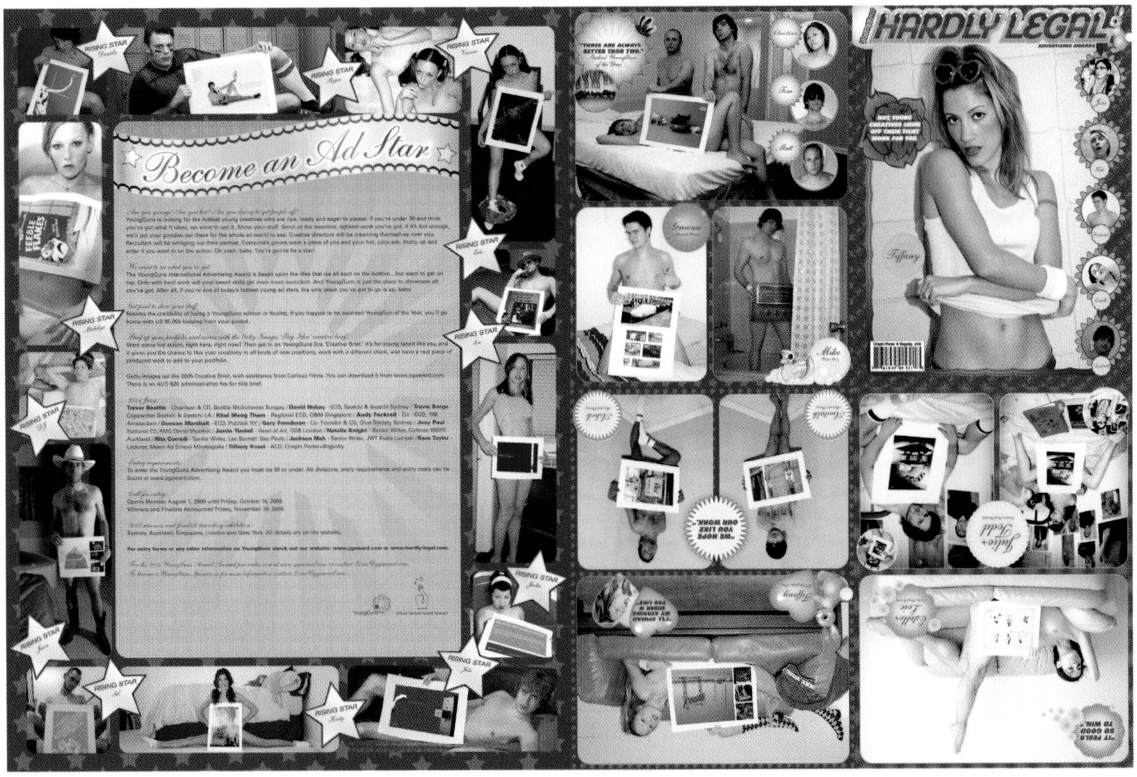
RISING STAR
Become an Ad Star
HARDLY LEGAL
ADVERTISING AWARDS
Tiffany
Mike

MERIT

ART DIRECTORS
Jed Grossman
Kevin Koller

WRITERS
David Povill
Larry Corwin

PHOTOGRAPHERS
Sara Padgett
Andy Benson
Various

PROGRAMMER
Adam Paul

AGENCY PRODUCER
Neil D'Amico

CREATIVE DIRECTORS
Alex Bogusky
Jeff Benjamin
Tiffany Kosel

CLIENT
Young Guns International Advertising Awards

AGENCY
Crispin Porter + Bogusky/Miami

ANNUAL ID
06305G

MERIT

ART DIRECTORS
Mehdi Dewalle

CREATIVE DIRECTORS
Jens Mortier
Joost Berends
Philippe Deceuster

CONTENT STRATEGIST
Tom Himpe

CLIENT
Le Soir Newspaper

AGENCY
Mortierbrigade/Brussels

ANNUAL ID
06308G

AIDEZ LE TIERS-MONDE
ACHETEZ-Y VOS ORGANES
UN ORGANE PEUT SAUVER PLUS D'UNE VIE.
WWW.GIVELIFE.BE
GIVE LIFE

AIDEZ LE TIERS-MONDE
LE SOIR SE LEVE
CONTRE L'INACCEPTABLE
CHAQUE JOUR, DANS LES PAYS DU TIERS-MONDE, DES GENS SONT PRÊTS À VENDRE UN DE LEURS ORGANES
POUR AMÉLIORER LEUR CONDITION DE VIE. INACCEPTABLE ! Changeons notre quotidien.
LE SOIR
GIVE LIFE

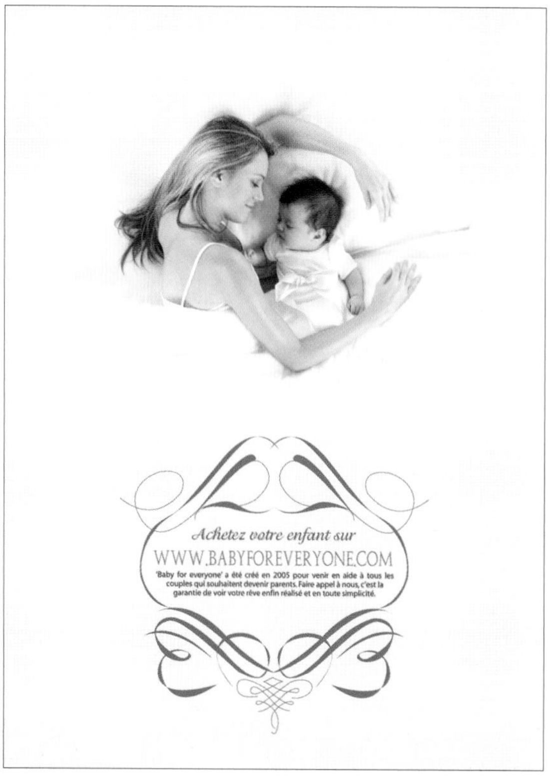
Achetez votre enfant sur
WWW.BABYFOREVERYONE.COM
'Baby for everyone' a été créé en 2005 pour venir en aide à tous les couples qui souhaitent devenir parents. Faire appel à nous, c'est la garantie de voir votre rêve enfin réalisé et en toute simplicité.

LE SOIR SE LEVE
CONTRE L'INACCEPTABLE
Chaque jour dans le monde, des familles vendent leur enfant contre une poignée de dollars et chez nous, il y a quelques mois, une
femme vendait son enfant sur Internet. Inacceptable ! Changeons notre quotidien.
LE SOIR
Achetez votre enfant sur
WWW.BABYFOREVERYONE.COM
'Baby for everyone' a été créé en 2005 pour venir en aide à tous les couples qui souhaitent devenir parents. Faire appel à nous, c'est la garantie de voir votre rêve enfin réalisé et en toute simplicité.

INTEGREZ-VOUS A 100%
www.institut-integration.be

LE SOIR SE LEVE
CONTRE L'INACCEPTABLE
LE SOIR
US A 100%
egration.be

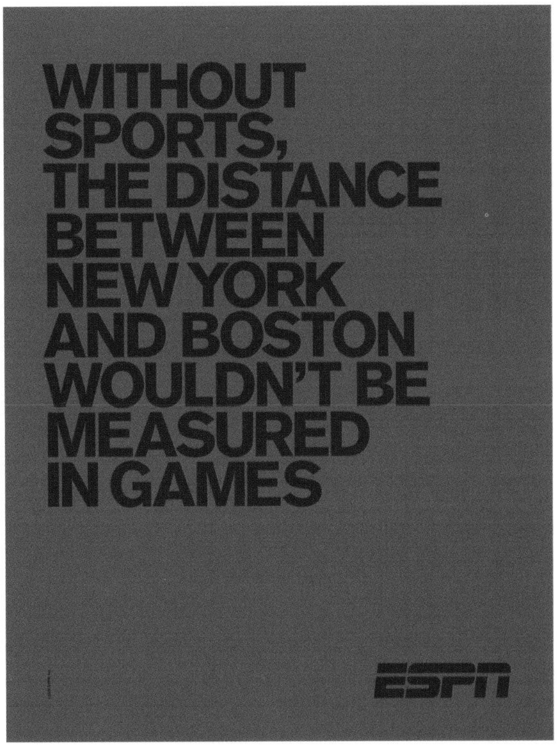
WITHOUT SPORTS, THE DISTANCE BETWEEN NEW YORK AND BOSTON WOULDN'T BE MEASURED IN GAMES
ESPN

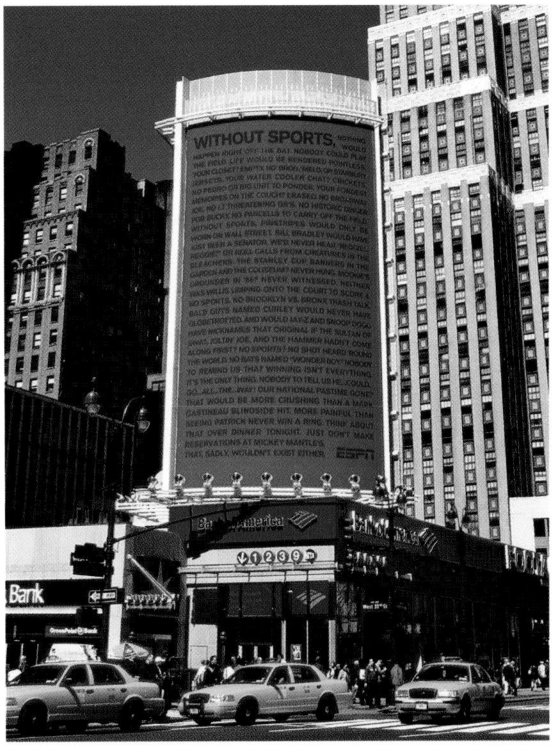
WITHOUT SPORTS,

WITHOUT SPORTS, WE'D STOP BELIEVING

WITHOUT SPORTS, CINDERELLA WOULDN'T WEAR SNEAKERS

WITHOUT SPORTS, HOW WOULD WE ESCAPE?

WITHOUT SPORTS, WHAT WOULD WE HOLD ON TO?

WITHOUT SPORTS, THIS WOULD BE A WALK IN THE PARK

WITHOUT SPORTS, THE WORLD WOULD BE A BIGGER PLACE

WITHOUT SPORTS, WHERE WOULD WE FIND OURSELVES?

WITHOUT SPORTS, THERE'D BE NOTHING TO SAY

WITHOUT SPORTS, 32-00-33 WOULDN'T BE CONSIDERED BEAUTIFUL.
ESPN

WITHOUT SPORTS, TAKING TWO STEPS WOULDN'T BE CONSIDERED TRAVELING
ESPN

WITHOUT SPORTS, WHICH SECTION WOULD YOU READ FIRST?
ESPN

Merit

ART DIRECTORS
Alan Buchanan
Stuart Jennings
Jesse Coulter
Eric Stevens

WRITERS
Andy Carrigan
Lisa Topol
Scott Hayes
Greg Kalleres

DESIGNER
Nelson Lowry

AGENCY PRODUCERS
Gary Krieg
Temma Shoaf
Jesse Wann

PRODUCTION COMPANIES
Anonymous Content
Laika House
RSA Films
Smuggler
Chelsea Pictures

DIRECTORS
Robert Logevall
Mark Gustafson
The Malloys
Chris Smith
David Gordon Green
Filip Engstrom
Mark Romanek

CREATIVE DIRECTORS
Todd Waterbury
Kevin Proudfoot
Paul Renner
Derek Barnes

CLIENT
ESPN

AGENCY
Wieden+Kennedy/ New York

ANNUAL ID
06309G

MERIT

DESIGN

MERIT

DESIGNERS
Jill Misawa
Don Emery

CREATIVE DIRECTORS
Liz Haldeman
Brock Haldeman

CLIENT
Feinberg School of Medicine at Northwestern University

AGENCY
Pivot Design/Chicago

ANNUAL ID
06064D

ANNUAL REPORT 2003–04
Anatomy
of Northwestern University's
Feinberg School of Medicine

THE PEOPLE
Body of the School
Students and faculty and staff members interact to create an environment conducive to learning and the advancement of science. For many, this environment is at the heart of their decision to choose the Feinberg School.

= 12 PERSONS

– Isaac Asimov –
Research

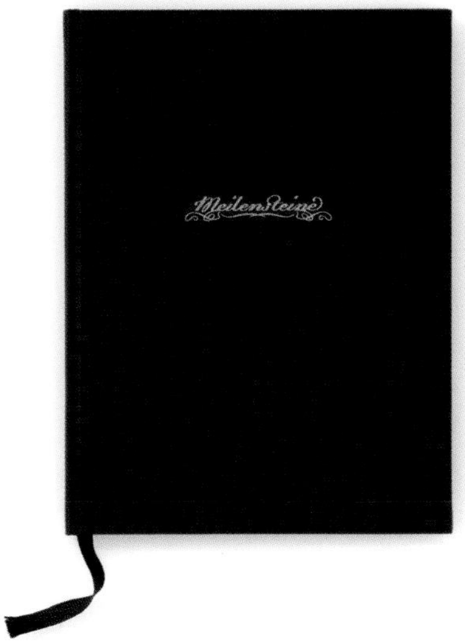

CASLON
WILLIAM 1692 - 1766

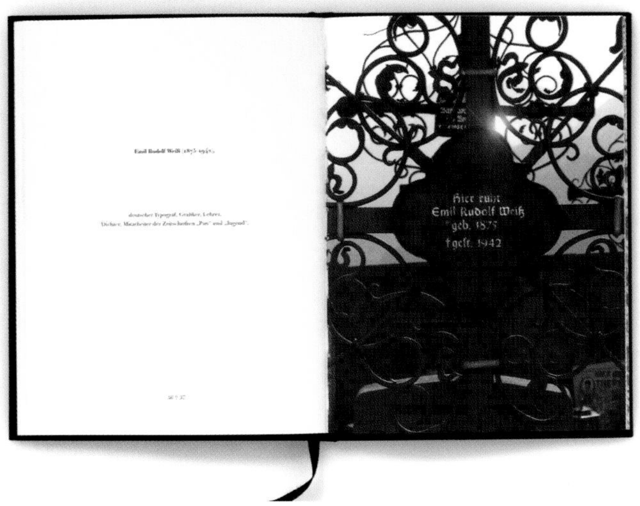
Hier ruht
Emil Rudolf Weiß
geb. 1875
† gest. 1942

BOSSONI
1880
GIAMBATTISTA
BODONI
1740 1813

MERIT

DESIGNER
Wolfgang Schif

ART DIRECTORS
Armin Jochum
Joerg Bauer

WRITER
Andreas Rell

CREATIVE DIRECTORS
Armin Jochum
Andreas Rell
Joerg Bauer

CLIENT
Cicero Werkstudio

AGENCY
BBDO/Stuttgart

ANNUAL ID
06065D

ALSO AWARDED
Merit:
Direct Mail - Single

Merit

DESIGNER
Charlie Ross

WRITER
Eric Luoma

CREATIVE DIRECTORS
Bill Thorburn
Michael Skjei

CLIENT
Formica

AGENCY
Carmichael Lynch
Thorburn/Minneapolis

ANNUAL ID
06066D

Surfacing Healthcare

Merit

DESIGNERS
Marie-Elaine Benoit
Jonathan Nicol
Laurence Pasteels

WRITERS
Marieve Blanchette-Guertin
Jonathan Rosman

PHOTOGRAPHER
Raoul Manuel Schnell

CREATIVE DIRECTOR
Helene Godin

CLIENT
Saputo

AGENCY
Diesel/Montreal

ANNUAL ID
06067D

PORTNEUF
Mon âme est aux
TERRES DE PORTNEUF
ce que mon cœur d'artisan est au
FROMAGE.
My soul belongs to Portneuf, yet my heart belongs to cheese

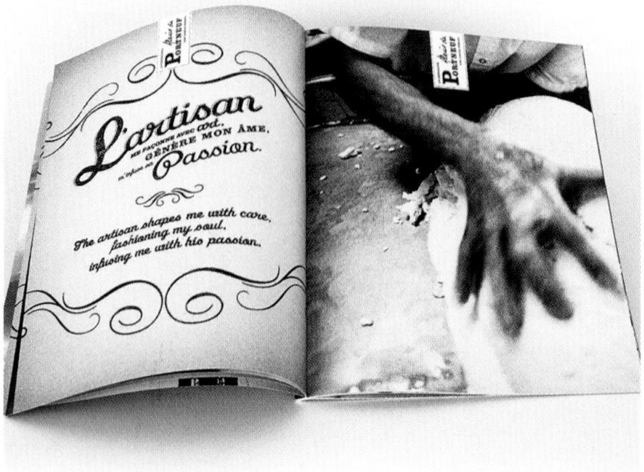
L'artisan
me façonne avec soin, génère mon âme, m'infuse sa Passion.
The artisan shapes me with care, fashioning my soul, infusing me with his passion.
PORTNEUF

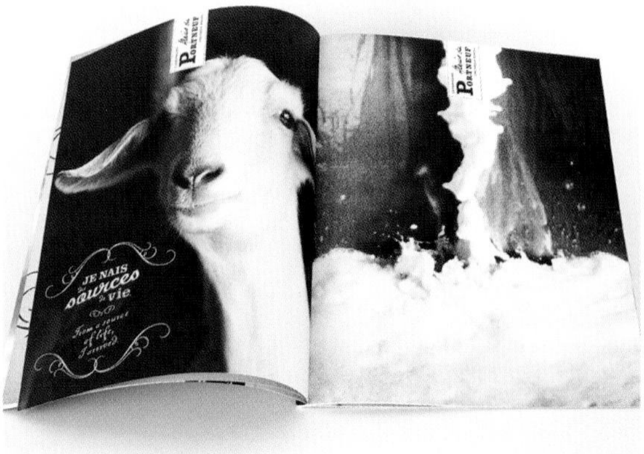
PORTNEUF
JE NAIS
vie

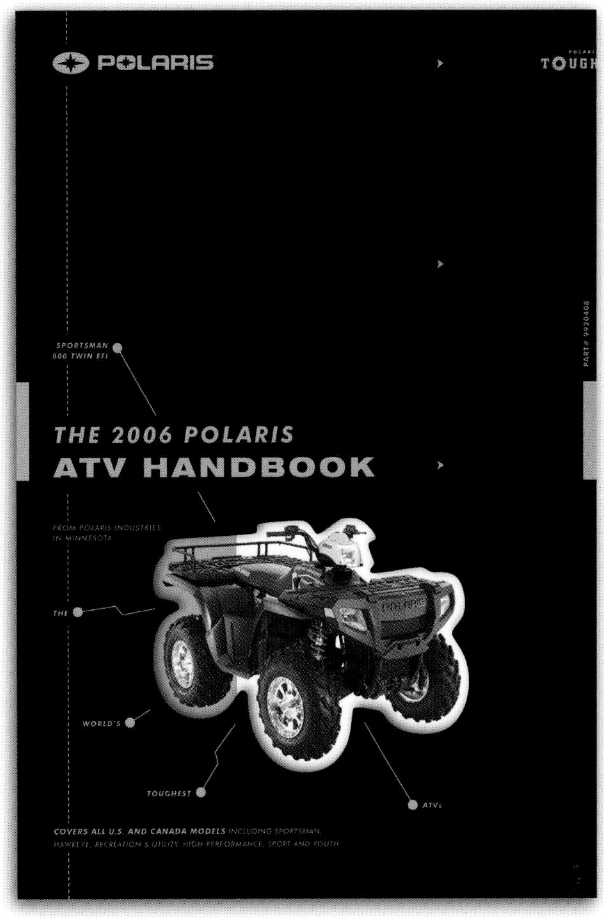
POLARIS
THE 2006 POLARIS
ATV HANDBOOK
SPORTSMAN 800 TWIN EFI
FROM POLARIS INDUSTRIES IN MINNESOTA
THE
WORLD'S
TOUGHEST
ATVs
COVERS ALL U.S. AND CANADA MODELS INCLUDING SPORTSMAN, HAWKEYE, RECREATION & UTILITY, HIGH-PERFORMANCE, SPORT AND YOUTH

MERIT

DESIGNER
Scott Pridgen

ART DIRECTOR
Scott Pridgen

WRITER
Brian Murray

PHOTOGRAPHER
David Perry

CREATIVE DIRECTORS
Liz Paradise
David Baldwin

CLIENT
Polaris Industries

AGENCY
McKinney/Durham

ANNUAL ID
06068D

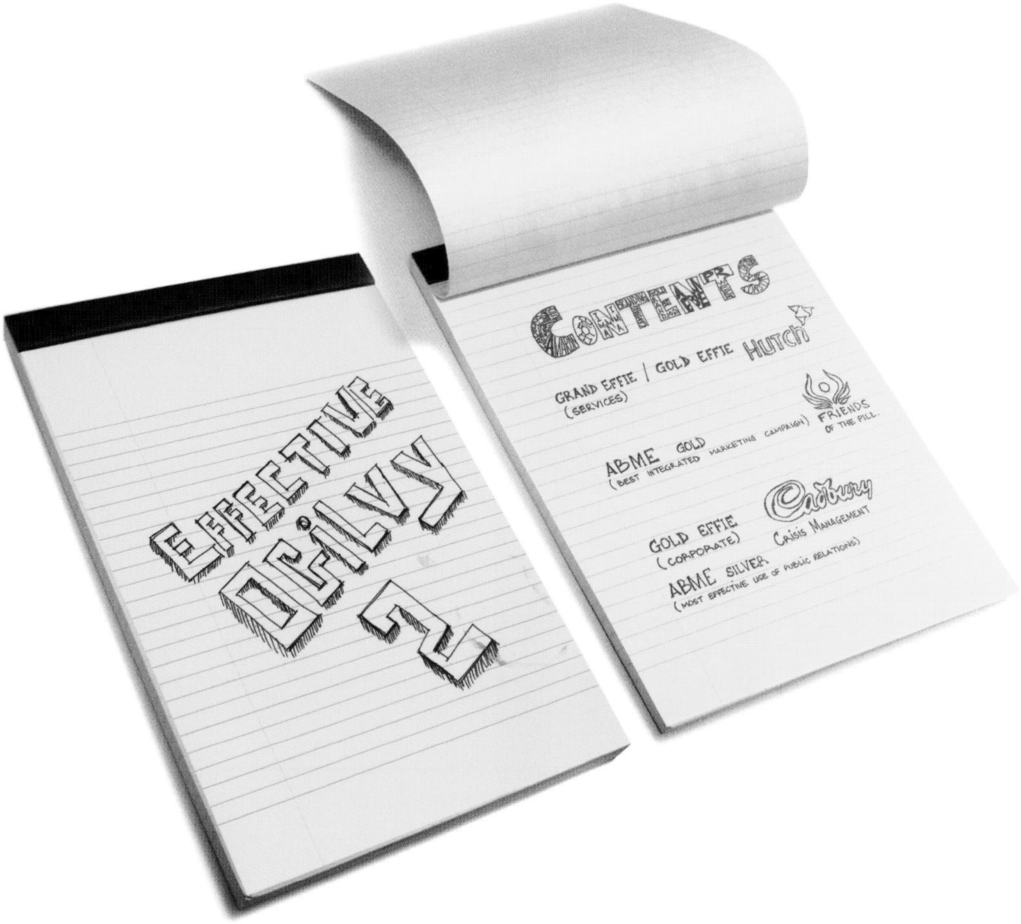
EFFECTIVE
OGILVY
2
CONTENTS
GRAND EFFIE / GOLD EFFIE
(SERVICES)
HUTCH
ABME GOLD
(BEST INTEGRATED MARKETING CAMPAIGN)
FRIENDS OF THE PILL
GOLD EFFIE
(CORPORATE)
Cadbury
Crisis Management
ABME SILVER
(MOST EFFECTIVE USE OF PUBLIC RELATIONS)

MERIT

DESIGNERS
Yogesh Mani Pradhan
Samir Sojwal

ART DIRECTORS
Yogesh Mani Pradhan
Samir Sojwal

ILLUSTRATOR
Nandu Mistry

CREATIVE DIRECTORS
Abhijit Avasthi
Piyush Pandey

CLIENT
Ogilvy & Mather

AGENCY
Ogilvy & Mather/ Mumbai

ANNUAL ID
06069D

Merit

DESIGNERS
Steve Sandstrom
Kristin Anderson

ART DIRECTOR
Steve Sandstrom

WRITER
Jim Moore

PHOTOGRAPHER
Michael Jones

CREATIVE DIRECTOR
Steve Sandstrom

CLIENT
Converse

AGENCY
Sandstrom Design/
Portland

ANNUAL ID
06072D

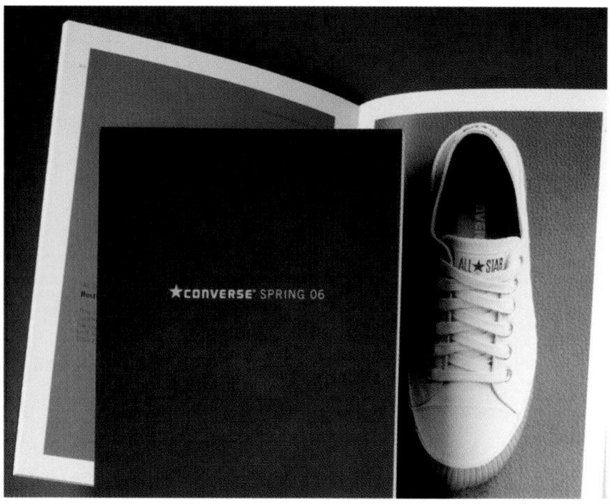
★CONVERSE SPRING 06
ALL★STAR

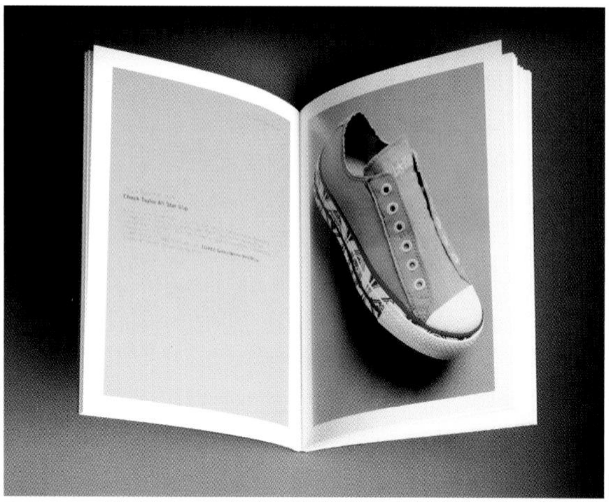

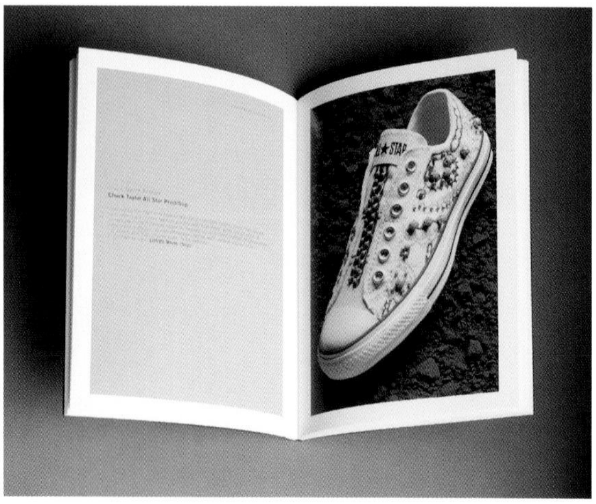

GO
PREMIER
ISSUE
ARRIVES
FALL
2005

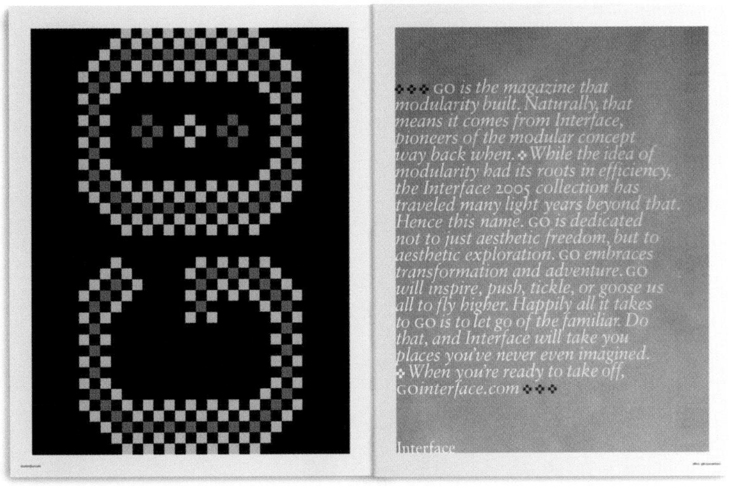
GO
GO is the magazine that modularity built. Naturally, that means it comes from Interface, pioneers of the modular concept way back when. While the idea of modularity had its roots in efficiency, the Interface 2005 collection has traveled many light years beyond that. Hence this name. GO is dedicated not to just aesthetic freedom, but to aesthetic exploration. GO embraces transformation and adventure. GO will inspire, push, tickle, or goose us all to fly higher. Happily all it takes to GO is to let go of the familiar. Do that, and Interface will take you places you've never even imagined.
When you're ready to take off, GOinterface.com
Interface

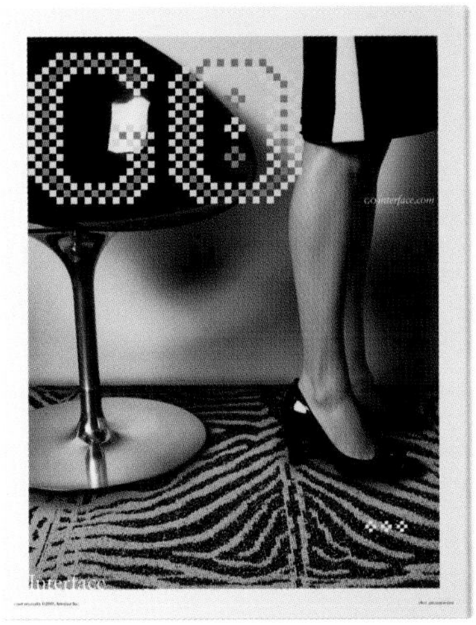
GO
GOinterface.com
Interface

GO takes flights of fancy fall
GO

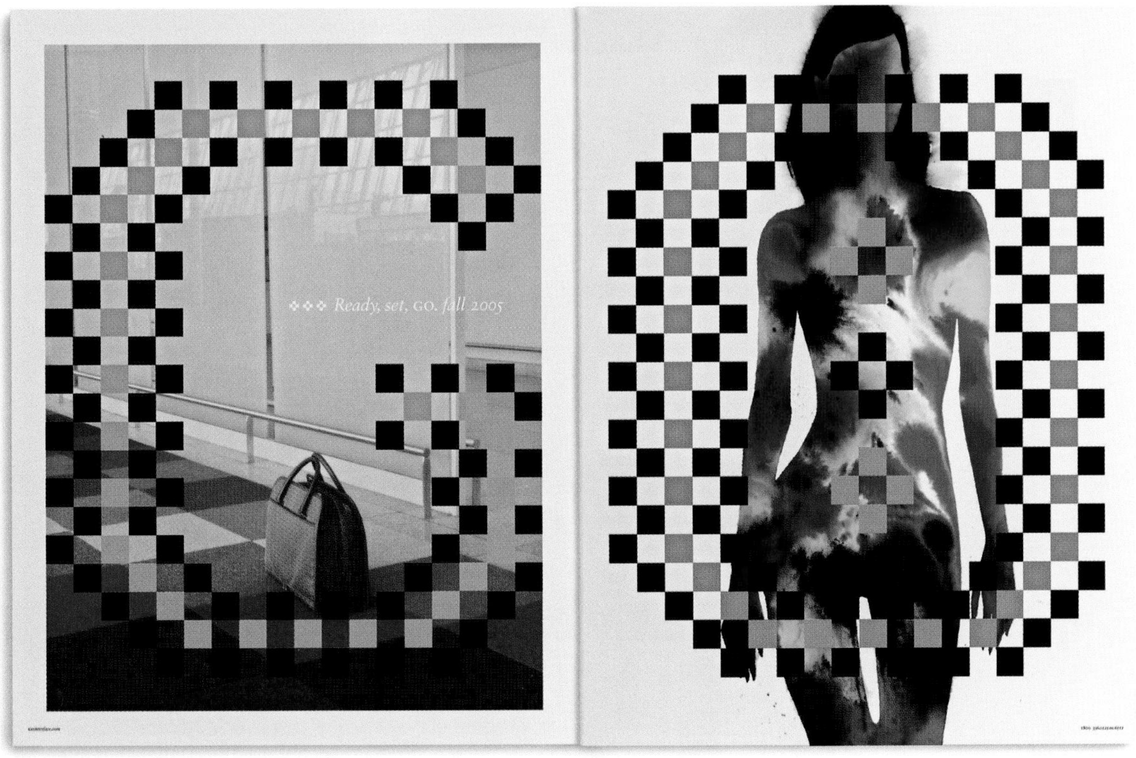
GO
Ready, set, GO. fall 2005

Merit

DESIGNERS
Brooke Romney
Aaron Amaro

WRITER
Dianna Edwards

PHOTOGRAPHER
Roland Bello

CREATIVE DIRECTOR
Robert Valentine

CLIENT
Interface

AGENCY
The Valentine Group/ New York

ANNUAL ID
06073D

MERIT

ART DIRECTORS
Uschi Henkes
Marcos Fernandez

CREATIVE DIRECTORS
Uschi Henkes
Urs Frick
Manolo Moreno

CLIENT
CdC - Club de Creativos de España

AGENCY
Zapping/Madrid

ANNUAL ID
06074D

MERIT

ART DIRECTORS
Uschi Henkes
Jenny Nerman

WRITER
Manolo Moreno

CREATIVE DIRECTORS
Uschi Henkes
Manolo Moreno
Urs Frick

CLIENT
Disney/Buenavista España

AGENCY
Zapping/Madrid

ANNUAL ID
06075D

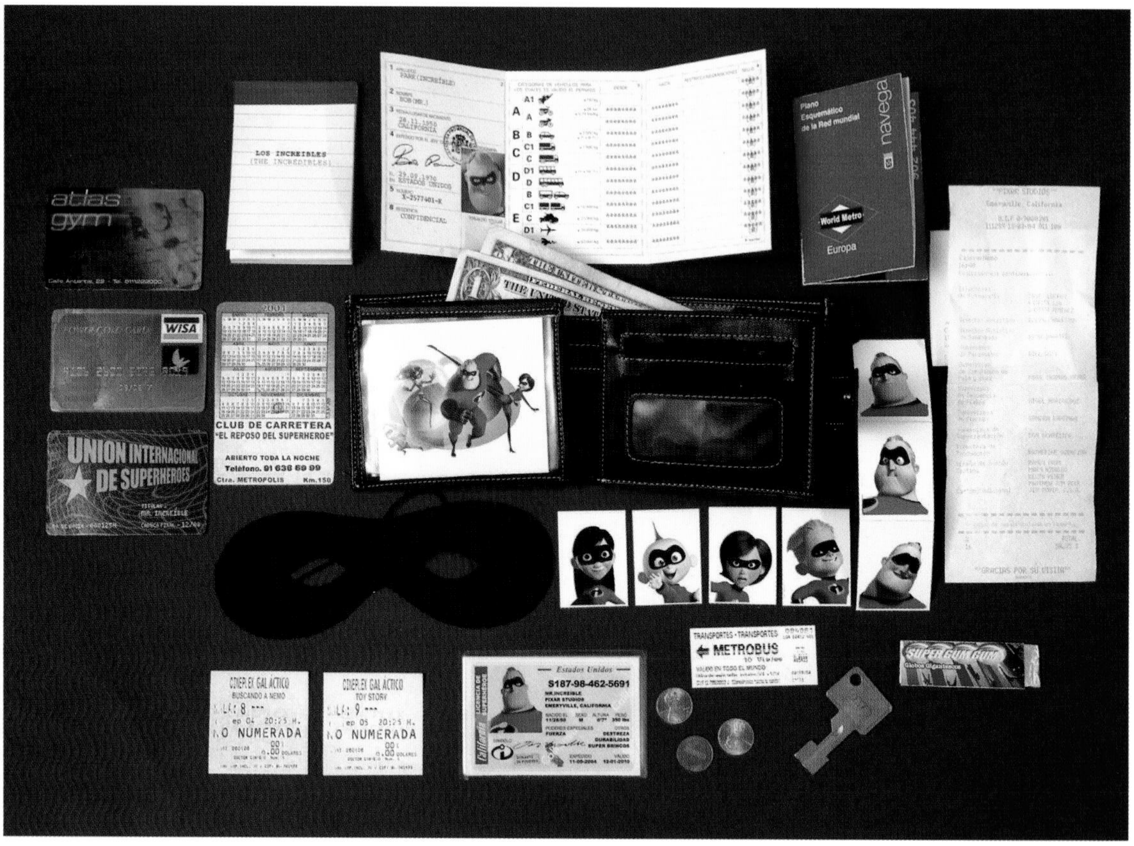
LOS INCREIBLES
(THE INCREDIBLES)
navega
World Metro
Europa
CLUB DE CARRETERA
"EL REPOSO DEL SUPERHEROE"
UNION INTERNACIONAL DE SUPERHEROES
METROBUS
S187-98-462-5691
NO NUMERADA
NO NUMERADA

ASYLUM

CHRISTOPHER LEE
Creative Director

FIERCELY DEMANDING

PAINFULLY METICULOUS

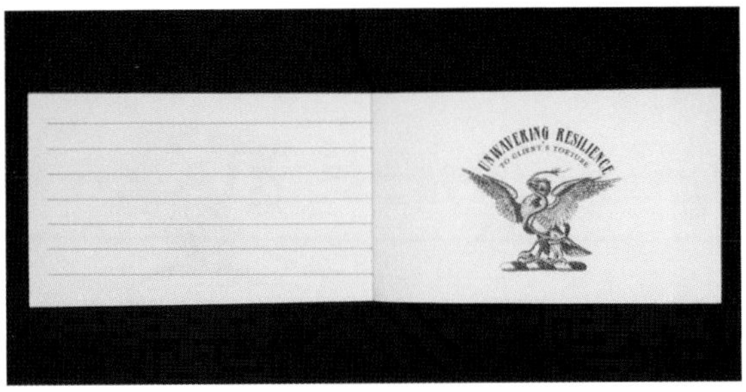
UNWAVERING RESILIENCE

DEDICATED COMMITMENT

MERIT

DESIGNERS
Cara Ang
Bel Ong

CREATIVE DIRECTOR
Christopher Lee

CLIENT
Asylum

AGENCY
Asylum Creative/ Singapore

ANNUAL ID
06076D

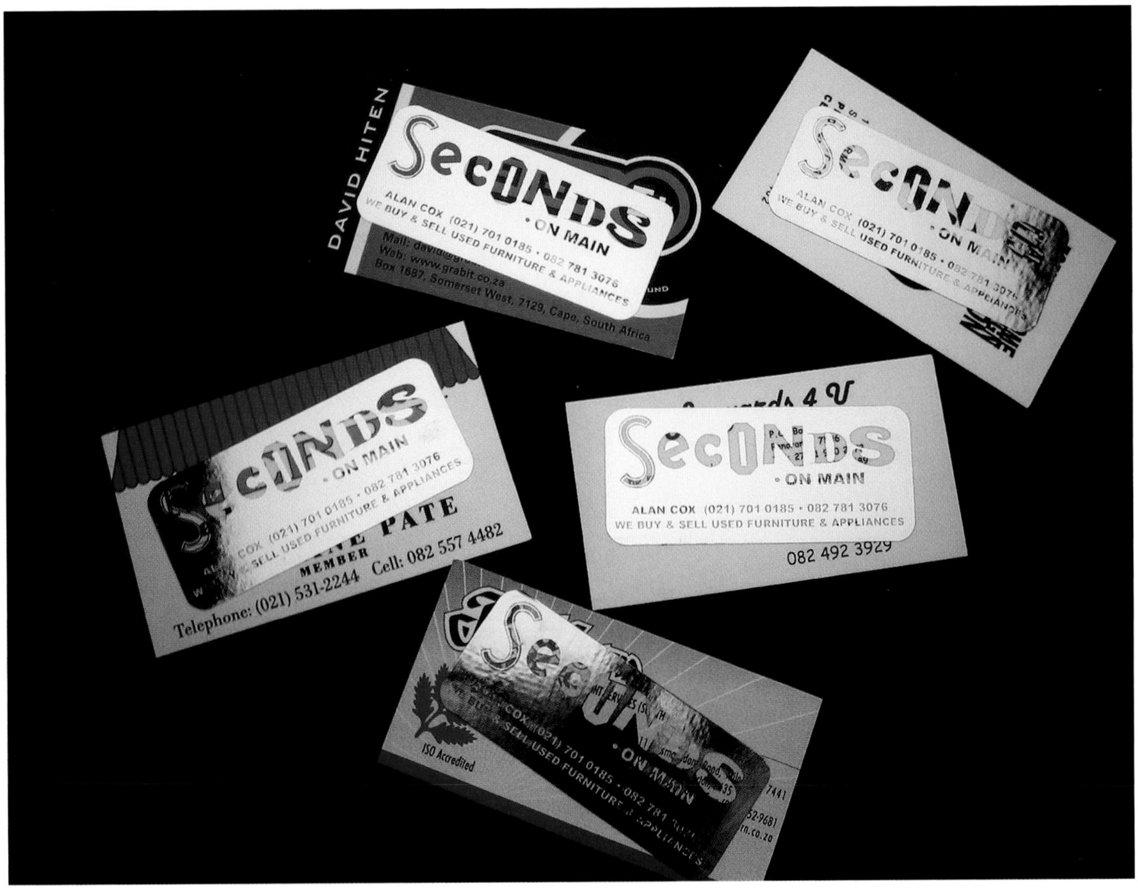
SecONDS
· ON MAIN
ALAN COX (021) 701 0185 · 082 781 3076
WE BUY & SELL USED FURNITURE & APPLIANCES
DAVID HITEN
Web: www.grabit.co.za
Box 1687, Somerset West, 7129, Cape, South Africa
MEMBER
Telephone: (021) 531-2244 Cell: 082 557 4482
082 492 3929
ISO Accredited

MERIT

DESIGNER
Tandy van Schalkwyk

CREATIVE DIRECTOR
Paul Carstens

CLIENT
Seconds on Main

AGENCY
FCB South Africa/ Cape Town

ANNUAL ID
06077D

MERIT

ART DIRECTOR
Sanket Pathare

WRITER
Parixit Bhattacharya

CLIENT
Ninad Kamat

AGENCY
idiots/Mumbai

ANNUAL ID
06078D

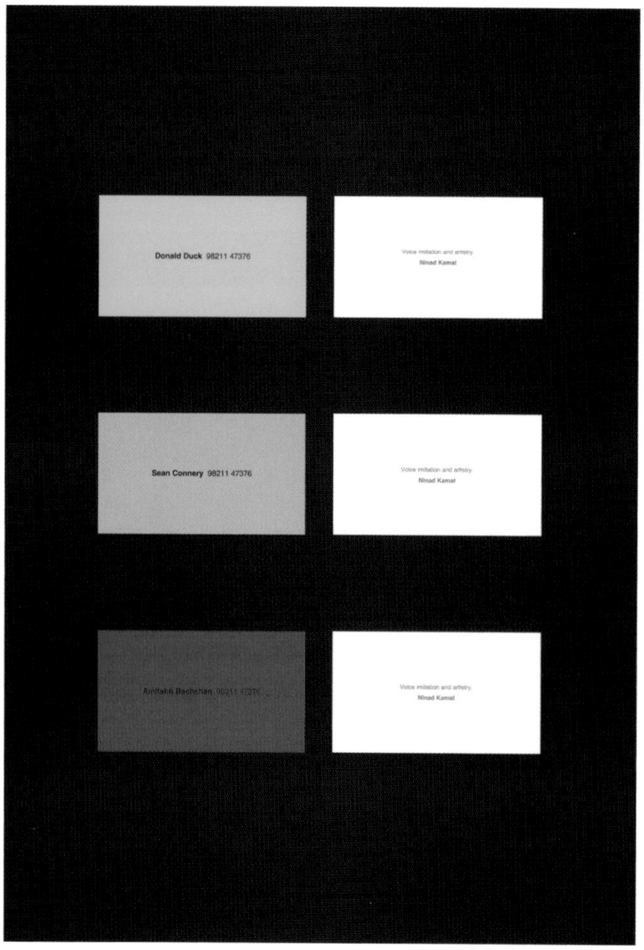
Donald Duck 98211 47376
Voice imitation and artistry.
Ninad Kamat
Sean Connery 98211 47376
Voice imitation and artistry.
Ninad Kamat
Amitabh Bachchan
Voice imitation and artistry.
Ninad Kamat

MERIT

ART DIRECTORS
Roy Poh
Pann Lim
Leng Soh

WRITER
Alex Goh

CLIENT
Holmes Private Investigators

AGENCY
Kinetic/Singapore

ANNUAL ID
06079D

HOLMES PRIVATE INVESTIGATORS
MIKE LOW
(65) 9781 8795

VITOOL VIRAPONSAVAN
PRESIDENT AND CEO
PLAN CREATION CO., LTD.
114/1 SOI SATHORN 10,
BANGKOK 10500, THAILAND
T:66(0)2237-9070
F:66(0)2237-9247

MERIT

ART DIRECTORS
Khomson Poopijit
Saharath Sawadatikom

WRITER
Mantira Srichandra

CREATIVE DIRECTOR
Saharath Sawadatikom

CLIENT
Plantoys

AGENCY
OgilvyOne Worldwide/Bangkok

ANNUAL ID
06080D

MELANGE
FINE ACCESSORIES
Gormannstr.23 - Berlin

MERIT

ART DIRECTOR
Maja Mack

WRITER
Felix John

CREATIVE DIRECTOR
Constantin Kaloff

CLIENT
Melange Accessories

AGENCY
Scholz & Friends/Berlin

ANNUAL ID
06081D

Merit

ILLUSTRATOR
Paul Arkle

CREATIVE DIRECTORS
Todd Waterbury
Kevin Proudfoot
Paul Renner

CLIENT
ESPN

AGENCY
Wieden+Kennedy/
New York

ANNUAL ID
06082D

THE ESPN BRAND
ISN'T KEPT IN A BOX, OR A SAFE, OR OWNED BY SOME CRAZY SPORTS COLLECTOR LIKE THIS BALL, IT'S OWNED BY YOU AND IS IN YOUR HANDS.
THIS IS A
BIG RESPONSIBILITY.
SO HERE ARE A COUPLE OF THINGS TO KEEP IN MIND WHEN COMMUNICATING WITH AND SERVING THE
ESPN
THE WORLD'S BIGGEST SPORTS FAN
SPORTSCENTER

Merit

DESIGNER
Tim McGrath

WRITER
Sam Maclay

CREATIVE DIRECTOR
Sam Maclay

CLIENT
3

AGENCY
3/Albuquerque

ANNUAL ID
06083D

MELISSA GEORGE
3 THINGS YOU SHOULD KNOW ABOUT MELISSA
www.whois3.com

PANDIT HARIPRASAD CHAURASIA
FLUTIST
VRINDABAN GURUKUL, JUHU VERSOVA LINK ROAD ANDHERI (W) MUMBAI 400 053 TEL: +91 - 22 - 26212121 E-MAIL: INFO@HARIPRASADCHAURASIA.COM

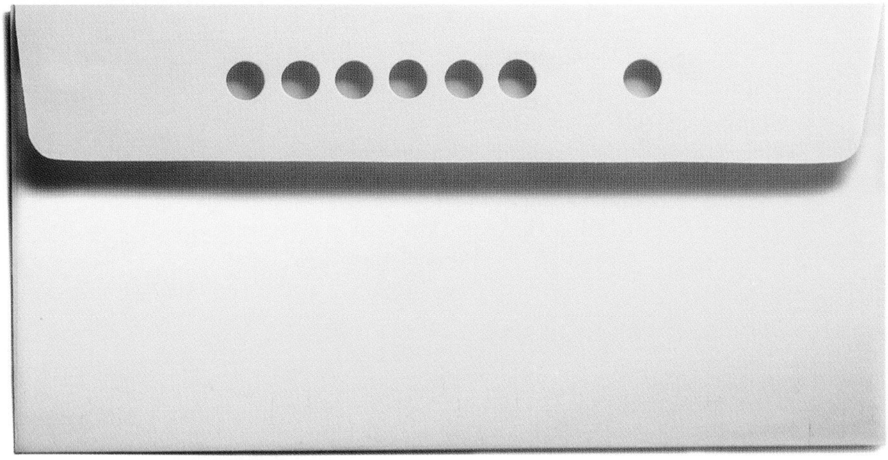

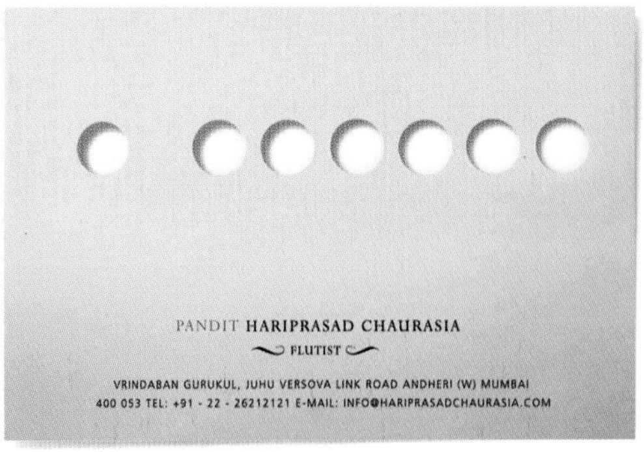
PANDIT HARIPRASAD CHAURASIA
FLUTIST
VRINDABAN GURUKUL, JUHU VERSOVA LINK ROAD ANDHERI (W) MUMBAI
400 053 TEL: +91 - 22 - 26212121 E-MAIL: INFO@HARIPRASADCHAURASIA.COM

Merit

ART DIRECTOR
Abhijit Karandikar

WRITER
Abhijit Karandikar

CREATIVE DIRECTOR
Abhijit Karandikar

CLIENT
Pandit Hariprasad Chaurasia

AGENCY
Abhijit/Mumbai

ANNUAL ID
06084D

Merit

DESIGNER
Goh Wee Kim

ART DIRECTOR
Goh Wee Kim

WRITER
Andrew McKechnie

CREATIVE DIRECTOR
Francis Wee

CLIENT
Ella Cheong Spruson & Ferguson

AGENCY
BBDO/Singapore

ANNUAL ID
06085D

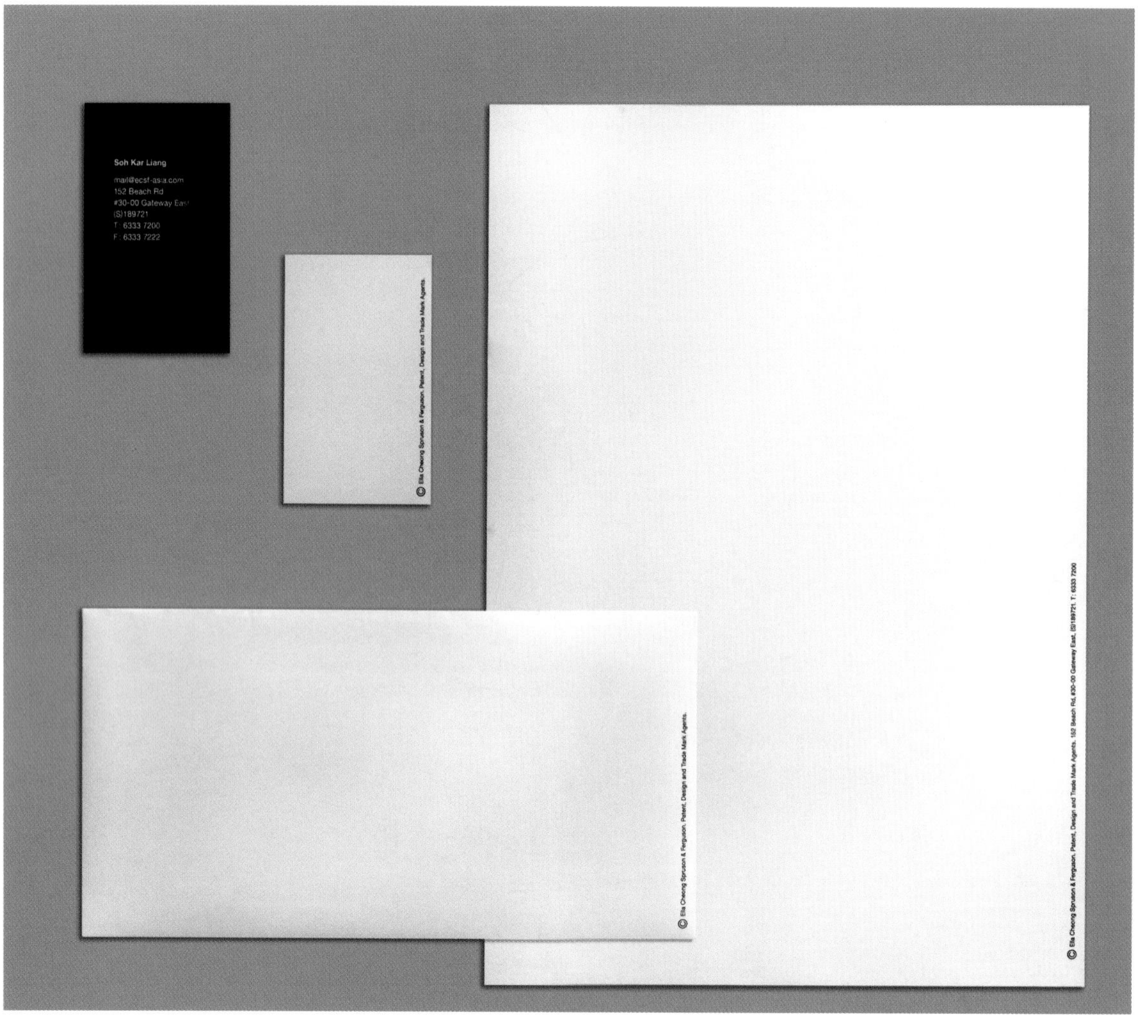
Soh Kar Liang
mail@ecsf-asia.com
152 Beach Rd
#30-00 Gateway East
(S)189721
T: 6333 7200
F: 6333 7222
© Ella Cheong Spruson & Ferguson. Patent, Design and Trade Mark Agents.
© Ella Cheong Spruson & Ferguson. Patent, Design and Trade Mark Agents.
© Ella Cheong Spruson & Ferguson. Patent, Design and Trade Mark Agents. 152 Beach Rd, #30-00 Gateway East, (S)189721. T: 6333 7200

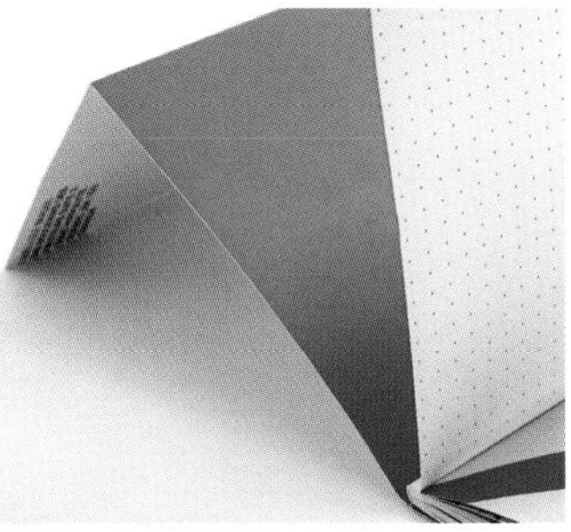

MERIT

DESIGNER
Laurence Pasteels

ART DIRECTOR
Laurence Pasteels

WRITERS
Thierry De Greef
Crystal Beliveau

PHOTOGRAPHER
André Rider

CREATIVE DIRECTOR
Thierry De Greef

CLIENT
Libellule Images

AGENCY
Nonante/Montreal

ANNUAL ID
06086D

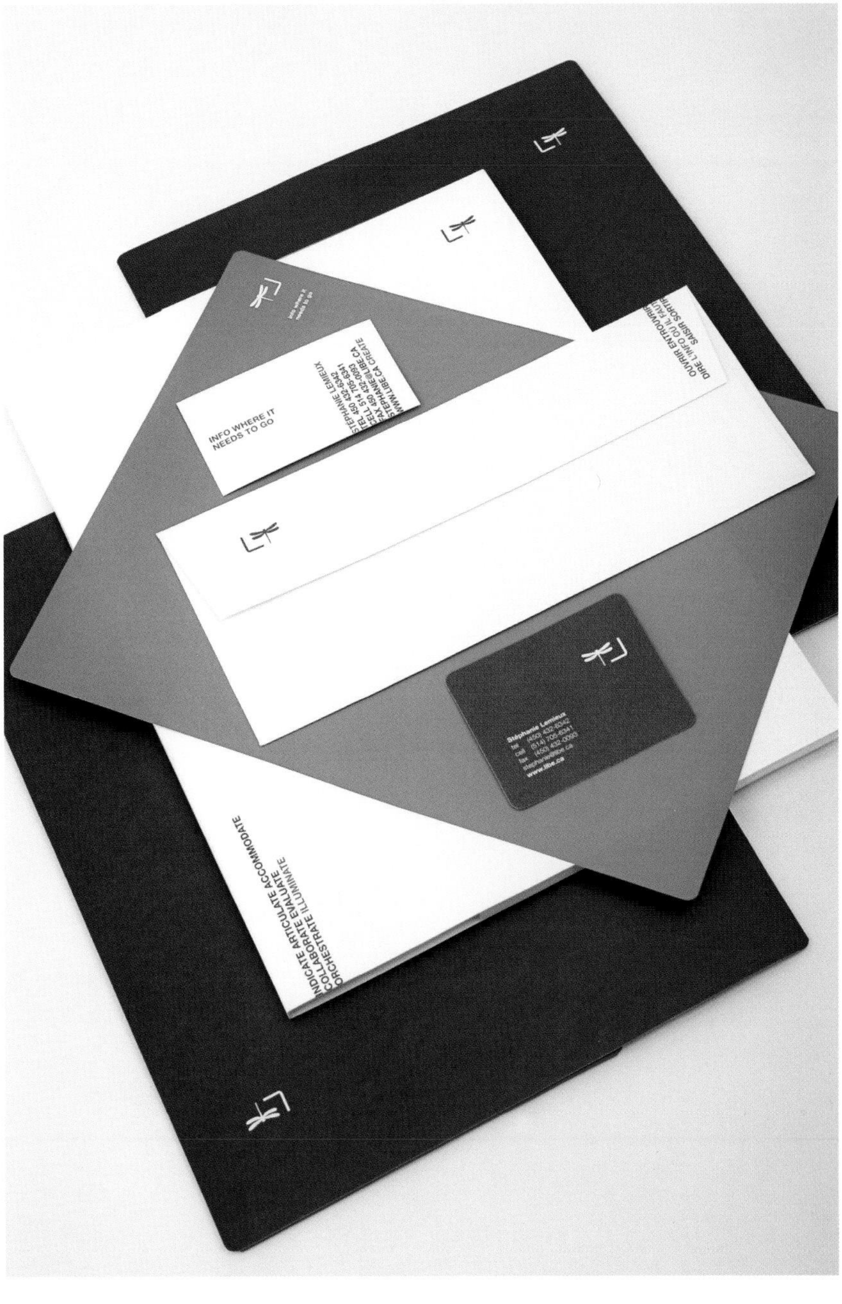
INFO WHERE IT
NEEDS TO GO
INDICATE ARTICULATE ACCOMMODATE
COLLABORATE EVALUATE
ORCHESTRATE ILLUMINATE
Stéphanie Lemieux

MERIT

DESIGNERS
Satian Pengsathapon
Apirat Infahsaeng

CREATIVE DIRECTORS
Weston Bingham
Brian Collins

CLIENT
American Express/
Tribeca Film Festival

AGENCY
Ogilvy & Mather/
New York

ANNUAL ID
06087D

TRIBECA
FILM
FESTIVAL
APR 19 - MAY 1

TRIBECA
FILM
FESTIVAL
APR 19 - MAY 1

TRIBECA
FILM
FESTIVAL
APR 19 - MAY 1

I am fresh.
HANAMOTO

I am fresh.
HANAMOTO

I am fresh.
HANAMOTO

MERIT

DESIGNER
Kazuto Nakamura

ART DIRECTOR
Kazuto Nakamura

WRITER
Tomiko Nakamura

ILLUSTRATOR
Tomiko Nakamura

CREATIVE DIRECTOR
Kazuto Nakamura

CLIENT
Hanamoto

AGENCY
Penguin Graphics/ Hiroshima

ANNUAL ID
06088D

MERIT

DESIGNER
Peter Bell

ART DIRECTORS
Peter Bell
Michael Kriefski

CREATIVE DIRECTOR
Michael Kriefski

CLIENT
Umi

AGENCY
Shine Advertising/
Madison

ANNUAL ID
06089D

umi

MERIT

DESIGNER
Tony Thielen

ART DIRECTOR
Tony Thielen

CLIENT
Thielen Designs

AGENCY
Thielen Designs/
Albuquerque

ANNUAL ID
06090D

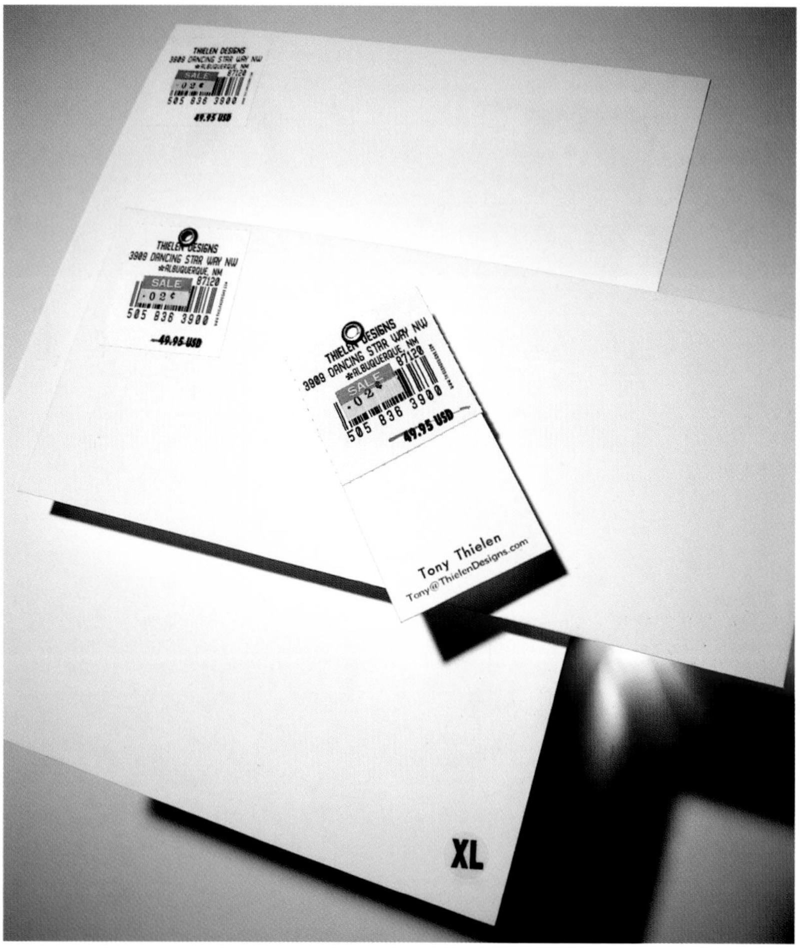
THIELEN DESIGNS
3909 DANCING STAR WAY NW
ALBUQUERQUE, NM 87120
SALE
505 836 3900
49.95 USD
Tony Thielen
Tony@ThielenDesigns.com
XL

Merit

DESIGNER
Ken Sakurai

CREATIVE DIRECTOR
Dan Olson

CLIENT
Good Day Cafe

AGENCY
Duffy & Partners/
Minneapolis

ANNUAL ID
06091D

Merit

DESIGNER
Mark Stead

CREATIVE DIRECTORS
Jenny Ehlers
Mark Stead

CLIENT
Flat Stanley

AGENCY
King James RSVP/
Cape Town

ANNUAL ID
06092D

MERIT

DESIGNER
Jon Ritt

CREATIVE DIRECTOR
Jon Ritt

CLIENT
Birdie

AGENCY
Pool/San Francisco

ANNUAL ID
06093D

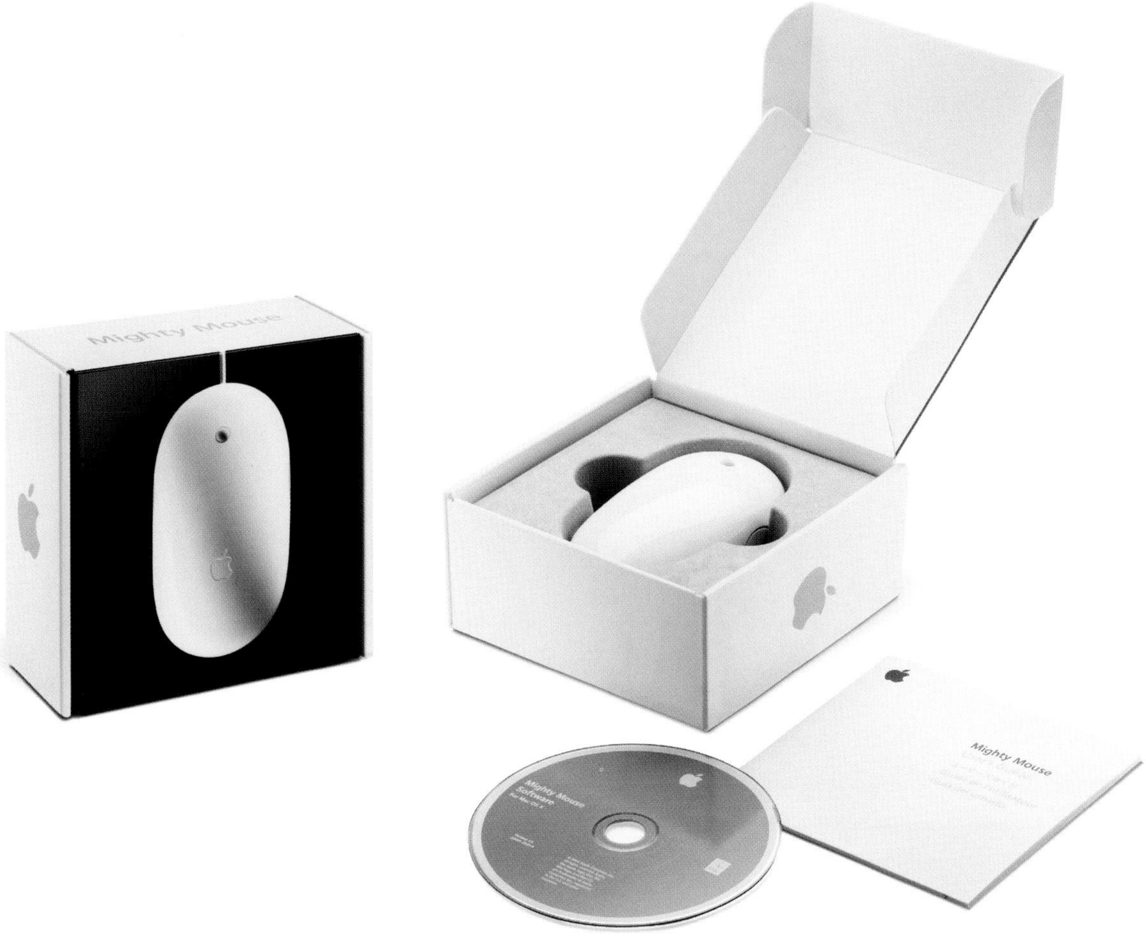
Mighty Mouse
Mighty Mouse
Software
Mighty Mouse

Merit

DESIGNERS
Apple Graphic Design
Apple Industrial Design
Apple Packaging Engineering

CLIENT
Apple Computer

AGENCY
Apple Computer/ Cupertino

ANNUAL ID
06094D

Merit

DESIGNER
Edwin Tan

CREATIVE DIRECTOR
Christopher Lee

CLIENT
Auric Pacific

AGENCY
Asylum Creative/ Singapore

ANNUAL ID
06095D

MERIT

DESIGNER
Ryota Sakae

ART DIRECTOR
Kenjiro Sano

CLIENT
Uplink

AGENCY
Hakuhodo/Tokyo

ANNUAL ID
06096D

毛皮族
DVD

毛皮族
dvd
1_kichiku roman 2_bowling
DVD

MERIT

DESIGNER
Friederike Coninx

ART DIRECTOR
David Mously

WRITER
Jan Harbeck

PHOTOGRAPHER
Michael Tewes

CREATIVE DIRECTORS
Burkhart von Scheven
David Mously
Jan Harbeck

CLIENT
Schaefer Pharma

AGENCY
Jung von Matt/Berlin

ANNUAL ID
06097D

Nail biter?
stop'n grow
helps.

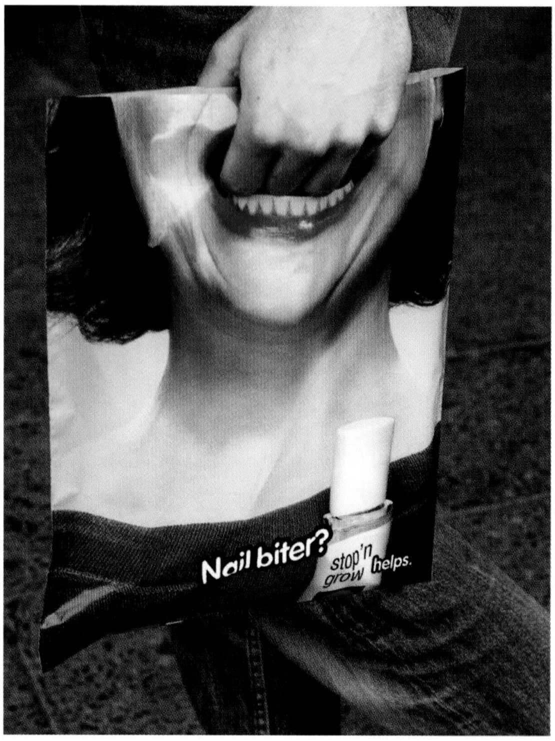
Nail biter?
stop'n grow
helps.

Session
PREMIUM
LAGER
11 FLUID OZ

MERIT

DESIGNERS
Steve Sandstrom
James Parker

ART DIRECTOR
Steve Sandstrom

WRITER
Mark Waggoner

CREATIVE DIRECTORS
Steve Sandstrom
Mark Waggoner

CLIENT
Full Sail Brewery

AGENCY
Sandstrom Design/ Portland

ANNUAL ID
06099D

INDEPENDENT
EMPLOYEE-OWNED
Full Sail
PALE ALE
12
TWELVE FLUID OZ. BOTTLES
AMERICAN PALE ALE
FULL SAIL BREWING COMPANY, HOOD RIVER, OREGON

MERIT

DESIGNERS
Steve Sandstrom
James Parker

ART DIRECTOR
Steve Sandstrom

WRITER
Mark Waggoner

CREATIVE DIRECTORS
Steve Sandstrom
Mark Waggoner

CLIENT
Full Sail Brewery

AGENCY
Sandstrom Design/ Portland

ANNUAL ID
06098D

Merit

DESIGNER
Shawn Rosenberger

CREATIVE DIRECTORS
David Turner
Bruce Duckworth

CLIENT
Click Wine Group

AGENCY
Turner Duckworth/
San Francisco

ANNUAL ID
06100D

Root: 1
CABERNET SAUVIGNON

Merit

ART DIRECTOR
Stuart Jennings

WRITER
Greg Kalleres

ILLUSTRATOR
Urs Althaus

CREATIVE DIRECTORS
Todd Waterbury
Kevin Proudfoot

CONTENT STRATEGIST
Dan Cherry

CLIENT
Nike Brand Jordan -
Work'm Sneaker

AGENCY
Wieden+Kennedy/
New York

ANNUAL ID
06101D

Motion 2
HD

Shake 4

DVD Studio Pro 4
HD

Soundtrack Pro
HD

Aperture

Logic Pro 7

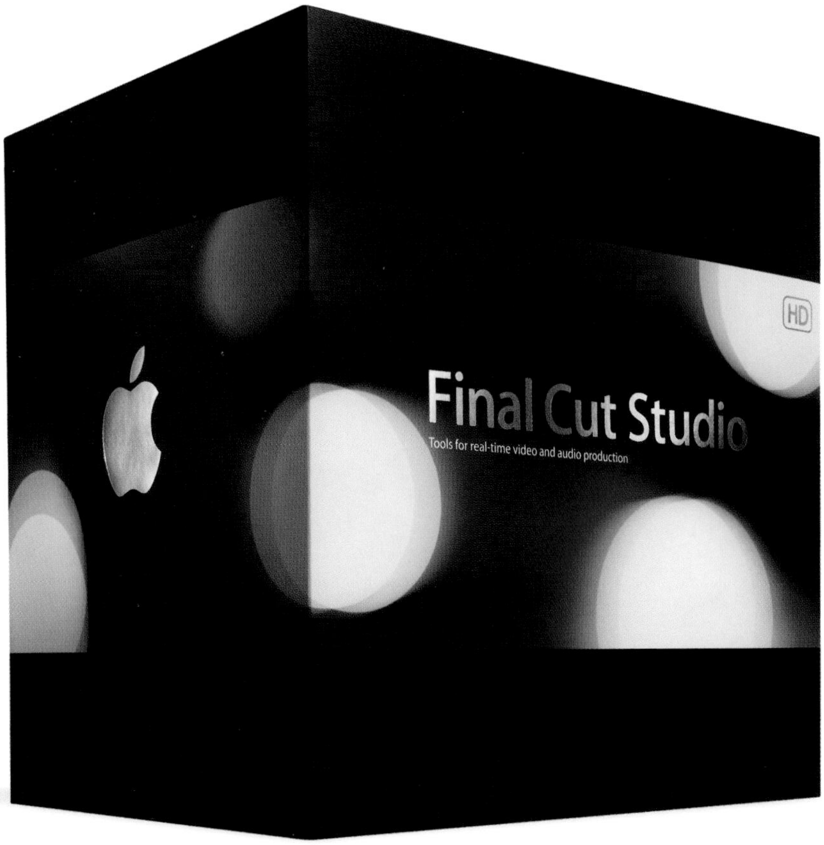
Final Cut Studio
Tools for real-time video and audio production
HD

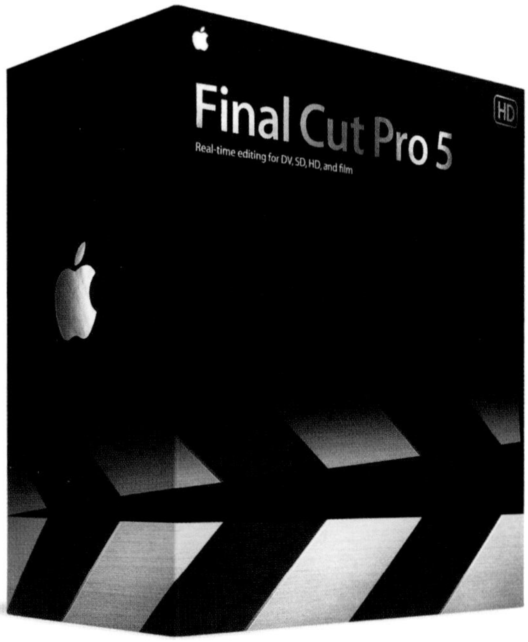
Final Cut Pro 5
Real-time editing for DV, SD, HD, and film
HD

Merit

DESIGNERS
Apple Graphic Design
Apple Packaging Engineering

CLIENT
Apple Computer

AGENCY
Apple Computer/ Cupertino

ANNUAL ID
06102D

Merit

DESIGNER
Linda Fahrlin

ILLUSTRATOR
Linda Fahrlin

CREATIVE DIRECTORS
Michael Faudet
Christy Peacock

CLIENT
PZ Cussons

AGENCY
DDB/Melbourne

ANNUAL ID
06103D

GRAPHITE
DEODORANT BODY SPRAY
SKULL / 100g
GRAPHITE
DEODORANT BODY SPRAY
CAUTION / 100g

Merit

DESIGNER
Alan Leusink

WRITER
Lisa Pemrick

CREATIVE DIRECTOR
Dan Olson

CLIENT
Thymes

AGENCY
Duffy & Partners/ Minneapolis

ANNUAL ID
06104D

THYMES
AU CHOCOLAT
AROMATIC CANDLE

giraffe®
Foot Soap
giraffe®
Brushing Toner
giraffe®
Tea Tree Care Cream
giraffe®
Tea Tree Conditioner

MERIT

DESIGNER
Tomoko Komazawa

ART DIRECTOR
Takahito Noguchi

CLIENT
Park Project

AGENCY
Dynamite Brothers Syndicate/Tokyo

ANNUAL ID
06105D

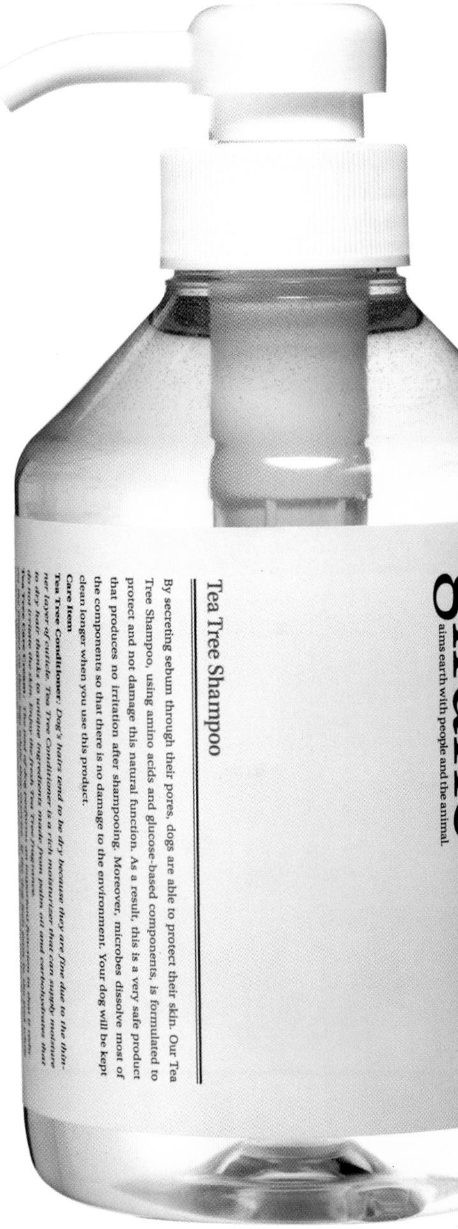
giraffe®
aims earth with people and the animal.
Tea Tree Shampoo
By secreting sebum through their pores, dogs are able to protect their skin. Our Tea Tree Shampoo, using amino acids and glucose-based components, is formulated to protect and not damage this natural function. As a result, this is a very safe product that produces no irritation after shampooing. Moreover, microbes dissolve most of the components so that there is no damage to the environment. Your dog will be kept clean longer when you use this product.
Care Item

MERIT

DESIGNERS
Ryo Miyawaki
Mai Inayoshi

ART DIRECTOR
Chie Morimoto

WRITER
Masaki Yoshimizu

CREATIVE DIRECTOR
Masaki Yoshimizu

CLIENT
The University of Tokyo

AGENCY
Hakuhodo Creative Vox/ Tokyo

ANNUAL ID
06106D

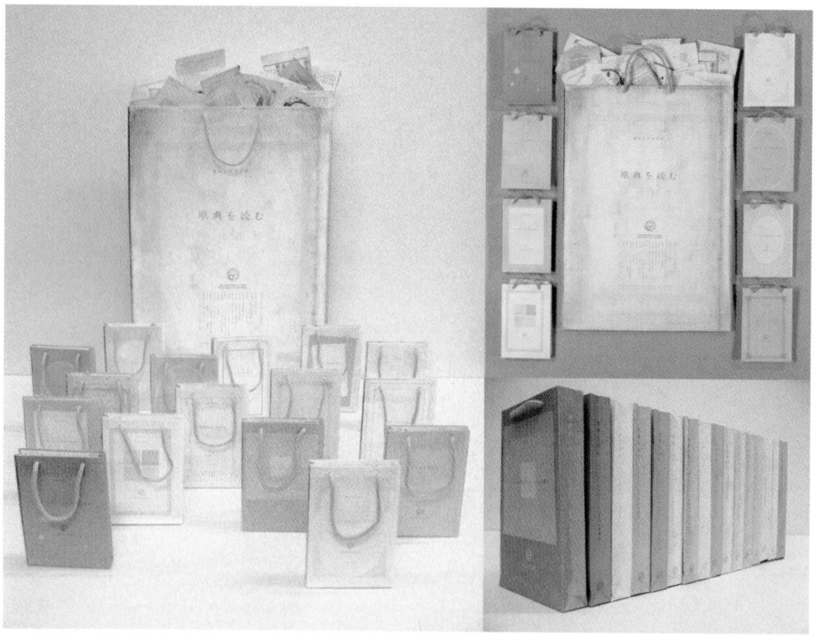

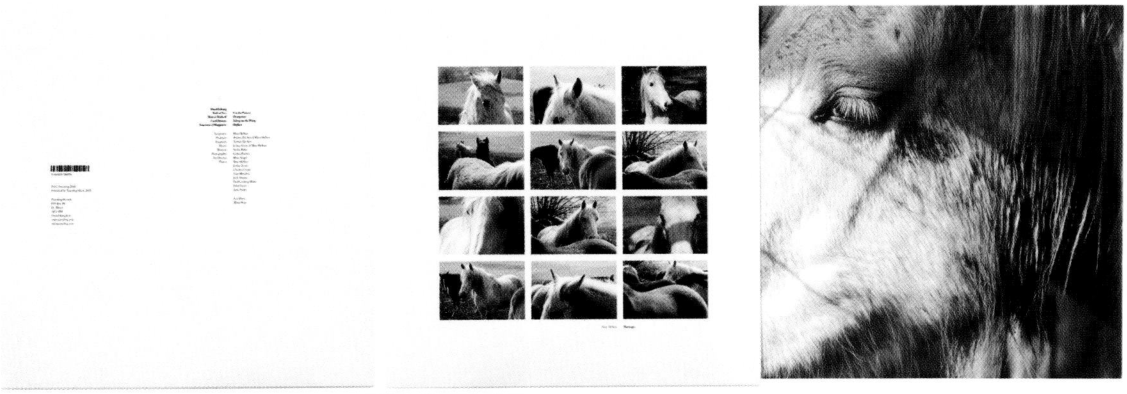

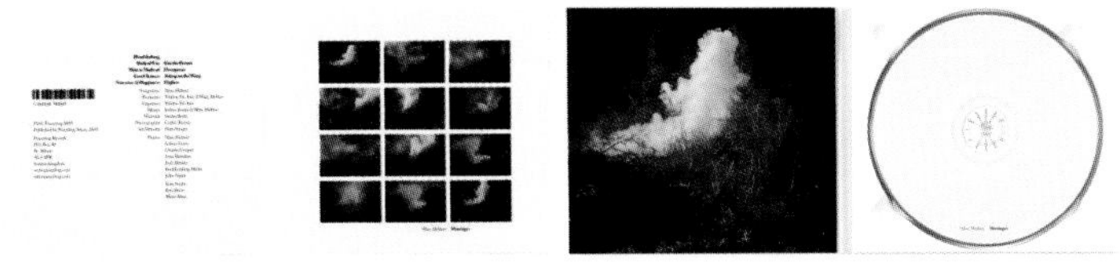

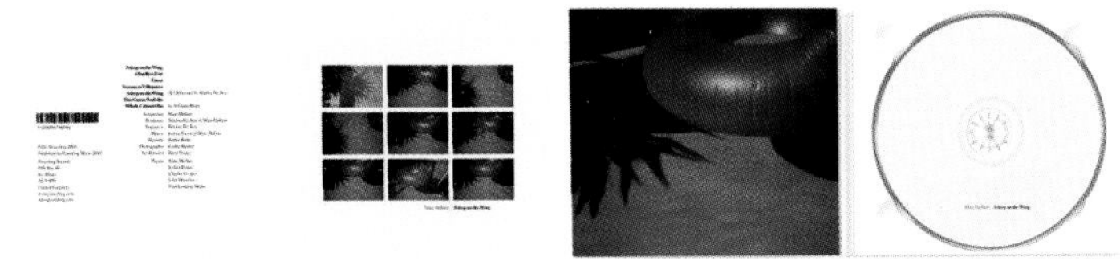

MERIT

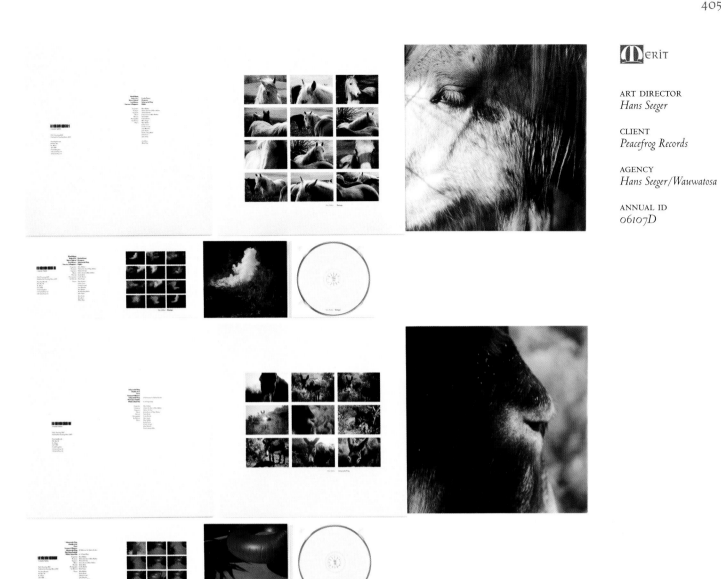

ART DIRECTOR
Hans Seeger

CLIENT
Peacefrog Records

AGENCY
Hans Seeger/Wauwatosa

ANNUAL ID
06107D

MERIT

ART DIRECTOR
Sara Sandstrom

WRITER
Emma Zetterholm

CREATIVE DIRECTOR
Anders Kornestedt

CLIENT
Triumfglass

AGENCY
Happy Forsman & Bodenfors/Gothenburg

ANNUAL ID
06108D

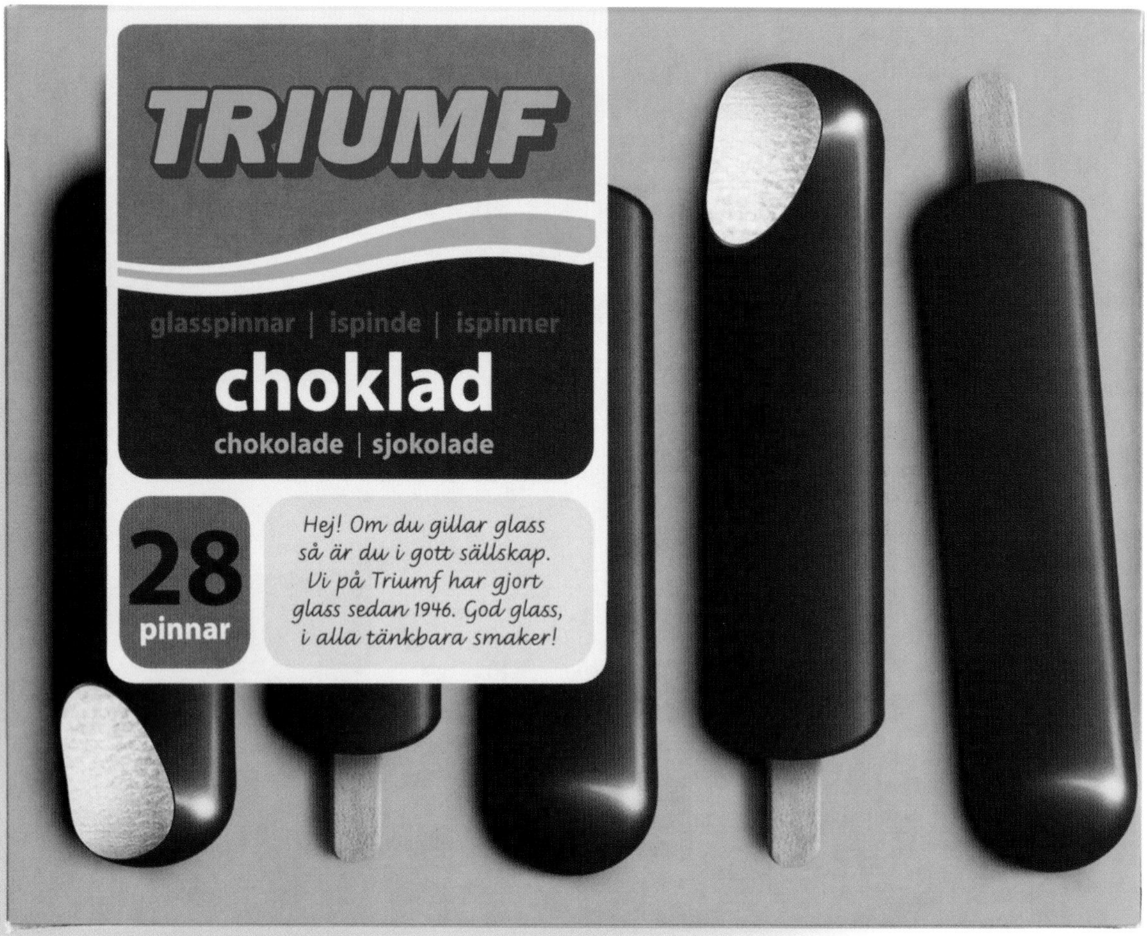
TRIUMF
glasspinnar | ispinde | ispinner
choklad
chokolade | sjokolade
28
pinnar
Hej! Om du gillar glass så är du i gott sällskap. Vi på Triumf har gjort glass sedan 1946. God glass, i alla tänkbara smaker!

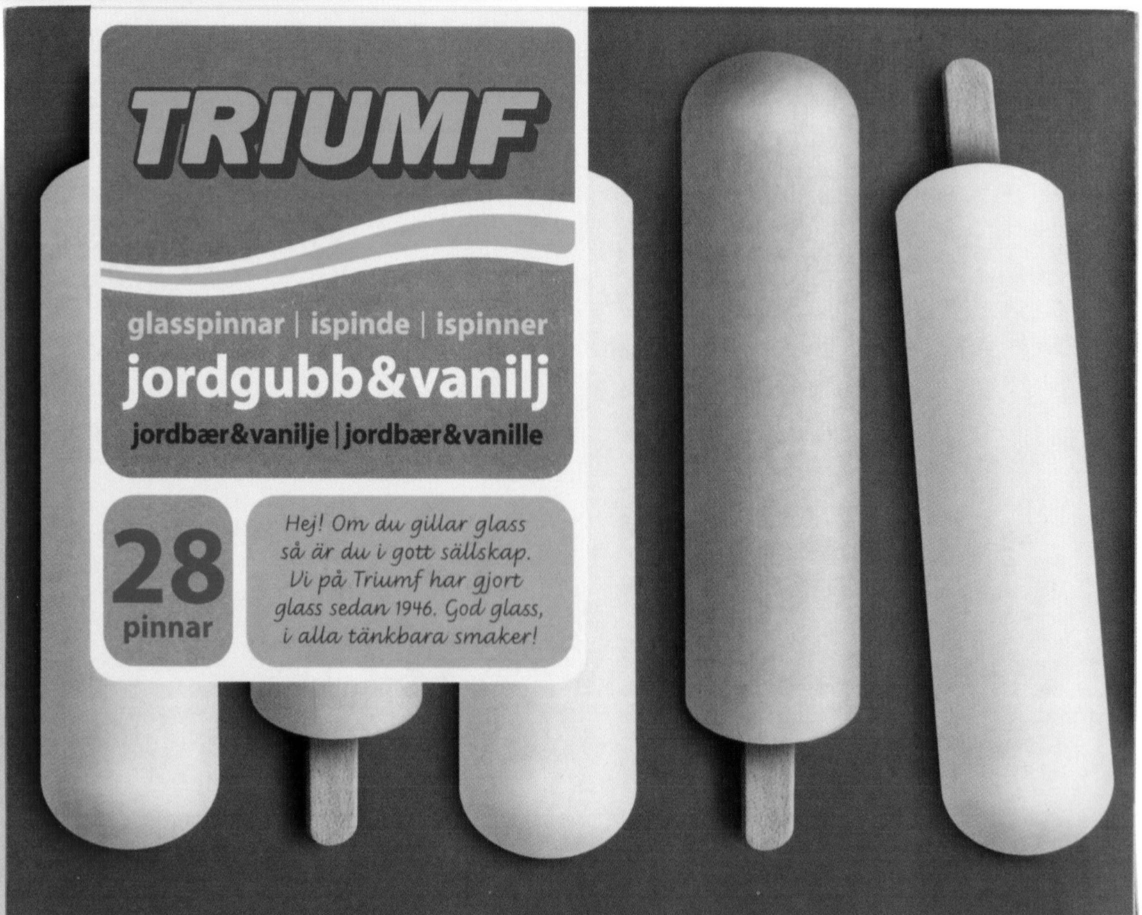
TRIUMF
glasspinnar | ispinde | ispinner
jordgubb&vanilj
jordbær&vanilje | jordbær&vanille
28
pinnar
Hej! Om du gillar glass så är du i gott sällskap. Vi på Triumf har gjort glass sedan 1946. God glass, i alla tänkbara smaker!

Your Vehicle
JUST APPRECIATED
IN VALUE.
WHATABURGER
SINCE 1950
THERE'S ONE NEAR YOU

Merit

ART DIRECTOR
Michael Anderson

WRITER
Brooks Jackson

CREATIVE DIRECTOR
James Mikus

CLIENT
Whataburger

AGENCY
McGarrah/Jessee/Austin

ANNUAL ID
06109D

WAITING
FOR YOUR
Burger
IS MUCH BETTER THAN
YOUR BURGER WAITING
FOR
You.
WHATABURGER
SINCE 1950
THERE'S ONE NEAR YOU
Rarely
DO THE FRIES
MAKE IT ALL
THE WAY HOME.
WHATABURGER
SINCE 1950
THERE'S ONE NEAR YOU

MERIT

BARK MULCH
ORGANIC AND NUTRITIOUS
TOP SOIL
FERTILE AND NUTRITIOUS
OREGON GARDEN
STEER MA
MUSHROOM
PLANT
GARDEN COMPOST
BALANCED AND NUTRITIOUS
PREMIUM ORGANIC COMPOST
AGED 100 DAYS (AT LEAST)
THREEMILE CANYON FARMS

DESIGNERS
Marc Cozza
Brad Engle

ART DIRECTORS
Marc Cozza
Brad Engle

WRITER
Leslee Dillon

ILLUSTRATORS
Marc Cozza
Brad Engle

CREATIVE DIRECTOR
Marc Cozza

CLIENT
Threemile Canyon Farms

AGENCY
Sandstrom Design/Portland

ANNUAL ID
06110D

MERIT

ART DIRECTORS
Masaya Maruta
Ryoko Nagamatsu

WRITER
Soichiro Suzuki

PHOTOGRAPHER
Minoru Mitsui

CREATIVE DIRECTOR
Jiro Akefuji

CLIENT
Mercian

AGENCY
Tokyu Agency/Tokyo

ANNUAL ID
06111D

Drink generously
heavenly
Devilishly Good Red
Cielo e Terra,
Valpolicella 2003
13.5% vol 75cl
Drink generously
Drink generously
Drink generously

MERIT

DESIGNER
Sam Lachlan

CREATIVE DIRECTORS
David Turner
Bruce Duckworth

CLIENT
Heavenly Marketing

AGENCY
Turner Duckworth/
San Francisco

ANNUAL ID
06112D

heavenly™
Remain standing...
THIS WAY UP
...Drink responsibly
Avoid feeling...
FRAGILE
...Drink responsibly
Drink generously
100% heavenly

MERIT

DESIGNERS
Christian Eager
Paula Talford
Mike Harris
Charlotte Barres

CREATIVE DIRECTORS
David Turner
Bruce Duckworth

CLIENT
Homebase Stores

AGENCY
Turner Duckworth/
San Francisco

ANNUAL ID
06113D

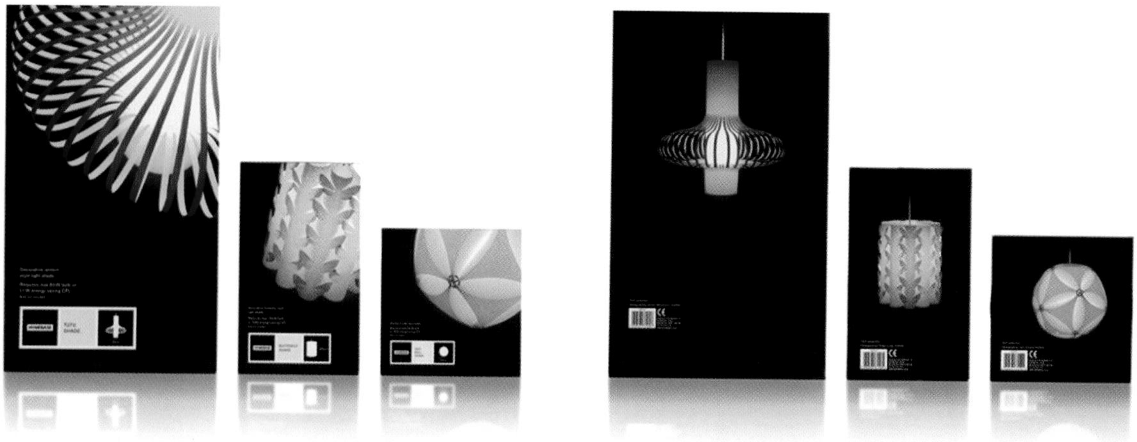

non stick
non stick
non stick

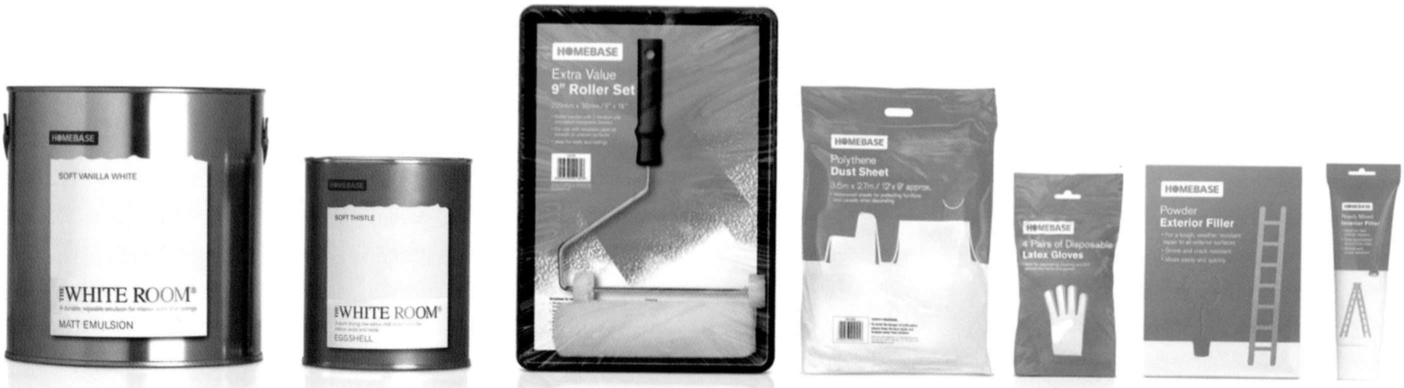
HOMEBASE
SOFT VANILLA WHITE
THE WHITE ROOM®
MATT EMULSION
SOFT THISTLE
THE WHITE ROOM®
EGGSHELL
HOMEBASE
Extra Value
9" Roller Set
HOMEBASE
Polythene
Dust Sheet
HOMEBASE
4 Pairs of Disposable
Latex Gloves
HOMEBASE
Powder
Exterior Filler

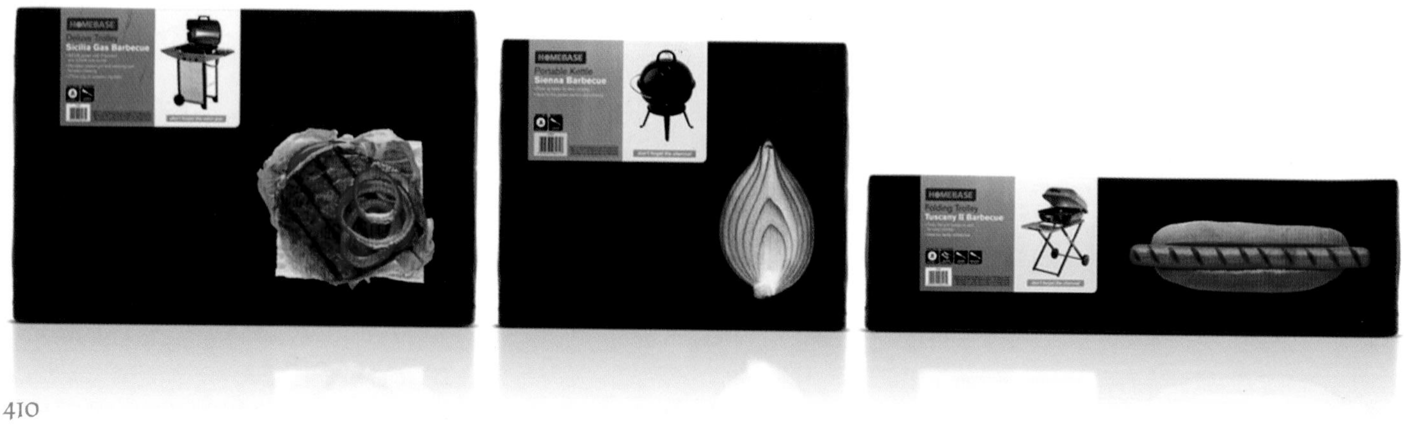
HOMEBASE
Sicilia Gas Barbecue
HOMEBASE
Portable Kettle
Sienna Barbecue
HOMEBASE
Folding Trolley
Tuscany II Barbecue

Red-breasted Snipe and the GEnx Jet Engine
Lessus Pollutantus
The cleaner GEnx aircraft engine. Just one way ecomagination is creating a better world.
imagination at work

MERIT

ART DIRECTOR
Jean Robaire

WRITER
Kara Goodrich

ILLUSTRATORS
John James Audubon
John Perlock

CREATIVE DIRECTORS
Don Schneider
David Lubars

CLIENT
GE

AGENCY
BBDO/New York

ANNUAL ID
06117D

SWISS
NIGHT
SWISS-AMERICAN
SOCIETY OF PITTSBURGH
ANNUAL SWISS NIGHT
DINNER AND FUND RAISER
SUNDAY APRIL 24, 2005
TIME: 5:00-12:00
TEUTONIA MÄNNERCHOR
FOR RESERVATIONS
CALL 724.869.3961

MERIT

DESIGNER
Dave Vissat

CREATIVE DIRECTORS
Dave Kwasnick
Jay Giesen

CLIENT
Swiss-American Society of Pittsburgh

AGENCY
Blattner Brunner/ Pittsburgh

ANNUAL ID
06114D

MERIT

DESIGNER
Jagjit Singh

ART DIRECTOR
Prasad Raghavan

WRITER
Emmanuel Upputuru

CREATIVE DIRECTORS
Ramesh Narayanaswamy
Emmanuel Upputuru

CLIENT
A:Door

AGENCY
Ogilvy & Mather/
New Delhi

ANNUAL ID
06119D

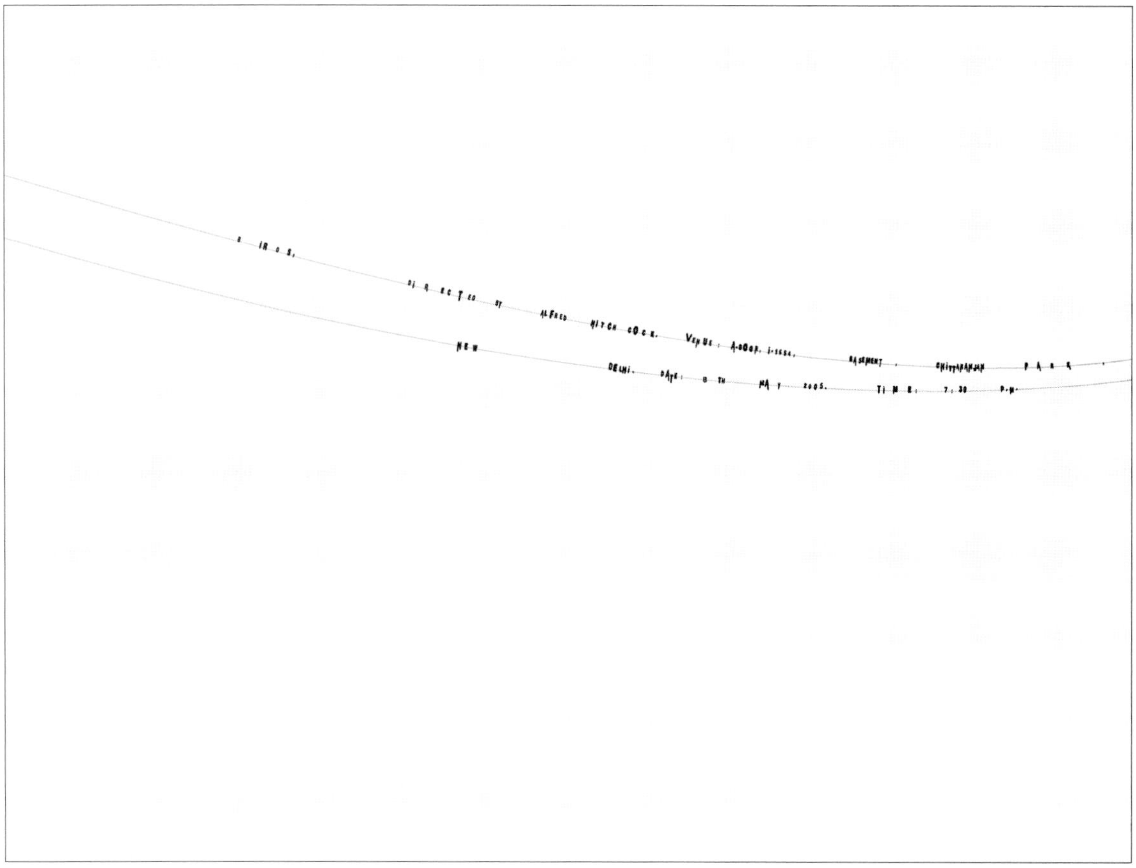
DIRECTED BY ALFRED HITCHCOCK.
NEW DELHI.
TIME: 7:30 P.M.

MERIT

DESIGNER
Dan Richards

CREATIVE DIRECTORS
Dan Richards
Michael Verdine

CLIENT
ESPN

AGENCY
Opolis/Portland

ANNUAL ID
06120D

IT'S THE
YEAR OF THE:
A. HORSE
B. TIGER
C. LEFTY
D. ROCKET
E. BODE
F. 49 TD PASSES
G. LADY BEARS
H. MANNINGS
I. HEELS
J. YELLOW BRACELET
K. LOCKOUT
L. 262 HITS
M. TROJANS
N. SUMMITT
O. RUSSIAN BEAUTY
P. TELL-ALL
Q. BLOODY SOCK
R. 8 GOLDS
S. SISTERS
T. NATIONALS
U. DYNASTY
V. JUICE
W. BIG BEN
X. 97 CAR
Y. UNDERDOG
Z. UNCURSED
AA. LAMBEAU MOON
BB. 700TH HOMER
CC. SWISS NETTER
DD. BIG UNIT
EE. BIRDIE ON 16
FF. SERIES SWEEP
FOR CORRECT ANSWERS
WATCH SUNDAY, JULY 17 9PM ET ESPN
ESPY AWARDS
KODAK THEATRE - HOLLYWOOD, CA

HAPPY HAPPY NEW YEAR! HAPPY HAPPY NEW YEAR! HAPPY HAPPY NEW YEAR! HAPPY HAPPY NEW YEAR!
2005 NEW YEAR SALE
2005.1/4tue.START LAST SALE.50%OFF
EVE GROUP CO.,LTD. ROUEN VIA LUISA GALAXY FIA DONNE
Neil Barrett John Galliano MARNI STELLA McCARTNEY DOLCE & GABBANA JILSANDER
HELMUT LANG BALENCIAGA ADAM JONES ERMANNO SCERVINO VALENTINO DSQUARED²
DOLCE & GABBANA JILSANDER DRIES VAN NOTEN HELMUT LANG BALENCIAGA ADAM JONES
miu miu D&G CIVIDINI L.G.B. SARTORE Chloé RENA LANGE ANN-LOUISE ROSWALD catherine malandrino
ERMANNO SCERVINO VALENTINO DSQUARED² miu miu D&G CIVIDINI L.G.B. SARTORE
McCARTNEY DOLCE & GABBANA JILSANDER DRIES VAN NOTEN HELMUT LANG BALENC
本年モ皆様ニ「福」来タレ。「服」着タレ。

MERIT

ART DIRECTOR
Kazuto Nakamura

CLIENT
Eve Group

AGENCY
Penguin Graphics/ Hiroshima

ANNUAL ID
06121D

Nice to meat you.
HANA MOTO
cresson
HANAMOTO

MERIT

DESIGNER
Kazuto Nakamura

ART DIRECTOR
Kazuto Nakamura

WRITER
Tomiko Nakamura

ILLUSTRATOR
Tomiko Nakamura

CREATIVE DIRECTOR
Kazuto Nakamura

CLIENT
Hanamoto

AGENCY
Penguin Graphics/ Hiroshima

ANNUAL ID
06122D

MERIT

DESIGNERS
Dan Solen
Lindsay Rabe

WRITER
Kyle Snarr

CLIENT
AIGA Salt Lake Chapter

AGENCY
Struck Design/
Salt Lake City

ANNUAL ID
06123D

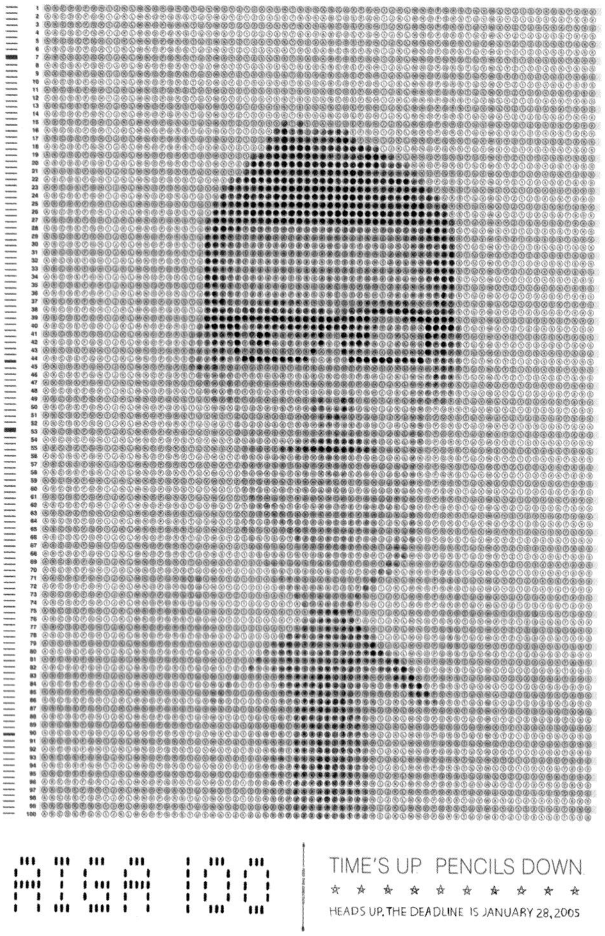
AIGA 100
TIME'S UP PENCILS DOWN
HEADS UP. THE DEADLINE IS JANUARY 28, 2005

MERIT

ART DIRECTOR
Sachin Ambekar

WRITER
Parag Tembulkar

PHOTOGRAPHER
Charles Chua

ILLUSTRATOR
Rhypsody Digital Art

CREATIVE DIRECTOR
Saad Hussein

CLIENT
Sony PlayStation2

AGENCY
TBWA/Singapore

ANNUAL ID
06124D

PS2
PlayStation 2

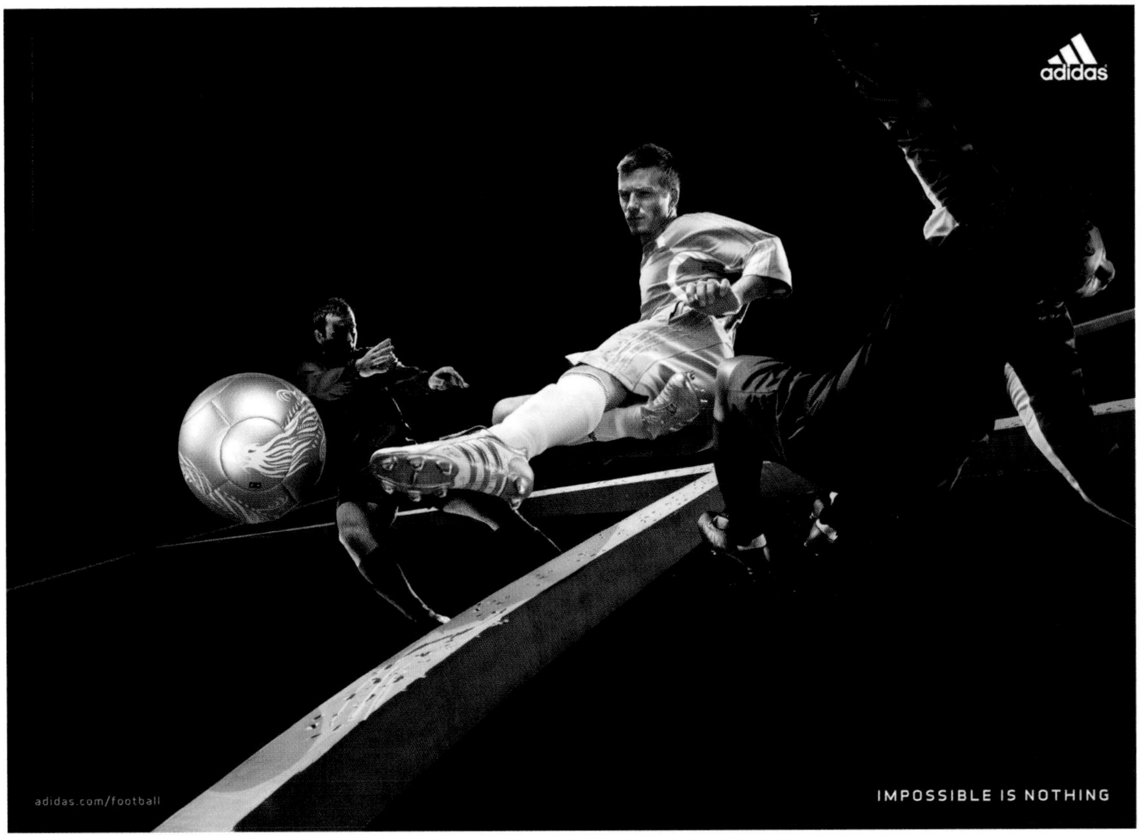
adidas
adidas.com/football
IMPOSSIBLE IS NOTHING

Merit

ART DIRECTOR
Dean Maryon

WRITER
Ben Abramowitz

PHOTOGRAPHER
Tom van Heel

CREATIVE DIRECTORS
Andy Fackrell
Dean Maryon

CLIENT
adidas

AGENCY
180 Amsterdam
(180\TBWA)

ANNUAL ID
06125D

adidas
IMPOSSIBLE IS NOTHING

adidas
IMPOSSIBLE IS NOTHING

adidas
IMPOSSIBLE IS NOTHING

adidas
IMPOSSIBLE IS NOTHING

Merit

ART DIRECTOR
Sissy Estes

WRITER
Ken Marcus

ILLUSTRATOR
Michael Schwab

CREATIVE DIRECTORS
Ron Lawner
Woody Kay
Fred Burgos

CLIENT
Amtrak

AGENCY
Arnold/McLean

ANNUAL ID
06126D

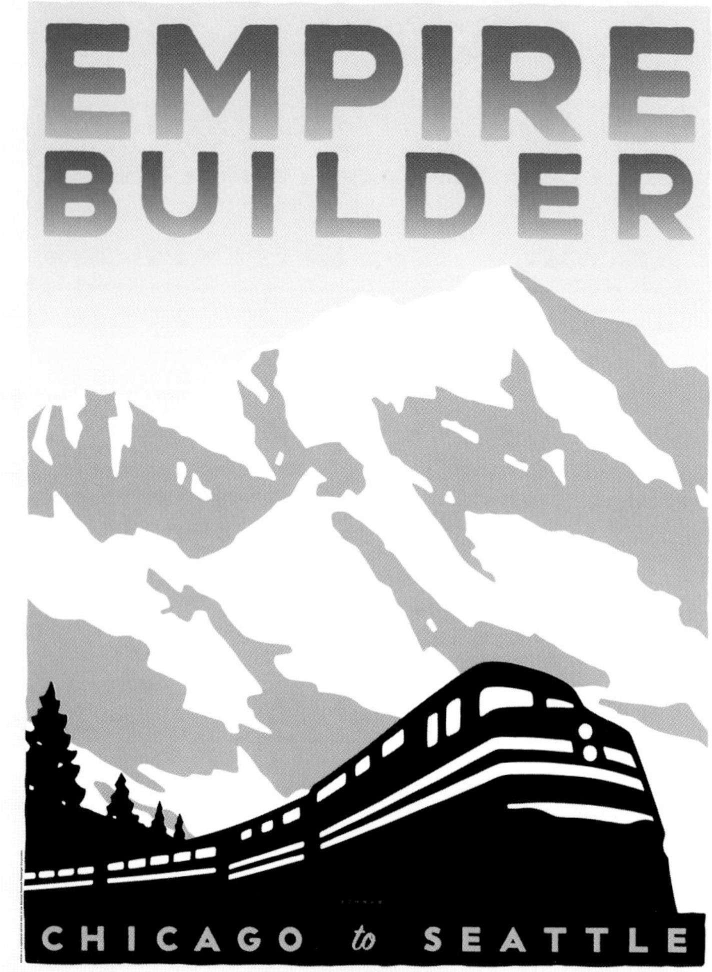
EMPIRE BUILDER
CHICAGO to SEATTLE

SILVER STAR
NEW YORK CITY to MIAMI

CAPITOL LIMITED
WASHINGTON, DC to CHICAGO

Stay in tune. Drink with care.
TENNESSEE
WHISKEY
OLD TIME

Merit

DESIGNER
Corey Favier

ART DIRECTOR
Corey Favier

WRITER
Greg Vogler

PHOTOGRAPHER
Jay Baker

CREATIVE DIRECTOR
Mark Ray

CLIENT
Jack Daniel's Tennessee Whiskey

AGENCY
Arnold/St. Louis

ANNUAL ID
06127D

WHIS
DISTILLED AND B
JACK DANIEL D
LEM MOTLOW, PR
LYNCHBURG (POP. 361)
40% ALC BY VOL. (80 PR
Stay in tune. Drink with care.

Tennessee
WHISK
Stay in tune. Drink with care.

MERIT

DESIGNERS
Bel Ong
Jeanna Seow

CREATIVE DIRECTOR
Christopher Lee

CLIENT
Asylum

AGENCY
Asylum Creative/
Singapore

ANNUAL ID
06128D

The Dinner Party

The Dinner Party
An exhibition on salvaged furniture by Asylum and friends. From 16th - 30th Nov 2005, Asylum, 22 Ann Siang Road
www.theasylum.com.sg

The Dinner Party

Merit

ART DIRECTOR
James Clunie

WRITER
Tim Cawley

CREATIVE DIRECTOR
David Lubars

CLIENT
Dexter Russell

AGENCY
BBDO/New York

ANNUAL ID
06134D

ALSO AWARDED
Merit:
Collateral Design:
Posters - Single

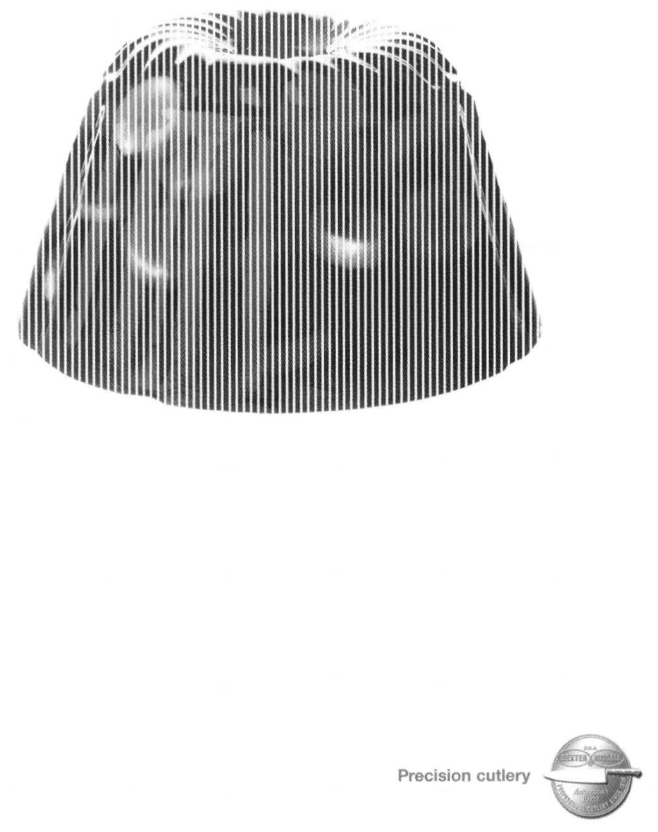
Precision cutlery

Merit

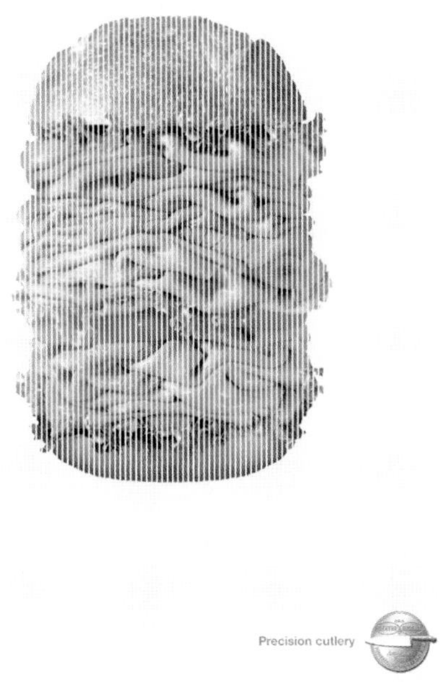
Precision cutlery

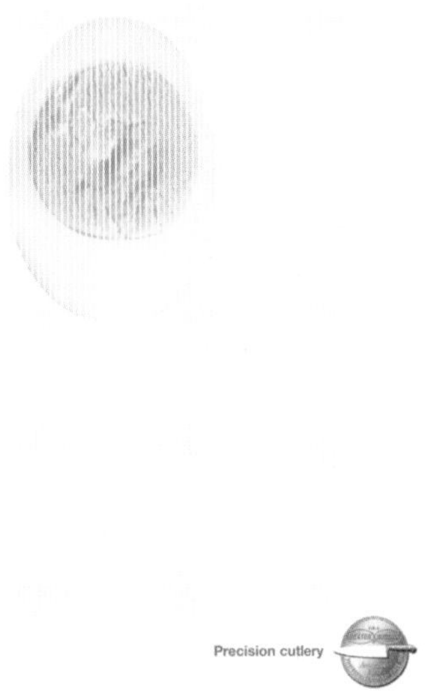
Precision cutlery

MERIT

DESIGNERS
Sven Gareis
Tang Kee Hong
Alex Lim Thye Aun

ART DIRECTOR
Alex Lim Thye Aun

WRITER
Farrokh Madon

PHOTOGRAPHER
Jeremy Wong

ILLUSTRATOR
Raul

CREATIVE DIRECTORS
Francis Wee
Farrokh Madon
Alex Lim Thye Aun

CLIENT
W.S. Papers

AGENCY
BBDO/Singapore

ANNUAL ID
06129D

conqueror
white paper

conqueror
white paper

conqueror
white paper

2005 MINNESOTA
fringe
AUG. 4-14
fringefestival.org
GET TICKETS: @ THE DOOR OR IN ADVANCE
UPTOWN TICKETS
651-209-6799
UPTOWNTIX.COM
BUENO
LIVE
Romance
NAUGHTY
Mind Blown
SPICY
CULT-TURE
MIS-ADVENTUROUS
fresh
No Strings
HEARTS ON FIRE
Swerving
Budding Minds
ELECTRIC

MINNESOTA
fringe
AUG. 4-14 2005
WRITE IN THE NAME, DATE & TIME OF ANY FRINGE EVENT
PRINTED PROGRAM AVAILABLE IN CITYPAGES THE AUG. 3RD
fringefestival.org
CALIENTE
I ♥ DRAMA
manic
good VIBES
SEE NO EVIL
TICKETS: @ THE DOOR OR IN ADVANCE
UPTOWN TICKETS
651-209-6799
UPTOWNTIX.COM
COMEDY 1*
LIVE
Romance
Flavor Savior
SUPER fresh
100% SNORE PROOF
lucygoosey

MINNESOTA
fringe
05
VISUAL ARTS
KIDS SHOWS ★ SPOKEN WORD ★ & MORE
THEATER ★ MUSIC ★ DANCE
August 4-14
fringefestival.org
COMEDY 1*
I ♥ DRAMA
TICKETS: @ THE DOOR OR IN ADVANCE
UPTOWN TICKETS
651-209-6799
UPTOWNTIX.COM
ON THE LIPS
CALIENTE
SWEET
TAKING YOU HIGHER
good VIBES
LOUD
Flavor Savior

Merit

Merit

DESIGNER
Steve Jockisch

WRITER
Jonathan Graham

CREATIVE DIRECTOR
Bill Thorburn

CLIENT
Fringe Festival

AGENCY
Carmichael Lynch Thorburn/Minneapolis

ANNUAL ID
06130D

ALSO AWARDED
Merit: Collateral Design: Posters - Single

MERIT

DESIGNERS
Naomi Sakamoto
Chihiro Hane

ART DIRECTOR
Tatsuo Ebina

WRITERS
Takehiko Iwasaki
Hitoshi Ono

PHOTOGRAPHER
Tadashi Tonomo

CREATIVE DIRECTORS
Takehiko Iwasaki
Yoshinori Tanaka

CLIENT
Miwa Lock

AGENCY
E.Co./Tokyo

ANNUAL ID
06131D

MIWA

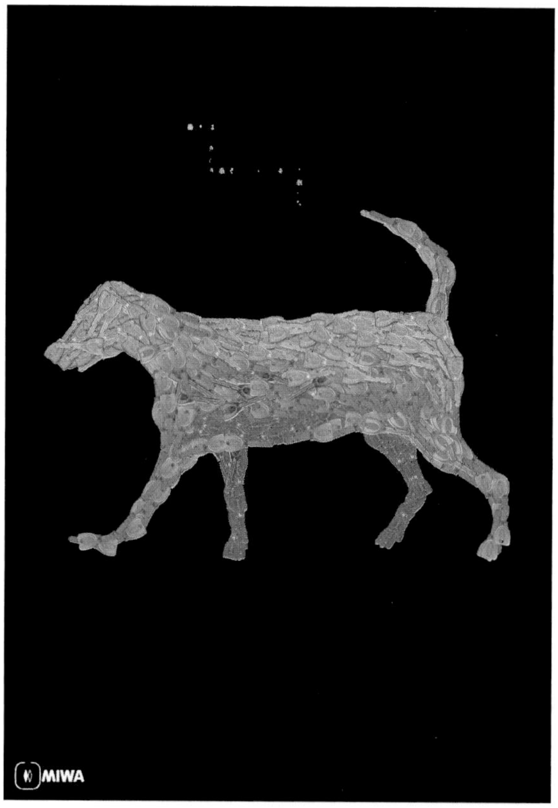
MIWA

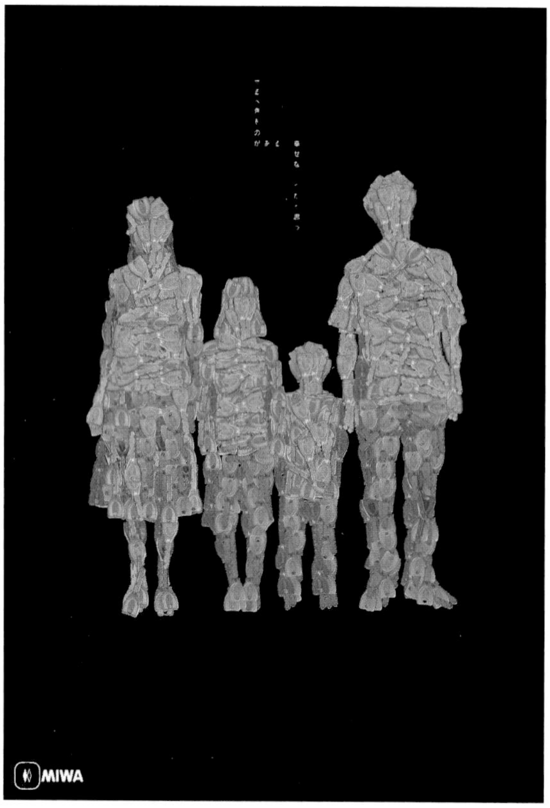
MIWA

MIWA

NORDSTROM
SILVERSCREEN
"I'LL TUMBLE 4 YA"
CULTURE CLUB
MUSIC REMIX BY JXL • VIDEO REMIX BY OLIVIER GONDRY
DECEMBER 2005 RELEASE

NORDSTROM
SILVERSCREEN
CULTURE CLUB "I'LL TUMBLE 4 YA"
MUSIC REMIX BY JXL · VIDEO REMIX BY OLIVIER GONDRY
• DECEMBER 2005 RELEASE •

THE
GO-GO'S
"OUR LIPS ARE SEALED"
MUSIC REMIX BY FATBOY SLIM
VIDEO REMIX BY OLIVIER GONDRY
NORDSTROM
SILVERSCREEN
NOVEMBER 2005 RELEASE

The
GO-GO'S
"OUR LIPS ARE SEALED"
MUSIC REMIX BY FATBOY SLIM • VIDEO REMIX BY OLIVIER GONDRY
NORDSTROM
SILVERSCREEN
November 2005
RELEASE

the
go-go's
"OuR Lips ArE sEaLEd"
SILVERSCREEN

MERIT

DESIGNERS
Anchalee Chambundabongse
Mary Lam
Dan Broad
Aesthetic Apparatus

CREATIVE DIRECTORS
Paul Silburn
Susan Treacy

CLIENT
Nordstrom

AGENCY
Fallon/Minneapolis

ANNUAL ID
06132D

Merit

ART DIRECTOR
Brett Stiles

WRITER
Chad Berry

ILLUSTRATOR
Brett Stiles

CREATIVE DIRECTORS
David Crawford
Luke Sullivan

CLIENT
American Legacy Foundation

AGENCY
GSD&M/Austin

ANNUAL ID
06133D

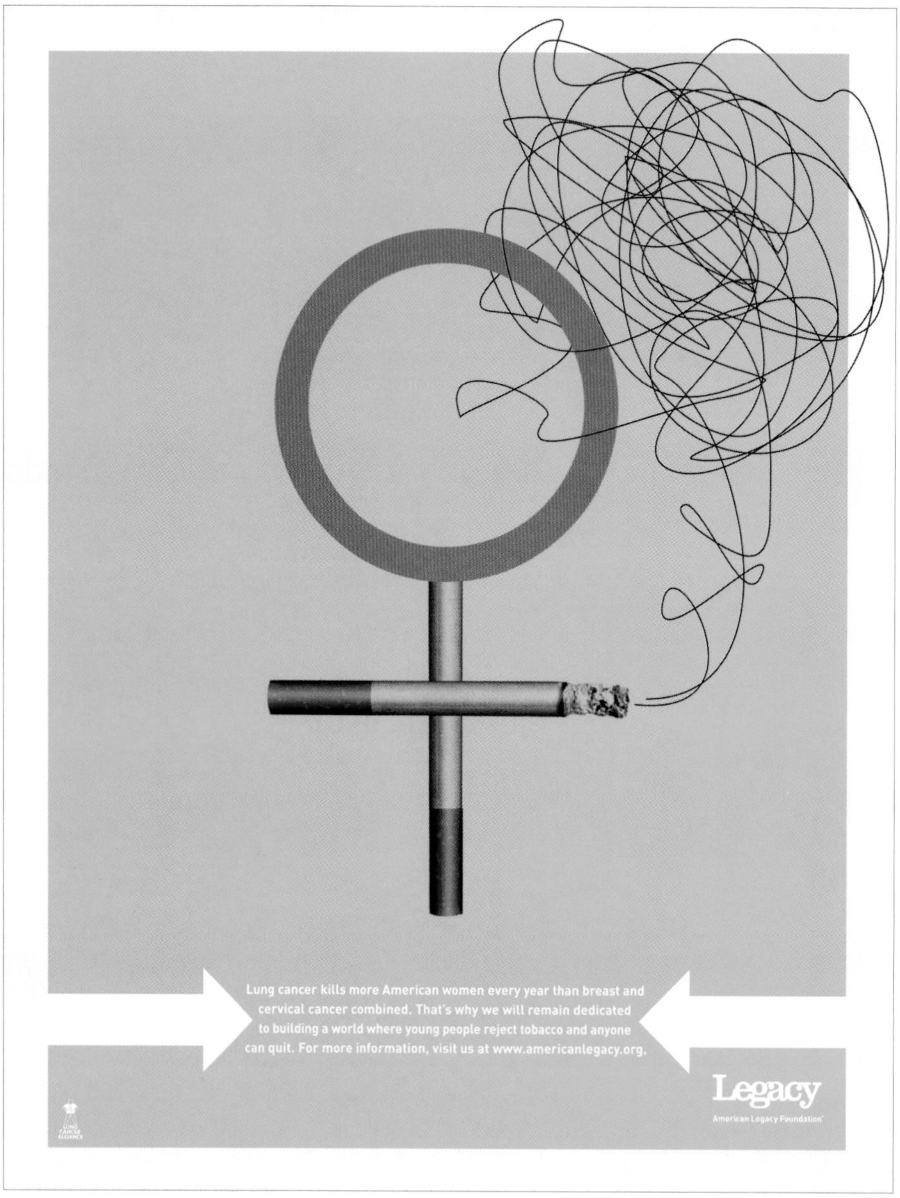
Lung cancer kills more American women every year than breast and cervical cancer combined. That's why we will remain dedicated to building a world where young people reject tobacco and anyone can quit. For more information, visit us at www.americanlegacy.org.
Legacy
American Legacy Foundation

Studies show that girls may develop symptoms of nicotine dependence more quickly than boys. That's why we are dedicated to building a world where young people reject tobacco and anyone can quit. For more information, visit our website at www.americanlegacy.org.
Legacy

Each day two thousand teenagers become trapped by a deadly addiction that kills over 400,000 people a year—cigarettes. That's why we will remain dedicated to building a world where young people reject tobacco and anyone can quit. To find out more, visit us at www.americanlegacy.org.
Legacy
American Legacy Foundation

DIAL 9
OR
YELL FOR THE MAID
MRS. KAPUR'S GUESTHOUSE
A home away from home. No, really!
+91 11 51642790

A sob story
will always get you
a discount.
MRS. KAPUR'S GUEST HOUSE
A home away from home. No, really!
+91 11 51642790

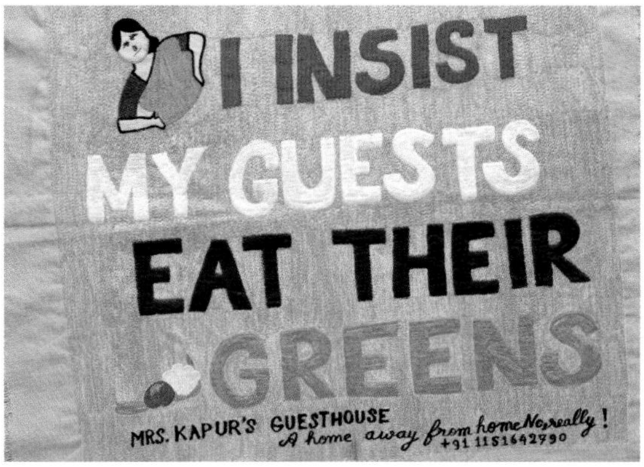
I INSIST
MY GUESTS
EAT THEIR
GREENS
MRS. KAPUR'S GUESTHOUSE
A home away from home No, really!
+91 1151642790

Of course there's housekeeping
But don't you think
you're old enough to make your own bed?
MRS. KAPUR'S GUESTHOUSE
A HOME AWAY FROM HOME
NO, REALLY

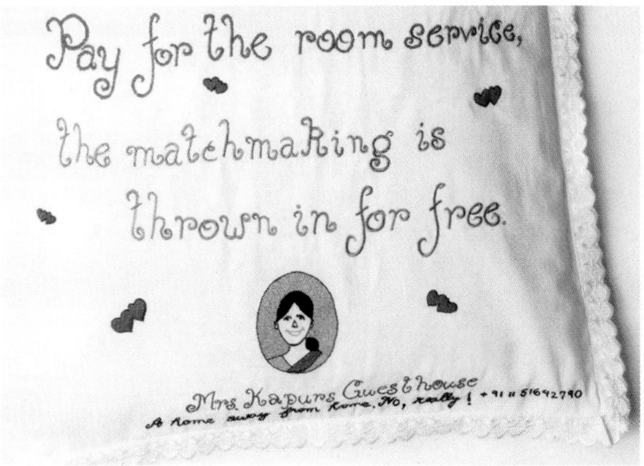
Pay for the room service,
the matchmaking is
thrown in for free.
Mrs Kapurs Guesthouse
+91 11 51642790
A home away from home. No, really!

MERIT

ART DIRECTOR
Pooja Trehan Theeng

WRITER
Radhika Kapur

PHOTOGRAPHER
Pankaj Arora

ILLUSTRATOR
Pooja Trehan Theeng

CREATIVE DIRECTORS
Rupam Borah
Santosh Padhi

CLIENT
Mrs. Kapoor Guest House

AGENCY
Leo Burnett/Mumbai

ANNUAL ID
06136D

Merit

ART DIRECTOR
Felipe Massis

WRITER
Alexandre Scaff

PHOTOGRAPHER
Du Ribeiro

CREATIVE DIRECTOR
Ruy Lindenberg

CLIENT
Fiat

AGENCY
Leo Burnett Publicidade/ São Paulo

ANNUAL ID
06137D

You had no idea
that it had
so much space.
Fiat Ducato Cargo
Fiat Ducato

Merit

ART DIRECTOR
Felipe Massis

WRITER
Alexandre Scaff

PHOTOGRAPHER
Du Ribeiro

CREATIVE DIRECTOR
Ruy Lindenberg

CLIENT
Fiat

AGENCY
Leo Burnett Publicidade/ São Paulo

ANNUAL ID
06138D

You had no idea
that it had
so much space.
Fiat Ducato Cargo
OFERTA
Fiat Ducato

MERIT

ART DIRECTOR
Walter Teoh

WRITER
Ivan Yeo

PHOTOGRAPHER
Kenny of DL Studio

CREATIVE DIRECTORS
Alex Lim
Chan Lee Shon
Ali Ahmad
Yasmin Ahmad

CLIENT
Kinokuniya Bookstore

AGENCY
Leo Burnett/
Kuala Lumpur

ANNUAL ID
06139D

MERIT

ART DIRECTORS
Graham Lamont
Vanessa Gibson

WRITER
Fran Luckin

CREATIVE DIRECTORS
Graham Lamont
Gerry Human

CLIENT
Exclusive Books

AGENCY
Ogilvy South Africa/
Johannesburg

ANNUAL ID
06140D

Merit

ART DIRECTOR
Ray Andrade

WRITER
James Robinson

CREATIVE DIRECTORS
Greg Bell
Paul Venables

CLIENT
HBO Home Video OZ Season 5

AGENCY
Venables Bell & Partners/San Francisco

ANNUAL ID
06142D

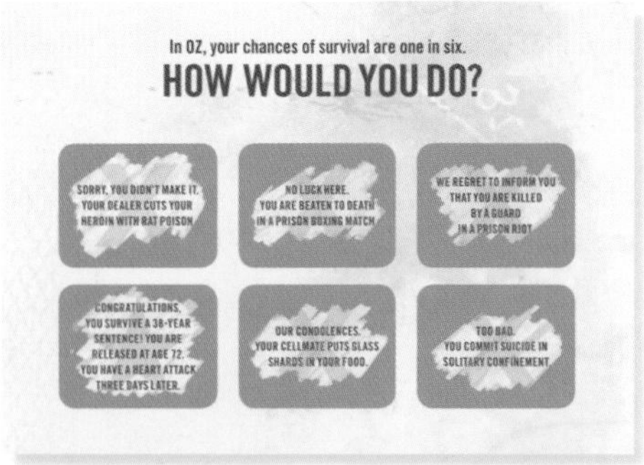
In OZ, your chances of survival are one in six.
HOW WOULD YOU DO?
SORRY, YOU DIDN'T MAKE IT. YOUR DEALER CUTS YOUR HEROIN WITH RAT POISON
NO LUCK HERE. YOU ARE BEATEN TO DEATH IN A PRISON BOXING MATCH
WE REGRET TO INFORM YOU THAT YOU ARE KILLED BY A GUARD IN A PRISON RIOT
CONGRATULATIONS, YOU SURVIVE A 38-YEAR SENTENCE! YOU ARE RELEASED AT AGE 72. YOU HAVE A HEART ATTACK THREE DAYS LATER.
OUR CONDOLENCES. YOUR CELLMATE PUTS GLASS SHARDS IN YOUR FOOD.
TOO BAD. YOU COMMIT SUICIDE IN SOLITARY CONFINEMENT

OZ
THE COMPLETE FIFTH SEASON
EIGHT HOURS OF CHOICES YOU'LL NEVER WANT TO MAKE.
Own The Complete Fifth Season of OZ on DVD.
HBO VIDEO

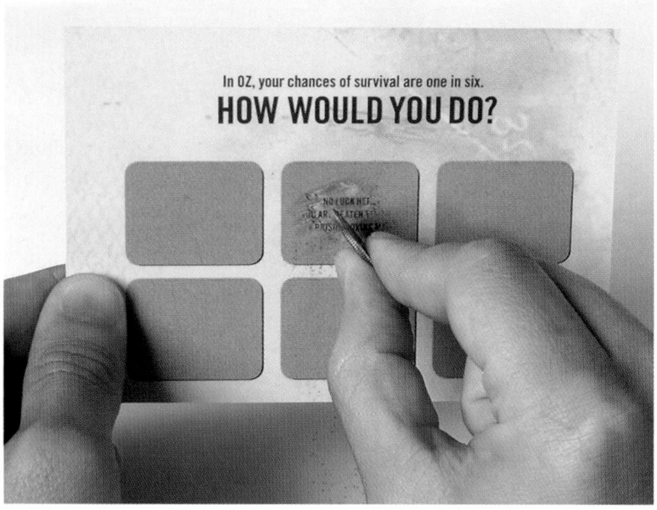
In OZ, your chances of survival are one in six.
HOW WOULD YOU DO?

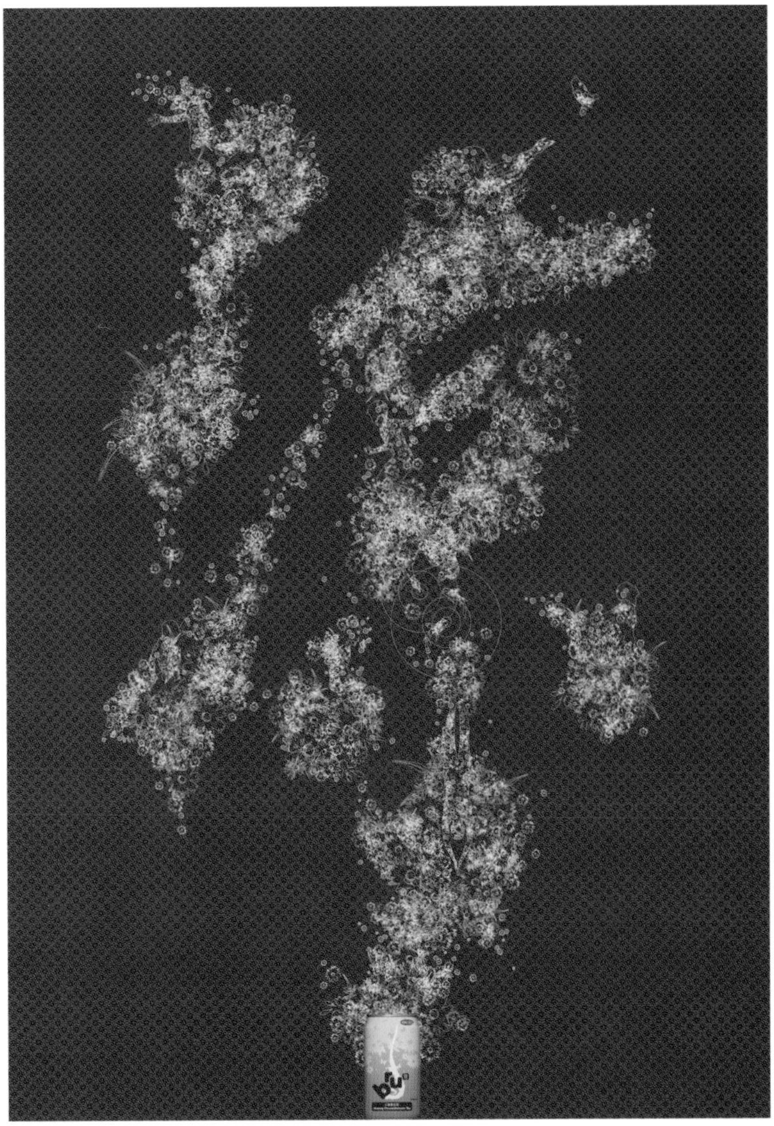

MERIT

ART DIRECTORS
Jonathan Yuen
Roy Poh
Pann Lim

WRITERS
Pann Lim
Roy Poh

PHOTOGRAPHER
Jeremy Wong

CLIENT
Wong Coco

AGENCY
Kinetic/Singapore

ANNUAL ID
06143D

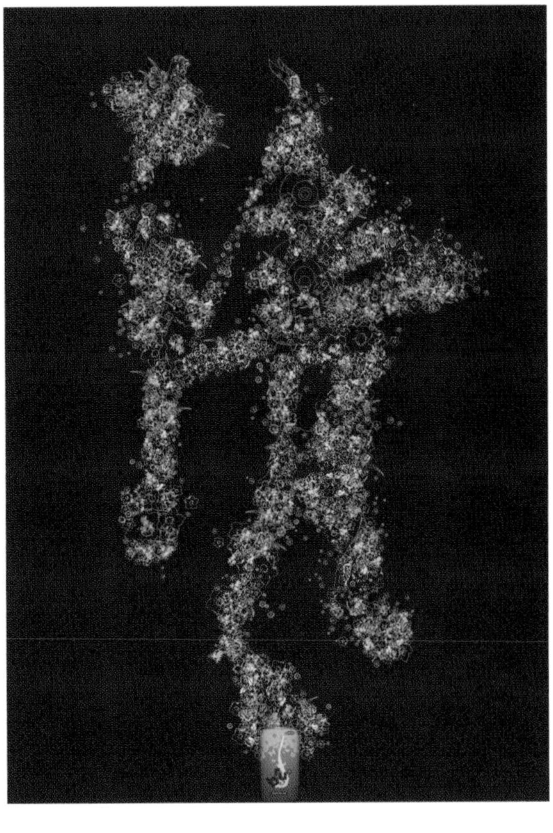

MERIT

ART DIRECTOR
Birger Linke

WRITERS
Audra Tan
Roger Makak

PHOTOGRAPHER
Jean Leprini

CREATIVE DIRECTOR
Andy Greenaway

CLIENT
Weston Corporation - Reebok

AGENCY
Saatchi & Saatchi/ Singapore

ANNUAL ID
06144D

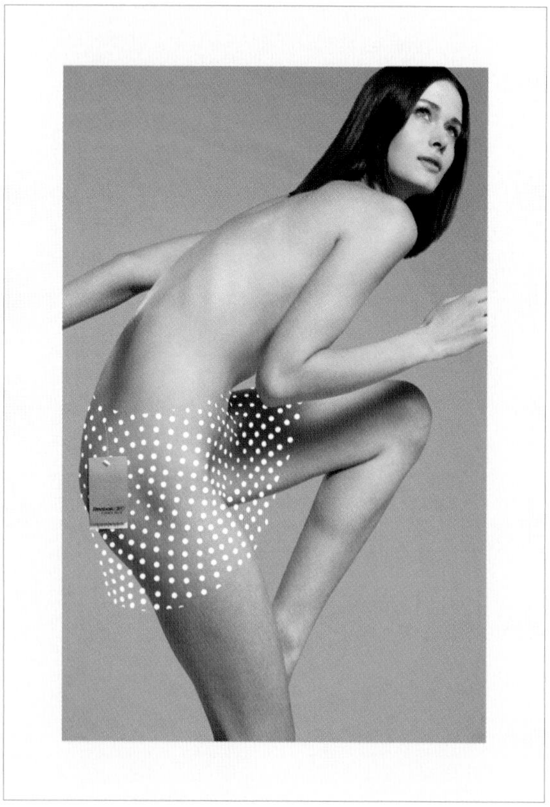

A
B
Hilton
Travel should take you places

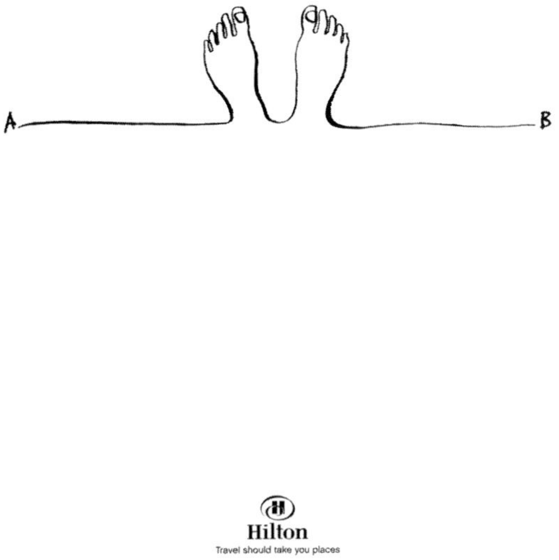
A
B
Hilton
Travel should take you places

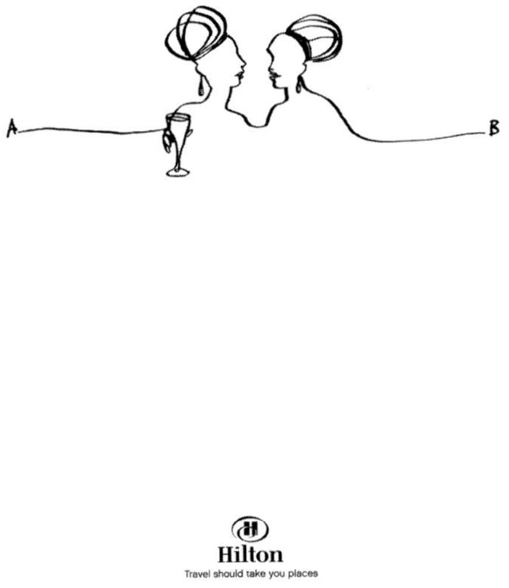
A
B
Hilton
Travel should take you places

A
B
Hilton
Travel should take you places

Merit

ART DIRECTOR
Sonya Grewal

WRITER
Ken Erke

ILLUSTRATOR
Greg Stevenson

CREATIVE DIRECTORS
Ken Erke
Sonya Grewal
Mark Figliulo

CLIENT
Hilton

AGENCY
Young & Rubicam/ Chicago

ANNUAL ID
06145D

Merit

DESIGNERS
Cathy Solarana
Michah Schmiedeskamp
Randall Myers

CREATIVE DIRECTOR
Marty Amsler

CLIENT
Bailey Lauerman

AGENCY
Bailey Lauerman/
Omaha

ANNUAL ID
06146D

MIXER
MIXER

Merit

DESIGNERS
Florian Schoffro
Julia Otten

ART DIRECTORS
Florian Schoffro
Arne Schultchen

CREATIVE DIRECTORS
Arne Schultchen
Andre Feldmann

CLIENT
Feldmann+Schultchen
Design Studios

AGENCY
Feldmann+Schultchen
Design Studios/Hamburg

ANNUAL ID
06147D

DEUTSCHBAND®

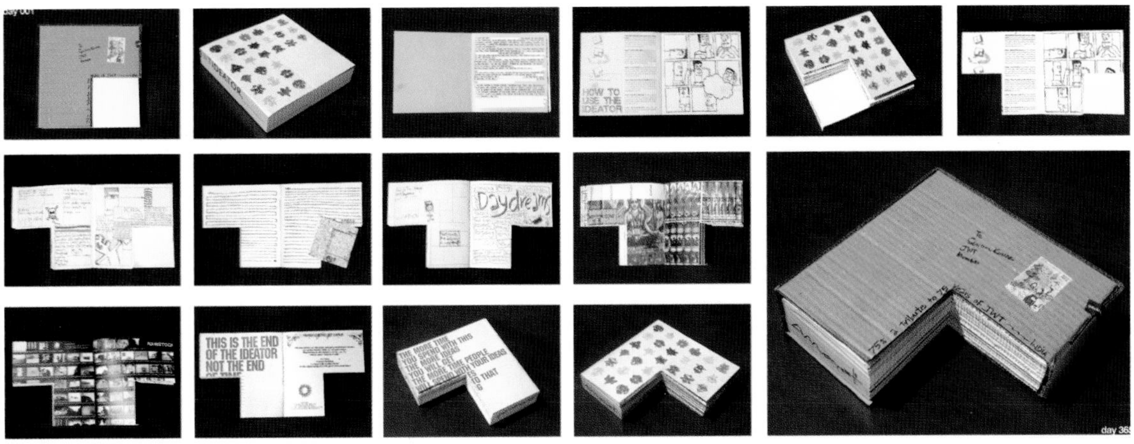
THIS IS THE END
OF THE IDEATOR
NOT THE END

fig A
fig B
fig C
75%
a tribute to 75 years of JWT India
HOW TO USE THE IDEATOR
THE IDEATOR (each one get one on a daily basis): invites you to take the leap into that almost god-like trance, every day. to create something original, a new idea on any of our brands. a new strategy, a new plan, a new business, a new vision, a new whatever. here's how you do it...
step1 - think of the idea :) use 75% of the daily page in the ideator as your scribbling pad. do it on your way to work. do it first thing in the morning. do it on the pot. do it while waiting for a meeting. do it whenever but ensure that you spend a few minutes ideating every day. use the boxes to remind yourself that you have to think out of the box.
step2 - put it down ;) use the blank remaining 25% of the daily page to put the idea down in one line, as a scribble, as a rough layout, as a thought. because every idea, when you first get it, is usually a diamond in the rough.
step3 - write your name on the idea :} become the ideator. take a hard look at your daily quarter. have you filled in something that'll make you proud? if you're sure, put your name on it, cut the corner, fold it or make a rocket of it and put it in the **quarterbox** in your office.
step4 - bite your nails :D the idea is read by colvyn & ramki. they love it. they give you a call. you are rocking. you've just used the official patli gully to the top. expect an instant raise, promotion, even that elusive trip to cannes.
step5 - the execution B-) whatever your idea was, you'll have to lead its execution with unabashed support from everyone.
LET YOUR IDEA SPIN OUT OF THE BOX

MERIT

DESIGNERS
Debu Purkayastha
Senthil Kumar

ART DIRECTORS
Debu Purkayastha
Hital Pandya
Bosky Cherin
Abhay Arekar
Joseph De Souza
Malini Chandrasekar

WRITERS
Senthil Kumar
Arkadyuti Basu
Karan Amin

PHOTOGRAPHERS
Senthil Kumar
Debu Purkayastha

ILLUSTRATORS
Debu Purkayastha
Hital Pandya
Bosky Cherin

CREATIVE DIRECTORS
Debu Purkayastha
Senthil Kumar
Bruce Matchett
Agnello Dias

CLIENT
JWT India

AGENCY
JWT/Mumbai

ANNUAL ID
06148D

MERIT

DESIGNER
Gurdish Kaur

ART DIRECTOR
Gurdish Kaur

WRITER
Nitin Adake

ILLUSTRATOR
Gurdish Kaur

CREATIVE DIRECTOR
Nitin Adake

CLIENT
Latitude 23

AGENCY
Latitude 23 Communications/ New Delhi

ANNUAL ID
06149D

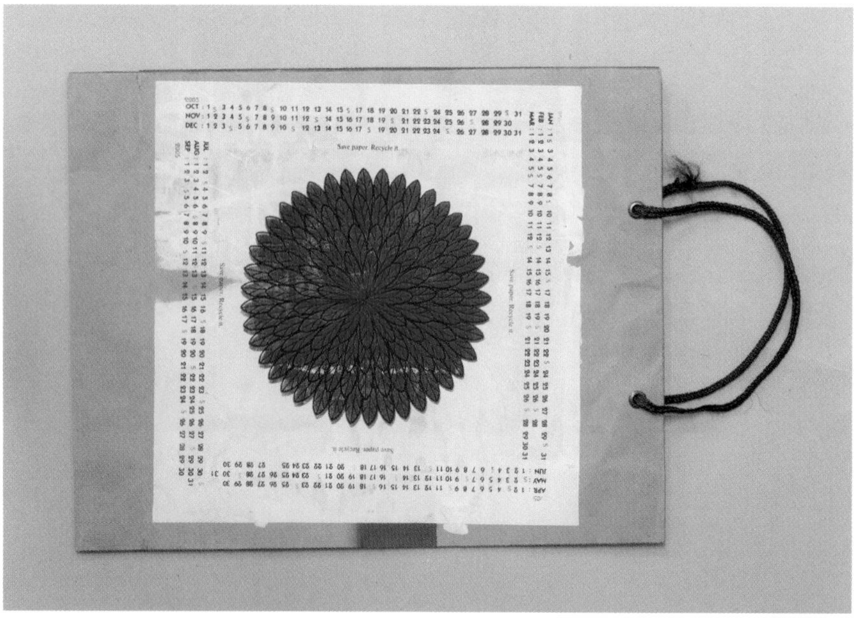
Save paper. Recycle it.

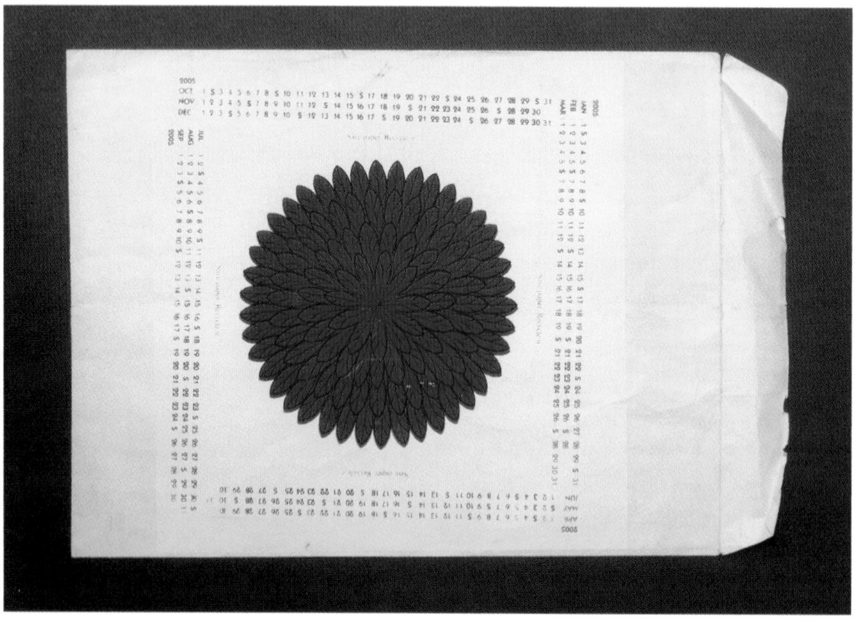

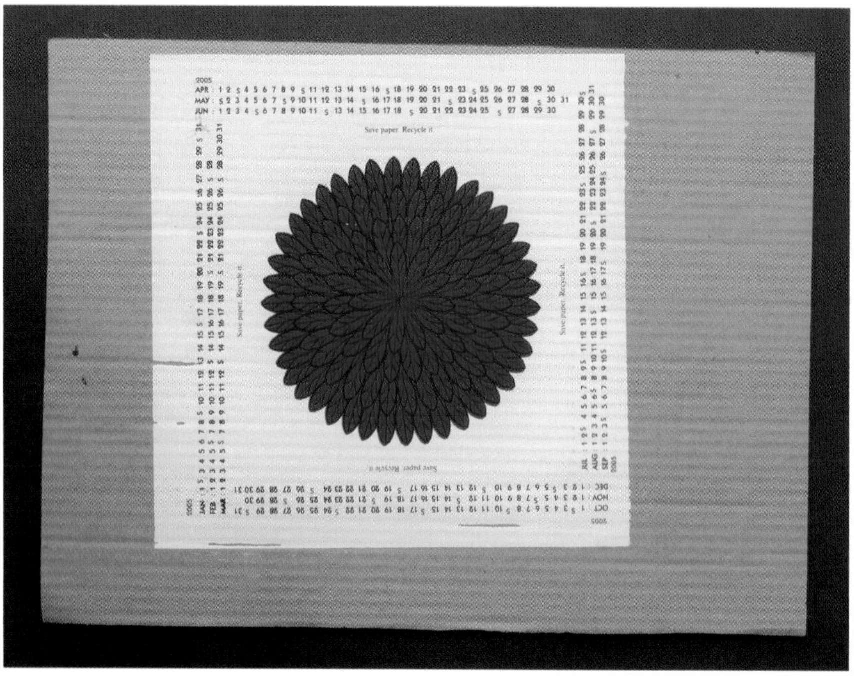
Save paper. Recycle it.

11.06
Pentagram
2006 Typography Calendar
365

MERIT

DESIGNERS
Kit Hinrichs
Jessica Siegel

CLIENT
Pentagram

AGENCY
Pentagram/San Francisco

ANNUAL ID
06150D

Mother's Christmas Gift
THIS CERTIFIES THAT
is the proud owner of one
share of a fully certified greyhound purchased "Just For Christmas"
MOTHER'S CHRISTMAS GIFT
"Just For Christmas" Shareholders' Report
VOL. MMV ISSUE I

MERIT

DESIGNER
Harrimansteel

ART DIRECTOR
Piers North

WRITER
Erik Enberg

CREATIVE DIRECTORS
Robert Saville
Mark Waites

CLIENT
Mother

AGENCY
Mother/London

ANNUAL ID
06151D

Merit

DESIGNERS
Tan Yee Kiang
Chiw Mun Yew

ART DIRECTORS
Tan Yee Kiang
Alvin Teoh
Mun

WRITERS
Raymond Ng
Ted Lim

CREATIVE DIRECTORS
Ted Lim
Alvin Teoh

CLIENT
Naga DDB Malaysia

AGENCY
Naga DDB Malaysia/ Petaling Jaya

ANNUAL ID
06152D

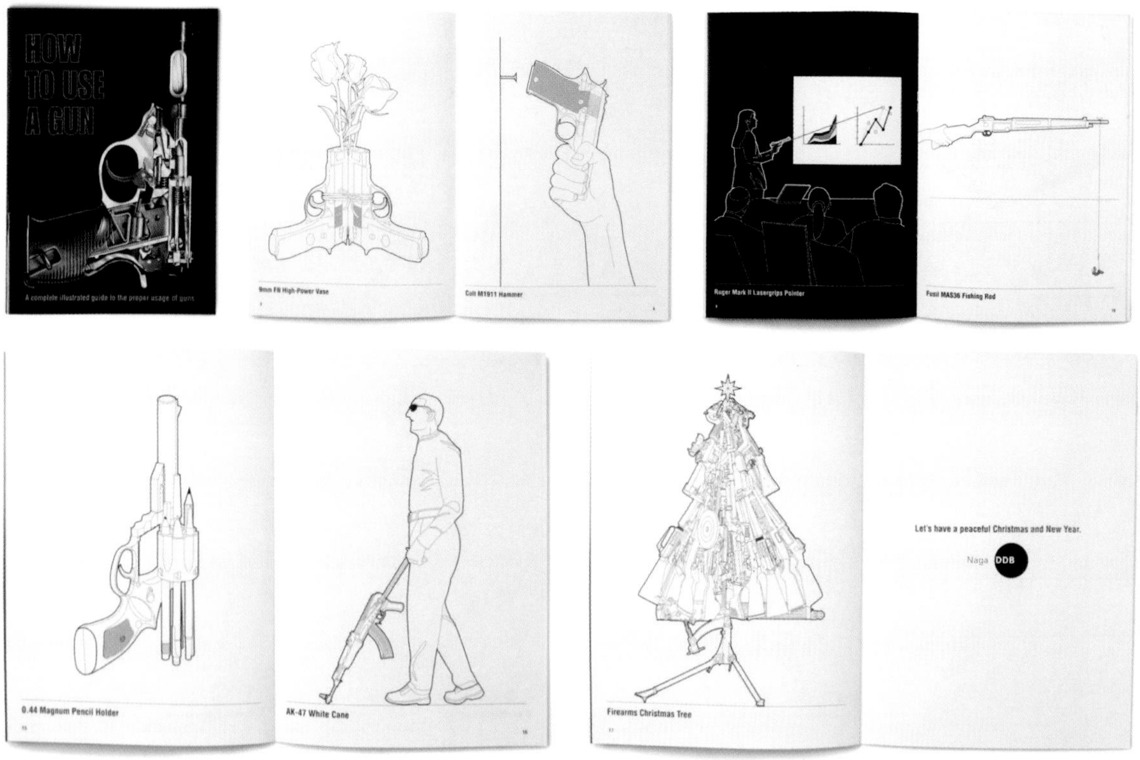
HOW TO USE A GUN
A complete illustrated guide to the proper usage of guns.
9mm FN High-Power Vase
Colt M1911 Hammer
Ruger Mark II Lasergrips Pointer
Fusil MAS36 Fishing Rod
0.44 Magnum Pencil Holder
AK-47 White Cane
Firearms Christmas Tree
Let's have a peaceful Christmas and New Year.
Naga DDB

Merit

DESIGNERS
Jon Olsen
Kristin Anderson

ART DIRECTOR
Jon Olsen

WRITER
Austin Howe

CREATIVE DIRECTORS
Jon Olsen
Austin Howe

CLIENT
Sandstrom Design

AGENCY
Sandstrom Design/ Portland

ANNUAL ID
06153D

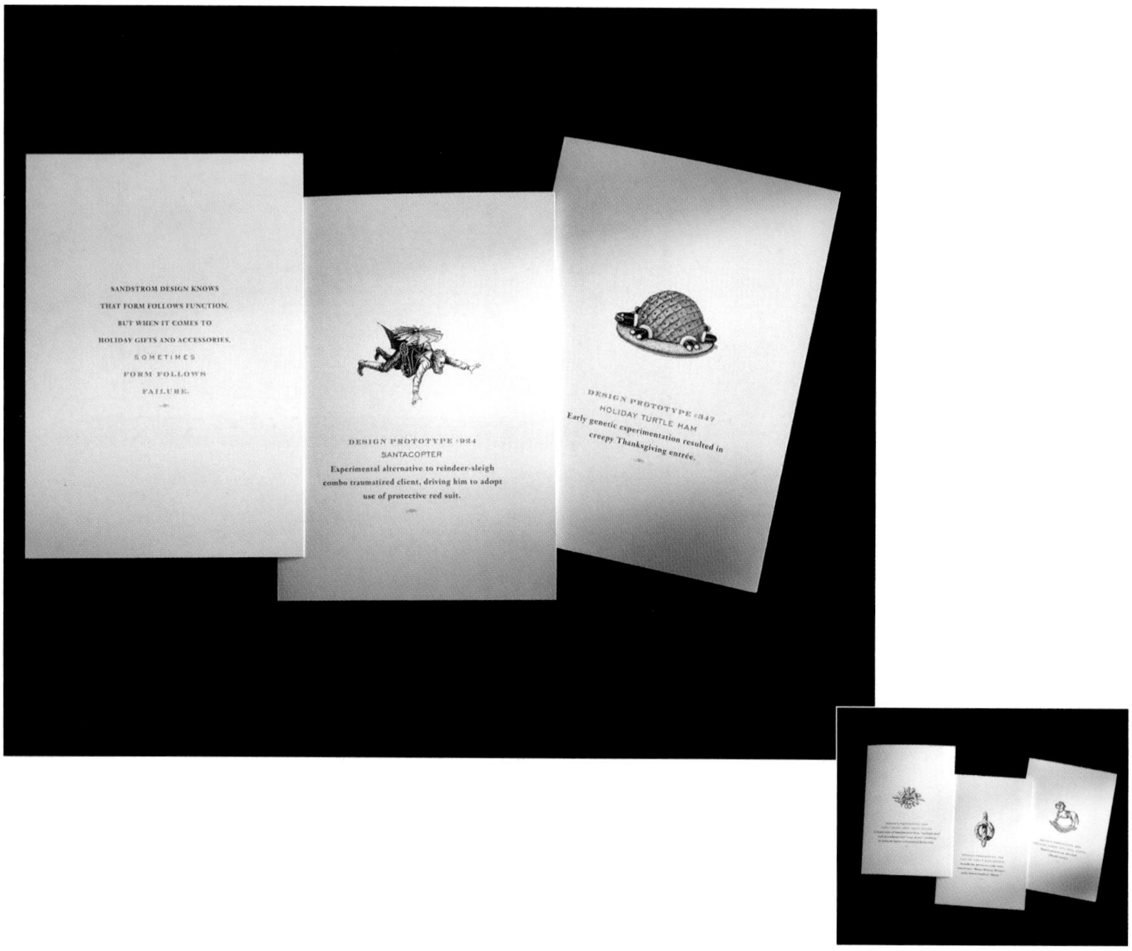
SANDSTROM DESIGN KNOWS THAT FORM FOLLOWS FUNCTION. BUT WHEN IT COMES TO HOLIDAY GIFTS AND ACCESSORIES, SOMETIMES FORM FOLLOWS FAILURE.
DESIGN PROTOTYPE #924
SANTACOPTER
Experimental alternative to reindeer-sleigh combo traumatized client, driving him to adopt use of protective red suit.
DESIGN PROTOTYPE #347
HOLIDAY TURTLE HAM
Early genetic experimentation resulted in creepy Thanksgiving entrée.

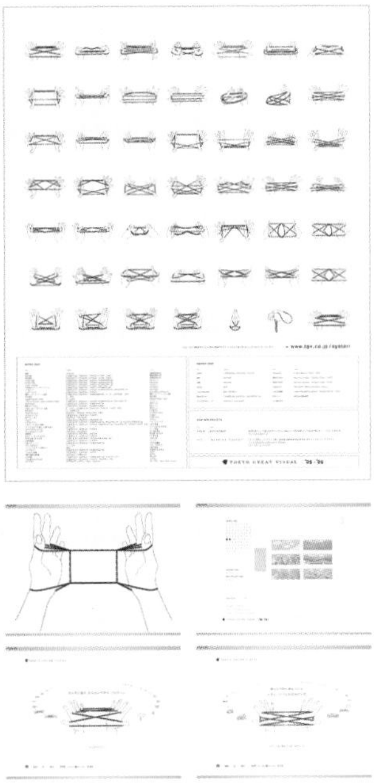

MERIT

DESIGNERS
Akihiro Oyama
Takahiro Fuke
Daisuke Shimokawa
Yoshiko Okamoto
Fumihito Usukura
Takahiro Mikuni
Akira Kumagai

ART DIRECTOR
Hisamoto Naito

WRITERS
Tetsuo Nishii
Takahiro Fuke

ILLUSTRATORS
Akihiro Oyama
Takahiro Mikuni

CREATIVE DIRECTOR
Hisamoto Naito

CLIENT
Tokyo Great Visual

AGENCY
Tokyo Great Visual/ Tokyo

ANNUAL ID
06154D

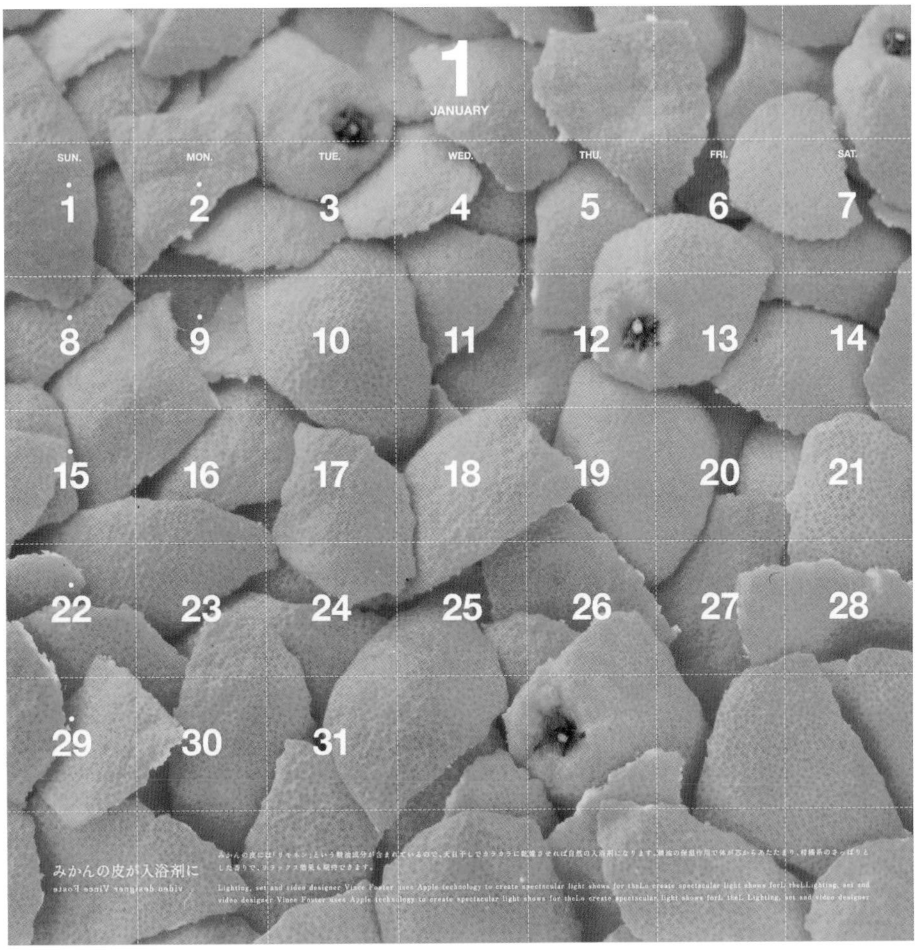
1
JANUARY
SUN. MON. TUE. WED. THU. FRI. SAT.
1 2 3 4 5 6 7
8 9 10 11 12 13 14
15 16 17 18 19 20 21
22 23 24 25 26 27 28
29 30 31
みかんの皮が入浴剤に

MERIT

DESIGNERS
Yukio Anazawa
Noriko & Don Carrol
Kiyoshi Nakayama
Yutaka Yasunaga

ART DIRECTORS
Yuji Nagase
Wakako Endo

PHOTOGRAPHER
Yukikazu Ito

ILLUSTRATOR
Masaharu Ohsuga

CREATIVE DIRECTOR
Minoru Fujisaki

CLIENT
Yomiko

AGENCY
Yomiko Advertising/ Tokyo

ANNUAL ID
06155D

Merit

ART DIRECTOR
Guy Rooke

WRITER
Keith Scott

CREATIVE DIRECTORS
Alex Bogusky
Andrew Keller
Rob Strasberg

CLIENT
MINI

AGENCY
Crispin Porter + Bogusky/Miami

ANNUAL ID
06156D

MOTORING WILL RESUME IN
0:36
MINIUSA.COM
MINI
INSERT VALID COINS ONLY
DISPLAY INDICATES TIME PURCHASED

Merit

ART DIRECTOR
Thomas Mitoh

WRITER
Elena Tresnak

CREATIVE DIRECTOR
Michael Hoinkes

CLIENT
www.fairlines.de

AGENCY
He Said She Said/ Hamburg

ANNUAL ID
06157D

WWW.FAIRLINES.DE

MERIT

ART DIRECTOR
Robin Clark

WRITER
Katie Edwards

CREATIVE DIRECTORS
Shirley Walker
Peter Higgins

CLIENT
UK Government, Foreign & Commonwealth Office

AGENCY
Land Design Studio/ London

ANNUAL ID
06158D

Merit

DESIGNERS
Rebeca Mendez
Roxane Zargham

ART DIRECTOR
Rebeca Mendez

WRITERS
Adam Eeuwens
Rebeca Mendez

PHOTOGRAPHER
Rebeca Mendez

CREATIVE DIRECTOR
Rebeca Mendez

CLIENT
Morphosis

AGENCY
Rebeca Mendez
Communication Design/
Altadena

ANNUAL ID
06159D

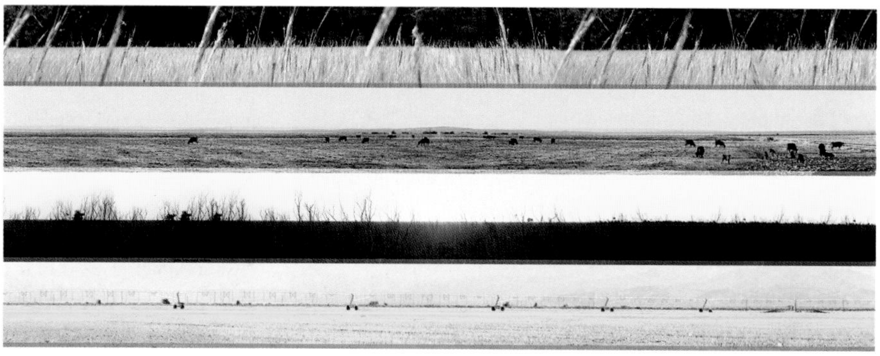

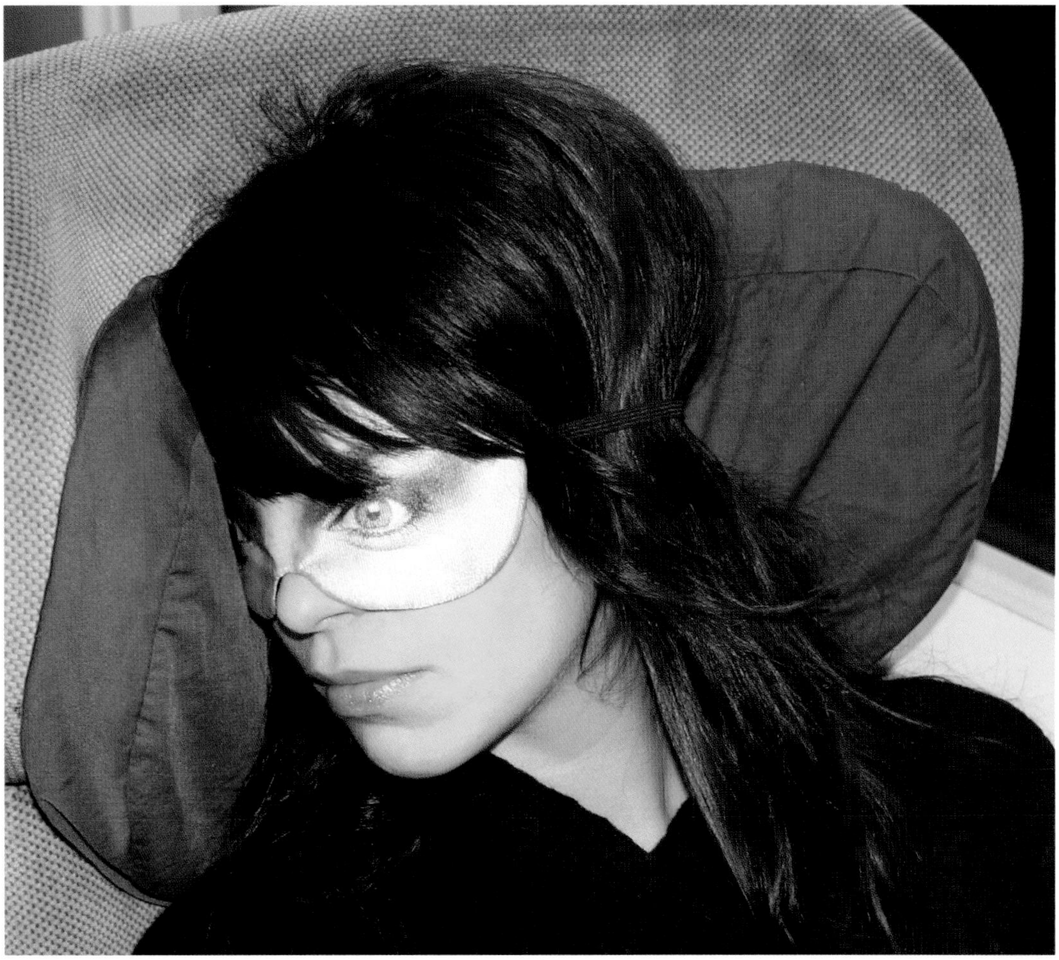

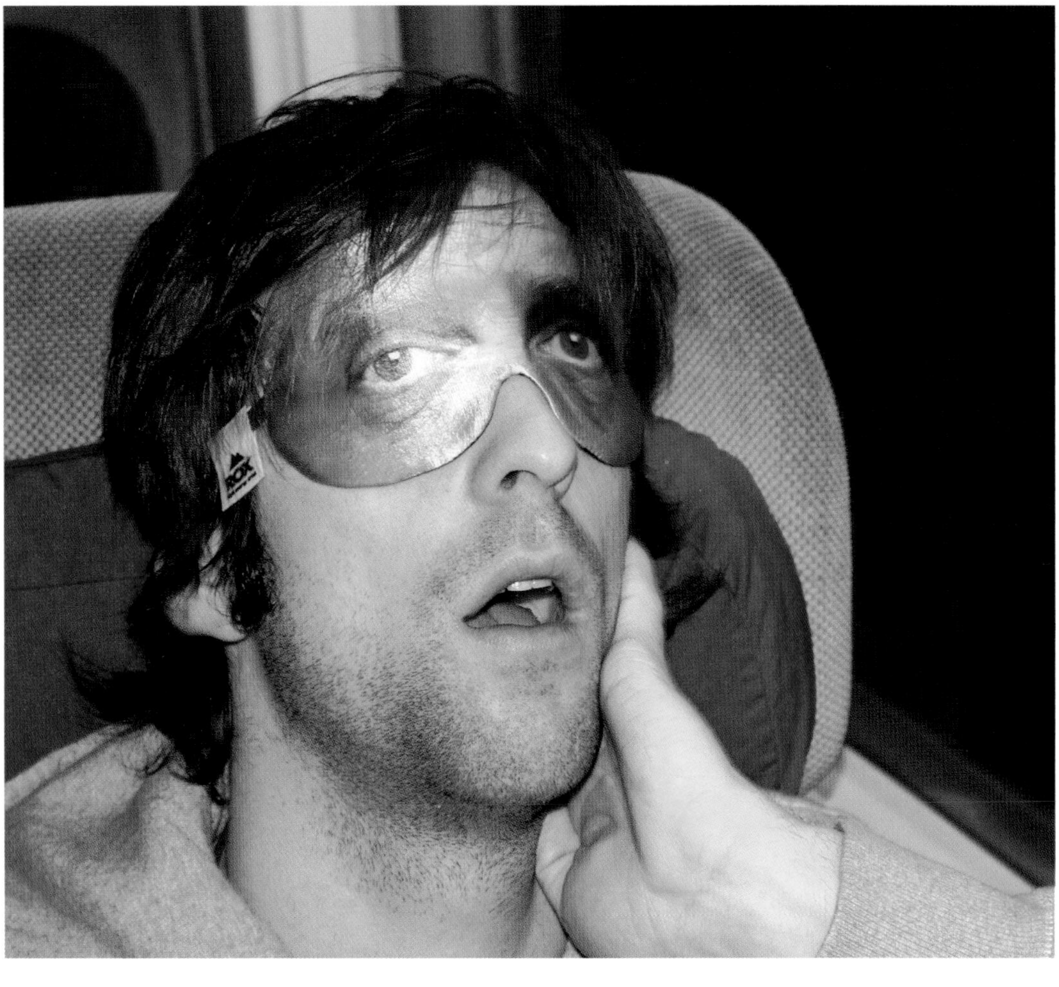

Merit

ART DIRECTOR
Johannes Hicks

WRITER
Stuart Kummer

CREATIVE DIRECTORS
Matthias Spaetgens
Jan Leube

CLIENT
Zebra Vertriebs

AGENCY
Scholz & Friends/Berlin

ANNUAL ID
06160D

Merit

CREATIVE DIRECTOR
Scott Willy

CLIENT
Indianapolis Cultural Development Commission

AGENCY
Three-sixty Group/ Indianapolis

ANNUAL ID
06161D

IMA

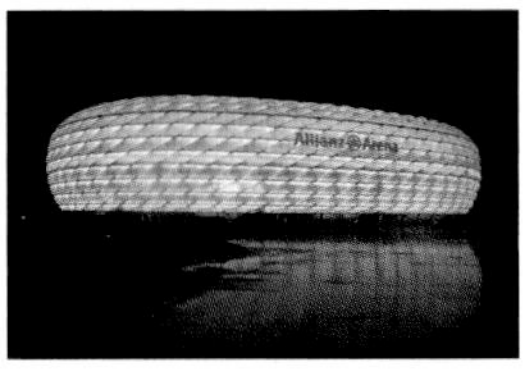

Allianz Arena

MERIT

DESIGNER
Ansgar Seelen

CREATIVE DIRECTORS
Claus Koch
Dirk Thieme

CLIENT
Allianz - Allianz München Stadium

AGENCY
Claus Koch Identity/ Duesseldorf

ANNUAL ID
06162D

308-310

Allianz Arena
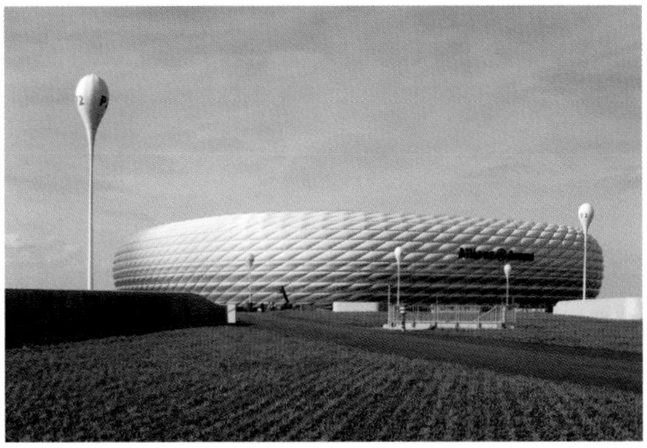

03/01
04/01
06
04/01
07

Allianz Global Investors
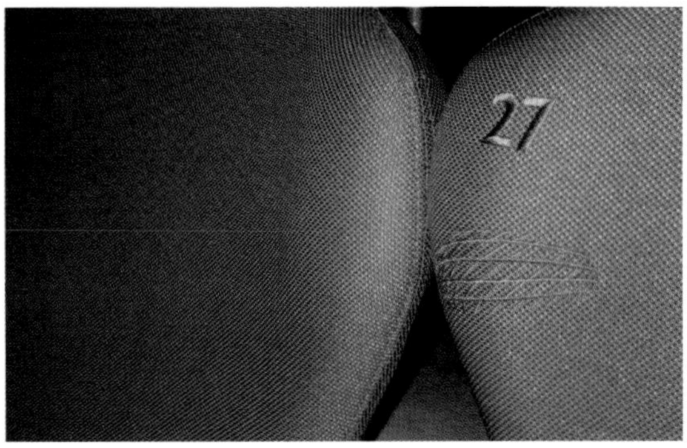
27

MERIT

DESIGNERS
Toshikazu Minatomura
Yasunari Mori

ART DIRECTORS
Koichi Sawada
Hirofumi Watanabe

WRITER
Hiroki Fukue

PHOTOGRAPHERS
Takashi Seo
Makoto Okamoto

CREATIVE DIRECTOR
Koichi Sawada

CLIENT
Ascot Corporation

AGENCY
Dentsu/Tokyo

ANNUAL ID
06163D

ごまのドレッシング

ブルーベリージャム
四季の桜ジャム

高尾そば
八割そば
茶そば
とろろそば

茶そば

MERIT

DESIGNERS
Toshihiro Onimaru
Graphics & Designing

ART DIRECTOR
Toshihiro Onimaru

CREATIVE DIRECTOR
Takanori Aiba

CLIENT
World Co.

AGENCY
Graphics & Designing/
Tokyo

ANNUAL ID
06165D

MEDITERRASSE

MERIT

DESIGNER
Simon Grendene

CREATIVE DIRECTOR
Alon Shoval

CLIENT
Blue Man Group

AGENCY
Hill Holliday/New York

ANNUAL ID
06166D

ACE

ANSWER
YOUR
CRAVINGS
PRICES TO
HOWL
ABOUT

MERIT

DESIGNERS
Nicole Flores
Jason Schulte

ART DIRECTORS
Mike Rice
Jason Schulte

WRITERS
Jason Schulte
Nicole Flores
Jeff Mueller

ILLUSTRATOR
Jason Schulte

CREATIVE DIRECTOR
Tim Murray

CLIENT
Target

AGENCY
Office: Jason Schulte Design/San Francisco

ANNUAL ID
06167D

COUNT DOWN
12
DAYS TO
HALLOWEEN
PRICES TO
HOWL
ABOUT
BONE
CHILLING
PRICES
EXCLUSIVE
EYE-TEM

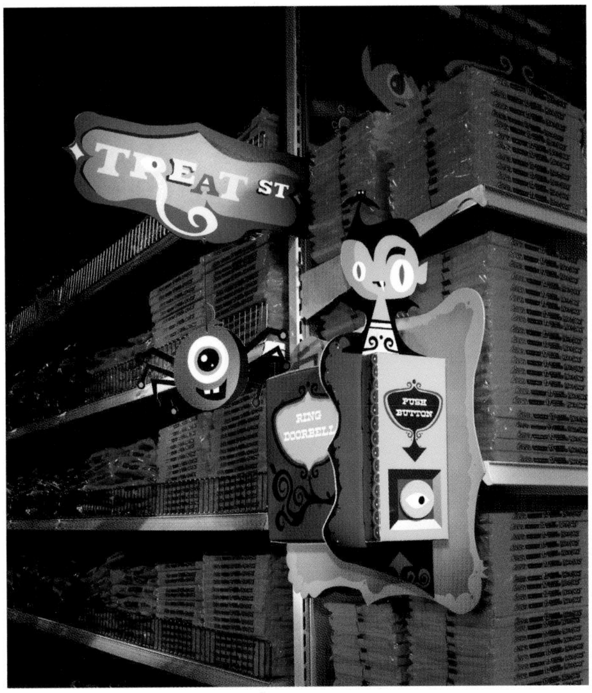
TREAT ST
RING
DOORBELL
PUSH
BUTTON

PREPARE
TO SCARE
COUNT DOWN

MONSTER
VALUE
X-LARGE
VALUE
LARGE
VALUE
JUMBO
SNACK
SIZE

Merit

DESIGNERS
Pamela Okecki
Emre Veryeri

WRITERS
Anne Geri
Andy Ure

CREATIVE DIRECTORS
Jakob Trollback
Joe Wright

CLIENT
Court TV

AGENCY
Trollback + Company/
New York

ANNUAL ID
06168D

THE LOOKOUT
courtTV
Seriously Entertaining
COMMAND

THE STASH
courtTV
Seriously Entertaining
Arresting Documentaries, Movies and Series
Nights + Weekends
www.courttv.com

WITNESS RELOCATION

THE COVER-UP
THE COVER-UP
THE COVER-UP
courtTV
NERVES OF STEAL.
THEY LIE, THEY CHEAT, THEY STEAL
Miami Ink
TAKEDOWN
COLDPLAY
06.07.05
jealousy
hunger

GETAWAY CAR
courtTV
elevato
N.Y.C. TAXI
1P96
TAXI FARE

トイレ川柳大賞
TOTO

MERIT

DESIGNERS
Tomoki Uematsu
Miyuki Sugawara

ART DIRECTOR
Ryosuke Sakaki

WRITERS
Yasushi Takimura
Masahiro Imai
Taichi Tanigawa
Saori Watanabe

CREATIVE DIRECTORS
Yuki Abe
Shigenobu Yamamoto

CLIENT
TOTO

AGENCY
Dentsu/Tokyo

ANNUAL ID
06169D

MERIT

DESIGNER
Masayoshi Kodaira

ART DIRECTOR
Masayoshi Kodaira

PHOTOGRAPHER
Taiji Matsue

CLIENT
Daiwa Radiator Factory

AGENCY
Flame/Tokyo

ANNUAL ID
06170D

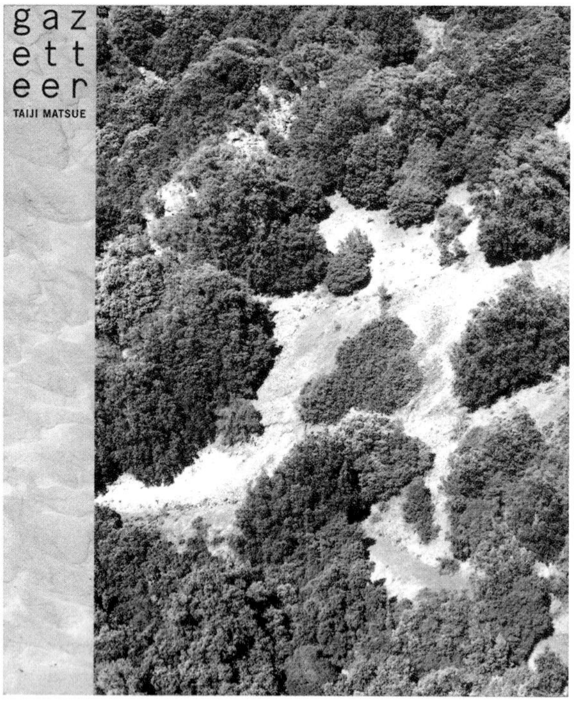
gaz
ett
eer
TAIJI MATSUE

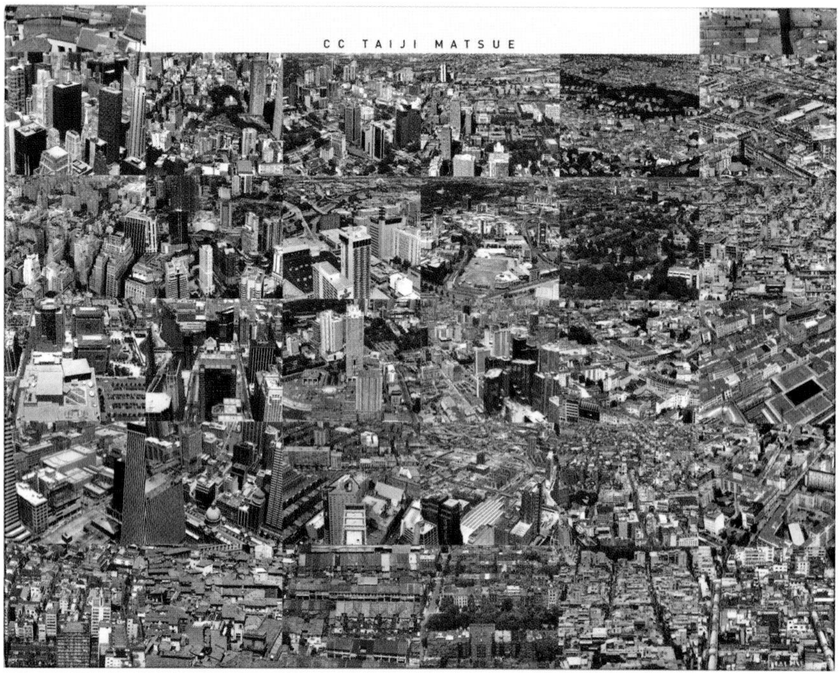
CC TAIJI MATSUE

BAUHAU
US DESS
SAU :: MI
KIYA TA
KIMOTO

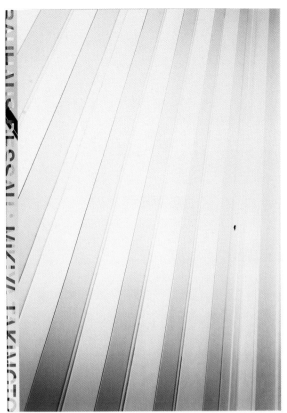

MERIT

DESIGNERS
Masayoshi Kodaira
Emi Ikami

ART DIRECTOR
Masayoshi Kodaira

PHOTOGRAPHER
Mikiya Takimoto

CLIENT
Pie Books

AGENCY
Flame/Tokyo

ANNUAL ID
06171D

Merit

DESIGNERS
Eric Tong
Azazaa Dai
Roy Yeo

CREATIVE DIRECTORS
Bill Chan
Nick Lim
SheungYan Lo

CLIENT
Nike

AGENCY
JWT/Shanghai

ANNUAL ID
06172D

Just Do It
in China
JWT
NIKE
Estrelas
SINCE 1972

sva
YEARBOOK
2005

SVA
Valerie
Puks

William Baughman
Marlie Decopain

Machine wash warm, inside out, with like colors. Only non-chlorine bleach. Tumble dry medium. Medium/hot iron. Do not iron decoration.
Laver à la machine à l'eau tiède, vêtement à l'envers, avec couleurs semblables. Agent de blanchiment sans chlore seulement. Sécher à température moyenne. Fer moyen ou chaud: ne pas repasser les décorations.
Lavar a mano o en lavadora con agua tibia, lavar por el revés, con colores similares. Solo blanqueador sin cloro. Secar a temperatura baja. Planchar a temperatura media o alta, no planchar el estampado.
RN 93846
CA 25181
40°C
BOOK OF THE YEAR
05
20
05

Merit

DESIGNERS
Ha Do
Lisa Sobcynski
Lenny Naar
Chris Spooner
Ana Pavlovic

PHOTOGRAPHER
David Maio

CREATIVE DIRECTORS
Genevieve Williams
Richard Wilde

CLIENT
School of Visual Arts

AGENCY
School of Visual Arts/ New York

ANNUAL ID
06173D

MERIT

DESIGNERS
Guy Pask
Kerry Argus

PHOTOGRAPHER
Guy Pask

CREATIVE DIRECTOR
Guy Pask

CLIENT
Te Runanga O Ngai Tahu

AGENCY
Strategy Advertising & Design/Christchurch

ANNUAL ID
06174D

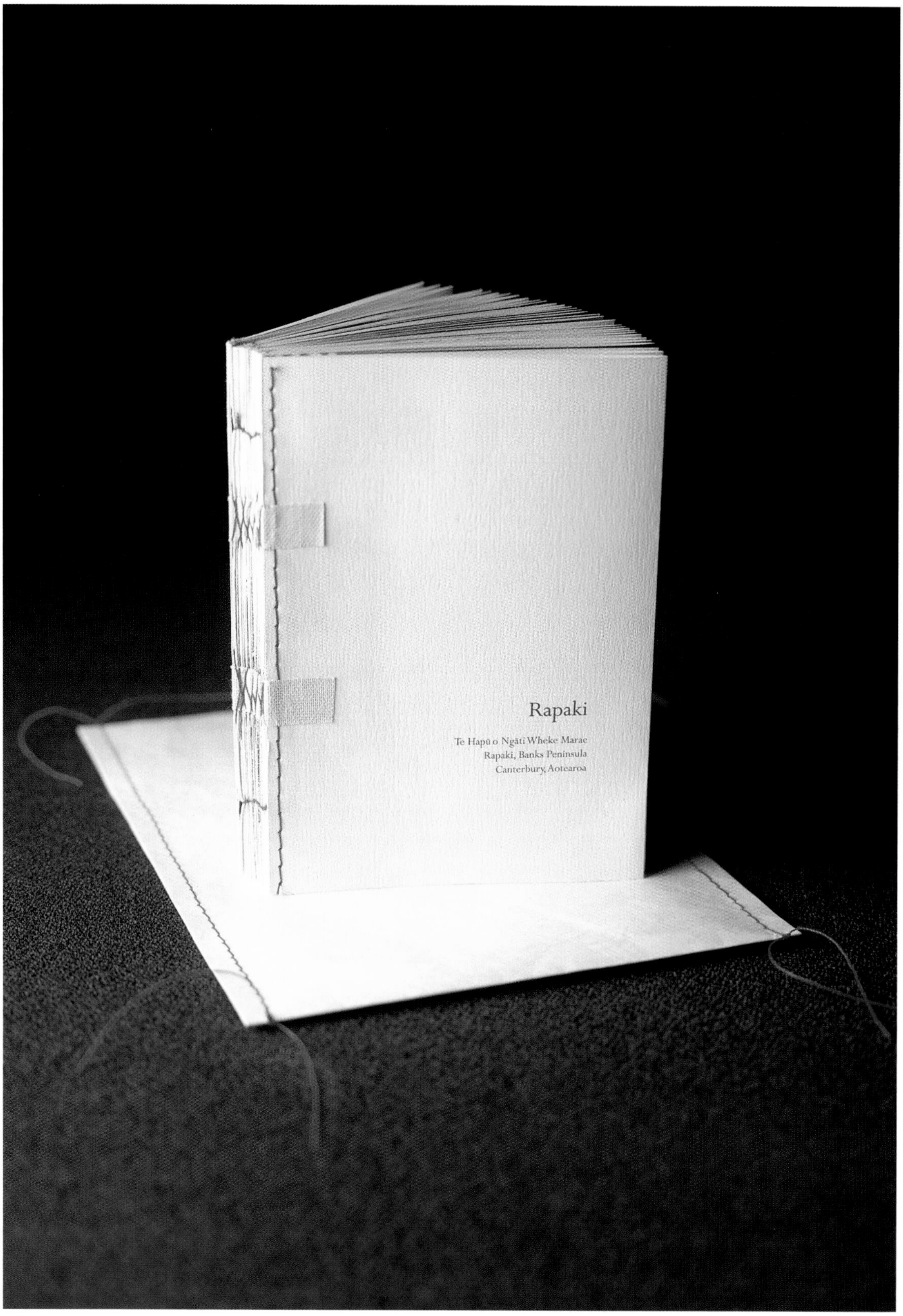
Rapaki
Te Hapū o Ngāti Wheke Marae
Rapaki, Banks Peninsula
Canterbury, Aotearoa

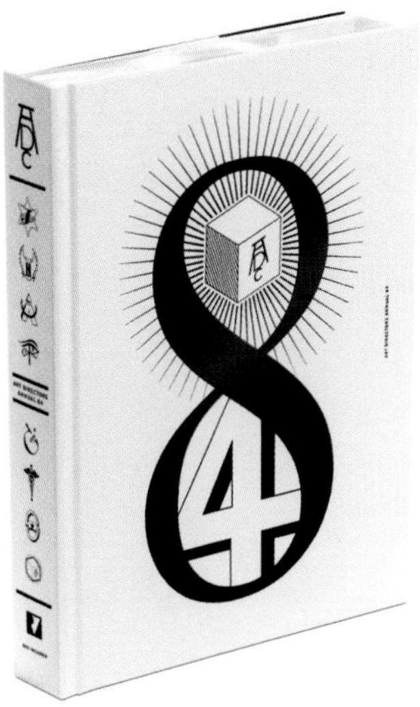

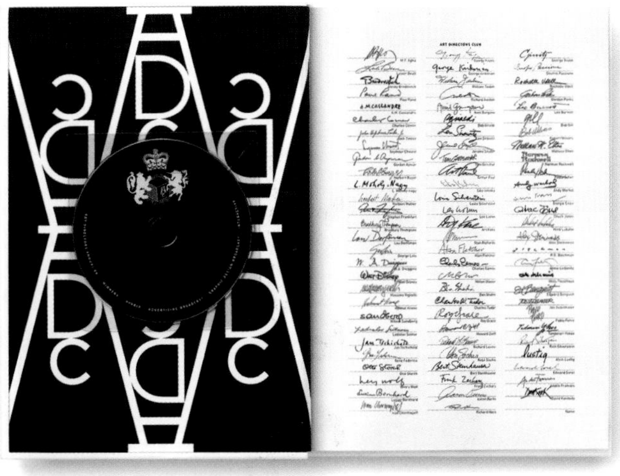

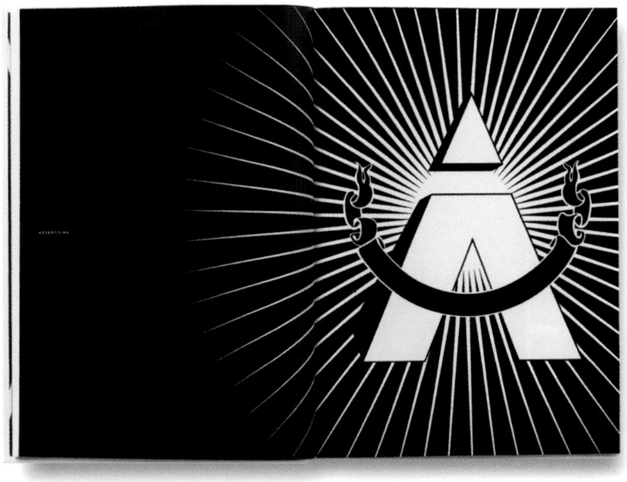

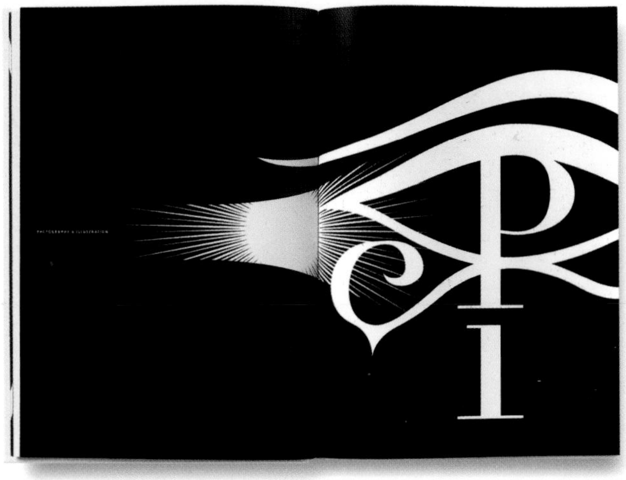

Merit

DESIGNERS
Stephanie Yung
Louis Hess

ART DIRECTOR
Stephanie Yung

WRITER
Jason McCann

ILLUSTRATORS
Stephanie Yung
Brad Kumaraswamy

CREATIVE DIRECTOR
Jane Hope

CLIENT
ADC

AGENCY
Taxi/New York

ANNUAL ID
06175D

MERIT

DESIGNERS
Eric Heiman
Elizabeth Fitzgibbons
Akiko Ito

ART DIRECTOR
Eric Heiman

WRITERS
Shoshana Berger
Grace Hawthorne

PHOTOGRAPHER
Jeffery Cross

ILLUSTRATOR
Kate Francis

CREATIVE DIRECTORS
Adam Brodsley
Eric Heiman

CLIENT
ReadyMade

AGENCY
Volume/San Francisco

ANNUAL ID
06176D

ReadyMade
HOW TO MAKE
{ALMOST} EVERYTHING
A Do-It-Yourself Primer

MERIT

DESIGNER
W+K 12

ART DIRECTOR
W+K 12

WRITER
W+K 12

ILLUSTRATOR
W+K 12

CREATIVE DIRECTOR
W+K 12

CLIENT
W+K 12

AGENCY
W+K 12/Portland

ANNUAL ID
06177D

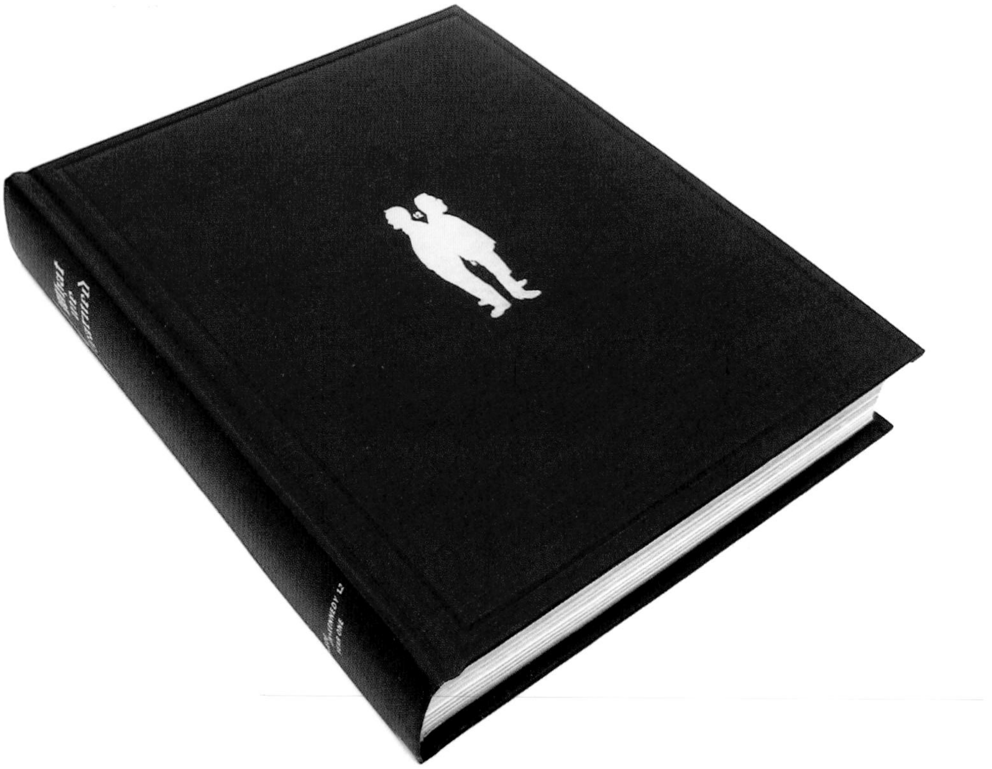

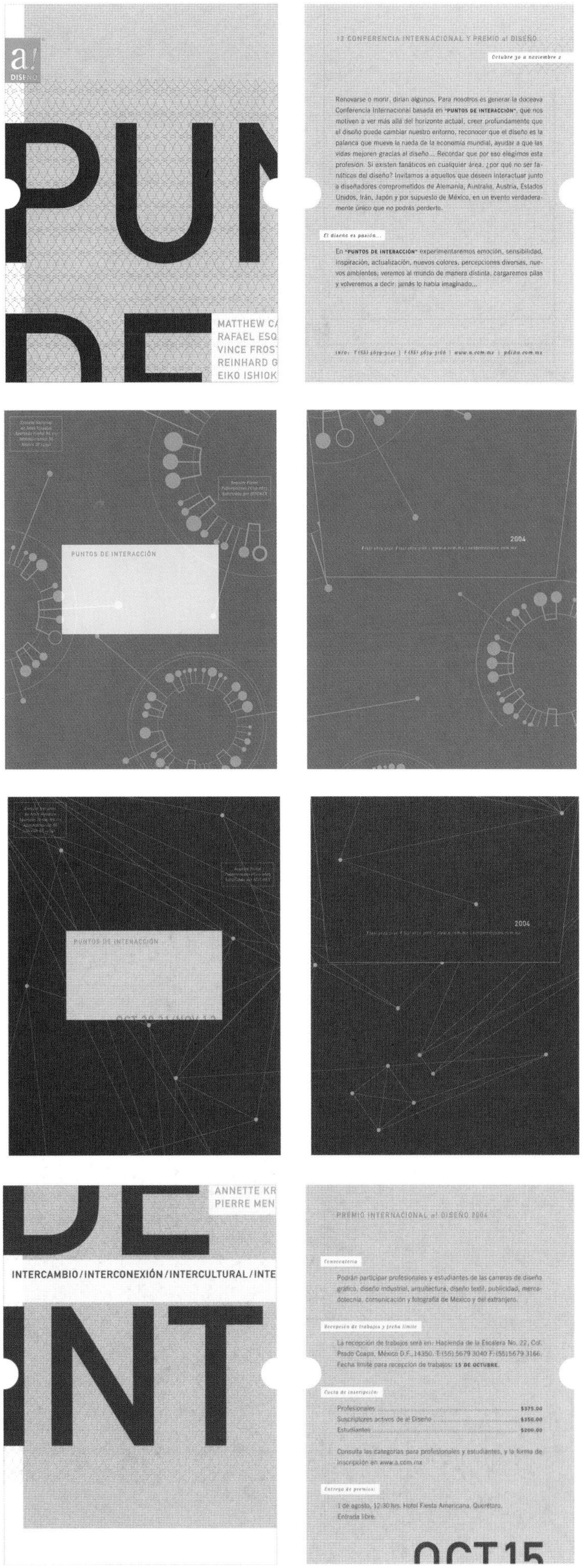
a! DISEÑO
PUN
DE
MATTHEW C
RAFAEL ESQ
VINCE FROST
REINHARD G
EIKO ISHIOK
12 CONFERENCIA INTERNACIONAL Y PREMIO a! DISEÑO
PUNTOS DE INTERACCIÓN
2004
ANNETTE KR
PIERRE MEN
INTERCAMBIO/INTERCONEXIÓN/INTERCULTURAL/INTE
INT
PREMIO INTERNACIONAL a! DISEÑO 2004
OCT15

MERIT

DESIGNERS
Vanessa Eckstein
Vanesa Enriquez

ART DIRECTOR
Vanessa Eckstein

CLIENT
a! diseno

AGENCY
Blok Design/Mexico

ANNUAL ID
06179D

Merit

DESIGNERS
Heidi Chisholm
Peet Pienaar

CLIENT
Afro Magazine

AGENCY
daddy buy me a pony
– a 9Nov Union Co/
Cape Town

ANNUAL ID
06180D

ROLEX

Merit

DESIGNER
Heidi Chisholm

ILLUSTRATOR
Peet Pienaar

CLIENT
Interactive Africa

AGENCY
daddy buy me a pony
– a 9Nov Union Co/
Cape Town

ANNUAL ID
06181D

you

Jan
1

Aug
8

Sep
9

Oct
10

MERIT

DESIGNER
Shiho Shimizu

ART DIRECTORS
Shotaro Sakaguchi
Mari Konishi

PHOTOGRAPHER
Kazunari Koyama

CREATIVE DIRECTOR
Shotaro Sakaguchi

CLIENT
Pierre Fabre Japon

AGENCY
Dentsu/Tokyo

ANNUAL ID
06182D

MERIT

DESIGNERS
Masayoshi Kodaira
Namiko Otsuka

ART DIRECTOR
Masayoshi Kodaira

CLIENT
Magnum

AGENCY
Flame/Tokyo

ANNUAL ID
06183D

Men's shoes: PREMIATA UOMO
PREMIATA WHITE / CROCKETT
& JONES
BADOUR / DIGGER / RUBBERS
Ladies' shoes: PREMIATA DON
L'HEURE BLEUE Men's & Ladies'
accessories: BETONY VERNON
DAZZLING M·A·R·S Men's belts:
ENZO BONAFE / MAGNUM Men's
& Ladies' gloves: FILO D'ORO
Buyers
Press & Friends
MAGNUM
AUTUMN/WINTER

MAGNUM
AUTUMN
/WINTER

MERIT

DESIGNER
Lian Siah

ART DIRECTOR
Herbie Phoon

WRITER
Herbie Phoon

PHOTOGRAPHER
Kenny Chai@Studio DL

ILLUSTRATOR
Lian Siah

CREATIVE DIRECTOR
Nana Tan

CLIENT
Dasein Academy of Art

AGENCY
Grass/Dasein/Kuala Lumpur

ANNUAL ID
06184D

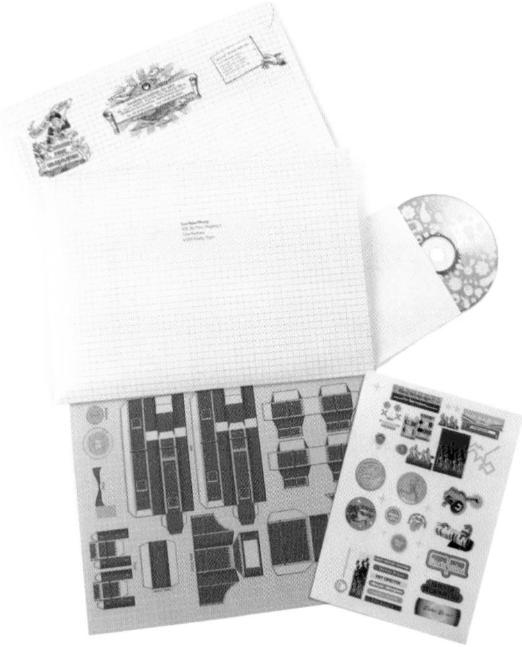

GREY

MERIT

ART DIRECTORS
Andreas Kittel
Lisa Careborg

WRITER
Lars Forsberg

PHOTOGRAPHER
Atelje Marie

ILLUSTRATORS
Jonas Rathsman
Ylva Smedberg

CREATIVE DIRECTOR
Anders Kornestedt

CLIENT
Klippan

AGENCY
Happy Forsman & Bodenfors/Gothenburg

ANNUAL ID
06185D

MERIT

DESIGNERS
Yao-Feng Chou
Ken-Tsai Lee

ART DIRECTOR
Ken-Tsai Lee

CLIENT
Fonso Interprise

AGENCY
Ken-Tsai Lee Design Studio/Taipei

ANNUAL ID
06186D

Merit

DESIGNERS
Karin Fong
Stan Lim
Ronnie Kauf

CREATIVE DIRECTOR
Karin Fong

CLIENT
Discovery Communications

AGENCY
Imaginary Forces/ Los Angeles

ANNUAL ID
06188D

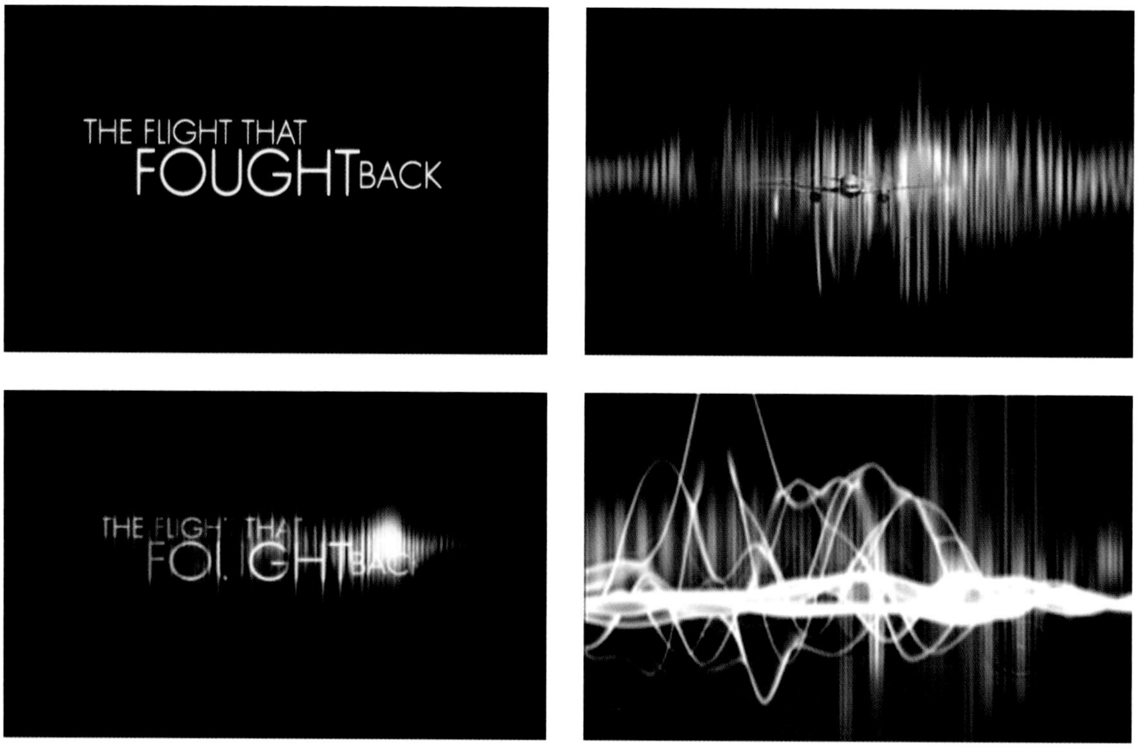
THE FLIGHT THAT
FOUGHTBACK

Merit

DESIGNERS
Carlos Bela
Gabriel Dietrich
Paula Nobre
Rafael Grampa
Raquel Falkenbach
Roger Marmo

ART DIRECTOR
Luciane Vieira

WRITER
Marcello "Droopy" Almeida

AGENCY PRODUCER
Maria Herminia Weinstock

DIRECTOR
Mateus de Paula Santos

CREATIVE DIRECTOR
Joao Livi

CLIENT
Banco Real

AGENCY
Lobo/São Paulo

ANNUAL ID
06189D

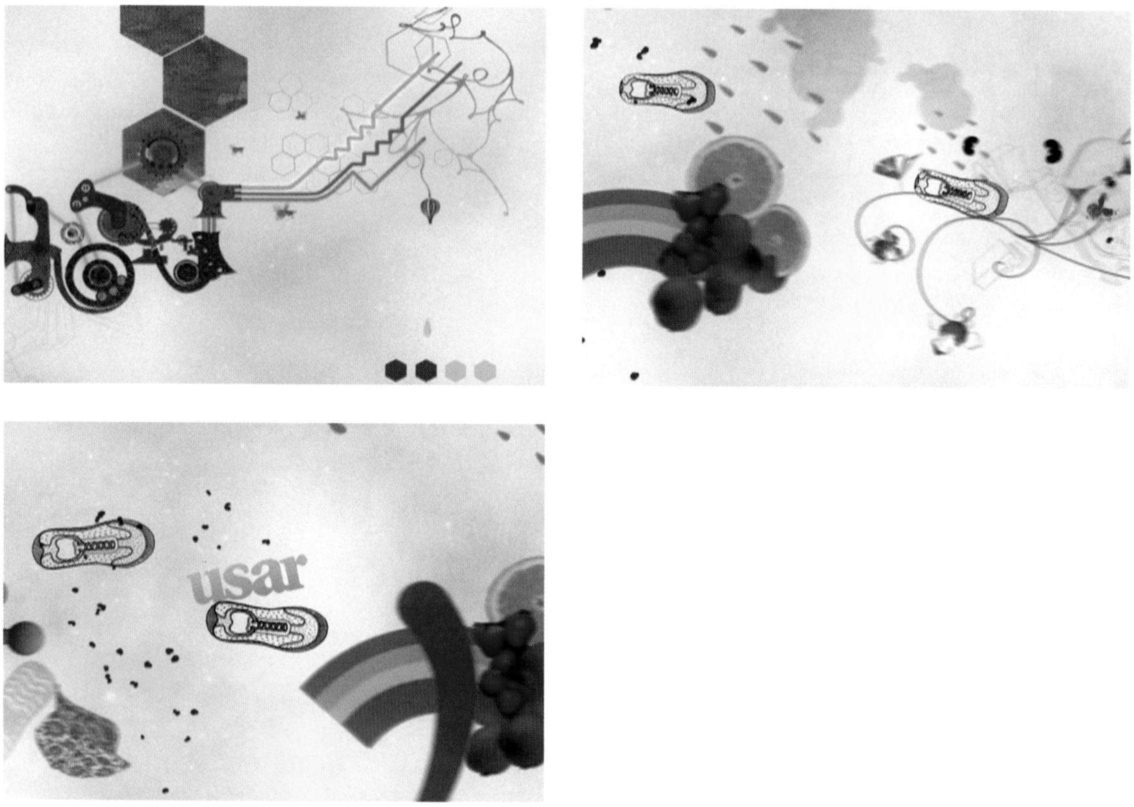
usar

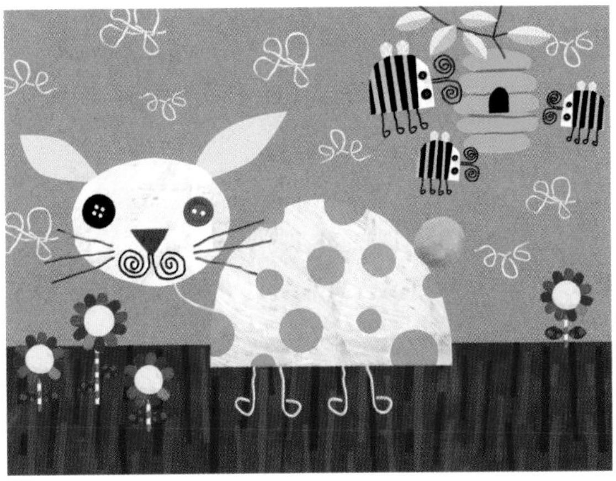

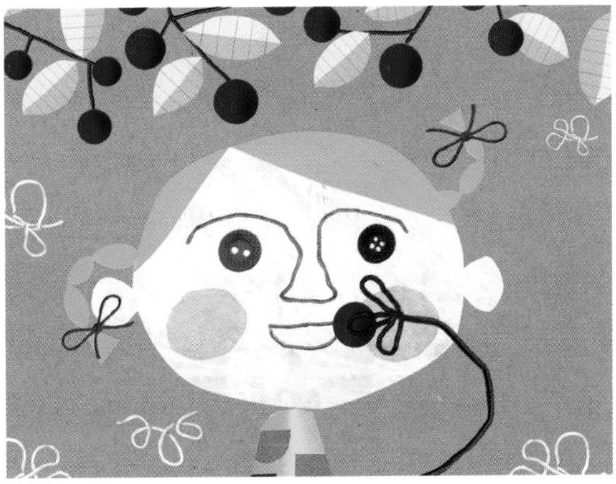

NOGGIN
noggin.com

MERIT

DESIGNER
Melinda Beck

ART DIRECTOR
Matthew Duntemann

WRITER
Dixie Feldman

ILLUSTRATOR
Melinda Beck

AGENCY PRODUCER
Clark Stubbs

CREATIVE DIRECTOR
Matthew Duntemann

CLIENT
Noggin

AGENCY
MTV Networks/ New York

ANNUAL ID
06190D

NOGGIN
noggin.com

MERIT

DESIGNER
Melinda Beck

ART DIRECTOR
Matthew Duntemann

WRITER
Matt Perreault

ILLUSTRATOR
Melinda Beck

AGENCY PRODUCER
Matt Perreault

CREATIVE DIRECTOR
Matthew Duntemann

CLIENT
Noggin

AGENCY
MTV Networks/ New York

ANNUAL ID
06191D

Merit

ART DIRECTOR
Pam Fujimoto

WRITER
Matt McCain

ILLUSTRATOR
Tim Silbaugh

AGENCY PRODUCER
Dax Estorninos

CREATIVE DIRECTOR
Tracy Wong

CLIENT
Seattle International Film Festival

AGENCY
Wongdoody/Seattle

ANNUAL ID
06194D

ALSO AWARDED
Merit:
Broadcast Design - Single

Merit:
Broadcast Design - Single

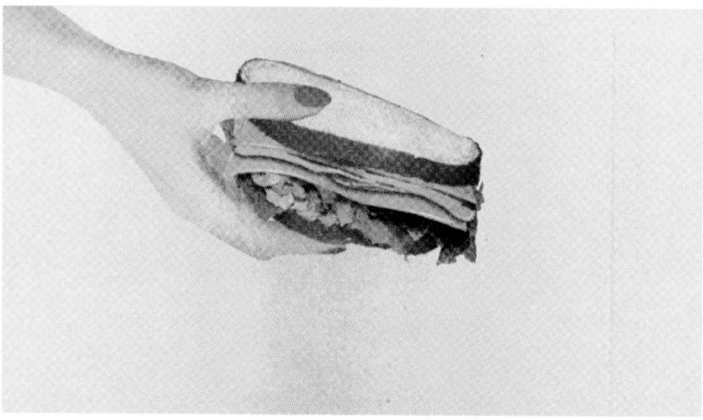

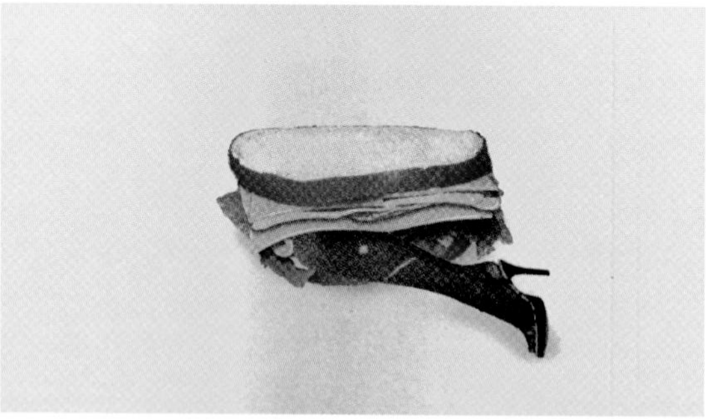

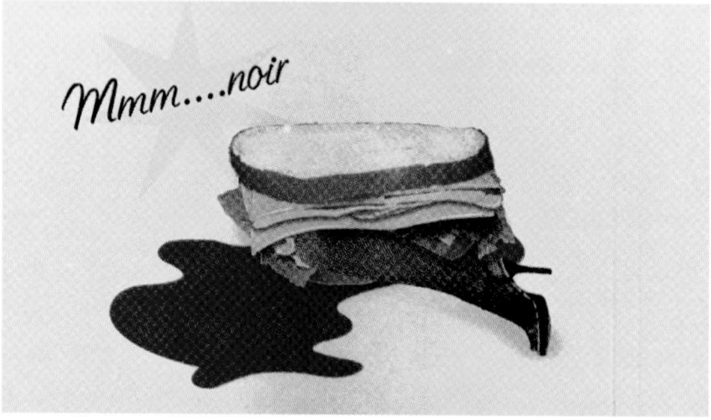
Mmm....noir

Seattle International Film Festival
MAY 19 - JUNE 12 2005

Feast Your Eyes

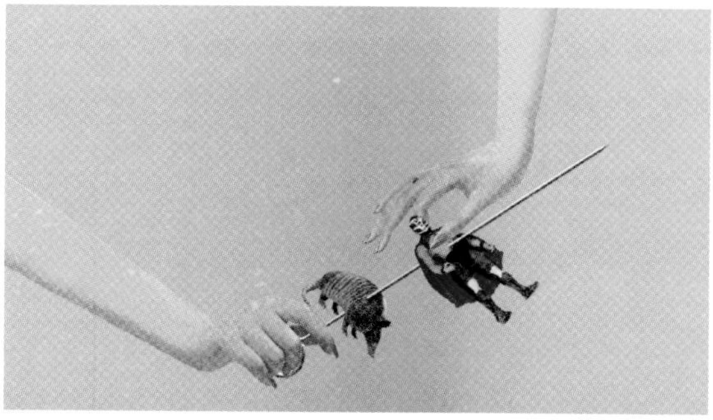

Obskewer!

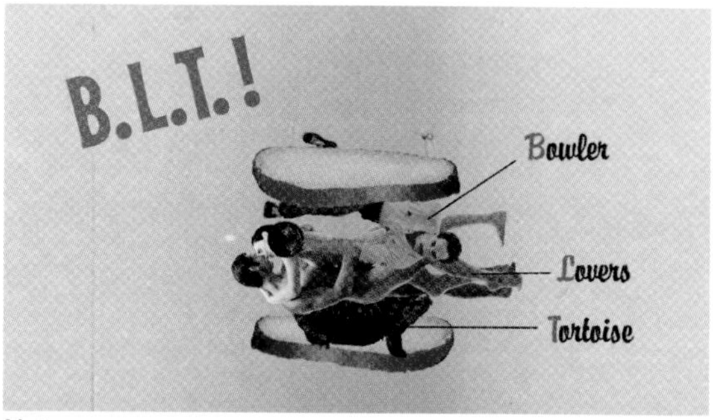
B.L.T.!
Bowler
Lovers
Tortoise

Merit

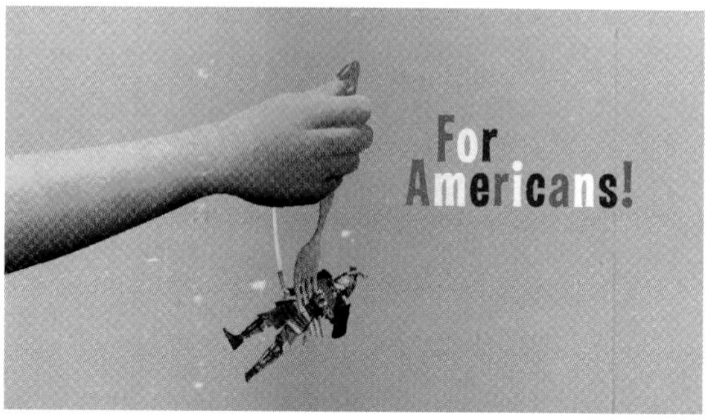
For Americans!

FOREIGN DELITES!

Merit

MERIT

Southwark
Council
Please recycle your Christmas tree.
Call 020 7525 2000 for information.

DESIGNER
Nils Leonard

ART DIRECTOR
Alexander Holder

WRITER
Oliver Kellett

ILLUSTRATORS
Oli Kellett
Nils Leonard

CREATIVE DIRECTORS
Daryl Corps
Ben Kay

CLIENT
Southwark Partnership

AGENCY
Lunar/London

ANNUAL ID
06195D

MERIT

DESIGNER
Paul Belford

ART DIRECTOR
Paul Belford

CREATIVE DIRECTORS
Paul Belford
Nigel Roberts

CLIENT
Type Museum

AGENCY
Abbott Mead Vickers BBDO/London

ANNUAL ID
06196D

A good
tpyeafce
mkaes
ahnytnig
eeisar
to raed.
typemuseum
.org

MERIT

DESIGNER
Michael Braley

ART DIRECTOR
Michael Braley

CLIENT
Creative Circus

AGENCY
Braley Design/New York

ANNUAL ID
06197D

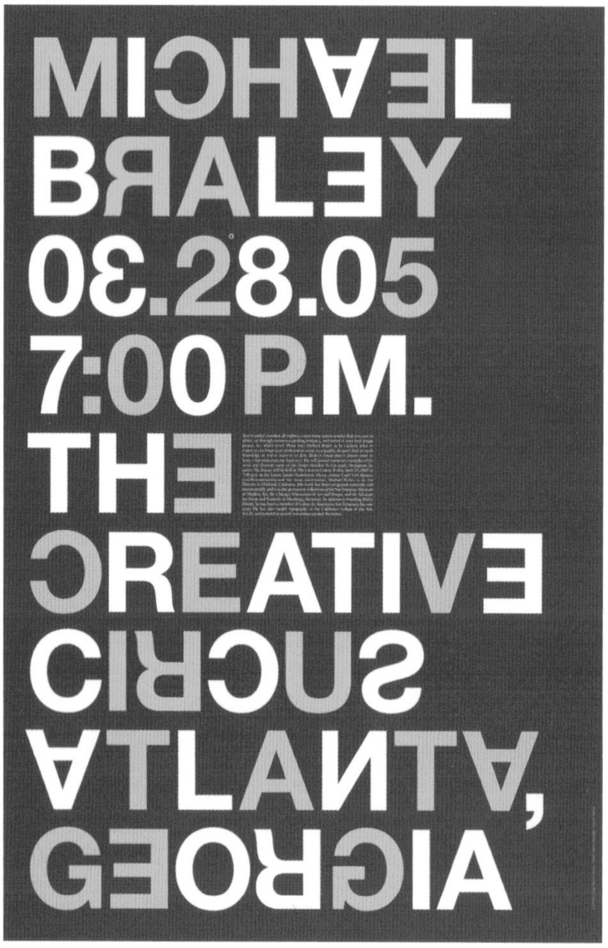
MICHAEL
BRALEY
03.28.05
7:00 P.M.
THE
CREATIVE
CIRCUS
ATLANTA,
GEORGIA

Michael Braley
Poster Design Workshop
Wichita State University
November 11-12, 2005

MERIT

DESIGNER
Michael Braley

ART DIRECTOR
Michael Braley

CLIENT
Wichita State University

AGENCY
Braley Design/New York

ANNUAL ID
06198D

MERIT

ART DIRECTOR
Kamal Bhatnagar

WRITER
Navajyoti Pegu

ILLUSTRATORS
Navajyoti Pegu
Kamal Bhatnagar
Gurdev Singh

CREATIVE DIRECTORS
Vineet Mahajan
Ashish Chakravarty

CLIENT
ICARE

AGENCY
Contract Advertising/
New Delhi

ANNUAL ID
06199D

MERIT

DESIGNERS
Masaki Idera
Chihiro Shiraishi

ART DIRECTOR
Tsubasa Adachi

WRITER
Hiroko Yamamoto

PHOTOGRAPHER
Naonori Kohira

CREATIVE DIRECTOR
Ryo Honda

CLIENT
World Swim for Malaria

AGENCY
Dentsu/Tokyo

ANNUAL ID
06200D

世界一小さな「大量破壊兵器」を、知っていますか？
泳ぐことで救える命がある。
WORLD SWIM FOR MALARIA
www.world swim for malaria.com

The world's smallest Weapon of Mass Destruction.

In Africa, every 30 seconds someone dies from Malaria.
The World Swim for Malaria is a global fundraising event from which 100% of the money raised is spent on preventing malaria. Join us in the fight against this deadly disease.

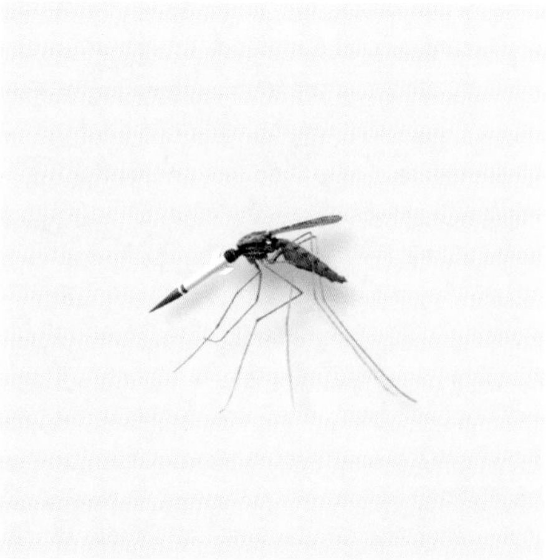

MERIT

DESIGNER
Masayoshi Kodaira

ART DIRECTOR
Masayoshi Kodaira

PHOTOGRAPHER
Mikiya Takimoto

CLIENT
NPO Harappa

AGENCY
Flame/Tokyo

ANNUAL ID
06202D

NARA YOSHITOMO
HIROSAKI
NARA YOSHITOMO
HIROSAKI

Torsten och Wanja Söderbergs pris 2005
VOLVO YCC (Your Concept Car)
Anna Rosén, Cynthia Charwick, Maria Uggla, Maria Widell Christiansen, Camilla Palmertz, Eva-Lisa Andersson, Elna Holmberg, Lena Ekelund samt Tatiana Butovitsch Temm.
RÖHSSKA MUSEET 4 NOVEMBER 2005–8 JANUARI 2006
Vasagatan 37–39, Göteborg www.designmuseum.se

MERIT

ART DIRECTOR
Andreas Kittel

WRITERS
Elsebet Welander-Berggren
Penny Sparke

ILLUSTRATOR
Fredrik Persson

CREATIVE DIRECTOR
Anders Kornestedt

CLIENT
The Röhsska Museum

AGENCY
Happy Forsman & Bodenfors/Gothenburg

ANNUAL ID
06203D

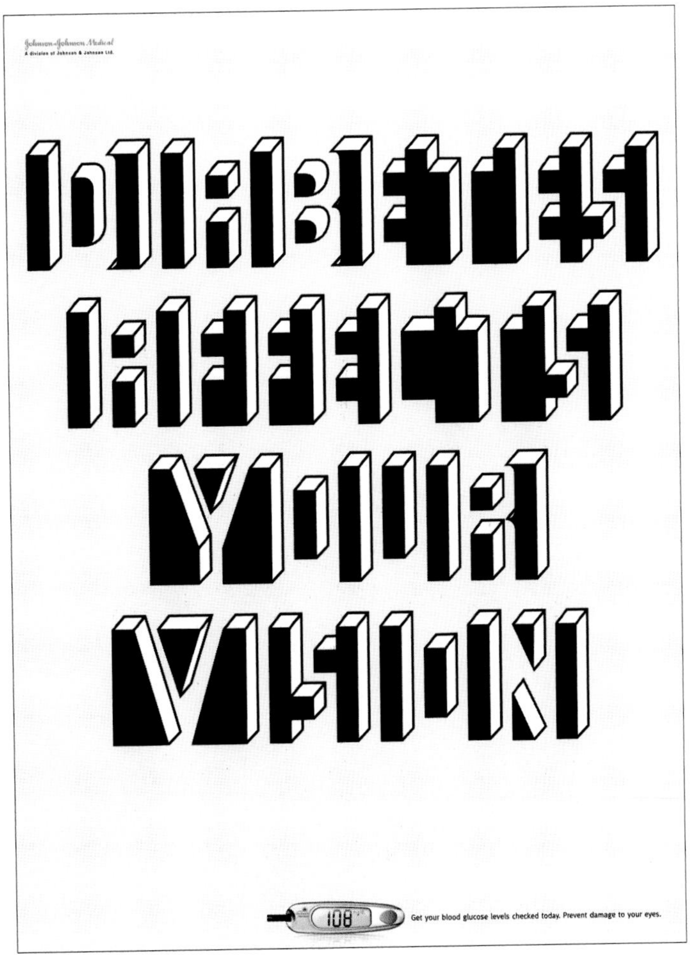
Johnson & Johnson Medical
A division of Johnson & Johnson Ltd.
108
Get your blood glucose levels checked today. Prevent damage to your eyes.

MERIT

ART DIRECTOR
Zahid Shaikh

WRITER
Hemal Jhaveri

ILLUSTRATOR
Mahesh Bolaikar

CLIENT
Johnson & Johnson Medical India

AGENCY
OgilvyOne/Mumbai

ANNUAL ID
06204D

MERIT

ART DIRECTOR
Tim Stuebane

WRITER
Birgit van den Valentyn

ILLUSTRATOR
Carolina Cwiklinska

CREATIVE DIRECTORS
Julia Schmidt
Matthias Schmidt
Constantin Kaloff

CLIENT
Aktionsbuendnis
Landmine.de

AGENCY
Scholz & Friends/Berlin

ANNUAL ID
06206D

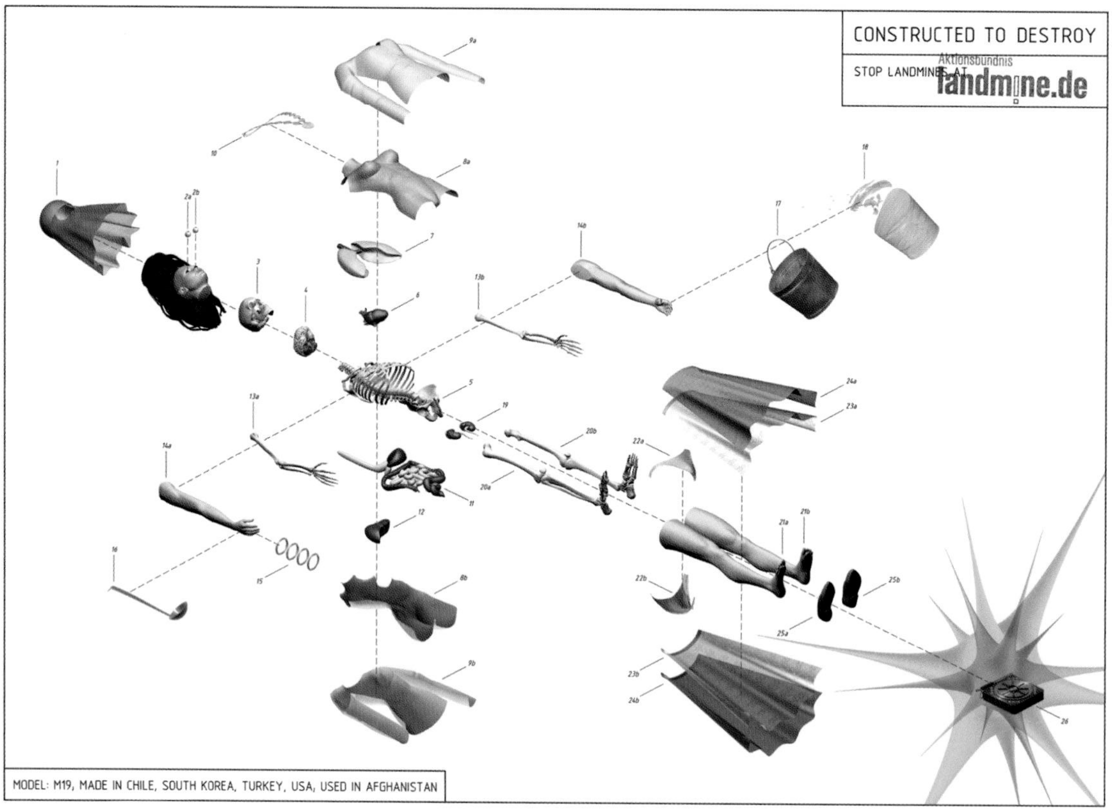
CONSTRUCTED TO DESTROY
STOP LANDMINES AT
Aktionsbundnis
landmine.de
MODEL: M19, MADE IN CHILE, SOUTH KOREA, TURKEY, USA, USED IN AFGHANISTAN

MERIT

ART DIRECTOR
Tim Stuebane

WRITER
Birgit van den Valentyn

ILLUSTRATOR
Carolina Cwiklinska

CREATIVE DIRECTORS
Julia Schmidt
Matthias Schmidt
Constantin Kaloff

CLIENT
Aktionsbuendnis
Landmine.de

AGENCY
Scholz & Friends/Berlin

ANNUAL ID
06205D

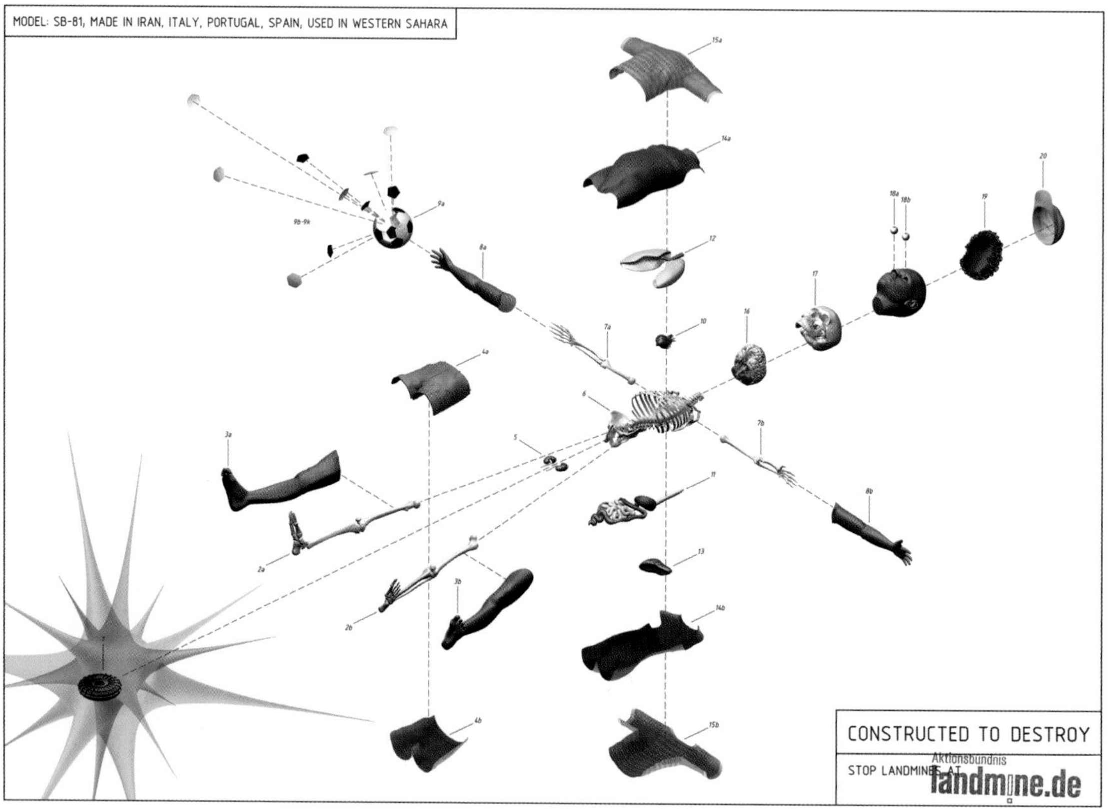
MODEL: SB-81, MADE IN IRAN, ITALY, PORTUGAL, SPAIN, USED IN WESTERN SAHARA
CONSTRUCTED TO DESTROY
STOP LANDMINES AT
Aktionsbundnis
landmine.de

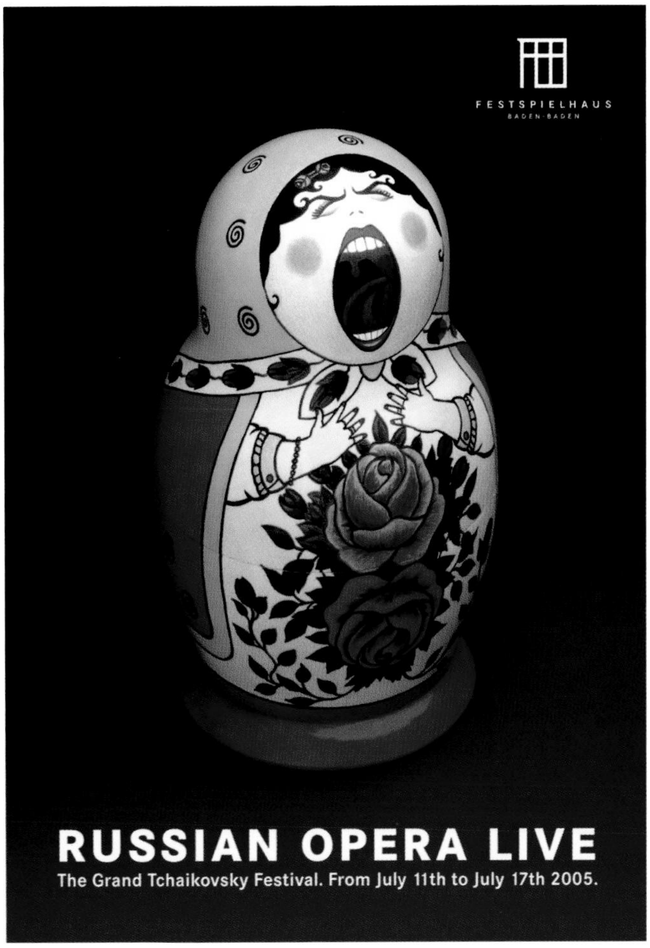
FESTSPIELHAUS
BADEN-BADEN
RUSSIAN OPERA LIVE
The Grand Tchaikovsky Festival. From July 11th to July 17th 2005.

MERIT

ART DIRECTOR
Stefanie Flaig

WRITER
Christopher Ruckwied

PHOTOGRAPHER
Philipp Goetz

ILLUSTRATOR
Jan Hoffmann

CREATIVE DIRECTORS
Martin Pross
Mario Gamper
Stefan Leick
Michael Winterhagen

CLIENT
Festspielhaus und Festspiele Baden-Baden

AGENCY
Scholz & Friends/Berlin

ANNUAL ID
06207D

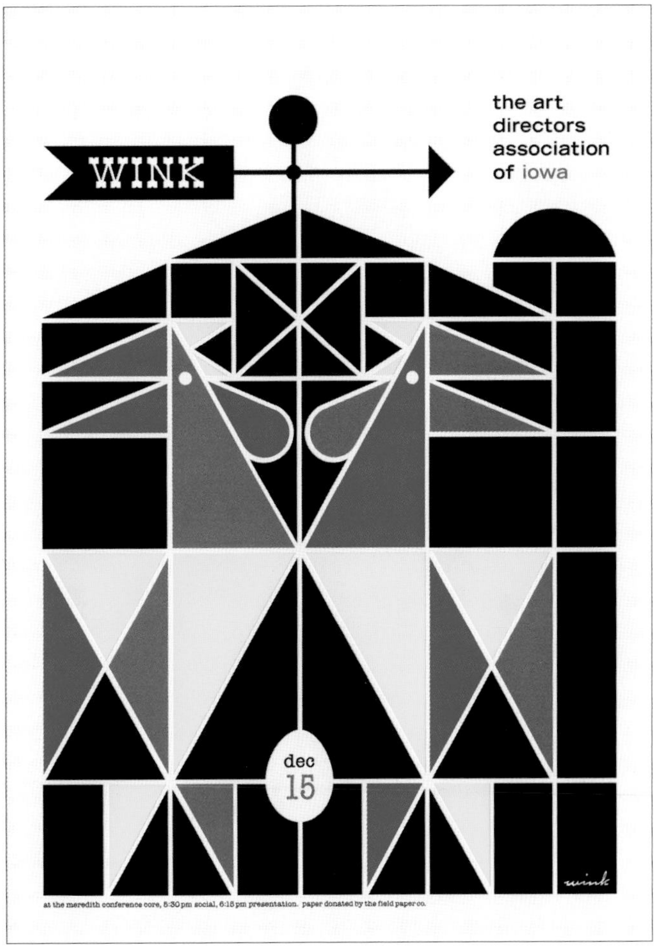
WINK
the art directors association of iowa
dec
15
wink
at the meredith conference core, 5:30 pm social, 6:15 pm presentation. paper donated by the field paper co.

MERIT

DESIGNERS
Richard Boynton
Scott Thares

ILLUSTRATORS
Scott Thares
Richard Boynton

CREATIVE DIRECTORS
Scott Thares
Richard Boynton

CLIENT
The Art Directors Association of Iowa

AGENCY
Wink/Minneapolis

ANNUAL ID
06208D

MERIT

DESIGNER
Scott Thares

ILLUSTRATOR
Scott Thares

CREATIVE DIRECTORS
Scott Thares
Richard Boynton

CLIENT
The Hurricane Poster Project

AGENCY
Wink/Minneapolis

ANNUAL ID
06209D

wink

MERIT

DESIGNER
Richard Boynton

ILLUSTRATOR
Richard Boynton

CREATIVE DIRECTORS
Richard Boynton
Scott Thares

CLIENT
The Hurricane Poster Project

AGENCY
Wink/Minneapolis

ANNUAL ID
06210D

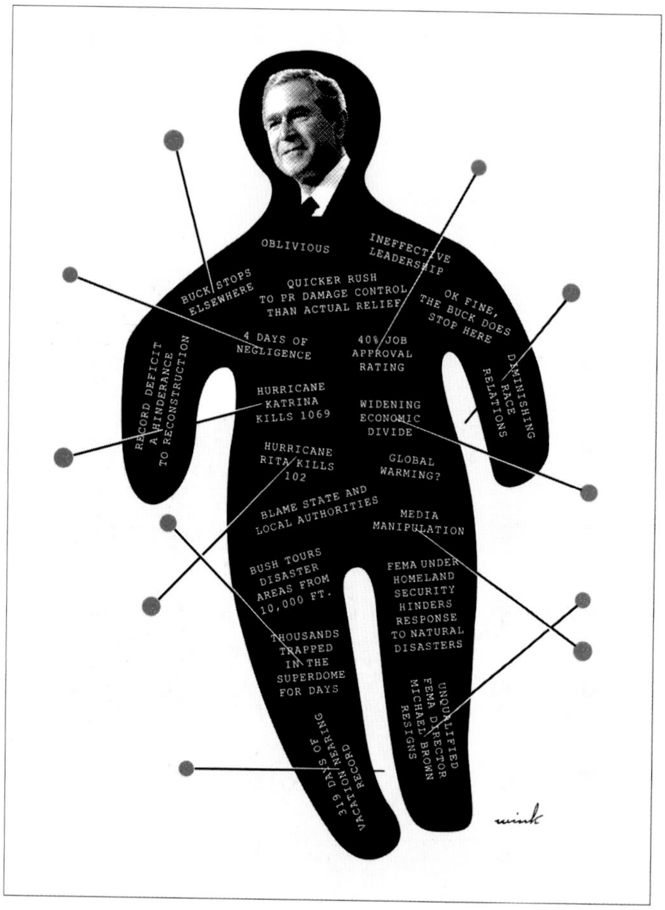
OBLIVIOUS
INEFFECTIVE LEADERSHIP
BUCK STOPS ELSEWHERE
QUICKER RUSH TO PR DAMAGE CONTROL THAN ACTUAL RELIEF
OK FINE, THE BUCK DOES STOP HERE
4 DAYS OF NEGLIGENCE
40% JOB APPROVAL RATING
RECORD DEFICIT A HINDERANCE TO RECONSTRUCTION
DIMINISHING RACE RELATIONS
HURRICANE KATRINA KILLS 1069
WIDENING ECONOMIC DIVIDE
HURRICANE RITA KILLS 102
GLOBAL WARMING?
BLAME STATE AND LOCAL AUTHORITIES
MEDIA MANIPULATION
BUSH TOURS DISASTER AREAS FROM 10,000 FT.
FEMA UNDER HOMELAND SECURITY HINDERS RESPONSE TO NATURAL DISASTERS
THOUSANDS TRAPPED IN THE SUPERDOME FOR DAYS
319 DAYS OF VACATION NEARING RECORD
UNQUALIFIED FEMA DIRECTOR MICHAEL BROWN RESIGNS
wink

TOMMY LEE MARRIED STRIPPER CANDICE STARREK FOR ONE MONTH THEN DATED FORMER O.J. LOVER TAWNY KITAEN MARRIED HEATHER LOCKLEAR DIVORCED HER MET PAMELA ANDERSON MARRIED HER AFTER 4 DAYS OF KNOWING HER THEN HAD KIDS WITH HER PUNCHED HER RELEASED A PORN VIDEO OF HER GAVE HER HEPATITIS-C AND DIVORCED HER TO HOOK UP WITH PORN STAR JENNA JAMESON WHO HE CHEATED ON WITH DENNIS RODMAN'S 3-WEEK WIFE CARMEN ELECTRA DID DRUGS WENT TO JAIL GOT BUSTED WITH HOOKERS GOT ENGAGED AGAIN BROKE UP DATED SINGER PINK WHO DUMPED HIM FOR AN EX. STILL WANT TO GET RELATIONSHIP ADVICE FROM THE ENTERTAINMENT INDUSTRY?
STEP UP SPEAK OUT .COM

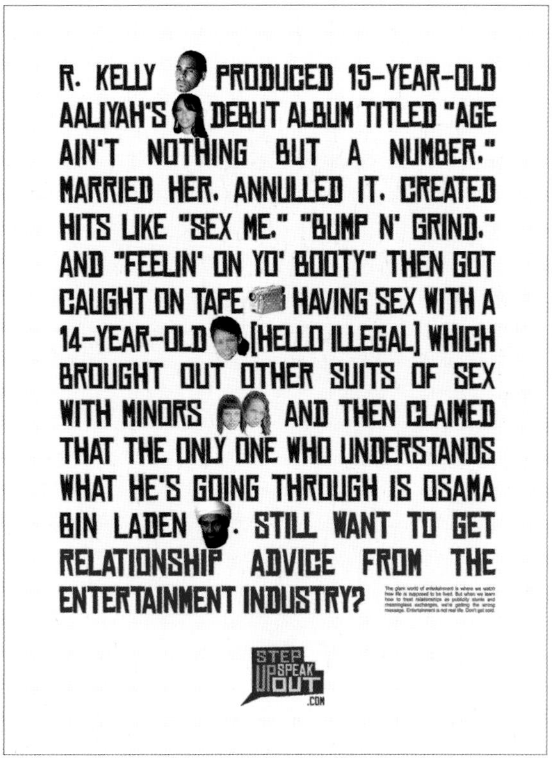
R. KELLY PRODUCED 15-YEAR-OLD AALIYAH'S DEBUT ALBUM TITLED "AGE AIN'T NOTHING BUT A NUMBER." MARRIED HER. ANNULLED IT. CREATED HITS LIKE "SEX ME," "BUMP N' GRIND," AND "FEELIN' ON YO' BOOTY" THEN GOT CAUGHT ON TAPE HAVING SEX WITH A 14-YEAR-OLD [HELLO ILLEGAL] WHICH BROUGHT OUT OTHER SUITS OF SEX WITH MINORS AND THEN CLAIMED THAT THE ONLY ONE WHO UNDERSTANDS WHAT HE'S GOING THROUGH IS OSAMA BIN LADEN. STILL WANT TO GET RELATIONSHIP ADVICE FROM THE ENTERTAINMENT INDUSTRY?
STEP UP SPEAK OUT .COM

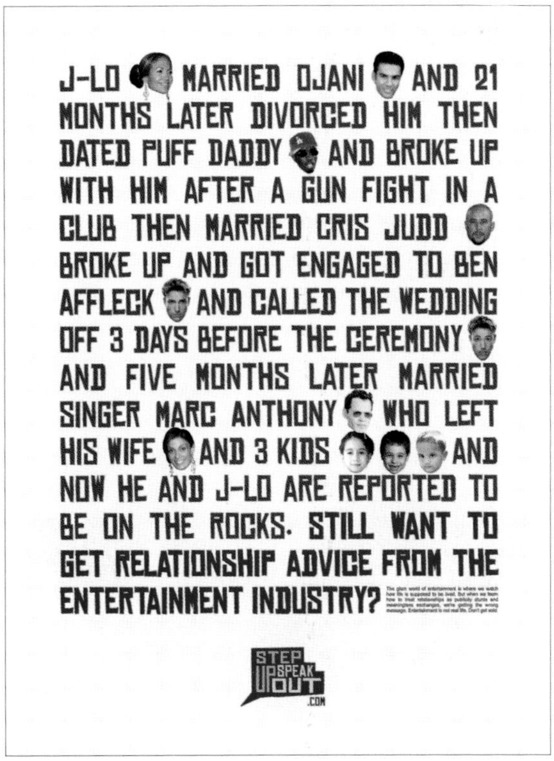
J-LO MARRIED OJANI AND 21 MONTHS LATER DIVORCED HIM THEN DATED PUFF DADDY AND BROKE UP WITH HIM AFTER A GUN FIGHT IN A CLUB THEN MARRIED CRIS JUDD BROKE UP AND GOT ENGAGED TO BEN AFFLECK AND CALLED THE WEDDING OFF 3 DAYS BEFORE THE CEREMONY AND FIVE MONTHS LATER MARRIED SINGER MARC ANTHONY WHO LEFT HIS WIFE AND 3 KIDS AND NOW HE AND J-LO ARE REPORTED TO BE ON THE ROCKS. STILL WANT TO GET RELATIONSHIP ADVICE FROM THE ENTERTAINMENT INDUSTRY?
STEP UP SPEAK OUT .COM

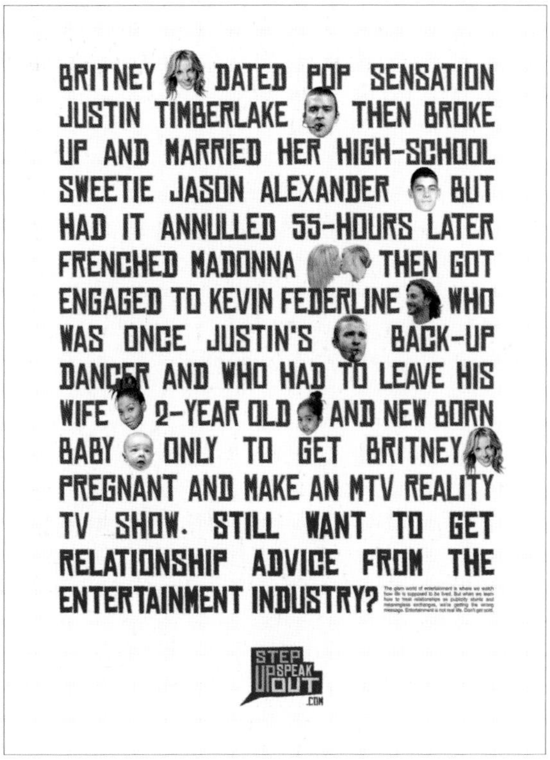
BRITNEY DATED POP SENSATION JUSTIN TIMBERLAKE THEN BROKE UP AND MARRIED HER HIGH-SCHOOL SWEETIE JASON ALEXANDER BUT HAD IT ANNULLED 55-HOURS LATER FRENCHED MADONNA THEN GOT ENGAGED TO KEVIN FEDERLINE WHO WAS ONCE JUSTIN'S BACK-UP DANCER AND WHO HAD TO LEAVE HIS WIFE 2-YEAR OLD AND NEW BORN BABY ONLY TO GET BRITNEY PREGNANT AND MAKE AN MTV REALITY TV SHOW. STILL WANT TO GET RELATIONSHIP ADVICE FROM THE ENTERTAINMENT INDUSTRY?
STEP UP SPEAK OUT .COM

MERIT

WRITER
Clint! Runge

ILLUSTRATORS
Carey Goddard
Cassidy Kovanda

CREATIVE DIRECTOR
Clint! Runge

CLIENT
Nebraska Domestic Violence Council

AGENCY
Archrival/Lincoln

ANNUAL ID
06211D

MERIT

ART DIRECTORS
Tetsu Goto
Shizuko Goto

WRITER
Tetsu Goto

ILLUSTRATOR
Tetsu Goto

CREATIVE DIRECTOR
Tetsu Goto

CLIENT
National Federation of UNESCO Associations in Japan

AGENCY
Dentsu/Tokyo

ANNUAL ID
06212D

Change your viewpoint. Change the world.
UNESCO
If you change your viewpoint, you can often find something completely different.

Change your viewpoint. Change the world.
UNESCO
If you change your viewpoint, you can often find something completely different.

Change your viewpoint. Change the world.
UNESCO
If you change your viewpoint, you can often find something completely different.

Change your viewpoint. Change the world.
UNESCO
If you change your viewpoint, you can often find something completely different.

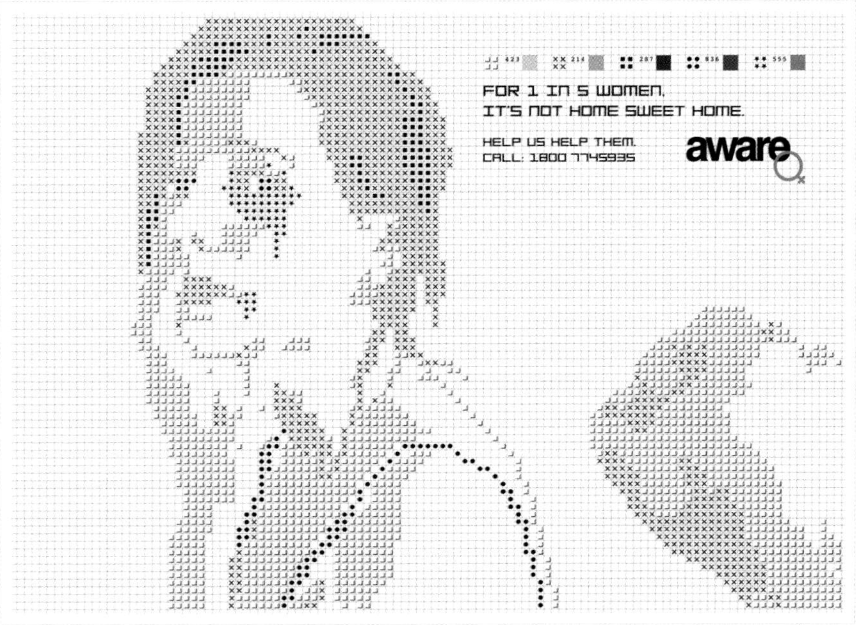
FOR 1 IN 5 WOMEN,
IT'S NOT HOME SWEET HOME.
HELP US HELP THEM.
CALL: 1800 7745935
aware

Merit

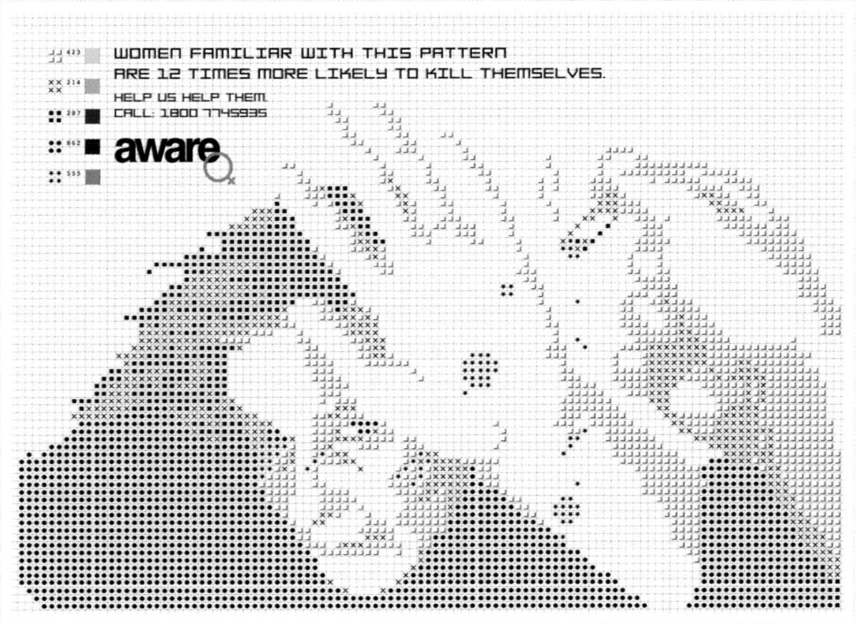
WOMEN FAMILIAR WITH THIS PATTERN
ARE 12 TIMES MORE LIKELY TO KILL THEMSELVES.
HELP US HELP THEM.
CALL: 1800 7745935
aware

EVERY 3 DAYS,
A WOMAN GETS
STITCHED UP.
HELP US HELP THEM.
CALL: 1800 7745935
aware

MERIT

DESIGNER
Aaron Phua

ART DIRECTOR
Aaron Phua

WRITER
Raymond Chin

ILLUSTRATOR
Aaron Phua

CREATIVE DIRECTORS
Calvin Soh
Yang Yeo

CLIENT
Aware Singapore

AGENCY
Fallon/Singapore

ANNUAL ID
06213D

ALSO AWARDED
Merit:
Public Service/Non-Profit/Educational: Posters – Single

Merit

DESIGNER
Masayoshi Kodaira

ART DIRECTOR
Masayoshi Kodaira

PHOTOGRAPHER
Mikiya Takimoto

CLIENT
Organaizing Comittee for the Exhibition Bauhaus Dessau: Mikiya Takimoto

AGENCY
Flame/Tokyo

ANNUAL ID
06214D

ALSO AWARDED
Merit: Environmental Design - Single

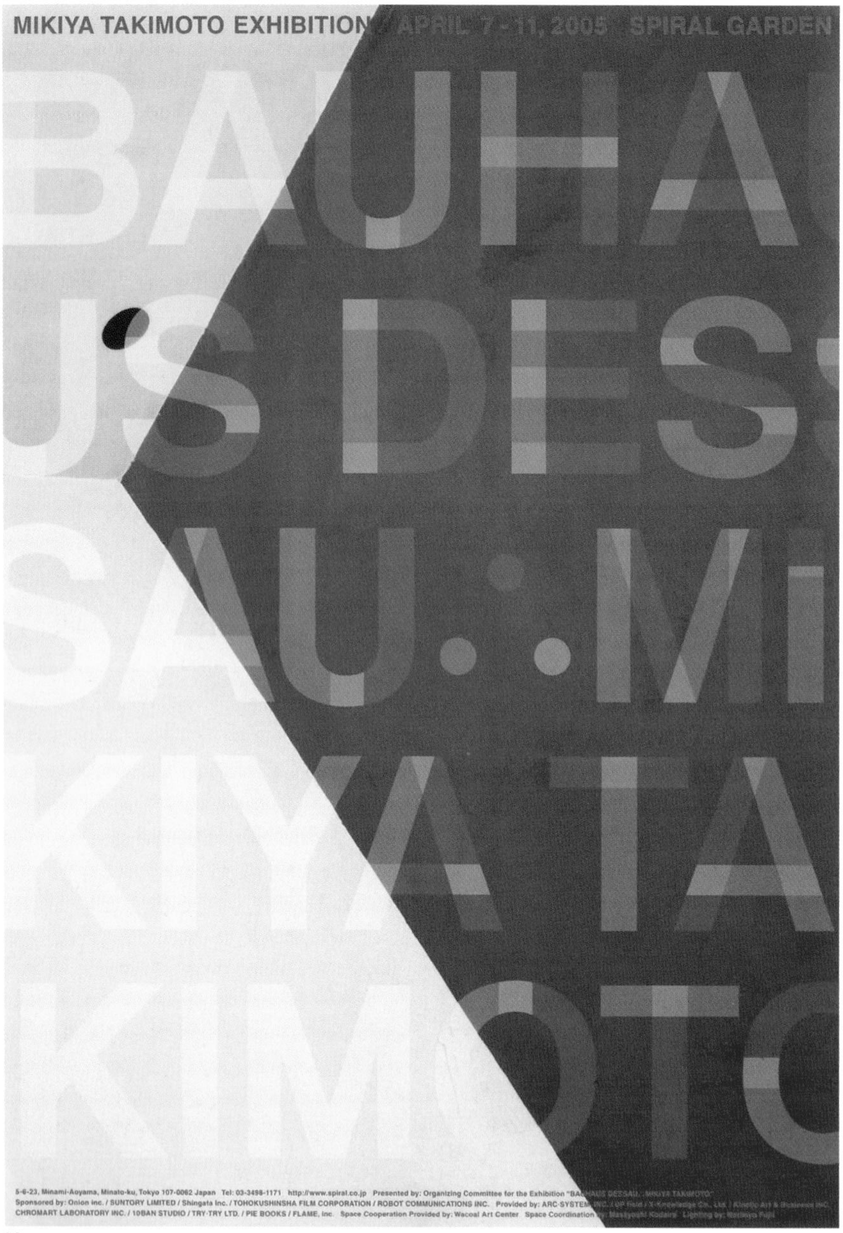
MIKIYA TAKIMOTO EXHIBITION APRIL 7 - 11, 2005 SPIRAL GARDEN
BAUHAUS DESSAU: MIKIYA TAKIMOTO
5-6-23, Minami-Aoyama, Minato-ku, Tokyo 107-0062 Japan Tel: 03-3498-1171 http://www.spiral.co.jp Presented by: Organizing Committee for the Exhibition
Sponsored by: Onion inc. / SUNTORY LIMITED / Shingata Inc. / TOHOKUSHINSHA FILM CORPORATION / ROBOT COMMUNICATIONS INC. Provided by: ARC-SYSTEM
CHROMART LABORATORY INC. / 10BAN STUDIO / TRY-TRY LTD. / PIE BOOKS / FLAME, Inc. Space Cooperation Provided by: Wacoal Art Center Space Coordination

Merit

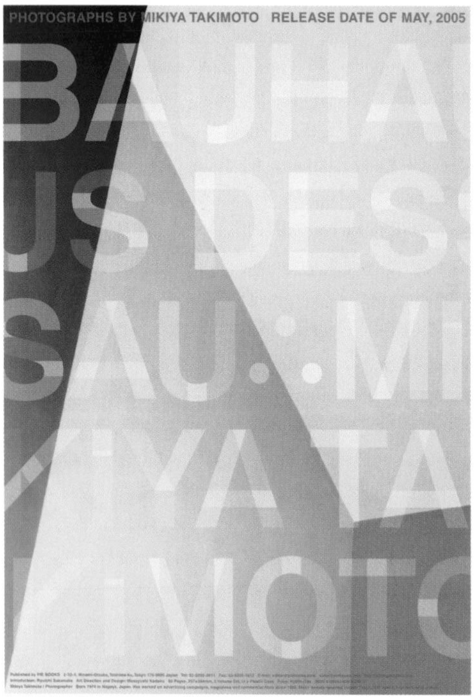
PHOTOGRAPHS BY MIKIYA TAKIMOTO RELEASE DATE OF MAY, 2005
BAUHAUS DESSAU: MIKIYA TAKIMOTO

NOTHING COULD STOP THE JAPANESE.
NOT EVEN A PREGNANT WOMAN.
WORLD WAR II
THE EURASIAN STORY

THE ONLY HOPE OF ESCAPE FROM THE JAPANESE WAS TO RAM A CONCRETE WALL WITH YOUR OWN SKULL.
WORLD WAR II
THE EURASIAN STORY

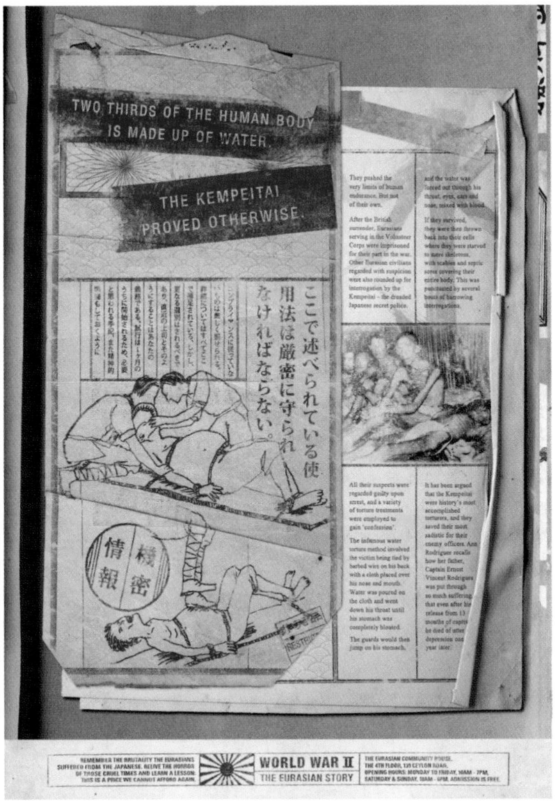
TWO THIRDS OF THE HUMAN BODY IS MADE UP OF WATER.
THE KEMPEITAI PROVED OTHERWISE.
ここで述べられている使用法は厳密に守られなければならない。
WORLD WAR II
THE EURASIAN STORY

AT THE COST OF 300 DEATHS PER KILOMETRE, THE JAPANESE COMMAND CONSIDERED THE RAILWAY A CHEAP BARGAIN.
WORLD WAR II
THE EURASIAN STORY

Merit

ART DIRECTORS
Francis Ooi
Agnes Lee
Irene Lau

WRITER
Alvin Wong Twei

CREATIVE DIRECTORS
Francis Ooi
Alvin Wong Twei

CLIENT
The Eurasian Association Singapore

AGENCY
The Alchemy Partnership/Singapore

ANNUAL ID
06215D

Merit

ART DIRECTOR
Denison Kusano

WRITER
Greg Christensen

ILLUSTRATOR
Alan Daniels

CREATIVE DIRECTORS
Dave Loew
Jon Wyville

CLIENT
National Parks Conservation Association

AGENCY
Young & Rubicam/ Chicago

ANNUAL ID
06216D

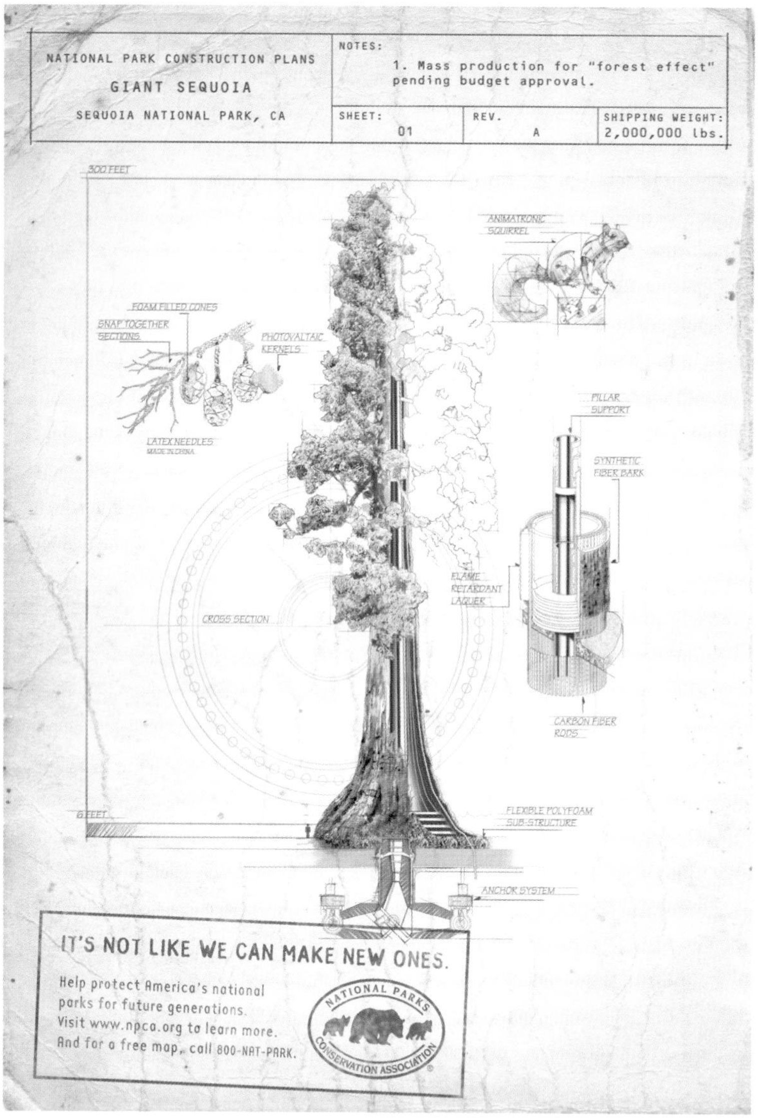
NATIONAL PARK CONSTRUCTION PLANS
GIANT SEQUOIA
SEQUOIA NATIONAL PARK, CA
NOTES:
1. Mass production for "forest effect" pending budget approval.
SHEET: 01
REV. A
SHIPPING WEIGHT: 2,000,000 lbs.
300 FEET
ANIMATRONIC SQUIRREL
FOAM FILLED CONES
SNAP TOGETHER SECTIONS
PHOTOVALTAIC KERNELS
LATEX NEEDLES
PILLAR SUPPORT
SYNTHETIC FIBER BARK
FLAME RETARDANT LAQUER
CROSS SECTION
CARBON FIBER RODS
FLEXIBLE POLYFOAM SUB-STRUCTURE
ANCHOR SYSTEM
IT'S NOT LIKE WE CAN MAKE NEW ONES.
Help protect America's national parks for future generations.
Visit www.npca.org to learn more.
And for a free map, call 800-NAT-PARK.
NATIONAL PARKS CONSERVATION ASSOCIATION

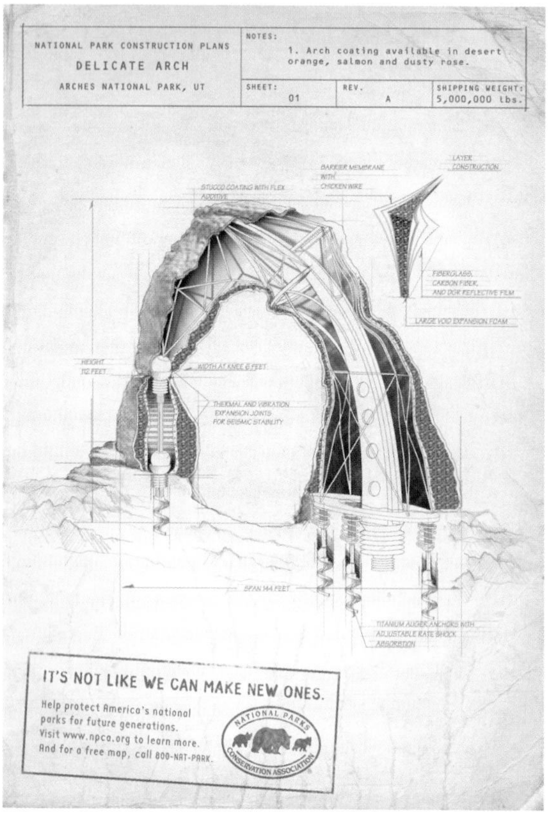
NATIONAL PARK CONSTRUCTION PLANS
DELICATE ARCH
ARCHES NATIONAL PARK, UT
NOTES:
1. Arch coating available in desert orange, salmon and dusty rose.
SHEET: 01
REV. A
SHIPPING WEIGHT: 5,000,000 lbs.
IT'S NOT LIKE WE CAN MAKE NEW ONES.
Help protect America's national parks for future generations.
Visit www.npca.org to learn more.
And for a free map, call 800-NAT-PARK.
NATIONAL PARKS CONSERVATION ASSOCIATION

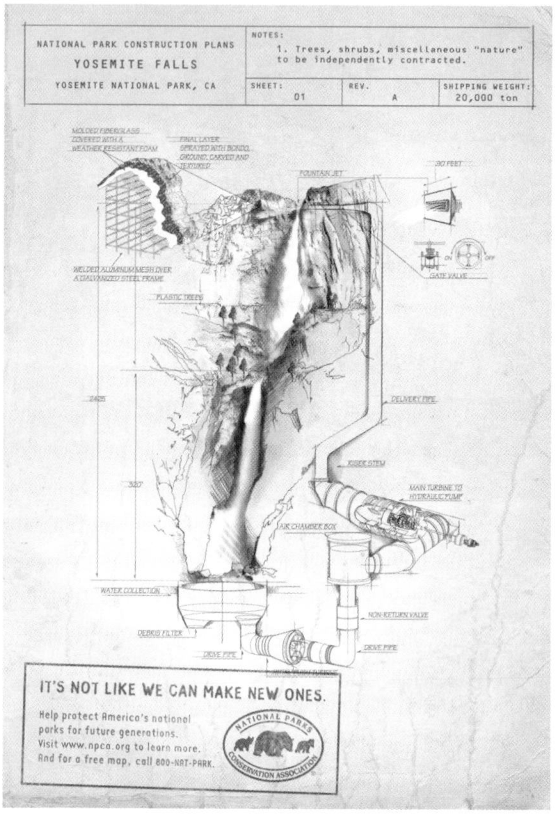
NATIONAL PARK CONSTRUCTION PLANS
YOSEMITE FALLS
YOSEMITE NATIONAL PARK, CA
NOTES:
1. Trees, shrubs, miscellaneous "nature" to be independently contracted.
SHEET: 01
REV. A
SHIPPING WEIGHT: 20,000 ton
IT'S NOT LIKE WE CAN MAKE NEW ONES.
Help protect America's national parks for future generations.
Visit www.npca.org to learn more.
And for a free map, call 800-NAT-PARK.
NATIONAL PARKS CONSERVATION ASSOCIATION

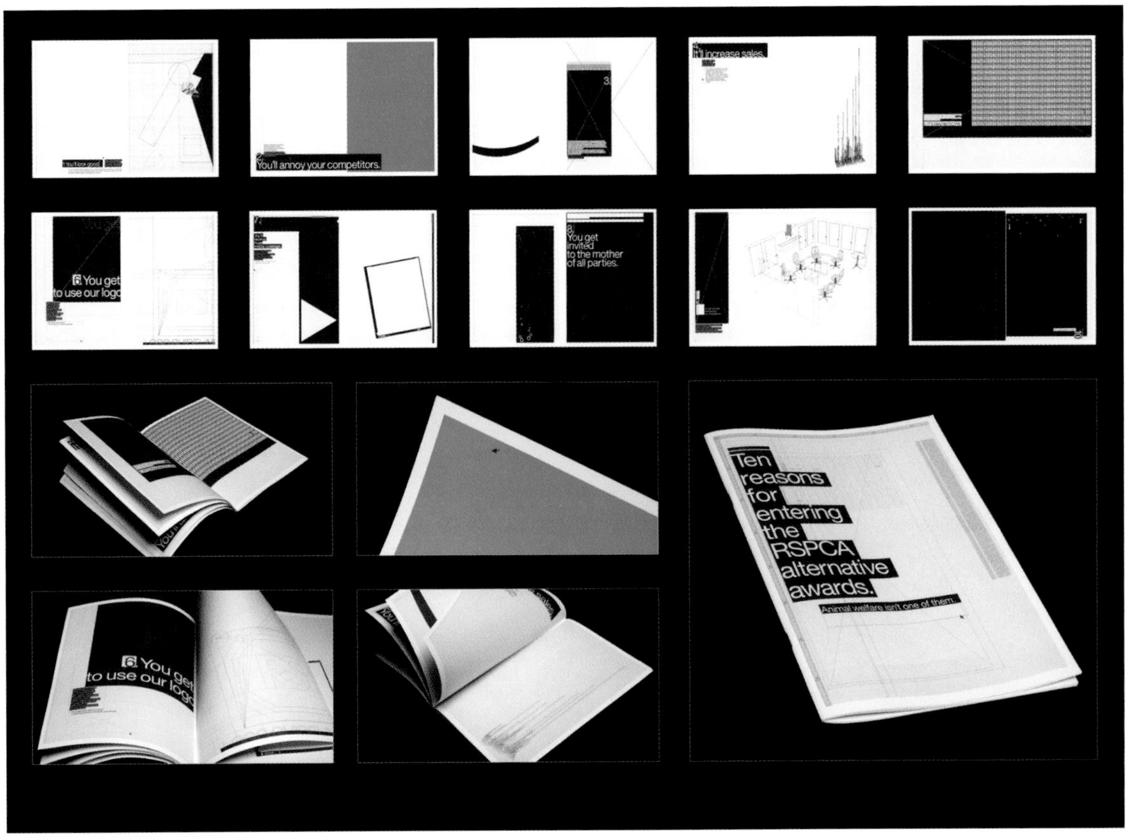
You'll annoy your competitors.
increase sales.
8. You get invited to the mother of all parties.
6. You get to use our logo
Ten reasons for entering the RSPCA alternative awards.
Animal welfare isn't one of them.

MERIT

DESIGNER
Nils Leonard

ART DIRECTORS
Sonny Adorjan
Milo Campbell

WRITERS
Sonny Adorjan
Milo Campbell

CREATIVE DIRECTORS
Nigel Roberts
Paul Belford

CLIENT
RSPCA

AGENCY
Abbott Mead Vickers BBDO/London

ANNUAL ID
06217D

You useless BITCH!

MERIT

ART DIRECTOR
Theresa Tsang

WRITER
Valerie Chen

PHOTOGRAPHER
Allen Dang

CREATIVE DIRECTOR
Kien Eng Tan

CLIENT
Women's Aid Organisation

AGENCY
Arc Worldwide/Leo Burnett/Kuala Lumpur

ANNUAL ID
06218D

MERIT

DESIGNERS
Vanessa Eckstein
Mariana Contegni

ART DIRECTOR
Vanessa Eckstein

CLIENT
Marco

AGENCY
Blok Design/Mexico

ANNUAL ID
06219D

smith /tercerunquinto /emanuel tovar /pablo vargas lugo /
sólo los personajes cambian

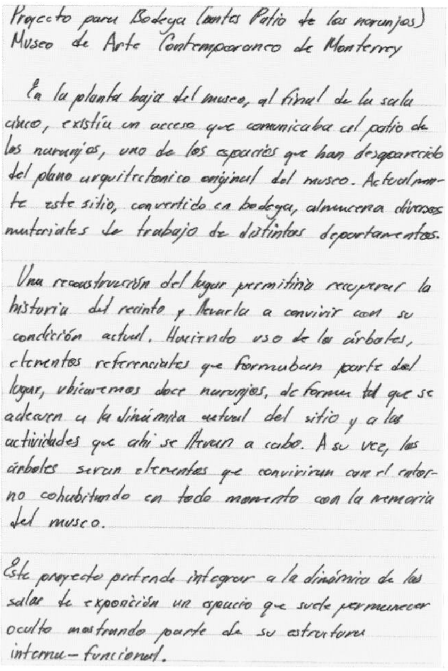

Proyecto para Bodega (antes Patio de los naranjos)
Museo de Arte Contemporaneo de Monterrey

En la planta baja del museo, al final de la sala cinco, existía un acceso que comunicaba al patio de los naranjos, uno de los espacios que han desaparecido del plano arquitectonico original del museo. Actualmente este sitio, convertido en bodega, almacena diversos materiales de trabajo de distintos departamentos.

Una reconstrucción del lugar permitiria recuperar la historia del recinto y llevarla a convivir con su condición actual. Haciendo uso de los árboles, elementos referenciales que formaban parte del lugar, ubicaremos doce naranjos, de forma tal que se adecuen a la dinámica actual del sitio y a las actividades que ahí se llevan a cabo. A su vez, los árboles serán elementos que convivirán con el entorno cohabitando en todo momento con la memoria del museo.

Este proyecto pretende integrar a la dinámica de las salas de exposición un espacio que suele permanecer oculto mostrando parte de su estructura interna-funcional.

MARCO
Proyecto para Bodega
(antes Patio de los naranjos)
Mesas para recepciones

MERIT

DESIGNER
Lydia Lim

ART DIRECTORS
Lydia Lim
Gigi Lee

WRITER
Primus Nair

PHOTOGRAPHER
Yuk Hou Chong

ILLUSTRATOR
Lydia Lim

CREATIVE DIRECTORS
Steve Hough
Henry Yap

CLIENT
Amnesty International Malaysia

AGENCY
Saatchi & Saatchi/Petaling Jaya

ANNUAL ID
06220D

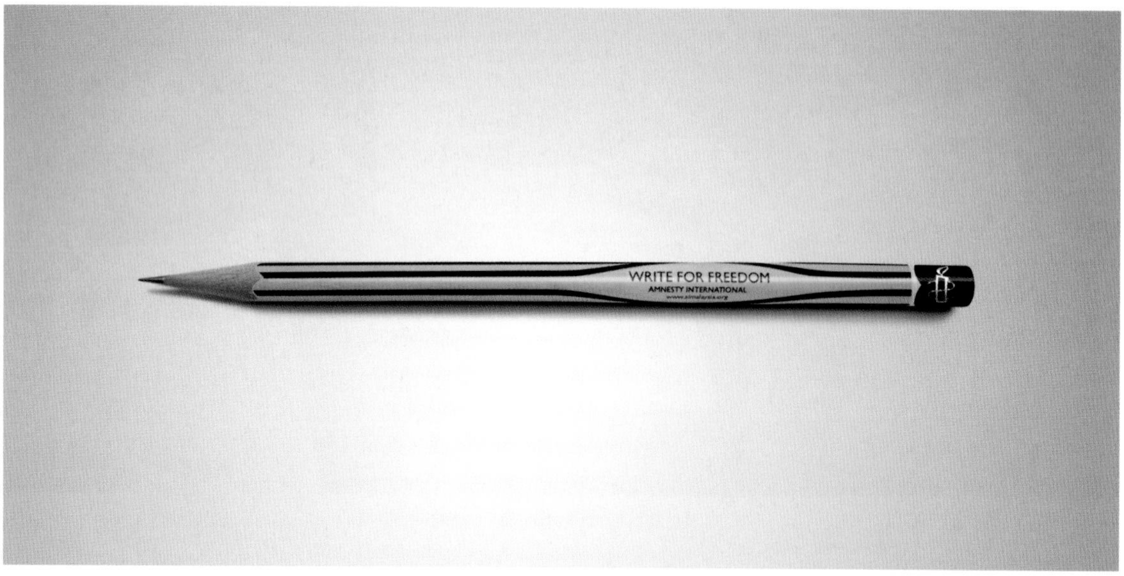
WRITE FOR FREEDOM
AMNESTY INTERNATIONAL

IF YOU'RE THIS COLD AFTER FOUR MINUTES,
IMAGINE HOW YOU'D FEEL AFTER A WHOLE NIGHT.

PLEASE DONATE BLANKETS

Merit

DESIGNER
Debbie Gyngell

ART DIRECTORS
Alan Lewus
Debbie Gyngell

WRITER
Stefanus Nel

PHOTOGRAPHER
Michael Meyersfeld

ILLUSTRATOR
Belinda Leontsinis

CREATIVE DIRECTOR
Vanessa Pearson

CLIENT
Salvation Army

AGENCY
Lobedu Leo Burnett/ Sunninghill

ANNUAL ID
06221D

Sallie's
WonderfullyWarm
TEL 011 718 8746
A
B
B

SUPPORT THE
HOMELESS
THIS WINTER.

SUPPORT THE
HOMELESS
THIS WINTER.

MERIT

COLLEGE

MERIT

ART DIRECTOR
Punita Tanna

WRITER
Punita Tanna

SCHOOL
Academy of Art
University/San Francisco

CCA004

By 2015, we might view the world differently.
Hybridcenter.org
Cleaner technology for a better tomorrow.

CRAYONS
By 2015, we might view the world differently.
Hybridcenter.org
Cleaner technology for a better tomorrow.

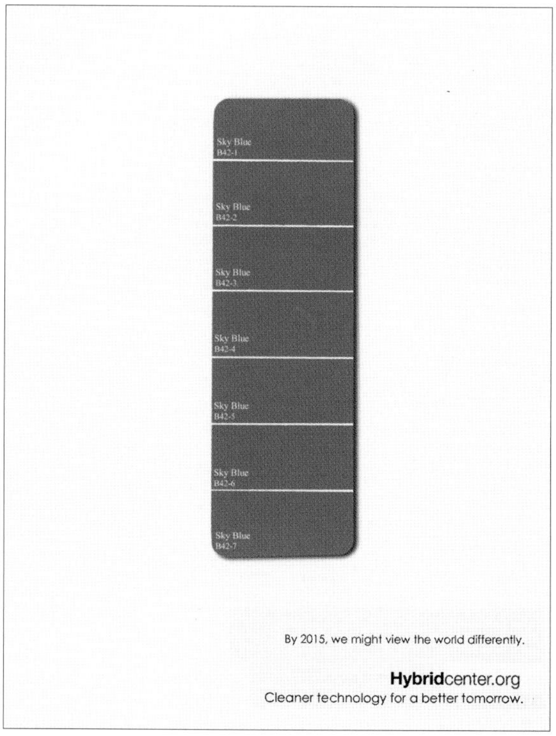
Sky Blue B42-1
Sky Blue B42-2
Sky Blue B42-3
Sky Blue B42-4
Sky Blue B42-5
Sky Blue B42-6
Sky Blue B42-7
By 2015, we might view the world differently.
Hybridcenter.org
Cleaner technology for a better tomorrow.

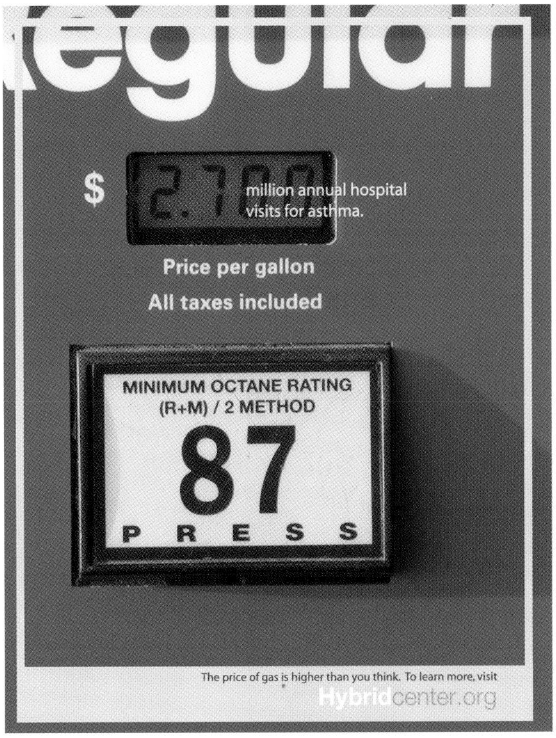
egular
$
2.700
million annual hospital
visits for asthma.
Price per gallon
All taxes included
MINIMUM OCTANE RATING
(R+M) / 2 METHOD
87
P R E S S
The price of gas is higher than you think. To learn more, visit
Hybridcenter.org

76
%
of drivers spend
more on gas
than food.
The price of gas is higher than you think. To learn more, visit
Hybridcenter.org

100,000 troops
Mobil
ized for war.
The price of gas is higher than you think. To learn more, visit
Hybridcenter.org

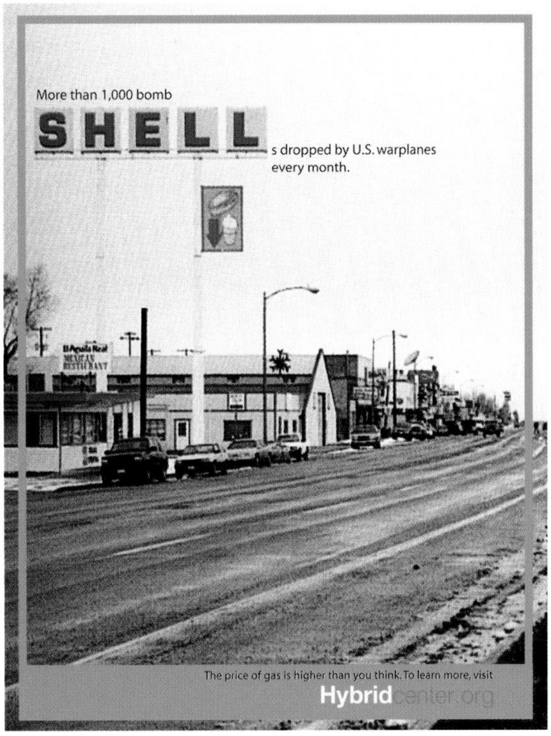
More than 1,000 bomb
SHELL
s dropped by U.S. warplanes
every month.
The price of gas is higher than you think. To learn more, visit
Hybridcenter.org

MERIT

ART DIRECTORS
Tiffany Stark
Charles D'Attilio

WRITERS
Yama Rahyar
Tiffany Stark

SCHOOL
The Book Shop/ Culver City

CCA005

MERIT

ART DIRECTOR
Amanda Sinele

WRITERS
Jennifer O'Brien
Howard Shur

SCHOOL
The Book Shop/
Culver City

CCA006

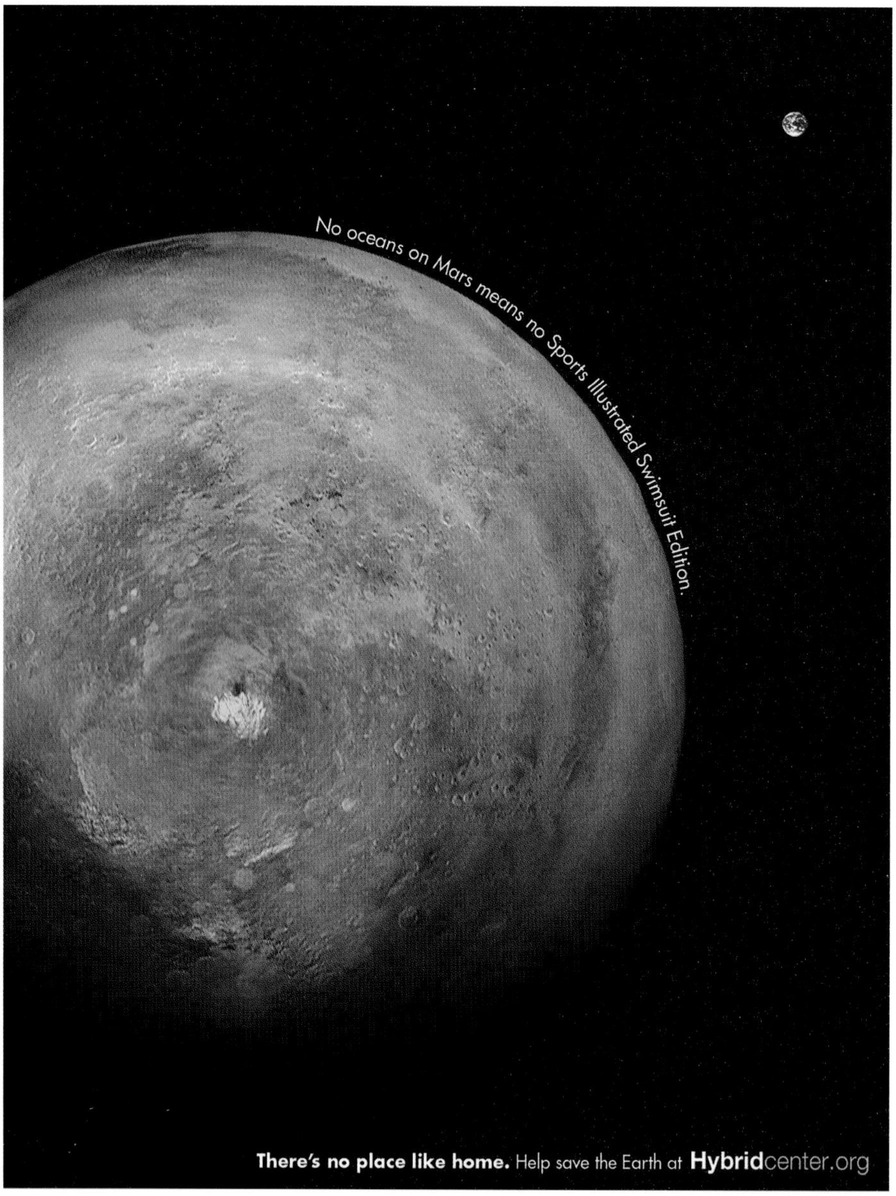
No oceans on Mars means no Sports Illustrated Swimsuit Edition.
There's no place like home. Help save the Earth at Hybridcenter.org

Jupiter. Gassier than your Uncle Morty.
There's no place like home. Help save the Earth at Hybridcenter.org

With Mercury topping 800° F, there would be no marching and definitely no penguins.
There's no place like home. Help save the Earth at Hybridcenter.org

_z_ne
If you think O_2 isn't that important, think again.
Earth first. Hybridcenter.org

w_rkf_rce
Destroy the O_2 and you also hurt those who depend on it.
Earth first. Hybridcenter.org

MERIT

ART DIRECTOR
Mariam Farooq

WRITER
Lisa Boosin

SCHOOL
The Book Shop/ Culver City

CCA007

ec_l_gy
When you deplete the O_2, look at what else you ruin.
Earth first. Hybridcenter.org

MERIT

ART DIRECTOR
Mariam Farooq

WRITER
Lisa Boosin

SCHOOL
*The Book Shop/
Culver City*

CCA008

WHEN YOU BRING TOGETHER A ZEAL FOR TECHNOLOGY AND A LOVE OF HUMANITY, IT JUST MIGHT BE POSSIBLE TO SAVE THE WORLD.
WHAT IF. Hybridcenter.org

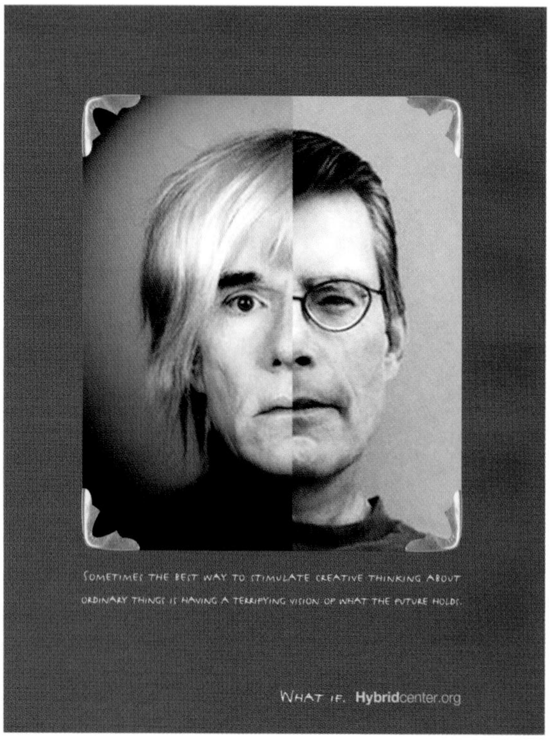
SOMETIMES THE BEST WAY TO STIMULATE CREATIVE THINKING ABOUT ORDINARY THINGS IS HAVING A TERRIFYING VISION OF WHAT THE FUTURE HOLDS.
WHAT IF. Hybridcenter.org

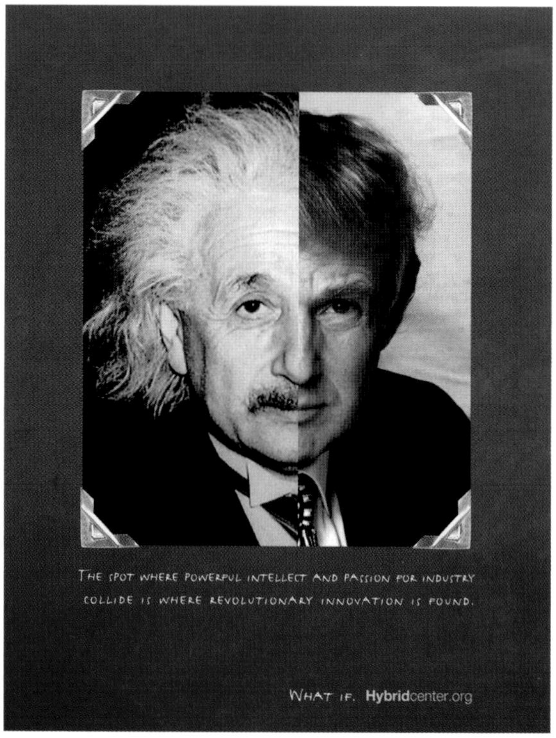
THE SPOT WHERE POWERFUL INTELLECT AND PASSION FOR INDUSTRY COLLIDE IS WHERE REVOLUTIONARY INNOVATION IS FOUND.
WHAT IF. Hybridcenter.org

TRAIL BEGINS
TRAIL ENDS
Limit emissions, before it limits your lifestyle.
Hybridcenter.org

10
20
10
Limit emissions, before it limits your lifestyle.
Hybridcenter.org

Limit emissions, before it limits your lifestyle.
Hybridcenter.org

MERIT

ART DIRECTOR
Shevaun Seene

WRITER
Shannon Duffy

SCHOOL
The Book Shop/ Culver City

CCA009

Merit

ART DIRECTOR
Hunter Sebresos

WRITERS
Hunter Sebresos
Spencer Hansen

PHOTOGRAPHER
Kyle Morgan

SCHOOL
Brigham Young University/Provo

CC010

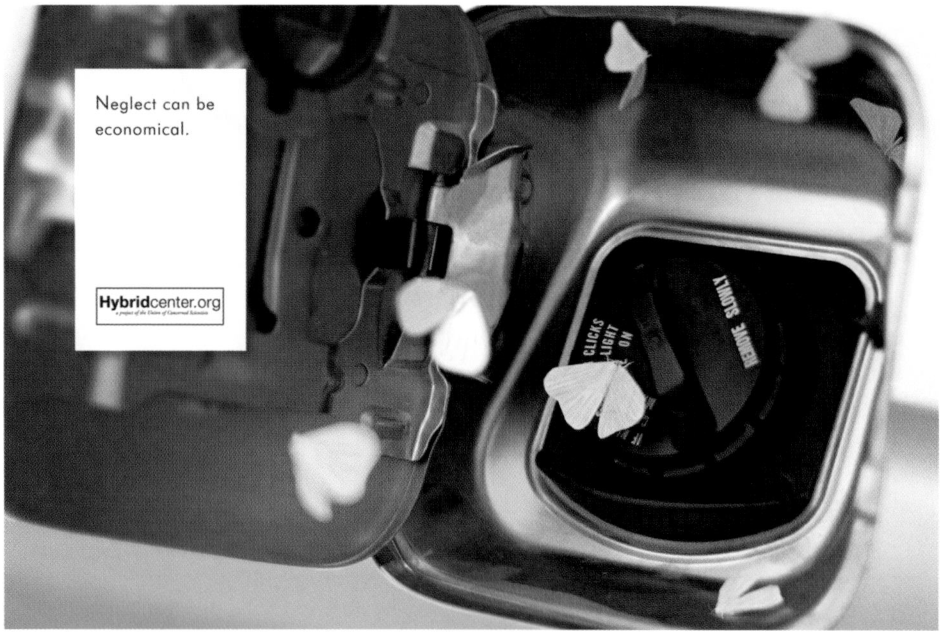
Neglect can be economical.
Hybridcenter.org

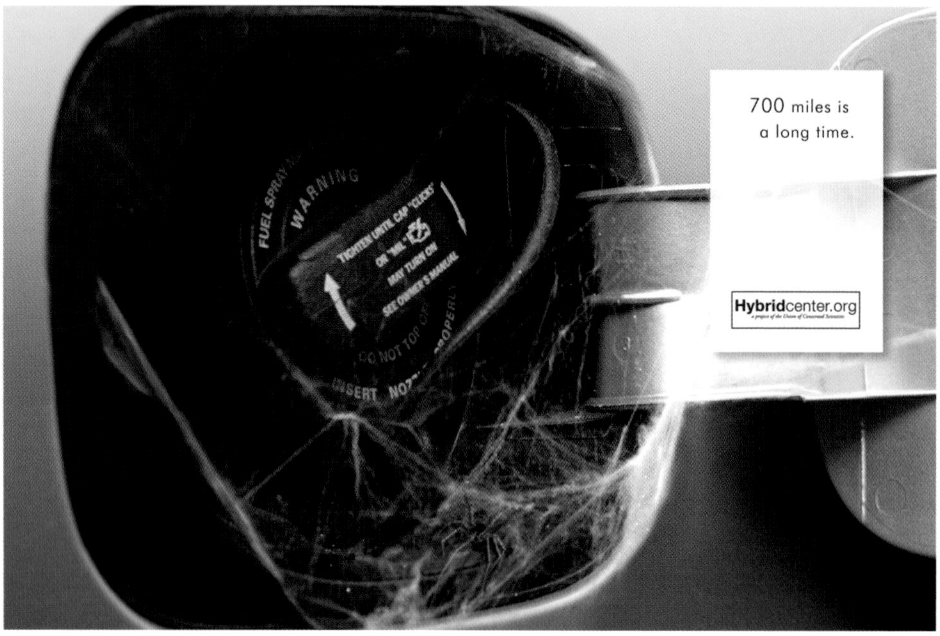
700 miles is a long time.
Hybridcenter.org
WARNING

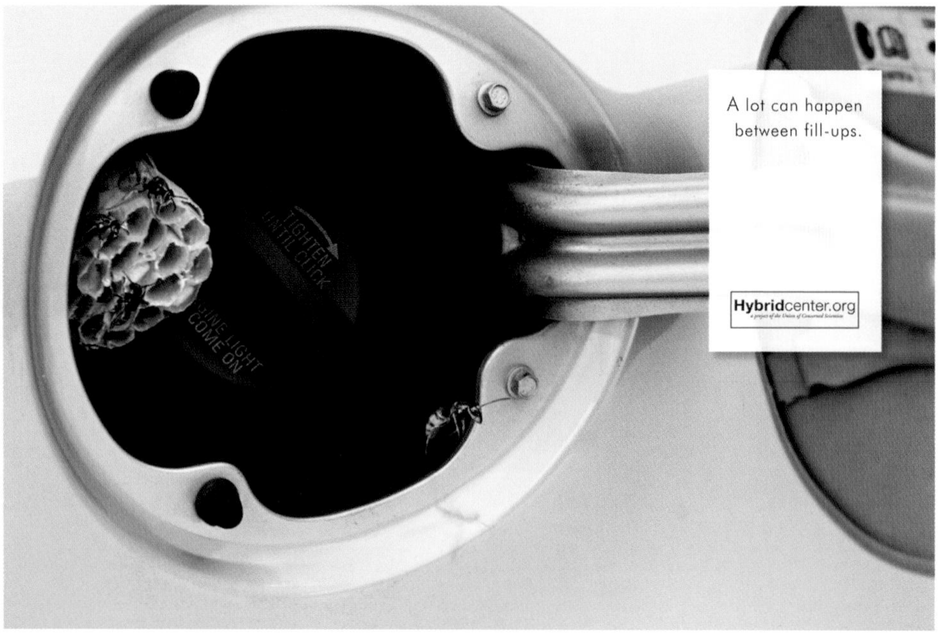
A lot can happen between fill-ups.
Hybridcenter.org

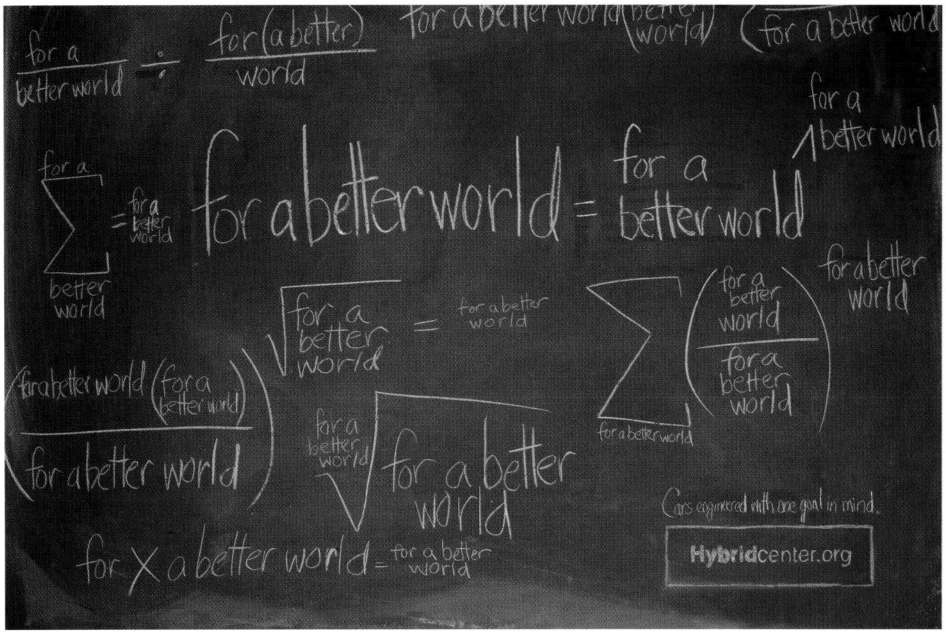
for a better world
for (a better) world
for a better world
for a better world
for a better world = for a better world
for a better world
Cars engineered with one goal in mind.
Hybridcenter.org

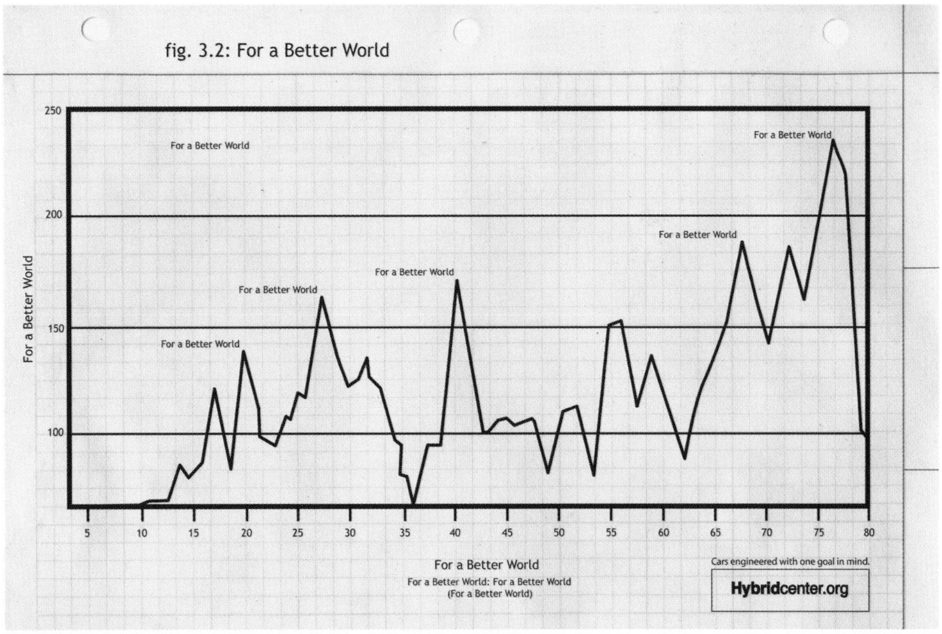
fig. 3.2: For a Better World
For a Better World
250
200
150
100
5
10
15
20
25
30
35
40
45
50
55
60
65
70
75
80
For a Better World
For a Better World: For a Better World
(For a Better World)
Cars engineered with one goal in mind.
Hybridcenter.org

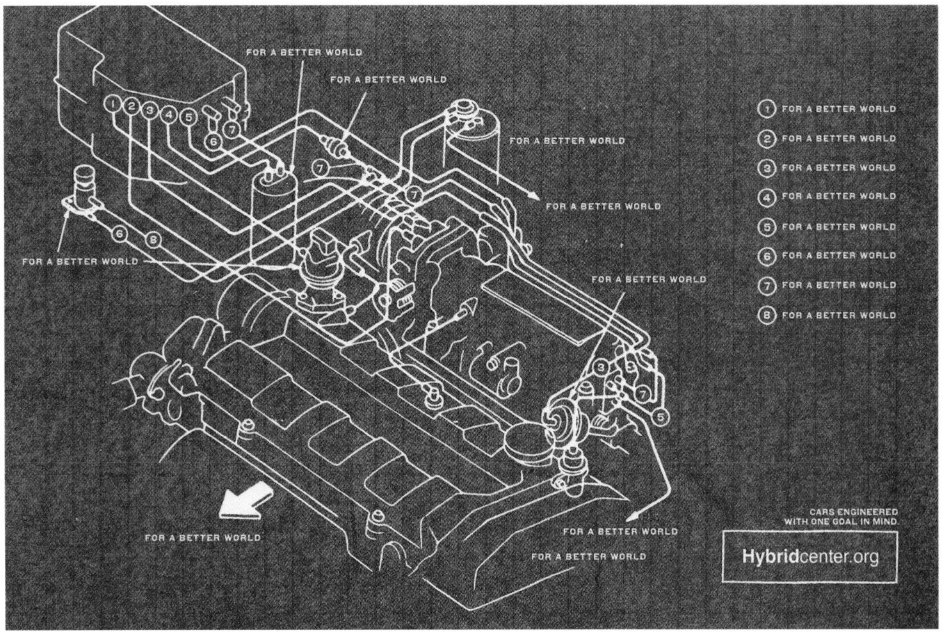
FOR A BETTER WORLD
1 FOR A BETTER WORLD
2 FOR A BETTER WORLD
3 FOR A BETTER WORLD
4 FOR A BETTER WORLD
5 FOR A BETTER WORLD
6 FOR A BETTER WORLD
7 FOR A BETTER WORLD
8 FOR A BETTER WORLD
CARS ENGINEERED WITH ONE GOAL IN MIND.
Hybridcenter.org

MERIT

ART DIRECTOR
Aimee Roberge

WRITER
Nick Zafonte

SCHOOL
The Creative Circus/ Atlanta

CCA011

MERIT

WRITER
Alicia Dotter

ART DIRECTOR
Paula Cristalli

SCHOOL
The Creative Circus/ Atlanta

CCA012

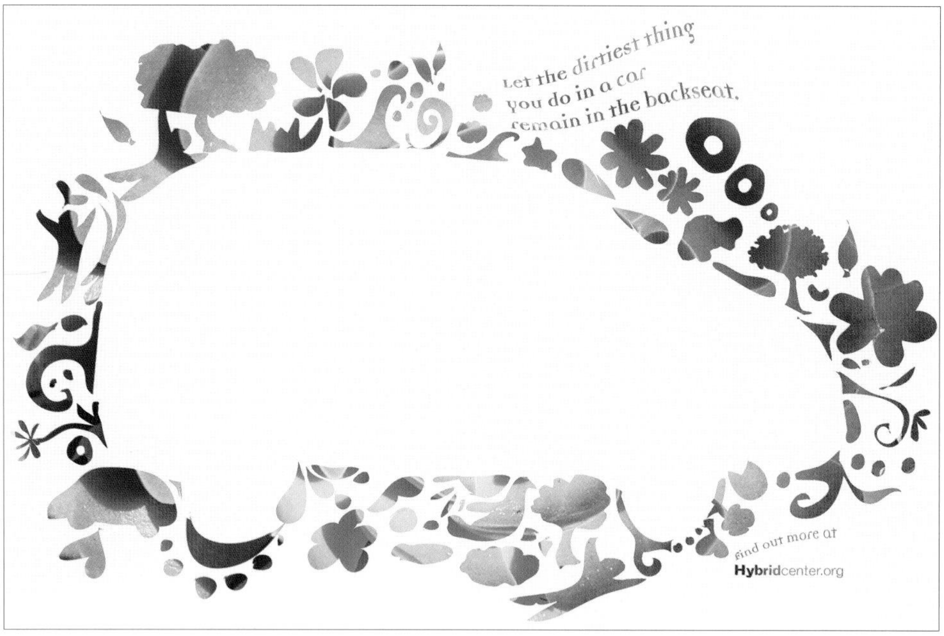
Let the dirtiest thing you do in a car remain in the backseat.
find out more at
Hybridcenter.org

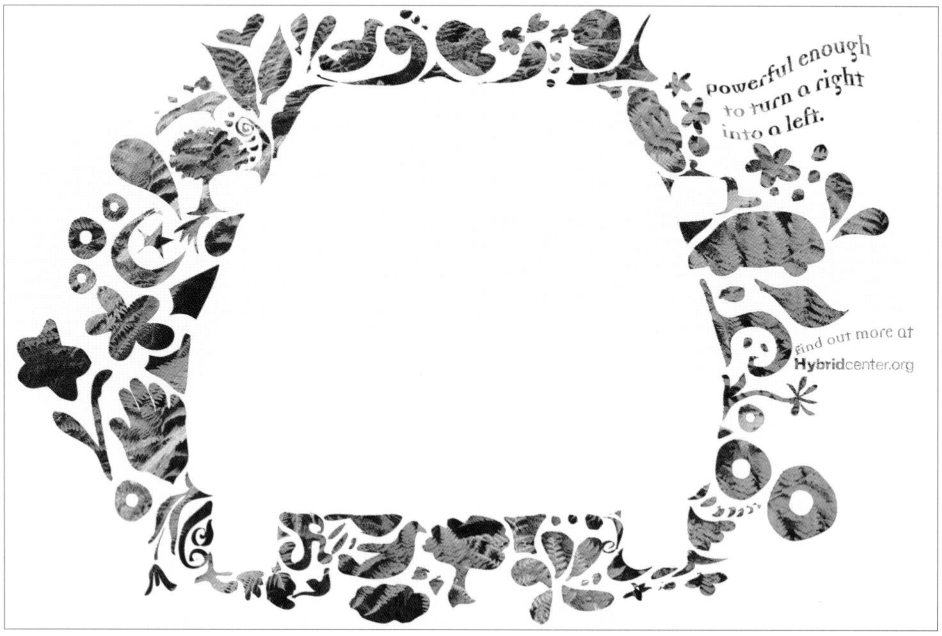
Powerful enough to turn a right into a left.
find out more at
Hybridcenter.org

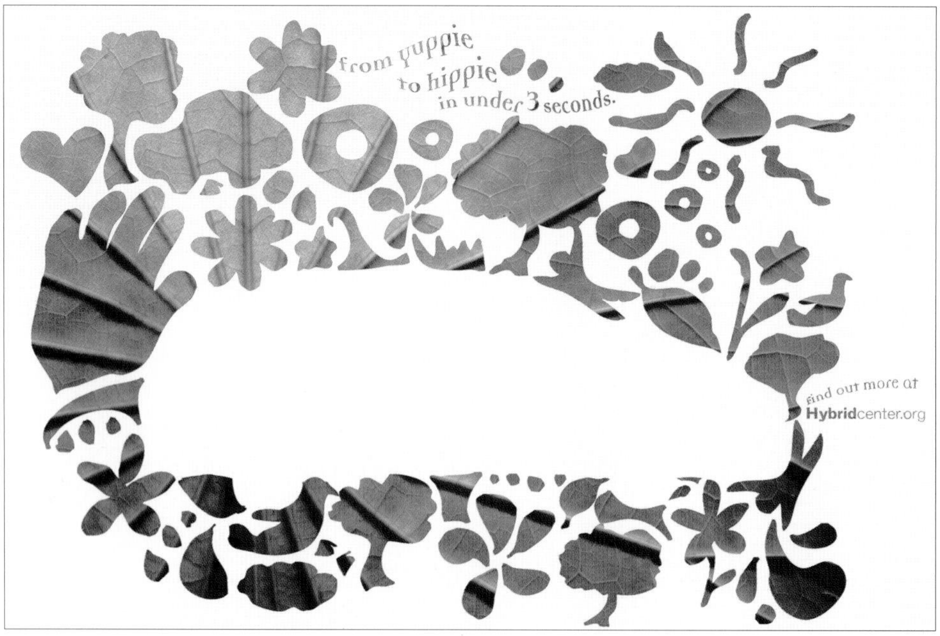
from yuppie to hippie in under 3 seconds.
find out more at
Hybridcenter.org

MERIT

ART DIRECTORS
Adris Kamuli
Yashika Punjabi

WRITER
Kevin Klumpyan

SCHOOL
Miami Ad School/
Minneapolis

CCA013

WHEN YOU HELP THE EARTH, THE EARTH HELPS YOU.
Hybrid cars can improve everyone's environment. To learn more, visit Hybridcenter.org

WHEN YOU HELP THE EARTH, THE EARTH HELPS YOU.
Hybrid cars can improve everyone's environment. To learn more, visit Hybridcenter.org

WHEN YOU HELP THE EARTH, THE EARTH HELPS YOU.
Hybrid cars can improve everyone's environment. To learn more, visit Hybridcenter.org

MERIT

ART DIRECTOR
Shaun Bruce

WRITER
David Roth

SCHOOL
Texas Creative-
The University of Texas
at Austin

CCA020

HELP MAKE HONKING THE LEADING SOURCE OF POLLUTION.
Drive Motor
Gearbox
Drive Motor
www.HybridCenter.org
Where cars are going.

THE FUEL GAUGE ISN'T BROKEN. IT JUST TAKES AWHILE TO GET MOVING.
ENGINE
www.HybridCenter.org
Where cars are going.

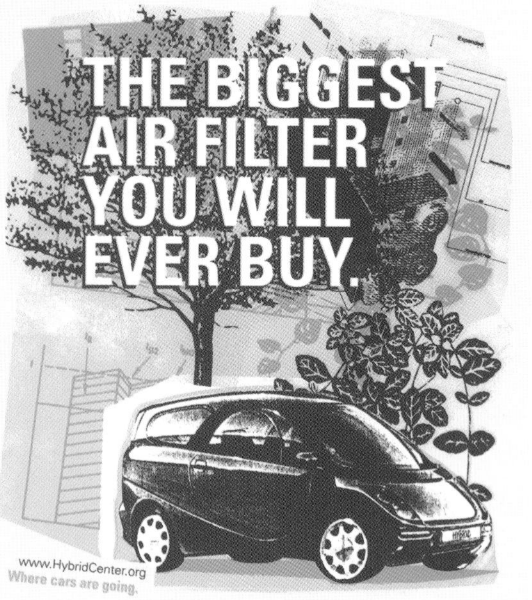
THE BIGGEST AIR FILTER YOU WILL EVER BUY.
www.HybridCenter.org
Where cars are going.

Hybridcenter.org
make a right turn
WM
WASTE MANAGEMENT
4311

Hybridcenter.org
make a right turn

280
Plus
250
Unleaded
220
Hybridcenter.org
make a right turn

MERIT

ART DIRECTOR
Chase Quarterman

WRITER
Shannon Burke

SCHOOL
Texas Creative-
The University of Texas
at Austin

CCA015

MERIT

ART DIRECTOR
Maxime Jenniss

SCHOOL
Université du Québec á Montréal/Montreal

CCA016

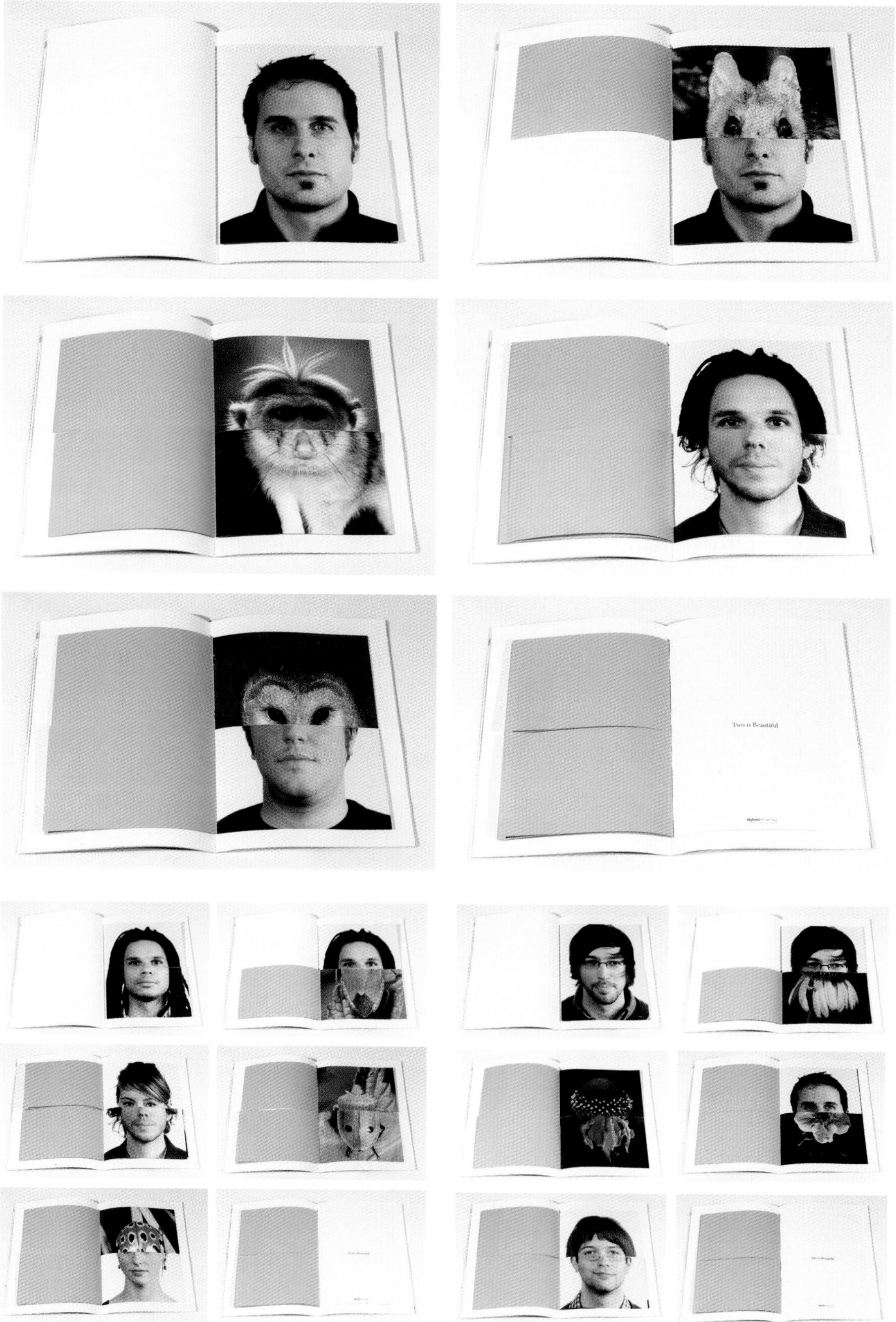
Two is Beautiful

FUEL MAINTENANCE SCHEDULE
Hybridcenter.org
CAUTION
A helpful reminder from Hybridcenter.org

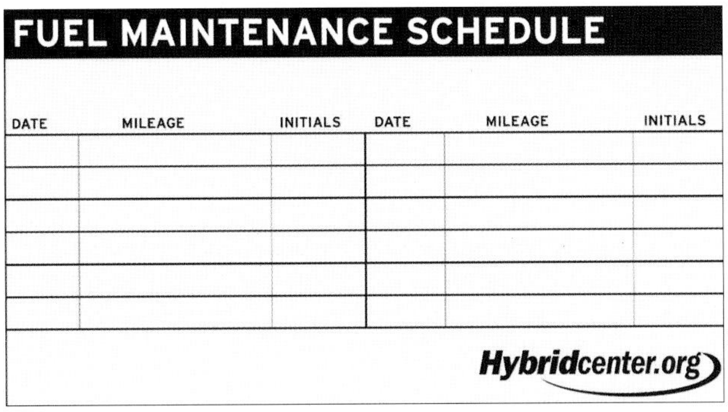
FUEL MAINTENANCE SCHEDULE

DATE	MILEAGE	INITIALS	DATE	MILEAGE	INITIALS

Hybridcenter.org

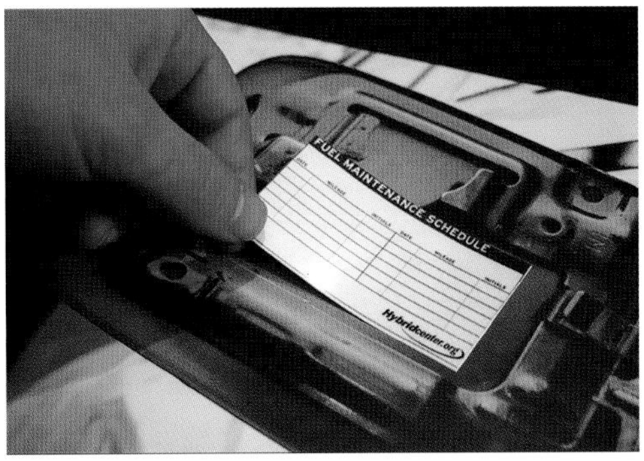
FUEL MAINTENANCE SCHEDULE
Hybridcenter.org

MERIT

ART DIRECTOR
Will Geddes

WRITERS
Mike King
Justin Horrigan

SCHOOL
University of Colorado/ Boulder

CCA017

MERIT

ART DIRECTOR
Will Geddes

WRITERS
Mike King
Justin Horrigan

SCHOOL
University of Colorado/ Boulder

CCA018

UNDERSTANDING YOUR FUEL GAUGE

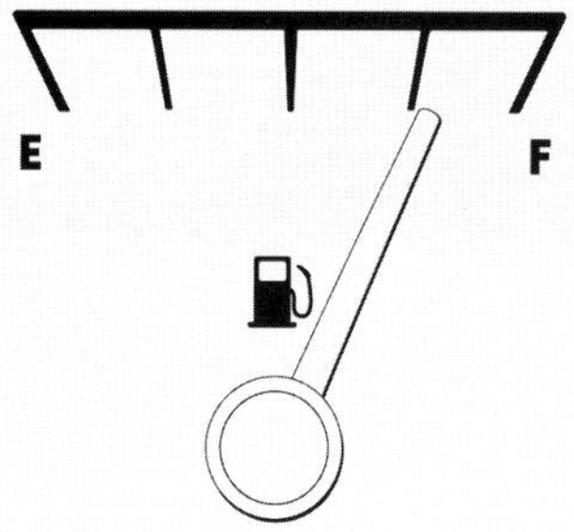
E
F

Checking fuel level

Your fuel gauge indicates the approximate fuel level in your tank. Over time, you may notice the fuel level decreasing. This is normal and should not be reported to your mechanic.

- **If your gauge registers E, or Empty, your gas tank simply needs to be refilled.**
- **Make an appointment with a nearby gas station for a fill-up.**

3.15

You just might forget. **HYBRID**CENTER**.**ORG

INDICATOR LIGHTS

Low fuel warning light

In rare cases, you may see this light illuminate. Do not be alarmed: You are low on gas.

- **If you have called a tow-truck, make the needed cancellation.**
- **Proceed to the nearest gas station.**
- **Refill your gas tank.**

2.6

You just might forget. **HYBRID**CENTER**.**ORG

REFUELING YOUR VEHICLE

Locating the fuel door

Before you can refuel your vehicle, you must first locate and open the fuel door. It can be found at the rear-left end of your vehicle, as shown in this diagram.

Fuel door

- **For easy reference, if you are in the driver's seat, it's on your side.**
- **If you have trouble locating the fuel door, ask a gas station attendant to help you.**

4.19

You just might forget. **HYBRID**CENTER**.**ORG

ANTIQUES
Things are changing.
Learn more at hybridcenter.org

DIAMOND SHAMROCK
Things are changing.
Learn more at hybridcenter.org

Things are changing.
Learn more at hybridcenter.org

MERIT

ART DIRECTORS
Ian Tulk
Pat Donaldson

WRITERS
Brad Phifer
Zac Chester

SCHOOL
University of Colorado/ Boulder

CCA019

MERIT

ART DIRECTORS
Amanda Cohen
Cassandra DiCesare

PHOTOGRAPHER
HumanDescent.com

SCHOOL
Syracuse University/
Syracuse

CCA014

The definition of a hybrid has become unclear. Find out more information at **hybridcenter.org**
PASSED

The definition of a hybrid has become unclear. Find out more information at **hybridcenter.org**
APPROVED

The definition of a hybrid has become unclear. Find out more information at **hybridcenter.org**
CERTIFIED

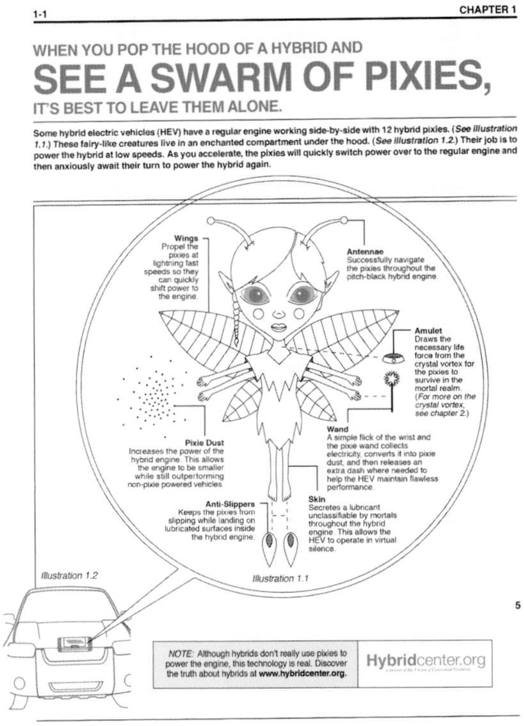

1-1
CHAPTER 1
WHEN YOU POP THE HOOD OF A HYBRID AND
SEE A SWARM OF PIXIES,
IT'S BEST TO LEAVE THEM ALONE.
Some hybrid electric vehicles (HEV) have a regular engine working side-by-side with 12 hybrid pixies. (See illustration 1.1.) These fairy-like creatures live in an enchanted compartment under the hood. (See illustration 1.2.) Their job is to power the hybrid at low speeds. As you accelerate, the pixies will quickly switch power over to the regular engine and then anxiously await their turn to power the hybrid again.
Wings
Propel the pixies at lightning fast speeds so they can quickly shift power to the engine.
Antennae
Successfully navigate the pixies throughout the pitch-black hybrid engine.
Amulet
Draws the necessary life force from the crystal vortex for the pixies to survive in the mortal realm. (For more on the crystal vortex, see chapter 2.)
Wand
A simple flick of the wrist and the pixie wand collects electricity, converts it into pixie dust, and then releases an extra dash where needed to help the HEV maintain flawless performance.
Pixie Dust
Increases the power of the hybrid engine. This allows the engine to be smaller while still outperforming non-pixie powered vehicles.
Anti-Slippers
Keeps the pixies from slipping while landing on lubricated surfaces inside the hybrid engine.
Skin
Secretes a lubricant unclassifiable by mortals throughout the hybrid engine. This allows the HEV to operate in virtual silence.
Illustration 1.2
Illustration 1.1
5
NOTE: Although hybrids don't really use pixies to power the engine, this technology is real. Discover the truth about hybrids at www.hybridcenter.org.
Hybridcenter.org

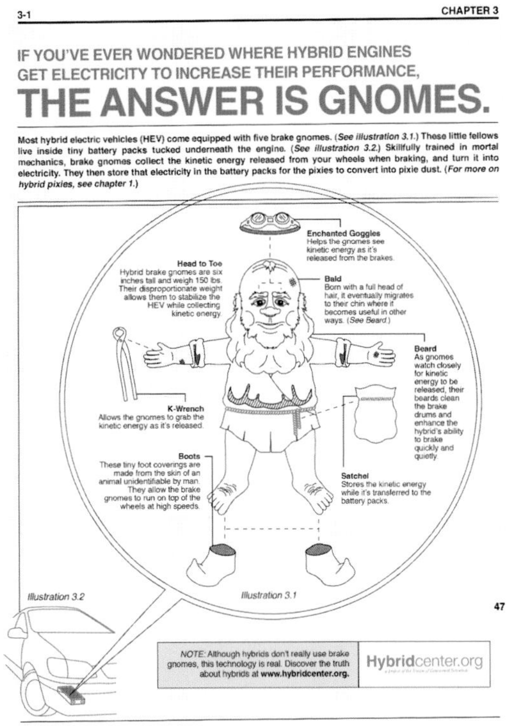

3-1
CHAPTER 3
IF YOU'VE EVER WONDERED WHERE HYBRID ENGINES GET ELECTRICITY TO INCREASE THEIR PERFORMANCE,
THE ANSWER IS GNOMES.
Most hybrid electric vehicles (HEV) come equipped with five brake gnomes. (See illustration 3.1.) These little fellows live inside tiny battery packs tucked underneath the engine. (See illustration 3.2.) Skillfully trained in mortal mechanics, brake gnomes collect the kinetic energy released from your wheels when braking, and turn it into electricity. They then store that electricity in the battery packs for the pixies to convert into pixie dust. (For more on hybrid pixies, see chapter 1.)
Enchanted Goggles
Helps the gnomes see kinetic energy as it's released from the brakes.
Head to Toe
Hybrid brake gnomes are six inches tall and weigh 150 lbs. Their disproportionate weight allows them to stabilize the HEV while collecting kinetic energy.
Bald
Born with a full head of hair, it eventually migrates to their chin where it becomes useful in other ways. (See Beard.)
Beard
As gnomes watch closely for kinetic energy to be released, their beards clean the brake drums and enhance the hybrid's ability to brake quickly and quietly.
K-Wrench
Allows the gnomes to grab the kinetic energy as it's released.
Boots
These tiny foot coverings are made from the skin of an animal unidentifiable by man. They allow the brake gnomes to run on top of the wheels at high speeds.
Satchel
Stores the kinetic energy while it's transferred to the battery packs.
Illustration 3.2
Illustration 3.1
47
NOTE: Although hybrids don't really use brake gnomes, this technology is real. Discover the truth about hybrids at www.hybridcenter.org.
Hybridcenter.org

Merit

ART DIRECTOR
David Grindon

WRITER
Patrick Maravilla

SCHOOL
VCU Adcenter/ Richmond

CCA021

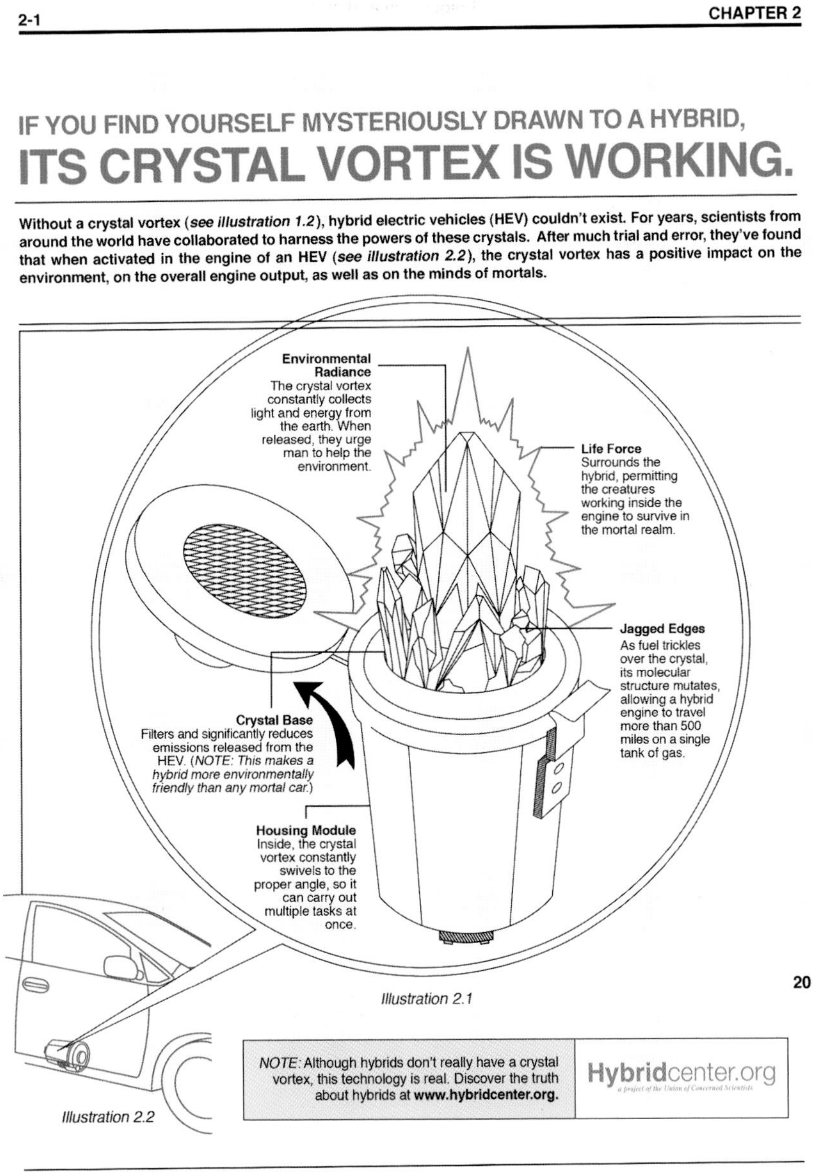

2-1
CHAPTER 2
IF YOU FIND YOURSELF MYSTERIOUSLY DRAWN TO A HYBRID,
ITS CRYSTAL VORTEX IS WORKING.
Without a crystal vortex (see illustration 1.2), hybrid electric vehicles (HEV) couldn't exist. For years, scientists from around the world have collaborated to harness the powers of these crystals. After much trial and error, they've found that when activated in the engine of an HEV (see illustration 2.2), the crystal vortex has a positive impact on the environment, on the overall engine output, as well as on the minds of mortals.
Environmental Radiance
The crystal vortex constantly collects light and energy from the earth. When released, they urge man to help the environment.
Life Force
Surrounds the hybrid, permitting the creatures working inside the engine to survive in the mortal realm.
Jagged Edges
As fuel trickles over the crystal, its molecular structure mutates, allowing a hybrid engine to travel more than 500 miles on a single tank of gas.
Crystal Base
Filters and significantly reduces emissions released from the HEV. (NOTE: This makes a hybrid more environmentally friendly than any mortal car.)
Housing Module
Inside, the crystal vortex constantly swivels to the proper angle, so it can carry out multiple tasks at once.
20
Illustration 2.1
Illustration 2.2
NOTE: Although hybrids don't really have a crystal vortex, this technology is real. Discover the truth about hybrids at www.hybridcenter.org.
Hybridcenter.org

MERIT

ART DIRECTOR
Thompson Harrell

WRITER
Chris Guichard

SCHOOL
VCU Adcenter/ Richmond

CCA022

I STARTED USING WHEN I WAS ONLY SIXTEEN YEARS OLD.
Whether it's our environment, foreign policy or pocketbooks, oil addiction affects every American. There is help.
GET CLEAN
Hybridcenter.org

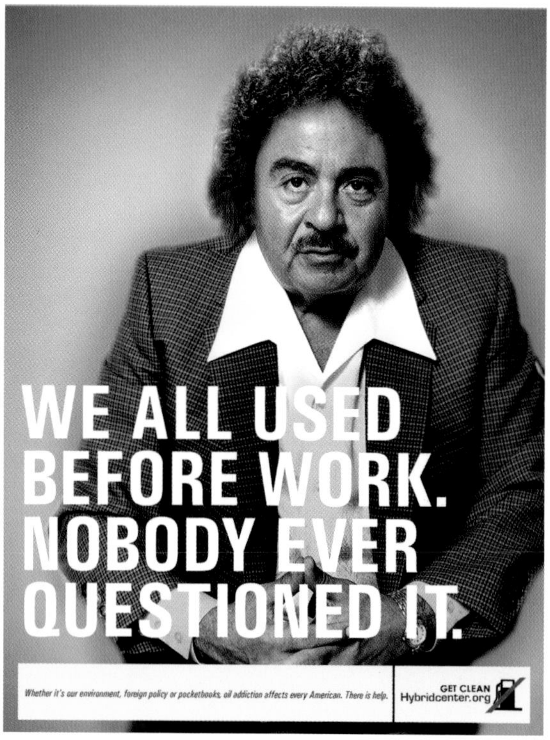
WE ALL USED BEFORE WORK. NOBODY EVER QUESTIONED IT.
Whether it's our environment, foreign policy or pocketbooks, oil addiction affects every American. There is help.
GET CLEAN
Hybridcenter.org

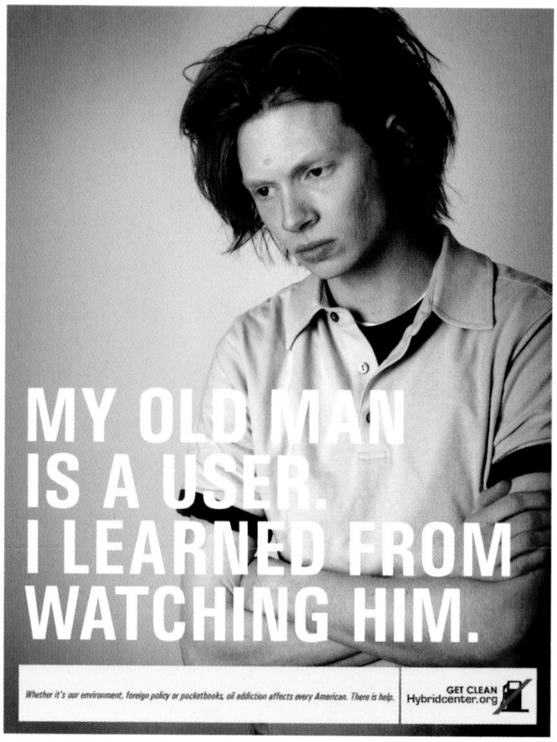
MY OLD MAN IS A USER. I LEARNED FROM WATCHING HIM.
Whether it's our environment, foreign policy or pocketbooks, oil addiction affects every American. There is help.
GET CLEAN
Hybridcenter.org

Calvin Klein
Hybridcenter.org

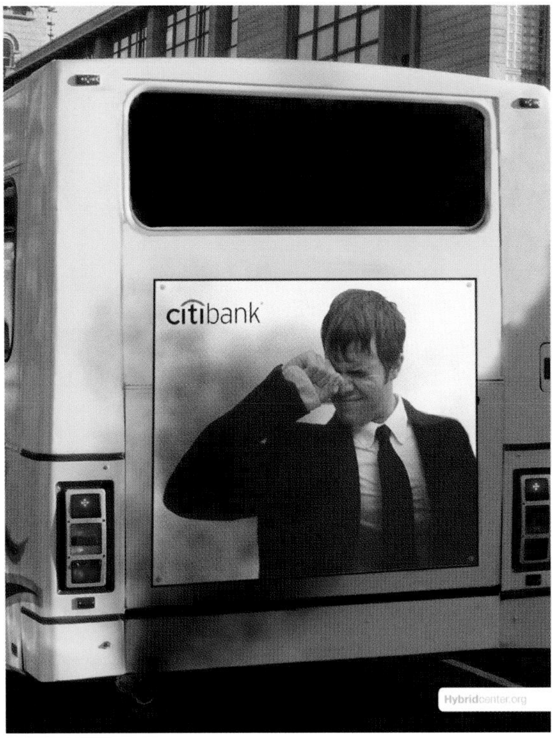
citibank
Hybridcenter.org

ve
Hybridcenter.org

Merit

ART DIRECTOR
Emily Delayen

WRITER
Mike Ng

SCHOOL
Virginia Commonwealth University-School of Mass Communications/ Richmond

CCA023

MERIT

ART DIRECTOR
Yoon Kyung Bae

WRITER
Keri Zierler

DIRECTORS
Hoon Kim
Austin Hilde

SCHOOL
Art Center College of Design/Pasadena

CCT005

Not every hybrid is
a friend of nature.
hybridcenter.org

HYBRID

MERIT

ART DIRECTOR
Sungho So

DIRECTOR
Sungho So

SCHOOL
Art Center College of Design/Pasadena

CCT004

Not all Hybrids are as clean as you think.

Respects life

MERIT

ART DIRECTOR
Javier de Vega

WRITERS
Mario Gomez
Alfonso Rivera

DIRECTORS
Alvaro Lopez
Jorge Gomez

SCHOOL
Miami Ad School/
Madrid

CCT006

Plus

Spend less time at the pump.

MERIT

ART DIRECTOR
Kait Deloof

WRITERS
Mike King
Justin Horrigan

DIRECTOR
Justin Horrigan

SCHOOL
University of Colorado/
Boulder

CCT007

MERIT

ART DIRECTOR
Brian Popko

WRITERS
Ian Hart
Adam Rosenberg

SCHOOL
Miami Ad School/
San Francisco

CCN006

CONDITIONS IN MIRROR ARE
CLOSER THAN THEY APPEAR
Hybridcenter.org
FULL/SELF SERVE GASOLINE
Unleaded Plus 1249 9/10
Performance Plus 1259 9/10
High Performance 1269 9/10

MERIT

WRITER
Francis Chung

SCHOOL
Miami Ad School/
San Francisco

CCN007

Neutrogena
ACTIVE
BREATHABLE
SUNBLOCK
SPF
4455
ALLOWS SKIN TO BREATHE
sweatproof, waterproof
resists running into eyes
Broad Spectrum UVA/UVB
4.0 FL OZ (118 mL)

MERIT

ART DIRECTOR
Ned Sundby-Munson

WRITER
Lindsay Cliett

SCHOOL
Miami Ad School/ Minneapolis

CCN005

Adopt every highway.
Adopt hybrid technology
86

Adopt every mile.
Adopt hybrid technology
Hybridcenter.org

Adopt every road.
Adopt hybrid technology
WISDOM

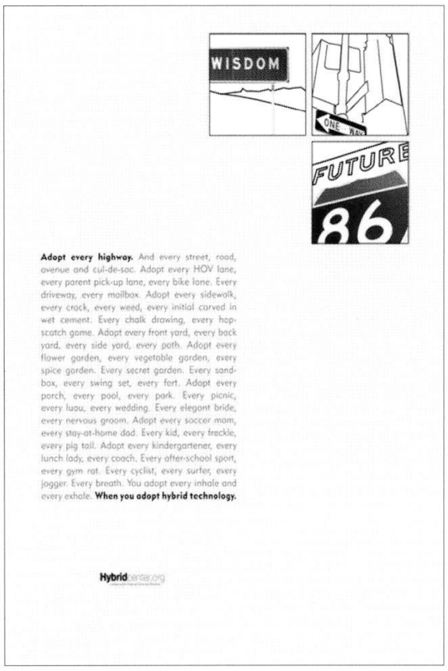
WISDOM
ONE WAY
FUTURE
86
Adopt every highway. And every street, road, avenue and cul-de-sac. Adopt every HOV lane, every parent pick-up lane, every bike lane. Every driveway, every mailbox. Adopt every sidewalk, every crack, every weed, every initial carved in wet cement. Every chalk drawing, every hop-scotch game. Adopt every front yard, every back yard, every side yard, every path. Adopt every flower garden, every vegetable garden, every spice garden. Every secret garden. Every sand-box, every swing set, every fort. Adopt every porch, every pool, every park. Every picnic, every luau, every wedding. Every elegant bride, every nervous groom. Adopt every soccer mom, every stay-at-home dad. Every kid, every freckle, every pig tail. Adopt every kindergartener, every lunch lady, every coach. Every after-school sport, every gym rat. Every cyclist, every surfer, every jogger. Every breath. You adopt every inhale and every exhale. **When you adopt hybrid technology.**
Hybridcenter.org

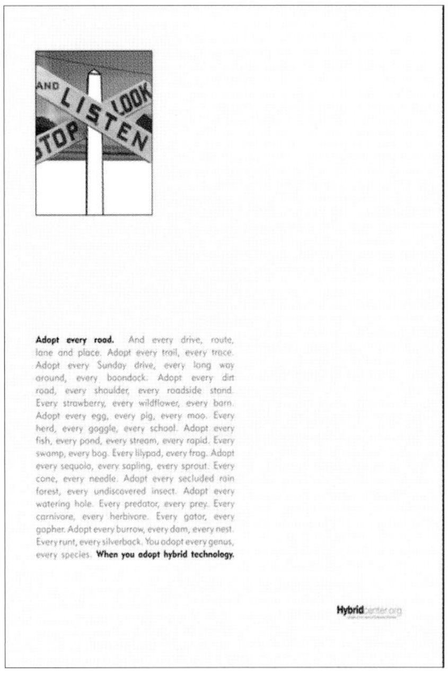
AND
LISTEN
LOOK
STOP
Adopt every road. And every drive, route, lane and place. Adopt every trail, every trace. Adopt every Sunday drive, every long way around, every boondock. Adopt every dirt road, every shoulder, every roadside stand. Every strawberry, every wildflower, every barn. Adopt every egg, every pig, every moo. Every herd, every goggle, every school. Adopt every fish, every pond, every stream, every rapid. Every swamp, every bog. Every lilypad, every frog. Adopt every sequoia, every sapling, every sprout. Every cone, every needle. Adopt every secluded rain forest, every undiscovered insect. Adopt every watering hole. Every predator, every prey. Every carnivore, every herbivore. Every gator, every gopher. Adopt every burrow, every dam, every nest. Every runt, every silverback. You adopt every genus, every species. **When you adopt hybrid technology.**
Hybridcenter.org

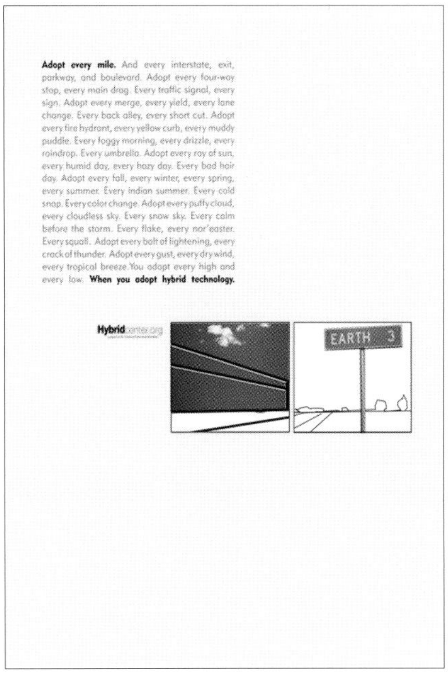
Adopt every mile. And every interstate, exit, parkway, and boulevard. Adopt every four-way stop, every main drag. Every traffic signal, every sign. Adopt every merge, every yield, every lane change. Every back alley, every short cut. Adopt every fire hydrant, every yellow curb, every muddy puddle. Every foggy morning, every drizzle, every raindrop. Every umbrella. Adopt every ray of sun, every humid day, every hazy day. Every bad hair day. Adopt every fall, every winter, every spring, every summer. Every indian summer. Every cold snap. Every color change. Adopt every puffy cloud, every cloudless sky. Every snow sky. Every calm before the storm. Every flake, every nor'easter. Every squall. Adopt every bolt of lightening, every crack of thunder. Adopt every gust, every dry wind, every tropical breeze. You adopt every high and every low. **When you adopt hybrid technology.**
Hybridcenter.org
EARTH 3

ADOPT
EVERY
HIGHWAY
NEXT 2 MILES
Hybridcenter.org
a project of the Union of Concerned Scientists

ADOPT EVERY HIGHWAY
PROGRAM
NEXT 2.5 MILES
DRYDEN DEMOCRATS
366
Hybridcenter.org

Merit

ART DIRECTOR
Katharine Wolfe

WRITER
Patrick Conlon

SCHOOL
The Creative Circus/ Atlanta

CCN002

www.hybridcenter.org

www.hybridcenter.org

SW 82
www.hybridcenter.org

test
drive
The Selling Power

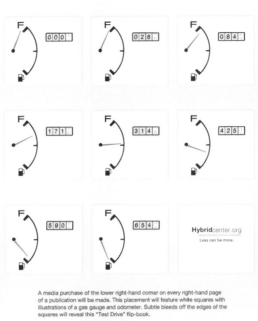

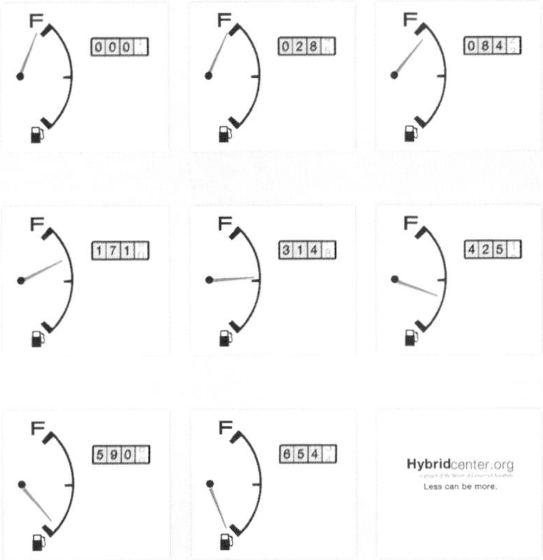
F
000
028
084
171
314
425
590
654
Hybridcenter.org
Less can be more.

A media purchase of the lower right-hand corner on every right-hand page of a publication will be made. This placement will feature white squares with illustrations of a gas gauge and odometer. Subtle bleeds off the edges of the squares will reveal this "Test Drive" flip-book.

When the reader quick-flips the pages it will give the illusion of the gas gauge and odometer moving in unison. The miles will rack up very quickly, illustrating the truth of how much farther a hybrid can go on a single tank of gas.
The last square will feature the hybridcenter.org logo/website, as well as the call to action, "Less can be more".

MERIT

ART DIRECTORS
Chris Milne
Paulo Cruz

WRITERS
Chris Milne
Philip Henson

SCHOOL
The Creative Circus/ Atlanta

CCN003

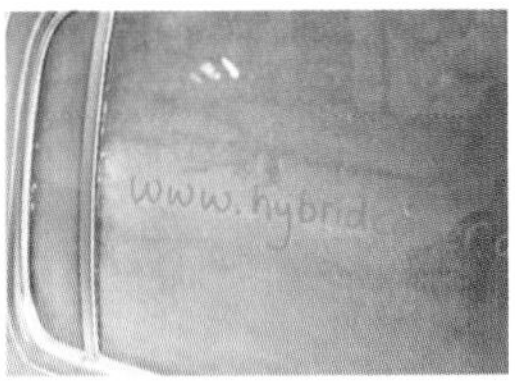
www.hybrid

CTA Bus & Rail Map
www.hybridcenter.org

MERIT

ART DIRECTOR
Jesse Juriga

WRITER
Ted Kapusta

SCHOOL
The Creative Circus/ Atlanta

CCN004

Merit

ART DIRECTORS
Molly Gannon
Vanessa Lozano
Sheena Brown

SCHOOL
University of Colorado/ Boulder

CCN008

Hybridcenter.org

Merit

ART DIRECTOR
Trevor Hubbard

SCHOOL
Academy of Art University/San Francisco

CCI004

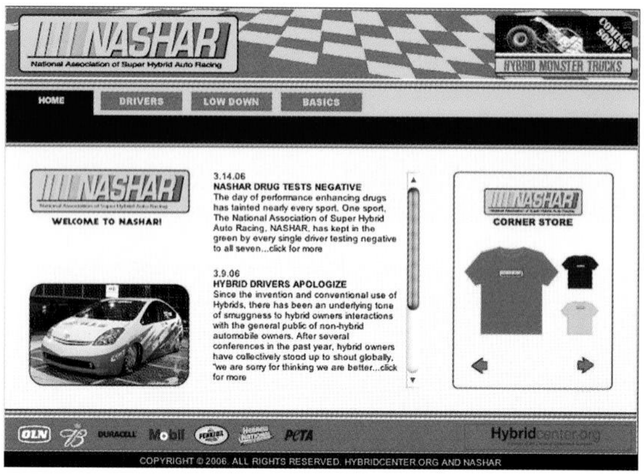
NASHAR
National Association of Super Hybrid Auto Racing
COMING SOON
HYBRID MONSTER TRUCKS
HOME
DRIVERS
LOW DOWN
BASICS
WELCOME TO NASHAR!
3.14.06
NASHAR DRUG TESTS NEGATIVE
The day of performance enhancing drugs has tainted nearly every sport. One sport, The National Association of Super Hybrid Auto Racing, NASHAR, has kept in the green by every single driver testing negative to all seven...click for more
3.9.06
HYBRID DRIVERS APOLOGIZE
Since the invention and conventional use of Hybrids, there has been an underlying tone of smuggness to hybrid owners interactions with the general public of non-hybrid automobile owners. After several conferences in the past year, hybrid owners have collectively stood up to shout globally, "we are sorry for thinking we are better...click for more
CORNER STORE
OLN
DURACELL
Mobil
PETA
Hybridcenter.org
COPYRIGHT © 2006. ALL RIGHTS RESERVED. HYBRIDCENTER.ORG AND NASHAR

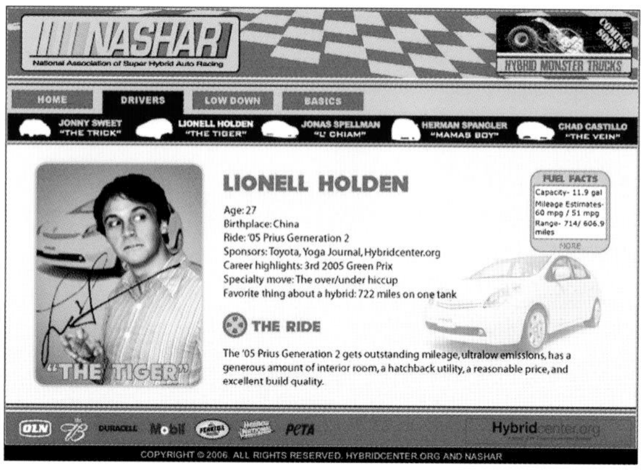
NASHAR
National Association of Super Hybrid Auto Racing
COMING SOON
HYBRID MONSTER TRUCKS
HOME
DRIVERS
LOW DOWN
BASICS
JONNY SWEET "THE TRICK"
LIONELL HOLDEN "THE TIGER"
JONAS SPELLMAN "L' CHIAM"
HERMAN SPANGLER "MAMAS BOY"
CHAD CASTILLO "THE VEIN"
"THE TIGER"
LIONELL HOLDEN
Age: 27
Birthplace: China
Ride: '05 Prius Gerneration 2
Sponsors: Toyota, Yoga Journal, Hybridcenter.org
Career highlights: 3rd 2005 Green Prix
Specialty move: The over/under hiccup
Favorite thing about a hybrid: 722 miles on one tank
FUEL FACTS
Capacity- 11.9 gal
Mileage Estimates- 60 mpg / 51 mpg
Range- 714/ 606.9 miles
MORE
THE RIDE
The '05 Prius Generation 2 gets outstanding mileage, ultralow emissions, has a generous amount of interior room, a hatchback utility, a reasonable price, and excellent build quality.
OLN
DURACELL
Mobil
PETA
Hybridcenter.org
COPYRIGHT © 2006. ALL RIGHTS RESERVED. HYBRIDCENTER.ORG AND NASHAR

NASHAR
National Association of Super Hybrid Auto Racing
COMING SOON
HYBRID MONSTER TRUCKS
HOME
DRIVERS
LOW DOWN
BASICS
Hybridcenter.org
Who's Got Hybrids? Take the Earth Day Challenge with Bill Nye
News: 2006 hybrid sales jump over 40%
Hybridblog: Hybrid Sales Stats and the State of the Market
Hybrid Watchdog: 2006 Legislative Outlook
Take the HybridCenter Earth Day Challenge
Welcome to Who's Got Hybrids hosted by Bill Nye the Science Guy. Take a look at real world hybrid owners, submit testimonials, and join our new HybridCenter Driving Change Network.
Tech Center
Hybrids Under the Hood
A New Road: Hybrid Tech Report
Watchdog: Hollow Hybrids
Hybrid Transit Buses
CLICK HERE FOR MORE
OLN
DURACELL
Mobil
PETA
Hybridcenter.org
COPYRIGHT © 2006. ALL RIGHTS RESERVED. HYBRIDCENTER.ORG AND NASHAR

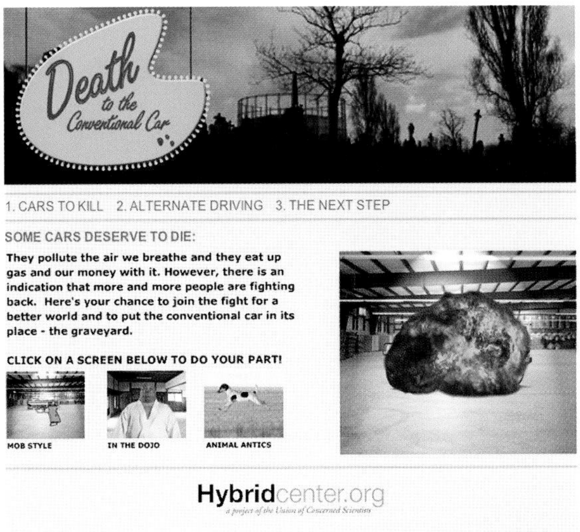
Death to the Conventional Car
1. CARS TO KILL 2. ALTERNATE DRIVING 3. THE NEXT STEP
SOME CARS DESERVE TO DIE:
They pollute the air we breathe and they eat up gas and our money with it. However, there is an indication that more and more people are fighting back. Here's your chance to join the fight for a better world and to put the conventional car in its place - the graveyard.
CLICK ON A SCREEN BELOW TO DO YOUR PART!
MOB STYLE
IN THE DOJO
ANIMAL ANTICS
Hybridcenter.org

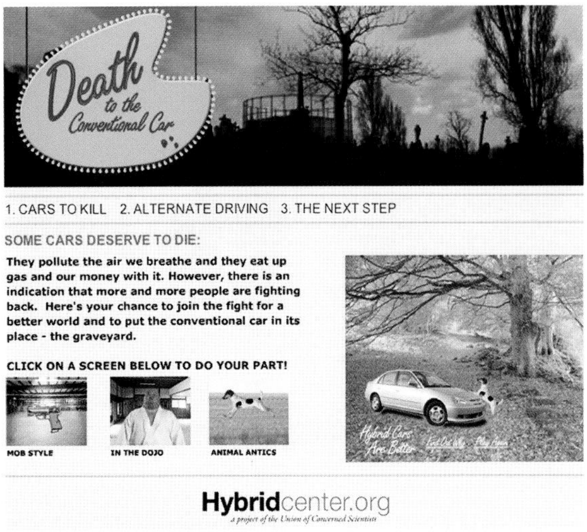
Death to the Conventional Car
1. CARS TO KILL 2. ALTERNATE DRIVING 3. THE NEXT STEP
SOME CARS DESERVE TO DIE:
They pollute the air we breathe and they eat up gas and our money with it. However, there is an indication that more and more people are fighting back. Here's your chance to join the fight for a better world and to put the conventional car in its place - the graveyard.
CLICK ON A SCREEN BELOW TO DO YOUR PART!
MOB STYLE
IN THE DOJO
ANIMAL ANTICS
Hybridcenter.org

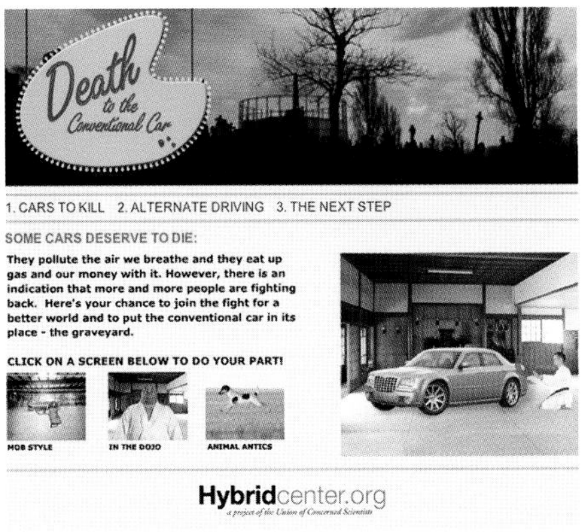
Death to the Conventional Car
1. CARS TO KILL 2. ALTERNATE DRIVING 3. THE NEXT STEP
SOME CARS DESERVE TO DIE:
They pollute the air we breathe and they eat up gas and our money with it. However, there is an indication that more and more people are fighting back. Here's your chance to join the fight for a better world and to put the conventional car in its place - the graveyard.
CLICK ON A SCREEN BELOW TO DO YOUR PART!
MOB STYLE
IN THE DOJO
ANIMAL ANTICS
Hybridcenter.org

MERIT

ART DIRECTOR
Mike Brenner

WRITER
Inseeyah Barma

DESIGNER
Brent Pocker

SCHOOL
Academy of Art University/San Francisco

CCI005

Recognize Your Revolution.
hyspace.com

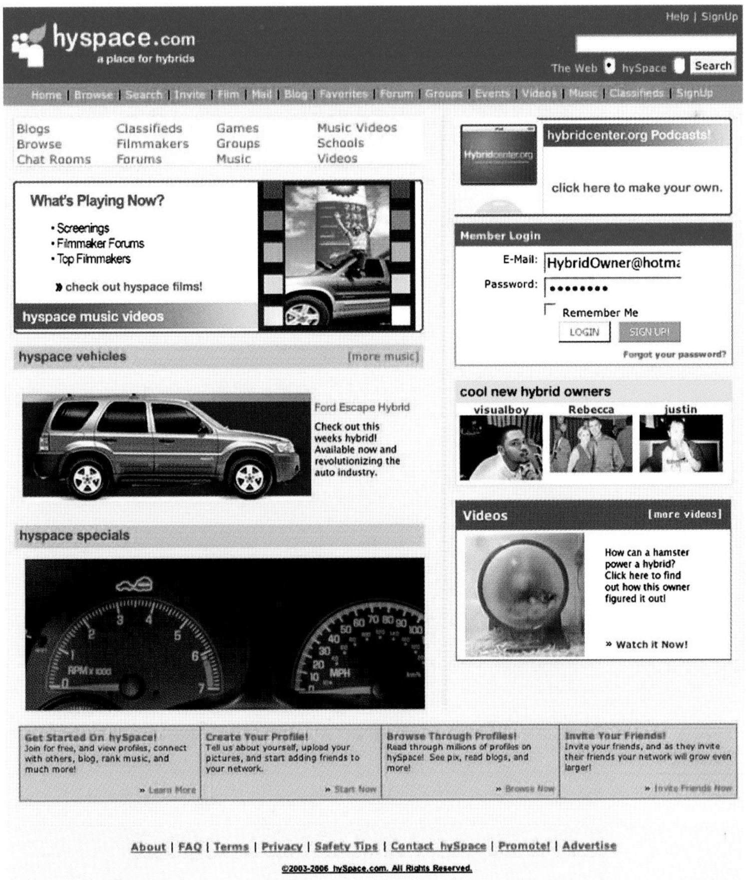
hyspace.com
a place for hybrids
Help | SignUp
Search
Blogs
Browse
Chat Rooms
Classifieds
Filmmakers
Forums
Games
Groups
Music
Music Videos
Schools
Videos
What's Playing Now?
• Screenings
• Filmmaker Forums
• Top Filmmakers
check out hyspace films!
hyspace music videos
hyspace vehicles
Ford Escape Hybrid
Check out this weeks hybrid! Available now and revolutionizing the auto industry.
hyspace specials
hybridcenter.org Podcasts!
click here to make your own.
Member Login
E-Mail:
Password:
Remember Me
LOGIN
SIGN UP!
Forgot your password?
cool new hybrid owners
visualboy
Rebecca
justin
Videos
[more videos]
How can a hamster power a hybrid? Click here to find out how this owner figured it out!
» Watch it Now!
About | FAQ | Terms | Privacy | Safety Tips | Contact hySpace | Promote! | Advertise
©2003-2006 hySpace.com. All Rights Reserved.

MERIT

ART DIRECTORS
Bob Basiewicz
Tia Harper

WRITERS
Bob Basiewicz
Tia Harper

PHOTOGRAPHER
Rob Dawson

SCHOOL
College for Creative Studies/Detroit

CCI006

MERIT

ART DIRECTOR
Drew Shamen

WRITER
John Paquette

SCHOOL
Miami Ad School/ Minneapolis

CCI007

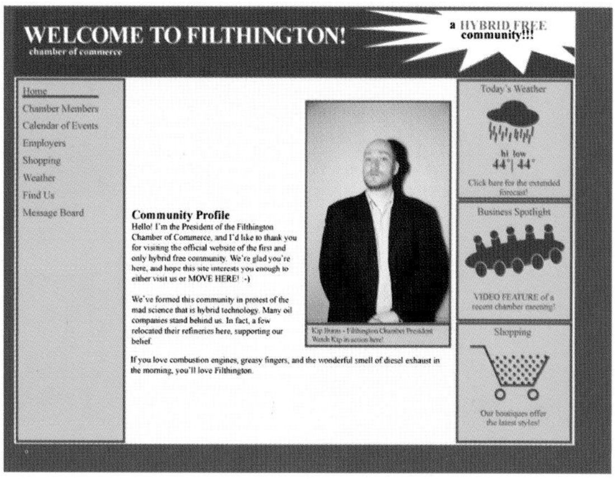
WELCOME TO FILTHINGTON!
chamber of commerce
a HYBRID FREE community!!!
Home
Chamber Members
Calendar of Events
Employers
Shopping
Weather
Find Us
Message Board
Community Profile
Today's Weather
Business Spotlight
Shopping

WELCOME TO FILTHINGTON!
chamber of commerce
a HYBRID FREE community!!!
APRIL EVENTS
Piston Parade
ATV Drag Races
Demo Derby
Tractor Pull
Crowbar Days
Today's Weather
Business Spotlight
Shopping

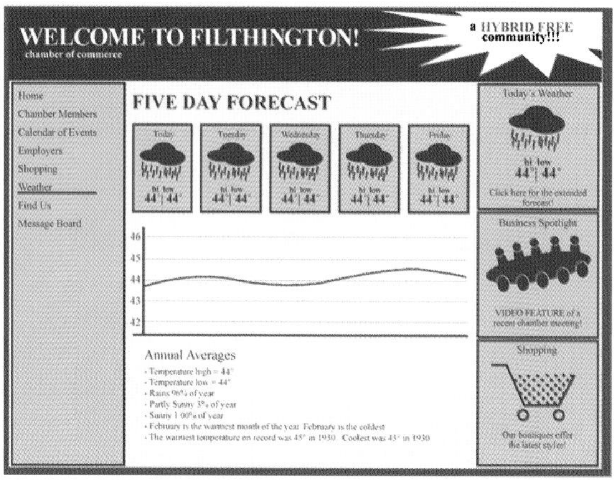
WELCOME TO FILTHINGTON!
chamber of commerce
a HYBRID FREE community!!!
FIVE DAY FORECAST
Today
Tuesday
Wednesday
Thursday
Friday
Annual Averages
Today's Weather
Business Spotlight
Shopping

MERIT

DESIGNER
Heidi Min

ART DIRECTOR
Heidi Min

SCHOOL
California State University/Long Beach

CCD004

hybrid

MERIT

DESIGNER
Chun-Pin Grace Cho

SCHOOL
California State University/Long Beach

CCD005

MERIT

DESIGNER
Peter Kim

SCHOOL
California State University/Long Beach

CCD006

MERIT

DESIGNER
Dilshad Bhangu

SCHOOL
Columbus College of Art & Design/Columbus

CCD007

MERIT

DESIGNER
Chad Price

SCHOOL
Corcoran College of Art
+ Design/Washington

CCD008

MERIT

DESIGNER
Hooh Oi Leng

ART DIRECTOR
Herbie Phoon

SCHOOL
Dasein Academy of Art/
Kuala Lumpur

CCD009

MERIT

ART DIRECTOR
Andrea Jaimes Tello

SCHOOL
Miami Ad School/
Miami Beach

CCD010

MERIT

DESIGNER
Boriana Mintcheva-Strzok

SCHOOL
Minneapolis College of Art and Design/Minneapolis

CCD011

MERIT

DESIGNER
Cesar R. Torres

SCHOOL
Texas Creative-The University of Texas at Austin

CCD012

MERIT

DESIGNER
Nathalie Lavoie

SCHOOL
Université du Québec á Montréal/Montreal

CCD013

INDEX

AGENCIES

A

Abbott Mead Vickers BBDO/ London: 14, 41, 71, 120, 137, 148, 181, 466, 479
Abhijit/Mumbai: 389
Alchemy Partnership, The/ Singapore: 287, 477
AlmapBBDO/São Paulo: 182, 183
Ando BV/The Hague: 105
Anothermountainman Communications/Hong Kong: 102, 144
Apple Computer/Cupertino: 86, 87, 156, 397, 401
Arc Worldwide/Leo Burnett Advertising/Kuala Lumpur: 479
Archrival/Lincoln: 141, 473
Arnika/Hopewell Junction: 288
Arnold/McLean: 203, 208, 416
Arnold/St. Louis: 417
Arnold Australia/Sydney: 276
Arnold Worldwide/Boston: 35, 38, 39, 136, 184, 227, 289, 304, 335, 369, 370
Arnold Worldwide/Toronto: 161
Asylum Creative/Singapore: 385, 397, 418

B

Bailey Lauerman/Omaha: 432
Bartle Bogle Hegarty/New York: 17, 185, 307, 323, 324, 340, 341, 342, 371
Bassat Ogilvy & Mather S.A./ Barcelona: 186
Bates/Singapore: 165
Batey/Singapore: 200
BBDO/New York: 26, 66, 77, 99, 101, 141, 227, 228, 245, 311, 411, 419
BBDO/Atlanta: 264, 267
BBDO/Bangkok: 94, 143, 224
BBDO Campaign/Stuttgart: 379
BBDO Guerrero Ortega/ Makati City: 290
BBDO Malaysia/Kuala Lumpur: 239, 360
BBDO/Singapore: 390, 420
BBDO West/San Francisco: 276
Beijing Creative World Advertising/Beijing: 246
BETC EURO RSCG/Paris: 299
Big Bang/Seattle: 336
Blattner Brunner/Pittsburgh: 411
Blok Design/Mexico: 457, 480
Blue Sky Advertising/Atlanta: 228
BMF/Pyrmont: 326
Borders Perrin Norrander/ Portland: 229
Bradley And Montgomery/ Indianapolis: 336
Braley Design/New York: 466, 467
Brooklyn Brothers, The/ New York: 36

C

Cahan & Associates/ San Francisco: 107, 108
Campbell Doyle Dye/London: 223
Carmichael Lynch Thorburn/ Minneapolis: 380, 421
Clarity Coverdale Fury/ Minneapolis: 34, 337
Claus Koch Identity/Duesseldorf: 443
Clemenger BBDO/Wellington: 290, 350
Colenso BBDO/Auckland: 247, 281, 356
Contract Advertising/New Delhi: 467
Contrapunto/Madrid: 172, 211
Creative Juice/GI/Bangkok: 50
Creature/Seattle: 61, 139, 152
Crispin Porter + Bogusky/ Miami: 6, 25, 35, 38, 39, 44, 60, 67, 68, 69, 134, 136, 139, 147, 154, 174, 289, 312, 334, 369, 372, 373, 438

D

Daddy Buy Me A Pony - A 9nov Union Co/Cape Town: 106, 458
davidandgoliath/Los Angeles: 313
DDB/Amsterdam: 321
DDB/Auckland: 366
DDB/Berlin: 305, 327, 332, 334, 337
DDB/Brussels: 174
DDB/Chicago: 71, 140, 307, 334, 337
DDB/Dallas: 84, 142
DDB/London: 4, 22, 147
DDB/Los Angeles: 49, 137
DDB/Madrid: 175
DDB/Melbourne: 402
DDB/Mexico City: 308
DDB/Paris: 47, 137, 187, 188, 308
DDB/San Francisco: 330
DDB/São Paulo: 173
DDB/Seattle: 291
DDB/Singapore: 342
DDB/Toronto: 30, 153, 221, 229
DDB/Vancouver: 40, 260, 282, 334
Dentsu/Tokyo: 357, 444, 449, 459, 468, 474
Dentsu Young & Rubicam/ Singapore: 109, 175
Devilfish/London: 112
Devito/Verdi/New York: 71, 140, 335
Diesel/Montreal: 380
DiMassimo/New York: 230
Duffy & Partners/Minneapolis: 82, 89, 143, 395, 402
Dynamite Brothers Syndicate/ Tokyo: 403

E

E.Co./Tokyo: 96, 422
Epoch Films/New York:
Euro RSCG India/Mumbai: 268
Everest Brand Solutions/ Mumbai: 33

F

F/Nazca Saatchi & Saatchi/São Paulo: 176
Fallon/London: 151, 212, 300, 367
Fallon/Minneapolis: 231, 300, 423
Fallon/Singapore: 189, 350, 475
FCB/Cape Town: 78, 85, 385
FCB/Johannesburg: 161, 343
Feldmann+Schultchen Design Studios/Hamburg: 432
Flame/Tokyo: 104, 117, 450, 451, 460, 468, 476
Foote Cone & Belding/New York: 239, 334
Forsman & Bodenfors/ Gothenburg: 162, 362
Fort Franklin/Boston: 190, 318

G

George Patterson Y&R/ Melbourne: 42, 136, 148
Good Design Company Co./ Tokyo: 116, 145
Goodby, Silverstein & Partners/ San Francisco: 29, 51, 283, 314, 335, 337
Graphics & Designing Inc./ Tokyo: 445
Grass/Dasein/Kuala Lumpur: 460
Grey/Oslo: 176
Grey Worldwide/Auckland: 213
Grey Worldwide/Crows Nest: 291
Grey Worldwide/Duesseldorf: 100, 351
Grey Worldwide/Johannesburg: 343
Grey Worldwide/Melbourne: 71, 140
Ground Zero Advertising/ Los Angeles: 152, 325, 360
GSD&M/Austin: 424

H

Hakuhodo Creative Vox/Tokyo: 404
Hakuhodo/Tokyo: 87, 99, 156, 398
Hanft Raboy and Partners/ New York: 336
Hans Seeger/Wauwatosa: 405
Happy Forsman & Bodenfors/ Gothenburg: 97, 118, 119, 121, 123, 406, 461, 469
He Said, She Said/Hamburg: 438
Head Gear Animation/Toronto:

113, 145, 157
Henderson Advertising/ Greenville: 284
Hill Holliday/New York: 446
Hungry Man/New York: 315
HunterGatherer/New York: 111, 115, 145

i
Iconologic/Atlanta: 109
idiots/Mumbai: 386
Imaginary Forces/Los Angeles: 462

J
John St./Toronto: 28
Jung Von Matt/Berlin: 162, 214, 327, 351, 398
Jung Von Matt/Hamburg: 24
Jung Von Matt/Zurich: 62
Jupiter Drawing Room, The/ Johannesburg: 5
JWT/Kuala Lumpur,: 248
JWT/Lisbon: 264
JWT/London: 53, 138, 150, 204, 336, 348
JWT/Makati City: 29
JWT/Mexico City: 234
JWT/Mumbai: 163, 352, 433
JWT/New York: 71, 295, 334
JWT/Paris: 192, 352
JWT/São Paulo: 191
JWT/Shanghai: 452
JWT/Singapore: 288

k
Ken-Tsai Lee Design Studio/ Taipei: 461
Kinetic/Singapore: 386, 429
King James RSVP/Cape Town: 395
KNSK/Hamburg: 193
Kolle Rebbe/Hamburg: 20

L
la comunidad/Miami Beach: 316
Land Design Studio/London: 439
Latitude 23 Communications/ New Delhi: 434
Leo Burnett/Chicago: 7, 8, 36, 134, 163, 166, 225, 364, 426, 427
Leo Burnett/Frankfurt: 215, 332
Leo Burnett/Kuala Lumpur: 93
Leo Burnett/London: 210, 361
Leo Burnett/Mumbai: 167, 425
Leopold Ketel & Partners/ Portland: 334
Ligalux/Hamburg: 83
LKM/Charlotte: 209, 222
Lobedu Leo Burnett/Sunninghill: 277, 481
Lobo/São Paulo: 114, 462
Lowe/Dubai: 65, 171
Lowe/New York: 11, 135, 147, 168, 216, 240
Lowe/Shanghai: 364
Lowe Bull/Cape Town: 160, 244
Lowe Bull/Johannesburg: 353
Lowe Bull Truth/Durban: 335
Lowe Hunt/Sydney: 70, 154
Lunar/London: 465

M
Martin Agency, The/Richmond: 13, 206, 207, 265, 266
M&C Saatchi/New York: 232
M&C Saatchi/Santa Monica: 328
McCann Erickson/Kuala Lumpur: 25, 92
McCann Erickson/New York: 333
McCann Erickson/San Francisco: 46
McCann Erickson/Singapore: 329, 344
McGarrah/Jessee/Austin: 407
McKinney/Durham: 64, 381
Middle Child/Lake Forest: 269
Modernista/Boston: 306
Mortierbrigade/Brussels: 374
Mother/London: 27, 135, 292, 435
Mother/New York: 55, 73, 75, 141, 333
MTV Networks/New York: 463
Mullen/Wenham: 205, 260

N
Naga DDB Malaysia/Petaling Jaya: 240, 241, 436
Neiman Group/Harrisburg: 91
Net#work BBDO/Hyde Park: 361
Nonante/Montreal: 391
Nordpol+/Hamburg: 74, 98, 155, 157

O
180 Amsterdam: 180, 298, 415
Office: Jason Schulte Design/ San Francisco: 95, 144, 447
Ogilvy/Beijing: 164, 279
Ogilvy/London: 177
Ogilvy & Mather/Bangkok: 252, 253, 285
Ogilvy & Mather/Buenos Aires: 277
Ogilvy & Mather/Frankfurt: 254, 271, 286
Ogilvy & Mather/Guangzhou: 345, 346
Ogilvy & Mather/Hong Kong: 235
Ogilvy & Mather/Kuala Lumpur: 21, 250
Ogilvy & Mather/Makati City: 242
Ogilvy & Mather/Mexico: 194, 344
Ogilvy & Mather/Mumbai: 31, 249, 270, 381
Ogilvy & Mather/New Delhi: 78, 124, 241, 251, 278, 412
Ogilvy & Mather/New York: 331, 392
Ogilvy & Mather/Santiago: 15
Ogilvy & Mather/Singapore: 18, 21, 23, 62, 177, 178, 232, 345
Ogilvy Groep Nederland/ Amsterdam: 265
Ogilvy South Africa/Cape Town: 365
Ogilvy South Africa/ Johannesburg: 10, 169, 255, 427
OgilvyOne/Bangkok: 387
OgilvyOne/London: 280
OgilvyOne/Mumbai: 443
Oink Ink Radio/New York: 336
Opolis/Portland: 80, 142, 412
Opto Design/New York: 72

p
Penguin Graphics/Hiroshima: 393, 413
Pentagram/San Francisco: 435
Pivot Design/Chicago: 378
Pool/San Francisco: 396
Publicis/Frankfurt Am Main: 353
Publicis/New York: 301
Publicis Mojo/Melbourne: 59
Publicis Mojo/Walsh Bay: 242, 243, 293
Publicis West/Seattle: 217

R
R/GA/New York: 354
Rebeca Mendez Communication Design/Altadena: 440
Rediffusion DYR/Mumbai: 110
Remerinc/Seattle: 226
Rethink/Vancouver: 334
Richards Group, The/Dallas: 336
Rodgers Townsend/St. Louis: 122
R&R Partners/Las Vegas: 317

S
72andSunny/El Segundo: 46, 299
Saatchi & Saatchi/Frankfurt: 346
Saatchi & Saatchi/London: 334, 335
Saatchi & Saatchi/Los Angeles: 100, 233
Saatchi & Saatchi/Mumbai: 201, 256
Saatchi & Saatchi/New York: 12, 195, 196, 272, 273
Saatchi & Saatchi/Petaling Jaya: 274, 309, 480
Saatchi & Saatchi/Singapore: 9, 32, 134, 197, 198, 202, 257, 258, 355, 430
Saatchi & Saatchi/Sydney: 236, 237, 261, 294, 329, 336, 365
Sandstrom Design/Portland: 382, 399, 408, 436

Scholz & Friends/Berlin: 19, 218, 335, 387, 441, 470, 471
Scholz & Friends/Hamburg: 16
School Of Visual Arts/ New York: 103, 144, 453
Sci Fi Channel/New York: 111
Sedgwick Rd./Seattle: 336
Serviceplan Gruppe Für Innovative Kommunikation/ München: 238
Shine Advertising/Madison: 394
Strategy Advertising & Design/ Christchurch: 454
Struck Design/Salt Lake City: 414

T

3/Albuquerque: 388
Taxi/New York: 455
Taxi/Toronto: 52, 54, 138, 219, 222, 233, 322, 358
TBWA\Chiat\Day/New York: 57, 71, 151, 280, 310, 335, 336
TBWA\Chiat\Day/ San Francisco: 45
TBWA\Germany/Berlin: 210
TBWA\GI/Paris: 178, 179
TBWA\Hunt\Lascaris - Johannesburg/Sandton: 335, 359
TBWA\Paris/Boulogne-Billancourt: 37, 71, 199, 233, 275, 337
TBWA\Raad/Dubai: 347
TBWA/Singapore: 414
Thielen Designs/Albuquerque: 394
Think Tank 3/New York: 363
Three-Sixty Group/Indianapolis: 442
Tokyo Great Visual/Tokyo: 437
Tokyu Agency/Tokyo: 408
Tonic Communications/Dubai: 170
Trollback + Company/ New York: 448
Turner Duckworth/ San Francisco: 90, 156, 400, 409, 410

V

Valentine Group, The/ New York: 383
Vegaolmosponce/Acassuso: 302
Venables Bell & Partners/ San Francisco: 428
Volume/San Francisco: 456

W

W+K 12/Portland: 456
Wax Partnership/Calgary: 81, 142
Whybin\TBWA/Auckland: 63
Wieden+Kennedy/London: 56, 138, 149
Wieden+Kennedy/New York: 4, 149, 154, 302, 319, 368, 375, 388, 400
Wieden+Kennedy/Portland: 45, 48, 303, 320, 349
Wieden+Kennedy/Tokyo: 88
Wink/Minneapolis: 76, 471, 472
Wirz/BBDO/Zurich: 48
Wongdoody/Seattle: 464

Y

Y&R/Kuala Lumpur: 259
Y&R/Generator/Auckland: 220
Yomiko Advertising/Tokyo: 437
Young & Rubicam/Chicago: 58, 151, 337, 431, 478

Z

Zapping/Madrid: 384
Zig/Toronto: 336

ART DIRECTORS

A

Abrams, Rachel: 153, 229
Achterberg, Jakko: 321
Adachi, Tsubasa: 468
Adorjan, Sonny: 479
Ahmed, Shani: 85
Ajmal, Mohammad: 270
Alam, Moyeenul: 130, 160
Alcorn, David: 354
Allen, Craig: 57, 151
Allpress, Myles: 261
Allwardt, Benjamin: 20
Alvarado, Sebastian: 15
Ambekar, Sachin: 414
Ambrose, Jason: 35, 38, 39, 68, 69, 136, 147, 289, 369
Anantananukun, Kornthon: 252
Anderson, Michael: 407
Andery, Julio: 183
Andrade, Ray: 428
Andrews, Mike: 330
Arbez, Joel: 153, 229
Ardito, Richard: 311
Arekar, Abhay: 433
Arzu, Joel: 126
Ashley, Michael: 288
Assawanapanon, Aniruth: 224
Astorgue, Eric: 299
Auer, Greg: 8, 134

B

Bae, Yoon Kyung: 504
Bailes, Darren: 292
Baird, Rob: 55
Bakay, Chris: 35, 38, 136, 147, 369
Bamfield, Mark: 200
Barlock BV: 105
Barry, Karin: 169
Bartholomew, Ben: 162
Basiewicz, Bob: 511
Bates, Sarah May: 49, 137
Bathwal, Anil: 232
Batis, Angie: 361
Bauer, Joerg: 379
Baumhugger, Verena: 83
Bayractar, Birol: 346
Belford, Paul: 120, 466
Bell, Peter: 394
Bergdahl, John: 362
Bergmann, Robyn: 10
Best, Wayne: 300
Bhatnagar, Kamal: 467
Bianca, Farrah: 360
Bianrosa, Richard: 125
Biehler, Franois: 352
Bielefeldt, Christoph: 98, 157
Bindi, Adrien: 8, 134
Bioty, Anne: 313
Bjurman, Markus: 27, 135
Blom, Mikael: 118
Blumentritt, Jan: 193
Bobst, Christian: 214
Boland, Jeremy: 229
Bonnery, Phillip: 17
Bonnery, Philip: 306
Boothroyd, Anne: 247
Bootlis, Paul: 276
Borgen, Anne-Lise: 313
Bower, Nicola: 343
Bradbourne, Tony: 220
Braley, Michael: 466, 467
Brandse, Simone: 70, 154
Brazier, Paul: 181
Brenner, Christian: 305
Brenner, Mike: 511
Brooks, Christiane: 49, 137
Broughton, Eron: 365
Brown, Sheena: 155, 510
Bruce, Shaun: 494
Bryan, Marion: 353
Bryant, Rick: 317
Buchanan, Alan: 154, 375
Burnett, Leo: 361
Butori, Rodrigo: 360

C

Cabral, Juan: 151, 300, 367
Cahan, Bill: 108
Campbell, Jason: 71, 334
Campbell, Keith: 226
Campbell, Milo: 479
Caravedo, Beatriz: 36
Careborg, Lisa: 119, 121, 461
Carlson, Tobias: 27, 135
Carmody, Sean: 75
Chalermwong, Jon: 50
Chandrasekar, Malini: 433
Chaturvedi, Juhi: 270
Chaudhury, Somak: 364
Chaumont, Santiago: 234
Cheah, Im Im: 360
Chen, Johe: 345
Chen, Shengxiong: 279
Cherin, Bosky: 433
Cheung, Simon: 345
Chiew Chiew, Neo: 288
Chin, Richard: 248
Chong, Richard: 259
Chung, KC: 25, 92
Ciszek, Corey: 58, 151
Clark, Robin: 439
Clement, Joel: 274, 355
Clunie, James: 227, 228, 419
Cohen, Amanda: 500
Cohen, Peter: 196

Copeland, Greg: 324
Copping, Richard: 32, 197, 257, 258, 355
Correa, Nicolle: 164
Costarides, Nicholas: 228
Costello, Mike: 39, 289, 369
Coulter, Jesse: 4, 149, 154, 302, 368, 375
Covitz, Phil: 39, 369
Cox, Simon: 242, 243
Cozza, Marc: 408
Cremer, Petra: 20
Cristalli, Paula: 492
+cruz: 88
Cruz, Paulo: 509
Curtis, Hal: 303

D

Daz, Ismael: 344
Dorner, Philipp: 98, 157
D'attilio, Charles: 485
Davidson, Tony: 56, 138, 149
Davila, Cristina: 175
Davis, Al: 212
Dawsonhollis, James: 68
Day, Larry: 225
Deboey, Yves-Eric: 178, 179
De Dios, Ivan: 166, 172
Degryse, Mathieu: 178, 179
De Klerk, Anthony: 78
Delayen, Emily: 503
Deloof, Kait: 505
Deng, Bo: 164
De Souza, Joseph: 433
De Vega, Javier: 505
Dewalle, Mehdi: 374
Dias, Mario: 256
Diaz, Pierrette: 188
Dicesare, Cassandra: 500
Dishack, Sawzer: 126
Doman, Lisa: 164
Doman, Matt: 41, 137, 148
Donaldson, Pat: 499
Duering, Anja: 68
Dufils, Cecilia: 27, 135
Dugas, Matthew: 363
Duke, Dustin: 240
Duntemann, Matthew: 463
Durham, Peter: 128
Dye, Dave: 223

E

Ebenwaldner, Marc: 16
Ebina, Tatsuo: 422
Eckstein, Vanessa: 457, 480
Edwards, Clark: 7, 134, 163
Eghammer, Johan: 162
Endo, Wakako: 437
Engle, Brad: 408
Erasmo, Juan: 277
Estes, Sissy: 203, 208, 416

F

Fairbanks, Mark: 14
Farooq, Mariam: 487, 488
Favier, Corey: 417
Fernandez, Marcos: 384
Fernandez, Renato: 182
Ferrer, Dave: 29, 290
Figliulo, Mark: 58, 151
Finamori, Cesar: 182
Fischer, David: 218
Flaig, Stefanie: 471
Fonseca, Jose Carlos: 264
Forbes, Shane: 5
Ford, Hannah: 204
Forsythe, Liz: 122
Foulkes, Paul: 29, 283
Frenkler, Ekkehard: 238
Friedel, Daniela: 286
Frykholm, Steve: 107, 108
Fujimoto, Pam: 464
Fukuda, Susan: 49, 137

G

Ga, Naoki: 62
Gabaldoni, Ian: 53, 138, 150, 348
Gallucci, Marc: 318
Gannon, Molly: 155, 510
Gardiner, Daryl: 40, 282
Gates, Bob: 260
Gaul, Colin: 71, 295, 334
Geddes, Will: 497, 498
Gentile, Kevin: 230
Gerard-Huet, Jessica: 199
Ghazali, Ashidiq: 18, 21, 178
Ghidotti, Luis: 316
Gibson, Vanessa: 10, 427
Gigante, Arturo: 331
Gilmour, Matt: 236
Goh, Justin: 250
Goh, Pebble: 360
Goldberg, Carin: 103, 144
Goldblatt, Stephen: 51
Gooden, Matt: 56, 138, 149
Goto, Shizuko: 474
Goto, Tetsu: 474
Grafton, Regan: 366
Gressbach, Michaela: 238
Grewal, Sonya: 431
Grindon, David: 501
Groenewald, Mike: 255
Groom, Chris: 56, 138, 149
Grossman, Jed: 68, 69, 373
Grskovic, Steven: 217
Guillon, Romain: 299
Gyngell, Debbie: 277, 481

H

Hofvner, Pontus: 123
Haegerling, Stefan: 20
Hall, Chris: 161
Hall, Tarsha: 217
Han, Xin-An: 246
Hanrahan, Rory: 73, 141, 333
Hanselmann, David: 62
Hare, Gareth: 210
Harper, Tia: 511
Harrell, Thompson: 502
Harricks, Stuart: 202, 355
Harris, Joe: 213
Heilemann, Kristoffer: 327, 332
Heiman, Eric: 456
Heimann, Jochen: 351
Henderson, Scott: 290, 350
Heng, Eddie Wong Yew: 109, 175
Henkes, Uschi: 384
Henniger Von Wallersbrunn, Ulf: 215
Hernandez, Bernardo: 175
Heshui, Wang: 364
Hicks, Johannes: 441
Hobbs, John: 323, 324, 371
Hohalek, Xanthe: 152, 309, 325
Holder, Alexandre: 465
Holmes, Tim: 291
Hor, Gary: 21
Hor, Wing Kit: 239
Horton, Simon: 204
Hough, Steve: 274
Huang, Ean-Hwa: 25, 92
Hubbard, Trevor: 510
Huse, Tim: 281

I

Iacobelli, Sergio: 15
Inpornvichitr, Kajnarong: 94, 143
Israel, Aramis: 68

J

Jacobs, Jan: 273
Jain, Hemant: 110
James, Shawn: 222
Jeffery, Colin: 304, 370
Jenkins, Jayanta: 320
Jenkins, Kim: 12
Jennings, Stuart: 154, 319, 375, 400
Jenniss, Maxime: 496
Jethi, Nishant: 33
Jochum, Armin: 379
Johnson-Pond, Rebecca: 247
Jones, Steve: 4
Jue, Hewaed: 276
Juenger, Nico: 353
Juriga, Jesse: 509

K

Kaemmerer, Hans Juergen: 332
Kaleli, Ece: 363
Kamble, Raj: 11, 135, 147, 168
Kamuli, Adris: 493
Kamzelas, Paul: 232
Kanjanapokin, Gun: 224
Kappes, Thomas: 83
Karandikar, Abhijit: 249, 389
Kashima, Emi: 96
Kaur, Gurdish: 434
Kavina, Roshni: 268
Kayser, Joe: 45
Khambekar, Sharmad: 201
Khan, Husen Baba: 65, 171
Kim, Jin: 350
Kim, Nellie: 28
King, Malcom: 343
Kittel, Andreas: 118, 461, 469
Klinkert, Nick: 185
Klintworth, Anni: 160
Kodaira, Masayoshi: 104, 117, 450, 451, 460, 468, 476
Koller, Kevin: 68, 373
Komatsu, Yoichi: 357

Konishi, Mari: 459
Kortemeier, Pia: 20
Kosel, Tiffany: 6, 25, 44, 60, 67, 68, 134, 139, 149, 154, 372
Kottkamp, Rob: 35, 38, 136, 147, 289, 369
Kriefski, Michael: 394
Kroijer, Mikkel: 128
Kusano, Denison: 478
Kwong, Paul: 12

L

Lad, Ashok: 163, 352
Lagana, Vince: 237
Laksanajinda, Gumpon: 285
Lamont, Graham: 427
Landry, Jim: 34
Langlais, Clement: 233
Larppitakpong, Kittitat: 50
Lau, Irene: 287, 477
Lee, Agnes: 287, 477
Lee, Gigi: 480
Lee, James: 350
Lee, Ken-Tsai: 461
Lee, Paul: 370
Leong, Edwin: 248
Leong, Kelvin: 360
Lesinski, Justin: 264
Leung, Owen: 346
Lewus, Alan: 481
Li, Hua: 246
Li, Jian: 246
Lim, Clement: 360
Lim, Lydia: 480
Lim, Pann: 386, 429
Lim Thye Aun, Alex: 420
Lin, Melissa: 216
Linke, Birger: 258, 430
Lishman, Maria: 247, 356
Lok, Ng See: 93
Lopez, Paulo: 370
Lossgott, Nadja: 359
Lozano, Vanessa: 155, 510
Luebke, Kay: 19

M

Mendez, Rebeca: 440
Maccuish, Al: 292
Macgregor, Callum: 36
Mack, Maja: 387
Mackler, Jonathan: 311
Manger, Christine: 193
Manosalvas, Alex: 317
Marchal, Benjamin: 47, 137, 308
Marucci, Jerome: 26
Maruta, Masaya: 408
Maryon, Dean: 298, 415
Massis, Andre: 340, 341, 342
Massis, Felipe: 426
Maurice-O'Leary, Karen: 63
McArthur, Hamish: 196
McCoy Kelly, Buffy: 91
McCracken, Todd: 213
McGuinness, Dale: 326
McGuinness, Troy: 233
McKay, Andy: 71
McKenzie, Selena: 59
Medeiros, Marcos: 173
Meimberg, Florian: 100
Melvin, Sherrod: 99
Miller, Matt: 8, 134
Miller, Tony: 324
Mills, Stuart: 21
Milne, Chris: 509
Mimaki, Phil: 267
Min, Heidi: 512
Min Jung, Ko: 165
Mitoh, Thomas: 438
Mizuno, Manabu: 116, 145
Mongkolsaetarin, Sakol: 276
Montanez, Daniela: 239
Montesano, Julian: 316
Morelle, Keka: 191
Morimoto, Chie: 404
Morris, Kat: 174, 372
Morrison, Jae: 356
Mously, David: 162, 398
Muk: 177
Mun: 240, 241, 436
Munoz, Nick: 372
Musante, Jason: 64

N

Nagai, Kazufumi: 99
Nagamatsu, Ryoko: 408
Nagase, Yuji: 437
Naito, Hisamoto: 437
Nakamura, Kazuto: 393, 413
Navas, Antonio: 314
Nazli, Naz: 210
Nerman, Jenny: 384
Nobay, David: 329
Noguchi, Takahito: 403
North, Piers: 435
Nucci, Dario: 298

O

Olsen, Jon: 436
Olson, Larry: 291
Ong, Edward: 259
Ong, Joey: 29
Ong, Kien Hoe: 309
Onimaru, Toshihiro: 445
Ooi, Francis: 287, 477
Oppmann, Simon: 254, 271, 286
Osman, Khalid: 342

P

Padgett, Dave: 265, 266
Padhi, Santosh: 167
Padin, Aaron: 195
Pafenbach, Alan: 304
Pagano, Alexandre: 176
Pandya, Hital: 433
Parker, John: 301, 372
Pasteels, Laurence: 391
Pathare, Sanket: 386
Patris, Carles: 186
Pay, Caroline: 292
Pedersen, Doug: 209, 222
Peterson, Matt: 61, 139, 152
Petri, Anne: 346
Phoon, Herbie: 460, 514
Phua, Aaron: 189, 475
Pierre, Sebastien: 187
Poh, Roy: 386, 429
Pok, Ching Hai: 189
Pollock, Keli: 81, 142
Poopijit, Khomson: 387
Popko, Brian: 506
Porky Hefer: 244
Pradhan, Yogesh Mani: 381
Presiado, Arnie: 184
Pridgen, Scott: 381
Pringle, Nicholas: 7, 134, 163
Punjabi, Yashika: 493
Purkayastha, Debu: 433

Q

Qi, Xingsheng: 279
Qiu, Lei: 246
Quarterman, Chase: 495

R

Ragan, Kimberley: 247
Raghavan, Prasad: 412
Ramos, Alvaro: 36
Rasic, Dejan: 70, 154
Rebeschini, Marcus: 280
Reginelli, Michael: 100, 233
Reinhart, Andrea: 48
Rekoumis, John: 128
Renbaum, Leah: 125
Renner, Paul: 4, 149, 388
Reveman, Joakim: 275
Rice, Mike: 447
Richards, Todd: 107, 108
Robaire, Jean: 411
Roberge, Aimee: 491
Roberts, Guy: 63
Robinson, Nick: 70, 154
Rodriguez, Javier: 199
Rodriguez, Pres: 372
Rooke, Guy: 438
Rosen, Josh: 331
Rothwell, James: 195
Royer, Ted: 301
Ruehmann, Bjoern: 275
Russo, Davi: 349
Rutherford, Grant: 42, 136, 148

S

Sanchez, Diego: 302
Sakaguchi, Shotaro: 459
Sakaki, Ryosuke: 449
Sakamoto, Dave: 328
Sanders, Paul: 365
Sandstrom, Sara: 406
Sandstrom, Steve: 382, 399
Sano, Kenjiro: 87, 99, 156, 398
Saruwatari, Javier: 194
Sawada, Koichi: 444
Sawada, Makoto: 357
Sawadatikom, Saharath: 387
Sawant, Kunal: 31
Sawant, Vijay: 270
Schilling, Axel: 16
Schmidt, Arne: 83
Schoffro, Florian: 432
Schreiber, Gunther: 74, 155
Schultchen, Arne: 432
Schulte, Jason: 447
Schutte, Eric: 77, 141
Schweder, Hendrik: 62

Seah, David: 189
Sebresos, Hunter: 490
Seeger, Hans: 405
Seene, Shevaun: 489
Selman, James: 48
Sethi, Kanika: 278
Settesoldi, Giovanni: 192
Shah, Amee: 17, 307, 323, 324
Shaikh, Zahid: 443
Shamen, Drew: 512
Shaughnessy, Mike: 205
Sheen, Heather: 242, 243, 293
Shiman, Jennifer: 305
Siddique, Zayed: 63
Sides, Brandon: 304
Siegal, Meghan: 369
Simon, Brad: 72
Simpson, Gavin: 242
Sinele, Amanda: 486
Sloan, Tom: 284
Smith, Markham: 14
Smits, Jan-Willem: 265
Smrczek, Ron: 52, 54, 138, 322
So, Sungho: 504
Soh, Leng: 386
Sojwal, Samir: 381
Sommalardpun, Nirun: 94, 143
Spinadel, Cody: 206
Squier, Phillip: 304, 370
St. John, Todd: 115
Stark, Tiffany: 485
Stechschulte, Paul: 6, 25, 44, 60, 67, 69, 134, 139, 154
Stempel, Sybille: 238
Stephens, Geordie: 39, 289, 369, 372
Stevens, Eric: 154, 375
Stiles, Brett: 424
Strasser, Dan: 307
Stuebane, Tim: 470
Sumedi, Din: 9, 134
Sundby-Munson, Ned: 507
Sutherland, Shannon: 294
Sutton, Eric: 190

T

Tan, Aaron: 198
Tan, Elisa: 288
Tanapatanakul, Thirasak: 50
Tanna, Punita: 484
Tansrikeat, Watchara: 253
Tan Yee Kiang: 240, 241, 436
Taroux, Philippe: 233, 37
Taylor, Mark: 68, 312
Taylor, Monica: 45
Techera, Manuel: 234
Teng, Run Run: 329, 344
Teo, Carina: 248
Teoh, Alvin: 240, 241, 436
Teoh, Walter: 427
Tham, Khai Meng: 21
Tham, Shannon: 235
Thielen, Tony: 394
Thoem, Kevin: 13, 207
Timonen, Mikko: 162
Tindall, Justin: 22, 147
Tomar, Mohit: 251
Tranter, Gary: 235
Trehan Theeng, Pooja: 425
Triechel, Dan: 71, 334
Tsang, Theresa: 479
Tso, Chuck: 66, 77, 101, 141, 245
Tulk, Ian: 499
Tung, Diana: 288

V

Vaccarino, Tim: 306
Van Den Broeck, Tim: 174
Vangelder, Jules: 208
Veeramachineni, Shruti: 128
Vieira, Luciane: 462
Villagrán, Alberto: 194
Vining, Lance: 161
Vior, Ricky: 316
Vitrone, Scott: 310
Vladusic, Alan: 23
Voehringer, Mark: 272
Vrdoljak, Andre: 353

W

W+K 12: 456
Wachter, Paul: 127
Waernes, Jens Petter: 24
Walker, Peter: 170
Wallace, Paul: 221, 30
Ware, Dan: 8, 134
Watanabe, Hirofumi: 444
Wee, Maurice: 232
Wee Kim, Goh: 390
Weeks, Dan: 269
Wells, Jen: 227
Whitlow, Mike: 512
Wielopolski, Liam: 5
Williams, Jason: 59
Wilson, Charlie: 280
Wittenmark, Jonas: 27, 135
Wolfe, Katharine: 508
Wong, Craig: 232
Wong, James: 21
Wong, Stanley: 102, 144

Y

Yemma, Dawn: 68
Yeo, Eric: 177, 345
Yew Pong, Hor: 259
Yu, Caprice: 180
Yu, Peng: 279
Yuen, Jonathan: 429
Yung, Stephanie: 455
Yunus, Shehzad: 347

Z

Zenas Upputuru, Daniel: 78, 124, 241
Zentil, Jaimes: 219, 358
Zheng, Wing: 346
Zunini, Alvaro: 234

Clients

A

a! diseo: 457
A:Door: 412
AC Delco Shock Absorbers: 165
ACE Hardware: 51
ADC: 455
Adcock Ingram: 343, 359
ADENA: 172
adidas: 45, 63, 180, 298, 415
Afro Magazine: 458
AIGA Salt Lake Chapter: 414
Airbus: 164
Aktionsbuendnis Landmine.de: 335, 470
Alexandria Real Estate Equities: 72
Allianz AG - Allianz München Stadion: 443
Altoids: 8, 134
American Cancer Society: 280
American Express/Tribeca Film Festival: 392
American Legacy Foundation: 35, 38, 39, 136, 147, 289, 335, 369, 424
American Red Cross: 284
American Society for the Prevention of Cruelty to Animals (ASPCA): 272
Ameriquest Mortgage: 49, 137
Amnesty International: 37, 269, 274, 292, 480
Amtrak: 203, 416
Ando BV: 105
Anheuser-Busch: 71, 140, 307, 334, 337
APAV: 264
Apollo Tyres: 163
Apple Computer: 86, 87, 156, 397, 401
Art Directors Association of Iowa, The: 471
Art Tower Mito: 117
Ascot Corporation: 444
ASICS: 98, 157
Asylum: 385, 418
Atlanta Braves: 228
Audi: 64, 246
Auric Pacific: 397
Aware Singapore: 475

B

Bailey Lauerman: 432
Banco Real: 462
Bangkok Insurance: 50
BBC Television: 181
Bendon Lingerie: 347
Birdie: 396
Bisley: 20
Black Rep: 122
Blue Man Group: 446
British Airways: 232
BSH Bosch und Siemens: 16
Burger King: 68, 312, 334

C

C. Roy: 78
California Coastal Commission: 29, 283
CANAL+: 299
Cancer Patients Aid Association: 33, 268
Cancer Research UK: 280
Care International: 332
Carlton Draught: 42, 136, 148

Cars-and-Boxes: 24
CBS: 206
CdC (Club de Creativos de España): 384
Change the Policy: 264
Church of Sweden: 123
Cicero Werkstudio: 379
Citibank: 231
Click Wine Group: 400
Colonial Williamsburg: 208
Columbia Sportswear: 229
Comedy Central: 315
Converse: 382
Cooper Carry: 109
Corbis: 226
Court TV: 448
Creative Brands: 242, 243
Creative Circus: 466

D

D&AD: 120
Daimler Chrysler: 94, 143
Dairy Queen: 337
Daiwa Radiator Factory: 450
Dasein Academy of Art: 460
DC Shoes: 299
DDB Canada: 260
Department for Transport: 71
Dexter Russell: 227, 228, 419
DHL: 18, 162, 177, 327, 351
Diageo - Smirnoff: 348
Diakonie Katastrophenhilfe (Emergency Aid): 346
Dinopolis Teruel: 186
Discovery Communications: 241, 462
Disney/Buenavista España: 384
Dog House, The: 84, 142
Drive Alive: 335
Duracell: 232
Durex: 244
Dutch Association for Traffic Victims (Vereniging Verkeersslachtoffers): 265
Duvel/Moortgat Brewery: 230

E

E.Co.: 96
Eagle, Idaho Volunteer Firefighters Association: 334
eBay: 245
Economist, The: 14, 21, 178, 242
Editora Abril: 182
Ella Cheong Spruson & Ferguson: 390
Energizer Malaysia: 240
Ephydrol: 199
ESPN: 4, 149, 152, 154, 190, 309, 318, 319, 325, 375, 388, 412
Eurasian Association Singapore, The: 287, 477
Eve Group: 413
Exclusive Books: 427

F

Federated Department Stores: 168
FedEx: 77, 141, 311
FedEx/Kinko's: 66, 101
Feinberg School of Medicine at Northwestern University: 378
Feldmann+Schultchen Design Studios: 432
Festspielhaus und Festspiele Baden-Baden: 471
Fiat: 166, 215, 426
Figueroa Brothers: 214
Flat Stanley: 395
Fonso Interprise: 461
Ford / Lo Jack: 234
Ford Multi-State Working Group: 371
Formica: 380
FOX Sports: 329
Franc franc: 87, 156
Fringe Festival: 421
Fruit of the Loom: 336
Full Sail Brewery: 399
Fundacion Vida Silvestre: 277

G

Gap: 301, 372
GE: 411
General Mills - Wheaties: 12
General Motors - HUMMER Division: 306
George Simhoni Photography: 222
German Foundation for Monument Protection (Deutsche Stiftung Denkmalschutz): 271
Gillette: 21
Golden Gate Fields: 330
Golden Star Gifts & Stationery: 329
Golite: 197
Good Day Cafe: 395
Greek Restaurant: 78
Greenpeace: 29, 32
Groupe SEB Singapore: 344
Guinness: 26, 41, 99, 137, 148

H

Hachi Tei Restaurant: 175
Hanamoto: 393, 413
Happy Forsman & Bodenfors: 97
Harley Davidson: 10, 255
Harrods: 177
Harvey Nichols: 22, 147
Hasbro: 9, 134, 198, 257
HBO - OZ Season 5: 428
Heavenly Marketing: 409
Heineken: 301
Heinz: 7, 134, 163
Herman Miller: 107, 108
Hertz Theatre: 267
Hewlett Packard: 314, 335
Hifana: 88
Hilton: 431
Hindustan Times: 270
Holmes Private Investigators: 386
Homebase Stores: 410
Honda: 56, 138, 149
Hurricane Poster Project, The: 472

I

I-Jusi Magazine: 85
ICARE: 467
ICBC: 40, 334
IKEA Sweden: 362
Illustration Growers of America: 225
Independent Newspapers: 160
Indian Association For Promotion Of Adoption & Child Welfare (IAPA): 31
Indianapolis Cultural Development Commission: 442
Innocence in Danger: 273
Interactive Africa: 458
Interface: 383
International Campaign to Ban Landmines: 276
Ionique Fertilizer: 252
Isoldit on eBay: 336

J

J H Kim Taekwondo Institute Singapore: 342
Jack Daniel's Tennessee Whiskey: 417
James Mahon: 28
JFK Library: 265, 266
Jim Aitchison: 345
Jim Esch for Congress: 141
jobsintown.de: 218
Johnson & Johnson Medical India: 443
Joshua Dalsimer: 260
Jumeirah Music Equipment: 171
JWT India: 433

K

Kaiser Family Foundation: 291
Kellogg's: 210, 352
Kimberly-Clark: 191, 248
Kinokuniya Bookstore: 427
Kiwicare: 213
Klippan: 461
Kodak Germany: 254
Koleman: 253
Kraft / Milk-Bone: 239

L

L'Equipe: 47, 137, 308
Land Transport NZ: 290, 350
Las Vegas Convention and Visitors Authority: 317
Latitude 23: 434
Le Soir Newspaper: 374
Lego: 15, 161, 202
Leo Burnett / Comic Relief: 361
Levi's: 324, 333
Lexus Australia: 236
Libellule Images: 391
Lion Nathan: 237
LVMH: 75

M
MADD: 34
Magnum: 460
Mamamoto: 83
Maneland Jungle Lodge: 167
Marco: 480
Marshall Field's: 76
Masterfoods: 57, 71, 151, 310, 335, 336
Match.com: 336
MCCM Creations / Anothermountainman Communications: 102, 144
Meat & Livestock Australia: 326
Melange Accessoires: 387
Mercedes-Benz: 211
Mercian: 408
Merrydown: 223
Metropolitan TV: 250
Microsoft XBOX: 46
Midland Bookshop: 110
MilkPEP - Milk Processor Education Program: 216
Miller Brewing Company: 55, 58, 151
MINI: 6, 25, 44, 60, 62, 67, 69, 134, 139, 154, 174, 233, 356, 438
MIWA Lock: 422
Monaco: 247
Monster: 335
MORI Art Museum: 116, 145
Morphosis: 440
Mother: 27, 135, 435
Motorola: 344
Mrs. Kapoor Guest House: 425
MTV: 115
Multichoice DSTV: 169
Museum of Sex: 240

N
Nadezhda Russian Restaurant: 109
Naga DDB Malaysia: 436
National Aids Trust: 334
National Federation of UNESCO Associations in Japan: 474
National Parks Conservation Association: 478
National Thoroughbred Racing Association: 71, 140, 335
Nebraska Domestic Violence Council: 473
Nestlé: 23
New York Mets: 331
New Zealand Book Council: 281
Nike: 45, 48, 59, 62, 111, 114, 145, 187, 219, 302, 303, 320, 349, 354, 358, 368, 400, 452
Nikon Malaysia: 241
Ninad Kamat: 386
Nissan: 178, 179
NOGGIN Brand: 463
Nokia: 220
Nordstrom: 423
North Carolina Travel & Tourism: 209, 222
NPO Harappa: 468
NTT-Resonant: 357
nzgirl: 366

O
Office: Jason Schulte Design: 95, 144
Ogilvy & Mather, India: 381
Olympus: 239
Onion, The: 13, 207
Open Family: 71, 140
Opolis: 80, 142
ORBO: 124
Oregon Coast Aquarium: 334
Organizing Committee for the Exhibition Bauhaus Dessau: Mikiya Takimoto: 476
Oslo Hudpleiesenter: 176

P
P&G Rejoice: 364
Pandit Hariprasad Chaurasia: 389
Paramount Comedy: 112
Park Project Inc.: 403
Partnership For A Drug Free America: 71, 295, 334
Peacefrog Records: 405
Pentagram Design: 435
PepsiCo International: 360
Permark International: 5
PetsUnite: 93
Pfizer Canada: 52, 54, 138, 322
Philips: 173, 221
PIE Books: 104, 451
Pierre Fabre Japon: 459
Plantoys: 387
Playstation: 337
Polaris Industries: 381
Pon's Automobielhandel: 321
Ponle Corazon (Foundation Against Cancer): 36
Procter & Gamble: 195, 196, 201, 256, 351, 365
PZ Cussons: 402

R
ReadyMade: 456
Reckitt Benckiser O Cedar: 192
Renault: 74, 155, 210
Republic of Singapore Navy: 355
Robert Bosch: 175
Röhsska Museum, The: 118, 469
Royal Ontario Museum: 30
RSPCA: 479

S
Saatchi & Saatchi/Sydney: 261
Salvation Army: 277, 481
San Francisco Zoological Society: 276
Sandstrom Design: 436
SANTA (South African National Tuberculosis Association): 365
Saputo: 380
Schaefer Pharma: 398
School of Visual Arts: 103, 144, 453
SCI FI Channel: 111
Science World: 334
Seagram India: 278
Seattle International Film Festival: 464
Seconds on Main: 385
Shenzhen Mobile: 345
Shipra Estate Private Limited: 251
Sony: 25, 92, 151, 170, 212, 300, 414
Soon Hin Sportsbikes: 258
Southwark Partnership: 465
Sphere: 200
Spier: 106
Spontex: 233
Sport Graphics: 336
Starbucks: 61, 139, 152, 300
Stella Artois: 11, 135, 147
Sundance Channel, The: 113, 145, 157
Superdrug: 90, 156
Surfrider Foundation: 100, 233
Sustagen: 176
Swedish Museum of Architecture, The: 119, 121
Swiss Assurance Mobiliar: 48
Swiss-American Society of Pittsburgh: 411

T
3: 388
3M Reclosable Fasteners: 343
Takeo Company: 99
Target: 447
Tate: 367
Te Runanga O Ngai Tahu: 454
Texwood: 235
Thielen Designs: 394
Think Centre: 288
Think Tank 3: 363
Three Bond VIV Sales: 224
Threemile Canyon Farms: 408
Thymes: 82, 89, 143, 402
Tokai Germany: 353
Tokyo Great Visual: 437
TorchBearer Sauces: 91
Toronto Plastic Surgery: 153, 229
Total Fitness Club: 364
Toto: 449
Tower Records: 336
Toyota Motor Corporation of Australia: 336
Toys "R" Us: 100
Trader Media - Autotrader: 204
Transport Accident Commission (TAC): 291
Travel Channel: 337
Triumfglass: 406
Turner Broadcasting System (TBS): 73, 141, 333
Type Museum: 466

U
UK Government, Foreign & Commonwealth Office: 439
Umi: 394

UMW Toyota Motor: 309
UNICEF / Consuelo Foundation: 290
UNIFEM: 294
Unilever: 17, 65, 70, 154, 185, 302, 307, 323, 340, 341, 342, 353
United Airlines Hong Kong: 350
United Breweries India: 352
United Nations Mine Action Service: 36
United Way: 282
Universal Orlando: 313
University of Tokyo, The: 404
Uplink: 398

V
VCU Adcenter: 288
Verlagsgruppe Lübbe: 238
Virgin Atlantic Airlines: 361
Virgin Digital: 360
Virgin Mobile: 316
Visage Images: 249
Vodafone: 53, 138, 150, 336
Volkswagen: 4, 161, 174, 183, 184, 188, 189, 227, 304, 305, 308, 327, 332, 334, 337, 370
Volvo: 162, 194

W
W Network: 336
W+K 12: 456
W.S. Papers: 420
Washington's Lottery: 217
WaterAid Australia: 293
WAX partnership: 81, 142
web.com: 328
Weru: 19
Weston Corporation - Reebok: 430
Whataburger: 407
Wheel of Fortune: 336
Wichita State University: 467
WMF: 193
Women's Aid Organisation: 479
Wonderbra: 335
Wong Coco: 429
World: 445
World Swim for Malaria: 468
Worldwide Fund for Nature (WWF): 279, 285, 286
www.fairlines.de: 438

X
XM Satellite Radio: 205

Y
YLAT (Young Lungs Against Tobacco): 71, 275
Yomiko Itself: 437
Young Guns International Advertising Awards: 373
Yser Marketing: 259

Z
Zebra Vertriebs: 441
Zhujiang Beer: 346

COLLEGES

A
Academy of Art University/ San Francisco: 129, 484, 510, 511
Art Center College of Design/ Pasadena: 504
The Book Shop/Culver City: 485, 486, 487, 488
Brigham Young University/ Provo: 490
California State University/ Long Beach: 512, 513
College for Creative Studies/ Detroit: 511
Columbus College of Art & Design/Columbus: 513
Corcoran College of Art + Design/Washington: 514
Creative Circus, The/Atlanta: 131, 491, 492, 508, 509
Dasein Academy of Art/ Kuala Lumpur: 514
Fashion Institute of Technology/ New York: 125, 126
Miami Ad School/Madrid: 505
Miami Ad School/Miami Beach: 129, 130, 514
Miami Ad School/Minneapolis: 493, 507, 512
Miami Ad School/San Francisco: 128, 506
Miami Ad School/Stockholm: 128
Minneapolis College of Art and Design/Minneapolis: 131, 515
School of Visual Arts/New York: 129
Syracuse University/Syracuse: 500
Texas Creative, The University of Texas/Austin: 128, 494, 495, 515
Université du Québec á Montréal/Montreal: 131, 496, 515
University of Colorado/Boulder: 155, 497, 498, 499, 505, 510
University of Delaware/Newark: 127
VCU Adcenter/Richmond: 501, 502
Virginia Commonwealth University-School of Mass Communication/Richmond: 503

CREATIVE DIRECTORS

A
Abe, Yuki: 449
Adake, Nitin: 434
Adams, Tom: 35, 38, 39, 136, 147, 289, 335, 369
Agnihotri, Amitabh: 163, 352
Agost Carreno, Cesar: 15
Ahmad, Ali: 427
Ahmad, Yasmin: 93, 427
Aiba, Takanori: 445
Akefuji, Jiro: 408
Alexander, Joe: 265, 266
Alvarez, Javier: 166
Ammanath, Manoj: 65, 171
Amsler, Marty: 432
Ancevic, Michael: 205
Andersson, Nils: 164, 279
Andrew, Philip: 290, 350
Angelo, David: 313
Apicella, David: 331
Aranguena, Yosu: 308
Arnold, Ron: 12
Arrechedera, Sebastian: 308
Ashley, Michael: 288
Astorga, Alberto: 175
Avasthi, Abhijit: 270, 381

B
Bahu, Tales: 183
Baldwin, David: 64, 381
Bamfield, Mark: 200
Banny, Rudy: 91
Barlow, Toby: 71, 113, 145, 157, 295, 334
Barnes, Derek: 154, 319, 375
Barnwell, Mike: 343
Bascope, Felipe: 100, 233
Basu, Juju: 201, 256
Bauer, Joerg: 379
Becker, Chris: 239, 334
Belford, Paul: 14, 71, 120, 466, 479
Bell, Greg: 428
Bell, Nick: 53, 138, 150, 204, 348
Benjamin, Jeff: 67, 68, 69, 139, 154, 372, 373
Bennett, Lisa: 330
Berends, Joost: 374
Beverley, Dave: 210
Bidenko, Peter: 70, 154
Bindra, Siddhartha: 268
Bingham, Weston: 392
Blood, Andy: 63
Blore, Michael: 5
Boches, Edward: 205, 260
Bogusky, Alex: 6, 25, 35, 38, 39, 44, 60, 67, 68, 69, 134, 136, 139, 147, 154, 174, 289, 301, 312, 334, 335, 369, 372, 373, 438
Boiler, John: 46, 299
Boler, Brenda: 21
Borah, Rupam: 425
Boyle, Barbara: 196
Boynton, Richard: 76, 471, 472
Bradbourne, Tony: 220
Bradley, Chris: 370
Bradley, Mark: 336
Brazier, Paul: 41, 137, 148, 181
Brodsley, Adam: 456
Brown, Warren: 326
Bruce, Bill: 311
Buceta, Rich: 230
Bullock, Richard: 180
Burgdorf, Knut: 210

Burgos, Fred: 203
Burgos, Fred: 416
Byrne, Mike: 45, 48, 303, 320

C

Cardenas, Ricardo: 344
Cacciatore, Mark: 12
Cahan, Bill: 107, 108
Caizergues, Olivier: 194
Campo, Martin: 308
Cappeletti, Pedro: 173
Carl, Chris: 370
Carstens, Paul: 385
Catmur, Paul: 366
Cavanah, Earl: 240
Cawley, Tim: 205
Chakravarty, Ashish: 467
Chan, Bill: 452
Chanen, Rowan: 259
Chattopadhyay, Sumanto: 31
Chaumont, Santiago: 234
Chavarri, Jaime: 172
Chax, Ks: 110
Cheong, Eugene: 21
Chiu, Chris: 364
Choe, Edmund: 309
Chow, Wilson: 164
Cianfrone, Bob: 334
Clark, Brian: 64
Clark, Greg: 76
Clow, Lee: 45
Cole, Glenn: 299, 46
Collins, Brian: 392
Comar, Daniel: 21, 250
Connelly, Walt: 71, 295, 334
Connelley, Walt: 295
Cook, Dave: 64
Cooper, Craig: 84, 142
Corps, Daryl: 465
Cote, Helene: 49, 137
Coverdale, Jac: 34, 337
Cozza, Marc: 408
Craigen, Jeremy: 4
Crandall, Court: 152, 309, 325, 360
Crawford, David: 424
Cude, Jonathan: 64
Cullen, Matt: 235
Curtis, Hal: 45, 48, 303, 320

D

D'Alvia, Rafael: 302
Dabral, Sonal: 18, 23, 62, 177, 178, 232, 345
Daniels, James: 255
Davidson, Tony: 56, 138, 149
Dawson, Nigel: 291
De Almeida, Rodrigo: 183
Deceuster, Philippe: 374
De Dios, Ivan: 172
De Greef, Thierry: 391
Detweiler, Curt: 178, 179
De Villiers, Francois: 78
DeVito, Sal: 71, 140, 335
Dhaimade, Milind: 33
Dias, Agnello: 163, 352, 433
Digeorge, Arnie: 317
DiMassimo, Mark: 230
Dix, Martin: 328
Dong, Li: 364
Droga, David: 301
Duchon, Scott: 46
Duckworth, Bruce: 90, 156, 400, 409, 410
Duntemann, Matthew: 463
Dye, Dave: 223

E

Ebina, Tatsuo: 96
Eduardo, Ramiro: 186
Edwards, Geoff: 46
Ehlers, Jenny: 395
Erke, Ken: 431

F

Fackrell, Andy: 180, 298, 415
Faudet, Michael: 402
Favat, Pete: 35, 38, 39, 136, 147, 289, 335, 369
Feldmann, André: 432
Fernandes, Fabio: 176
Ferreira, Theo: 359
Ferrer, Dave: 29
Figliulo, Mark: 58, 151, 337, 431
Fischer-Appelt, Claudia: 83
Fisher, Mark: 365
Flintham, Richard: 151, 212, 300, 367
Fong, Karin: 462
Francucci, Atila: 191
French, Neil: 110
Frenkler, Ekkehard: 238
Freuler, Matthias: 48
Frick, Urs: 384
Fujisaki, Minoru: 437
Furby, Jay: 276

G

Gadallah, Khaled: 170
Gallucci, Marc: 190, 318
Gamache, Monique: 81, 142
Gamper, Mario: 471
Gangaram, Kamal: 343
Ganser, Stephan: 214
Gaxiola, Robert: 165
Gelner, William: 17, 185, 307, 323, 340, 341, 342
Geyer, Andreas: 20
Gibbons, Brendan: 315
Giesen, Jay: 411
Godbole, Prashant: 110
Godin, Helene: 380
Gomez De La Torre, Juan Carlos: 36
Goodby, Jeffrey: 29, 51, 283, 337
Goto, Tetsu: 474
Graf, Gerry: 57, 71, 151, 280, 310, 335, 336
Grais, Ian: 334
Granger, Tony: 12, 195, 196, 272, 273
Greenaway, Andy: 197, 198, 202, 257, 258, 274, 355, 430
Greenberg, Sandy: 239
Grewal, Sonya: 431
Gross, Mark: 71, 140, 307, 334, 337
Guan Hin, Tay: 288
Guerrero, David: 290
Guillen, Roger: 111
Gumbinner, Liz: 313
Gutierrez, Eric: 291

H

Haan, Noel: 8, 134, 225
Hacohen, Dean: 240
Hahn, Greg: 245
Haldeman, Brock: 378
Haldeman, Liz: 378
Hammond, William: 30, 153, 221, 229
Handlos, Oliver: 327
Harada, Asako: 87, 156
Harbeck, Jan: 162, 351, 398
Hargreaves, Paul: 280
Haven, Jim: 61, 139, 152
Hayo, Thomas: 324, 371
Heath, Lynton: 335
Hefer, Porky: 160, 244
Heiman, Eric: 456
Henderson, Ron: 336
Henkes, Uschi: 384
Herberstein, Camilla: 335
Hervé, Alexandre: 47, 137, 187, 188, 308
Hess, Toni: 334
Higgins, Peter: 439
Hobbs, John: 11, 135, 147, 168, 216
Hogshead, Sally: 230
Hogya, Bernie: 216
Hoinkes, Michael: 438
Holman, Richard: 112
Honda, Ryo: 468
Hope, Jane: 455
Hotz, Chris: 114
Hough, Steve: 274, 480
Howe, Austin: 436
Howlett, Brett: 232
Huang, Ean-Hwa: 25, 92
Hudder, Tom: 122
Huggins, Jeff: 46
Hughes, Mike: 13, 207
Human, Gerry: 10, 169, 255, 427
Hussein, Saad: 414

I

Indravudh, Annop: 94, 143
Iwasaki, Takehiko: 422

J

Jacobs, Jan: 272, 273
Jaggy, Alexander: 62
Jay, John C.: 88
Jeffery, Colin: 184, 227, 304, 370
Jensen, Lance: 306
Jeske, Andrew: 195
Jochum, Armin: 379
Johansen, Jo Espen: 176
Johnson, Joe: 331
Johnson, Neil: 342
Junker, Robert: 332
Jurisic, Stephen: 28

K

Kaemmerer, Hans Juergen: 332
Kaloff, Constantin: 387, 470
Kamzelas, Paul: 232
Karandikar, Abhijit: 389
Karlsson, Linus: 55, 73, 75, 141, 333
Karnik, Ashok: 268
Kassaei, Amir: 305
Kavander, Tim: 161
Kay, Ben: 465
Kay, Woody: 203, 208, 416
Kayser, Joe: 45
Kearse, John: 35, 38, 39, 136, 147, 289, 335, 369
Keenan, Kerry: 275
Kelleher, Dan: 26, 99
Keller, Andrew: 6, 25, 44, 60, 67, 68, 69, 134, 139, 154, 174, 301, 312, 372, 438
Kelly, Graham: 9, 32, 134
Kemp, Marcus: 264, 267
Kennedy, Maria: 260
Ketel, Jerry: 334
Kleman, Robert: 280
Klotnia, John: 72
Koch, Claus: 443
Koepke, Gary: 306
Koniakowsky, Wade: 336
Kornestedt, Anders: 118, 119, 121, 123, 406, 461, 469
Kosel, Tiffany: 373
Kriefski, Michael: 394
Kuhn, Bastian: 337
Kumar, Senthil: 433
Kwasnick, Dave: 411

L

Labounty, Sean: 336
Lad, Ashok: 163, 352
Lamont, Graham: 427
Lance, Adam: 70, 154
Lawner, Ron: 35, 38, 39, 136, 147, 184, 203, 208, 227, 289, 304, 335, 369, 370, 416
Lear, Mike: 13, 207
Le Blond, Carl: 265
Lee, Christopher: 385, 397, 418
Lee, Szu-Hung: 25, 92
Leick, Stefan: 471
Leong, Edwin: 248
Leong, Tan Yew: 93
Lesser, Jim: 276
Lessing, Gareth: 353
Leube, Jan: 19, 218, 335, 441
Leung, Owen: 345, 346
Lewis, Kyle: 264, 267
Li, Hua: 246
Li, Jian: 246
Lim, Alex: 427
Lim, Nick: 452
Lim, Ted: 240, 241, 436
Lima, Eduardo: 176
Lim Thye Aun, Alex: 420
Lindenberg, Ruy: 426
Lineberry, Veronika: 336
Linneu, Joao: 191
Livi, Joao: 462
Lo, Sheungyan: 452
Loeser, Gunnar: 16
Loew, Dave: 58, 151, 337, 478
Lok, Andrew: 345, 346
Low, Patrick: 109, 175
Lubars, David: 26, 66, 77, 99, 101, 141, 227, 228, 245, 311, 411, 419
Luckin, Fran: 10, 169
Lumsiricharoenchoke, Wisit: 285
Lung, Jacky: 279
Lynn, Elspeth: 336

M

Méndez, Rebeca: 440
Maclay, Sam: 388
Maddocks, Richard: 247, 281, 356
Madon, Farrokh: 420
Mahabaleshwarkar, Sagar: 249
Mahajan, Vineet: 467
Makarechi, Sharoz: 363
Malmstrom, Paul: 55, 73, 75, 141, 333
Manry, Pascal: 192, 352
Marco, Harvey: 100, 233
Markus, Craig: 333
Martin, Greg: 336
Martin, Lance: 52, 54, 138, 219, 322, 358
Maryon, Dean: 298, 415
Matchett, Bruce: 163, 352, 433
Matejczyk, John: 335
Matouschek, Petra: 83
McBride, Chuck: 45
McCoy Kelly, Buffy: 91
McCracken, Todd: 213
McGrath, James: 42, 136, 148
McKenna, Mike: 336
McLennan, Rob: 335, 353
McLeod, Andy: 151, 212, 300, 367
McNeil, John: 46
Meimberg, Florian: 100
Merkin, Ari: 300
Meyer, G. Andrew: 8, 134, 225
Meyer, Terri: 239
Mikus, James: 407
Mizuno, Manabu: 116, 145
Mogrelia, Hanoz: 201, 256
Mohamed, Ali: 93
Mohd. Samidin, Hasnah: 248
Molla, Joaquin: 316
Molla, Jose: 316
Monteiro, Mark: 49, 137
Montero, Antonio: 172
Montgomery, Scott: 336
Moore, Bob: 217
Moore, Dave: 336
Moreno, Manolo: 384
Morris, Brett: 161, 343
Mortier, Jens Mortier: 374
Mountjoy, Jim: 209, 222
Mously, David: 162, 351, 398
Mroueh, Zak: 52, 54, 138, 219, 222, 233, 322, 358
Murray, Tim: 447

N

Nagai, Kazufumi: 99
Naito, Hisamoto: 437
Nakamura, Kazuto: 393
Narayanaswamy, Ramesh: 412
Newbery, Bill: 161
Ng, Ronald: 239, 360
Ng, Tian It: 329, 344
Nimick, Colin: 280
Nobay, David: 236, 237, 261, 294, 329, 336, 365
Nobre, Fernando: 191

O

O'Connell, Steve: 6, 44, 60, 67, 69, 134, 139, 154
Olsen, Jon: 436
Olson, Dan: 82, 89, 143, 395, 402
Ong, Edward: 259
Ooi, Francis: 287, 477
Oppmann, Simon: 254, 271, 286

P

Padhi, Santosh: 167, 425
Pafenbach, Alan: 184, 227, 304, 370
Pagel, Florian: 346
Pandey, Piyush: 31, 249, 270, 381
Papworth, Kim: 56, 138, 149
Paradise, Liz: 381
Pask, Guy: 454
Pauli, Andreas: 215
Peacock, Christy: 59, 402
Pearson, Vanessa: 277, 481
Peterson, Matt: 61, 139, 152
Petri, Anne: 346
Pfeiffer-Belli, Michael: 327
Pollmann, Torsten: 100
Ponce, Hernan: 302
Praditpong, Prangthip: 50
Prat, Leo: 316
Premutico, Leo: 272, 273
Pross, Martin: 471
Proudfoot, Kevin: 4, 149, 154, 302, 319, 368, 375, 388, 400
Purkayastha, Debu: 433

R

Roffen, Kai: 210
Ruhmann, Lars: 74, 98, 155, 157
Rabosky, Steve: 100, 233
Raboy, Doug: 336
Raffray, Vincent: 170
Rao, Kumuda: 364
Ratcliffe, Ken: 301
Ray, Mark: 417
Rebeschini, Marcus: 280
Reichenthal, Ian: 57, 71, 151, 310, 335, 336
Reilly, Rob: 68, 312, 372
Rell, Andreas: 379
Remer, Dave: 226
Renner, Paul: 154, 319, 375
Rettig-Falcone, Lisa: 240
Rexhausen, Jan: 24
Rich, Rob: 217
Richards, Dan: 80, 142, 412

Riebartsch, Lars: 351
Ritt, Jon: 396
Roberts, Nigel: 14, 71, 120, 466, 479
Roemmelt, Peter: 254, 271, 286
Rollins, Matt: 109
Romano, Fernanda: 11, 135, 147, 168, 216
Rosch, Peter: 11, 135, 147, 168, 216
Rottmann, Michael: 62
Royer, Ted: 301
Runge, Clint!: 473
Russell, Alan: 40, 260, 282, 334

S

Sakaguchi, Shotaro: 459
Sanchez, Juan: 175
Sandstrom, Steve: 382, 399
Sarff, Noah: 336
Sato, Sumiko: 88
Saville, Robert: 27, 135, 292, 435
Sawada, Koichi: 444
Sawadatikom, Saharath: 387
Schalit, Mike: 361
Schiff, Doug: 279
Schmidt, Julia: 470
Schmidt, Matthias: 470
Schneider, Don: 411
Schneider, Silke: 16
Schneider, Terry: 229
Schneider, Wolfgang: 327, 332, 334
Schoeffler, Eric: 305
Schultchen, Arne: 432
Schulte, Jason: 95, 144
Seisser, Tod: 12
Serpa, Marcello: 182
Setzkorn, Stefan: 16
Shabaz, Ali: 288
Shannon, Ant: 71, 140, 291
Shen Guan, Tan: 259
Sherman, Derek: 269
Shiman, Jennifer: 305
Shon, Chan Lee: 427
Shoval, Alon: 446
Silburn, Paul: 423
Silver, Eric: 26, 66, 77, 99, 101, 141, 311
Silverstein, Rich: 29, 283, 314
Simon, Andrew: 30, 153, 221, 229
Simpson, Gavin: 242
Simpson, Steve: 314, 335
Sin, David: 239
Singer, Vappu: 193
Skjei, Michael: 380
Sloan, Tom: 284
Smith, Craig: 62
Smith, Tim: 228
Snow, Randy: 317
Soares, Alexandre: 191
Soh, Calvin: 189, 350, 475
Sorah, Cliff: 206
Spaetgens, Matthias: 19, 218, 335, 441
Spengler-Ahrens, Doerte: 24
Spiller, Darren: 59, 242, 243, 293
Sridhar, K.V.: 167
Srikieatikajohn, Nopadol: 252, 253
St. John, Todd: 115
Stagno, Sebastian: 302
Staples, Chris: 334
Stapleton, Damon: 335
Stead, Mark: 395
Stillacci, Andrea: 192, 352
Stiller, Mathias: 327, 332, 334
Stolz, Mirko: 162
Stout, Gethin: 217
Strasberg, Rob: 438
Sucharittanonta, Suthisak: 94, 143, 224
Sullivan, Luke: 424
Sunol, Alvar: 234

T

Takamatsu, Satoshi: 357
Tan, Kien Eng: 479
Tan, Nana: 460
Tan, Terrence: 342
Tanaka, Yoshinori: 422
Tanapatanakul, Thirasak: 50
Tao, Lorraine: 336
Taretto, Gustavo: 277
Tavlin, Josh: 331
Techera, Manuel: 234
Teoh, Alvin: 240, 241, 436
Tham, Khai Meng: 21
Thares, Scott: 76, 471, 472
Thieme, Dirk: 443
Thirache, Sylvain: 47, 137, 187, 188, 308
Thorburn, Bill: 380, 421
Thornton, Jim: 7, 134, 163, 210, 361
Tindall, Justin: 22, 147
Ting, Richard: 354
Tranter, Gary: 235
Treacy, Susan: 423
Trollback, Jakob: 448
Tucker, Adam: 22, 147
Tucker, Angus: 28
Turner, David: 90, 156, 400, 409, 410
Tutssel, Mark: 210
Twei, Alvin Wong: 287, 477

U

Upputuru, Emmanuel: 78, 124, 241, 251, 278, 412

V

Valente, Sergio: 173
Valentine, Robert: 383
Van Doormaal, Dominique: 174
Vazquez, Gabriel: 277
Venables, Paul: 428
Verdine, Michael: 80, 142, 412
Vervroegen, Erik: 37, 71, 199, 233, 275, 337
Vior, Ricky: 316
Vitrone, Scott: 57, 71, 151, 310, 335, 336
Von Scheven, Burkhart: 162, 214, 398

W

W+K 12: 456
Waggoner, Mark: 399
Waites, Mark: 27, 135, 292, 435
Wakefield, Rich: 264
Walker, Dennis: 336
Walker, Jim: 336
Walker, Shirley: 439
Wannavalee, Sirin: 364
Warsop, Graham: 5
Waterbury, Todd: 4, 149, 154, 302, 319, 368, 375, 388, 400
Weber-Gruen, Alexander: 337
Wee, Francis: 390, 420
Weeks, Dan: 269
Weist, Dave: 184, 227, 304, 370
Wilde, Richard: 103, 144, 453
Williams, Genevieve: 453
Willvonseder, Claudia: 353
Willy, Scott: 442
Winschewski, Anke: 193
Winterhagen, Michael: 471
Wnek, Mark: 11, 135, 147, 168, 216
Wong, Stanley: 102, 144
Wong, Tracy: 464
Wright, Bill: 334
Wright, Joe: 448
Wyville, Jon: 58, 151, 478

X

Xiberras, Stephane: 299

Y

Yamamoto, Shigenobu: 449
Yap, Henry: 309, 480
Yeo, Yang: 189, 350, 475
Yoshimizu, Masaki: 404
Yunus, Shehzad: 347

Z

Zuenkeler, Ulrich: 20
Zunini, Alvaro: 234

DESIGNERS

A

Ahmed, Shani: 85
Aizawa, Chiaki: 116, 145
Albee, Floyd: 372
Amaro, Aaron: 383
Anazawa, Yukio: 437
Anderson, Kristin: 382, 436
Ang, Cara: 385
Apparatus, Aesthetic: 423
Argus, Kerry: 454
Atkins, Kelly: 72

B

Bela, Carlos: 462
Barlock: 105
Barres, Charlotte: 410
Bauer, Matt: 112
Bayractar, Birol: 346
Beck, Melinda: 463
Belford, Paul: 120, 466
Bell, Peter: 394
Benoit, Marie-Elaine: 380

Benzel, Gary: 111, 115, 145
Benzur, Gabriel H.: 109
Bessen, Neal: 369
Bhangu, Dilshad: 513
Bohl, Kara: 260
Boudrias, Brigitte: 131
Boynton, Richard: 471, 472
Braley, Michael: 466, 467
Broad, Dan: 423
Buck: 372
Buckingham, Nic: 237

C

Caal, Nancy: 72
Carmody, Sean: 75
Carrel, Ginny: 367
Chambundabongse, Anchalee: 423
Chapman, Greg: 84, 142
Chin, Richard: 248
Chisholm, Heidi: 106, 458
Chiw Mun Yew: 436
Cho, Chun-Pin Grace: 513
Chou, Yao-Feng: 461
Christopher, Samuel: 112
Chung, KC: 25, 92
Coninx, Friederike: 398
Contegni, Mariana: 480
Cozza, Marc: 408
+Cruz: 88

D

Dagnell, Erik: 24
Dai, Azazaa: 452
Davidson, Nicholas: 107, 108
Dietrich, Gabriel: 462
Do, Ha: 453

E

Eager, Christian: 410
Eckstein, Vanessa: 457, 480
Emery, Don: 378
Engle, Brad: 408
Enriquez, Vanesa: 457
Erdil, Guenduez: 351

F

Fahrlin, Linda: 402
Falkenbach, Raquel: 462
Favier, Corey: 417
Ferrare, Michael: 67, 139, 154
Fitzgibbons, Elizabeth: 456
Flores, Nicole: 95, 144, 447
Fong, Karin: 462
Friedman, Lea: 109
Fuke, Takahiro: 437

G

Gamache, Monique: 81, 142
Gareis, Sven: 420
Garton, Matt: 354
Genco, Chuck: 354
Goh, Justin: 250
Goh, Pebble: 360
Goldberg, Carin: 103, 144
Gramp·, Rafael: 462
Graphics & Designing Inc.: 445
Grendene, Simon: 446
Gyngell, Debbie: 481

H

Hane, Chihiro: 422
Harrimansteel: 435
Harris, Mike: 410
Heiman, Eric: 456
Hemphill, Martha: 109
Hess, Louis: 455
Hillier, Dave: 361
Hinrichs, Kit: 435
Hofler, Mark: 98, 157

I

Idera, Masaki: 468
Igarashi, Junko: 357
Ikami, Emi: 451
Ikeda, Masayuki: 357
Inayoshi, Mai: 404
Infahsaeng, Apirat: 392
Ito, Akiko: 456

J

Jain, Hemant: 110
Jockisch, Steve: 421

K

Kalil, Diogo: 114
Karpinska, Aya: 354
Kashima, Emi: 96
Kauf, Ronnie: 462
Kaur, Gurdish: 434
Kee Hong, Tang: 420
Kim, Peter: 513
Kimgym: 88
Kirschenhofer, Bertrand: 74, 155
Kodaira, Masayoshi: 104, 117, 450, 451, 460, 468, 476
Komazawa, Tomoko: 403
Kooper, Troy: 354
Kreutzer, Joel: 141
Kuhn, Michael: 98, 157
Kumagai, Akira: 437
Kumar, Senthil: 433
Kwok, Wai-Ki: 102, 144

L

Lachlan, Sam: 90, 156, 409
Lam, Mary: 423
Lavoie, Nathalie: 515
Lee, Ken-Tsai: 461
Leonard, Nils: 465, 479
Leung, Dick: 350
Leusink, Alan: 402
Lim, Lydia: 480
Lim, Stan: 462
Lim Thye Aun, Alex: 420
Liu, Davi Sing: 88
Lowry, Nelson: 154, 375

M

Marmo, Roger: 462
Mashburn, David: 75
Méndez, Rebeca: 440
McGrath, Tim: 388
Mikuni, Takahiro: 437
Min, Heidi: 512
Minatomura, Toshikazu: 444
Mintcheva-Strzok, Boriana: 131, 515
Misawa, Jill: 378
Mitt Out Sound: 372
Miyawaki, Ryo: 404
Mori, Yasunari: 357, 444
Mun, Esther: 89, 143
Myers, Randall: 432

N

Naar, Lenny: 453
Nakamura, Kazuto: 393
Nakayama, Kiyoshi: 437
Ng, Eileen: 102, 144
Nicol, Jonathan: 380
Nobre, Paula: 462
Noriko&Don Carrol: 437

O

Oi Leng, Hooh: 514
Okamoto, Kazuki: 99
Okamoto, Yoshiko: 437
Okecki, Pamela: 448
Oldorp, Bernd: 83
Olsen, Jon: 436
Ong, Bel: 385, 418
Onimaru, Toshihiro: 445
Otsuka, Namiko: 104, 117, 460
Otten, Julia: 432
Oyama, Akihiro: 437

P

Panchal, Rahul: 67, 69, 139, 154, 372
Parker, James: 399
Pask, Guy: 454
Pasteels, Laurence: 380, 391
Pavlovic, Ana: 453
Pence, Laura: 354
Pengsathapon, Satian: 392
Pfennighaus, Max: 369
Phua, Aaron: 475
Pienaar, Peet: 106, 458
Pinto, Phil: 115
Pocker, Brent: 511
Practise: 367
Pradhan, Yogesh Mani: 381
Price, Chad: 514
Pridgen, Scott: 381
Purkayastha, Debu: 433

R

Rabe, Lindsay: 414
Rees, Kris: 70, 154
Richards, Dan: 412
Richards, Todd: 107, 108
Richardson, Iain: 212, 367
Ritt, Jon: 396
Romney, Brooke: 383
Rosenberger, Shawn: 400
Ross, Charlie: 380
Ross, Hayo: 238
Rustia, Johanna: 354

S

Sakae, Ryota: 398
Sakamoto, Naomi: 422
Sakurai, Ken: 82, 395

Sandstrom, Steve: 382, 399
Santi, Luis: 67, 68, 139, 154
Sawada, Makoto: 357
Schif, Wolfgang: 379
Schmiedeskamp, Michah: 432
Schneider, Pia: 16
Schoffro, Florian: 432
Schulte, Jason: 447
Schwartz, Molly: 115
Sedelmayer, Hana: 83
Seelen, Ansgar: 443
Seow, Jeanna: 418
Shimizu, Shiho: 459
Shimokawa, Daisuke: 437
Shiraishi, Chihiro: 468
Siah, Lian: 460
Siegal, Meghan: 369
Siegel, Jessica: 435
Singh, Jagjit: 412
Sjovall, Jonas: 362
Smith, Justin: 64
Sobcynski, Lisa: 453
Sojwal, Samir: 381
Solarana, Cathy: 432
Solen, Dan: 414
Spooner, Chris: 453
St. John, Todd: 111, 115, 145
Stan Winston Studios: 68
Stead, Mark: 395
Stipinovitch, Mario: 115
Sugawara, Miyuki: 449
Szulborski, Dave: 64

T
Takada, Yui: 116, 145
Talford, Paula: 410
Tan, Edwin: 397
Tan Yee Kiang: 436
Templar Studios: 369
Teo, Carina: 248
Thares, Scott: 76, 471, 472
Thielen, Tony: 394
Tisdall, John: 14, 120
Tomiyama, Shotaro: 88
Tong, Eric: 452
Torres, Cesar R: 515
Tsang, Winnie: 73, 141

U
Uematsu, Tomoki: 449
Usukura, Fumihito: 437

V
Valencius, Chris: 369
Van Schalkwyk, Tandy: 385
Verdine, Michael: 80, 142
Veryeri, Emre: 448
Vissat, Dave: 411
Votaw, Brian: 354

W
W+K 12: 456
Wee Kim, Goh: 390
Williams, Molly: 131

Y
Yasunaga, Yutaka: 437
Yeo, Roy: 452
Yung, Stephanie: 455

Z
Zargham, Roxane: 440

WRITERS

A
Abramowitz, Ben: 298, 415
Abrams, Rachel: 153, 229
Adake, Nitin: 434
Adorjan, Sonny: 479
Agnihotri, Amitabh: 163, 352
Alexander, Joe: 265, 266
Almeida, Marcello: 462
Alshin, Adam: 300
Amin, Karan: 433
Andersen, Mark: 8, 134
Aranguena, Yosu: 308
Arbez, Joel: 153, 229
Ashley, Michael: 288
Askelof, Oscar: 162
Atkinson, Michael: 34, 337
Auslander, Shalom: 333
Avasthi, Abhijit: 270
Azadi, Eddie: 25, 92

B
Bailes, Darren: 292
Baker, John: 71, 140, 334
Ballada, Matias: 316
Ballard, Dustin: 35, 38, 39, 69, 136, 147, 289, 335, 369
Barma, Inseeyah: 511
Barnes, Derek: 4, 45, 149
Barnett, Guy: 36
Bartels, Ingmar: 74, 155
Basiewicz, Bob: 511
Basu, Arkadyuti: 433
Baxter, Jeff: 205
Baynham, Richard: 53, 138, 150, 348
Bechus, Clint: 5
Beliveau, Crystal: 391
Bell, Scott: 71, 334
Benjamin, Jake: 272
Benzur, Gabriel H.: 109
Berger, Shoshana: 456
Berndl, Ludwig: 327, 332, 334
Berry, Chad: 424
Bhattacharya, Parixit: 386
Bialik, Stephanie: 128
Billows, Mark: 227, 304
Bindra, Siddhartha: 268
Bjurman, Markus: 27, 135
Black, Rich: 231
Blanchette-Guertin, Marieve: 380
Bletterman, Josh: 354
Bloomfield, William: 328
Bongiovanni, Maureen: 174, 372
Boosin, Lisa: 487, 488
Boothroyd, Anne: 247
Bootlis, Paul: 276
Bottkol, Matthew: 239
Bouchet, Jean-Francois: 199
Branning, Matthew: 337
Brasil, Joao Caetano: 191
Bray, James: 231
Brioul, Thierry: 352
Browne, Claudette: 160
Brusnighan, Todd: 13
Buckhorn, Dean: 231
Bunnell, Mat: 46
Burke, Pat: 337
Burke, Shannon: 495
Burnett, Leo: 361
Bursky, Rick: 49, 137
Burton, Trent: 81, 142
Busch, Akiko: 103, 144
Butt, Verity: 63
Byrne, Mike: 48

C
Cardenas, Ricardo: 344
Cabral, Juan: 151, 300, 367
Cade, Nick: 8, 134
Cain, Brian: 64
Calabro, Robert: 71, 140, 334
Caldeira, Dulcidio: 182
Campbell, Milo: 479
Canning, Michael: 70, 154
Careless, Jonathan: 336
Carl, Chris: 370
Carlin, Steve: 336
Carlson, Tobias: 27, 135
Carraway, Chris: 337
Carrigan, Andy: 154, 375
Casarotti, Flavio: 173
Cawley, Tim: 419
Chambliss, Will: 28, 35, 38, 136, 147, 289, 369
Charoenwiwatchai, Wirat: 224
Chattopadhyay, Sumanto: 31
Chaudhury, Somak: 364
Chaumont, Santiago: 234
Chavarri, Jaime: 172
Chen, Ning: 164
Chen, Valerie: 479
Cheong, Eugene: 21
Chess, Luke: 237
Chester, Zac: 499
Chew, Donevan: 93
Chia, Yvonne: 62
Chiao Woon, Lim: 165
Chiaphanumas, Nutchanun: 50
Childress, Stephen: 284
Chin, Raymond: 350, 475
Chochinov, Allan: 108
Chong, Richard: 259
Chowdhury, Nrusingha: 256
Christensen, Greg: 478
Chung, Francis: 506
Cianfrone, Bob: 68, 312
Clark, Dave: 55, 73, 141, 333
Clarke, Phil: 335
Clement, Joel: 274
Clement, John: 71, 140, 335
Cliett, Lindsay: 507
Clunie, James: 227, 228
Collinge, Howard: 70, 154
Collins, Billy: 113, 145, 157
Conlon, Patrick: 508
Cook, Adam: 317
Copeland, Paul: 324
Corbelle, Matìas: 302
Corbitt, Carl: 68
Corbo, Bruno: 205, 260

Corcoran, Colin: 231
Corwin, Larry: 68, 69, 373
Coulibaly, Sergi: 186
Cousteau, Clemence: 71
Covington, Matt: 228
Crocker, Andrew: 330
Cronin, Dan: 71, 335, 336
Culberson, Bart: 337
Cullen, Matt: 235
Curtis, Glenn: 5

D

D'Ambrosio, Juliet: 109
Dao, Andy: 8, 134
Davis, Ashley: 57, 151
Dawood, Sumeera: 106
Dawson, Nigel: 291
Deboey, Yves-Eric: 178, 179
De Greef, Thierry: 391
Degryse, Mathieu: 178, 179
Deinhart, Christine: 238
De La Fosse, Emma: 280
Del Gobbo, Luissandro: 192
Derrick, Dave: 8, 134
Detweiler, Curt: 178, 179
DeVito, Sal: 335
De Vries, Fred: 106
Dias, Agnello: 167
Dildarian, Steve: 337
Dillon, Leslee: 408
Djelaj, Karin: 84, 142
Doksroy, Kulvadee: 285
Dong, Li: 364
Dotter, Alicia: 492
Doucette, Jordan: 233
Doyle, Sean: 223
Driggs, Steve: 231
Duffy, Shannon: 489
Dufils, Cecilia: 27, 135
Dustin, Ballard: 334
Dzakaria, Zamri: 360

E

Ebner, Ryan: 337
Eckloff, Bill: 122
Edwards, Clark: 7, 134, 163
Edwards, Dianna: 383
Edwards, Katie: 439
Eeuwens, Adam: 440
Einhorn, Marc: 39, 289, 369
Elkaim, Matthieu: 188
Emmett, Brad: 71, 140
Enberg, Erik: 435
Erbe, Pamela: 107
Erke, Ken: 58, 151, 431
Ernsting, Daniel: 337
Ewen, Paul: 335

F

Fackrell, Andy: 298
Fairbanks, Mark: 14
Fallon, Joe: 306
Faria, Andre: 183
Fass, Philippe: 334
Feldman, Dixie: 463
Fell, Josh: 49, 137
Ferguson, Andy: 319, 368
Fernandes, Sandeep: 65, 171
Figel, Pete: 58, 151, 337
Fischvogt, Matt: 64
Flint, Alex: 306
Flores, Nicole: 447
Flory, Neil: 23
Foley, Charles: 161
Ford, Brian: 320
Ford, Hannah: 204
Forsberg, Lars: 461
Foster, Richard: 14
Frank, Nathan: 340, 341, 342
Friedrich, Brian: 17
Fry, Evan: 301, 372
Fuke, Takahiro: 437
Fukue, Hiroki: 444

G

Gahlot, Suchitra: 78, 124, 241
Gallucci, Marc: 190
Galvin, Justin: 190, 318
Garbutt, Chris: 337
Gauthier, Shawn: 195
Geoghegan, Tim: 180
Geri, Anne: 448
Giachetti, Daniel: 71, 140, 335
Gibbons, Brendan: 315
Goh, Alex: 386
Golder, Jeff: 232
Gomez, Mario: 505
Gomez De La Torre, Juan Carlos: 36
Goodman, Matthew: 128
Goodrich, Kara: 411
Gordon, Lauren: 343
Goto, Tetsu: 474
Gotz, Chris: 365
Graham, Jonathan: 421
Graham, Paul: 350
Grunden, Sara: 13, 207
Guerrero, David: 290
Guichard, Chris: 502
Gunshanon, Jim: 64
Guthrie, Brendan: 71, 140
Guzman, Juan: 130, 160

H

Hackemer, Heidi: 239
Haensell, Lars: 62
Haeussler, Michael: 19
Hale, Gregg: 64
Hampton, Tyler: 29, 283
Hansen, Spencer: 490
Harbeck, Jan: 162, 214, 398
Hardy, Stacy: 106
Hare, Gareth: 210
Harper, Tia: 511
Harricks, Stuart: 202
Harris, Brian: 336
Hart, Ian: 506
Hart, Michael: 231
Harwood, Chris: 226
Haven, Jim: 61, 139, 152
Hawthorne, Grace: 456
Hayes, Scott: 154, 375
Heartfield, Ian: 41, 137, 148
Henderson, Ron: 336
Hennah, Angus: 290, 350
Henson, Philip: 509
Hernandez, Luis: 194
Herrera, Rick: 46
Hill, Howard: 264
Hindley, Stephen: 336
Hirsch, Chris: 28
Hirthler, Jason: 109
Hoff, Jason: 99
Holm, Dick: 107, 108
Holmes, Tim: 71, 140
Honey, Juliet: 335
Horn, Marlo: 351
Horrigan, Justin: 497, 498, 505
Horton, Simon: 204
Hosokawa, Naoya: 357
Hospodarec, Joe: 81, 142
Hough, Steve: 274
Houston, Mike: 334
Howard, Mike: 372
Howe, Austin: 436
Hower, Reuben: 231
Howie, Craig: 189
Howlett, Brett: 232

I

Ian, Matt: 17, 307, 323, 324
Illes, Sandra: 305
Imai, Masahiro: 449
Israel, Aramis: 372
Iwasaki, Takehiko: 422
Iyer, Sundar: 33

J

Jackson, Brooks: 407
Jackson, Steve: 59
Jacobs, Tim: 305
Jaen, Alberto: 166
Jain, Hemant: 110
Jalfen, Martin: 316
Jansson, Fredrik: 362
Janzen, Paul: 267
Jennions, David: 343
Jhaveri, Hemal: 443
John, Felix: 387
Johnson, Bridget: 10
Johnson, Donnell: 68
Johnson-Pond, Rebecca: 247
Junker, Robert: 332

K

Kalleres, Greg: 4, 149, 154, 302, 375, 400
Kapoor, Dinesh: 288
Kapur, Priti: 342
Kapur, Radhika: 425
Kapusta, Ted: 509
Karandikar, Abhijit: 389
Kayenburg, Hanna: 20
Keenan, Kerry: 275
Kellen, Pete: 269
Kellett, Oliver: 465
Kemeny, Thomas: 68
Kempen, Jason: 335
Kennedy, Dave: 335, 369
Keogh, Ant: 42, 136, 148
Khambekar, Sharmad: 201
Khan, Irfan: 52, 54, 138, 322
King, Mike: 497, 498, 505
Kleinhans, Ole: 62
Kleman, Robert: 200, 280

Klepka, Marina: 83
Klumpyan, Kevin: 493
Knight, Natalie: 281
Koutoulogenis, Dennis: 326
Kraemer, Tom: 185
Kriel, Hanlie: 78
Kumar, Senthil: 433
Kummer, Stuart: 441
Kurzmeyer, Thomas: 48

L

Lamb, Todd: 75
Lambert, Claire: 112
Lancaric, Jon: 330
Landa, Celine: 47, 137, 308
Lane, Greg: 217
Langlade, Jerome: 187
Larkin, Brian: 106
Larsen, Ernie: 64
Lear, Mike: 13
Lecocq, Carol: 107, 108
Lee, Darren: 250
Lee, Dylan: 303
Lee, James: 260
Lee, Mabel: 350
Lee, Szu-Hung: 25, 92
Lemaitre, Jim: 311
Lemmon, Todd: 335
Leong, Edwin: 248
Leong, Terence: 350
Leroux, Benoit: 37, 233
Leung, Owen: 345, 346
Levy, Glen: 12
Levy, Neil: 276
Lewman, Mark: 114
Li, Hua: 246
Li, Jian: 246
Lieberman, Ann: 55
Lim, Gayle: 329, 344
Lim, Pann: 429
Lim, Renee: 232
Lim, Ted: 240, 241, 436
Linnen, Scott: 68, 372
Lishman, Maria: 247, 356
Little, Paul: 334
Loew, Dave: 337
Lok, Andrew: 345, 346
Loong, Serene: 177
Loperena, Pablo: 277
Loraine, Martin: 4
Love, Craig: 12
Low, Danny: 21
Lowe, Mark: 336
Luckin, Fran: 427
Luijten, Ad: 174
Lundberg, Stephen: 168
Lung, Jacky: 279
Luoma, Eric: 380

M

Méndez, Rebeca: 440
MacCuish, Al: 292
Mackenzie, Carey: 102, 144
Maclay, Sam: 388
Madon, Farrokh: 420
Mahoney, John: 206
Maiorino, Chris: 245
Makak, Roger: 258, 430
Makarechi, Sharoz: 363
Manalich, Felipe: 15
Manikas, Konstantinos: 353
Manske, Nathan: 336
Maravilla, Patrick: 501
Marcus, Ken: 416
Marshall, Noah: 213
Matejczyk, John: 231
Matteucci, Liber: 264
Mattick, Kathy: 294
Mau, Brant: 319
May, Steve: 365
McBride, Chuck: 45
McCabe, Steve: 220
McCain, Matt: 464
McCann, Jason: 455
McCoy Kelly, Buffy: 91
McIntosh, Craig: 219, 358
McKechnie, Andrew: 390
Meimberg, Claudia: 100
Miller, Tony: 324
Milne, Chris: 509
Miranda, Adam: 239
Mitra, Kaushik: 167
Moehrle, Armin: 108
Mohd. Samidin, Hasnah: 248
Moore, Jim: 382
Moore, Toby: 59
Moreno, Manolo: 384
Morgan, Brad: 337
Morris, Peter: 106
Morrison, Jae: 356
Moss, Anthony: 236
Mueller, Curtis: 331
Mueller, David: 222
Mueller, Jeff: 447
Muhlenfeld, Dave: 265, 266
Murray, Brian: 381

N

Naidu, Asheen: 353
Nair, Primus: 309, 480
Nakamura, Tomiko: 393
Nanfeldt, Mikael: 97
Nazli, Naz: 210
Nel, Stefanus: 277, 481
Nelson, Jacob: 162
Ng, Mike: 503
Ng, Raymond: 240, 241, 436
Nhlapo, Mbulelo: 335
Nishii, Tetsuo: 437
Nobay, David: 329
Nobili, Simone: 24
Nogueira, Marcelo: 176
Northrop, Ronny: 174

O

O'Connell, Steve: 174
O'Brien, Jennifer: 486
Ohlson, Johan H.: 16
Oink Ink Radio: 336
Olivas, Cesar: 175
Oliver, Lauren: 351
Ong, Joey: 29
Ono, Hitoshi: 422

P

Pandey, Nikhil: 251
Pang, Sunny: 102, 144
Papworth, Kim: 56, 138, 149
Paquette, John: 512
Paulse, Roger: 244
Pay, Caroline: 292
Pegu, Navajyoti: 467
Pemrick, Lisa: 82, 89, 143, 402
Pendleton, Aaron: 71, 140
Perreault, Matt: 463
Phifer, Brad: 499
Phoon, Herbie: 460
Pipeling, Melissa: 313
Pithey, Michele: 361
Poh, Roy: 429
Pollmann, Torsten: 100
Povill, David: 373
Praditpong, Prangthip: 50
Prat, Leo: 316
Premutico, Leo: 273
Prenger, Deborah: 336
Prince, Rachel: 350
Pringle, Nicholas: 7, 134
Pringle, Nick: 163
Pulickal, Nirmal: 109, 175
Puls, Christian Ole: 335
Putter, Kelly: 178

Q

Quaid, Jeb: 71, 140

R

Rachford, Chuck: 334
Raffray, Vincent: 170
Ragan, Kimberley: 247
Rahyar, Yama: 485
Ramakrishnan, Jagdish: 32, 197, 257, 258, 355
Ramos, Anselmo: 11, 135, 147, 216
Rampolokeng, Lesego: 106
Rao, Gururaj: 352
Ratcliffe, Ken: 301
Rathgeber, Kevin: 40, 282
Reichenthal, Ian: 57, 310
Reilly, Rob: 6, 25, 44, 60, 67, 134, 139, 154
Rell, Andreas: 379
Remias, Lee: 209, 222
Resch, Gary: 334
Reveman, Joakim: 275
Ridl, Julie: 107, 108
Riess, Pierre: 299
Riley, Tim: 14
Rivera, Alfonso: 505
Rivera, Rebecca: 49, 137
Roan, Tim: 334
Roberts, Nigel: 120
Robinson, James: 428
Rockowitz, Glenn: 217
Roe, Chris: 334
Roemmelt, Peter: 254, 271, 286
Rollins, Matt: 109
Rooney, Rob: 315
Rosch, Peter: 323, 324, 371
Rosenberg, Adam: 506
Rosman, Jonathan: 380
Ross, Charlie: 261
Ross, David: 30, 221

Roth, David: 494
Rouzier, Luc: 299
Ruben, Justin: 293
Ruckwied, Christopher: 471
Ruddy, Braden: 106
Ruehmann, Bjoern: 275
Runge, Clint!: 473
Russoff, Michael: 56, 138, 149

S

Saling, Dean: 291
Sanchez, Juan: 175
Sander, Emily: 71, 295, 334
Sawant, Kunal: 31
Scaff, Alexandre: 426
Schierl, Alexander: 16
Schiff, Doug: 279
Scholes, Adam: 336
Schrack, Joe: 71, 140
Schulte, Jason: 447
Schutte, Edsard: 265
Schutte, Eric: 66, 101
Scott, Keith: 438
Sebresos, Hunter: 490
Sels, Veronique: 71
Sethi, Kanika: 278
Sgro, Joe: 307
Shabaz, Ali: 288
Shamon, Pete: 184, 318
Shazlina, Sharin: 360
Sherman, Derek: 269
Shevel, Derek: 169
Short, Bridget: 366
Shur, Howard: 486
Silver, Harris: 363
Simpson, Gavin: 242
Simpson, Steve: 314
Skolar, Matthew: 334
Skonvitayanon, Bhakpong: 252, 253
Slade, Kristina: 360
Smith, Grant: 311
Smith, Markham: 14
Smith, Mike: 231
Smith, Xander: 275
Snarr, Kyle: 414
Soh, Calvin: 189
Song, Andy: 279
Sorensen, Dan: 107
Soskin, Chris: 240
Sparke, Penny: 469
Spencer, Hamish: 242, 243, 293
Spiegel, Mike: 354
Srichandra, Mantira: 387
Sridhar, K.V.: 167
Stalder, Andreas: 215
Stark, Tiffany: 485
Stassen, Anna: 231
Stolz, Mirko: 162, 214
Subramanian, Ramamurthy: 249
Sucharittanonta, Suthisak: 94, 143, 224
Sutter, Mick: 203, 208
Suzuki, Soichiro: 408
Svartz, Mark: 331
Syberg-Olsen, Matt: 161

T

Takamatsu, Satoshi: 357
Takimura, Yasushi: 449
Tan, Aaron: 198
Tan, Audra: 258, 430
Tanigawa, Taichi: 449
Tanna, Punita: 484
Tarry, Rob: 334
Tatarka, Allon: 231
Taub, Jay: 196
Tay, Allen: 345
Taylor, Mark: 317
Techera, Manuel: 234
Tembulkar, Parag: 414
Teo, Mikael: 9, 134
Terchila, Eric: 229
Tham, Yin May: 62
Thoem, Kevin: 13
Thompson, Sean: 56, 138, 149
Tipton, Franklin: 6, 25, 39, 44, 60, 67, 69, 134, 139, 154, 289, 369, 372
Tischer, Axel: 218
Todd, Hugh: 336
Topol, Lisa: 154, 375
Tresnak, Elena: 438
Tucker, Adam: 22, 147
Tufts, Scott: 354
Turner, Stuart: 359
Twei, Alvin Wong: 287, 477

U

Ugaeri, Yohei: 357
Upputuru, Emmanuel: 412
Ure, Andy: 448

V

Van Den Valentyn, Birgit: 470
Van Huyssteen, Konstant: 255
Vij, Sean: 152, 309, 325
Vining, Lance: 161
Vitrone, Scott: 57, 151
Vogler, Greg: 417

W

W+K 12: 456
Wa Bofelo, Mphutlane: 106
Wachter, Paul: 127
Waggoner, Mark: 399
Walker, Ben: 56, 138, 149
Ward, Mike: 231
Watanabe, Saori: 449
Waterhouse, Scot: 336
Watkins, Zach: 109
Wear, Mary: 71
Weber Neidhart, Sandy: 230
Weeraworawit, Weerachon: 94, 143
Weiss, Ari: 26
Weist, Dave: 304, 370
Welander-Berggren, Elsebet: 469
Westra, Niels: 321
Wilkesmann, Dirk: 210
Willett, David: 108
Willy, Jez: 212
Winter, Bob: 51
Wittenmark, Jonas: 27, 135
Wong, Phoebe: 102, 144
Wong, Stanley: 102, 144

X

Xu, Qing: 246

Y

Yamamoto, Hiroko: 468
Yeo, Ivan: 427
Yew Pong, Hor: 259
Yong, May: 259
Yoshimizu, Masaki: 404
Yun, Jason: 335, 369
Yunus, Shehzad: 347

Z

Zafonte, Nick: 491
Zetterholm, Emma: 406
Zhao, Fei: 279
Zhuwo, Phillip: 106
Zierler, Keri: 504
Zunini, Alvaro: 234

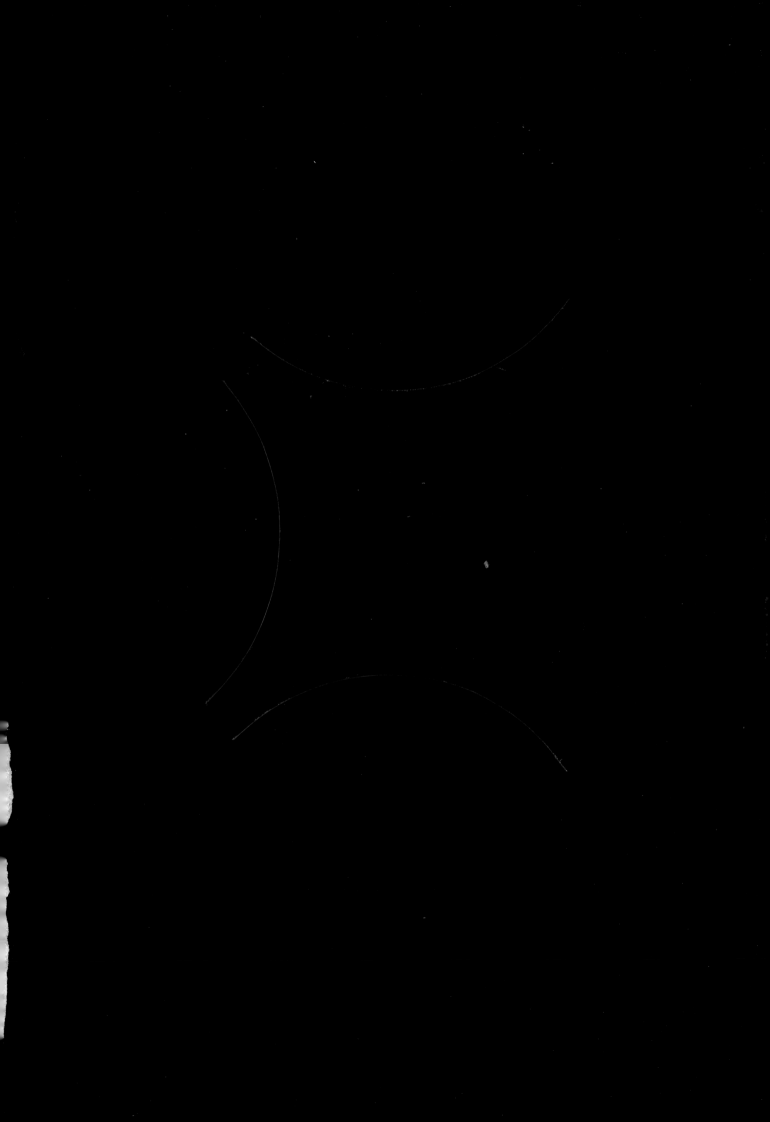